# The Wilson Chronology of Women's Achievements

## Other Titles in the Wilson Chronology Series

# The Wilson Chronology of Women's Achievements

Irene M. Franck and David M. Brownstone

The H. W. Wilson Company

New York • Dublin

1998

Library of Congress Cataloging-in-Publication Data

Franck, Irene M.
    The Wilson chronology of women's achievements: a record of
    women's achievements from ancient times to the present / by
    Irene M. Franck and David M. Brownstone.
       p.    cm.
    Includes index.
    ISBN 0-8242-0936-2
    1. Women—History—Chronology.   I. Brownstone, David M.
    II. H. W. Wilson Company. III. Title.
HQ1121.F65   1998
305.4'02'02—dc21                     94-34394
                                    CIP

Printed in the United States of America

07 06 05 04 03 02 01 00 99 98  10 9 8 7 6 5 4 3 2 1

The H. W. Wilson Company
950 University Avenue
Bronx, NY 10452

http://www.hwwilson.com

Also by Irene M. Franck and David M. Brownstone

*Timelines of the 20th Century*

*Timelines of the Arts and Literature*

*Timelines of War*

*People in the News*

*Sports People in the News*

*Parent's Desk Reference (2nd ed.: Parenting A–Z)*

*Women's Desk Reference*

*Dictionary of 20th Century History*

*20th Century Culture: A Dictionary of the Arts and Literature of Our Time*

*The Green Encyclopedia*

*Island of Hope, Island of Tears: The Great Migration Through Ellis Island to America Told by Those Who Made the Passage*

*The Silk Road: A History*

*To the Ends of the Earth: The Great Travel and Trade Routes of Human History*

*America's Ethnic Heritage series*

*Work Throughout History series*

*Great Historic Places of America*

*Natural Wonders of America*

*Historic Places of Early America*

*What's New for Parents*

*Where to Find Business Information*

*On the Tip of Your Tongue: The Word/Name/Place Finder*

*The Dictionary of Publishing*

# Contents

# Preface

This book is a chronology of women's history, from the Venus figurines of the dawn, the Egyptian queen Nefertiti, the Greek poet Sappho, and the alchemist Mary of Alexandria all the way to Susan B. Anthony and the Woman Suffrage Amendment, Marie Curie, Eleanor Roosevelt, Marian Anderson, Marilyn Monroe, *Roe v. Wade*, Aung San Suu Kyi, Anita Faye Hill, and Janet Reno. Thousands of other key women, works, and events—many of them long obscured and only now emerging—are included.

A chronology is a particularly useful way of looking at women in history, because it makes key people, works, and events so easy to reach and to see in the context of their times. That is extraordinarily important for women, who for so long were ignored by history and historians—so much so that many thought they had no history. Not so; women and their history are a massive part of the human experience. Our aim here has been to provide a useful—and browsable—way of illuminating the role of women in history that will appeal to readers of every age and background, and especially to the millions of women who feel that they want to know more—indeed, have a right to know more—about a history of their own.

The reader will find thousands of quite extraordinary women here, many of them people who broke their bonds to become major figures in their own times, many others whose stature became known only to later generations. Here are Assyrian princess Enheduanna, the earliest known poet of either sex; Hypatia, the Alexandrian mathematics professor murdered by a mob for her "pagan" views; Aphra Behn, the first woman to become a professional writer; Margaret of Denmark, who united Norway, Sweden, and Denmark in the 14th century; Hildegard of Bingen, the abbess and scholar known as the Sybil of the Rhine; Ellen Swallow Richards, notable founder of both ecology and home economics; and Madeleine Albright, the first woman to become U.S. secretary of state.

Here, too, are many notable women encountered in the course of developing our own historical works, especially in the sciences, in premodern history, and in non-Western civilizations—women such as Lei-tzu, the Chinese empress credited with discovering silkmaking techniques; Mary the Jewess, the 1st-century Alexandrian alchemist who laid the basis for modern laboratory chemistry; Irene of Athens, powerful regent of the Byzantine empire, who became a Greek Orthodox saint; Arabian queen Zubaydah (wife of caliph Harun al-Rashid), who founded numerous oasis towns en route to Mecca; Laura Bassi, the first woman to become a professor of physics; and Okuni, the Japanese dancer who founded the first kabuki company.

*The Wilson Chronology of Women's Achievements* covers the entire range of women's activity. Coverage is worldwide and spans all of human history, becoming deepest in recent centuries, where so much more reliable information is available.

The early part of the work (through 1499) is in simple chronological form, with subheads to indicate time periods, but with entries all in order by date. From 1500 through 1829, entries are grouped by decade and subdivided into four categories: Politics/Law/War, Religion/Education/Everyday Life, Science/Technology/Medicine, and Arts/Literature; within each category entries are given in chronological order. From 1830 on, entries are grouped year-by-year and subdivided into the same four categories; within those categories, general entries appear first, followed by birth entries and then death entries.

Throughout the work, in addition to the main chronological entries, we have also included sidebars:

- Quotations from women over the centuries, such as English mystic Julian of Norwich on writing her revelations, Dutch poet Ann Bijns on being single, Mary Wollstonecraft on women's rights, Angelina Grimké on abolition as a women's cause, Mattie Knight on inventing machines, Emmeline Pankhurst on women's militancy, Josephine St. Pierre Ruffin on black women's clubs, and Gloria Steinem on being 40.

- Excerpts from notable documents in women's history, such as Jacoba Felicie's defense of her practice of medicine in 14th-century Paris, Abigail Adams's request to "remember the Ladies" (and her husband's reply), Sojourner Truth's famous "Ain't I a Woman?" speech, and the Declaration of Sentiments and Resolutions passed at the 1848 Seneca Falls Women's Rights Convention.

- Descriptions or discussions of women's experiences or events that have helped shape women's lives, on topics as various as early priestesses, midwifery, attempted bans on women's religious singing, witch-hunting, childbed fever (which killed many women, including Mary Wollstonecraft), and equal rights vs. protective legislation for women.

Running heads on each page give the year (or time period) for ready reference. An index provides an additional way to locate women of interest. Throughout the book, we have kept abbreviations to a minimum, notably b. for born, d. for died, r. for reigned, c. for century, and ca. for circa, in addition to the standard B.C. and A.D. Where a birth or death date is unknown, we have used a ca. or ?; where neither date is known, we simply say "active" and give the general time period.

*The Wilson Chronology of Women's Achievements* is a revised and updated edition of our earlier *Women's World*. Our thanks to Wilson publications director Michael Schulze and editors Hilary Claggett, Joseph Sora, and Frank McGuckin for so capably seeing this book through the production process; to Mary Racette for her help in organizing the material; and as always to librarians throughout

the northeastern library network, in particular to the staff of the Chappaqua
Library—director Mark Hasskarl; the expert reference staff, including Martha
Alcott, Teresa Bueti, Maryann Eaton, Sue Farber, Carolyn Jones, Jane Peyraud,
Paula Peyraud, Carolyn Reznick, and Michele Snyder; and the circulation staff,
headed by Marilyn Coleman—for fulfilling our wide-ranging research needs.

IRENE FRANCK
DAVID BROWNSTONE
Chappaqua, New York

## 35,000 B.C.–2501 B.C.

Venus figurines—small statues of faceless pregnant women, with greatly exaggerated breasts and buttocks—were among the small carvings (*mobilier,* or portable art) created in Eurasia and Africa (from ca. 35,000 B.C. or earlier). Some have taken these as evidence of fertility cults, and of early goddess worship.

Both women and men were employed as professional dancers, attached to Egyptian temples (as early as 3000 B.C.).

Techniques of raising silkworms and spinning silk thread were developed in China; in ancient China, discoveries were traditionally credited to the emperor, at this time Huang Ti, but silk making (as well as weaving) was credited to the emperor's chief wife, Lei-tzu (ca. 2600 B.C.), popularly called Si Ling-chi (Lady of the Silkworm). She is supposed to have discovered the art after picking up a silkworm's cocoon in her mulberry garden and idly pulling it apart. China would keep silk making techniques secret for millennia.

## 2500 B.C.–2001 B.C.

Ritual dances involving sophisticated acting by professional performers, both women and men, seem to have been important in Egypt's religious observance (by 2500 B.C.). By that time, Egyptian records also suggest a dancing tradition outside Egypt, probably in Ethiopia; certainly professional dancers were employed by royal courts in China and India.

Enheduanna (active ca. 2300 B.C.), Assyrian princess, priestess, and poet, daughter of King Sargon of Akkad; she is the earliest writer, male or female, whose name and work have survived.

## 2000 B.C.–1501 B.C.

Oldest references to contraception found in Egyptian manuscripts (ca. 1900 B.C.), though how widely it was used, and how effective or harmful, is unclear.

The law code of the Middle Assyrian empire (ca. 1750 B.C.) was the first known regulation requiring women to be veiled, including daughters, wives, widows, concubines, and sacred prostitutes,

---

# Early Priestesses

In the second and third millennia B.C. in Mesopotamia, daughters of kings were, like Enheduanna, appointed to be moon-priestesses of Inanna-Ishtar, wearing special garments, living in and managing the temple, and performing religious ceremonies. The goddess Ishtar was herself possibly derived from the earlier Egyptian goddess Isis. Priestesses operated in other temples as well; some participated in an annual "Sacred Marriage," related to fertility rites, probably the origin of later "temple prostitution." They generally came from wealthy families, joining the temple when young and bringing to it a dowry. Generally unmarried and forbidden to bear children, they would often adopt daughters, to whom they would leave their dowries, often much increased through their commercial activities. With activities at different levels, a major temple might include several hundred women. Though such worship would gradually decline, priestesses continued to operate in the Mediterranean region for many centuries, perhaps mostly notably the Greeks' powerful Delphic oracle—called Pythia, Dragon Priestess of Earth (always a woman of at least 50)—and the Romans' Vestal virgins, who tended the sacred hearth of Vesta, goddess of the hearth.

even those who later married; common prostitutes, however, were not allowed to wear a veil but were obliged to leave their heads uncovered.

Hatshepsut (1503–1482 B.C.), Egyptian queen, daughter of Thutmose I; wife of her half-brother Thutmose II; regent for her son, Thutmose III; and then herself pharaoh, ruling Egypt for 21 years, one of the most powerful and historically important women of the Bronze Age. Among her accomplishments were the establishment of trading relations with Punt, on the Red Sea, and the commissioning of several massive monuments.

## 1500 B.C.–1001 B.C.

At least some women studied medicine at the medical school in Heliopolis, Egypt (by ca. 1500 B.C.). One female physician, Peneshet, became director of physicians; other women are shown preparing drugs. In addition, some women worked as embalmers, especially to handle the bodies of aristocratic women; before the advent of female embalmers, some families would hold women's bodies in the home for several days so they would not be misused by male embalmers, some with necrophiliac tastes.

Secular professional dancers, many of them women, were employed in Egypt, primarily to entertain the nobility (by ca. 1500 B.C.); they were often imported from Africa and India, many probably as slaves.

Nefertiti (active ca. 1379 B.C.), Egyptian queen, wife of King Akhenaton and a supporter of his new religion, worshiping the sun-god Aton.

The oldest books in the Old Testament of the Bible—Genesis, Exodus, Leviticus, Numbers, and Deuteronomy, collectively called the Pentateuch or (among Jews) the Torah—were written (by ca. 1200 B.C.). These introduced the story of Eve, Adam, and the Garden of Eden, which would help shape social attitudes toward women in the Judeo-Christian tradition, and codified various social assumptions about women, including the idea that a wife was her husband's property, as much as were his ox, his ass, and his servants; that a woman had virtually no independent legal standing; and that women's bodily processes were "unclean," with ritual purification required after menstruation, sexual intercourse, and childbirth. These and later books of the Bible also introduced many other women, some of them historical (or historically based) figures. Among those from this shadowy period were:

- Sarah, Abraham's wife, who pretended to be his sister so he would not be killed for her beauty; both Sarah and Abraham were sent away when her true identity was revealed; long childless, she bore Isaac and was later called "mother of the nation."

- Deborah, who as a prophet warned of an impending Canaanite invasion, and then with her general, Barak, led Israeli troops against a Canaanite army; another Israeli woman, Jael, reportedly killed the Canaanite general.

- Ruth, a widow who cared for her widowed mother-in-law, Naomi, and arranged for her welfare, only then herself remarrying, becoming the ancestor of King David. It was to Naomi that Ruth said the famous lines: "Whither thou goest, I will go; and where thou lodgest, I will lodge: thy people shall be my people, and thy God my God: Where thou diest, will I die, and there will I be buried: the Lord do so to me, and more also, if aught but death part thee and me." (Ruth 1:16–17)

Agamede (active 12th c. B.C.), Greek physician who, according to Homer, lived before the Trojan War and was skilled in using plants for medicinal purposes.

## 1000 B.C.–751 B.C.

Jezebel (active ca. 9th c. B.C.), princess of Tyre, who, according to the Old Testament, married Ahab, who became king of Israel; their daughter was Athaliah. A worshiper of the Phoenician gods, Jezebel was murdered by Israeli army commander Jehu.

Troupes of secular dancers, many of them women, worked as independent professionals in Egypt, touring to perform in the major cities (1st millennium B.C.).

Companies of dancers, mimes, acrobats, and jugglers toured Greece (as early as 9th c. B.C.); these included both men and women, though women would be barred from the stage in Greece's classic era.

d. Athaliah (?–ca. 837 B.C.), queen of Judah, daughter of Jezebel and Ahab, king of Israel, and wife of Jeham, king of Judah. According to the Old Testament, she took power after the death of her son, Ahaziah, and ruled for seven years, becoming Judah's only queen. Racine's 1691 play *Athalie* was based on this biblical story.

Sammuramat (Semiramis, active ca. 800 B.C.), possibly mythical queen of Assyria, wife of King Shamsi-Adad V and mother of King Adad-nirari III. Historian Diodorus Siculus identified her as Semiramis, who allegedly ruled alone for decades, founding Babylon.

Dido (active ca. 800 B.C.), princess of Tyre who, according to the *Aeneid*, fled to North Africa, there founding the city of Carthage; archaeological evidence suggests that the Phoenician city was founded between the traditional date (814 B.C.) and the mid-8th century B.C.

## 750 B.C.–501 B.C.

Early Hindu religious texts criticized prostitution (ca. 8th c. B.C.); women were generally regarded as sources of temptation and pollution, but prostitutes were involved in some religious rituals, notably in fertility cults.

Sappho (active ca. 610 B.C.–ca. 580 B.C.), Greek poet from the island of Lesbos, the best known of all the early Greek women who woe poets, though only fragments of her work survive, most notably *Hymn to Aphrodite*, seeking that goddess's help in seducing a young girl. Women-loving women are named lesbians after her.

Surviving pillars called *Asherahs* suggest that the ancient moon-goddess Ishtar was still worshiped in Jerusalem (586 B.C.).

Theano (active late 6th c. B.C.), Greek philosopher, mathematician, and physician; none of her original writings survive, but some (believed apocryphal) have been ascribed to her; she is thought to have been the wife or daughter of Pythagoras, and possibly to have run the Pythagorean school after his death.

Myrtis (active 6th–5th c. B.C.), Greek poet from Boeotia, said to have been the teacher of the male lyric poet Pindar; her work has been lost, except for paraphrases in Plutarch.

## 500 B.C.–401 B.C.

With the rise of Buddhism in India (ca. 500 B.C.) came nunneries for women, reportedly in response to a request by Buddha's aunt Mahaprajapati for a nunnery where women could lead an ascetic life of religious study and contemplation, free from family demands. The nuns were not considered equal within the faith, however, being subordinate to monks. Buddhist nuns (*theris*) began to write the poems that would later be collected in the *Therigatha* (ca. 80 B.C.). Though apparently restricted from higher religious learning, some women participated in religious and philosophical discussions in this period, including Gargi and Maitreyi.

Corinna (active 5th c. B.C.), Greek poet from Tanagra, noted for her choral lyric poems, who according to Pausanias (2nd c. B.C.) was considered a rival to her male contemporary Pindar.

Cleopatra (active ca. 5th c. B.C.), a physician, probably of Greek ancestry and possibly working in Alexandria; Hippocrates wrote of a physician named Cleopatra being concerned with the reproductive process.

Diotima of Mantinea (active ca. 5th c. B.C.), Greek philosopher who, according to Plato, was a priestess and a teacher of the philosopher Socrates.

Greek poet Telesilla, noted for her choral poetry, reportedly mobilized the women of Argos to resist invaders from Sparta (494 B.C.).

At the Battle of Marathon (490 B.C.), where the Greeks defeated the far more numerous Persian forces, Artemisia of Halicarnassus, a Greek ally, commanded several ships, according to Herodotus; she is the first female sea captain known by name.

Phaenarate began working as a midwife in Athens. Athenian midwives were required to have delivered children themselves before working as midwives. Phaenarate's son was Socrates (b. ca. 469 B.C.), who would call himself a "midwife to truth."

Aspasia of Miletos (5th c. B.C.), Greek courtesan whose home in Athens became a center for philosophical, artistic, and political discussion, reportedly including both Socrates and Plato, who said she had taught him the theory of love. Aspasia married Athens's powerful ruler Pericles, who personally and successfully defended her in the city-state's high court against charges of atheism and procuring.

Praxilla (active 5th c. B.C.), Greek poet from Sicyon, noted for her drinking songs and hymns, only fragments of which survive.

In Greek states of the 5th century, women's rights and lives were generally defined by their relationships to men—their fathers, husbands, and sons—with upper-class women often living in some seclusion in isolated women's quarters. Though they could sometimes hold property in their own name, notably as heiresses, women were unable to vote or hold public office. Said Athenian leader Pericles (430 B.C.): "The greatest glory of a woman is to be least talked about by men, whether they are praising you or criticizing you." Women did, however, exercise some public power as priestesses, in 5th-century B.C. Attica alone serving in some 40 cults.

*Lysistrata*, Aristophanes' comedy, introduced the idea of women using—or, rather, withholding—sex to try to force an end to war (411 B.C.). Ironically, no women appeared in the play; they were barred from the Greek stage, meaning that all the great women's roles of the classic Greek theater, including Antigone, Medea, Clytemnestra, and the rest, were originated by men. Women did, however, perform in touring companies, as dancing mimes, as temple dancers, and as dancer-prostitutes, called *heterae*.

---

## 400 B.C.–301 B.C.

Arete of Cyrene (active late 5th-early 4th c. B.C.), Greek philosopher of the Cyrenaic school of hedonism, founded by her father and teacher Aristippus, a student of Socrates; at her father's

---

# Early Midwives

For how many thousands of years no one knows, almost all babies were delivered by midwives; the Latin word obstetrix means simply "she who is present." In biblical times, a birthing stool—a semicircular *obstetrical* chair with the seat open in the middle—was used, though in some cultures the mother sat on the lap of the midwife, who was then able to knead the mother's belly, attempting to hasten birth, often while singing sacred songs. Midwives were generally older women, the main requirements being that she be honest, have a good character, have small hands with well-trimmed and clean nails, and have borne at least one child herself.

Greek midwives (perhaps working with male physicians) developed the technique of podalic version, in which the midwife manipulated a crosswise or feet-down infant in the womb into the proper position for normal headfirst birth. This technique saved the lives of thousands of mothers and infants in the Greek and Roman worlds; but in other parts of the world it was unknown, and in Europe during the Middle Ages it was forgotten, causing many to die in agony. If the child died in the womb, "child-breakers" were called in with knives, hooks, and forceps to remove the body piecemeal. If the mother died first, the child would be cut from the womb—but not while she lived, for the operation in those centuries caused virtually certain death.

Midwives were also often charged with taking the child to the father for acknowledgment; where the father did not accept the child, the midwife "exposed" the child in a public place, where it either died or was adopted by a passerby. Midwives also checked for virginity and fertility in young women, often as part of a sideline in matchmaking. In some places, they were also charged with cutting away parts of a girl's external sexual organs, a procedure called clitoridectomy or female genital mutilation, still performed in some cultures today.

Midwives also assessed whether a pregnancy existed, predicted the due date of the baby, and sometimes acted as abortionists. After the birth, midwives often stayed with the mother for a few weeks, advising on diet and child care. From such activities, some "medical midwives" developed into general medical advisers, often in consultation with male physicians, for women who for reasons of modesty felt unable to consult a male physician directly.

death she became the school's leading teacher, credited with more than 40 works, all now lost. Her son, also named Aristippus, was nicknamed "Mother-taught."

In India, the earlier practice of a bride and groom's families exchanging gifts equally with each other gave way (from ca. 400 B.C.) to the practice of the groom and his family giving the bride *stridhana* (specified maintenance, clothing, and adornments) and *sulka* (a bride price).

Agnodike (active last third of 4th c. B.C.), Greek physician who reportedly disguised herself as a man to study medicine under the physician Herophilus, at a time when Athenian women were barred from practicing medicine. After aiding a woman in labor, who had accepted help only after being assured that the physician was a woman, Agnodike was brought to trial for breaking the law, the penalty being death. But, reportedly, so many women protested that the judge changed the law, not only allowing women to practice medicine, but paying stipends to those who were most skilled.

Hipparchia (Hipparchus, active mid-4th c. B.C.), Greek philosopher of the Cynic school, as were her husband Crates and brother Metrocles; credited with writing philosophical treatises and also tragedies, and noted for wearing male attire, she is the only women to be profiled in Laertius's *Lives of the Philosophers* (3rd c. A.D.).

Axiothea of Phlius (active ca. 350 B.C.), Greek philosopher who, dressed in men's clothing, was one of two female pupils of Plato and later of his nephew and successor Speusippus.

Erinna (active 4th c. B.C.?), Greek poet from the island of Telos, best known for her poem *The Distaff*.

Anyte (active 4th c. B.C.), Greek poet noted for her pastoral epigrams.

According to Greek records, Krpi assumed power in northwest India after her husband's death, leading resistance to Alexander the Great (ca. 327–326 B.C.).

Nossis (active 4th-3rd c. B.C.), Greek poet from Locri, in southern Italy, noted for her epigrams.

Moero (Myro, active 4th-3rd c. B.C.), Greek poet from Byzantium, noted for her epigrams and lyric poetry.

In the Hellenistic world that survived Alexander the Great's death (ca. 323 B.C.), women had somewhat greater freedom in their personal lives, to move about in society, to act independently in economic and legal affairs, to obtain a divorce, and to become educated.

## 300 B.C.–201 B.C.

Buddhist hospitals developed a class of trained nurses; most were young men, but elderly women were trained to care for female patients (3rd c. B.C.).

The worship of Isis, dating back to at least 2500 B.C. in Egypt, reached Rome (by 200 B.C.), giving rise to the related worship of Vesta, whose sacred hearth would be tended by Vestal Virgins; these women served from childhood for 30 years, then were given dowries and allowed to marry, though most chose not to do so. If a Vestal Virgin lost her virginity while serving as a priestess, she could be buried alive.

## 200 B.C.–101 B.C.

Rome's Oppian Law (195 B.C.) attempted to restrict ownership and wearing of clothing and adornments, such as jewelry, that openly displayed wealth; many affluent women publicly protested the law and won its repeal.

Cho (Chuo) Wen-chün (179? B.C.–117? B.C.), Chinese poet; sale of her love poems helped support herself and her husband, poet Ssu-ma Hsiang-ju.

Rome's Voconian law (169 B.C.) prohibited a father, guardian, or husband from making a woman his heir, or from leaving her an amount greater than that of other joint heirs, though the law was often circumvented; before then daughters and sons traditionally were treated equally in a family inheritance.

Hsi-chün (active ca. 105 B.C.), Chinese poet, who wrote in lamentation after being cut off from her culture by a politically arranged marriage with an elderly Central Asian nomad king, K'un Mo, of the Wu-sun.

## 100 B.C.–51 B.C.

Elephantis (active ca. 1st c. B.C.), Greek physician, probably a courtesan. Pliny wrote of her skills as a midwife and her disagreements with midwife and physician Laïs; Galen noted her ability to cure baldness; possibly they were describing two different people of the same name.

Laïs (active ca. 1st or 2nd c. B.C.), Greek midwife and physician mentioned in Pliny's *Natural History* as disagreeing with the midwife Elephantis on the use of abortive drugs, on the causes of sterility or fertility, and the like; Laïs was said to have developed a treatment for rabies and fevers.

Sotira (active 1st c. B.C.), Greek physician who, according to Pliny, was noted for her remarkable cures; possibly the author of a surviving manuscript, *Gynaecia*.

Metrodora (active 1st or 2nd c. B.C.), Greek midwife whose writings survive in a work titled *Extracts from the Works of Metrodora Concerning the Diseases of Women*.

Salpe (active ca. 1st c. B.C.), Greek midwife from Lemnos whose remedies for various problems were described by Pliny.

*Natya-sastra* was produced in India (ca. 100 B.C.), outlining the stylized forms and gestures to be used by performers, many of them women, who combined music, drama, and dance in a single art form. Temple dancers called *devadasi* performed in Hindu temples of southern India and at various ceremonies, processions, and rites; they are best known for the Dance of Creation; they also acted as prostitutes in the service of Shiva, god of dance.

With the rise of the Mahayana strain of Buddhism (ca. 100 B.C.–ca. A.D.100), women—long regarded among Hindus as potential temptresses and polluters—came to be viewed as capable of living spiritually pure religious lives.

Poems by various Buddhist nuns (*theris*), some dating back to the 6th c. B.C., were collected in a work called the *Therigatha* (ca. 80 B.C.), in the first known anthology of women's literature.

d. Berenice II (?–80 B.C.), Greek-Egyptian queen, who survived her husband, Ptolemy XI, to briefly rule Egypt; she was murdered when she resisted Ptolemy Alexander, sent by the Romans to marry her and take power.

b. Cleopatra VII (69 B.C.–30 B.C.), Greek-Egyptian queen.

b. Drusilla Livia (later Julia Augusta, ca. 55 B.C.–A.D. 29), Roman empress and politician.

## 50 B.C.–1 B.C.

Olympias of Thebes (active 1st c. B.C.), Greek midwife who, according to Pliny, wrote various works, notably on the medicinal properties of various plants that could induce abortion or cure infertility.

Sulpicia (active 1st c. B.C.–1st c. A.D.), Roman poet, six of whose elegies survive.

b. Ban Jieyu (ca. 48 B.C.–ca. 6 B.C.), Chinese poet.

Egyptian forces of Cleopatra VII and her younger brother, Ptolemy, were defeated by Roman forces led by Julius Caesar at the Battle of the Nile (47 B.C.); Cleopatra and Ptolemy XIII remained corulers of Egypt under Rome.

Hortensia, daughter of orator Quintus Hortensius, made a public speech protesting the proposed taxing of women's property to support Rome's civil war, on the grounds that women were unable to participate in political life (42 B.C.); the speech itself survived only as described by others.

Roman general Marc Antony met Egyptian queen Cleopatra VII and followed her back to Egypt, beginning their liaison (42 B.C.). After they married (36 B.C.), the Roman Senate revoked all of his powers and ultimately went to war against Egypt (32 B.C.). Antony responded by sending a fleet and army to Greece, quartered near Actium. In a decisive sea battle off Actium, Antony and Cleopatra's forces were defeated by the Romans (31 B.C.), their remaining forces fleeing to Egypt, where their army defected to the Romans (30 B.C.).

d. Cleopatra VII (69 B.C.–30 B.C.), Greek-Egyptian queen, wife of Roman leader Marc Antony. Cleopatra and Antony committed suicide after losing their war with the Romans (31–30 B.C.).

b. Mary (ca. 20 B.C.–?), Jewish woman who became the mother of Jesus Christ, founder of Christianity; over the centuries, Mary herself became the object of great devotion, a female "role model" in an otherwise male-dominated Christian religion, especially after suppression of many earlier religions with their female deities.

Under Roman emperor Augustus, marriage laws (18 B.C., A.D. 9) required women ages 20 to 50 to marry and bear children, with penalties being imposed for those who did not; previously married women were to remarry 18 months after being divorced or 24 months after being widowed. Wives brought a dowry to the marriage, all or part of which might be returned in case of a divorce, depending on the circumstances. Either wife or husband could obtain a divorce without the consent of the other. Only a women, however, could be charged with adultery; if she was caught, her husband was obliged to divorce her or himself risk being prosecuted for "pandering." An adulterous woman could be killed by her husband. Rape was considered a crime against the family, represented by a woman's husband or father, and only they had the right to prosecute, an attitude that would persist into the 20th century.

b. Agrippina I (14 B.C.–A.D.33), Roman noblewoman and politician, granddaughter of the emperor Augustus.

*Lienu Zhuan*, a collection of biographies of noted Chinese women, was written by Liu Xiang (before 6 B.C.).

# A.D.

## 1–49

b. Agrippina II (15–59), empress of Rome, daughter of Agrippina I and Germanicus.

Agrippina I, granddaughter of the Roman emperor Augustus, accused the new emperor, Tiberius (19), of ordering the death of her husband, Germanicus, his adopted son; she became leader of the opposition to the emperor.

b. Valeria Messalina (22–48), Roman empress, wife of Claudius.

Mary Magdalene (active 1st c.), an early follower of Jesus Christ, according to New Testament accounts, present at key events, including the Crucifixion and the Resurrection. Modern biblical scholars find no textual support for the idea that she was a reformed prostitute.

Emperor Tiberius banished opposition leader Agrippina I from Rome (29).

d. Drusilla Livia (later Julia Augusta, ca. 55 B.C.–A.D. 29), Roman empress and politician, wife of the emperor Octavius (later Augustus) and mother of Tiberius; she held great power during the reigns of Augustus and Tiberius.

d. Agrippina I (14 B.C.–A.D. 33), Roman noblewoman and politician, granddaughter of the emperor Augustus; after unsuccessfully challenging the emperor Tiberius (19), she was banished from Rome (29), dying in exile.

b. Ban Zhao (Pan Chao, ca. 45–115), Chinese scholar and historian.

d. Valeria Messalina (22–48), Roman empress, wife of Claudius, who ordered her execution for allegedly plotting his overthrow. Her sexual life, in its main outlines rather typical of the male Roman nobility of her time, apparently contributed greatly to her adverse reputation, then and afterward.

Agrippina II married the Roman emperor Claudius (49 B.C.).

## 50–99

A Jewish women's ascetic monastic community was described as existing outside Alexandria, Egypt, near Lake Mareotis (ca. 50).

Pamphila, a historian working in Greek during the reign of the Roman emperor Nero (r. ca. 54–68), best known for her *Miscellaneous History*, which survives only in summaries by others.

d. Agrippina II (15–59), Roman empress, daughter of Agrippina I and Germanicus, sister of Caligula, wife of emperor Claudius, and mother of Nero, who ultimately ordered her murder.

d. Boudicca (Boadicea) (?–62), Icenian queen, who reportedly led an insurrection of the Iceni and Trinobantes peoples against Roman rule in southern England, achieving early successes but ultimately being defeated. She has been variously reported as dying in battle and taking poison after defeat.

Ascetic orders of widows apparently existed by the time of Timothy I (64–66) in the New Testament. From this period on, the ascetic life would exert a strong pull, and many other orders would be founded by women who chose sexual abstinence, either before marriage or after it.

## 100–149

Mary (Maria; Miriam) the Jewess (active 1st or 2nd c.), Alexandrian alchemist, who wrote as a prophet under the name "Miriam, sister of Moses." Her written works, the *Maria Practica*, survive only in fragments, but her practical laboratory inventions laid the basis for later chemistry. Her theories that metals were male and female, and that chemical processes were akin to sexual reproduction, had far less long-term impact.

During the great age of Sanskrit drama in India (ca. 100–ca. 800), women and men shared the stage, sometimes playing roles written for the opposite sex. Women would remain equals on the Indian stage until the arrival of the Muslims (after A.D. 1000), when they would be forced off the stage, until modern times.

Aspasia (active 1st c. or later), Greek physician whose work in obstetrics and gynecology, especially her emphasis on prevention, are known only through fragmentary references in the works of others.

Cecilia (active 2nd or 3rd c.), Roman Christian martyr who became the patron saint of music.

In India, the practice of a groom and his family giving the bride money and gifts gave way (by 2nd c.) to the practice of a bride's family supplying the groom and his family with a dowry. In the same period, divorce (always rare) came to be prohibited, remarriage of widows was discouraged, and women were barred from inheriting property.

d. Ban Zhao (Pan Chao, ca. 45–115), Chinese scholar and historian who completed the great *History of the Han Dynasty* after the successive deaths of the original authors, her father and brother (92). She also published a classic Confucian work on women's behavior, *Nu Chien (Advice for Women)*, and works of poetry. Skilled in astronomy and mathematics, Ban Zhao was teacher to the young Empress Teng.

b. Anna Galeria Faustina (ca. 125–176), Roman empress, daughter of the Roman emperor Antoninus Pius and Faustina (the elder).

## 150–199

b. Ts'ai Yen (Cai Yen; Cai Wenji, 162?–239?), Chinese poet.

d. Anna Galeria Faustina (ca. 125–176), Roman empress, wife of Emperor Marcus Aurelius, whom she accompanied on campaigns (170–174); she died en route to Rome's eastern provinces. He founded the Puellae Faustinanae, a school for poor girls, in her honor.

# Alchemy: Women's Work

Alchemy, basically the search for ways to make precious metals out of base ones, was from early times strongly associated with women and was held to have been founded by the goddess Isis. Perhaps the bestknown of the early alchemists, and one of the most notable early scientists, was Mary the Jewess, some of whose laboratory inventions are still used today. These include the three-part still, the *tribikos*, constructed of pottery and copper tubing, probably the world's first distillation device; the *kerotakis*, a device for creating and capturing vapors of metals such as mercury and arsenic; a metal alloy coated with black sulfide, still called *Mary's Black*; and the *balneum mariae*, also named for her, the prototype of the double boiler or autoclave.

## 200–249

The semilegendary Jingu ruled a kingdom in Japan (200–270) after the death of her husband, the emperor, according to the Japanese chronicle *Nihon shoki* (720).

d. Julia Domna (?–217), Roman empress and politician, second wife of the Emperor Septimius Severus, sister of Julia Maesa, and the mother of emperors Geta and Caracalla; during Caracalla's reign she held great power (212–217), taking over many imperial functions during his military campaigns; she was murdered or committed suicide the year he died.

d. Julia Maesa (?–ca. 226), Roman politician, sister of Julia Domna, mother of Julia Mamaea, and grandmother of emperors Elagabaeus and Alexander Severus. She strongly influenced the accession of each in turn, and held considerable power in Rome, although her daughter Julia Mamaea held far more power during the reign of Alexander Severus.

d. Julia Mamaea (?–235), Roman politician, daughter of Julia Maesa; she ruled as regent for her son, the emperor Alexander Severus. Both were assassinated by Roman soldiers, the army having blamed them for a Roman defeat in Persia (232).

d. Ts'ai Yen (Cai Yen; Cai Wenji, 162?–239?), Chinese poet, daughter of scholar-poet Ts'ai I; captured by Central Asian nomads, the Hsiung-nu, she was later ransomed back to China, but was forced to leave two sons behind, experiences about which she wrote in *Lamentations*. Her story was later much retold by others.

b. Helena (ca. 248–ca. 328), Roman saint.

## 250–299

In the Christian sect of Montanism, Priscilla and Maximilla were held to be prophets directly transmitting revelations of the Holy Spirit (mid-2nd c.).

Queen Zenobia took control of Palmyra (267), a city within the Roman sphere of influence, first as regent for her son, Vaballathus, then as full ruler, after the murder of her husband, King Odaenathus. Zenobia's forces took Egypt and defeated a Roman army sent against them.

Queen Zenobia's Palmyran forces were defeated by Roman forces under Aurelian at Immae, near Antioch, and at Emesa. After a siege of Palmyra, Zenobia surrendered, with all Palmyra's territories coming under Roman control (271–272).

Palmyra's Queen Zenobia again warred with Rome (272); Aurelian's Roman forces took and sacked Palmyra, taking Zenobia and her son, Vaballathus, to Rome as prisoners.

d. Zenobia (?–274), queen of Palmyra. After losing finally to the Romans (272), she had been taken to Rome, where she remarried and later died in exile.

b. Eulalia of Mérida (ca. 291–304), Spanish child martyr and saint.

Himiko, an unmarried priestess, ruled a kingdom in Japan (before 297), according to a Chinese chronicle.

## 300–349

Nina (Christiana; Christina, early 4th c.), Georgian saint, a slave who is credited with introducing Christianity to Georgia, inducing King Mirian to send for Christian missionaries.

Cleopatra (active 3rd or 4th c.), an alchemist, probably of Greek ancestry, working in Alexandria, described as a follower of the Alexandrian alchemist Mary the Jewess; Cleopatra's manuscript *Chrysopeia* (*Goldmaking*) survives in a later copy (10th-11th c.).

Theosobeia worked as an alchemist in Alexandria, with her brother Zosimus, author of an encyclopedia of alchemy (ca. 300).

d. Eulalia of Mérida (ca. 291–304), Spanish child martyr and saint believed to have been burned on a pyre under the anti-Christian edicts of Diocletian (303–304); she became patron saint of Oviedo and Mérida.

d. Eulalia of Barcelona (?–304), Spanish virgin saint martyred under Diocletian's anti-Christian edicts; patron saint of Barcelona and of sailors.

Lady Wei Shao wrote the first known Chinese treatise on calligraphy (320).

d. Helena (ca. 248–ca. 328), Roman saint, mother of the emperor Constantine, who made Christianity the Roman state religion (313); divorced by her husband (ca. 292), in her 80s she traveled to Palestine, building a basilica at Bethlehem and a monument at the Mount of Olives.

b. Paula (347–404), Roman saint.

## 350–399

Wealthy Christians often set aside a *diakonus* (Christ room), where they would help the ill, abandoned, or infirm (ca. 4th c.); the church also delegated men and women, deacons and deaconesses, to provide care in the patient's home, the origin of both modern nursing and social work.

Faltonia Betitia Proba (active 4th c.), Roman poet, whose only surviving work is a poem on the life of Jesus Christ.

Prabhavati Gupta served as regent in northwest India (ca. 365–ca. 440).

b. Hypatia of Alexandria (ca. 370–415), Egyptian-born mathematician and philosopher.

Fabiola, a convert to Christianity, founded a hospital at Ostia (390), Rome's port, with cofounders Paula and Paula's son-in-law Pammachius. This is the best-known of many public institutions (*hospices*) that Christians began to found (late 4th c.) to provide free care for the sick and needy; though these often provided more custodial than medical care and were largely staffed by untrained women volunteers, they were the forerunners of modern hospitals.

Etheriae Silviae wrote *Peregrinatio*, describing her pilgrimage to Jerusalem (late 4th c.).

b. Galla Placidia (Augusta) (ca. 390–450), empress of Western Rome, daughter of Theodosius I (the Great) and half-sister of emperor Honorius.

Vestal Virgins, who had tended the sacred hearth in Rome's Temple of Vesta, were formally disbanded (ca. 394) with the rise of Christianity.

b. Pulcheria (399–453), Eastern Orthodox saint, regent and then empress of the Eastern Roman Empire, daughter of Arcadius and sister of Theodosius II.

d. Fabiola (?–ca. 399), Roman nurse and physician, who founded a hospital at Ostia (390); she is also noted for her scholarship, especially her reading of Homer and Hebrew writings.

## 400–449

The Christian church, at its First Council of Toledo, attempted (without notable success) to ban women from religious singing, except where supervised by a priest or bishop (400).

---

# Hymns for Her

Early Christians generally disapproved of and often banned women's religious singing, probably continuing an earlier Jewish prohibition. Although St. Paul had said in *Ephesians* and *Colossians* (ca. 60–61) that Christians should glorify their Lord with "psalms, hymns, and spiritual songs," more weight seemed to be given to his comment in *1 Corinthians* (ca. 56): "The voice of woman leads to licentiousness." Despite this, women's choruses were found in many churches from at least the 3rd century. Bishop Paulus of Samosata (ca. 230–290) routinely led women's religious choirs, though only fragments of their music survive. A major figure in fighting against the prohibition was St. Ambrose of Milan (ca. 340–397), who stressed religious singing by the whole community, men and women. In *Peregrinatio* (late 4th c.), about her pilgrimage to Jerusalem, Etheriae Silviae described a nun's choir, an example of segregated male and female choirs in religious communities. Not all religious music was found in churches; St. John of Chrysostom, for example, praised private singing of hymns as soothing to mothers, children, workers, and weary travelers (ca. 407). Women also formed their own religious singing circles, a development the church found threatening; as a result the First Council of Toledo (400) attempted to ban women—even "consecrated virgins or widows"—from religious singing, except in the presence of a bishop or priest.

Hypatia of Alexandria reportedly became director of the Neoplatonic school at Alexandria, at age 31 (ca. 400).

The West finally learned the technique of making silk, kept secret within China for many centuries; according to tradition, a Chinese princess en route westward to marry a Central Asian prince (ca. 400), having been warned that only this way would she have silk for her wardrobe, hid silkworms' eggs and mulberry seeds in her headdress, where Chinese border guards did not dare search.

d. Paula (347–404), Roman saint who turned to religion after losing her husband and eldest child, and who traveled to Syria, Egypt, and Palestine in search of religious guidance, inspired by St. Marcella. Accompanied by her daugher Eustochium, Paula settled near Bethlehem, founding two monasteries, one for her spiritual guide St. Jerome, the other for herself and her companions.

Roman aristocrat Galla Placidia was taken by Visigoth leader Alaric, when his forces sacked Rome (410). After his death later that year, he was succeeded by Ataulf, whom she married (414).

d. Marcella (?–410), Roman saint, an early patrician Christian who much influenced other Roman women, notably St. Paula. She died from beatings suffered when Alaric's Goths sacked Rome.

Pulcheria became regent of the Eastern Roman Empire for her brother, Theodosius II (414–416).

d. Hypatia of Alexandria (ca. 370–415), Egyptian-born mathematician, philosopher, and teacher.

Roman aristocrat Galla Placidia returned to Rome after the death of her husband, Visigoth leader Ataulf, and married Roman general Constantius (417).

b. Genevieve (ca. 420–ca. 500), Frankish saint.

Roman emperor Honorius named his halfsister, now Galla Placidia Augusta, as empress of the Western Roman Empire; her husband became the co-emperor Constantius III (421).

## 450–499

On the death of her brother Theodosius II, Pulcheria became empress of the Eastern Roman Empire, ruling jointly with her husband, Marcian (450–453).

Theodosia (active 5th c.), Roman physician and saint, a Christian martyr who ministered especially to the poor.

In Hindu India, the cult of individual devotion (*bhakti*) developed (5th c.), a movement producing female saints such as Avvaiyar and Karaikkal Ammaiyar, and also inspiring *bhakti* poetry. However, access to higher religious learning was restricted to the male Brahman priests.

d. Galla Placidia (Augusta) (ca. 390–450), empress of the Western Roman Empire, daughter of Theodosius I (the Great), halfsister of the emperor Honorius, and successively wife of Visigoth

# Hypatia of Alexandria

Daughter of Theon, a mathematician-astronomer who worked at Alexandria's famous museum, Hypatia studied at Athens with Plutarch the Younger and his daughter, Asclepegeneia, before herself becoming a teacher in Alexandria (ca. 400). She lectured widely, on mathematics, astronomy, and philosophy, including the teachings of Plato and Aristotle, and was especially talented in dealing with algebra. She wrote at least three books on mathematics and astronomy, most notably a commentary on the algebra of Diophantus, but nothing survives. She is also credited with mechanical and technological skill; Synesius of Cyrene described two devices he said he invented with her assistance: a hydrometer (hydroscope) for measuring the specific gravity of liquids and a silver astrolabe to fix the positions of the sun and the stars. Hypatia has also been credited with developing a device for measuring water level and another for distillation. Accused of pagan, anti-Christian teaching, she was killed by an Alexandrian mob, traditionally said to have been whipped into a frenzy by Bishop Cyril of Alexandria.

leader Ataulf and Constantius III, with whom she became co-emperor (421). She continued to exercise considerable influence after being succeeded by her son, Valentinian (425).

With Attila and his Hun forces threatening Paris (451), Genevieve persuaded the city's inhabitants that flight would gain them nothing, as their proposed places of refuge would be devastated, while Paris would survive, as it did; she was later regarded as Paris's patron saint.

b. Brigid (of Kildare) (ca. 452–ca. 523), Irish abbess and saint.

d. Pulcheria (399–453), regent and then empress of the Eastern Roman Empire, daughter of Arcadius and sister of Theodosius II; a devout and very orthodox Christian who strongly opposed Nestorius and other Christian dissidents, she became an Eastern Orthodox saint.

b. Clotilda (470–545), Frankish queen and saint.

b. Scholastica (ca. 480–543), Italian saint.

Clotilda succeeded in converting her husband, the Frankish king Clovis, to Christianity. He and some thousands of his followers were baptized in a mass ceremony at Rheims (495).

b. Theodora (497–548), Byzantine actress and dancer who became an empress of the Eastern Roman Empire, as wife of Justinian.

## 500–549

d. Genevieve (ca. 420–ca. 500), Frankish saint who is credited with inspiring Parisians to hold out against the attacking Huns (451), becoming the city's patron saint.

b. Radegunde (ca. 519–ca. 587), German-born Frankish queen and saint.

d. Brigid (of Kildare) (ca. 452–ca. 523), Irish abbess and saint, who founded schools and convents, including the first Irish women's religious community at Kildare, also noted for treating victims of leprosy.

d. Scholastica (ca. 480–543), Italian saint, twin sister of St. Benedict, who founded the first known Benedictine monastery for nuns, near her brother's famous monastery at Monte Cassino. Under her brother's influence, many monasteries founded infirmaries to care for the ill and the poor.

d. Clotilda (470–545), Frankish queen and saint, who converted her husband, Clovis, and many of his people to Christianity (495).

d. Theodora (497–548), Byzantine actress and dancer who became an empress of the Eastern Roman Empire, as wife of Justinian. From the time of his accession (527), she played a substantial role in Byzantine affairs, with special emphasis on improving the status of women and children and protecting them from predators.

## 550–599

b. Khadijah (ca. 564–619), Arabian first wife of Mohammed.

b. Al-Khansa (Tumadir bint Amr ibn al Harith ibn al Sharid, 575–646), Arabian poet.

A Turkish princess, coming to China as a bride (ca. 586), helped introduce Persian and Central Asian modes of music to East Asia, bringing with her a Persian musician who played the short lute, supplemented by various Central Asian ensembles ("Seven Orchestras").

d. Radegunde (ca. 519–ca. 587), German-born princess who was captured by and then married to

# Theodora: Superstar

Before her marriage to emperor Justinian, Theodora was a noted pantomimist, a superstar of the Eastern Roman theater. Working as soloists on stage, these performers—in masks and elaborate costumes—wordlessly acted out stories, accompanied by dancers and musicians. Unlike the theater of ancient Greece, women shared the stage with men in Rome, the emphasis over the centuries being less on great plays than on variety entertainment, including dance, mime, acrobatics, juggling, animal training, and gymnastics.

Clotaire, the Frankish king of Neustria; fleeing his violence, she found sanctuary in a monastery, later founding the Holy Cross Monastery at Poitiers and hospitals for the poor and the ill.

d. Agnes (?–before 589), Frankish saint who joined Queen Radegunde in retreat at Poitiers, becoming abbess of the Holy Cross convent; her fame was spread in the writings of poet Venentius Fortunatus.

According to tradition, an Irish princess, St. Dymphna, first began caring for mentally ill and mentally retarded people in Gheel, Belgium (late 6th c.), still a center for such care.

## 600–649

The two wives of King Srong Tsan Gampo, one Chinese and the other Nepalese, are by tradition credited with introducing sculpture to Tibet (ca. 7th c.).

b. Fatimah (Al-Zahra) (ca. 606–632), Arabic religious figure, daughter of Mohammed and his first wife, Khadijah.

b. 'A'ishah Bint Abi Bakr (613–678), Arabian Muslim religious and political figure, the third wife of the prophet Mohammed.

b. Hilda of Whitby (616–680), Northumbrian princess, abbess, and saint.

d. Khadijah (ca. 564–619), Arabian first wife of Mohammed, whom she supported after his first vision (ca. 610), which led him to found the Islamic religion. Already twice-widowed, she was a wealthy trader who had employed Mohammed, 15 years her junior, to lead her caravans, later marrying him (ca. 604) and bearing him six children, including Fatimah.

b. Wu Hou (Wu Chao) (625–705), empress of China.

Suiko was purported to be the first of six female rulers in Japan to use the title *tenno* (emperor) (592–628).

b. Bathildis (Balthilde, ca. 630–680), English-born saint, queen, and then regent of Neustria, the western Frankish kingdom.

d. Fatimah (Al-Zahra, ca. 606–632), Arabic religious figure, daughter of Islam's founder, Mohammed, and Khadijah, and wife of 'Ali; after a later schism in the Muslim world, she would become revered by the Shi'ite sect, who believed hers to be the true line of descent; her descendants, the Fatimids, established a caliphate (10th–11th c.).

Kogyoku was said to be the second of six Japanese female rulers to use the title *tenno* (emperor) (642–645), and again (655–661) under the name Saimei.

d. Al-Khansa (Tumadir bint Amr ibn al Harith ibn al Sharid, 575–646), Arabian poet noted for the poems lamenting the death in battle of two brothers, Sakhr and Muawiya.

## 650–699

Paris's famous hospital Hôtel Dieu was founded (ca. 650) by the Augustinian Sisters, a nursing order.

Wu Hou, originally the concubine of emperor T'ai Tsung, married his successor, Kao Tsung (655), systematically removed all opposition, and then emerged as de facto ruler of China (by 660).

Muslim leader 'A'ishah Bint Abi Bakr, Mohammed's widow, led an army against the forces of Caliph Ali; she was defeated and captured at the Battle of the Camel (656), near Basra, then retired from politics.

# Muslim Women Out in the World

'A'ishah Bint Abi Bakr, widow of Mohammed, was not rare in taking the field and participating fully in the life of her time. In early Muslim times, women were not veiled or secluded but lived in the world, as poets, nurses, warriors, and the like. Mohammed's wives were, shortly before his death (632), veiled and secluded, apparently to protect them after he became famous. But the general veiling and exclusion of Muslim women came only later, after the main early Islamic conquests in the century after Mohammed's death.

On the death of her husband, Neustrian ruler Clovis II, Bathildis became regent (ca. 656); she attempted unsuccessfully to unify the western Frankish kingdoms of Neustria, Burgundy, and Austrasia. She later retired from power to the convent of Notre Dame de Chelles (ca. 664), which she had founded.

d. 'A'ishah Bint Abi Bakr (613–678), Arabian Muslim religious figure, third wife of Mohammed, who lost the Battle of the Camel (656).

d. Audrey (Ethelreda, ?–679), English saint, sister of Sts. Withburga, Sexburga, and Ethelburga; she founded two abbeys at Ely, one for men and one for women (ca. 672), serving as abbess until her death.

d. Hilda of Whitby (616–680), Northumbrian princess, abbess, and saint, founder of a monastery for both men and women at Whitby (Streaneshalch), in Yorkshire, on land donated by King Osiwin; among the people to live and work at the monastery were St. John of Beverley and the poet Caedmon.

Aelfleda succeeded Hilda as abbess of Whitby (680); her own mother joined the convent under Aelfleda's rule.

d. Bathildis (Balthilde, ca. 630–680), English-born saint and queen of Neustria, wife of Clovis II, after his death regent and effective ruler of this and other western Frankish territories (ca. 656–ca. 664). She had come to Clovis's house originally as a slave, captured by pirates and sold to the Franks.

Wu Hou, long de facto ruler of China, deposed her son, Chung Tsung, soon after he succeeded to the throne (683), replacing him with another son, Jui Tsung, who was entirely malleable, continuing her de facto rule.

d. Wandru (Waldetrude, ?–688), Frankish saint who founded a convent at Mons, where several of her family also served, devoting her life to helping the poor.

Wu Hou openly took control as empress of China, ruling alone (690–705), the first woman ever to do so in China.

Jito was the third of six female rulers of Japan said to have used the title *tenno* (emperor) (690–697).

St. Adela founded a convent at Palatiolum (Pfalsel) (690), becoming its first abbess.

Laila Akhyaliyya (active late 7th c.), Arabian poet noted for her poems lamenting the death of her lover, the robber chief Tauba.

## 700–749

During the T'ang dynasty in China, when westward routes were reopened (ca. 700), many musicians, dancers, and other performers traveled eastward to China, where Persian and Central Asian modes of music and dress became the fashion; among the most popular were Sogdian "twirling girls," who danced atop a series of rolling balls, dressed in brightly colored robes and loose trousers.

b. Komyo (701–760), Japanese empress.

d. Wu Hou (Wu Chao, 625–705), empress of China, wife of Emperor Kao Tsung, long de facto ruler, and later the only woman to rule directly as empress of China (690–705). She was eventually deposed by a palace coup that reinstalled Chung Tsung as emperor (705) but was unharmed and died later in the year.

Gemmei was said to be the fourth Japanese female ruler to use the title *tenno* (emperor) (707–715); she was succeeded by the fifth woman, Gensei (715–724).

b. Rabi'ah al-'Adawiyyah (ca. 712–ca. 801), Arabian religious scholar, a Sunni Muslim.

d. Aelfleda (?–713), English saint, abbess of Whitby; daughter of Northumbrian king Oswy and granddaughter of St. Edwin.

China's first national school of the performing arts (714), called the School of the Pear Garden, was founded by Emperor Hsüan Tsung. There men and women (some destined to be courtesans) learned all the performing arts, including acting, singing, and dancing. Chinese female and male performers would have such professional training for centuries.

d. Irmina (?–716), Frankish saint, daughter of Dagobert II and sister of St. Adela; after her fiancé's death, Irmina founded a convent under Benedictine rule at Trier.

d. Adela (?–735), Frankish saint, daughter of Dagobert II; inspired by her sister, St. Irmina, she founded a convent at Palatiolum (Pfalsel) (690).

Koken was the last of the six Japanese female rulers said to have used the title *tenno* (emperor) (749–758), and again (764–770) under the name of Shotoku.

## 750–799

Karraikal Ammaiyar (active 8th c.), Indian religious poet, specializing in *bhakti* (devotional) poetry, a popular form among Indian women for centuries.

b. Irene of Athens (ca. 752–803), wife of Byzantine emperor Leo IV, regent on his death, and then emperor and sole ruler of Byzantium.

d. Komyo (701–760), Japanese empress noted for establishing temples, nunneries, and charitable homes for the sick and poor.

b. Hsüeh T'ao (768–831), Chinese poet and singer.

Al-Khaizuran became the wife and queen of Al-Mahdi, when he took power as caliph (774), emerging as a considerable political figure in her own right; originally a slave, she had already borne him three children.

Irene of Athens became regent for her son, Constantine VI, on the death of her husband, the Byzantine emperor Leo IV (780).

d. Lioba (Truthgeba; Liobgetha, ?–782), Anglo-Saxon abbess and saint, whose correspondence with Boniface led to her and 30 other nuns joining him at Mainz; she became abbess of the convent of Tauberbischofsheim, making it an important center and establishing numerous daughter-houses.

Irene of Athens, then regent of Byzantium, caused the Greek Orthodox Church Council of Nicaea to restore the use of icons in church practice (787). She ultimately became a saint of the Greek Orthodox Church.

Constantine VI of Byzantium came of age to take the throne and banished his mother, Irene of Athens, previously regent, from the Byzantine court (790–792).

d. Al-Khaizuran (?–790), Arabian queen, originally a Yemeni slave of Al-Mahdi, then his wife and queen, a considerable political figure; she was the mother of caliphs Al-Hadi and Harun al-Rashid.

Irene of Athens, who had been allowed to return to the Byzantine court (792), mounted a palace coup against her son, Constantine VI, had him blinded, and took power as empress, ruling for five years (797–802).

## 800–849

*Wulf and Eadwacer*, the lament of an anonymous female poet, was written in Anglo-Saxon England (ca. 800).

d. Rabi'ah al-'Adawiyyah (ca. 712–ca. 801), Arabian religious scholar, a Sunni Muslim whose influential writings centered on mystical love in the Sufi tradition; she spent her later years living as an ascetic.

d. Irene of Athens (ca. 752–803), empress of Byzantium, wife of the Byzantine emperor Leo IV, regent on his death, and eventually sole ruler of Byzantium (797), before being deposed in a palace coup (802), dying in exile on the island of Lesbos.

b. Ono no Komachi (ca. 810?–ca. 880), Japanese poet.

d. Zubaydah (?–831), Arabian queen, wife of caliph Harun al-Rashid; as presented in *The Thousand and One Nights* a semilegendary figure, but in actuality a very real patron of the arts. She is perhaps best remembered for having built numerous oasis towns on the road to Mecca, around which grew several surviving cities, some named after her.

d. Hsüeh T'ao (768–831), Chinese poet and singer, a "singing girl" at the imperial court from her youth; her *Chin River Collection* of some 500 lyrics survived into the 14th century but was then lost.

d. Alfrida (Etheldreda, ?–ca. 840), Mercian princess and saint, daughter of King Offa; she was a religious recluse on the island of Croyland for four decades.

b. Yü Hsüan-chi (ca. 843–868), Chinese poet, nun, and courtesan.

## 850–899

d. Pope Joan (?–858), purported German-English pope; according to medieval chronicles, she was a northern European scholar who, disguised as a man, was made a cardinal and then pope (855), reportedly being stoned to death when her sex was revealed after she gave birth to a child. Pope Clement VIII declared the story apocryphal (1601); later commentators have suggested that the story was inspired by tales of some powerful 10th-century women, notably Theodora the Senatrix and her daughter Marozia, who influenced papal elections.

d. Yü Hsüan-chi (ca. 843–868), Chinese poet, a noted literary courtesan, who lived for a time as a Taoist nun.

b. Lade Ise (875?–938?), Japanese poet.

d. Ono no Komachi (ca. 810?–ca. 880), Japanese poet who was portrayed in at least three Noh plays.

b. Olga (890–969), Russian ruler and saint.

## 900–949

Aethelflaed, called "Lady of the Mercians," became sole ruler of West Mercia on the death of her husband, Ethelred (911); she had effectively ruled the region for some years by then.

Aethelflaed's forces defeated Danish occupying armies in eastern England, retaking Derby and Leicester (917).

d. Aethelflaed (Lady of the Mercians, ?–918), Saxon queen, who ruled West Mercia with her husband, Ethelred, until his death (911), then alone; daughter of Alfred the Great, she and her brother, Wessex King Edward, co-commanded English forces engaged in reconquering parts of England from the Danes, until her death.

b. Hrotsvitha (Roswitha) of Gandersheim (ca. 953–972), Saxon abbess and writer.

d. Lade Ise (875?–938?), Japanese poet and lady-in-waiting to Empress Onshi; many of her poems were included in the imperial anthology *Kokinshu* (ca. 905).

b. Adelaide (931–999), Italian queen and saint, later regent of Germany.

Olga became regent of Kiev (945–964), after the assassination of her husband, Prince Igor I, ruling for his son Svyatoslav.

## 950–999

Olga, regent of Kiev, was baptized, playing a major role in bringing Christianity to Russia. She later became the first Russian saint of the Orthodox Church. Her grandson, Vladimir, carried forward the transition to Christianity.

b. Sei Shonagon (ca. 966–ca. 1013), Japanese writer.

d. Olga (890–969), regent of Kiev (945–964) and first Russian saint of the Orthodox Church.

d. Hrotsvitha (Roswitha) of Gandersheim (ca. 953–972), Saxon abbess and writer, the writer of the six plays *Gallicanus, Dulcitius, Callimachus, Abraham, Pafnutius,* and *Sapientia,* as well as many poems, including verse histories of her convent and of Holy Roman Emperor Otto the Great.

b. Murasaki Shikibu (ca. 978–ca. 1030), Japanese writer.

As regent, the Italian queen Adelaide became effective ruler of the Holy Roman Empire (991–994).

d. Adelaide (931–999), Italian ruler and saint, queen of Italy (947–950) until the death of her husband, Lothair; ruler of Italy again, this time as Holy Roman Empress beside her second husband, Otto I of Germany (962–973), and later viceroy of Italy and regent (991–994), effective ruler of the Holy Roman Empire. She was a prime force in the development of the Clunaic monastic order.

## 1000–1024

*The Wife's Lament,* an anonymous Old English poem, survives in a manuscript (ca. 1000).

b. Sarashina (ca. 1008–1060), Japanese diarist.

d. Sei Shonagon (ca. 966–ca. 1013), Japanese writer best known for her *Makura no sashi* (ca. 1000–1013), a diverse body of material described as a "pillow book," for browsing.

d. Adelaide (Alice of Guelders, ?–ca. 1015), Frankish saint, abbess of the convents of Villich, near Bonn, and of Our Lady of the Capitol, at Cologne.

Murasaki Shikibu published *The Tale of Genji* (*Genji monogatari*), often regarded as the world's first complete novel and perhaps the most notable of all Japanese literary works (ca. 1020).

Japanese diarist Sarashina wrote *Sarashina Nikki* (1021).

b. Agnes of Poitou (1024–1077), empress and later regent of the Holy Roman Empire (1056–1062).

## 1025–1049

Aelgifu (active ca. 1010–1037), Saxon aristocrat, regent of Norway (ca. 1030–1035); the companion of Canute the Great, king of Denmark and England, she became regent when their young son, Sweyn, was named king of Norway, but was deposed by an insurrection (1035), then returning to England.

d. Murasaki Shikibu (ca. 978–1030), Japanese novelist, diarist, and poet who created *The Tale of Genji*.

b. Ma-gcig Lab-sgron (1044–1131), Tibetan Buddhist nun.

b. Matilda ("La Gran Contessa," 1046–1115), Countess of Tuscany.

## 1050–1074

Walladah bint al-Mustakfi (active 11th c.), Spanish Muslim poet.

Upon the death of her husband, Holy Roman Emperor Henry III, Agnes of Poitou became regent (1056–1062), ruling on behalf of her young son, Henry IV, until deposed by an insurrection.

d. Sarashina (ca. 1008–1060), Japanese diarist who wrote *Sarashina Nikki* (1021).

## 1075–1099

On the death of her mother, Beatrice of Bar, with whom she had ruled jointly, Matilda ruled Tuscany and related territories on her own (1076).

At Canossa, the seat of Matilda of Tuscany, Holy Roman Emperor Henry IV and Pope Gregory VII met in a classic confrontation (1077). Matilda of Tuscany continued to strengthen her alliance with Gregory.

d. Agnes of Poitou (1024–1077), empress of the Holy Roman Empire, wife of Henry III and mother of Henry IV; as regent she ruled the empire (1056–1062).

Matilda of Tuscany, in alliance with the papacy, led her forces in the field against those of excommunicated Holy Roman Emperor Henry IV (1080–1106).

---

# Footbinding

The practice of footbinding—tightly wrapping young girls' feet to stunt growth and produce small feet—developed in China by the 11th century, small feet being regarded as attractive, erotic, and a sign of status and wealth. Starting at ages four to eight, a girl's four smaller toes would be bent and bound backward under her feet, sometimes so tightly as to lead to atrophy, putrefaction, and infection. The feet would then be permanently crippled, their arches broken, and for life the woman would have difficulty walking without help, meaning she was also largely confined to women's quarters. Footbinding was generally practiced in wealthier families, since poorer families generally could not afford the loss of a girl's labor, but some poor families also bound the feet of girl children, hoping to make an advantageous match for them. Most widespread in China from the 16th to 19th centuries, the practice of footbinding was not outlawed until 1911, with the revolution that produced the Chinese Republic.

b. Anna Comnena (1083–1153), Byzantine historian and writer, daughter of Irene Dukas and the Byzantine emperor Alexius Comnenus.

b. Li Ch'ing-chao (1084?–ca. 1151), Chinese poet.

d. Trotula (?–1097?), Italian physician, among the best-known and most influential teachers at Salerno's famed medical school.

b. Hildegard of Bingen (1098–ca. 1178), German abbess, scholar, and saint.

## 1100–1124

b. Héloïse (1101–1164), French abbess and writer.

b. Matilda of England (1102–1167), daughter of Henry I of England, designated by him as his rightful heir to the English throne.

b. Melisend (ca. 1105–1160), queen of the crusader state of Jerusalem, daughter of Morphia and Baldwin II of Jerusalem.

d. Matilda ("La Gran Contessa," 1046–1115), Countess of Tuscany, daughter of Boniface of Tuscany and Beatrice of Bar; she was a key Italian ally of the papacy in its struggle with the Holy Roman emperors.

b. Eleanor of Aquitaine (1122–1202), duchess of Aquitaine, who became successively queen of France and of England, also mother of England's kings Richard (the Lion-Hearted) and John.

d. Frau Ava (?–1127), the first known German woman to become an author; she wrote religious poetry and books based on the New Testament, such as *The Life of Jesus*.

## 1125–1149

b. Rosalia (ca. 1130–ca. 1160), Sicilian saint.

As provided for by Baldwin II, on his death his daughter Melisend and her husband, Fulk V of Anjou, jointly ruled the crusader state of Jerusalem as his successors (1131).

d. Ma-gcig Lab-sgron (1044–1131), Tibetan Buddhist nun, a noted spiritual leader.

On the death of Henry I of England, Stephen I seized power, opposing the claim of Henry's daughter, Matilda, whom Henry had designated as his rightful heir to the throne. A series of dynastic conflicts began (1135–1154).

Hildegard became abbess of Diessem (1136), later moving her convent to Bingen, and founding several other convents.

On the death of her father, William X, Eleanor of Aquitaine inherited Aquitaine and Poitiers. She soon married Louis VII and became queen of France, beginning her career as one of the most astute practitioners of statecraft in her time (1137).

Matilda's army invaded England, pressing her claim to the throne; after early victories, including the capture of rival claimant Stephen, Matilda's forces were defeated (1139–1148). She retired

# Dame Trot

The 11th-century physician Trotula was known to generations of students as "Dame Trot." A pioneer in the area of preventive health, she emphasized the importance of cleanliness and stressed nonradical treatments such as baths, ointments, massages, and balanced diet. Her works embodying these ideas, notably *Practica Brevis* and *De Compositione Medicamentorum*, were hand-copied throughout Europe for several centuries, and her ideas were later incorporated into the widely popular medical work *Regimen sanitatis salernitatum* (13th c.), a basic medical reference used for at least four centuries after her death. Trotula also wrote a work specifically on women's health, *Passionibus Mulierum Curandorum* (*The Diseases of Women*), a work nicknamed *Trotula Major*. She has been credited with pioneering in the surgical repair of the perineum, the tissue often ruptured in childbirth.

to Normandy, though the dynastic wars continued in England.

b. Marie de France (ca. 1140–1200), French poet.

b. Countess Beatriz de Die (ca. 1140–?), Provençal poet and troubadour, five of whose poems survive.

Melisend of Jerusalem jointly ruled Jerusalem with her son, Baldwin III (1143–1160).

Eleanor of Aquitaine and her husband, Louis VII of France, fought together during the Second Crusade; her retinue included several hundred female soldiers and nurses (1147–1149).

Anna Comnena published the *Alexiad* (after 1148), her 15-volume prose-poem history of the reign of her father, Byzantine Emperor Alexius I (Comnenus).

## 1150–1174

Melisend of Jerusalem founded the abbey at Bethany (ca. 1150).

Hildegard of Bingen produced *Scivias*, the best known of her several works on cosmology (1151).

d. Li Ch'ing-chao (1084?–ca. 1151), Chinese poet; some 50 of her estimated six volumes of lyrics survive.

Ultimately irreconcilable, Eleanor of Aquitaine and Louis VII of France had their marriage annulled. Within two months, she married Henry of Normandy (1152), who would found England's Plantagenet line.

d. Anna Comnena (1083–1153), Byzantine historian and writer, daughter of Irene Dukas and Byzantine Emperor Alexius Comnenus; she was the author of the *Alexiad* (after 1148).

Henry of Normandy, son of Matilda and grandson of Henry I, won the Battle of Wallingford (1154), finally making good Matilda's claim to the English throne and ending the dynastic wars. He became Henry II of England, making Eleanor of Aquitaine, his wife, queen of England. Their own long personal and political contest would end only with his death (1189).

b. Hojo Masako (1154–1225), Japanese religious figure, wife of the shogun.

d. Rosalia (ca. 1130–ca. 1160), Sicilian saint, niece of King William II, who at age 14 left her home to live as a religious hermit; the patron saint of Palermo.

d. Melisend (ca. 1105–1160), queen of the crusader state of Jerusalem, daughter of Morphia and Baldwin II of Jerusalem, wife of Fulk of Anjou and Jerusalem, and mother of Baldwin III.

d. Héloïse (1101–1164), French abbess and writer, best known for her love of Abelard, known to the world largely through their letters to one another.

d. Elizabeth of Schönau (?–1164), German saint, a nun at Schönau Abbey on the Rhine, who recorded her visions in *The Book of the Ways of God*.

d. Matilda of England (1102–1167), daughter of Henry I of England, designated by him as his rightful heir to the English throne; her claim ultimately failed, but that of her son succeeded; he became England's Henry II.

Eleanor of Aquitaine took the side of her sons Richard (the Lion-Hearted) and John against her

---

# Héloïse and Abelard

While being educated at the University of Paris, a rarity for women at the time, Héloïse began a love affair with her teacher Abelard, a leading philosopher of the day and, like all European university teachers of the time, supposedly a celibate cleric. After she bore him a son, they secretly married; even so her uncle and guardian, canon Fulbert, became so enraged at the affair that he had Abelard castrated. Abelard then entered the abbey at St. Denis and convinced Héloïse to enter a convent, becoming abbess of Paraclete. A dozen years later she came upon *Historia calamitatum Abaelardi*, Abelard's autobiographical work in letter form, which described his tragic love for Héloïse. This triggered a famous series of letters between the two, first published in Latin as *Lettres d'Abelard et d'Héloïse* in 1616, about their love and despair and their attempts to rebuild their lives under spiritual discipline.

husband, Henry II of England, and lost (1173). Captured while fleeing England, she was imprisoned (1174–1189) by Henry II until his death.

## 1175–1199

d. Hildegard of Bingen (1098–ca. 1178), German abbess, scholar, and saint who headed the convent at Bingen; known as the "Sibyl of the Rhine," she produced several volumes of revelations, poetry, a morality play, hymns—including the earliest extant Mass music by a woman—and scientific works, many of them joint efforts with nuns in her convent.

Marie de France published the poetry collection *Isopet* (ca. 1180).

The Beguines, a secular women's nursing order, was founded in Flanders, Belgium (1184); they worked in communal cottage settlements, caring for the sick, sometimes building hospitals nearby.

b. Blanche of Castile (1188–1252), French queen, wife of Louis VIII and mother of Louis IX, twice regent of France (1226–1234; 1248–1252).

Freed from prison after the death of her husband, Henry II of England, Eleanor of Aquitaine gained great power during the reign of her son, Richard I (the Lion-Hearted) (1189–1199); while he was away fighting in the Crusades, she ruled England as regent.

Marie de France published *L'espurgatoire Seint Patriz* (ca. 1190).

Hadewijch (active late 12th or early 13th c.), Dutch mystic and poet who led a group associated with the Beguines, a lay religious community; her mystical poems, in Provençal forms and possibly set to music, were collected in *Strophische Gedichten*.

b. Jacoba (Jacqueline; Jacoba de Settesoli, ca. 1190–ca. 1273), Italian saint.

Eleanor of Aquitaine ransomed England's King Richard I (the Lion-Hearted) after his capture in Austria returning from the Crusades; she brought him back to England (1194), then arranged a reconciliation between him and his brother John.

b. Clare of Assisi (ca. 1194–1253), Italian saint and founder of the Poor Clares.

d. Herrade of Landsburg (?–1195), German abbess and artist.

## 1200–1224

Eleanor of Aquitaine suppressed a rebellion in Anjou by her grandson Arthur against her son, King John of England (1200). In the same year, she arranged the marriage of Blanche of Castile to Louis of France, later Louis VIII.

d. Marie de France (ca. 1140–1200), earliest known French female poet, best known for *Le lai de Lanval*, one of her many short narrative works (*lais*).

Chu Shu-chen (active ca. 1200), Chinese poet whose work was burned after her death by her parents, some surviving only in friends' copies.

Eleanor of Aquitaine retired to the abbey at Fontrevault (1201).

d. Eleanor of Aquitaine (1122–1202), successively duchess of Aquitaine, queen of France, queen of England, and queen mother of England in a public career that spanned 65 years; she was one of the most powerful and astute women of her age.

b. Elizabeth of Hungary (1207–1231), Hungarian princess and saint, daughter of Andrew II of Hungary.

b. Mechtild of Magdeburg (1210–1282), German nun and mystic.

Poor Clares (Order of Poor Ladies) was founded by St. Clare of Assisi (1212), inspired by St. Francis of Assisi; she was joined by her widowed mother, Ortolana, and her sisters, St. Agnes and Beatrice. Living entirely on alms, the Poor Clares spread throughout Europe.

In Paris, an edict restricted the practice of medicine to people who were members of the University of Paris's faculty of medicine (1220), a ban effectively barring women, though at first widely ignored.

## 1225–1249

b. Isabel of France (Blessed Isabel, 1225–1270), French princess and religious figure.

d. Hojo Masako (1154–1225), influential wife of Japanese shogun Minamoto Yoritomo, called the

"Nun Shogun" after adopting the tonsure (partly shaved head) to show the strength of her religious beliefs. Like many aristocratic women in this era, she became a nun for a time.

On the death of France's Louis VIII, his wife, Blanche of Castile, became regent (1226–1234), ruling France alone until the accession of her son, Louis IX.

d. Elizabeth of Hungary (1207–1231), Hungarian princess and saint, daughter of Andrew II of Hungary; she devoted her life to the Catholic Church after the death of her husband, Ludvig IV of Thuringia.

Muslim Queen Razia Sultana ruled the Delhi sultanate in India (1236–1240), though most other women of the time were sequestered in private quarters, including imperial harems, which sometimes held thousands of women.

Blanche of Castile again ruled France as regent (1248–1252), while her son, Louis IX, was on the Seventh Crusade (1248); he was captured at Fariskur (1250) and was ransomed by Blanche.

Hersend, a woman physician, served France's Louis IX and the royal family on Crusade in the Holy Land (1249).

## 1250–1274

d. Blanche of Castile (1188–1252), French queen, wife of Louis VIII and mother of Louis IX, twice regent of France (1226–1234; 1248–1252).

d. Clare of Assisi (ca. 1194–1253), Italian saint who founded the Poor Clares (1212); the monastic rules she wrote for her order (1252), calling for stricter enclosure of women, were the first known to have been written by a woman.

b. Gertrud von Helfta (Gertrud die Grosse; Gertrude the Great, 1256–1302), German nun and mystical writer.

b. Fu-Jen Kuan (1262–1319), Chinese painter and calligrapher.

After 40 years as a Beguine at Magdeburg (1230–1270), Mechtild of Magdeburg was forced from her order after her visions were criticized; she took refuge in a Cistercian convent at Helfra.

d. Isabel of France (Blessed Isabel, 1225–1270), French princess and religious figure, youngest sister of St. Louis; she founded the abbey of Longchamp on the Seine and served there with the Poor Clares.

b. Elizabeth (Isabella) of Portugal (1271–1336), Portuguese queen and saint, daughter of Peter III of Aragon.

---

# Doors Close

Paris's attempt to restrict the practice of medicine to University of Paris faculty (1220) was not immediately effective; both men and women widely ignored it. But such prohibitions would come to be increasingly issued and enforced and would spread to other European countries. Where women were barred from universities—virtually everywhere in Europe except Italy (and after several centuries there as well)—it meant they were also barred from professions such as medicine. Midwives and healers who were women would continue to practice, as they had for thousands of years, with greater or lesser skill, depending on their background, intelligence, and luck at finding experienced teachers. But these lay healers would be increasingly disadvantaged by being cut off from the developing body of scientific and technical knowledge that would advance medicine. That is one reason why female lay healers and midwives would, over the coming centuries, be replaced by academically trained male obstetricians and gynecologists, sometimes called "male midwives."

A corollary to this, as Dr. Jacoba's Defense (1322) suggests, is that women would be increasingly shortchanged in medical care, until modern times. Considerations of modesty were so great that few doctors, especially not males, ever visually or manually examined their female patients. As late as the 18th century, a blind obstetrician from Philadelphia had a booming practice among women, largely because he could not *see* what he was doing and so protected the modesty of women in childbirth.

d. Jacoba (Jacqueline; Jacoba de Settesoli, ca. 1190–ca. 1273), Italian saint, a member of the third order much influenced by St. Francis of Assisi, who nicknamed her "Brother Jacoba."

## 1275-1299

b. Jacoba (Jacobina) Félicie (ca. 1280–?), French physician, possibly Italian-born.

d. Agnes of Bohemia (Blessed Agnes, ?–ca. 1280), daughter of Bohemia's king Ottokar I, who refused several proposed state marriages to serve as a Poor Clare in Prague.

Gertrud von Helfta had a vision of Christ (1281), which turned her from secular scholarship to religious writings, notably of her visions, as in *Exercitia spiritualia septem* and *Legatio divinae pietatis*.

d. Mechtild of Magdeburg (1210–1282), German nun and mystic known for her extraordinary visions, described in her *Das fliessende Licht des Gottheit* (*Light of My Divinity Flowing*); she was the model for Matelda in Dante's *Purgatorio*, which was influenced by her visions.

An anonymous woman was the first female doctor recorded as practicing in Germany, in Mainz (1288).

Pope Boniface III, in his papal bull *Periculoso* (1298), mandated strict enclosure for women in monastic orders. Previously, many women in religious orders worked in a wide variety of activities, many of them out in the world. From this period on, the activities of nuns would be increasingly restricted, and women's religious orders would gradually lose much of their independence.

b. Janabai (ca. 1298–ca. 1350), Indian poet.

d. Yolanda (Helen, ?–1299), Hungarian saint, daughter of King Bela IV and niece of St. Elizabeth of Hungary, who joined the Poor Clares after being widowed (1279), becoming abbess at Gnesen.

## 1300-1324

Lalla (active ca. 1300), Kashmiri poet.

Abella (active 14th c.), Italian physician who taught at the famed medical school in Salerno; her written works, including the two treatises *De atrabile* and *De natura seminis humani*, have not survived.

Mercuriade (active 14th c.), Italian physician and surgeon, one of several female physicians who taught at Salerno's noted medical school; she also wrote on various topics, including fever crises, ointments, and the healing of wounds.

b. Bridget (Bridget [Birgit; Birgitta] Persson Godmarsson, ca. 1302–1373), Swedish saint.

d. Gertrud von Helfta (Gertrud die Grosse; Gertrude the Great, 1256–1302), German nun, who became a mystical writer after a having a vision (1281).

d. Angela of Foligno (Blessed Angela, ?–1309), Italian Catholic mystic, who after an unbridled life became a religious recluse; best known for her *Book of the Experiences of the True Faithful*.

b. Agnes, countess of Dunbar (Black Agnes, ca. 1312–1369), Scottish defender, the granddaughter

---

# A-Barbering We Shall Go

In many trades and occupations during medieval times, wives, daughters, and sisters often learned skills otherwise reserved for males, working alongside their husbands, fathers, or brothers—and after their deaths, sometimes working alone. A well-known case is that of barbers. According to the Paris tax rolls, for example, 12 *barbières* (female barbers) were working in the city in 1292. In 1413, England's archbishop of Canterbury directed that barbers, their wives, sons, daughters, apprentices, or servants should not work at haircutting or shaving on Sundays. Records from Lincoln, England, refer to "brothers and sisters of the [barbers'] guild," and a popular London song celebrated five female barbers working in Drury Lane.

of King Robert Bruce.

Alessandra Giliani (Alexandra Galiani, active ca. 1318), Italian anatomist, assistant to the University of Bologna's famous anatomy professor Mondino de' Luzzi. Noted as a dissector, Giliani is credited with developing the technique of injecting dyes into blood vessels, to make veins and arteries easier to trace.

d. Fu-Jen Kuan (1262–1319), Chinese painter and calligrapher.

Francesca de Romana was certified as a surgeon, having passed an examination from the University of Salerno (1321).

Jacoba (Jacobina) Félicie was prosecuted several times under Paris's 1220 law for practicing medicine without a license, despite testimony as to her skills as a doctor and her own eloquent defense (see box). In the same year (1322), the surgeon Marguerite de Ypra was fined and barred from practicing, under threat of excommunication. Through cases such as these, women were increasingly barred from practicing medicine in France.

Alice Kyteler (Kettle, active 1324), reputed Irish witch. A wealthy woman whose first three (of four) husbands died mysteriously and whose children accused her of using "magic" to cheat them of their inheritance, she was accused of witchcraft by the bishop of Ossory. In defiance, she threw him into prison and fled to England, but others associated with her were punished, her maid Petronilla being burned at the stake..

## 1325–1349

b. Giovanna I (1326–1382), queen of Naples (1342–1382).

d. Novella d'Andrea (?–1333), Italian scholar, who reportedly sometimes lectured on canon law in place of her father, Giovanni d'Andrea, at the University of Bologna (1333).

d. Elizabeth (Isabella) of Portugal (1271–1336), Portuguese queen and saint, wife of King Dinis and mother of King Alfonso; daughter of Peter III of Aragon; she focused on church-connected good works.

Agnes Dunbar directed the successful six-month-long Scottish defense of Dunbar Castle (1337), besieged land and sea by English forces, until the English withdrew.

b. Julian of Norwich (1342–1443), English mystic.

After her husband's death, St. Bridget retired to a monastery (1344), there dictating her controversial book of revelations and visions.

b. Catherine of Siena (Caterina Benincasa, 1347–1380), Italian saint.

b. Dorothea Swartz (1347–1394), German saint.

While the Black Death was raging through Europe (1348), the Sisterhood of the Hôtel Dieu, Paris's great hospital, continued their nursing services, though many lay doctors and nurses fled.

## 1350–1374

d. Janabai (ca. 1298–ca.1350), Indian poet.

Rebecca Guarna (active ca. mid-14th c.), Italian teacher of medicine at Salerno's noted medical

---

# Dr. Jacoba's Defense

It is better and more honest that a wise and expert woman in this art visit sick women, and inquire into the secret nature of their infirmity, than a man to whom it is not permitted to see, inquire of, or touch the hands, breasts, stomach, etc. of a woman; nay rather ought a man shun the secrets of women and their company and flee as far as he can. And a woman before now would permit herself to die rather than reveal the secrets of her infirmity to any man, because of the honor of the female sex and the shame which she would feel. And this is the cause of many women and also men dying of their infirmities, not wishing to have doctors see their secret parts.

school; she is said to have known "all medicine, herbs, and roots," and to have written on topics such as the embryo, urine, and fevers.

b. Margaret of Denmark (1353–1412), queen of Norway and Sweden as wife of Haakon of Norway, later herself regent and effective ruler of Norway, Sweden, and Denmark.

Catherine of Siena joined the Third Order of St. Dominic (ca. 1363), winning many followers, especially from the aristocracy.

b. Christine de Pisan (ca. 1364–ca. 1430), Italian writer and composer.

d. Agnes, countess of Dunbar (Black Agnes, ca. 1312–1369), Scottish defender, the granddaughter of King Robert Bruce; she commanded the successful defense of Dunbar Castle against English invaders (1337).

St. Bridget founded the Bridgettines (Order of the Most Holy Savior) (1370), after one of her revelations.

b. Giovanna II (1371–1435), queen of Naples (1414–1435).

After a severe illness, Julian of Norwich experienced a series of religious revelations (1373), about which she would two decades later write in her *XVI Revelations Divine Love.*

b. Margery Kempe (ca. 1373–ca. 1440), English mystic.

d. Bridget (Bridget [Birgit; Birgitta] Persson Godmarsson, ca. 1302–1373), Swedish saint who founded a new order, the Bridgettines (1370).

b. Jadwiga (1374–1399), queen of Poland, daughter of Louis d'Anjou, king of Poland and Hungary, and sister of Maria, queen of Hungary.

## 1375–1399

Five years after the death of her father, Valdemar IV of Denmark, Margaret of Denmark succeeded in having her five-year-old son, Olaf, declared king of Denmark, and became regent for him (1375).

Catherine of Siena began her successful campaign to convince Pope Gregory XI to return from

# Witch-hunting

From the 14th to the 17th centuries, Europe and later the American colonies as well were swept by a craze of witch-hunting. While some women had earlier been accused of using magic and being in league with the devil, it was only in the 14th century, with official sanction from the Catholic church, that large numbers of women were accused, tortured, tried, and murdered, in the name of the church, as part of a wider inquisition that also encompassed other perceived threats to the church, including Jews and homosexuals. In 1320 the church granted inquisitors in southern France permission to prosecute anyone who used magic or worked with demons. In 1484 Pope Innocent VIII published *Summis desiderentes affectibus,* his papal bull asserting the church's opposition to witchcraft. Close on its heels came publication of *Malleus Maleficarum (Hammer of Witch)*, a witch-hunting manual by Heinrich Kramer (Institoris), a Dominican inquisitor, and Jacob Sprenger, which was reprinted numerous times over the next two centuries. This book defined witches as heretics, asserted that most witches were women, described how to identify witches (including mischief after anger, "witchmarks" such as a mole or wart, familiars, specters, and confessions), and outlined how to prosecute them. Many of the women persecuted were midwives or healers, charged with causing harm, strife, sickness, or death, all under the heading of *maleficia.* As witch-hunting developed into a craze, which would later involve Protestants as well, some thousands of women were murdered. No serious estimate is possible; guesses have ranged as high as several hundred thousand even to nine million. Some modern theorists regard the attacks as focusing on women practicing an "Old Religion," while others focus on the sociological marginality of single women as making them convenient scapegoats for the social and political turbulence of the time.

Avignon to Rome (1375–1377) and helped his successor, Pope Urban VI, heal divisions in the church (1378–1380).

After the death of her husband, Haakon of Norway, Margaret of Denmark became regent in Norway for her son, Olaf (1380).

d. Catherine of Siena (Caterina Benincasa, 1347–1380), Italian saint, who worked to bring the pope back from Avignon to Rome, and to resolve the Great Schism.

b. Colette (1381–1447), Flemish nun and saint.

d. Giovanna I (1326–1382), queen of Naples (1342–1382), whose rule was shaped by the complex southern European politics of her time. Ultimately, she supported France against the papacy, disinherited her heir, Charles of Durazzo, and was murdered after having managed to survive for almost four decades when his papacy-supported forces took Naples.

After the death of her father, Louis d'Anjou, king of Poland and Hungary, Jadwiga succeeded to the Polish throne (1384).

Jadwiga of Poland married Jagiello, prince of Lithuania, who became Wladyslaw II (1386); together they established the Jagiellan dynasty and laid the basis for a flowering of the arts, literature, and humanities in Poland.

Margaret of Denmark succeeded in bringing together Denmark, Sweden, and Norway in the Union of Kalmar, with her nephew Erik of Pomerania as king (1387). However, she continued to rule all three countries until her death (1412).

Margaret of Denmark's forces defeated and captured Albert of Mecklenburg, ending a dispute over the Swedish throne, confirming her regency in Sweden (1389–1396).

Lal-Ded (active late 14th c.), Kashmiri mystic and poet, author of *The Songs of Lal*.

Dorotea Bocchi (Bucca) was appointed her father's successor as professor of medicine at the University of Bologna (1390) and would remain there for 40 years.

An anonymous female doctor practiced in Frankfurt, the first on record there (1393).

d. Dorothea Swartz (1347–1394), German saint, a visionary who had spent her last year immured in a 6-by-9-foot cell at the Marienwerder cathedral; she became the patron saint of Prussia.

Christine de Pisan published *Epistre au dieu d'amour*, on feminist themes (1399).

d. Jadwiga (1374–1399), queen of Poland, daughter and successor of Louis d'Anjou, king of Poland and Hungary, and wife of Wladyslaw II of Poland, with whom she established the Jagiellan dynasty.

## 1400–1424

St. Cecilia was adopted as patron saint by various musicians' guilds (15th c.), though in earlier centuries she had been seen as disapproving of secular music.

Christine de Pisan published *Letters on the Debate on the Romance of the Rose* and the biography *The Book of the Deeds and Morals of the Wise King Charles V* (both 1404).

Christine de Pisan published the *The Book of the City of Ladies* and *The Treasure of the City of Ladies*, landmark works on the history and status of women; and also her autobiography, *Avision Christine* (all 1405).

Christine de Pisan published *Le livre de Duc des vrais amants* (1407).

b. Joan of Arc (Jeanne d'Arc; Maid of Orléans, ca. 1412–1431), French general and saint.

d. Margaret of Denmark (1353–1412), queen of Norway and Sweden as wife of Haakon of Norway, and herself later regent and, until her death, effective ruler of Norway, Sweden, and Denmark, for Olaf and then for Erik, who became king of all three countries under the Union of Kalmar.

b. Catherine of Bologna (Caterina Vigri, 1413–1463), Italian saint.

b. Isotta Nogarola (Divine Isotta, 1418–1466), Italian scholar.

b. Agnes Sorel (1422–1450), French mistress of France's Charles VII.

Constanza Calenda was a lecturer on medicine at the University of Naples (1423), where her father was dean of the faculty.

An anonymous female Jewish doctor, an oculist, practiced in Frankfurt, Germany (1423); she is one of a number of Jewish women who became physicians, including three oculists, recorded in 15th-century Frankfurt. They are believed to have brought Muslim medical traditions to Central Europe from Spain.

b. Margaret Paston (1423–1484), English estate and business manager.

## 1425–1449

Having convinced supporters to give her arms, a horse, and men's clothing, Joan of Arc led French forces in raising the English siege of Orléans (1429) as part of the Hundred Years' War; she then helped to retake much of the Loire Valley, ensuring the coronation of Charles VII (the Dauphin), an early supporter, who then abandoned her. She later tried but failed to take Paris.

Christine de Pisan published her last known work, *Le Ditié de Jehanne d'Arc* (1429), in praise of Joan of Arc.

b. Margaret of Anjou (1430–1482), queen of England, leader of Lancastrian forces during England's Wars of the Roses.

d. Christine de Pisan (ca. 1364–ca. 1430), Italian writer and composer, a leading feminist of her time, known for such works as *La cité des dames* and *Trésor des dames*.

d. Joan of Arc (Jeanne d'Arc; Maid of Orléans, ca. 1412–1431), French general and saint who, still in her teens, rallied the French against the English late in the Hundred Years' War, helping to ensure France's ultimate victory and becoming a popular national hero; captured at Compiègne (1430), she was tried, convicted, and burned as a heretic, a judgment later reversed (1456). She was eventually canonized (1920).

Henriette de Craus, a female healer in Chamars (Besançon), France, was burned as a witch, accused of healing with the help of devils (1434).

d. Giovanna II (1371–1435), queen of Naples (1414–1435), an astute practitioner of statecraft who managed to keep her crown and her life in an extraordinarily complex and turbulent period, as French Anjou and Spanish Aragonese forces contested for dominance in Naples.

d. Margery Kempe (ca. 1373–ca. 1440), English mystic, probably illiterate, who dictated her *Boke of Margery Kempe* (ca. 1432–ca. 1436), one of the earliest autobiographical works in English, describing her religious pilgrimages.

b. Hino Tomiko (1440–1496), wife of Japanese shogun Yoshimasa.

b. Margaret Beaufort (1443–1509), English scholar and philanthropist, mother of Henry Tudor, later Henry VII of England.

d. Julian of Norwich (1342–1443), English mystic noted for the *Revelations* that record her ecstatic religious experiences (1373).

b. Catherine of Genoa (Caterina Fieschi, 1147–1510), Italian saint.

d. Colette (1381–1447), Flemish nun and saint who brought a stricter rule, including the veil, to many Poor Clare convents (Colettine Poor Clares), over whom she was made superior general.

## 1450–1474

d. Agnes Sorel (1422–1450), French mistress of France's Charles VII, becoming highly influential (from 1444); called "Dame de Beauté" after the estates of Beauté-sur-Marne given to her by the king, she is said to have been poisoned by her enemies at court.

---

# On Writing Her *Revelations*

I am a woman, ignorant, weak and frail. But I know very well that what I am saying I have received by the revelation of Him who is the sovereign teacher. But because I am a woman, ought I therefore to believe that I should not tell you of the goodness of God when I saw at the same time that it is His will that it be known?

— Julian of Norwich

Isotta Nogarola published *De pari aut impari Evae atque Adae peccato*, a work defending Eve in the loss of Eden (1451).

b. Isabella I of Castile (1451–1504), queen of Spain.

Isotta Nogarola published *Oratio in laudem beati Hieronymis*, her work on Saint Jerome (1453).

b. Caterina Cornaro (1454–1510), Venetian-born Cypriot queen, wife of James II of Cyprus.

Margaret of Anjou, who had been effective ruler of England, triggered the Wars of the Roses by dismissing Richard, Duke of York, from his position as Protector during the insanity of her husband, Henry VI. Margaret then led Lancastrian forces in the long war that they ultimately lost (1455–1485).

b. Veronica of Binasco (1455–1497), Italian saint.

b. Gwerfyl Mechain (ca. 1460–1500), Welsh poet.

In England's Wars of the Roses, Lancastrian forces under Margaret of Anjou won a key battle over the Yorkists at St. Albans (1461) but were forced to retreat when Edward, who had succeeded his father as Duke of York, proclaimed himself Edward IV. After some later losses, Margaret took refuge in France (1464–1471).

b. Anne of France (1461–1522), French princess, oldest daughter of Louis XI of France and Charlotte of Savoy.

b. Philippa of Guelders (Blessed Philippa, 1462–1547), French religious figure.

d. Catherine of Bologna (Caterina Vigri, 1413–1463), Italian saint who was founder and abbess of a Poor Clare convent at Bologna; among her written works were *Treatise on Spiritual Weapons* and *Revelations*.

d. Isotta Nogarola (Divine Isotta, 1418–1466), Italian scholar noted in her teens for her classical learning, who after anonymous charges (1438) of homosexuality and incest involving Isotta and her sister and brother, also scholars, became a reclusive religious scholar.

Isabella I of Castile married Ferdinand III of Aragon; they were to become the rulers of a united Spain (1469).

In England's Wars of the Roses, Margaret of Anjou returned from refuge in France to lead her Lancastrian forces against those of Edward IV's Yorkists, but lost disastrously at Tewkesbury (1471). Her son, Prince Edward, was killed in battle; her husband, England's Henry VI, was taken, later to be executed; and she herself was captured, eventually ransomed by France's Louis IX (1475), and returned to France.

Catherine of Genoa underwent a religious conversion, soon converting her husband, Julian Adorno, as well; they devoted the rest of their lives to care of the patients at Genoa's Pammatane hospital, where Catherine became matron (1490–1496).

b. Angela of Brescia (Angela Merici) (ca. 1474–1540), Italian nun and saint.

b. Beatriz Galindo (La Latina, 1474–1534), Spanish scholar.

b. Isabella d'Este (1474–1539), marquesa and regent of the Italian state of Mantua.

## 1475–1499

b. Louise of Savoy, Duchesse D'Angoulême (1476–1531), daughter of the duke of Savoy and Marguerite de Bourbon, and mother of Francis I of France and Marguerite of Navarre.

b. Anne of Brittany (1477–1514), duchess of Brittany and queen of France.

Isabella of Castile took the Castilian throne (1479) after defeating Portuguese forces contesting her accession.

Guillemette Du Luys was a female healer in service to France's Louis XI (1479).

A papal decree barred both men and women from practicing medicine in Rome without a license (ca. 1480), an indication that women were still able to attend universities and become licensed in Italy, probably in the traditional centers: Florence, Venice, Naples, and Rome.

b. Lucrezia Borgia (1480–1519), a highly visible member of the Spanish-Italian Borgia family, sister of Cesare Borgia and daughter of Cardinal Rodrigo Borgia, later Pope Alexander VI.

d. Margaret of Anjou (1430–1482), queen of England, wife of Henry VI, and head of Lancastrian forces in England's Wars of the Roses (1455–1485), sparked by her dismissal of Richard, Duke of York. She was ultimately defeated at Tewkesbury (1471) and imprisoned until ransomed by France's Louis XI (1475), returning to Anjou.

d. Margaret Paston (1423–1484), English estate and business manager, who handled the family farm and wool and malt businesses after her husband, John Paston, was elected to Parliament (1460); she was made famous later by the lively and detailed collection of 15th-century Paston family letters, many by her.

b. Catherine of Aragon (1485–1536), queen of England, first wife of Henry VIII.

Julyans Bernes published *The Boke of St. Albans* (1486), including treatises on hawking, hunting, and fishing, among her favorite diversions. She is believed to have been Juliana Barnes (Berners), prioress of Britain's Sopewell nunnery.

Cypriot queen Caterina Cornaro, a Venetian who had nominally ruled Venetian-controlled Cyprus since the death of her husband, James II of Cyprus (1460–1473), abdicated under Venetian pressure and returned home to Venice, where she became a celebrated patron of the arts and humanities.

Isabella d'Este married Francesco Gonzaga, the marquis of Mantua, beginning her long career in statecraft and as a leading Italian patron of the arts and literature (1490).

In an attempt to save Brittany from absorption into France, Anne of Brittany married Maximilian of Austria by proxy (1490).

b. Vittoria da Colonna (1490–1547), Italian poet.

With French forces attacking her duchy, Anne of Brittany gave way, renouncing her 1490 proxy marriage to Maximilian of Austria and marrying Charles VIII of France (1491).

Granada fell to the Catholic forces of Ferdinand and Isabella, who then ruled a united Spain. In the same year, Ferdinand and Isabella forced the expulsion of Spain's Jews and funded the first voyage of Christopher Columbus (1492).

b. Marguerite (Margaret) of Navarre (Angoulême; 1492–1549), French writer and patron of the arts.

b. Anna Bijns (1493–1575), Dutch poet and teacher.

d. Hino Tomiko (1440–1496), influential wife of Japanese shogun Yoshimasa, who built an independent fortune through commerce and influenced the succession.

b. Katharine Schutz Zell (1497–1562), German Protestant leader.

d. Veronica of Binasco (1455–1497), Italian saint known for her ecstasies and visions, as recorded in her *Revelations*.

On the death of her husband, Charles VIII of France, Anne of Brittany was obliged to marry his successor, Louis XII (1498), though still vainly striving to keep Brittany's independence.

Spanish women first arrived in the Americas, on Christopher Columbus's third voyage (1498).

b. Mira Bai (ca. 1498–ca. 1565), Indian poet.

b. Diane de Poitiers, Duchesse de Valentinois (1499–1566), mistress of Henry II of France.

## 1500–1509

### POLITICS/LAW/WAR

b. Malintzin (Marina de Jaramillo, ca. 1501–1550), Tabascan Indian aristocrat, guide, interpreter, and mistress to Hernan Cortés during the Spanish conquest of Mexico.

d. Isabella I of Castile (1451–1504), queen of Spain, wife of Ferdinand III of Aragon, with whom she united Spain; she was instrumental in encouraging an expansion of the Inquisition, in forcing the expulsion of Spain's Jews, and in funding Christopher Columbus's voyages.

b. Anne Boleyn (1507–1536), second wife of Henry VIII of England and mother of Elizabeth I.

b. Inés de Suárez (1507–1572), Spanish-Chilean adventurer and nurse.

### RELIGION/EDUCATION/EVERYDAY LIFE

b. Margaret More Roper (1505–1544), English scholar.

d. Margaret Beaufort (1443–1509), English scholar and philanthropist, mother of Henry Tudor, who with her support became Henry VII of England; a scholar and translator, she funded professorships and colleges at Oxford and Cambridge.

### Arts/Literature

Hubb Khatun (active ca. 1500), Kashmiri female poet.

d. Gwerfyl Mechain (ca. 1460–1500).

## 1510–1519

### Politics/Law/War

d. Caterina Cornaro (1454–1510), Cypriot queen, a Venetian who became the wife of James II of Cyprus, ruling Cyprus after his death (1474–1489).

b. Catherine Parr (1512–1548), queen of England, the sixth wife of Henry VIII.

d. Anne of Brittany (1477–1514), duchess of Brittany and twice queen of France, once by her marriage to Charles VIII (1491) and on his death to Louis XII (1498); she made a failed lifelong attempt to save Brittany from absorption into France. A noted patron of the arts, she commissioned Jean Baudichon's *Book of Hours*.

b. Mary I (1516–1558), queen of England (1553–1558), daughter of Henry VIII and Catherine of Aragon.

b. Elizabeth Talbot, countess of Shrewsbury (Bess of Hardwick, 1518–1608), English aristocrat.

After the death of her husband, Isabella d'Este ruled Mantua as regent for her son Frederico (1519).

b. Catherine de Medicis (1519–1589), queen of France, wife of Henry II and mother of Henry III.

d. Lucrezia Borgia (1480–1519), a highly visible member of the Italian Borgia family, sister of Cesare Borgia and daughter of Cardinal Rodrigo Borgia, later Pope Alexander VI, whose three marriages served family political interests.

Malintzin (Marina), like many other Tabascan Indian women, was given as a slave to the Spanish (1519); she became Hernan Cortés's guide, interpreter, and mistress during the conquest of Mexico; they had one son. She later married a Spanish soldier and went to Spain as Doña Marina de Jaramillo.

### Religion/Education/Everyday Life

d. Catherine of Genoa (Caterina Fieschi, 1147–1510), Italian saint noted for her service to Genoa's Pammatane Hospital.

b. Teresa of Ávila (Teresa De Cepeda y Ahumada; Teresa of Jesus, 1515–1582), Spanish nun and saint.

### Science/Technology/Medicine

Britain's Parliament passed a law (1511) against a "great multitude of ignorant persons," including "smythes, weavers, and women," practicing healing, charging that they "partly use sorcerye, and witchcrafte."

*The Garden of Roses for Pregnant Women and for Midwives* was published, commissioned by Duchess Catherine of Brunswick (1513).

### Arts/Literature

b. Tullia d'Aragona (1510–1556), Italian poet.

b. Levina Benninck Teerling (1515–1576), Flemish artist.

## 1520–1529

### Politics/Law/War

d. Anne of France (1461–1522), French princess, oldest daughter of Louis XI of France and Charlotte of Savoy, and wife and political partner of Pierre de Bourbon, who with him exerted great power in France during the early years of the reign of Charles VIII (1491–1498).

b. Jeanne d'Albret (1528–1572), queen of Navarre (1555–1572), the daughter of Marguerite of Navarre and Henri d'Albret, and mother of Henry IV of France.

### RELIGION/EDUCATION/EVERYDAY LIFE

b. Anne Askew (1521–1546), English royal attendant and Protestant martyr.

b. Olympia Fulvia Morata (1526–1555), Italian scholar.

Katharine Schutz married a priest, Matthew Zell, who was then excommunicated; their home became a haven for other early Protestants (1527) just 10 years after Martin Luther had posted his 95 Theses at Wittenberg, effectively beginning the Reformation.

### SCIENCE/TECHNOLOGY/MEDICINE

Dr. Wertt, a male physician from Hamburg, disguised himself as a female midwife to be able to observe and learn from the childbirth process; for breaking the law that barred all males (except astrologers) from delivery rooms, he was burned at the stake (1522).

### ARTS/LITERATURE

b. Gaspara Stampa (1523–1554), Italian poet.

b. Gul-Badan Begum (1523–1603), Indian writer, sister of Mughal ruler Humayun.

b. Louise Labé (ca. 1524–1566), French poet.

b. Caterina van Hemessen (1528–1587), Flemish painter.

## 1530–1539

### POLITICS/LAW/WAR

b. Grace O'Malley (Graine Mhaol, ca. 1530–ca. 1600), Irish seafarer.

d. Louise of Savoy, Duchesse D'Angoulême (1476–1531), daughter of the Duke of Savoy and Marguerite de Bourbon, and mother of Francis I of France and Marguerite of Navarre; she attained great power in France during her son's reign, and in two periods acted as his regent.

Anne Boleyn secretly married England's Henry VIII (1533), who had for her repudiated his first wife, Catherine of Aragon, and begun the divorce process (against the will of the Catholic church) that would make him an excommunicated Protestant.

b. Elizabeth I (1533–1603), queen of England and Ireland (1558–1603), daughter of Henry VIII and Anne Boleyn.

d. Catherine of Aragon (1485–1536), queen of England, first wife of Henry VIII, who later repudiated her to marry Anne Boleyn (1533), triggering England's split with the Roman Catholic church; a Spanish Catholic, she became a factor in the long Protestant-Catholic struggle for Europe and the Spanish-English wars.

d. Anne Boleyn (1507–1536), second wife of Henry VIII of England and the mother of Elizabeth I. She was imprisoned and then executed, and their three-year marriage was pronounced invalid, though Henry's charges of adultery and incest were unsubstantiated. Henry quickly married a new favorite, Jane Seymour, who became the third of his six wives. With the execution of Anne Boleyn, Elizabeth of England was declared illegitimate; the long struggle over the succession to the throne of Henry VIII had begun.

Jane Seymour, third wife of England's Henry VIII, died (1537) soon after bearing him a long-sought son, Edward, who became heir to the throne, ahead of his older half sisters, Mary and Elizabeth.

Inés de Suárez sailed from Spain to South America (1537). Seeking her husband, she tracked him from Venezuela to Peru, only to find he had died in a siege; she settled for a time near Cuzco, working as a nurse and later joining an expedition to Chile—officially as nurse, unofficially as mistress of Francisco Pizarro's lieutenant, Pedro de Valdivia; she helped found Santiago (1539).

b. Lady Jane Grey (1537–1554), queen of England for nine days (1553).

b. Diane of France (1538–1619), French princess, later duchess of Angoulême.

d. Isabella d'Este (1474–1539), wife of Francesco Gonzaga, the marquis of Mantua; after his death (1519) She was regent and effective ruler of Mantua; she became a leading Renaissance patron of the arts and literature.

### RELIGION/EDUCATION/EVERYDAY LIFE

Early German Protestant Katharine Schutz Zell edited a religious songbook (1534).

d. Beatriz Galindo (La Latina, 1474–1534), Spanish scholar who was professor of philosophy, rhetoric, and medicine at Salamanca, and tutor to Queen Isabella I.

Responding to a vision that she would found a society of virgins at Brescia, Angela of Brescia led a group in establishing the Company of St. Ursula, the first religious order devoted to educating young girls (1535).

### ARTS/LITERATURE

Marguerite of Navarre published the religious poetry *Le miroir de l'âme pécheresse* (*The Mirror of the Sinner's Soul*) (1531), criticized by some Catholic theologists as pro-Lutheran.

b. Sofonisba Anguissola (ca. 1535–1625), Italian painter.

## 1540–1549

### POLITICS/LAW/WAR

Catherine Howard became the fifth wife of England's Henry VIII (1540), shortly after the annulment of his brief marriage to Anne of Cleves. Two years later, Catherine would be beheaded on charges of adultery (1542).

b. Mary (1542–1587), queen of Scotland (1542–1567), daughter of James V of Scotland and Mary of Guise; she succeeded to the throne when she was six days old.

Parliament declared Elizabeth of England a legitimate successor to the throne (1544), after her half brother, Edward, and her older halfsister, Mary.

d. Catherine Parr (1512–1548), queen of England, the sixth wife of Henry VIII, a poet and patron of the arts and humanities who played a considerable role in the education of Elizabeth and Mary, both later queens of England. She was widowed twice before her marriage to Henry (1543), but survived him and later married Thomas Seymour; she died following the birth of their only child. She is credited with having edited *Prayers and Meditations*, thereafter called the *Queen's Prayers*. The poetic work *Lamentation or Complaint of a Sinner* was published posthumously.

Jeanne d'Albret, then princess of Navarre, married Antoine de Bourbon, Duc de Vendôme (1548); they were to move apart during the Huguenot Wars, she to the Protestant side, he to the Catholic.

### RELIGION/EDUCATION/EVERYDAY LIFE

d. Angela of Brescia (Angela Merici, ca. 1474–1540), Italian nun and saint who founded the Company of St. Ursula (1535).

d. Margaret More Roper (1505–1544), English scholar, educated by her father, Sir Thomas More, whom she strongly defended during his imprisonment in the Tower of London, being herself briefly imprisoned. She translated Erasmus's *Treatise on the Lord's Prayer*.

d. Anne Askew (1521–1546), English Protestant martyr, who had been an attendant at Queen Catherine Parr's court; for her religious views she was judged a heretic, tortured, and then burned at the stake.

d. Philippa of Guelders (Blessed Philippa, 1462–1547), French religious figure, who after the death of her husband, René II, duke of Lorraine, with whom she had had 12 children, entered the convent of the Poor Clares at Pont-à-Mousson.

### ARTS/LITERATURE

b. Maddalena Mezzari Casulana (ca. 1540–1583), Italian composer and singer.

Marguerite of Navarre published the poetry collection *Les Marguerites* (1547).

Tullia d'Aragona published the poetry collection *Rime* (1547).

d. Mira Bai (ca. 1498–ca. 1565), Indian poet, among the finest *bhakti* (devotional) poets, whose work was meant to be sung.

d. Vittoria da Colonna (1490–1547), Italian poet known for her sonnets.

Elizabeth of England translated Marguerite of Navarre's *Le miroir de l'âme pécheresse* from the

French into English (1548).

d. Marguerite (Margaret) of Navarre (Angoulême; 1492–1549), French writer and patron of the arts, daughter of Louise of Savoy and Charles of Orleâns, duke of Angoulême, and sister of Francis I of France.

# 1550–1559

## POLITICS/LAW/WAR

d. Malintzin (Marina de Jaramillo, ca. 1501–1550), Tabascan Indian aristocrat, guide, interpreter, and mistress of Hernan Cortés during the conquest of Mexico.

At the death of England's Edward VI, his half sister, Lady Jane Grey, took the throne for nine days (1553). She was a Protestant named heir to the English throne by Edward VI and confirmed by the Privy Council after his death (1553), bypassing his elder half sister, Mary, a Catholic, who had earlier been named heir by Parliament. But Mary raised an army and popular support, forcing Lady Jane Grey off the throne and into prison. Mary then took the throne, the first woman to rule England in her own right. She reintroduced Catholicism to England, accompanied by the bloody persecution of Protestants.

Catholic Mary I of England married Catholic Philip I of Spain (1554), precipitating a near-crisis in largely Protestant England and setting the stage for the long Spanish-English wars.

Elizabeth of England, the focus of Protestant English hopes, was imprisoned by Mary I (1554), using the pretext provided by Thomas Wyatt's plot to overthrow the Catholic queen.

d. Lady Jane Grey (1537–1554), briefly queen of England (1553), forced to abdicate after nine days by Mary's supporters. Jane Grey and her husband, Guildford Dudley, were executed after a plot against Mary, although they apparently had no direct hand in it.

Jeanne d'Albret became queen of Navarre (1555–1572), and a Protestant leader during the French Huguenot Wars.

d. Mary I (1516–1558), queen of England (1553–1558), daughter of Henry VIII and Catherine of Aragon, and wife of Philip I of Spain; she restored Catholicism to England and persecuted Protestants so severely that she was known as "Bloody Mary."

Elizabeth of England succeeded her half sister, Mary I, becoming Elizabeth I (1558). Quickly demonstrating her grasp of statecraft, she ended the war with France (1559) and attempted to reassure Catholics that she would not mount a reign of terror against them. But the Protestant-Catholic contest for Europe and the expanding colonial world would dominate her reign.

## RELIGION/EDUCATION/EVERYDAY LIFE

*Vita e dottrina* was published (1551), outlining the spiritual doctrine of Catherine of Genoa, though probably not written by her; *Dialogues on the Soul and the Body* and *Treatise on Purgatory* were drawn from it.

d. Olympia Fulvia Morata (1526–1555), Italian scholar, daughter of scholar Pellegrino Morata, teacher and companion to the princesses of Ferrara, until banished for her independent religious views; she later taught classics at Heidelberg and published dialogues in Greek and Latin.

## ARTS/LITERATURE

b. Lavinia Fontana (1552–1614), Italian painter.

b. Marguerite de Valois (Margaret of France, 1553–1615), French princess and writer, daughter of Henry II and Catherine de Medicis.

d. Gaspara Stampa (1523–1554), Italian poet; her poetry collection, *Rime*, was published posthumously (1554).

Louise Labé published her *Works*, most notable for her sonnets (1555).

d. Tullia d'Aragona (1510–1556), Italian poet and a notable Florentine hostess.

Marguerite of Navarre's story collection *Heptaméron*, modeled on Boccaccio's *Decameron*, was published posthumously (1558–1559).

Italian painter Sofonisba Anguissola became a portrait painter in the court of Spain's Philip II (1559).

## 1560–1569

### Politics/Law/War

d. Diane de Poitiers, Duchesse de Valentinois (1499–1566), mistress of Henry II of France, a dominant figure in the life of his court until his death (1559); she was a leader of the Catholic faction and a patron of the arts and humanities.

Mary of Scotland was imprisoned and forced to abdicate after her forces were defeated at Carberry Hill (1567) by Scottish forces supporting her son, who became James VI of Scotland (later James I of England).

After the final defeat of her forces, at Langside (1568), Mary of Scotland fled to England and would be imprisoned for 19 years, under the guise of being given refuge.

### Religion/Education/Everyday Life

b. Mary Herbert, countess of Pembroke (1561–1621), English writer, editor, and literary patron.

Teresa of Ávila founded the Reformed Carmelite convent of St. Joseph's at Ávila, the first of 18 such highly disciplined communities she would found (1562–1582).

b. Maria Victoria Fornari (1562–1617), Italian religious leader.

b. Oliva Sabuco (1562–1625), Spanish scholar.

d. Katharine Schutz Zell (1497–1562), German religious figure, an early Protestant.

Teresa of Ávila wrote *Camino de perfección* (*Way of Perfection*) (1565).

b. Barbe (Jeanne Avrillot) Acarie (Marie de l'Incarnation, 1566–1618), French religious leader.

### Science/Technology/Medicine

b. Louyse Bourgeois (1563–1636), French midwife.

### Arts/Literature

Tullia d'Aragona published the poem *Il meschino d'il guerino* (1560).

b. Isabella Canali Andreini (1562–1604), Italian commedia dell'arte actress, manager, and writer.

b. Marie le Jars de Gournay (1566–1645), French writer and editor.

d. Louise Labé (ca. 1524–1566), French poet, center of a Lyon literary circle.

Maddalena Casulana began to publish what would ultimately become her three-volume collection of madrigals (1568; 1570; 1583).

## 1570–1579

### Politics/Law/War

Pope Pius V excommunicated Elizabeth I of England (1570) as the worldwide Protestant-Catholic conflict continued and further developed.

b. Nur Jahan (Mihr-ur-Nisa, 1571–1634), Moghul Indian empress, wife of Emperor Jahangir.

d. Jeanne d'Albret (1528–1572), queen of Navarre (1555–1572), the daughter of Marguerite of Navarre and Henri d'Albret, and mother of Henry IV of France. She became a Protestant leader during the French Huguenot Wars and was a leading patron of the humanities.

d. Inés de Suárez (1507–1572), Spanish-Chilean adventurer and nurse, who helped found Santiago, Chile.

b. Marie de Médicis (1573–1642), queen of France, wife of Henry IV and mother of Louis XIII.

### Religion/Education/Everyday Life

b. Jane Frances Frémyot de Chantal (Baroness de Chantal, 1572–1641), French religious leader and saint.

### Arts/Literature

Catherine de Medicis sponsored the dance performance *Ballet de Polonais*, developed as an entertainment for Polish diplomats in France (1573).

Okuni, a Japanese dancer, founded the first Kabuki company (1575). The government soon banned women from practicing the art form they had created, and they were replaced by men.

d. Anna Bijns (1493–1575), Dutch poet and teacher, an independent woman who headed her own school and wrote three collections of poems, some notable for their acerbity.

d. Levina Benninck Teerling (1515–1576), Flemish artist, long resident in England as a painter at the royal court.

## 1580–1589

### POLITICS/LAW/WAR

Diane of France became duchess of Angoulême (1582), working for Protestant-Catholic reconciliation, with some temporary success but no lasting effect; she was notably influential with Henry of Navarre.

d. Mbanda Nzinga (?–ca. 1663), queen of Ndongo and Matamba.

d. Mary (1542–1587), queen of Scotland (1542–1567), daughter of James V of Scotland and Mary of Guise, who had succeeded to the throne when six days old but was forced out by forces favoring her son (1567). A strong claimant to the English throne, she was imprisoned by Elizabeth I of England for 19 years and then executed.

Elizabeth I gathered an army at Tilbury to defend against a threatened invasion of England by the Spanish Armada (1588) and, in a moving speech, promised to live or die with her forces and offered "to lay down for my God, and for my Kingdom, and for my people, my honor and my blood, even in the dust. I know I have the body of a weak and feeble woman, but I have the heart and stomach of a King, and a King of England too." The Armada was defeated by an English fleet, and by bad weather in the English Channel.

d. Catherine de Medicis (1519–1589), queen of France, wife of Henry II and mother of Henry III, regent after the death of her husband, an astute politician who continued to hold great power throughout her lifetime, as the Huguenot Wars continued to tear France apart.

### RELIGION/EDUCATION/EVERYDAY LIFE

d. Teresa of Ávila (Teresa De Cepeda y Ahumada; Teresa of Jesus, 1515–1582), Spanish saint, a Carmelite nun (from 1533) who founded 18 Reformed Carmelite convents (1562–1582). She was one of the first two women officially named a doctor of the Roman Catholic church (1970). Various of her writings were published posthumously.

b. Mary (Joan) Ward (1585–1645), British religious leader.

b. Rose of Lima (Isabel de Flores, 1586–1617), Peruvian saint.

Gul-Badan Begum published *Humayun Nama* (1587), a history of the reign of her brother, Mughal ruler Humayun.

Oliva Sabuco was shown as author of the seven-volume *Nueva filosofía de la naturaleza del hombre, no conocida ni alcanzada de los grandes filósofos antiguos, la quae mejora la vida y salud humana* (1587); some modern historians suggest that the collection of philosophical dialogues was actually written by her father, Miguel Sabuco.

Teresa of Ávila's *Castillo interior* (*The Interior*) and *Relaciones espirituales* (1588) were published

---

Heed my advice: take care
For I divine, often having perceived,
That when a woman marries, even though she be of noble blood
And well off, her feet will be
In fetters. But should she remain single,
And keep herself pure and clean,
She is lord and mistress, none ever lived better.

— Anna Bijns

posthumously.

b. Marquise de Rambouillet (Catherine de Vivonne, 1588–1665), French salon hostess.

### ARTS/LITERATURE

Catherine de Medicis organized the *Ballet Comique de la Reyne Louise*, often described as the first full ballet, complete with music, dance, and drama (1581).

Lavinia Fontana painted *The Visit of the Queen of Sheba* (1581).

d. Maddalena Mezzari Casulana (ca. 1540–1583), Italian composer and singer; the last of her three volumes of madrigals was published the year of her death.

Actresses were first permitted to work on stage in Spain, all the roles previously having been played by men (1587).

b. Francesca Caccini (1587–1640?), Italian musician, a composer, singer, and instrumentalist.

d. Caterina van Hemessen (1528–1587), one of the earliest known Flemish women who painted, largely a portraitist.

## 1590–1599

### POLITICS/LAW/WAR

b. Catalina de Erauzo (1592–1650?), Spanish soldier.

The forces of Elizabeth I suppressed an Irish uprising led by Hugh O'Neill, earl of Tyrone (1598–1603). Elizabeth accelerated the "plantation" of Ireland with Scottish settlers, laying the basis for the Catholic-Protestant conflict that would convulse Ireland for four centuries. Robert Devereux, Earl of Essex, whom she had sharply criticized for his initial failure against Tyrone, raised a rebellion of his own against her in London, which she put down, later executing him (1601).

### RELIGION/EDUCATION/EVERYDAY LIFE

b. Mary Frith (Moll Cutpurse, ca. 1590–1659), British thief.

b. Angélique (Jacqueline Marie) Arnauld, (1591–1661) French abbess.

b. Anne Marbury Hutchinson (1591–1643), British-American midwife and religious leader.

d. Agnes Sampson (?–1592), Scottish lay healer and reputed witch who was labeled "eldest witch" of the 70 people named by Geillis Duncan, herself accused of witchcraft. Sampson was tortured and eventually confessed; she and many of the others were executed.

b. Pocahontas (Matoaka; Rebecca, 1596–1617), Native American princess.

b. Marie Guyard (1599–1672), French Ursuline sister and missionary.

### SCIENCE/TECHNOLOGY/MEDICINE

b. Louise de Marillac (1591–1660), French nursing order founder and saint.

### ARTS/LITERATURE

Lavinia Fontana painted the altarpiece *The Holy Family with the Sleeping Christ Child* (ca. 1590–1599) for the Escorial in Spain.

b. Maria de Zayas y Sotomayor (1590–ca. 1660), Spanish writer.

Mary Herbert, countess of Pembroke, published her editions of *The Countess of Pembroke's Arcadia* (1593, 1596), written earlier by her brother, Philip Sidney, at her suggestion.

Raffaella Aleotti composed *Sacrae cantiones* (1593).

b. Artemisia Gentileschi (1593–ca. 1653), Italian painter.

b. Clara Peeters (1594–after 1657), Dutch painter.

## 1600–1609

### POLITICS/LAW/WAR

d. Grace O'Malley (Graine Mhaol, ca. 1530–ca. 1600), Irish seafarer, a rebel and pirate who effectively opposed the English until the mid-1580s.

b. Anne of Austria (1601–1666), queen of France.

b. Margaret Brent (ca. 1601–1671), Maryland colony landowner and, after his death, executor for Governor Calvert (1647).

d. Elizabeth I (1533–1603), queen of England and Ireland (1558–1603), called "Gloriana" and the "Virgin Queen," one of the most astute and powerful rulers—and certainly the most powerful woman—of her time, whose life and work did much to set the course of European and world history until the present. She was also a massive figure in the development of the arts, literature, and humanities, as the chief patron of the English Renaissance; her England was also Shakespeare's England.

d. Elizabeth Talbot, countess of Shrewsbury (Bess of Hardwick, 1518–1608), English aristocrat, several times married and widowed, a powerful figure who gathered considerable estates, especially in Derbyshire, living most notably at Chatsworth and Hardwick.

## RELIGION/EDUCATION/EVERYDAY LIFE

In a list of publishers in England's Stationers' Company (ca. 1600), a surprising 10 percent were women, generally widows or daughters who had learned the business from their husbands or fathers.

Inspired by the work of Teresa of Ávila, Barbe Acarie (Marie de l'Incarnation) introduced the Carmelite order into France (1603).

Maria Victoria Fornari founded a new religious order, the Celestial Annunciades (1604).

b. Alexandra Mavrokordatou (1605–1684), Constantinople-born Greek intellectual and salon hostess.

Native American princess Pocahontas reportedly saved the life of English settler John Smith (1607), according to later tales doing it out of love; she also attempted to protect her own people from English attack.

b. Anna Maria van Schurman (1607–1678), Dutch philologist and theologian.

Angélique Arnauld, abbess at Port-Royal-les-Champs, near Versailles, France, introduced radical changes in her convent, including silence, abstinence, communal sharing of material goods, and enclosure from the outside world (1608), helping spread such changes to other religious foundations.

b. Bathshua Pell Makin (1608–1675), British educator.

## SCIENCE/TECHNOLOGY/MEDICINE

Among the earliest settlers of North America, at Habitation (Port Royal), Nova Scotia (1605), was the first French nurse, Marie Hebert (later Hobou).

French midwife Louyse Bourgeois began publication of her noted three-part text on gynecological-obstetrical problems, *Observations diverses sur la stérilité, perte de fruice, fécondité, accouchements et maladies des femmes, et des enfants nouveaux naiz* (*Various Observations on Sterility, Miscarriage, Fecundity, Confinements and Illnesses of Women and Newborn Infants*) (1608).

## ARTS/LITERATURE

Marie le Jars de Gournay published *De l'education des enfants de France* (*On the Education of the Children of France*) (1600).

Italian dramatist Suor Annalena Odaldi wrote *The Comedy of Nannuccio and Fifteen Stepdaughters* (1600).

Isabella Andreini published the poetry collection *Rime* (1601).

b. Sor Violante do Céu (1602?–1693?), Portuguese poet, playwright, and nun.

d. Gul-Badan Begum (1523–1603), Indian writer, sister of Mughal ruler Humayun, author of the *Humayun Nama* (1587).

d. Isabella Andreini (1562–1604), a leading commedia dell'arte actress, manager, and writer, who with her husband, Francesco Andreini, co-managed the Gelosi Company.

b. Madeleine de Scudéry (1607–1701), French writer.

Virginia Andreini created the title role in Claudio Monteverdi's opera *Arianna* (1608).

b. Judith Leyster (1609–1660), Dutch artist.

## 1610–1619

### POLITICS/LAW/WAR

After Henry IV of France was assassinated, his queen, Marie de Medicis, took power as regent for her son, Louis XIII (1610–1617).

d. Diane of France (1538–1619), French princess, later duchess of Angoulême, daughter of Henry II of France, who with her husband, Francois de Montmorency, led moderate-minded French Catholic opinion during part of the Huguenot Wars.

### RELIGION/EDUCATION/EVERYDAY LIFE

Inspired by St. Francis de Sales, Jane Frances Frémyot, baroness de Chantal, founded the Order of the Visitation of Mary (1610), a voluntary association of women serving as "friendly visitors" and home nurses, with her as director.

Teresa of Ávila's *Libro de las fundaciones* (*Book of Foundations*) (1610) and *Libro de su vida* (1611) were published posthumously.

Marquise de Rambouillet began to hold intellectual and cultural gatherings at her house, the Hôtel de Rambouillet (from ca. 1610); these developed into France's first great salon, prototype of many to follow.

*The Roaring Girl, or Moll Cutpurse*, by Thomas Middleton and Thomas Dekker, was based on the life of Mary Frith; she herself was arrested in St. Paul's Cathedral for dressing like a man (1611).

After her husband's death, Barbe Acarie (Marie de l'Incarnation) joined the Carmelite order (1613), which she had introduced into France.

Powhatan princess Pocahontas was taken as a hostage by the English at Jamestown and held for ransom. While imprisoned, she met John Rolfe, whom she later married (1614).

b. Margaret Askew Fell (1614–1702), British religious figure.

*Lettres d'Abelard et d'Héloïse*, correspondence between the tragic lovers Héloïse (1101–1164) and Abelard, was first published, in Latin (1616).

d. Rose of Lima (Isabel de Flores, 1586–1617), Peruvian saint noted for her visions, serving with extreme austerity in the Dominican third order; patron saint of South America, the first saint born in the Americas.

d. Pocahontas (Matoaka; Rebecca, 1596–1617), Native American princess, daughter of Chief Powhatan, who married John Rolfe; she died of smallpox in England, after having been presented at court to King James I.

d. Maria Victoria Fornari (1562–1617), Italian religious leader who founded the Celestial Annunciades (1604).

d. Barbe (Jeanne Avrillot) Acarie (Marie de l'Incarnation, 1566–1618), French religious leader who introduced the Carmelite order into France (1603).

### SCIENCE/TECHNOLOGY/MEDICINE

b. Maria Cunitz (1610–1664), German astronomer.

St. Vincent de Paul established the Dames de Charity (ca. 1617–ca. 1627), an order of community nurses caring for the ill in their homes.

b. Elizabeth of Bohemia (1618–1680), student of natural philosophy.

### ARTS/LITERATURE

b. Anne Dudley Bradstreet (1612–1672), American writer.

d. Lavinia Fontana (1552–1614), Italian painter who worked in the papal court, one of the leading artists of her time, noted for her portraiture, group work, and altarpieces.

d. Marguerite de Valois (Margaret of France, 1553–1615), French princess and writer, daughter of Henry II and Catherine de Medicis, wife of Henry of Navarre, and sister of Charles IX and Henry III. She was best known for her *Memoires*, which detailed her liaisons, and for her poems and letters.

b. Madeleine Béjart (1618–1672), French actress.

b. Barbara Strozzi (1619–after 1663), Italian singer and composer.

## 1620–1629

### POLITICS/LAW/WAR

Elizabeth of Portugal was canonized (1625), becoming Saint Elizabeth, like her great aunt Saint Elizabeth of Hungary.

Unable to successfully resist expanding Portuguese forces, Queen Mbanda Nzinga of Ndongo retreated east with substantial forces and took Matamba (1626), there establishing a state that continued to resist Portuguese penetration during the rest of her long reign (1618–1663), although in the 1650s she became a Portuguese partner in the slave trade.

b. Anne-Marie-Louise d'Orléans de Montpensier (La Grande Mademoiselle, 1627–1693), French duchess.

### RELIGION/EDUCATION/EVERYDAY LIFE

b. Ninon (Anne) de Lenclos (1620–1705), French courtesan and salon hostess.

English Catholic leaders attempted to suppress the English Ladies (1621), a lay organization founded by Mary Ward, modeled on the Dutch beguines, working in the community, especially in improving women's education, but subject not to local bishops but directly to the pope. Ward founded other schools in Italy, Germany, Austria, and Hungary, but the order was finally suppressed (1629).

b. Rebecca Towne Nurse (1621–1692), American victim of the Salem witch trials.

d. Mary Herbert, countess of Pembroke (1561–1621), English writer, editor, translator, and literary patron, sister of Philip Sidney, whose work she edited after his death.

d. Oliva Sabuco (1562–1625), Spanish scholar and author.

### SCIENCE/TECHNOLOGY/MEDICINE

The first midwife in the Puritan settlement at Plymouth (1620), Mrs. Samuel Fuller, was the wife of the deacon-physician.

### ARTS/LITERATURE

b. Anna Renzi (ca. 1620–1660 or later), Italian soprano.

b. Leonarda Isabella (1620–ca. 1700), Italian composer.

Marie le Jars de Gournay published *Égalité des hommes et des femmes* (*Equality of Men and Women*) (1622).

b. Margaret Cavendish, duchess of Newcastle (ca. 1623–1674), British writer.

d. Sofonisba Anguissola (ca. 1535–1625), Italian painter, a well-known Renaissance figure after 1559, while a Spanish Court portrait painter. She is credited with being a model for several later women painters, and during the late 20th century has drawn great attention as a trailblazer, although little of her work has survived.

Marie le Jars de Gournay published *Le Grief des dames* (*The Ladies' Grievance*) and the essay collection *A L'ombre de la demoiselle de Gournay* (*In the Shadow of Mademoiselle de Gournay*) (1626).

b. Marie de Rabutin Chantal Sévigné (1626–1696), French essayist and letter writer.

Judith Leyster painted *The Gay Cavaliers* (1628–1629).

Women were banned from the Kabuki stage—from the art they had created—by Japan's shogunate (1629); until 1868, their roles would be taken by men, the biggest stars being female impersonators (*onnagata*).

## 1630–1639

### POLITICS/LAW/WAR

Marie de Medicis was banished from the French court by her son, King Louis XIII, and went into exile abroad (1631).

d. Nur Jahan (Mihr-ur-Nisa, 1571–1634), Moghul Indian empress, the wife of Emperor Jahangir; a very powerful figure during the last years of his reign, she took on many administrative and political functions as he became more deeply addicted to opium and alcohol.

b. Françoise Augigné de Maintenon (Madame de Maintenon, 1635–1719), second wife of Louis XIV of France.

French queen Anne of Austria was accused of treason (1637); pardoned by her husband, Louis XIII, she remained his opponent until his death (1643).

Deborah Moody became the first known woman to lead a colonial settlement in America, at Gravesend, Long Island, in what is now New York (1639).

## RELIGION/EDUCATION/EVERYDAY LIFE

b. Kaibara Ekken (1630–1714), Japanese essayist.

b. Marquise de Brinvilliers (Marie-Madeleine Marguerite Aubray, 1630–1676), French poisoner.

Massachusetts Puritans made a capital crime of adultery, defined as sexual relations between a man and a married woman (1631).

Newly arrived in Massachusetts, Anne Hutchinson began holding twice-weekly religious meetings in her home (1634), originally recitations of sermons for women, but gradually developing into religious discussion groups for both men and women. The Puritan clergy tried Hutchinson (1637) on charges of having "troubled the peace of the commonwealth" through actions "not fitting for [her] sex." Found guilty, she was banished from Massachusetts and settled in Rhode Island.

By special arrangement, and hidden from male students, Anna Maria van Schurman was allowed to attend theology and oriental language lectures at Utrecht University (ca. 1635); she studied Hebrew, Arabic, and Ethiopian, of which she wrote a grammar, and wrote *On the End of Life* and the *Amica dissertatio*, on education for Christian women.

Mary Dyer and her husband left the Puritan church (1638) in protest over the banishment of Anne Hutchinson from Massachusetts, and were themselves later excommunicated; they too went to Rhode Island.

Marie Guyard, Madame de la Peltrie, and two other nuns founded Quebec's Ursuline Convent (1639), opening a school for girls.

Mary Mandame was the first American woman recorded as having been publicly whipped and sentenced to wear a symbol of her sexual offense, "dallyance" with a Native American man (who was also whipped), in Massachusetts (1639).

## SCIENCE/TECHNOLOGY/MEDICINE

b. Anne Finch Conway (1631–1679), British scientific theorist.

Influenced by St. Vincent de Paul, Louise de Marillac established a training center for young women, mostly from farming or artisan backgrounds (1633); this would grow into the Daughters of Charity, a secular nursing order whose "convent is the sick-room, their chapel the parish church, their cloister the city streets."

Louyse Bourgeois published *A Collection of the Secrets of Louyse Bourgeois*, recipes for her remedies for various ailments (1635).

d. Louyse Bourgeois (1563–1636), French midwife who published a standard text on gynecological-obstetrical problems.

Quinine, a cure for malaria, was brought to Europe from South America by Ana de Osorio, countess of Chinchon, vicereine of Peru. She had been treated there with the medication (ca. 1638) made from the Chinchona bark (named for her) and for centuries called *pulvis comitessa* (the countess's powder).

Three Augustinian sisters, led by Jeanne Mance, emigrated from France to North America, founding the Hôtel Dieu (1639), a hospital in Quebec, funded by wealthy female patrons in France.

## ARTS/LITERATURE

b. Mlle. De Brie (Catherine Leclerc du Rozet, ca. 1630–1706), French actress.

Judith Leyster painted *The Proposition* (1631).

b. Katherine Fowler Philips (Orinda, 1631–1664), British poet.

b. Marie-Catherine-Hortense Desjardins (Madame de Villedieu, 1632–1683), French writer.

Marie le Jars de Gournay published the essay collection *Les advis ou les présens* (1634).

b. Comtesse de La Fayette (Marie Madeleine de la Vergne, 1634–1693), French novelist.

Maria de Zayas y Sotomayor published the group of novels collectively titled *Novelas amorosas y exemplares* (*Exemplary Love Stories*) (1635).

b. Elisabetta Sirani (1638–1665), Italian artist.

Madeleine de Scudéry published the novel *Artamène ou le grand Cyrus* (1649–1653).

## 1640–1649

### POLITICS/LAW/WAR

b. Françoise-Athenis de Rochechouart de Mortmart de Montespan (Madame de Montespan, 1641–1707), mistress of Louis XIV of France.

d. Marie de Medicis (1573–1642), queen of France, wife of Henry IV, then regent for her son, Louis XIII, after Henry's assassination; she held power until forced to give way (1617) and was then in and out of exile until going permanently into exile (1631).

On the death of Louis XIII, his estranged queen, Anne of Austria, became regent and ruler of France (1643–1651), strongly aided by her first minister, Cardinal Mazarin.

On being named executor for the estate of Maryland's governor Leonard Calvert (1647), Margaret Brent campaigned to have two votes, one as a freeholder, the other as an executor; the latter was granted, making her a very early American female voter.

### RELIGION/EDUCATION/EVERYDAY LIFE

d. Jane Frances Frémyot de Chantal (Baroness de Chantal, 1572–1641), French religious leader and saint who founded the Order of the Visitation (1610), which at her death had 86 houses.

d. Anne Marbury Hutchinson (1591–1643), British-American midwife and religious leader, who led opposition to Puritan strictures in Massachusetts.

d. Mary (Joan) Ward (1585–1645), British religious leader who founded the English Ladies (1621), an order later suppressed (1629).

b. Jeanne Marie (de Bouvier de la Mothe) Guyon (1648–1717), French Quietist and mystical author.

b. Tituba (1648?–1692), Carib (or Carib-African) slave.

### SCIENCE/TECHNOLOGY/MEDICINE

Jane Sharp (active ca. 1640–1671), British midwife who published *The Midwive's Book* (1671), the first known textbook by a British midwife.

b. Maria Sibylla Merian (1647–1717), German naturalist and illustrator.

### ARTS/LITERATURE

b. Aphra (Afra) Behn (1640–1689), British writer, playwright, and novelist.

d. Francesca Caccini (1587–1640?), Italian musician, a composer, singer, and instrumentalist attached to the court of Florence from 1607.

b. Armande-Grésinde-Claire-Élisabeth Béjart (1641–1700), French actress.

b. Marie Desmares Champmeslé (Madame Champmeslé, 1642–1698), French actress.

Madeleine Béjart and Molière founded the Illustre Théâtre (1643).

Barbara Strozzi published a madrigal collection, which included her own works (1644).

d. Marie le Jars de Gournay (1566–1645), French writer and editor, who wrote an early work on sexual equality (1622).

Sor Violante do Céu published her *Collected Poems* (1646).

d. Raffaella Aleotti (1570–ca. 1646), Italian composer, long the music director of the convent of St. Vito, at Ferrara.

## 1650–1659

### POLITICS/LAW/WAR

d. Catalina de Erauzo (1592–1650?), Spanish soldier, who saw service in Latin America during the early 17th century, later claiming to have engaged in a wide range of adventures, often disguised as a man, and to have been given special papal dispensation to dress as a man.

Anne-Marie-Louise de Montpensier supported the losing side in the mid-century French civil wars of the Fronde (1652) and then went into lifelong exile (except for 1657–1662).

### RELIGION/EDUCATION/EVERYDAY LIFE

Society of Friends (Quakers) was founded in England by George Fox (1652), notable in regarding women and men as spiritually equal. Among the early converts were Margaret Fell and her husband, Thomas Fell, whose Swarthmore Hall was open to all religious leaders. Quakers had no professional ministers, but—reportedly at Margaret Fell's suggestion—women and men equally served as lay ministers from the start.

Mary Dyer, who had become a Quaker, returned to Massachusetts (1657). Testing Puritan laws against Quakers, Dyer was arrested, then banished, then arrested and sentenced to death, but pardoned and banished again.

b. Damaris Cudworth Masham (Lady Masham, 1658–1708), British scholar.

Courtesan Ninon de Lenclos was banished to a convent for lack of religious respect by Anne of Austria, the Queen Mother (1659); on her release, de Lenclos published *La coquette vengée* in self-defense.

d. Mary Frith (Moll Cutpurse, ca. 1590–1659), British thief who dressed as a man; model for numerous literary characters, most notably *The Roaring Girl, or Moll Cutpurse* (1611).

### SCIENCE/TECHNOLOGY/MEDICINE

German astronomer Maria Cunitz published *Urania propitia sive tabulae astronomicae mire faciles*, a simplified version of Johannes Kepler's tables of planetary motion (1650).

b. Catharina Geertuida Schrader (1656–1745), German-Dutch midwife.

Jeanne Mance visited France to recruit the Nursing Sisters of St. Joseph de La Flèche to staff Montreal's Hôtel Dieu (1657), under her supervision.

### ARTS/LITERATURE

Anne Bradstreet published *The Tenth Muse Lately Sprung Up in America*, the first original poetic work written and published in English in North America (1650).

b. Nell (Eleanor) Gwynn (1650–1687), British actress.

b. Sor Juana Inés de la Cruz (Juana de Asbaje y Ramirez de Santillana, 1651–1695), Mexican nun, poet, and playwright.

Margaret Cavendish published *Philosophical Fancies* and *Poetical Fancies* (1653).

d. Artemisia Gentileschi (1593–ca. 1653), Italian painter, daughter of painter Orazio Gentileschi; her work included historical allegory and portraits.

Madeleine de Scudéry published the 10-volume novel *Clélie* (1654); the character of Clarisse is reportedly based on the life of Ninon de Lenclos.

Barbara Strozzi published *Cantate, ariette e duetti* (1655).

b. Mary Chudleigh (1656–1710), British writer.

d. Clara Peeters (1594–after 1657), Dutch painter, whose surviving work consists largely of still lifes.

b. Elizabeth Barry (1658–1713), British actress.

Barbara Strozzi composed the cantata *Lagrime mie* (1659).

## 1660–1669

### POLITICS/LAW/WAR

b. Sarah Jennings Churchill, Duchess of Marlborough (1660–1744), wife of English general John Churchill, Duke of Marlborough.

b. Mary II (1662–1694), queen of England, Scotland, and Ireland (r. 1689–1694), who ruled jointly with her husband, William of Orange.

b. Anne (1665–1714), queen of Great Britain (r. 1702–1714).

d. Anne of Austria (1601–1666), daughter of Philip III of Spain and Margaret of Austria, queen of France after marrying Louis XIII (1615), though they were bitter opponents from 1637; after his death, she was regent of France (1643–1651) until the accession of Louis XIV, remaining a major European figure until her own death. She figured in the 1844 Alexandre Dumas novel, *The Three Musketeers.*

### RELIGION/EDUCATION/EVERYDAY LIFE

Margaret Philipse became the first known female business agent in the North American colonies, working for Dutch merchants trading with New Netherland (1660).

d. Mary Dyer (?–1660), British-American Quaker martyr, who was hanged after her third defiance of the Massachusetts Puritans' ban against Quakers (1657). She was one of many Quaker missionaries in this period (ca. 1656–ca. 1664), most of them women, many of them severely persecuted.

d. Angélique (Jacqueline Marie) Arnauld (1591–1661), French abbess.

A probably apocryphal autobiography of Mary Frith (Moll Cutpurse) was published posthumously (1662).

British Quaker activist Margaret Fell was arrested and jailed (1663) for her beliefs, and her estates given to her son; she remained active on behalf of other imprisoned Quakers after her release.

d. Marquise de Rambouillet (Catherine de Vivonne, 1588–1665), French hostess who led France's first great salon (ca. 1610–1665), satirized in Molière's first comedy of manners, *Les precieuses ridicules* (1659).

Margaret Fell published *Women's Speaking Justified. Proved and Knowed of the Scriptures* (1666).

Using a poison (*aqua tofana*) about which her lover, Gaudin de Sainte-Croix, had learned in prison, Marquise de Brinvilliers killed her father (1666) and her two brothers (1670), though failing to kill her husband; she was found out only through papers discovered after Sainte-Croix was killed experimenting with the poison (1672).

Margaret Fell, who had been widowed and later married Quaker leader George Fox, was again arrested (1669), but on her release continued to allow Quaker meetings at her home, Swarthmore Hall.

### SCIENCE/TECHNOLOGY/MEDICINE

d. Louise de Marillac (1591–1660), French saint who founded the nursing order Daughters of Charity (1633).

d. Maria Cunitz (1610–1664), German astronomer noted for her astronomical tables.

### ARTS/LITERATURE

Women first appeared professionally on the British stage after the Puritan ban on the professional theater was lifted; previously, all professional stage roles had been taken by men.

Madeleine de Scudéry published the novel *Amalida, ou l'esclave riche* (1660–1663).

d. Anna Renzi (ca. 1620–1660 or later), Italian soprano, a leading figure in Venetian opera during the 1640s, credited with creating several roles, most notably the title role in Claudio Monteverdi's *The Coronation of Poppea.*

d. Judith Leyster (1609–1660), Dutch artist, a student of Franz Hals, who is best known for her genre paintings and portraiture.

d. Maria de Zayas y Sotomayor (1590–ca. 1660), Spanish writer known for her series of novels on love.

b. Anne Finch, countess of Winchelsea (Ardelia) (ca. 1661–1720), British poet.

Margaret Cavendish published *Playes* (1662).

Marie-Catherine-Hortense Desjardins published her play *Manlius* (1662).

Mlle. De Brie created the role of Agnès in Molière's *L'Ecole des Femmes* (1662).

b. Mary de la Rivière Manley (1663–1724), British writer, editor, and political satirist.

d. Barbara Strozzi (1619–after 1663), Italian singer and composer.

d. Katherine Fowler Philips (1631–1664), British poet who wrote under the pseudonym Orinda.

d. Elisabetta Sirani (1638–1665), Italian artist, a prolific painter in a wide range of forms and subjects.

Marie-Catherine-Hortense Desjardins published the play *Le Favory* (1665).

b. Elisabeth-Claude Jacquet de la Guerre (ca. 1666–1729), French composer and harpsichordist.

Madeleine de Scudéry published the novel *Mathilde d'Aguilan* (1667).

b. Susannah Centlivre (1667–1723), British playwright and actress.

French grammarian Marguerite Buffet published *New Observations on the French Language* (1668), "setting out to teach ladies the art of speaking and writing well on all subjects."

b. Mary Astell (1668–1731), British writer.

# 1670–1679

## POLITICS/LAW/WAR

d. Margaret Brent (ca. 1601–1671), Maryland colony landowner, influential because of her own holdings and as executor for former governor Calvert.

## RELIGION/EDUCATION/EVERYDAY LIFE

Ninon de Lenclos retired from life as a courtesan and began to hold salons (ca. 1671), whose habitués included Jean Racine and Marie La Fayette.

d. Marie Guyard (1599–1672), French Ursuline sister and missionary who cofounded a convent and school in Quebec (1639), preparing catechisms in Huron and Algonquin, and a French-Algonquin dictionary.

Anna Maria van Schurman joined the religious community of Jean de Labadie (1673), chosing spiritual fellowship over learning; rejecting her earlier *Amica dissertatio* (ca. 1635) on women's education, she published the autobiographical *Euklerion* (*Choice of a Better Part*).

Bathshua Makin published her *Essay to Revive the Ancient Education of Gentlewomen* (1673).

d. Bathshua Pell Makin (1608–1675), British educator, tutor of Charles I's daughters.

d. Marquise de Brinvilliers (Marie-Madeleine Marguerite Aubray, 1630–1676), French poisoner, convicted in a sensational trial and executed for killing her father and two brothers and for attempting to kill her husband.

d. Anna Maria van Schurman (1607–1678), Dutch philologist and theologist, who attended lectures at Utrecht University (1635) and wrote various books.

## SCIENCE/TECHNOLOGY/MEDICINE

b. Maria (Margaretha) Winkelmann Kirch (1670–1720), German astronomer.

Jane Sharp published her practical manual *The Midwives' Book; or, The Whole Art of Midwifery*, the first textbook by a British midwife (1671). It discussed anatomy, sterility, signs and diseases of pregnancy, labor, and post-childbirth disease, based on her three decades of experience, and was widely used well into the 18th century.

Anne Finch Conway developed a vitalist scientific philosophy in her notebooks (1671–1675); they would eventually be published posthumously in Latin (1690), then retranslated into English and published as *The Principles of the Most Ancient and Modern Philosophy, concerning God, Christ and the Creation; that is, concerning Spirit, and Matter in General* (1692).

d. Anne Finch Conway (1631–1679), British scientific theorist.

## ARTS/LITERATURE

Aphra Behn's first play was *The Forc'd Marriage; or, the Jealous Bridegroom* (1670).

Madame Champmeslé (Marie Desmares) created the title role in Jean Racine's *Bérénice* (1670).

Comtesse de La Fayette published the novels *La Princesse de Montpensier* and *Zaïde* (1670).

b. Henrietta Deering Johnston (1670–1728/9), American painter.

Madame Champmeslé (Marie Desmares) created the role of Atalida in Jean Racine's play *Bajazet*

(1672) and the title roles in Thomas Corneille's play *Ariadne* (1673) and in Racine's *Iphigénie* (1674) and *Phèdre* (1677).

d. Madeleine Béjart (1618–1672), French actress, Molière's colleague, sometime comanager of his company, and as an actress creator of several of his leading roles.

d. Anne Dudley Bradstreet (ca. 1612–1672), American writer, the first poet in English to be published in North America (1650).

Maria de Zayas y Sotomayor published the group of novels collectively titled *Parle segunda des sarao y entretenimientos honestos (Disillusionment in Love)* (1674).

d. Margaret Cavendish, duchess of Newcastle (ca. 1623–1674), English writer; a poet, playwright, essayist, and biographer.

b. Rosalba Giovanna Carriera (1675–1758), Italian painter.

Aphra Behn's comedy *The Rover, or The Banished Cavaliers, Part I* was produced in London (1677).

Comtesse de La Fayette published the novel *La Princesse de Clèves* (1678).

Anne Bradstreet's *Poems* were published posthumously (1678).

Aphra Behn's comedies were produced in London: *Sir Patient Fancy* (1678) and *The Feign'd Curtizans; or, a Night's Intrigue* (1679).

# 1680–1689

## POLITICS/LAW/WAR

Elizabeth Dormer Cellier (active 1680s), British midwife and social reformer, also a convert to Catholicism linked to an assassination conspiracy. Acquitted of charges that she hid assassination plans in a "meal tub" in her house, she then published a pamphlet, *Malice defeated; or a Brief Relation of the Accusation and Deliverance of Elizabeth Cellier*, criticizing conditions at Newgate Prison so severely that she was charged with and convicted of libel and fined £1,000, an enormous sum at the time.

Françoise de Maintenon founded a school (1686), the Maison Royale de Saint Louis, at St. Cyr, later a convent, to which she retired (1715).

Mary, daughter of England's James II, and her Protestant husband, William of Orange, overthrew her Catholic father with English Protestant support (1688) in what was later called the Glorious Revolution. They ruled jointly as Mary II (r. 1689–1694) and William III (r. 1689–1702).

## RELIGION/EDUCATION/EVERYDAY LIFE

b. Elizabeth Haddon Estaugh (ca. 1680–1762), British-born American Quaker.

In Pennsylvania's Quaker communities, founded by William Penn (1681), the secular government was male-dominated, but women retained equality within the religious community, also holding separate women's meetings.

French missionary Marie Guyard's letters were posthumously published (1681), as was her *Retraites* (1682), both key documents of early French Canada.

b. Elizabeth Elstob (1683–1756), British Anglo-Saxon scholar and teacher.

d. La Voisin (Catherine Deshayes Monvoisin, ?–1684), French midwife, fortune-teller, and reputed witch, whose clients included aristocrats such as the marquise de Montespan; convicted of selling poisons and charms, she was burned at the stake, as witch-hunting and the long attack on female healers continued.

d. Alexandra Mavrokordatou (1605–1684), Constantinople-born Greek intellectual and salon hostess who introduced Western European-style salons to the Turkish Empire; she died in prison, after the Turks accused her son, a diplomat in their service, of betrayal in the siege of Vienna (1683).

Jeanne Guyon published *Moyen court et très facile de faire oraison* (1685) and *Le Cantique des Cantiques* (1688).

*Advice to a Daughter*, by the marquis of Halifax (1688), was one of a long line of works telling young women how to act and think in society.

b. Mary Wortley Montagu (1689–1762), British traveler and writer.

### SCIENCE/TECHNOLOGY/MEDICINE

d. Elizabeth of Bohemia (1618–1680), student of natural philosophy; daughter of Frederick V, king of Bohemia and granddaughter of England's James I, she long corresponded on science and philosophy with René Descartes, who dedicated his *Principia philosophiae* (1644) to her.

Jeanne Dumée (active ca. 1680), French astronomer, widowed at age 17, who continued her astronomy studies, publishing *Entretiens sur l'opinion de Copernic touchant la mobilité de la terre*, a book explaining the Copernican system.

British midwife Elizabeth Dormer Cellier published a plan for a hospital that would care for mothers, provide training for midwives, and find homes for "foundling and exposed children" (1687). A strong advocate of education and merit-based licensing for midwives, she also compiled data on the high maternal and infant mortality rate, due to poor care.

### ARTS/LITERATURE

Aphra Behn's comedies were seen in London: *The Rover, or The Banished Cavaliers: Part II* (1680), *The Roundheads; or, the Good Old Cause* (1681), and *The City-Heiress, or, Sir Timothy Treat-all* (1682).

Elizabeth Barry starred opposite Thomas Betterton in the first London production of Thomas Otway's *Venice Preserved* (1682).

Francesca Caccini wrote the opera *La liberazione di Ruggiero* (1682).

d. Marie-Catherine-Hortense Desjardins (1632–1683), French writer who worked in various forms, best known for her plays.

b. Claudine-Alexandrine Guerin de Tencin (Madame de Tencin, 1685–1749), French novelist and salon hostess.

d. Nell (Eleanor) Gwynn (1650–1687), British actress, who played several roles on the London stage (1665–1671) before becoming the mistress of Charles II and giving up her career.

Aphra Behn published her antislavery novel *Oroonoko, or the History of the Royal Slave*, the first published English novel by a woman (1688); she also published *The Fair Jilt*.

Sor Juana Inés de la Cruz wrote the play *Love, the Greater Labyrinth* (1689).

d. Aphra (Afra) Behn (1640–1689), British author, the first woman to become a professional writer.

## 1690–1699

### POLITICS/LAW/WAR

b. Mary Read (1690–1720), English sailor and soldier.

Madame de Montespan, formerly mistress of Louis XIV of France, retired to St. Joseph's convent in Paris (1691), later becoming its mother superior.

d. Anne-Marie-Louise d'Orléans de Montpensier (La Grande Mademoiselle, 1627–1693), French duchess, who after supporting the losing side in the wars of the Fronde (1652) went into exile (except for 1657–1662).

## Salem Witch Trials

In 1692, a group of teenage girls in Salem, Massachusetts, accused Tituba, a Carib (or Carib-African) slave, of witchcraft; after she "confessed" to telling of voodoo rituals and the spirit life, a string of further accusations followed, mostly of women, some of men, who were brought before a special court in the Massachusetts Bay Colony. In the end, 19 people were executed in Salem (1692–1693), and the witchcraft hysteria spread elsewhere in Massachusetts, continuing until a new governor from England dismissed the witchcraft court and freed those imprisoned (not before his own wife was accused). Some have suggested that the original adolescent accusers had been made ill by hallucinogenic chemicals from ergot fungus in their grain-based foods.

d. Mary II (1662–1694), queen of England, Scotland, and Ireland (r. 1689–1694), who ruled jointly with her husband, William of Orange, after they had deposed her father, James II of England, in what would be called the Glorious Revolution (1688).

### RELIGION/EDUCATION/EVERYDAY LIFE

d. Rebecca Towne Nurse (1621–1692), a victim of the Salem witch trials in Massachusetts, later "posthumously rehabilitated."

d. Tituba (1648?–1692), a Carib (or Carib-African) slave whose tales of voodoo rituals and spirit life may have triggered the Salem witch trials; she herself was accused but after confessing was released as penitent.

Damaris Masham published *Occasional Thoughts in Reference to a Christian Life* (1694) and *Discourse Concerning the Love of God* (1696).

b. Marie-Thérèse Rodet de Geoffrin (1699–1777), French salon hostess.

### SCIENCE/TECHNOLOGY/MEDICINE

After the death of her husband, astronomer Johannes Hevelius, Elisabetha Koopman Hevelius edited and published his writings (1690), among them *Prodomus astronomiae*, a catalog of more than 1,500 stars; she had long assisted her husband, director of the Danzig observatory.

Catharina Schrader began working as a midwife to support her family after her husband's death (1692); before her retirement, at age 88, she would attend at 3,060 deliveries. In later years she specialized in difficult births, using manual techniques outlined in her *Notebook*, which stressed avoiding instruments and using traditional skills whenever possible.

### ARTS/LITERATURE

Sor Juana Inés de la Cruz wrote *Carta Atenagórica* (1690), a letter to a Mexican bishop opposing a Jesuit sermon. When he criticized her for writing such a letter, she wrote her famous *Reply to Sor Filotea* (1691), an autobiographical letter amounting to a call for greater freedom for women within the Catholic church, and more generally for greater educational and intellectual opportunities.

b. Adrienne Lecouvreur (1692–1730), French actress.

Anne Bracegirdle starred opposite William Betterton in William Congreve's play *The Old Bachelor* (1693).

b. Eliza Fowler Haywood (1693–1756), British writer and editor.

d. Comtesse de La Fayette (Marie Madeleine de la Vergne, 1634–1693), French novelist.

d. Sor Juana Inés de la Cruz (Juana de Asbaje y Ramirez de Santillana, 1651–1693), Mexican nun, poet, and playwright.

d. Sor Violante do Céu (1602?–1693?), Portuguese poet and playwright, a nun from 1630, whose play *Saint Eufemia* was produced before Spain's Philip III; some works were posthumously published in *Lusitanian Parnassus* (1733).

Anne Bracegirdle starred opposite William Betterton in William Congreve's play *The Double Dealer* (1694).

Elisabeth-Claude Jacquet wrote the opera *Cephale et Procris* (1694).

Mary Astell published *A Serious Proposal to the Ladies for the Advancement of their True and Greatest Interest* (1694), urging the founding of a women's education institution in England; a precurser

---

# On Women and Education

Women are from their very Infancy debarr'd those advantages [of education] with the want of which they are afterwards reproached, and nursed up in those vices with which will hereafter be upbraided them. So partial are Men as to expect Bricks when they afford no straw.

— Mary Astell, in *A Serious Proposal to the Ladies for the Advancement of their True and Greatest Interest* (1694).

of the women's educational movement that would flourish in the 19th century.

Anne Bracegirdle starred opposite William Betterton in William Congreve's play *Love for Love* (1695), originating the role of Angelica.

Mary Manley wrote the plays *The Lost Lover* and *The Royal Mischief* (1696).

d. Marie de Rabutin Chantal Sévigné (1626–1696), French essayist, the most notable of European letter writers.

Anne Bracegirdle created the part of Almeria in William Congreve's tragedy *The Mourning Bride* (1697).

b. Carolina Neuber (1697–1760), German actress and manager.

d. Marie Desmares (Madame Champmeslé, 1642–1698), French actress.

## 1700–1709

### POLITICS/LAW/WAR

Anne, younger daughter of James II and sister of Mary II, took the throne of Great Britain (r. 1702–1714); a major influence in her early reign (1702–ca. 1705) was her childhood friend and longtime confidante, Sarah Jennings Churchill, duchess of Marlborough.

d. Françoise-Athenis de Rochechouart de Mortmart de Montespan (Madame de Montespan, 1641–1707), mistress of Louis XIV of France, a powerful influence at court until involved in court scandals (ca. 1680); later mother superior of Paris's St. Joseph's convent.

b. Elizabeth of Russia (Yelizaveta Petrovna, 1709–1762), empress of Russia, daughter of Peter the Great and Catherine I.

### RELIGION/EDUCATION/EVERYDAY LIFE

Elizabeth Haddon (later Estaugh) founded a home for traveling ministers (1701) on land her father owned in New Jersey; married to a young preacher, John Estaugh, she managed the plantation and served as clerk of the Quaker women's meeting for over 50 years.

Elizabeth Mallet founded *The Daily Courant*, the first daily newspaper in England (1702–1732).

d. Margaret Askew Fell (1614–1702), British religious figure who was converted by Quaker leader George Fox (1652), who became her second husband (1669).

d. Ninon (Anne) de Lenclos (1620–1705), French courtesan and later salon hostess, who traveled in influential and intellectual circles; reportedly the model for Clarisse in Madeleine de Scudéry's novel *Clélie*.

b. Selina Huntingdon (Countess of Huntingdon, 1707–1791), British religious figure.

Elizabeth Elstob published her translations of Madeleine de Scudéry's *Essay on Glory* (1708).

b. Hannah Allgood Glasse (1708–1770), British cook.

d. Damaris Cudworth Masham (Lady Masham, 1658–1708), British scholar, a strong supporter of women's education, if only to make them good educators of their own children.

Elizabeth Elstob published *The Anglo-Saxon Homily on the Nativity of St. Gregory* (1709), with a preface defending women's right to study.

### SCIENCE/TECHNOLOGY/MEDICINE

German astronomer Maria Kirch discovered a comet (1702).

Maria Sibylla Merian and her two daughters published *De generatione et metamorphosibus instectorum surinamensium* (1705), a study of the flora and fauna collected, described, and illustrated from a trip to Surinam.

b. Gabrielle-Émilie Le Tonnelier de Breteuil, marquise du Châtelet (1706–1749), French writer on natural philosophy.

d. Tofana (?–ca. 1709/1730?), Italian herbalist who concocted a poison called *aqua tofana*, originally purporting to be a healing medicine called the "Mana of St. Nicholas of Bari." Probably an arsenic mixture, it is alleged to have been used by numerous women to poison their husbands.

## ARTS/LITERATURE

b. Faustina Bordoni (1700–1781), Italian mezzo-soprano.

d. Armande-Grésinde-Claire-Élisabeth Béjart (1641–1700), French actress, Molière's wife, creator of many of his major roles, and manager of their company after his death. She was the sister of Madeleine Béjart.

d. Leonarda Isabella (1620–ca. 1700), prolific Italian composer, whose published works included hundreds of motets, in more than 20 collections.

d. Madeleine de Scudéry (1607–1701), French writer.

Mary Astell published *The Christian Religion, as Professed by a Daughter of the Church of England* (1705).

Susannah Centlivre's play *The Gamester* was seen in London (1705).

d. Mlle. De Brie (Catherine Leclerc du Rozet, ca. 1630–1706), French actress, a leading player in Molière's company, and a founding member of the Comédie Francaise, who created several major roles, including that of Agnès in Molière's *L'Ecole des Femmes*.

b. Marie Sallé (1707–1756), French ballerina.

Elisabeth-Claude Jacquet published three collections of cantatas (1708–1715).

b. Lavinia Fenton (1708–1760), British actress.

Mary Manley published her best-known work, the political satire *The New Atlantis* (1709).

Susannah Centlivre's play *The Busie Body* was seen in London (1709).

# 1710–1719

## POLITICS/LAW/WAR

d. Anne (1665–1714), queen of Great Britain (r. 1702–1714), daughter of James II and last of the Stuart line. During her reign, England and Scotland were united as Great Britain (1707); at her death, succession passed to the Hanoverian line.

b. Maria Theresa (1717–1780), Holy Roman (Austrian) Empress, the archduchess of Austria and queen of Bohemia and Hungary.

d. Françoise Augigné de Maintenon (Madame de Maintenon, 1635–1719), second wife of Louis XIV of France, at first secretly, a powerful influence at court.

## RELIGION/EDUCATION/EVERYDAY LIFE

The Salem witch trial conviction of Rebecca Nurse (1692) was posthumously voided and her excommunication erased from the Massachusetts Puritan church records (1712).

b. Elizabeth Sampson Ashbridge (1713–1755), American Quaker preacher.

d. Kaibara Ekken (1630–1714), Japanese essayist, credited with writing *Onna Daigaku (The Greater Learning for Women)*.

Elizabeth Elstob published *Rudiments of Grammar for the English-Saxon Tongue, first given in English; with an Apology for the Study of Northern Antiquities* (1715).

d. Jeanne Marie (de Bouvier de la Mothe) Guyon (1648–1717), French Quietist and mystical author, whose views were sometimes regarded as heretical, leading to arrest and condemnation.

Anne Bonney (active ca. 1718–1720), Irish pirate, mistress of Atlantic and Caribbean pirate Captain Rackham (Calico Jack), with whom she made raids, during one of them taking Mary Read, with whom she formed a passionate partnership.

## SCIENCE/TECHNOLOGY/MEDICINE

b. Laura (Maria Caterina) Bassi (1711–1778), Italian physicist, anatomist, and natural philosopher.

German astronomer Maria Kirch wrote a paper on the coming conjunction of Jupiter and Saturn, with astrological commentary (1712).

b. Angélique (Marguerite le Boursier) du Coudray (1712–1789), French midwife and obstetrician.

Sybilla Righton Masters was the first American female inventor whose work was patented (1715); the British government, which still ruled her colony of New Jersey, granted to Thomas Masters a patent for a machine to prepare Indian corn, but clearly stating that it covered "a new Invencon found out by Sybilla, his wife."

b. Dorothea Christiana Leporin Erxleben (1715–1762), German physician.

Sybilla Righton Masters, under the name of her husband, Thomas Masters, received a second patent from the British government (1716) "for the Sole Working and Weaving in a New Method, Palmetto, Chips and Straw, for covering hats and bonnets, and other improvements in that ware." The invention was presumably later used in her London shop, where she briefly made and sold hats, bonnets, "child-bed baskets," and matting made of the fiber; she later returned to America.

b. Anna Morandi Manzolini (1716–1774), Italian anatomist.

d. Maria Sibylla Merian (1647–1717), German naturalist who with her two daughters became zoological collectors and illustrators, especially focusing on flora and insects, notably tracing the stages of insect growth.

Mary Wortley Montagu brought back to England the practice of inoculation for smallpox, about which she had learned on a trip to Turkey (1716–1718) with her husband, England's ambassador.

b. Maria Gaetana Agnesi (1718–1799), Italian mathematician.

b. Marie Catherine Biheron (1719–1786), French anatomist.

### ARTS/LITERATURE

b. Marie-Anne de Cupis de Camargo (1710–1770), French dancer.

b. Marie-Anne Le Page du Bocage (Madame du Bocage, 1710–1802), French playwright and poet.

d. Mary Chudleigh (1656–1710), British writer, author of the essay *The Ladies Defence*, rebutting a sermon attacking women on the question of marital obligations.

Isabella Girardeau created the role of Almirena in George Frideric Handel's opera *Rinaldo* (1711).

Mary Manley succeeded Jonathan Swift as editor of *The Examiner* (1711).

b. Hannah Pritchard (1711–1768), British actress.

b. Kitty Clive (Catherine Raftor Clive, 1711–1785), British actress.

Anne Finch published *Miscellany Poems on Several Ocasions*, including "A Nocturnal Reverie" and "To the Nightingale" (1713).

b. Marie-Françoise Dumesnil (1713–1803), French actress.

d. Elizabeth Barry (1658–1713), British actress, a major tragedian on the London stage.

Mary Manley published the autobiographical novel *The Adventures of Rivella* (1714).

b. Susannah Arne Cibber (1714–1766), British singer and actress.

Susannah Centlivre's play *The Wonder, a Woman Keeps a Secret* played in London (1714).

b. Elizabeth Carter (1717–1806), British writer.

Susannah Centlivre's play *A Bold Stroke for a Wife* was seen in London (1718).

b. Peg (Margaret) Woffington (ca. 1718–1760), Irish actress.

Eliza Haywood published her first novel, *Love's Excess* (1719).

## 1720–1729

### POLITICS/LAW/WAR

b. Jeanne Antoinette Poisson (Madame de Pompadour, 1721–1764), mistress of Louis XV of France.

b. Catherine II (the Great, 1729–1796), empress of Russia (1762–1796).

### RELIGION/EDUCATION/EVERYDAY LIFE

Anne Bonney and Mary Read fought alongside their male pirate colleagues, but their ship was captured by government forces. The men were hanged; Bonney and Read were spared, but their further lives are unclear.

b. Elizabeth Robinson Montagu (1720–1800), British intellectual and salon hostess.

b. Hannah (Cook) Heaton (1721–1794), American autobiographer.

　　b. Mercy Otis Warren (1728–1814), American playwright, poet, and historian.

**SCIENCE/TECHNOLOGY/MEDICINE**

　　d. Maria (Margaretha) Winkelmann Kirch (1670–1720), German astronomer who assisted her husband, Gottfried Kirch, in making observations and calculations for his calendars and ephemerides (tables showing the position of key celestial bodies for each day of the year), which she continued after his death, also doing her own astronomical work. Her daughter, Christine, and son, Christfried, also became astronomers.

　　d. Sybilla Righton Masters (?–1720), American inventor, who invented a machine to prepare Indian corn (1715) and a method of working and weaving palmetto and straw (1716).

　　b. Elizabeth (Eliza) Lucas Pinckney (1722–1793), American agricultural innovator.

　　b. Nicole-Reine Etable de la Brière Hortense Lepaute (1723–1788), French astronomer.

　　b. Jane Colden (1724–1766), American botanist.

**ARTS/LITERATURE**

Mary Manley published *The Power of Love* (1720).

　　d. Anne Finch, countess of Winchelsea (Ardelia) (ca. 1661–1720), British poet.

　　b. Anna (Dorothea) Lisiewska (1721–1782), German artist.

Eliza Haywood wrote the play *A Wife to be Left* (1723).

　　b. Mlle. Clairon (Claire-Josephe-Hippolyte Leris de La Tude, 1723–1803) French actress.

　　d. Susannah Centlivre (1667–1723), British playwright and actress.

Franceska Cuzzoni created the role of Cleopatra in George Frideric Handel's opera *Giulio Cesare* (1724), the role of Asteria in his opera *Tamburlaine* (1724), and the title role in his opera *Rodelinda* (1725).

　　d. Mary de la Rivière Manley (1663–1724), British writer, editor, and political satirist.

　　b. Maria Antonia Walpurgis (1724–1780), electress of Saxony, a composer, singer, poet, painter, and patron of the arts.

Eliza Haywood published her novel *Memoirs of a Certain Island* (1725).

　　b. George Anne Bellamy (1727–1788), British actress.

　　b. Jane Elliot (1727–1805), Scottish poet.

Lavinia Fenton created the role of Polly in John Gay's *The Beggar's Opera* (1728) at London's Lincoln's Inn Fields; Gay's play was the basis for the Bertolt Brecht—Kurt Weill musical *The Threepenny Opera* (1928).

　　d. Henrietta Deering Johnston (1670–1728/9), the earliest American professional female painter, who worked largely as a portraitist in pastels, mainly in Charleston, South Carolina.

　　d. Elisabeth-Claude Jacquet de la Guerre (ca. 1666–1729), French composer and harpsichordist whose patron was Louis XIV; she was an early composer of sonatas and cantatas.

---

# By a Woman Writ

Did I my lines intend for public view,
How many censures would their faults pursue. . .
True judges might condemn their want of wit,
And all might say, they're by a woman writ.
Alas a woman that attempts the pen, such an intruder on the rights of men,
Such a presumptuous creature is esteemed,
The fault can by no virtue be redeemed.

— Anne Finch (1671)

---

## 1730–1739

### POLITICS/LAW/WAR

b. Molly (Mary) Brant (1736–1796), Mohawk leader.

### RELIGION/EDUCATION/EVERYDAY LIFE

Giuseppa Eleonora Barbapiccola (active ca. 1731), Italian natural philosopher noted for her Italian translation of René Descartes' *Principles of Philosophy*.

b. Catharine Sawbridge Macaulay (1731–1791), British historian.

b. Julie (Jeanne-Eléanore) de Lespinasse (1732–1776), French salon hostess.

b. Ann Lee (1736–1784), British-American religious leader.

After her husband's death, Elizabeth Timothy supported her family by publishing alone their weekly newspaper, the *South-Carolina Gazette* (from 1738).

b. Mary Katherine Goddard (1738–1816), American postmaster, printer, publisher, and bookseller.

*Women Not Inferior to Men* was published anonymously in England (1739), probably written by Mary Wortley Montagu.

b. Suzanne Curchod Necker (1739–1817), Swiss writer and philanthropist.

### SCIENCE/TECHNOLOGY/MEDICINE

Laura Bassi received a doctorate from the University of Bologna (1731 or 1732), and remained there as a lecturer on anatomy, later on experimental physics (1745–1778).

Gabrielle-Émilie Le Tonnelier de Breteuil, marquise du Châtelet, wrote an essay on the nature of fire (1736), which Voltaire published (1739) with his own and several other essays submitted to an Académie des Sciences contest on the topic.

Italian mathematician Maria Agnesi published *Propositiones philosophicae*, her essays on science and philosophy (1738).

In French Canada, Madame d'Youville founded the Soeurs Grises (Grey Nuns) (1738), an order of uncloistered nurses who visited and cared for the sick in their homes; she also founded La Crèche d'Youville, a home for abandoned children.

### ARTS/LITERATURE

d. Adrienne Lecouvreur (1692–1730), French actress, long a leading player with the Comédie Française.

d. Mary Astell (1668–1731), British writer best known for her *A Serious Proposal . . .* (1694) on women's education.

Laura Monti created the role of Serpina in Giovannie Battista Pergolesi's opera *La Serva Padrona* (1733).

b. Anna Lucia De Amicis (1733–1816), Italian soprano.

Anna Strada created the role of Ginevra in *Ariodante* and the title role in *Alcina*, both George Frideric Handel operas (1735).

Madame de Tencin published the novel *Les mémoires du comte de Comminge* (*Memoirs of the Count of Comminge*) (1735).

b. Frances Abington (1737–1815), British actress.

Elisabeth Duparc created the role of Romilda in George Frideric Handel's opera *Xerxes* (1738).

Elizabeth Carter published *Poems Upon Particular Occasions* (1738).

Marquise de Tencin published the novel *Le siège de Calais* (1739).

## 1740-1749

### POLITICS/LAW/WAR

On the death of Holy Roman Emperor Charles VI, Maria Theresa succeeded to the throne (1740), able to do so because her only son, upon his death, had declared the "Pragmatic Sanction," allowing a woman to succeed where no man was in line. Her right to the succession was quickly challenged by Frederick II (the Great) of Prussia, triggering the War of the Austrian Succession (1740–1748).

Elizabeth of Russia took power by coup, deposing Empress Anna Elizabeth, regent for Ivan IV, then ruling Russia until her death (1741–1762).

b. Ekaterina (Yekaterina) Romanovna Dashkova (1743–1810), Russian princess.

b. Marie Jeanne Gomard de Vaubernier, comtesse du Barry (Madame du Barry, 1743–1793), mistress to Louis XV of France.

b. Abigail Adams (1744–1818), American First Lady, wife of President John Adams.

d. Sarah Jennings Churchill, duchess of Marlborough (1660–1744), wife of English general John Churchill, duke of Marlborough; childhood friend and longtime confidante to Anne of England, she was a powerful influence in Anne's court, until losing favor (ca. 1705).

b. Olympe de Gouges (Marie-Olympe Gouze, 1748–1793), French feminist and writer, a leading woman of the French Revolution.

### RELIGION/EDUCATION/EVERYDAY LIFE

Great Awakening of the 1740s, the first major religious revival in America, saw disproportionately large numbers of women join churches, a phenomenon some have called the "feminization of the church."

b. Hester Lynch Salisbury Thrale (Piozzi) (1741–1821), British salon hostess and writer.

b. Sarah Trimmer (1741–1810), British educator.

Moravians, German immigrant members of the Church of the United Brethren, founded a school in Germantown (later in Bethlehem), Pennsylvania (1742); this would grow into the Moravian Seminary for Young Females (from 1805, the Young Ladies Seminary), one of the earliest American girls' boarding schools.

After the death of her son, Elizabeth Montagu developed a literary salon (1744); her informal gatherings—which allowed the wearing of blue (instead of formal black) stockings—gave rise to the term *bluestocking* for a female intellectual.

b. Marie Madeleine Postel (1746–after 1836), French teacher and saint.

Marie-Thérèse Rodet de Geoffrin, long associated with Madame de Tencin's salon, established her own salon (ca. 1749), making it a leading gathering place for artistic and literary figures, with discussion of religion and politics banned.

### SCIENCE/TECHNOLOGY/MEDICINE

Gabrielle-Émilie Le Tonnelier de Breteuil, marquise du Châtelet, published *Institutions de physique* (1740), a textbook written for her son, aimed at reconciling Newtonian physics with Leibniz's metaphysics.

Trained at Paris's Hôtel Dieu School, Angélique du Coudray received her license as a midwife (*accoucheuse*) (1740); as a teacher she introduced the use of a model of the female body and an actual fetus, so students could practice delivery.

Women began to be barred from studying and practicing dentistry in France (from the 1740s), the leading country in the licensed dentistry movement; until then, they had been able to do so, despite being barred from universities.

Dorothea Erxleben obtained special permission from Prussia's Frederick II (the Great) to study medicine at the University of Halle (1741).

Jane Colden published her *Plantae Coldenghamae*, a book describing, illustrating, and cataloguing the plants found on her family's New York estate, Coldengham (1743), encouraged by Carolus Linnaeus, at whose system of classification she became expert; she later (1757) expanded her catalogue to cover over 300 plants.

Elizabeth Pinckney developed indigo as a commercial crop in the Carolinas (1744); despite the plant's sensitivity to soil and climate, she succeeded where other farmers, seven decades earlier, had failed.

Laura Bassi lectured on experimental physics at the University of Bologna (1745–1778), becoming the first female physics professor at any university; she also bore 12 children, after her 1738 marriage.

d. Catharina Geertuida Schrader (1656–1745), German-Dutch midwife.

b. Louise Elisabeth Félicité Pourra de la Madeleine du Pierry (1746–?), French astronomer who taught an astronomy course for women (1789) and did numerous astronomical calculations.

Italian mathematician Maria Agnesi published *Instituzioni Analitiche* (*Analytical Institutions*) (1748), her long-standard text on algebra, geometry, and the basics of what would become differential and integral calculus; trained at home by her father, she had begun the work by age 20.

Medical student Dorothea Erxleben published *Rational Thoughts on Education of the Fair Sex*, advocating university study for women (1749).

d. Gabrielle-Émilie Le Tonnelier de Breteuil, marquise du Châtelet (1706–1749), French writer on natural philosophy, a friend of Voltaire, notable for her work attempting to reconcile Newtonian physics and Leibniz's metaphysics. She died shortly after giving birth (the baby also died), having pressed to complete her annotated French translation of Newton's *Principia*, which she had begun in 1744 and which was published posthumously (1756–1759).

## ARTS/LITERATURE

b. (Magdeleine) Sophie Arnould (1740–1820), French soprano.

b. Angelica Kauffmann (1740–1807), Swiss painter.

b. Jane Pope (1742–1818), British actress.

Marie-Françoise Dumesnil created the title role in Voltaire's drama *Mérope* (1743).

b. Anna Letitia Aikin Barbauld (1743–1825), British writer and editor.

b. Françoise Vestris (1743–1804), French actress.

b. Hannah Cowley (1743–1809), British playwright.

b. Lucrezia Aguiari (1743–1783), Italian soprano.

Elisabeth Duparc created the title role in George Frideric Handel's opera *Semele* (1744).

Welsh poet Jane Hughes Brereton's *Poems on Several Occasions* was posthumously published (1744).

b. Anne Vallayer-Coster (1744–1818), French still-life painter.

b. Hannah More (1745–1835), British writer.

b. Sophia Snow (1745–1786), British actress.

Marquise de Tencin published the novel *Les malheurs de l'amour* (*The Misfortunes of Love*) (1747).

Madame du Bocage published her poem *Paradis Terrestre* (*The Earthly Paradise*) (1748).

Sarah Fielding published *The Governess*, the first English novel written expressly for children (1749). She was the sister of Henry Fielding.

Madame du Bocage's play *The Amazons* was performed at the Comédie Française (1749).

b. Adélaide Labille-Guiard (1749–1803), French painter.

d. Claudine-Alexandrine Guerin de Tencin (Madame de Tencin, 1685–1749), French novelist and salon hostess.

# 1750–1759

## POLITICS/LAW/WAR

b. Manon Roland (Marie-Jeanne Philpon, 1754–1793), French revolutionary.

b. Molly Pitcher (Mary Ludwig Hays McCauley, 1754–1832), reputed hero of the American Revolution.

b. Marie Antoinette (1755–1793), queen of France, daughter of Holy Roman Empress Maria Theresa and emperor Francis I.

Maria Theresa of Austria, pursuing territories lost during the War of the Austrian Succession and alliance with France and Russia, began the worldwide Seven Years War (1756–1763).

b. Pauline Léon (1758–?), French revolutionary and feminist, cofounder of the Republican Revolutionary Society (1792); originally a member of the Jacobins, but by 1792 strongly critical of them.

Mohawk leader Molly Brant became the companion and common-law wife of British Indian Affairs representative William Johnson (1759). She played a major role in developing the Iroquois-British alliance that continued through their joint defeat in the American Revolution and the flight to Canada, and into the following century.

b. Mary Wollstonecraft (Godwin; 1759–1797), British writer and women's rights advocate.

### RELIGION/EDUCATION/EVERYDAY LIFE

b. Joanna Southcott (1750–1814), British religious leader.

Hannah Glasse's *The Art of Cooking Made Plain and Simple* was published in its fourth edition (1751); this first British housewife's cooking guide would remain in print until 1824.

d. Elizabeth Sampson Ashbridge (1713–1755), American Quaker preacher, best known for her posthumously published autobiographical narrative (1774); she died in Ireland, where she had been preaching.

d. Elizabeth Elstob (1683–1756), British Anglo-Saxon scholar who published an early Anglo-Saxon grammar (1715) and several translations, later forced to earn her living as a governess (1738).

### SCIENCE/TECHNOLOGY/MEDICINE

Maria Agnesi was appointed to succeed her father as professor of mathematics at the University of Bologna (1750), but whether she actually assumed the chair is unclear.

b. Caroline Lucretia Herschel (1750–1848), German astronomer working largely in England.

Dorothea Erxleben received an M.D. degree from the University of Halle (1754), the first full medical degree awarded to a woman by a German university. She had begun her studies only after receiving royal permission (1741) and completed them after her 1742 marriage despite bearing four children, caring for four stepchildren, and being widowed; she was able to practice only eight years before her death, possibly of breast cancer.

Gabrielle-Émilie Le Tonnelier de Breteuil, marquise du Châtelet's annotated translation of Newton's *Principia*, on which she was working at her death after childbirth, was published in part (1756) and then whole (1759); the first version being available in French, it was reprinted in 1966.

Italian physicist and mathematician Maria Ardinghelli published her Italian translation of Stephen Hales's *Vegetable Staticks* (1756).

Nicole-Reine Lepaute and her husband, Jean André Lepaute, were engaged by astronomer Alexis Claude Clairaut (1757) to calculate exactly when in 1759 Halley's comet would reappear, with her performing most of the exacting calculations, figuring in the influence of Jupiter and Saturn.

b. Marie Anne Pierrette Paulze Lavoisier (1758–1836), French illustrator and editor.

French midwife Angélique du Coudray published *Abrégé de l'art des accouchements avec plusiers observations sur des cas singuliers*, her revised and expanded version of a 1667 midwifery textbook (1759).

### ARTS/LITERATURE

b. Fanny Burney (Madame d'Arblay, 1752–1840), British author.

b. Elizabeth Inchbald (1753–1821), British playwright and actress.

b. Phillis Wheatley (ca. 1753–1784), American poet.

b. Elizabeth (Ann) Linley (1754–1792), British soprano.

b. Sarah Kemble Siddons (1755–1831), British actress.

b. Marie-Louise Elisabeth Vigée-Lebrun (1755–1842), French painter.

Madame du Bocage published her epic poem *La Colombiade* (*The Journey of Columbus*) (1756).

d. Marie Sallé (1707–1756), French ballerina, one of the leading dancers of her time and the greatest rival of Marie-Anne Camargo.

d. Eliza Fowler Haywood (1693–1756), British writer and editor.

Charlotte Ramsay Lennox published the novel *Angelica; or, Quixote in Petticoats* (1758).

Elizabeth Carter began to publish her translations of the works of Epictetus (1758), ultimately in four volumes.

d. Rosalba Giovanna Carriera (1675–1758), Italian painter, one of the leading portraitists of her time, an internationally known figure especially noted for her pastels. She was a member of the French and Roman academies and worked throughout Europe.

b. Josepha Weber (1759–1819), German soprano.

b. Maria Theresia von Paradis (1759–1824), Austrian composer and pianist.

## 1760–1769

### POLITICS/LAW/WAR

b. Deborah Sampson (Gannett) (1760–1827), American Revolutionary War soldier (as Robert Shurtliff).

d. Elizabeth of Russia (Yelizaveta Petrovna, 1709–1762), empress of Russia, daughter of Peter the Great and Catherine I, who took power by coup (1741), pursued an expansionist foreign policy, had the Winter Palace built (1745–1762), and founded several institutions, including Moscow University (1755) and the National Academy of Fine Arts.

Shortly after her husband, Peter III, succeeded to the throne of Russia, Catherine of Russia deposed him, emerging as Empress Catherine II (the Great) (1762). Among her supporters was Ekaterina Romanovna Dashkova, who led an armed detachment on Catherine's side during the coup.

b. Théroigne Anne Josephe de Méricourt (1762–1817), French feminist, entertainer, journalist, and revolutionary.

d. Jeanne Antoinette Poisson (Madame de Pompadour, 1721–1764), mistress of Louis XV of France, a power at court and an influential patron of the arts, crafts, and humanities.

b. Claire Lacombe (1765–?), French actress who would emerge as a leading woman of the French Revolution.

Catherine the Great instituted major changes in the Russian legal code (1767).

b. Charlotte Corday (Marie Anne Charlotte Corday d'Armont, 1768–1793), French revolutionary.

b. Dorothea (Dolley) Payne Todd Madison (1768–1849), American politician, wife of President James Madison.

### RELIGION/EDUCATION/EVERYDAY LIFE

b. Mary Hays (1760–1843), British writer and feminist.

d. Mary Wortley Montagu (1689–1762), British traveler and writer, best known for introducing smallpox inoculation to England (ca. 1718), about which she had learned in Turkey (1716–1718); her letters and diaries from this period were published after her death (1763).

d. Elizabeth Haddon Estaugh (ca. 1680–1762), British-born American Quaker, who founded a ministers' home in New Jersey (1701).

Catharine Macaulay began publication of her eight-volume *History of England* (1763–1783).

After quarreling with salon leader Madame du Deffand, for whom she had worked (1754–1764), Julie de Lespinasse established her own salon, attracting key intellectuals, including the Encyclopedists.

Mary Katherine Goddard, with her mother and brother, began publishing the *Providence Gazette* in Rhode Island (1765).

Barbara Ruckle Heck and her cousin, Phillip Embury, founded a Methodist Society in New York City (1766) and sparked the building of the John Street Methodist Church.

b. Elizabeth Veale Macarthur (1767–1850), Australian pioneer and wool merchant.

Selina Huntingdon established Trevecca College, in Brecknockshire, for training evangelical ministers (1768), after Oxford University had expelled six theology students as suspected Methodists.

Academie de Coiffure was established in France by Legros de Rumigny (1769); he taught hairdressing and wig-making skills to both men and women, employing young women to "model" his creations in public. The large and elaborate arrangements (some reaching three feet high) were covered with flour and various oils; since these tended to attract lice and fleas, women often put a dab of honey and vinegar at the top, to draw the vermin away from the scalp.

b. Ann Royall (1769–1864), American journalist.

## SCIENCE/TECHNOLOGY/MEDICINE

After her husband's death, Anna Morandi was elected to his chair as professor of anatomy at the University of Bologna (1760), with the additional title of *modellatrice*, honoring her excellence at making precisely detailed wax models, which were widely displayed across Europe.

b. Margaret Bryan (ca. 1760–? [after 1815]), British teacher of natural philosophy, who published textbooks based on her lectures at her schools for girls.

Nicole-Reine Lepaute was engaged (1762) to calculate the exact time of an annular eclipse of the sun scheduled for 1764; she produced a map showing the time and extent of the eclipse across Europe at 15-minute intervals. Her tables of such calculations were given in *Connaissance des temps* (from 1763), annual almanacs published by the Academy of Sciences for astronomers and navigators, as were her calculations of ephemerides, tables showing the position of key celestial bodies for each day of the year.

d. Dorothea Christiana Leporin Erxleben (1715–1762), German physician, the first woman to receive a full medical degree from a German university (1754).

d. Jane Colden (1724–1766), American botanist whose work involved classification and cataloguing according to the Linnaean system; one of the first female scientists in America, she classified over 300 plant species and discovered and named the gardenia.

b. Jane Haldimand Marcet (1769–1858), British scientific writer.

b. Maria Louise Dugès La Chapelle (1769–1821), French midwife.

## ARTS/LITERATURE

d. Peg (Margaret) Woffington (ca. 1718–1760), Irish actress, best known by far for her "breeches," or male parts, the most notable of these being the role of Sir Harry Wildair in George Farquhar's play *The Constant Couple*.

d. Carolina Neuber (1697–1760), German actress and manager.

d. Lavinia Fenton (1708–1760), British actress.

b. Marie Grasholtz Tussaud (1761–1850), Swiss artist and entrepreneur.

b. Dorothy Jordan (1761–1816), British actress.

Hannah More wrote the play *A Search after Happiness* (1762).

b. Joanna Baillie (1762–1851), Scottish poet.

b. Mary Berry (1763–1852), British writer and editor.

Angelica Kauffmann painted *Bacchus and Chloë* (1764).

b. Ann Radcliffe (Ann Ward, 1764–1823), British Gothic novelist.

b. Elizabeth Billington (1765–1818), British soprano.

Welsh poet Anna Williams published *Miscellanies in Prose and Verse* (1766).

d. Susannah Arne Cibber (1714–1766), British singer and actress, a leading tragedian in David Garrick's company and interpreter of George Frideric Handel, perhaps most notably in the premiere of his *Messiah*.

Antonia Bernasconi created the title role in Christoph Gluck's opera *Alcestis* (1767).

b. Maria Edgeworth (1767–1849), Irish novelist.

Angelica Kauffmann was a founding member of the English Royal Academy (1768).

Fanny Burney began her diaries (1768), published posthumously in 1889 as her *Early Diary, 1768–1778*.

d. Hannah Pritchard (1711–1768), British actress.

Angelica Kauffmann painted *Interview of Hector and Andromache* (1769) and *Vortigern and Rowena* (1770).

## 1770–1779

### POLITICS/LAW/WAR

b. Laskarina Bouboulina (1771–1825), insurgent leader during the Greek War of Independence.

Catherine the Great took a major share of Poland, partitioning the country with Austria and Prussia in three stages (1772; 1793; 1794).

b. Thérésia de Cabarrus Tallien (Princess de Chimay, 1773–1835), French political figure and salon hostess.

As the Continental Congress was discussing the possibility of declaring independence from Britain, Abigail Adams urged her husband to do just that—and to free women as well (1776). The legislature of the new state of New Jersey gave women the right to vote (1776), later revoked (1807).

At the Battle of Monmouth (June 26, 1778), Mary Ludwig Hays carried water (and so was nicknamed Molly Pitcher) to the troops of the Pennsylvania Artillery, including her husband. She was said to have taken his place as a cannoneer after he was wounded; she became a Revolutionary hero and was later awarded a state pension (1822).

b. Rallou Karatza (ca. 1778–1830), Greek theater director, translator, and revolutionary.

### RELIGION/EDUCATION/EVERYDAY LIFE

Ann Lee had a vision that she was to spread word of Christ's second coming (1770), thereafter founding the Shakers, a celibate, communitarian Protestant sect.

d. Hannah Allgood Glasse (1708–1770), British cook who wrote *The Art of Cooking Made Plain and Simple*, considered Britain's first household cookbook, *The Compleat Confectioner*, and later the *The Servant's Directory or Housekeeper's Companion*.

---

# Remember the Ladies

**Abigail Adams to John Adams (Mar. 13, 1776)**

I long to hear that you have declared an independancy—and by the way in the new Code of Laws which I suppose it will be necessary for you to make I desire you would Remember the Ladies, and be more generous and favorable to them than your ancestors. Do not put such unlimited power into the hands of Husbands. Remember all Men would be tyrants if they could. If perticuliar care is not paid to the Ladies we are determined to foment a Rebellion, and will not hold ourselves bound by any laws in which we have no voice, or Representation.

**John Adams to Abigail Adams (Apr. 14, 1776)**

As to your extraordinary Code of Laws, I cannot but laugh. We have been told that our Struggle has loosened the bands of Government every where. That Children and Apprentices were disobedient—that schools and Colledges were grown turbulent—that Indians slighted their Guardians and Negroes grew insolent to their Masters. But your Letter was the first Intimation that another Tribe more numerous and powerfull than all the rest were grown discontented.—This is rather too coarse a Compliment, but you are so saucy, I wont blot it out.

Depend upon it, We know better than to repeal our masculine systems.

---

b. Rahel Levin Varnhagen von Ense (1771–1833), German salon hostess.

b. Marie (Anne Adelaide) Lenormand (1782–1843), French fortune-teller.

b. Jeanne-Elisabeth Bichier des Ages (1773–1838), French religious leader and saint.

Mother Ann Lee and her followers, known as Shakers, emigrated from England to America (1774), there still facing physical persecution.

*Some Account of the Fore-Part of the Life of Elizabeth Ashbridge,* the autobiographical work of the American Quaker preacher, was posthumously published (1774).

In France, women's lodges were routinely established, associated with many men's lodges, and were recognized as official Masonic institutions (1774), despite constitutional rules against female members. Attempts to establish official women's lodges in other countries generally failed, though some were founded in Germany and the Netherlands.

b. Elizabeth Ann Bayley Seton (1774–1821), American religious leader, the first American-born saint.

Anna Maria Swaegel was the last person executed as a witch in Germany (1775).

Mary Katherine Goddard became the first female postmaster in the American colonies, in Baltimore, Maryland (1775–1789).

Suzanne Necker, appalled by conditions in Paris hospitals, converted a former convent into a hospital (1776); named for her in 1820, it became an important pediatrics research center.

Betsy (Elizabeth) Griscom Ross is traditionally credited with designing the original American flag (ca. 1776).

b. Lady Hester Lucy Stanhope (1776–1839), British traveler.

d. Julie (Jeanne-Eléanore) de Lespinasse (1732–1776), French salon hostess (from 1764); she and her lover, mathematician Jean d'Alembert, were depicted in Denis Diderot's *Le rêve de d'Alembert*; her passionate letters to another lover, Comte de Guibert, would be published posthumously (1809).

Baltimore postmaster Mary Katherine Goddard was the first person to print the Declaration of Independence, in her *Maryland Journal* (1777).

b. Madame de Récamier (Jeanne-Françoise-Julie-Adelaide Bernard, 1777–1849), French salon hostess.

b. Mary Haydock Reibey (1777–1855), British-born Australian entrepreneur.

d. Marie-Thérèse Rodet de Geoffrin (1699–1777), French salon hostess.

## SCIENCE/TECHNOLOGY/MEDICINE

Jane Colden's discovery of the gardenia as a new genus, related to Old World plants, was posthumously recognized after publication of her botanical description in the Edinburgh Philosophical Society's journal *Observations, Physical and Literary* (1770). She had named it after 18th-century Scottish botanist Alexander Garden.

b. Claudine Poullet Picardet Guyton de Morveau (ca. 1770–ca. 1820), French scientific translator.

b. (Regina) Josepha Henning Siebold (1771–1849), German physician.

French midwife Angélique du Coudray published her *Oeuvres* (1773).

b. Marie (Anne Victoire) Gillain Boivin (1773–1841), French midwife.

d. Anna Morandi Manzolini (1716–1774), Italian anatomist, assistant to her husband, Giovanni Manzolini, professor of anatomy at the University of Bologna, succeeding him at his death (1760); she was especially expert at constructing precise wax models.

Nicole-Reine Lepaute assisted in writing and doing many calculations for *Traité de'horlogerie*, a work on pendulums published by her husband, Jean Lepaute (1775).

b. Sophie Germain (Le Blanc) (1776–1831), French mathematician.

After the Battle of Brandywine, Pennsylvania, wounded Revolutionary War soldiers were brought to the Ephrata Cloister to be cared for by the sisters there (1777).

b. Maria Dalle Donne (1778–1842), Italian physician.

d. Laura (Maria Caterina) Bassi (1711–1778), Italian physicist, anatomist, and natural philosopher, originally a lecturer in anatomy (1731), who became the first female professor of physics at any university, at the University of Bologna (1745–1778).

### ARTS/LITERATURE

d. Marie-Anne de Cupis de Camargo (1710–1770), French dancer, who introduced several steps for women that had previously been reserved for men, including entrechats and cabrioles.

Welsh poet Anne Penny published *Poems with a Dramatic Entertainment* (1771).

b. Dorothy Wordsworth (1771–1855), British writer.

Phillis Wheatley published *Poems on Various Subjects, Religious and Moral*, the first published works by an African-American poet (1773).

Sophie Arnould created the title role in Christoph Gluck's opera *Iphigenia in Aulis* (1774).

Hannah More wrote the play *The Inflexible Captive* (1774).

b. Jane Austen (1775–1817), British novelist.

Jane Elliot published the poem *The Flowers of the Forest* (1776), based on an old song.

Hannah Cowley's play *The Runaway* was seen in London (1776).

Frances Abington starred as Lady Teazle, Jane Pope as Mrs. Candour, and Robert Baddeley as Moses in Richard Brinsley Sheridan's play *The School of Scandal* (1777).

Hannah More wrote the plays *Percy* (1777) and *The Fatal Falsehood* (1779).

Fanny Burney published the novel *Evelina, or The History of a Young Lady's Entrance into the World* (1778). Her *Diaries and Letters, 1778–1840* would be posthumously published (1842–1848).

## 1780–1789

### POLITICS/LAW/WAR

d. Maria Theresa (1717–1780), Holy Roman (Austrian) Empress, the archduchess of Austria and queen of Bohemia and Hungary, oldest daughter of Holy Roman Emperor Charles VI, whom she succeeded (1740), ruling the Hapsburg empire for 40 years, through a series of dynastic wars that included the disastrous War of the Austrian Succession (1740–1748), the worldwide Seven Years War (1756–1763), and several other wars, in what amounted to a continuing European conflagration.

Catherine the Great's forces defeated Turkey and annexed the Crimea (1783).

Deborah Sampson (later Gannett) was discharged from the Revolutionary Army (1783) when it was discovered that she was a woman; as Robert Shurtliff she had enlisted and fought, sustaining wounds at Tarrytown.

Ekaterina Romanovna Dashkova was appointed by Catherine the Great to be director of Russia's Academy of Arts and Sciences and first president of the Russian Academy (1783).

b. Sacagawea (ca. 1786–1812), Shoshone Indian guide and interpreter, who accompanied the Lewis and Clark transcontinental expedition in North America (1804–1805).

In a major early legal breakthrough, the new state of Massachusetts began the long process that would ultimately give women full property rights by providing that women who had been abandoned by their husbands could sell property (1787).

Women were granted the right to be elected to office in the United States (1788), though in fact very few women would be elected until after women's suffrage was won (1919).

Dressed as an "Amazon," Théroigne de Méricourt helped lead the storming of the Bastille (July 1789). She was also among the many women of the markets (*dames des Halles*) who made up the Women's March to Versailles (October 1789).

### RELIGION/EDUCATION/EVERYDAY LIFE

Esther De Berdt Reed founded The Ladies Association of Philadelphia (1780), "George Washington's sewing circle," which raised money and supplies for the rebel side during the American Revolution.

b. Elizabeth Gurney Fry (1780–1845), British Quaker minister and social reformer.

Anna Goddi was the last person officially executed as a witch in Europe; she was hanged in Switzerland (1782).

British educator Sarah Trimmer published *An Easy Introduction to the Knowledge of Nature* (1782) and then a similar guide to Scripture.

Catharine Graham Macaulay completed publication of her eight-volume *History of England* (1763–1783).

d. Ann Lee (1736–1784), British-American religious leader, founder of the much-persecuted Shakers, of injuries received in a mob attack. After her death, the Shakers came to see "Mother Lee" as the female embodiment of Christ and the maternal component of a Mother/Father God, developing a tradition of dual male-female leadership.

Hester Lynch Thrale published *Anecdotes of the late Samuel Johnson* (1786).

Sarah Trimmer published the children's text *Fabulous Histories* (1786).

Suzanne Necker published *Mémoire sur l'établissement des hospices* (1786), describing her establishment of a Parisian hospital.

Mary Wollstonecraft published *Thoughts on the Education of Daughters*, a trailblazing call for women's educational opportunities (1787).

Young Ladies Academy of Philadelphia was founded to give girls an education equal to that of boys (1787). In *Thoughts on Female Education*, his commencement address that year, Benjamin Rush urged that women's education include substantive subjects such as geography and travel, history and biography, English language arts, basic mathematics and bookkeeping skills, and natural and physical sciences, not simply the usual vocal music and dancing. The school would draw students from as far away as the West Indies.

b. Emma Willard (1787–1870), American educator.

b. Sarah Josepha Buell Hale (1788–1879), American editor and author.

## SCIENCE/TECHNOLOGY/MEDICINE

French midwife Angélique du Coudray supervised the establishment of a course in practical obstetrics (1780)—though at the veterinary school at Alford, and though professors bitterly opposed her teaching there.

Maria Pettracini (active ca. 1780), Italian anatomist and physician; after receiving her medical degree from the University of Florence (1780), she taught anatomy and practiced as a physician in Ferrara, as did her daughter, Zaffira Peretti.

b. Mary Greig Fairfax Somerville (1780–1872), Scottish writer on science.

Astronomer Caroline Herschel discovered three new nebulae (1783), using a small refracting telescope given to her by her brother William, for whom she usually worked as assistant.

Elisabeth Thible became the first woman to go aloft, as a passenger, in a hot-air balloon, over Lyons, France (1784), only a few months after the first balloon flight.

Claudine Guyton de Morveau provided the first French translation of the chemistry work *Mémoires de chymie* of Karl Wilhelm Scheele (1785).

Astronomer Caroline Herschel discovered six new comets (1786–1797), usually during periods when her brother William was away, since she was otherwise fully engaged as his assistant. After she discovered her first comet, Britain's King George III granted her an independent salary of £50 a year.

d. Marie Catherine Biheron (1719–1786), French anatomist, noted for creating realistic anatomical models, which she sold to other teachers.

Marie Lavoisier published her French translation of Richard Kirwan's *Essay on Phlogiston*, a theoretical substance then believed to be important in the process of fire (1787).

b. Charlotte Heidenreich von Siebold (1788–1859), German physician.

d. Nicole-Reine Etable de la Brière Hortense Lepaute (1723–1788), French astronomer, who came to astronomy through her husband, Jean André Lepaute, France's royal clockmaker.

Hester Lynch Thrale Piozzi's descriptions of an earthquake from a book of her travels were published in American magazines (1789–1793).

Louise du Pierry taught an astronomy course for women (1789); the following year, Joseph Jérôme Lalande dedicated his *Astronomie des Dames* to her. She also performed numerous astronomical calculations for Lalande, such as historical data on eclipses and tables on the lengths of day and night.

Marie Lavoisier provided the illustrations for *The Elements of Chemistry* (1789), the classic treatise by her husband, Antoine Lavoisier.

d. Angélique (Marguerite le Boursier) du Coudray (1712–1789), French midwife-obstetrician.

### ARTS/LITERATURE

Hannah Cowley's play *The Belle's Stratagem* was seen in London (1780).

b. Angelica Catalani (1780–1849), Italian soprano.

b. Frances Trollope (1780–1863), British writer.

d. Maria Antonia Walpurgis (1724–1780), electress of Saxony, daughter of Maria Amalia of Austria and Karl Albert of Bavaria and wife of Saxony's elector Friedrich Christian; she was a composer, singer, poet, painter, and patron of the arts.

Dorothea Wendling created the role of Ilia and Elizabeth Wendling that of Electra in Wolfgang Amadeus Mozart's opera *Idomeneo* (1781).

b. Sophie Schröder (1781–1868), Austrian actress.

Katharina Cavalieri created the role of Constanze in Wolfgang Amadeus Mozart's opera *The Abduction from the Seraglio* (1782).

Fanny Burney published the novel *Cecilia, or Memoires of an Heiress* (1782).

Hannah Cowley's plays *Which Is the Man?* (1782) and *A Bold Stroke for a Husband* (1783) were seen in London.

d. Anna (Dorothea) Lisiewska (1721–1782), German artist.

d. Lucrezia Aguiari (La Bastardina, 1743–1783), Italian soprano, one of the leading European opera singers of her time.

d. Phillis Wheatley (ca. 1753–1784), American poet, the first published African-American poet.

Elizabeth Inchbald's plays *I'll Tell You What* (1785) and *The Widow's Vow* (1786) were seen in London.

b. Caroline Ponsonby Lamb (1785–1828), British writer.

d. Kitty Clive (Catherine Raftor Clive, 1711–1785), British actress, long associated with David Garrick at the Drury Lane Theater; one of the leading comedians of her time.

b. Ekaterina Semenova (1786–1849), Russian actress.

d. Sophia Snow (1745–1786), British actress, a leading player opposite David Garrick at the Drury Lane Theater in the late 1760s and the 1770s.

Teresa Saporiti created the role of Donna Anna in Wolfgang Amadeus Mozart's opera *Don Giovanni* (1787).

Mary Wollstonecraft published the novel *Mary* (1788).

b. Mary Prince (ca. 1788–?), one of the earliest black Caribbean female writers, noted for her autobiography (1831); in England (from 1827), she worked for the *Anti-Slavery Reporter*; her later life is unknown.

---

# Why They Should

Would man but generously snap our chains, and be content with rational fellowship instead of slavish obedience, they would find us more observant daughters, more affectionate sisters, more faithful wives, more reasonable mothers—in a word, better citizens. We should then love them with true affection, because we should learn to respect ourselves . . .

— Mary Wollstonecraft, in *A Vindication of the Rights of Woman* (1792)

b. Mme. Vestris (Lucy Elizabeth Bartolozzi, 1788–1856), British actress and manager.

d. George Anne Bellamy (1727–1788), British actress, a leading player on the London stage.

## 1790–1799

### POLITICS/LAW/WAR

French revolutionary Olympe de Gouges issued *Declaration of the Rights of Woman* (*Les Droits de la Femme*), her call for women's equality (1790).

Mary Wollstonecraft published *A Vindication of the Rights of Man* (1790).

Dutch feminist and revolutionary Etta Aelders Palm made a historic speech on the rights of women to the French Assembly (1791).

Pauline Léon called for the establishment of a Republican women's military organization but was rebuffed by the National Assembly (1791).

Mary Wollstonecraft published her landmark *A Vindication of the Rights of Woman* (1792), on male dominance and the need for complete education for women and the development of a fully equal society, a key document leading to the women's rights movement.

French actress Claire Lacombe became an active revolutionary, called the "heroine of August 10th" for her role in the storming of the Tuileries (1792). With Pauline Léon, she founded the radical and feminist Société des Républicaines Révolutionnaires (Republican Revolutionary Society).

Catherine the Great's forces continued their attack on Turkey, annexing portions of the Black Sea coast and winning long-sought Russian southern sea access (1792).

Olympe de Gouges published *Le Prince philosophe* (1792).

Théroigne de Méricourt organized revolutionary women's clubs in Paris (1792).

b. Sarah Moore Grimké (1792–1873), American abolitionist and feminist.

Société des Républicaines Révolutionnaires, France's first all-female revolutionary society, was founded (May 1793); among its most notable leaders were Claire Lacombe and Pauline Léon. It was quickly banned (October 1793), because of its militancy on women's freedom issues, including the right to serve in the military, to be active politically, and to wear nontraditional dress, including the revolutionary tricolor cockade.

Female Benevolent Society of St. Thomas was founded (1793).

d. Marie Antoinette (1755–1793), queen of France, daughter of Holy Roman Empress Maria Therese and emperor Francis I, and wife of Louis XV of France. Her extravagant lifestyle and Austrian origin made her a major target for French revolutionaries, as did her attempts to gain Austrian help for the French monarchy after the French Revolution. Ultimately, she was tried and convicted as "the widow Capet," and was guillotined. Her "Let them eat cake!" remark, purportedly directed at the poor, is of very doubtful attribution.

d. Olympe de Gouges (Marie-Olympe Gouze, 1748–1793), French feminist and writer, a leading woman of the French Revolution, executed during the Reign of Terror. She wrote the *Declaration of the Rights of Women and Citizens* (1790).

d. Charlotte Corday (Marie Anne Charlotte Corday d'Armont, 1768–1793), French revolutionary and Girondist, who assassinated Jacobin leader Jean-Paul Marat, an action for which she was guillotined.

d. Marie Jeanne Gomard de Vaubernier, comtesse du Barry (Madame du Barry, 1743–1793), mistress to Louis XV of France, an influence at court and patron of the arts; she had fled to England at the beginning of the French Revolution, but on a return visit was denounced and executed when her identity became known.

d. Manon Roland (Marie-Jeanne Philpon, 1754–1793), French revolutionary, a democrat and Girondist, who was executed during the Reign of Terror. While imprisoned (May–November 1793), she wrote her *Memoirs* and the *Appeal to an Impartial Posterity*.

Mary Wollstonecraft published *Historical and Moral View of the Origin and Progress of the French Revolution* (1794).

French revolutionary and feminist Pauline Léon and her husband, Théophile Leclerc, were imprisoned by the French government (1794); their later fate is unknown.

French revolutionary Claire Lacombe was imprisoned (1794–1795), her later fate unknown.

In Italy, Rosa Califronice published *Brief Defense of the Rights of Women* (1794).

d. Catherine II (the Great) (1729–1796), empress of Russia (r. 1762–1796), an absolute ruler who, after deposing her husband, Peter II, greatly expanded Russian power in Eurasia.

d. Molly (Mary) Brant (1736–1796), Mohawk leader, sister of Chief Joseph Brant, and companion and common-law wife of British Indian Affairs representative William Johnson.

*The Female Review; or, Life of Deborah Sampson* was published (1797), a greatly fictionalized biography of a woman who fought disguised as a man in the American Revolution.

b. Sojourner Truth (Isabella Van Wagener, ca. 1797–1883), African-American abolitionist and women's rights advocate, born into slavery.

d. Mary Wollstonecraft (Godwin; 1759–1797), British writer and pioneering women's rights advocate, best known for her *A Vindication of the Rights of Woman* (1792), whose very clearly stated body of thought on male-dominated society and call for full equality became basic to the 19th-century women's rights movement, and remains relevant in the late 20th century. Wife of political philosopher William Godwin, she died of complications after giving birth to her only child, their daughter, who would become the novelist Mary Wollstonecraft Godwin Shelley, author of *Frankenstein* (1818).

Mary Hays and her sister anonymously published *Appeal to the Men of Great Britain on Behalf of the Women* (1798).

### RELIGION/EDUCATION/EVERYDAY LIFE

Frances Dickinson and Ann Teresa Mathews founded a Carmelite convent in Maryland (1790), the first Roman Catholic convent in the United States.

Suzanne Necker published *Des inhumations precipitées* (1790).

d. Catharine Sawbridge Macaulay (1731–1791), British historian noted for her eight-volume *History of England* (1763–1783).

d. Selina Huntingdon (Countess of Huntingdon, 1707–1791), British religious figure, after her husband's death (1746) a key figure in spreading Methodism among the aristocracy.

Joanna Southcott began making religious prophesies (1792), claiming to have been sent to announce that Jesus Christ would shortly return to Earth; she gathered numerous followers in Britain.

Adviser to Britain's Queen Charlotte on Sunday schools (from 1786), Sarah Trimmer published *Reflection upon the Education of Children in Charity Schools* (1792).

# On Childbed Fever

Mary Wollstonecraft was one of the many victims of childbed (puerperal) fever, an infection following delivery, often deadly in the days before antibiotics. In her case, it seems to have been caused by incompletely expelled afterbirth; doctors in that era lacked the knowledge and skills to ensure that the uterus was fully cleared out after childbirth.

But many women were infected by the doctors themselves, who often worked in autopsy rooms while women were in labor and in any case did not wash their hands after either autopsy work or examination of other patients. This method of infection was independently identified by two physicians, Oliver Wendell Holmes in America and Jacob Semmelweiss in Europe, but most doctors rejected their ideas, believing that "a gentleman's hands could not spread disease." Ironically, Semmelweiss, who had been reviled for notions, himself died of childbed fever, infected during a cut received attending at a delivery.

Judith Sargent Murray published a regular series of essays titled "The Gleaner," under the guise of Mr. Vigillius, in the *Massachusetts Magazine* (1792–1794).

b. Anne Isabella, Lady Noel Byron (1792–1860), British philanthropist.

As a young bride, Madame de Récamier developed a political and literary salon (1793), until forced by Napoléon to leave Paris (1805).

Mary Hays and her sister published *Letters and Essays Moral and Miscellaneous* (1793).

b. Lucretia Coffin Mott (1793–1880), American Quaker minister, abolitionist, and pioneer women's rights leader.

Suzanne Necker published *Réflexions sur le divorce* (1794).

b. Rebecca Pennock Lukens (1794–1854), American industrial executive.

b. Zilpah P. Grant (1794–1874), American educator.

d. Hannah (Cook) Heaton (1721–1794), American autobiographer, whose memoir provided a unique glimpse of the religious wave called the Great Awakening (1740s).

b. Frances Wright (1795–1852), Scottish-American writer, editor, and social reformer.

b. Jane Griffin Franklin (Lady Franklin, 1795–1875), British reformer and traveler.

b. Henriette d'Angeville (1795–1871), French mountaineer.

Nicole-Barbe Clicquot (La Veuve [The Widow] Clicquot) developed a way of clearing sediment from champagne (1796), producing the first clear sparkling wines and champagnes, and later the first pink champagne.

Amelia Simmons wrote *American Cookery* (1796), among the earliest cookbooks to focus on American ingredients and dishes, including Indian pudding, johnnycake, and flapjacks.

b. Sophia Smith (1796–1870), American philanthropist.

b. Evanthia Kairi (1797–1866), Greek educator.

b. Nakayama Miki (1798–1887), Japanese religious leader.

b. Elizabeth Acton (1799–1859), British cookery writer.

#### SCIENCE/TECHNOLOGY/MEDICINE

Claudine Guyton de Morveau provided the first French translation of Abraham Gottlob Werner's work *Traité de charatères extérieurs des fossiles* (1790).

Marie Jeanne Amélie Harlay Lefrançais de Lalande (active 1790s), French astronomer who assisted both her husband, Michel de Lalande, and his cousin and mentor, Joseph Jérôme Lefrançais de Lalande, in their astronomical work, notably in calculating vital astronomical tables.

Catherine Littlefield Greene proposed to Eli Whitney that he develop a machine to separate seeds from cotton, providing him with workspace and financial assistance—some say also design assistance—for what became known as the cotton gin. Greene publicized the working model (1793) before Whitney and her partner Phineas Miller could obtain their own patent; Greene (who married Miller) later lost most of her family's resources in the legal fight to establish their title to the invention.

Mrs. Samuel Slater was the first woman ever granted a patent in the United States (1793), for a method of producing cotton sewing thread; it was, presumably, used in the successful New England mills run by her husband; her own first name has been lost.

Amélie Lefrançais de Lalande calculated the astronomical tables appended to Joseph Jérôme Lefrançais de Lalande's *Abrégé de navigation* (1793), designed so navigators could use the altitude of the sun and the stars to calculate the time at sea.

b. Almira Hart Lincoln Phelps (1793–1884), American science educator.

d. Elizabeth (Eliza) Lucas Pinckney (1722–1793), American agricultural innovator who developed indigo as a commercial crop in the Carolinas (1744).

Unable to study at Paris's new Ecole Centrale des Travaux Publics (later Ecole Polytechnique), because the school was restricted to male students, Sophie Germain arranged to obtain copies of student lecture notes and, under the pseudonym Le Blanc, submitted a paper to professor Joseph Lagrange (1794), who became her mentor. Still under the pseudonym, she maintained a long correspondence on mathematics with Karl Friedrich Gauss, who was for several years unaware that she was a woman.

British chemist Elizabeth Fulhame published *Essay on Combustion with a View to a New Art of Dying and Painting,* her exploration of the nature of fire, notable for her attempt to rest her theory on actual observations (1794); after her essay was reprinted in America (1810), she was made an honorary member of the Philadelphia Chemical Society.

During France's Reign of Terror, Marie Lavoisier campaigned unsuccessfully for the release of her husband, chemistry pioneer Antoine Lavoisier (1794); after his execution and her own brief imprisonment, she edited the finished portions of her husband's uncompleted memoirs and later led a scientific salon.

b. James Stuart (possibly Miranda Stuart [Barry], 1795?–1865), British physician.

British teacher Margaret Bryan published *A Compendious System of Astronomy* (1797), based on her lectures at her schools for girls.

Britain's Royal Society published Caroline Herschel's cross-indexed, corrected, and expanded version (1798) of the star catalogue originally published by Britain's first Astronomer Royal, John Flamsteed (1646–1719).

Betsey Metcalf invented a new method of braiding straw (1798), though she did not obtain a patent for it.

Maria Dalle Donne, originally educated by private tutors, was awarded a degree in philosophy and medicine from the University of Bologna (1799).

b. Mary Anning (1799–1847), British paleontologist.

d. Maria Gaetana Agnesi (1718–1799), Italian mathematician whose major work was *Instituzioni Analitiche* (1748); she was long known in English as the "witch of Agnesi" because a term for "curve" was mistranslated as "wife of the devil."

## ARTS/LITERATURE

Joanna Baillie published the poetry collection *Fugitive Verses* (1790).

Charlotte Ramsay Lennox published the novel *Euphemia* (1790).

Ho Xuan Huong (active end of 18th c.), Vietnamese female poet.

Anna Gottlieb created the role of Pamina and Josepha Weber that of the Queen of the Night in Wolfgang Amadeus Mozart's opera *The Magic Flute* (1791).

b. Anna Claypoole Peale (1791–1878), American painter.

Maria Theresia von Paradis composed the singspiel *Der Schulkandidat* (1792).

Anna Barbauld published *Civic Sermons to the People* (1792).

Anne-Louis Girodet de Roucy showed her painting *The Sleep of Endymion* (1792).

d. Elizabeth (Ann) Linley (1754–1792), British soprano, one of the leading opera singers of her time; daughter of composer Thomas Linley, she was married to playwright Richard Brinsley Sheridan.

Anna Barbauld published *Sins of Government* (1793).

Ann Radcliffe published the Gothic novels *The Mysteries of Udolpho* (1794) and *The Italian* (1796).

Hannah Cowley's play *The Town Before You* was seen in London (1794).

b. Anna Murphy Jameson (1794–1860), Irish writer.

b. Margaretta Angelica Peale (1795–1882), American painter.

Madame de Staël published *De l'influence des passions sur le bonheur des individuels et des nations (The Influence of Passions on the Happiness of Individuals and Nations)* (1796).

Fanny Burney published the novel *Camilla* (1796).

Elizabeth Inchbald's play *Wives as They Were and Maids as They Are* was seen in London (1797).

b. Mary Wollstonecraft Godwin Shelley (1797–1851), British writer and women's rights advocate, daughter of Mary Wollstonecraft.

b. Annette von Droste-Hülshoff (1797–1848), German writer.

b. Giuditta Negri Pasta (1797–1865), Italian soprano.

Joanna Baillie published a series of ten *Plays on the Passions*, in blank verse (1798–1812).

Mary Berry edited the works of Horace Walpole, in nine volumes (1798–1825).

b. Marie-Thomase-Amélie Dorval (1798–1849), French actress.

Claire Clairon published the autobiography *Mémoires et réflexions sur l'art dramatique* (1799).

# 1800–1809

## POLITICS/LAW/WAR

The Code Napoléon (1804), put into effect under Napoléon Bonaparte, reversed many liberalizations that had come with the French Revolution (1789), including liberalization of divorce and women's rights to inheritances and guardianship, making the power of the husband and father virtually absolute. Even though wife and husband were co-owners of community property, only he had the right to administer that property.

Shoshone Indian guide and interpreter Sacagawea accompanied the Lewis and Clark transcontinental expedition (1804–1805), with her husband, Toussaint Charbonneau, and her baby, born at Fort Mandan (1805). In the country of the Shoshone, she reportedly interceded with her brother, a Shoshone chief, to stop a planned attack on the expedition.

b. Angelina Emily Grimké (1805–1879), American abolitionist and feminist.

b. Maria Weston Chapman (1806–1885), American teacher, editor, and abolitionist.

New Jersey legislature revoked women's right to vote (1807), which it had granted in 1776.

b. Cristina Trivulzio (1808–1871), Italian writer and democratic revolutionary.

African Female Benevolent Society of Newport was founded (1809).

## RELIGION/EDUCATION/EVERYDAY LIFE

Boston Female Society for Missionary Purposes founded (1800), one of many such 19th-century organizations designed to fund the education of missionaries, initially male, but later also female.

Rahel Levin (later Varnhagen von Ense) established a salon in Berlin (ca. 1800), involving key figures in the Romantic movement; the salon ended after she lost her fortune (1806).

b. Catharine Esther Beecher (1800–1878), American educational reformer and writer.

d. Elizabeth Robinson Montagu (1720–1800), British intellectual and hostess of a notable literary salon (from 1744), the original *bluestocking*, so-called for the blue (rather than formal black) stockings allowed at her informal gatherings.

Sarah Trimmer published *The Economy of Charity* (1801).

Hester Stanhope served as hostess to British Prime Minister William Pitt, her uncle (1802–1806).

b. Dorothea Lynde Dix (1802–1887), American social reformer.

Mary Hays published her six-volume *Dictionary of Female Biography* (1803).

b. Flora (Célestine Thérèse) Tristan (1803–1844), French writer and socialist.

b. Elizabeth Palmer Peabody (1804–1894), American author and educator.

b. Prudence Crandall (1804–1889), American teacher and abolitionist.

Mercy Warren published a *History of the Rise, Progress, and Termination of the American Revolution* (1805).

b. Elizabeth Twining (1805–1889), British reformer and educator.

b. John Stuart Mill (1806–1873), British economist, philosopher, writer, and women's rights activist.

St. Marie Madeleine Postel founded the Poor Daughters of Mercy, a teaching and nursing order, at Cherbourg (1807).

b. Jane Digby El Mezrab (1807–1881), British adventurer and traveler.

b. Mary Carpenter (1807–1877), British social reformer.

b. Eliza Hart Spalding (1807–1851), American missionary.

Lucy Emerson published *New England Cookery* (1808), heavily plagiarizing from Amelia Simmons's *American Cookery* (1796).

b. Harriet Taylor (1808–1858), British writer and feminist.

d. Caroline Jones Chisholm (1808–1877), British philanthropist focusing primarily on Australia; reportedly the model for Mrs. Jellyby in Charles Dickens's *Bleak House*.

While her husband was away (1809–1817), Elizabeth Macarthur built up the flocks of sheep that made their Elizabeth Farm Australia's first great estate, foundation of its wool trade; after his death (1834), she and her sons further built the estate.

## SCIENCE/TECHNOLOGY/MEDICINE

Maria Dalle Donne was appointed director of midwives at the University of Bologna (1803), often lecturing in her own home.

b. Harriot Kezia Hunt (1805–1875), American physician.

b. Mary (Jane) Seacole (1805–1881), Jamaican nurse and hotel owner.

Jane Marcet published her first book, *Conversations on Chemistry* (1806); it was immensely popular and influential—the great Michael Faraday credited it with introducing him to electrochemistry.

British teacher Margaret Bryan published her *Lectures on Natural Philosophy* (1806), based on 13 lectures given at her girls' schools on hydrostatics, optics, pneumatics, and acoustics.

Josepha Siebold was granted permission to practice obstetrics and give smallpox vaccinations by the Archducal Medical College at Darmstadt (1807). She had served as midwife and assistant to her husband, Dr. Damian Siebold, and then studied obstetrics at Würzburg.

b. Jane Webb Loudon (1807–1858), British botanist and writer on horticulture.

The first known successful operation to remove an ovarian cyst was performed by Dr. Ephraim McDowell; the patient, Mrs. Jane Crawford, had ridden 60 miles on horseback to visit him (1809). This is regarded as the beginning of gynecological—or, more widely, abdominal—surgery, virtually all previous major abdominal operations having proved fatal.

Mary Kies, a Connecticut resident, was granted a patent for "a method to weave straw with silk and thread" (1809); it was used for about a decade, while straw bonnets were popular.

b. Marie (Josefina Mathilde) Durocher (1809–1893), French-Brazilian obstetrician.

## ARTS/LITERATURE

Madame de Staël published *De la littérature considérée dans ses rapports avec les institutions sociales* (1800).

Maria Edgeworth published the novel *Castle Rackrent*, about absentee landlords in Ireland (1800).

b. Sarah Miriam Peale (1800–1885), American painter.

Maria Edgeworth published the novel *Belinda* (1801).

b. Fredrika Bremer (1801–1865), Swedish novelist and travel writer.

b. Elisavet Moutza-Martinengou (1801–1821), Greek writer.

b. Harriet Martineau (1802–1876), British rationalist, feminist, writer, and political economist.

b. Lydia Maria Francis Child (1802–1880), American writer and abolitionist.

d. Marie-Anne Le Page du Bocage (Madame du Bocage, 1710–1802), French playwright and poet, nicknamed the French Milton.

Dorothy Wordsworth published her *Recollections of a Tour in Scotland* (1803).

Madame de Staël published the autobiographical novel *Delphine* (1803).

b. Karoline Unger (1803–1877), Austrian contralto.

b. Susanna Strickland Moodie (1803–1885), Canadian writer.

d. Marie-Françoise Dumesnil (1713–1803), French actress.

d. Mlle. Clairon (Claire-Josephe-Hippolyte Leris de La Tude, 1723–1803), French actress.

b. George Sand (Amandine Lucile Aurore Dupin, 1804–1876), French writer.

b. Marie Taglioni (1804–1884), ballet dancer, daughter of dancer-choreographer Filippo Taglioni and sister of dancer–ballet master Paul Taglioni.

d. Françoise Vestris (1743–1804), French actress, a tragedian who created several leading roles, including the title role in Voltaire's *Irene*.

d. Charlotte Ramsay Lennox (1720–1804), American writer.

Anna Milder created the role of Leonora in Ludwig van Beethoven's opera *Fidelio* (1805).

Elizabeth Inchbald's play *To Marry, or Not to Marry* was seen in London (1805).

Female artists began to exhibit at the Pennsylvania Academy of the Fine Arts (1805).

b. Giuditta Grisi (1805–1840), Italian mezzo-soprano.

b. Marie de Flavigny d'Agoult (1805–1876), French writer (as Daniel Stern).

d. Jane Elliot (1727–1805), Scottish poet noted for her poem "The Flowers of the Forest" (1776).

Anne-Louis Girodet de Roucy showed her painting *Deluge* (1806).

b. Elizabeth Barrett Browning (1806–1861), British poet.

b. Henriette Walpurgis Sontag (1806–1854), German soprano.

d. Elizabeth Carter (1717–1806), British writer.

Madame de Staël published the autobiographical novel *Corinne ou l'Italie* (1807).

Mary Lamb and her brother, Charles Lamb, published *Tales from Shakespeare*, their popular adaptation of the Bard for children (1807).

d. Angelica Kauffmann (1741–1807), Swiss painter.

Anne-Louis Girodet de Roucy showed her painting *The Entombment of Atala* (1808).

b. Caroline Elizabeth Sarah Sheridan Norton (1808–1877), British writer.

b. Maria Garcia Malibran (1808–1836), Spanish mezzo-soprano.

b. Fanny (Francis Anne) Kemble (1809–1893), British actress, daughter of actor-manager Charles Kemble and actress Maria De Camp.

d. Hannah Parkhouse Cowley (1743–1809), British playwright.

# 1810–1819

## POLITICS/LAW/WAR

b. Jeanne Deroin (1810–1894), French feminist, socialist, writer, and editor.

d. Ekaterina (Yekaterina) Romanovna Dashkova (1743–1810), Russian princess, who actively supported Catherine II of Russia during the 1762 coup that deposed Peter III. Later in her life, she became a Russian cultural official under Catherine. Her *Memoirs* were posthumously published (1840).

Lucy Brewer (later Louisa Baker) disguised herself as a man and enlisted in the marines as George Baker (1812), serving aboard the USS *Constitution*. Women were not openly allowed in the marines until 1918.

d. Sacagawea (ca. 1786–1812), Shoshone Indian guide and interpreter, who accompanied the Lewis and Clark transcontinental expedition (1804–1805).

b. Paulina Kellogg Wright Davis (1813–1876), American feminist, journalist, and organizer.

b. Jenny (Julia Joan Bertha) von Westphalen (1814–1881), German socialist, wife and aide of Karl Marx and mother of Eleanor Marx-Aveling.

b. Elizabeth Cady Stanton (1815–1902), American and worldwide women's rights movement leader.

d. Théroigne Anne Josephe de Méricourt (1762–1817), French feminist, entertainer, journalist, and revolutionary, who was among those who stormed the Bastille and led the women's march on Versailles (1789); she later emerged as a leading Girondist.

b. Lucy Stone (1818–1893), American abolitionist, feminist, and editor.

d. Abigail Adams (1744–1818), American First Lady, wife of John Adams; they were the first presidential couple to occupy the White House (1800).

b. Caroline Harper Dexter (1819–1884), Australian feminist, writer, and editor.

b. Julia Ward Howe (1819–1910), American abolitionist, social reformer, writer, and women's rights leader.

b. Luise Otto-Peters (1819–1895), German novelist and women's rights movement leader.

b. Victoria (1819–1901), queen of England (r. 1837–1901), who succeeded her uncle, William IV.

### RELIGION/EDUCATION/EVERYDAY LIFE

Elizabeth Seton and her community of sisters, which would become the Sisters of Charity, founded the first American Catholic parochial school, in Emmitsburg, Maryland (1810).

Hester Stanhope began the travels that would keep her abroad for the rest of her life (1810). After losing her baggage in a shipwreck, she adopted Arab male dress "for its splendour and convenience." She was among the earliest Britons to travel among the desert peoples of Egypt and Syria, often accompanied by a doctor, Charles Meryon, whose published *Memoirs* (1845) and *Travels* (1846) contain much of her writing.

b. Ernestine Rose (1810–1892), Polish-American social reformer and women's rights advocate.

b. Margaret Fuller (1810–1850), American transcendentalist writer, editor, and feminist.

d. Sarah Trimmer (1741–1810), British educator who inspired the foundation of many Sunday schools and charity schools, and wrote texts for children.

General Assembly of the Presbyterian Church in the United States formally stated its support for "pious females" (1811), who had begun organizing independent, female-run benevolent societies to support foreign and domestic missionaries, teachers, and doctors. The assembly stressed that "ladies" should provide services only for women and children; doing so for men was regarded as inappropriate.

After the death of her husband, Mary Reibey took over the Sydney-based international trading business she had helped build (1811), then much expanding it.

Elizabeth Seton formally established the Sisters of Charity (1812), the first Catholic sisterhood founded in America, from her earlier community (1809).

Ann (Nancy) Hesseltine Judson and Harriet Newell were the first two American women sent abroad as missionaries (1812), serving with their husbands in India, the Isle of France (Mauritius), and Burma (Myanmar).

b. Emma Bullock Martin (1812–1851), British freethinking lecturer, writer, and midwife.

Young female workers were first employed by Francis Cabot Lowell to work at the spinning frames and looms at his mill in Waltham, Massachusetts (1813), from 1822 followed by other more famous mills at Lowell. Living in boardinghouses established by Lowell, they became the first large-scale women's labor force in America.

b. Harriet Farley (1813–1907), American textile worker, teacher, writer, and editor.

Elizabeth Seton's Sisters of Charity took charge of orphanages in Philadelphia (1814) and New York (1817), establishing the first Catholic orphanages in America.

Rahel Levin Varnhagen von Ense reestablished her literary and cultural salon in Berlin (1814–1833), continuing until her death.

b. Angela (Georgina) Burdett-Coutts (1814–1906), British philanthropist.

d. Joanna Southcott (1750–1814), British religious leader who claimed she was sent to warn of Jesus Christ's return (1792), then that she was to give birth to the second Christ.

d. Mercy Otis Warren (1728–1814), American playwright, poet, and historian.

Returning to Paris, Madame Récamier reopened her salon (ca. 1815–1849), whose main figure would be the writer Châteaubriand.

b. Eliza Wood Burham Farnham (1815–1864), American feminist, prison reformer, and author.

b. Grace (Horsley) Darling (1815–1842), British hero.

b. Anne Ayres (1816–1896), English-American nun.

d. Mary Katherine Goddard (1738–1816), printer, publisher, bookseller, and the first American female postmaster.

British prison reformer Elizabeth Fry founded a pioneering prisoner's aid society (1817), focusing on the prison conditions of women and children.

d. Suzanne Curchod Necker (1739–1817), Swiss writer and philanthropist.

b. Amelia Jenks Bloomer (1818–1894), American reformer and feminist.

b. Susan King (1818–1880), American businesswoman.

## SCIENCE/TECHNOLOGY/MEDICINE

British paleontologist Mary Anning, then age 12, and her brother Joseph found the first complete *Ichthyosaurus* skeleton, 10 meters long (1811).

Calling herself James Barry, a woman (probably named Miranda Stuart) entered Edinburgh College of Medicine (1812), graduating and continuing to pose as a male throughout her medical career in Britain's colonial military service. In South Africa she discovered a plant used to treat syphilis and gonorrhea; she later became inspector general of all British hospitals in Canada.

French midwife Marie Gillain Boivin published her standard work on gynecology and obstetrics, *Mémorial de l'art des accouchements* (1812), long used as a standard text in Germany and France.

Mother Catherine Spalding founded the Sisters of Charity of Nazareth, Kentucky, a home-visiting order of nurses and teachers (1812).

b. Ann Preston (1813–1872), American physician and educator.

b. Clemence Sophia Lozier (1813–1888), American physician.

French midwife Marie Gillain Boivin was appointed codirector of the General Hospital for Seine and Oise (1814), the first of her many appointments as hospital director.

Josepha Siebold became the first woman to receive a doctoral degree in obstetrics from a Germany university, when she graduated from the University of Giessen (1815).

Sister Mary Aikenhead founded the Irish Sisters of Charity (1815).

British teacher Margaret Bryan published *An Astronomical and Geographical Class Book for Schools* (1815), based on her girls' school lectures.

b. (Augusta) Ada Byron, Countess of Lovelace (1815–1852), British mathematician.

Sophie Germain (Le Blanc) won the grand prize in a competition sponsored by the French Académie des Sciences on the mathematical theory of vibrations of elastic surfaces (1816), which would prove important to the modern study of acoustics and elasticity.

French midwife Marie Gillain Boivin published her gynecological-obstetrical text *Nouveau traité des maladies de l'uterus et des annexes* (1818).

b. Maria Mitchell (1818–1889), American astronomer.

b. Lydia Estes Pinkham (1819–1883), American medicine developer and distributor.

## ARTS/LITERATURE

b. Fanny (Franziska) Elssler (1810–1884), Austrian dancer.

b. Elizabeth Cleghorn Gaskell (1810–1865), British novelist.

b. Louise Colet (1810–1876), French poet and novelist.

Jane Austen published the novel *Sense and Sensibility* (1811), begun in 1797 under the title *Elinor*.

b. Harriet Beecher Stowe (1811–1896), American writer and women's rights leader.

b. Giulia Grisi (1811–1869), Italian soprano.

Maria Edgeworth published the novels *The Absentee* and *Vivian* (1812).

b. Fanny Tacchinardi-Persiani (1812–1867), Italian soprano.

Jane Austen published the novel *Pride and Prejudice*, introducing Elizabeth Bennet and Fitzwilliam Darcy (1813). She had originally written it in 1796 as *First Impressions* but could not find a publisher for the work, even as a subsidized publication, and later much revised it.

Madame de Staël published *De l'Allemagne* (*On Germany*) (1813).

Jane Austen published the novel *Mansfield Park*, creating Fanny Price (1814).

Fanny Burney published the novel *The Wanderer, or Female Difficulties* (1814).

b. Céline Céleste (1814–1882), French actress, dancer, and pantomimist.

b. Ellen Price Wood (Mrs. Henry Wood, 1814–1887), British writer.

Jane Austen published the novel *Emma*, creating Miss Woodhouse of Highbury (1815).

Isabella Colbran created the title role in Gioacchino Rossini's opera *Elizabeth, Queen of England* (1815).

b. Julia Margaret Cameron (1815–1879), British portrait photographer.

d. Frances Barton Abington (1737–1815), British actress, long associated with David Garrick at the Drury Lane Theater; she created Lady Teazle in Richard Brinsley Sheridan's *The School for Scandal* (1777).

Caroline Lamb published the autobiographical novel *Glenarvon* (1816).

b. Charlotte Brontë (1816–1855), British novelist and poet.

b. Charlotte Saunders Cushman (1816–1876), American actress.

b. Grace Aguilar (1816–1847), British author.

d. Anna Lucia De Amicis (1733–1816), Italian soprano.

d. Dorothy Jordan (1761–1816), British actress.

Isabella Colbran created the role of Anaïs in Gioacchino Rossini's opera *Moses in Egypt* (1817).

Maria Edgeworth published the novel *Ormond* (1817).

b. Fanny Cerrito (1817–1909), Italian dancer and choreographer.

b. Helen Faucit (1817–1898), British actress.

d. Jane Austen (1775–1817), British novelist; the novels *Northanger Abbey* and *Persuasion* were published the year of her death.

Mary Wollstonecraft Shelley published the novel *Frankenstein, or the Modern Prometheus* (1818).

b. Lola Montez (Maria Dolores Gilbert) (1818–1861), Irish dancer.

b. Emily Brontë (1818–1848) British novelist and poet.

b. Charlotte Mary Sanford Barnes (1818–1863), American actress and playwright.

d. Jane Pope (1742–1818), British actress who created the role of Mrs. Candour in Richard Brinsley Sheridan's *The School for Scandal* (1777).

d. Anne Vallayer-Coster (1744–1818), French still-life painter.

d. Elizabeth Billington (1765–1818), British soprano.

Isabella Colbran created the title role in Gioacchino Rossini's opera *The Lady of the Lake* (1819).

b. George Eliot (Mary Anne or Marian Evans, 1819–1880), British novelist.

b. Clara Wieck Schumann (1819–1896), German pianist, composer, and teacher, wife of Robert Schumann.

b. Carlotta Grisi (1819–1899), Italian ballerina.

b. Lucile Grahn (1819–1907), Danish ballerina.

d. Josepha Weber (1759–1819), German soprano, who created the role of the Queen of the Night in Wolfgang Amadeus Mozart's *The Magic Flute* (1791).

## 1820–1829

### POLITICS/LAW/WAR

b. Susan B. Anthony (1820–1906), American women's rights movement leader, social reformer, temperance movement activist, and abolitionist.

b. Mary Muller (1820–1902), New Zealand suffragist and writer.

Greek War of Independence leader Manto Mavrogenous acted as a general commanding guerrilla forces in the Peloponnesian peninsula (1821) and also mobilized international pro-Greek sentiment, helping to convince the western Great Powers to support the cause of Greek independence.

Connecticut passed a law (1821) against administering poison to produce an abortion after quickening (the first sign of fetal movement).

b. Harriet Tubman (ca. 1821–1913), African-American abolitionist, Underground Railroad conductor, and soldier.

Revolutionary War hero Molly Pitcher (Mary Ludwig Hays McCauley) was awarded a pension by the state of Pennsylvania (1822).

b. Harriet Hanson Robinson (1825–1911), American feminist, suffragist, and writer.

b. Jessie Boucherett (1825–1905), English feminist and suffragist.

d. Laskarina Bouboulina (1771–1825), insurgent leader during the Greek War of Independence, who funded and led modest Greek land and sea forces against Turkish forces.

b. Eugénie (Marie Eugénie de Montijo de Guzman, 1826–1920), wife of Napoléon III of France.

b. Henrietta Dugdale (1826–1918), Australian feminist, social reformer, suffragist leader, and writer.

b. Marie Pouchoulin Goegg (1826–1899), Swiss feminist and democratic revolutionary.

b. Lydia Ernestine Becker (1827–1890), British educator, writer, and suffragist.

b. Nathalie Lemel (1827–1921), French socialist, an activist of the Paris Commune (1871).

d. Deborah Sampson (Gannett) (1760–1827), Massachusetts soldier in the American Revolution, who enlisted and fought as Robert Shurtliff was wounded at Tarrytown, and was discharged (1783) when discovered to be a woman. She later received a soldier's pension.

b. Maria Deraismes (1828–1894), French feminist, women's rights leader, and writer.

Sarah Moore Grimké published *Epistle to the Clergy of the Southern States*, attacking religious rationalizations of slavery (1829).

## RELIGION/EDUCATION/EVERYDAY LIFE

b. Anne Jemima Clough (1820–1892), British educator.

b. Concepción Arenal (1820–1893), Spanish social scientist and journalist.

b. Louisa Twining (1820–1912), British reformer and feminist.

Troy Female Seminary (later the Emma Willard School) opened (1821), after Emma Hart Willard had convinced the city of Troy, New York, to fund the establishment of a girls' school; offering a rigorous education, it drew girls from across the young country.

Frances Wright published *Views of Society and Manners in America* (1821), giving impressions of her 1818 visit to New York.

b. Mary Baker Eddy (1821–1910), American religious leader.

d. Elizabeth Ann Bayley Seton (1774–1821), American religious leader, the first American-born saint, who established the first parochial school (1810), Catholic sisterhood (1812), and orphanage (1814) in America.

d. Hester Lynch Salisbury Thrale (Piozzi) (1741–1821), British salon hostess and writer, best known for her London salon and her friendship with Samuel Johnson, with whom she traveled in Wales and France (1774–1775) and about whom she wrote (1786); she introduced Fanny Burney to London's literary circles.

Frances Wright published *A Few Days in Athens*, an idiosyncratic view of philosophy (1822).

b. Elizabeth (Cabot) Cary Agassiz (1822–1907), American educator and scientist, the founder and first president of Radcliffe College (1893–1903).

b. Nadezhda Stasova (1822–1895), Russian feminist and social reformer.

b. Caroline Wells (Healey) Dall (1822–1912), American author.

b. Frances Power Cobbe (1822–1904), Irish writer, feminist, social reformer, and suffragist.

Catharine Beecher founded a girls' school at Hartford, Connecticut (1823).

b. Mary Ann Shadd (1823–1893), African-American antislavery and women's rights movement activist, teacher, writer, and editor.

New Harmony (1824–1827), a utopian community, was founded in Indiana by Robert Owen, who stressed equality of men and women and sought to redefine gender roles and marriage, believing it should be dissoluble.

Dorothea Dix authored a children's textbook, *Conversations on Common Things* (1824); she had earlier started a "dame school" for young girls in Boston (1821).

Emma Willard wrote the widely used textbook *Ancient Geography* (1824), which would be followed by several history texts.

New York United Tailoresses Society was organized (1824).

b. Julie-Victoire Daubie (1824–1874), French feminist and educational pioneer.

Rebecca Pennock Lukens took over the Brandywine Rolling Mill at the death of her husband (1825), becoming a rare and successful woman industrial entrepreneur; her father had been the mill's original founder.

Frances Wright funded an experiment in which slaves moved to a settlement in Nashoba, Tennessee (1825), intended as a "half-way house" on the way to establishing free colonies abroad; one group did move on to Haiti (1830).

b. Antoinette Brown Blackwell (1825–1921), American reformer, minister, and women's rights advocate.

b. Matilda Joslyn Gage (1826–1898), American women's rights organizer and writer.

b. Frances Auretta Fuller Victor (1826–1902), American historian and author.

Frances Wright founded the Women's Social Society at New Harmony, Indiana (1827), believed to be the first fully organized American women's club.

Joanne Bethune founded the Infant School Society, setting up her first of nine free schools for infants (1827), in New York City.

b. Barbara Leigh-Smith Bodichon (1827–1891), British feminist educator, writer, and artist.

b. Learmonth White Dalrymple (1827–1906), New Zealand educator and feminist.

Frances Wright began editing the *New Harmony Gazette* with Robert Dale Owen, founder of the utopian community (1828).

Zilpah Grant became head of the Ipswich Female Seminary (1828), building it into a select girls' boarding school; many of her students went on to become teachers themselves, moving West as the young country did.

b. Josephine Gray Butler (1828–1906), British feminist and social reformer.

The practice of suttee (*sati*)—burning a Hindu widow alive on her husband's funeral pyre—was outlawed in India (1829), though the practice continued to some extent, even into the 20th century. *Sati* (Sanskrit for "good wife") did not become common until medieval times, early Hindu texts simply calling for widows to be chaste and even sanctioning remarriage.

Mary Carpenter founded the Working and Visiting Society in Britain (1829).

b. Catherine Mumford Booth (1829–1890), British religious leader, co-founder of the Salvation Army.

b. Laura (Eliza Jane Seymour) Bell (1829–1894), Irish courtesan and missionary.

b. Maria Susan Rye (1829–1903), British social reformer and women's rights advocate.

### SCIENCE/TECHNOLOGY/MEDICINE

b. Florence Nightingale (1820–1910), British nurse and administrator.

d. Claudine Poullet Picardet Guyton de Morveau (ca. 1770–ca. 1820), French scientific translator.

b. Elizabeth Blackwell (1821–1910), British-American physician.

b. Louise Büchner (1821–1877), German nurse and women's rights activist.

b. Clara (Clarissa Harlowe) Barton (1821–1912), American nurse.

b. Amalie Nelle Dietrich (1821–1891), German naturalist.

d. Maria Louise Dugès La Chapelle (1769–1821), French midwife, daughter and granddaughter of midwives, who became head of the maternity department of Paris's Hôtel Dieu; after study in Heidelberg, she also founded a maternity and children's hospital at Port Royal, France. She is best known for her massive three-volume book, *Pratique des accouchements*, which became a standard text. It stressed obstetrical interference only when necessary, and introduced innovations such as repair of the perineum immediately after childbirth.

b. Lydia Folger Fowler (1822–1879), American physician.

British paleontologist Mary Anning discovered the almost-complete skeleton of a *Plesiosaurus*, a dinosaur (1824).

Madame Johnson (first name unknown) is believed to be the first American to fly a hot-air balloon solo, at an exhibition in New York (1825).

Mary Somerville wrote the paper "On the Magnetizing Power of the More Refrangible Solar Rays" (1826), the first of her many works on astronomy, mathematics, physics, chemistry, and geography. It was presented by her husband to the Royal Society and published in *Philosophical Transactions*.

b. Emily Blackwell (1826–1910), British-American physician.

For a catalogue of nebulae, not published but used by her nephew John Herschel for his own astronomical investigations, Caroline Herschel was awarded a gold medal by Britain's Royal Astronomical Society (1828).

British paleontologist Mary Anning discovered the skeleton of a *Pterodactyl* of the small *Dimorphodon* genus (1828).

b. Eleanor Anne Ormerod (1828–1901), British economic entomologist.

Physician and professor Maria Dalle Donne was honored with the title of "Academic" by Italy's Academia Benedettina (1829).

Almira Hart Lincoln Phelps published *Familiar Lectures on Botany*, the first of her many popular science textbooks (1829).

The Sisters of Our Lady of Mercy staffed the Hospital of the Society of Working Men in Charleston, South Carolina (1829).

b. Marie Elizabeth Zakrzewska (1829–1902), German-born Polish-American physician.

b. Mary Harris Thompson (1829–1895), American physician.

## ARTS/LITERATURE

b. Anne Brontë (1820–1849), British poet and novelist.

b. Rachel (1820–1858), French actress.

b. Laura Keene (1820–1873), British-American actress and theater manager.

b. Louise Lane Drew (Mrs. John Drew, 1820–1897), American actress and theater manager.

b. Jenny (Johanna Maria) Lind (1820–1887), Swedish soprano.

b. Alice Cary (1820–1871), American author.

d. (Magdeleine) Sophie Arnould (1740–1820), French actress and singer, a soprano who starred at the Paris Opéra (1757–1778), creating several major roles, including the title role in Christoph Gluck's *Iphegénie en Aulide* (1774).

Sophia Hewitt became the organist for Boston's Handel and Haydn Society (1820).

b. Anne Whitney (1821–1915), American sculptor, writer, abolitionist, feminist, and social reformer.

b. Pauline Garcia Viardot (1821–1910), French mezzo-soprano.

d. Elizabeth Inchbald (1753–1821), British actress and playwright.

d. Elisavet Moutza-Martinengou (1801–1821), Greek writer, a poet, dramatist, and translator of Greek classics; her autobiography was published posthumously (1881).

Catharine Maria Sedgwick published the novel *A New England Tale* (1822).

b. Rosa Bonheur (1822–1899), French artist.

b. Adelaide Ristori (1822–1906), Italian actress.

Mary Wollstonecraft Shelley published the novel *Valperga* (1823).

Henriette Sontag created the title role in Carl Maria von Weber's opera *Euryanthe* (1823).

b. Marietta Alboni (1823–1894), Italian contralto.

b. Mary Boykin Miller Chesnut (1823–1886), American writer.

d. Ann Radcliffe (Ann Ward, 1764–1823), British Gothic novelist best known for *The Mysteries of Udolpho* (1794).

Anna and Sarah Peale were the first female members of the Pennsylvania Academy of the Fine Arts (1824).

Karoline Unger and Henriette Sontag sang at the premieres of Ludwig van Beethoven's *Missa Solemnis* and *Ninth Symphony* (1824).

Lydia Maria Child published the novel *Habanok* (1824).

Catharine Maria Sedgwick published the novel *Redwood* (1824).

b. A(deline) D(utton) T(rain) Whitney (1824–1906), American novelist.

d. Maria Theresia von Paradis (1759–1824), Austrian composer and pianist, blind from her early years, who toured, composed, and wrote with the aid of innovative machines.

Lydia Maria Child published the novel *The Rebels* (1825).

b. Maria Firmina dos Reis (Uma Brasileira) (1825–1917), African-Brazilian teacher, novelist, and poet.

b. Adelaide Procter (1825–1864), British poet, writing as Mary Berwick.

b. Frances Ellen Harper (1825–1911), American poet, abolitionist, and social reformer.

b. Patience Lovell Wright (1825–1886) American portrait sculptor.

d. Anna Letitia Aikin Barbauld (1743–1825), British writer, editor, and critic.

Marie Taglioni created the title role in Filippo Taglioni's ballet *Danina, oder Jocko dre brasilianische Affe* (1826).

Elizabeth Barrett Browning published *Essay on Mind, with Other Poems* (1826).

Evanthia Kairi wrote the play *Nikiratos*, honoring the women who had fought to keep Missolonghi from falling to the Turks (1826).

Giuditta Pasta created the title role in Giovanni Pacini's opera *Niobe* (1826).

Mary Wollstonecraft Shelley published the novel *The Last Man* (1826).

Anna Jameson published the autobiographical novel *The Diary of an Ennuyée* (1826).

Anne Hall was the first female artist elected to the American National Academy of Design (1827); she later became the first female full member (1833).

Marie Taglioni made her Paris debut in Filippo Taglioni's version of the ballet *Le Sicilien* (1827).

Henriette Méric-Lalande created the role of Imogene in Vincenzo Bellini's opera *The Pirate* (1827).

Catharine Maria Sedgwick published the novel *Hope Leslie* (1827).

Sarah Josepha Hale published the novel *Northwood* (1827).

b. Maria Susanna Cummins (1827–1866), American author.

b. Mary Jane Peale (1827–1902), American painter.

Sarah Josepha Hale was editor-publisher of the *American Ladies' Magazine* in Boston (1828–1836).

Mary Berry published *Social Life of England and France, from Charles II to 1830* (1828–1831).

b. Margaret Wilson Oliphant (1828–1897), Scottish writer.

d. Caroline Ponsonby Lamb (1785–1828), British novelist.

Henriette Méric-Lalande created the title role in Vincenzo Bellini's opera *The Stranger* (1829).

# 1830

## Politics/Law/War

b. Belva Bennett Lockwood (1830–1917), American teacher, lawyer, feminist, suffragist, women's rights movement leader, presidential candidate, and pacifist.

b. Mary Harris "Mother" Jones (1830–1930), American teacher and labor organizer.

b. Louise Michel (1830–1895), French teacher, writer, and political activist.

d. Rallou Karatza (ca. 1778–1830), Greek theater director and translator, an active revolutionary during the Greek War of Independence.

## Religion/Education/Everyday Life

b. (Sarah) Emily Davies (1830–1921), British feminist, educator, and suffragist.

b. Clemence Augustine Royer (1830–1902), French scholar.

b. Emily Edson Briggs (Olivia) (1830–1910), American newspaper reporter.

## Science/Technology/Medicine

b. Harriet (Jemima Winifred) Clisby (1830–1931), Australian physician and feminist.

## Arts/Literature

Giuditta Grisi created the role of Romeo, opposite Rosalbina Caradori-Allan as Juliet, in Vincenzo Bellini's opera *The Capulets and the Montagues*.

Giuditta Pasta created the title role in Gaetano Donizetti's opera *Anna Bolena*.

Sarah Josepha Hale published *Poems for Our Children*, which included "Mary Had a Little Lamb."

b. Emily Elizabeth Dickinson (1830–1886), American poet.

b. Helen Maria Fiske Hunt Jackson (1830–1885), American writer and social reformer.

b. Christina Rossetti (1830–1894), British writer.

b. Francesca Romana Maddalena Janauschek (1830–1904), Czech actress.

b. Harriet Goodhue Hosmer (1830–1908), American sculptor.

# 1831

## Politics/Law/War

b. Myra Colby Bradwell (1831–1894), American social reformer, feminist, lawyer, and law publisher.

## Religion/Education/Everyday Life

*Godey's Lady's Book* began publication in Philadelphia, offering fashion plates, woodcuts, engraved pictures, poetry, and prose, largely a pastiche of British women's magazines, put together by Louis A. Godey.

Laure d'Abrantès published her 18-volume *Recollections of Napoléon, the Revolution, the Directory, and the Restoration* (1831–1834).

Mary Prince published *The History of Mary Prince, A West Indian Slave, Related by Herself*.

b. Helena Petrovna Blavatsky (1831–1891), Russian religious leader.

b. Dorothea Beale (1831–1906), British educator and feminist.

b. Isabel Arundell Burton (1831–1896), British traveler.

## Science/Technology/Medicine

Mary Somerville published *Mechanism of the Heavens*, her English translation of Laplace's *Mécanique céleste*, used as a college textbook into the early 20th century. Her preface was also published separately as *A Preliminary Dissertation on the Mechanism of the Heavens* (1832).

Mother Mary Catherine McAuley founded the Sisters of Mercy in Dublin, a nursing order that spread to England and America, also serving in various wars.

b. Isabella Lucy Bird Bishop (1831–1904), British naturalist, geographer, explorer, travel writer, and medical missionary.

b. Emily Howard Jennings Stowe (1831–1903), Canadian physician and suffrage advocate.

b. Harriet Mann (1831–1918), American writer of nature studies and children's books, writing as Olive Thorne Miller.

b. Rachel Bodley (1831–1888), American chemist and botanist.

d. Sophie Germain (Le Blanc) (1776–1831), French mathematician, largely self-taught against her parents' strong disapproval; her work on Fermat's last theorem was basic to 20th-century mathematicians' attempts to solve the notably intractable problem. Karl Friedrich Gauss recommended Germain for an honorary doctorate from the University of Göttingen, but she died of cancer before receiving it. Two posthumously published works were *Pensées diverses*, personal musings and thoughts on the work of great scientists and mathematicians, and *Considérations générales sur l'état des sciences et des lettres*, suggesting that the sciences and the humanities are not different in essentials.

### ARTS/LITERATURE

Frances Trollope published *The Domestic Manners of the Americans* after her tour of the United States.

Giuditta Pasta created the role of Amina in Vincenzo Bellini's opera *La sonnambula* and in the same year created the title role in his opera *Norma*.

b. Mary Mapes Dodge (1831–1905), American author.

b. Rebecca Harding Davis (1831–1910), American writer.

d. Sarah Kemble Siddons (1755–1831), a leading British tragedian and a very notable Lady Macbeth.

## 1832

### POLITICS/LAW/WAR

African-American women meeting in Salem, Massachusetts, founded the first Female Anti-Slavery Society. In the same year, Maria Chapman co-founded the Boston Female Anti-Slavery Society and William Lloyd Garrison founded the New England Anti-Slavery Society, including both men and women.

d. Molly Pitcher (Mary Ludwig Hays McCauley, 1754–1832), reputed hero of the American Revolution, lauded for her role at the Battle of Monmouth (1778).

### RELIGION/EDUCATION/EVERYDAY LIFE

Catharine Beecher founded and headed the Western Female Institute in Cincinnati, Ohio (1832–1837); she also worked with the Ladies' Society for Improving Education in the West, which recruited teachers and founded colleges in Milwaukee, Wisconsin, and elsewhere.

Caroline Chisholm founded the Female School of Industry for the Daughters of European Soldiers in Madras, India.

b. Henrietta Chamberlain King (1832–1925), American ranch manager.

### SCIENCE/TECHNOLOGY/MEDICINE

Jane Kilby Welsh published her two-volume textbook *Familiar Lessons in Mineralogy and Geology* (1832; 1833).

b. Mary Edwards Walker (1832–1919), American physician, suffragist, and dress-reform advocate.

### ARTS/LITERATURE

Marie Taglioni created the title role in Filippo Taglioni's *La Sylphide*, dancing *en pointe*, becoming the first great ballerina.

George Sand published the novels *Indiana* and *Valentine*, emerging as a major literary figure.

Harriet Martineau published *Illustrations of Political Economy*, a series of illustrative stories (1832–1834).

Sabina Heinefetter created the role of Adina in Gaetano Donizetti's opera *L'Eliser D'Amore*.

b. Louisa May Alcott (1832–1888), American writer.

## 1833

### POLITICS/LAW/WAR

American Anti-Slavery Society (AASS) was founded in Philadelphia; none of the four women attending the founding meeting were allowed to become members, though Lucretia Coffin Mott did speak, with the group's permission; Mott then led a group of antislavery women in founding the Philadelphia Female Anti-Slavery Society.

### RELIGION/EDUCATION/EVERYDAY LIFE

Oberlin Collegiate Institute (later Oberlin College) was founded in Cleveland, Ohio, as an experiment in "Christian living," being the first coeducational school to grant women undergraduate degrees and to accept students of all races. Women were, however, placed in a subservient role, obliged to clean rooms, wash clothing, and serve food for the male students. Notable early graduates included Antoinette Brown (later Blackwell) and Lucy Stone.

Inspired by William Lloyd Garrison's *Liberator*, Prudence Crandall admitted a young black student to the girls' school she had founded in Canterbury, Connecticut (1831). Many white parents withdrew their children and Connecticut passed its "black law," forbidding schools to teach black children from out of town without town approval. Crandall was arrested and convicted; though the decision was overturned (1834), continued harassment, including arson and armed mobs, forced her to close the school.

Abolitionist Lydia Maria Child published *An Appeal in Favour of the Class of Americans Called Africans*.

Abigail Goodrich Whittelsey became publisher-editor of *Mother's Magazine*, the first American journal for mothers.

b. Auguste Schmidt (1833–1902), German educator and feminist.

d. Rahel Levin Varnhagen von Ense (1771–1833), German salon hostess, whose Berlin salons (ca. 1800–1806; 1819–1833) attracted key figures of the Romantic movement. Some of her writings were posthumously published as *Rahel: Ein Buch des Andenkens für ihre Freunde* (1834).

### SCIENCE/TECHNOLOGY/MEDICINE

Mary Austin Holley published *Texas: Observations: Historical, Geographical, and Descriptive* (1833; 1836).

b. Lucy Hobbs (Taylor) (1833–ca. 1900), American dentist.

### ARTS/LITERATURE

George Sand published the novel *Lélia*, controversial for its eroticism.

Giuditta Pasta created the title role in Vincenzo Bellini's opera *Beatrice Di Tenda*.

Harriet Martineau published *Poor Laws and Paupers Illustrated*, a second series of illustrative stories (1833–1834).

b. Soledad Acosta de Samper (1833–1903), Colombian writer and editor.

## 1834

### POLITICS/LAW/WAR

b. Abigail Jane Scott Duniway (1834–1915), American women's rights advocate and suffragist.

### RELIGION/EDUCATION/EVERYDAY LIFE

Factory Girls' Association was organized in the textile mills of Lowell, Massachusetts. Female workers went on their first strike, after learning that the pay for some workers would be cut by 15 percent. The strike failed, with workers returning to their jobs within a day, after its leader was fired, but not before some 800 "mill girls" paraded in protest through the town.

New York Female Moral Reform Society was established at New York's Third Presbyterian Church, seeking to close the city's brothels and convert prostitutes to evangelical Protestantism, and also criticizing the sexual double standard that condemned women, not men, in such activities. The group had nationwide impact through its weekly publication, *The Advocate*.

b. Hetty (Henrietta Howland Robinson) Green (1834–1916), American financier.

## SCIENCE/TECHNOLOGY/MEDICINE

Marie Durocher received the first diploma granted by the new Medical School in Rio de Janeiro, becoming one of Latin America's first female doctors; she was much influenced by the work of French obstetrician Marie Boivin.

Mary Somerville published *On the Connexion of the Physical Sciences*.

Anne Isabella, Lady Noel Byron, founded an industrial and agricultural school at Ealing Grove, Britain.

## ARTS/LITERATURE

Marie Tussaud established her wax museum in London.

b. Louisa Atkinson (1834–1872), Australian novelist and naturalist.

## 1835

### POLITICS/LAW/WAR

b. Tz'u Hsi (1835–1908), dowager empress of China.

b. Lakshmi Bai (1835–1857), rani of Jhansi.

d. Thérésia de Cabarrus Tallien (Princess de Chimay, 1773–1835), French political figure and salon hostess, a revolutionary though the ex-wife of an aristocrat, imprisoned during the Reign of Terror; released with the death of Robespierre. She was later a leading Directoire hostess.

### RELIGION/EDUCATION/EVERYDAY LIFE

Henrietta Hall Shuck became the first American female missionary in China; aged 18, she accompanied her husband, J. Lewis Shuck, supported by the Southern Baptist Woman's Missionary Society.

First American women's prison, Mount Pleasant Female Prison, was founded in New York.

Lydia Maria Child published *History of the Condition of Women*.

Elizabeth Palmer Peabody published *Record of a School*, about her experiences working at Boston's Temple School.

b. Mariya (Vasilevna) Trubnikova (1835–1897), Russian feminist and educator.

### SCIENCE/TECHNOLOGY/MEDICINE

Britain's Royal Society awarded its first honorary memberships to two women: Caroline Herschel and Mary Somerville. The only other such award made before the 20th century was to feminist-pacifist educator Anne Sheepshanks (1862).

Harriot Hunt and her sister, Sarah, set up a medical practice in Boston; unable to attend medical school, they had studied anatomy and physiology privately. After numerous applications, Harriot Hunt was accepted to Harvard University (along with three black men); but male students rioted, protesting the "sacrifice of her modesty," and forced her to withdraw. She would later receive an honorary medical degree from Philadelphia's Female Medical College, after practicing for 18 years.

### ARTS/LITERATURE

Mary Wollstonecraft Shelley published the novel *Lodore*.

Fanny Tacchinardi-Persiani created the title role in Gaetano Donizetti's opera *Lucia di Lammermoor*.

Grace Aguilar published the poetry collecton *Magic Wreath*.

Lucile Grahn created the role of Astrid in August Bournonville's ballet *Valdemar*.

b. Adah Isaacs Menken (Dolores Adios Fuertes, 1835–1868), American actress.

b. Augusta Jane Evans (1835–1909), American author.

b. Rose Ettinge (1835–1911), American actress.

d. Hannah More (1745–1835), British playwright, poet, and educator.

## 1836

### POLITICS/LAW/WAR

Angelina Grimké published her *Appeal to the Christian Women of the South*, urging them to join in the fight to abolish slavery.

### RELIGION/EDUCATION/EVERYDAY LIFE

Women mill workers again struck at Lowell, again over a pay cut; this strike lasted a month, during which they were evicted from their boardinghouses, with some returning to work, others to their original homes.

Eliza Hart Spalding and Narcissa Whitman became the first women of European ancestry to cross the Rocky Mountains, en route with their husbands to found Presbyterian missions in the Oregon Territory: the Spaldings settled with the Nez Perce at Lapwai, now in Idaho; the Whitmans with the Cayuse near Fort Walla Walla, now in Washington, where they were later killed in an uprising (1847).

American journalist Ann Royall began publishing the periodical *The Huntress* (1836–1864).

Catharine Beecher published *Letters on the Difficulties of Religion*.

Lydia Maria Child published her *Anti-Slavery Catechism*.

b. Fannie Jackson Coppin (1836–1913), African-American educator.

b. Lucy Walker (1836–1916), British mountaineer.

b. Maria-Dominica Mazarello (1836–1881), Italian Catholic nun.

d. Marie Madeleine Postel (1746–after 1836), French teacher and saint who founded the Poor Daughters of Mercy (1807), which at her death had 37 houses.

### SCIENCE/TECHNOLOGY/MEDICINE

Frederika Münster Fliedner and her husband, Lutheran pastor Theodor Fliedner, founded the Kaiserswerth Institute for the Training of Deaconesses, a nurses' training center in Germany that would draw and inspire nurses throughout the world, the first graduate being Gertrude Reichard.

Felicia Dorothea Heman published the poem "Epitaph for a Mineralogist."

b. Elizabeth Garrett Anderson (1836–1917), Britain's first female physician.

b. Sarah Plummer Lemmon (1836–1923), American botanist.

d. Marie Anne Pierrette Paulze Lavoisier (1758–1836), French illustrator and editor, who assisted her husband, chemist Antoine Laurent Lavoisier, and later led a scientific salon.

### ARTS/LITERATURE

Clara Schumann composed her *Piano Concerto*.

Frances Trollope published the novel *The Life and Adventures of Jonathan Jefferson Whitlaw; or, Scenes on the Mississippi*.

Lucile Grahn created the title role in August Bournonville's ballet *La Sylphide*, opposite Bournonville.

Caroline Elizabeth Sarah Norton published the poetry collection *A Voice from the Factories*.

d. Maria Garcia Malibran (1808–1836), Spanish mezzo-soprano, sister of singer Pauline Viardot; one of the leading opera figures of her time.

---

# On Human Rights

I recognize no rights but *human rights*—I know nothing of men's rights and women's rights; for in Christ Jesus there is neither male nor female. It is my solemn conviction that, until this principle of equality is recognized and embodied in practice, the church can do nothing effectual for the permanent reformation of the world.

— Angelina Grimké (1836)

## 1837

### POLITICS/LAW/WAR

Radical abolitionists, led by William Lloyd Garrison, led the fight for women's full participation in the American Anti-Slavery Society (AASS), staging the fight around the right of Angelina and Sarah Grimké to speak against slavery to mixed (female and male) audiences.

The first Anti-Slavery Convention of American Women, a convention of the country's various Female Anti-Slavery Societies, was held in New York City.

Angelina Grimké published her *Appeal to Women of the Nominally Free States*.

b. Anna Diagileva Filosova (1837–1912), Russian social reformer and feminist.

b. Anna Maria Mozzoni (1837–1920), Italian socialist and women's rights movement leader.

### RELIGION/EDUCATION/EVERYDAY LIFE

Mount Holyoke Seminary (from 1893, College) was founded in South Hadley, Massachusetts, by Mary Lyon, who during her tenure (1837–1849) established a focus on preparing women to be educators; Lyon's fund-raising efforts kept tuition lower than at other women's schools, opening Mount Holyoke to less affluent women.

Angela Burdett-Coutts inherited an enormous fortune; over the next seven decades, she would give away nearly three million pounds, largely on projects for the poor, which included building houses and churches, providing public health works, aiding victims of Ireland's famine and Turkish refugees from the Russian-Turkish War, and funding women's emigration and African explorations.

b. Anne King Blunt (1837–1917), British traveler.

b. Isabella Mayson Beeton (1837–1865), British cookery writer.

b. Deguchi Nao (1837–1918), Japanese religious leader.

### SCIENCE/TECHNOLOGY/MEDICINE

b. Agnes McLaren (1837–1913), Scottish physician and nun.

### ARTS/LITERATURE

Harriet Martineau published *Society in America* after an extended tour of the United States (1834–1836).

---

# On Women and Abolition

I stand before you as a citizen, on behalf of the 20,000 women of Massachusetts, whose names are enrolled on petitions which have been submitted to the Legislature relating to the great and solemn subject of American slavery . . . because it is a *political* subject, it has often been tauntingly said, that *woman* has nothing to do with it. Are we aliens, because we are *women*? Are we bereft of citizenship, because we are the mothers, wives, and daughters of a mighty people? Have women *no* country— *no* interests staked in public weal—no liabilities in common peril—no partnership in a nation's guilt and shame? . . . I hold, Mr. Chairman, that Americans have to do with this subject, not only because it is moral and religious, but because it is *political*, inasmuch as we are citizens of this republic, and as such *our* honor, happiness, and well being, are bound up in its politics and government and laws.

I stand before you as a Southerner, exiled from the land of my birth, by the sound of the lash, and the pitious[sic] cry of the slave. I stand before you as a repentant slaveholder. I stand before you as a moral being, endowed with precious and inalienable rights, which are correlative with solemn duties and high responsibilities.

— Angelina Grimké, speaking to the Massachusetts legislature (1838)

Sarah Josepha Hale became editor of *Godey's Lady's Book* (1837–1877), after Louis Gadney bought *American Ladies' Magazine,* which she had founded in 1828. It would be the dominant American women's magazine until the Civil War, surviving into the 1890s.

Giuseppina Ronzi de Begnis created the role of Elizabeth I of England in Gaetano Donizetti's opera *Robert Devereux.*

Lucile Grahn created the role of Quiteria in August Bournonville's ballet *Don Quixote.*

Charlotte Saunders Cushman starred as Meg Merrilees in *Guy Mannering.*

Frances Trollope published the novel *The Vicar of Wrexhill.*

Fredrika Bremer published the novel *Grannarne.*

b. (Francesca Gaetana) Cosima Liszt Wagner (1837–1930), German musician and writer, daughter of Franz Liszt and Countess Marie D'Agoult, and the wife of composer Richard Wagner.

b. Mary Elizabeth Braddon (1837–1915), British writer and editor.

# 1838

## POLITICS/LAW/WAR

Angelina Grimké became the first woman ever to address an American legislature, speaking in Massachusetts on abolition.

Sisters Angelina and Sarah Grimké, the first female lecturers of the American Anti-Slavery Society, responded to criticism generated by their lectures to mixed audiences (women and men) with *Letters on the Equality of the Sexes and the Condition of Women.* This landmark defense of the right of women to engage in political action—in this case, the abolition movement—and call for full equality included Sarah's famous comment: "I ask no favors for my sex...All I ask of our brethren is that they will take their feet from off our necks." That same year the Grimkés also published *American Slavery as It Is: Testimony of a Thousand Witnesses,* written jointly; *The Condition of Women,* by Sarah; and *Letters to Catharine Beecher,* by Angelina.

Anti-Slavery Convention of American Women was held in Philadelphia (1838; also 1839).

Women won the right to vote in school board elections in Kentucky; it was the first grant of suffrage to American women since New Jersey had repealed the law granting votes for women (1807).

b. Victoria Claflin Woodhull (1838–1927), American feminist, reformer, stockbroker, spiritualist, and publisher.

b. Liliuokalani (Lydia Kamekeha; 1838–1917), the last queen of Hawaii (1891–1893).

## RELIGION/EDUCATION/EVERYDAY LIFE

Emma Martin gave a public lecture on education, the first of what would be many lectures around Britain (esp. 1838–1845) supporting women's rights and socialism, and attacking such institutions as marriage and religion.

Grace Darling and her father, a lighthouse keeper, rowed out off the Farne Islands in a great storm to rescue five survivors of the wrecked steamboat *Forfarshire,* their exploit winning them gold medals from the Humane Society and making Grace a national celebrity.

Henriette d'Angeville became the first woman to climb Mont Blanc in the French Alps, organizing her own expedition and completing the climb over three days; two other women had previously been carried to the summit.

Flora Tristan published *Peregrinations d'une paria,* describing her 14-year-long battle with her estranged husband over custody of their children and support (1824–1838).

b. Octavia Hill (1838–1912), British reformer.

b. Sarah Elizabeth van de Vort Emery (1838–1895), American writer.

d. Jeanne-Elisabeth Bichier des Ages (1773–1838), French religious leader and saint who founded the Daughters of the Cross, near Poitiers, for teaching poor rural children.

## SCIENCE/TECHNOLOGY/MEDICINE

Astronomer Caroline Herschel was elected to membership in the Royal Irish Academy.

b. Alice Cunningham Fletcher (1838–1923), American ethnologist and archaeologist.

b. Margaret (Mattie) E. Knight (1838–1914), American inventor.

### ARTS/LITERATURE

Elizabeth Barrett Browning published *The Seraphim and Other Poems*.

Helen Faucit created the role of Pauline opposite William Macready in Edward Bulwer Lytton's play *The Lady of Lyons*.

Caroline Norton published the novel *The Wife and Woman's Reward*.

Charlotte Guest translated *The Mabinogion*, a collection of medieval Welsh stories (1838–1849).

Frances Trollope published the novel *Widow Barnaby*.

## 1839

### POLITICS/LAW/WAR

Mississippi became the first state to recognize the right of women to hold property in their own names, though permission from their husbands was required. Several other states followed suit, women ultimately winning their rights to full and free ownership and transfer of property.

Women gained the right to vote at the annual convention of the American Anti-Slavery Society, providing additional strength for the radical abolitionist faction led by William Lloyd Garrison.

Maria Chapman was an editor of *The Liberator* and *Non-Resistant* (1839–1842), while an activist of the Massachusetts Anti-Slavery Society and the Non-Resistance Society.

b. Marianne Hainisch (1839–1936), Austrian women's rights movement leader and pacifist.

b. Paule (Paulina) Mekarska Mink (1839–1900), French writer, editor, socialist, and women's rights movement leader.

### RELIGION/EDUCATION/EVERYDAY LIFE

Elizabeth Palmer Peabody's Boston bookshop (1835–1845) became unofficial headquarters of the Transcendentalist Club; she was also a publisher, notably of the influential journal *The Dial* (1842–1843).

b. Frances E. Willard (1839–1898), American reformer, educator, and temperance advocate.

b. Kalliopi Kehajia (1839–1905), Greek educator.

d. Hester Lucy Stanhope (1776–1839), British traveler who traveled abroad for the last three decades of her life, notably in the Arab world.

### SCIENCE/TECHNOLOGY/MEDICINE

b. Mary Anna Palmer Draper (1839–1914), American benefactor of astronomy.

### ARTS/LITERATURE

Fredrika Bremer published the novel *Hemmet* (*The Home*).

Margaret Oliphant published the novel *Mrs. Maitland of Sunnyside* (ca. 1839).

b. Marie Louise de la Ramée (Ouida) (1839–1908), British writer.

## 1840

### POLITICS/LAW/WAR

Elizabeth Cady Stanton and Lucretia Coffin Mott were refused seating at the World Anti-Slavery Convention in London, beginning the train of events that would result in the landmark 1848 Seneca Falls Women's Rights Convention. As Stanton later described it: "As Mrs. Mott and I walked home, arm in arm, commenting on the incidents of the day, we resolved to hold a convention as soon as we returned home and form a society to advocate the rights of women." The "woman question" was resolved quite differently in the United States: At the annual convention of the American Anti-Slavery Society (AASS), an anti-woman group ultimately seceded in protest after pro-woman radical abolitionists elevated Abby Kelley to a leading position.

Ernestine Rose drafted a key petition for a married women's property law, presented to the New York State Legislature.

Lydia Maria Child and her husband, David Child, coedited the *Anti-Slavery Standard* (1840–1844).

Memoirs of Russian princess Ekaterina Romanovna Dashkova were posthumously published.

b. Amie (Amelia Jane) Hicks (1840–1917), British feminist, socialist, and trade unionist.

b. Matilde Bajer (1840–1934), Danish feminist and suffragist.

### RELIGION/EDUCATION/EVERYDAY LIFE

*Lowell Offering* began publication (1840–1845), edited by A. C. Thomas; it carried a variety of fiction and nonfiction written by women working in the Lowell, Massachusetts, textile mills.

Margaret Fuller became editor of *The Dial* (1840–1842).

Jane Franklin founded and endowed Tasmania's Christ's College.

Flora Tristan published *Promenades des Londres*, analyzing Chartism and British working life.

b. Emily (Emilia Francis Strong) Dilke (1840–1904), British feminist, social reformer, art critic, and writer.

b. Flora Adams Darling (1840–1910), American women's club leader.

### SCIENCE/TECHNOLOGY/MEDICINE

Elizabeth Gurney Fry inspired the founding of the Society of Protestant Sisters of Charity (Nursing Sisters), a secular nursing order in England.

b. Sophia Jex-Blake (1840–1912), British physician.

b. Ellen Mary Clerke (1840–1906), Irish writer on astronomy.

### ARTS/LITERATURE

b. Helena Modjeska (1840–1909), Polish actress.

b. Frances Raymond Ritter (1840–1890), American musician, writer, and teacher.

d. Fanny Burney (Madame d'Arblay, 1752–1840), British author best known today for her diaries.

d. Giuditta Grisi (1805–1840), Italian mezzo-soprano, sister of Giulia Grisi.

## 1841

### POLITICS/LAW/WAR

b. Minna (Wilhelmine) Cauer (1841–1922), German radical feminist, suffragist, and pacifist.

b. Sarah (Emma Evelyn) Edwards (Franklin Thompson) (1841–1898), American soldier.

### RELIGION/EDUCATION/EVERYDAY LIFE

Catharine Beecher published *A Treatise on Domestic Economy for the Use of Young Ladies at Home and at School*, her popular book on the "household arts," advising on how to set up and manage a household using scientific understanding and labor-saving technologies; the book helped establish "domestic science" as a proper course of study in girls' schools and enshrined the home as "woman's place."

Caroline Chisholm founded the Female Immigrants' Home in Sydney, Australia, to offer shelter to destitute immigrant women; she also founded for them the first free labor registry, later opened to all unemployed people, with agencies around Australia.

### SCIENCE/TECHNOLOGY/MEDICINE

Orra White Hitchcock illustrated publications of her husband, Edward Hitchcock, state geologist of Massachusetts (from at least 1841); many other women were employed the same way from the 1830s on.

Jane Webb Loudon published *The Ladies' Companion to the Flower Garden*.

Elizabeth Adams patented a corset for pregnant women.

d. Marie Anne Victoire Gillain Boivin (1773–1841), French midwife who became a hospital director, wrote a standard gynecology and obstetrics text, and invented two key devices: the pelvimeter, to measure the pelvis, and the vaginal speculum, to widen the vagina for examination. Unable to obtain a medical degree in France on account of her sex, Boivin was awarded an honorary M.D. by the University of Marburg.

### Arts/Literature

Carlotta Grisi created the role of Giselle opposite Lucien Petipa as Albrecht in Jean Coralli-Jules Perrot's ballet *Giselle*.

Harriet Martineau published *The Playfellow*, a collection of children's stories, and *The Hour and the Man*, a study of Toussaint l'Ouverture.

Rosa Bonheur began to exhibit annually at the Paris Salon.

Annette von Droste-Hülshoff published the novella *Die Judenbuche*.

b. Berthe Morisot (1841–1895), French painter.

b. Eliza Pawlowska Orzeszkowa (1841–1910), Polish novelist.

## 1842

### Politics/Law/War

American customs law banned the importation of indecent and obscene artworks, but exempted printed matter.

b. Helen Blackburn (1842–1903), Irish-English feminist, suffragist, social reformer, writer, and editor.

### Religion/Education/Everyday Life

Augusta Female Seminary (later Mary Baldwin Seminary, then College) was founded by Presbyterians in Staunton, Virginia, becoming one of the best-known early-19th-century girls' schools.

Daughters of Temperance was founded (ca. 1842), originally as an auxiliary to the Sons of Temperance, a New York fraternal temperance organization.

Harriet Farley became the second editor of the *Lowell Offering* (1842–1845).

Cristina Trivulzio published her four-volume *Essai sur la formation du dogme Catholique* (1842–1846).

Emma Hale Smith, who had long served as scribe to her husband, Mormon prophet Joseph Smith, headed the Mormons' Female Relief Society.

Grace Aguilar published *The Spirit of Judaism*.

b. Josephine St. Pierre Ruffin (1842–1924), African-American lecturer, journalist, philanthropist, and social activist.

b. Aikaterini Laskaridou (1842–1916), Greek educator, philanthropist, and writer.

d. Grace Horsley Darling (1815–1842), British hero famed for helping her father rescue survivors from a shipwreck (1838).

### Science/Technology/Medicine

b. Ellen Swallow Richards (1842–1911), American chemist, ecologist, and home economist.

b. Mary Corinna Putnam Jacobi (1842–1906), American physician.

b. Agnes (Mary) Clerke (1842–1907), Irish writer on astronomy.

d. Maria Dalle Donne (1778–1842), Italian physician who won a degree from the University of Bologna (1799), where she became director of midwives.

### Arts/Literature

George Sand published the novel *Consuelo*.

Louise Colet published *Poésies*.

b. Kate Josephine Bateman (1842–1917), American actress.

d. Marie-Louise Elisabeth Vigée-Lebrun (1755–1842), French painter, a portraitist whose subjects included Marie Antoinette, Madame de Staël, and Lord Byron.

## 1843

### Politics/Law/War

Flora Tristan published *Union ouvrière*, proposing the formation of a Socialist International, a single international union for all workers, and also the foundation of cooperative educational and welfare centers.

### RELIGION/EDUCATION/EVERYDAY LIFE

Margaret Fuller published the essay "The Great Lawsuit: Man versus Men, Woman versus Women," in *The Dial*, calling for equality.

Former slave Isabella Van Wagener changed her name to Sojourner Truth, and became a traveling evangelical preacher.

Jane Franklin started the Tasmanian Society for the Reformation of Female Prisoners, influenced by Elizabeth Fry.

Lydia Maria Child published *Letters from New York*.

Cristina Trivulzio founded the *Gazetta Italiana*.

b. Bertha Felicie Sophie Kinsky von Suttner (1843–1914), Austrian novelist and pacifist.

b. Josephine Shaw Lowell (1843–1905), American social reformer.

b. Susan Elizabeth Blow (1843–1916), American educator.

d. Marie (Anne Adelaide) Lenormand (1882–1843), French fortune-teller, "the Sybil of the Faubourg Saint-Germain," whose predictions were widely sought throughout the French Revolution and into the Napoleonic era, with clients ranging from Robespierre to Josephine Bonaparte.

d. Mary Hays (1760–1843), British writer and feminist.

### SCIENCE/TECHNOLOGY/MEDICINE

Ada Byron, countess of Lovelace, published *Sketch of the Analytical Engine*, an English translation of a work by Italian mathematician Luigi Menabrea on Charles Babbage's analytical engine, forerunner of the computer; with her numerous "annotations," some based on consultations with Babbage himself, she actually tripled the size of the original work. She was the first to formulate the computer law now known as GIGO (garbage in, garbage out), writing "The Analytical Engine has no pretensions whatever to originate anything. It can do whatever we know how to order it to perform. It can follow analysis; but it has no power to anticipate any analytical relationships or truths."

Harriot Hunt organized a Ladies' Physiological Society in Boston, giving talks on physiology and hygiene.

Nancy M. Johnson obtained a U.S. patent for a hand-cranked ice-cream freezer.

b. Gertrude Jekyll (1843–1932), British horticulturalist.

### ARTS/LITERATURE

Elizabeth Barrett Browning published the poem "The Cry of the Children."

Carlotta Grisi created the title role opposite Lucien Petipa in Jean Coralli's ballet *La Péri*.

Wilhelmine Schröder-Devrient created the role of Senta in Richard Wagner's opera *The Flying Dutchman*.

Helen Faucit starred in Robert Browning's play *A Blot in the 'Scutcheon*.

German women's rights leader Luise Otto (later Otto-Peters), writing as Otto Stern, published the novel *Ludwig der Kellner*.

b. Adelina Patti (1843–1919), Italian soprano.

Edmonia Lewis (active 1843–after 1911), American sculptor.

## 1844

### POLITICS/LAW/WAR

Maria Chapman became an editor of the *National Anti-Slavery Standard*.

b. Charlotte French Despard (1844–1939), British social reformer, suffragist, socialist, and activist in the Irish Republican cause.

b. Eugénie Potonie-Pierre (1844–1898), French feminist and socialist.

b. Sarah Winnemucca (Hopkins) (Thoc-me-tony; Shell-flower, 1844–1891), Paiute Indian rights advocate, author, and interpreter.

### RELIGION/EDUCATION/EVERYDAY LIFE

Dorothea Dix made a tour of mental asylums, prisons, and poorhouses, making a report to the Massachusetts legislature, as part of her lifelong campaign for reform of such institutions.

Eliza Farnham became matron of the women's prison at Sing Sing, and introduced a series of prison reforms during her tenure.

b. Bernadette of Lourdes (Marie Bernarde Soubirous, 1844–1879), French Catholic saint.

b. Edmonia Highgate (1844–1870), African-American teacher and lecturer.

d. Flora (Célestine Thérèse) Tristan (1803–1844), French writer and socialist whose battles over custody and child support, described in her *Peregrinations d'une paria* (1838), brought such topics into public discussion; she was grandmother of Paul Gauguin.

### SCIENCE/TECHNOLOGY/MEDICINE

b. Mary Katharine Layne Brandegee (1844–1920), American botanist.

### ARTS/LITERATURE

Elizabeth Barrett Browning published *Poems*, including "Lady Geraldine's Courtship."

Charlotte Barnes produced *The Forest Princess*, a play about Pocahontas.

Fanny Kemble published *Poems*.

Luise Otto (-Peters), writing as Otto Stern, published the novel *Kathinka*.

b. Sarah Bernhardt (1844–1923), French actress.

b. Elizabeth Stuart Phelps (1844–1910), American novelist and social reformer.

## 1845

### RELIGION/EDUCATION/EVERYDAY LIFE

Margaret Fuller published her major work, *Woman in the Nineteenth Century*, an expansion of her 1843 essay "The Great Lawsuit: Man versus Men, Woman versus Women." Her call for complete equality became one of the central works of the emerging women's movement. She also joined Horace Greeley's *New York Herald Tribune* (1845–1846) as a literary critic and then foreign correspondent.

Sarah G. Bagley founded and became first president of the Lowell Female Labor Reform Association, becoming the first notable female trade unionist in America, and soon leaving her job at the textile mill to become a full-time organizer.

Caroline Chisholm and her husband, Archibald Chisholm, returned to London, where they effectively ran an information service about Australia and worked for "family colonization," shipping the families of emancipated convicts out to Australia.

Anne Ayres founded the Sisters of the Holy Communion, an Episcopal nursing order, based in New York City.

Elizabeth Acton published *Modern Cookery*, a standard work for decades.

Women began to be employed as matrons in New York City prisons, in part at the urging of the American Female Reform Society.

Grace Aguilar published *The Jewish Faith*.

Elizabeth Palmer Peabody published *Chronological History of the United States*.

b. Ella Flagg Young (1845–1918), American educator.

d. Elizabeth Gurney Fry (1780–1845), British Quaker minister and social reformer, who also worked to improve the living conditions of the poor, focusing on prisons and hospitals.

### SCIENCE/TECHNOLOGY/MEDICINE

Vesico-vaginal fistula, a tear between the vagina and the bladder, was first surgically repaired by physician James Marion Sims of Montgomery, Alabama. Until then, women who had this problem, as after difficult childbirth, were subject to uncontrollable seepage of urine and largely had to withdraw from society.

Sarah Mather obtained a U.S. patent for a submarine telescope improved with a later patent (1864).

b. (Mary) Edith Pechey-Phipson (1845–1908), British physician.

b. Mary Ann Bird Scharlieb (1845–1930), British physician.

### ARTS/LITERATURE

Marie Taglioni, Carlotta Grisi, Lucile Grahn, and Fanny Cerito danced Jules Perrot's ballet *Pas de Quatre.*

Johanna Wagner created the role of Elisabeth in Richard Wagner's opera *Tannhäuser.*

Lucile Grahn created the title role in Jules Perrot's ballet *Eoline.*

Harriet Martindale published *Letters on Mesmerism* and *Forest and Game-Law Tales,* a third series of illustrative stories (1845–1846).

Erminia Frezzolini-Poggi created the title role in Giuseppe Verdi's opera *Joan of Arc.*

Fanny Cerrito danced the title role in Arthur Saint-Léon's ballet *La fille de marbre.*

Frances Harper published the poetry collection *Forest Leaves.*

George Sand published the novel *Le Meunier d'Angibault.*

Anna Cora Mowatt's comedy *Fashion; or, Life in New York,* was seen in Manhattan.

b. Mary Cassatt (1845–1926), American painter.

## 1846

### RELIGION/EDUCATION/EVERYDAY LIFE

American Missionary Association was founded, combining Protestant evangelicalism with abolitionism; missionaries, many of them New England women and (from the 1850s) many with medical training, were assigned to found schools and churches. Some were sent abroad, as single women or married to male missionaries, though many would work in the South after the Civil War.

Women at the Lowell mills again struck over a combination of wage cut and increased workload. Under the short-lived Lowell Female Labor Reform Association (LFLRA; 1845–1847), led by Sarah Bagley, the workers forced the mills to back down on increasing their workload. From this period on, the "mill girls" were gradually replaced by Irish immigrants willing to work for less pay, as the Lowell "experiment" come to an end.

Catharine Beecher published *Address on the Evils Suffered by American Women and American Children.*

Sarah Bagley was the first female telegrapher in America, becoming superintendent of the Lowell Telegraph Office.

b. Carry Amelia Moore Nation (1846–1911), American temperance activist.

b. Mary Seymour Foot (1846–1893), American publisher and entrepreneur.

### SCIENCE/TECHNOLOGY/MEDICINE

Caroline Herschel was awarded the King of Prussia's Gold Medal for science; she had returned to Hanover from England, after the death of her brother William (1822).

### ARTS/LITERATURE

George Sand published the novel *La Mare au diable.*

Daniel Stern (Marie d'Agoult) published the autobiographical novel *Nélida,* about her life with composer Franz Liszt.

Women became fully accepted students at New York's National Academy of Design.

Carlotta Grisi created the title role in Joseph Mazilier's ballet *Paquita.*

Lucile Grahn originated the title role in Jules Perrot's ballet *Catarina, ou La Fille du bandit.*

Sophie Loewe starred in the role of Odabella in Giuseppe Verdi's opera *Attila.*

Louise Colet published the poetry collection *Chant des armes.*

## 1847

### POLITICS/LAW/WAR

Daniel Stern (Marie d'Agoult) published the pro-Republican *Essai sur la liberté*.

b. Millicent Garrett Fawcett (1847–1929), British suffragist, politician, and writer.

b. Rose Scott (1847–1925), Australian feminist, suffragist, and pacifist.

### RELIGION/EDUCATION/EVERYDAY LIFE

Lowell Female Industrial Reform and Mutual Aid Society was founded, one of the first permanent American women's labor organizations, sparked by the earlier Lowell Female Labor Reform Association (LFLRA; 1845–1847). It took over the New England Workingman's Association's *Voice of Industry*, edited by LFLRA founder Sarah Bagley, pressing for the 10-hour day.

Rockford Female Seminary (later College) was founded in Rockford, Illinois, by a consortium of Congregational and Presbyterian churches. Modeled on Eastern women's colleges by its first principal, Anna Sill, it was called the "Mount Holyoke of the West."

b. Annie Wood Besant (1847–1933), British suffragist, socialist, and theosophist, latterly in India.

b. Anna Howard Shaw (1847–1919), British-born American minister and suffragist.

b. Sarah Jane Farmer (1847–1916), religious leader.

### SCIENCE/TECHNOLOGY/MEDICINE

The first known "painless childbirth" took place. Many religious leaders argued that using anesthetics was contrary to the Bible's statement that women should bring forth children in pain, but the practice would become popular after England's Queen Victoria used chloroform in giving birth to Prince Leopold (1853).

Maria Mitchell discovered a new comet, for which she was awarded a gold medal from the King of Denmark.

D. W. Godding published the children's textbook *First Lessons in Geology*.

Hannah Flagg Gould published the poem "The Mastodon."

b. Christine Ladd-Franklin (1847–1930), American psychologist and mathematician.

b. Vilma Hugonnai-Wartha (1847–1922), Hungarian physician.

b. Sarah Frances Whiting (1847–1927), American physicist and astronomer.

b. Mary Watson Whitney (1847–1921), American astronomer.

d. Mary Anning (1799–1847), British paleontologist who was inspired by her hobbyist father to collect fossils, making several important finds, starting in childhood.

### ARTS/LITERATURE

The Brontë sisters made their extraordinary literary debuts, all originally under male pseudonyms: Emily (as Ellis Bell) created Heathcliff and Cathy in *Wuthering Heights*; Charlotte (as Currer Bell) created Rochester and the governess of the title in *Jane Eyre*; and Anne (as Acton Bell) created another governess, *Agnes Grey*.

Anna Zerr created the title role in Friedrich von Flotow's opera *Martha*.

Clara Schumann composed her *Piano Trio*.

b. Ellen Alice Terry (1847–1928), British actress.

b. Charlotte "Lotta" Crabtree (1847–1924), American actress.

b. Alice Meynell (1847–1922), British writer.

b. Bertha Amalie Alver Skram (1847–1905), Norwegian novelist.

b. Mary Catherwood (1847–1902), American author.

b. Mary Hallock Foote (1847–1938), American writer and illustrator.

b. Vinnie Ream (Hoxie) (1847–1914), American sculptor.

d. Grace Aguilar (1816–1847), British essayist, novelist, and poet, best known for her romantic novels; her essays focused on Jewish themes.

<u>1848</u>

### POLITICS/LAW/WAR

Elizabeth Cady Stanton, Lucretia Mott, Martha C. Wright, Jane Hunt, and Mary Ann McClintock organized the landmark women's rights convention at Seneca Falls, New York (July 19–20), where the worldwide women's rights movement was born. Of the 100 to 300 attendees, 68 women and 32 men, including Frederick Douglass and Henry Stanton, signed the Declaration of Sentiments, a centrally important document in the history of women and the worldwide fight for women's rights. It was written by Elizabeth Cady Stanton, who also wrote the resolutions passed by that body (that on women's suffrage narrowly, the rest unanimously).

French feminist Jeanne Deroin published *Cours de droit social pour les femmes*.

b. Helene Lange (1848–1930), German educator and women's rights activist.

b. Hubertine (Marie-Anne) Auclert (1848–1924), French writer and editor, a socialist and feminist.

b. Kate Malcolm Sheppard (1848–1934), New Zealand feminist and suffragist leader.

b. Louisa Lawson (1848–1902), Australian feminist, editor, and suffragist.

b. Trinidad Tescon (1848–1928), Philippine soldier and nurse.

d. Manto Mavrogenous (?–1848), Greek War of Independence leader, a guerrilla leader who also mobilized Western support for the Greek freedom movement.

---

## *Declaration of Sentiments*

When, in the course of human events, it becomes necessary for one portion of the family of man to assume among the people of the earth a position different from that which they have hitherto occupied, but one to which the laws of nature and of nature's God entitle them, a decent respect to the opinions of mankind requires that they should declare the causes that impel them to such a course.

We hold these truths to be self-evident: that all men and women are created equal; that they are endowed by their Creator with certain inalienable rights; that among these are life, liberty, and the pursuit of happiness; that to secure these rights governments are instituted, deriving their just powers from the consent of the governed.—Whenever any form of Government becomes destructive of these ends, it is the right of those who suffer from it to refuse allegiance to it, and to insist upon the institution of a new government, laying its foundations on such principles, and organizing its powers in such form as to them shall seem most likely to effect their safety and happiness. Prudence, indeed, will dictate that governments long established should not be changed for light and transient causes; and accordingly, all experience hath shown that mankind are most disposed to suffer, while evils are sufferable, than to right themselves by abolishing the forms to which they are accustomed. But when a long train of abuses and usurpations, pursuing invariably the same object, evinces a design to reduce them under absolute despotism, it is their duty to throw off such government, and to provide new guards for their future security. Such has been the patient sufferance of the women under this government, and such is now the necessity which constrains them to demand the equal station to which they are entitled.

The history of mankind is a history of repeated injuries and usurpations on the part of men toward woman, having in direct object the establishment of an absolute tyranny over her. To prove this, let facts be submitted to a candid world.

He has never permitted her to exercise her inalienable right to the elective franchise.

He has compelled her to submit to laws, in the formation of which she had not voice.

He has withheld from her rights which are given to the most ignorant and degraded men—both natives and foreigners.

*continued next page*

---

*Declaration of Sentiments (cont.)*

Having deprived her of this first right of a citizen, the elective franchise, thereby leaving her without representation in the halls of legislation, he has oppressed her on all sides.

He has made her, if married, in the eye of the law, civilly dead.

He has taken from her all right in property, even to the wages she earns.

He has made her, morally, an irresponsible being, as she can commit many crimes with impunity, provided they be done in the presence of her husband. In the covenant of marriage, she is compelled to promise obedience to her husband, he becoming, to all intents and purposes, her master—the law giving him power to deprive her of her liberty, and to administer chastisement.

He has so framed the laws of divorce, as to what shall be the proper causes of divorce; in case of separation, to whom the guardianship of the children shall be given; as to be wholly regardless of the happiness of women—the law, in all cases, going upon the false supposition of the supremacy of man, and giving all power into his hands.

After depriving her of all rights as a married woman, if single and the owner of property, he has taxed her to support a government which recognizes her only when her property can be made profitable to it.

He has monopolized nearly all the profitable employments, and from those she is permitted to follow, she receives but a scanty remuneration.

He closes against her all avenues to wealth and distinction, which considers most honorable to himself. As a teacher of theology, medicine, or law, she is not known.

He has denied her the facilities for obtaining a thorough education—all colleges being closed against her.

He allows her in Church as well as State, but a subordinate position, claiming Apostolic authority for her exclusion from the ministry, and, with some exceptions, from any public participation in the affairs of the Church.

He has created a false public sentiment, by giving to the world a different code of morals for men and women, by which moral delinquencies which exclude women from society, are not only tolerated but deemed of little account in man.

He has usurped the prerogative of Jehovah himself, claiming it as his right to assign for her a sphere of action, when that belongs to her conscience and her God.

He has endeavored, in every way that he could, to destroy her confidence in her own powers, to lessen her self-respect, and to make her willing to lead a dependant and abject life.

Now, in view of this entire disfranchisement of one-half the people of this country, their social and religious degradation, in view of the unjust laws above mentioned, and because women do feel themselves aggrieved, oppressed, and fraudulently deprived of their most sacred rights, we insist that they have immediate admission to all the rights and privileges which belong to them as citizens of these United States.

In entering upon the great work before us, we anticipate no small amount of misconception, misrepresentation, and ridicule; but we shall use every instrumentality within our power to effect our object. We shall employ agents, circulate tracts, petition the state and national Legislatures, and endeavor to enlist the pulpit and the press on our behalf. We hope this Convention will be followed by a series of Conventions, embracing every part of the country.

Firmly relying upon the final triumph of the Right and the True, we do this day affix our signatures to this declaration.

— Elizabeth Cady Stanton, signed by 100 people—68 women and 32 men—at the Seneca Falls Women's Rights Convention (1848)

# Resolutions of the Seneca Falls Women's Rights Convention

Whereas, the great precept of nature is conceded to be, "that man shall pursue his own true and substantial happiness." Blackstone, in his Commentaries, remarks, that this law of Nature being coeval with mankind and dictated by God himself, is of course superior in obligation to any other. It is binding over all the globe, in all countries, and at all times; no human laws are of any validity if contrary to this, and such of them as are valid, derive all their force, and all their validity, and all their authority, mediately and immediately, from this origin; Therefore,

Resolved, That such laws as conflict, in any way, with the true and substantial happiness of woman, are contrary to the great precept of nature, and of no validity; for this is "superior in obligation to any other."

Resolved, That all laws which prevent women from occupying such a station in society as her conscience shall dictate, or which place her in a position inferior to that of man, are contrary to the great precept of nature, and therefore of no force or authority.

Resolved, That woman is man's equal—was intended to be so by the Creator, and the highest good of the race demands that she should be recognized as such.

Resolved, That the women of this country ought to be enlightened in regard to the laws under which they live, that they may no longer publish their degradation, be declaring themselves satisfied with their present position, nor their ignorance, by asserting that they have all the rights they want.

Resolved, That inasmuch as man, while claiming for himself intellectual superiority, does accord to woman moral superiority, it is pre-eminently his duty to encourage her to speak, and teach, as she has an opportunity, in all religious assemblies.

Resolved, That the same amount of virtue, delicacy, and refinement of behavior, that is required of woman in the social state, should also be required of man, and the same transgressions should be visited with equal severity on both man and woman.

Resolved, That the objection of indelicacy and impropriety, which is so often brought against a woman when she addresses a public audience, comes with a very ill grace from those who encourage, by their stance, her appearance on the stage, in the concert, or in the feats of the circus.

Resolved, That it is the duty of the women of this country to secure to themselves their sacred right to the elective franchise.

Resolved, That the equality of human rights results necessarily from the fact of the identity of the race in capabilities and responsibilities.

Resolved, there, That, being invested by the Creator with the same capabilities, and the same consciousness of responsibility for their exercise, it is demonstrably the right and duty of woman, equally with man, to promote every righteous case, by every righteous means; and especially in regard to the great subjects of morals and religion, it is self-evidently her right to participate with her brother in teaching them, both in private and in public, by writing and by speaking, by any instrumentalities proper to be used, and in any assemblies proper to be held; and this being a self-evident truth, growing out of the divinely implanted principles of human nature, any custom or authority adverse to it, whether modern or wearing the hoary sanction of antiquity, is to be regarded as self-evident falsehood, and at war with the interests of mankind.

Resolved, That the speedy success of our cause depends upon the zealous and untiring efforts of both men and women, for the overthrow of the monopoly of the pulpit, and for the securing to woman an equal participation with men in the various trades, professions, and commerce.

— Elizabeth Cady Stanton; resolutions passed at the 1848 Seneca Falls Women's Rights Convention

Oneida Community (1848–1881) was established by John Humphrey Noyes near Syracuse, New York; the first of the utopian communities to grant women full equality, it also rejected the notions of original sin and sexual shame.

### RELIGION/EDUCATION/EVERYDAY LIFE

Sarah Worthington Peter founded the Philadelphia School of Design to train women in commercial art skills; it later merged with the Moore College of Art and Design.

Working Women's Protective Union was founded in Rochester, New York, by middle- and upper-class reformers seeking to help working women; it was one of many such local unions founded around the country.

Elizabeth Lummis Ellet published her three-volume *The Women of the American Revolution* (1848–1850).

b. Belle Starr (1848–1889), American outlaw.

b. Emma (Anne) Smith Paterson (1848–1886), British trade unionist.

b. May French Sheldon (1848–1936), American traveler and writer.

### SCIENCE/TECHNOLOGY/MEDICINE

Margaret (Mattie) Knight, only ten years old, invented a stop-motion device for use in textile mills to keep shuttles from sliding out of the looms and injuring workers; it became widely used, though she never patented it.

Astronomer Maria Mitchell became the first woman to be elected a member of the American Academy of Arts and Sciences.

Emma Martin, who had become a midwife in London, published *The Most Common Female Complaints*; in the 1840s she also wrote essays and a novel, *The Exiles of Piedmont*, and published translations.

Lydia Fowler published *Familiar Lessons on Physiology, Designed for the Use of Children and Youth in Schools and Families*. These and other works made significant contributions to health and general science education among women.

Britain's Anglican Church established the Sisters of St. John's House nursing order.

Mary Somerville published *Physical Geography*, her most popular book.

b. Margaret Lindsay Murray Huggins (1848–1915), Irish astronomer.

d. Caroline Lucretia Herschel (1750–1848), German astronomer working largely in England, often assisting her brother, William, discoverer of the planet Uranus; on her own, she discovered three new nebulae (1783) and eight comets (1786–1797) and also published two key astronomical catalogues.

### ARTS/LITERATURE

George Sand published the novel *La Petite Fadette*.

Louisa May Alcott published *Flower Fables*.

b. Lilli Lehmann (1848–1929), German soprano.

d. Emily Brontë (1818–1848), British novelist and poet who created *Wuthering Heights*; sister of Charlotte and Anne Brontë.

d. Annette von Droste-Hülshoff (1797–1848), German writer, best known as a poet who focused on religious themes.

## 1849

### POLITICS/LAW/WAR

Jeanne Deroin became the first woman to declare her candidacy for France's National Assembly.

b. Vera Zasulich (1849–1919), Russian revolutionary.

d. Dorothea (Dolley) Payne Todd Madison (1768–1849), American political figure, the wife of President James Madison, who during the Jefferson and Madison administrations (1801–1817) became America's most notable political hostess, much influencing the nation's business.

### RELIGION/EDUCATION/EVERYDAY LIFE

Amelia Bloomer began publishing her temperance and increasingly feminist periodical, *The Lily* (1849–1855), moving it to Ohio (1853), and employing female typesetters despite a strike by males on the staff.

Women in the Oneida Community, in upstate New York, were among the first to adopt a new style of "reform dress"; instead of constricting corsets and layers of skirts, they wore a knee-length dress with a pair of loose trousers underneath, modeled on Muslim women's dress.

Caroline Chisholm and her husband, Archibald Chisholm, founded the Family Colonization Loan Society, providing loans of passage money to emigrants traveling to join family members, often freed convicts, in Australia; British philanthropist Angela Burdett-Coutts was a key figure in funding the project and guaranteeing it against losses.

Portuguese writer Antónia Gertrudes Pusich published *A Assembléia Literária*, one of the earliest magazines on women's issues.

b. Ellen Key (1849–1926), Swedish social feminist.

b. Harriet Hubbard Ayer (1849–1903), cosmetics entrepreneur.

d. Madame de Récamier (Jeanne-Françoise-Julie-Adelaide Bernard, 1777–1849), convent-educated French salon hostess who headed a notable political and literary salon, exiled from Paris under Napoléon (1805–1815); subject of a notable portrait by Jacques-Louis David (1800).

### SCIENCE/TECHNOLOGY/MEDICINE

Elizabeth Blackwell earned a medical degree from Geneva Medical College (later Hobart and William Smith Colleges), in Geneva, New York, becoming the first woman to graduate from an American medical school, writing a thesis on hygiene and typhus, then doing postgraduate study in Europe. The *Boston Medical & Surgical Journal* lamented: "It is to be regretted that she [Blackwell] has been induced to depart from the appropriate sphere of her sex and led to aspire to honors and duties which, by the order of nature and the common consent of the world, devolve alone upon men."

The Kaiserswerth tradition of nurses' training was established in Pittsburgh by four deaconesses (secular nurses) and Theodor Fliedner, who (with his late wife) had founded the original Kaiserswerth. The first American deaconess was Louisa Marthens.

Maria Mitchell began a 19-year job at the *American Ephemeris and Nautical Almanac*, calculating astronomical positions; she also began to work for the U.S. Coast Survey, making measurements for precise determination of time, latitude, and longitude.

Harriot Hunt's talks on physiology and hygiene (1843) developed into a series of public lectures in Boston.

American inventor Mary Ann Woodward patented a fan that attached to a rocking chair (1849).

b. Cornelia Maria Clapp (1849–1934), American zoologist.

d. (Regina) Josepha Henning Siebold (1771–1849), German physician, originally a midwife working with her doctor-husband. The first woman to gain a medical degree in obstetrics from a German university (1815), she also originally trained her daughter, physician Charlotte Siebold.

### ARTS/LITERATURE

Charlotte Brontë published the novel *Shirley*.

Pauline Viardot created the role of Fidès in Giacomo Meyerbeer's opera *Le prophéte* (*The Prophet*).

b. Emma Lazarus (1849–1887), American poet.

b. Frances Hodgson Burnett (1849–1924), American author.

b. Sarah Orne Jewett (1849–1909), American writer.

b. Virginia Zucchi (1849–1930), Italian dancer and choreographer.

d. Angelica Catalani (1780–1849), Italian soprano, long resident in London.

d. Ekaterina Semenova (1786–1849), Russian actress, a leading tragedian, most notably in Shakespeare.

d. Maria Edgeworth (1767–1849), Irish novelist, translator, and women's rights advocate.

d. Marie-Thomase-Amélie Dorval (1798–1849), French actress.

# 1850

## POLITICS/LAW/WAR

The first National Woman's Rights Convention was held in Worcester, Massachusetts, chaired by Paulina Davis, and attended by campaigners such as Lucretia Mott, Lucy Stone, and Harriot Hunt; Antoinette Brown (later Blackwell) made a speech refuting the Bible-based argument that women should not speak in public. The convention passed a resolution stating: "Women are clearly entitled to the right of suffrage, and to…equality before the law, without distinction of sex or color."

b. Elizaveta Kovalskaya (1850–1933), Russian anarchist.

b. Ellen Spencer Mussey (1850–1936), American lawyer, women's rights advocate, and educator.

b. Mary Clyens Lease (1850–1933), American teacher, labor journalist, feminist, writer, and politician.

## RELIGION/EDUCATION/EVERYDAY LIFE

Jane Franklin set out on the first of five voyages (1850–1857) seeking her husband, John Franklin, who had set off on an Arctic expedition (1845). She finally learned that he had died discovering the Northwest Passage, but she continued her own explorations.

O Jornal das Senhoras (The Journal for Ladies) was published in Brazil (1850s).

Elizabeth Lummis Ellet published Domestic History of the American Revolution.

Irish courtesan Laura Bell became known as the "Queen of London Whoredom" (ca. 1850).

b. (Maria) Francesca (Xavier) Cabrini (Mother Cabrini, 1850–1917), Italian-born American nun and saint.

b. Aline Valette (1850–1899), French teacher, writer, and union activist.

b. Annie Smith Peck (1850–1935), American mountaineer.

b. Jane Ellen Harrison (1850–1928), British classical scholar.

d. Margaret Fuller (1810–1850), New England Transcendentalist writer, editor, and early feminist, whose book Woman in the Nineteenth Century (1845) was a central work of the emerging worldwide feminist movement. She and her husband, Giovanni d'Ossoli, were active democratic revolutionaries in Italy; fleeing to America with their child, they died when their ship sank off Fire Island, New York.

d. Elizabeth Veale Macarthur (1767–1850), Australian pioneer and wool merchant, a key figure in early Australian society (from 1789), who helped build the country's wool trade and its first massive estate, Elizabeth Farm.

## SCIENCE/TECHNOLOGY/MEDICINE

Female Medical College (later Woman's Medical College of Pennsylvania) was founded in Philadelphia, originally with an all-male faculty; not until 1876 were there enough trained women to form an all-female faculty. Of the five American medical schools founded specifically to educate women, this would be the only one to survive (as the coeducational Medical College of Pennsylvania); the others closed down as male-dominated schools opened to women.

Lydia Fowler became the second woman (after Elizabeth Blackwell) and the first American woman to receive an American medical degree, from the Rochester Eclectic Medical College, a branch of the Central Medical College in New York State. On graduating, she became "demonstrator of anatomy" and then professor of midwifery and women's and children's diseases at the college, the only American medical school at the time to admit women on a regular basis (it closed in 1852).

Maria Mitchell became the first woman to be elected a member of the newly founded American Association for the Advancement of Science.

b. Sonya (Sofya) Vasilyevna Korvin-Krukovsky Kovalevsky (1850–1891), Russian mathematician.

## ARTS/LITERATURE

Elizabeth Barrett Browning published Sonnets from the Portuguese, which included the poem beginning "How do I love thee? Let me count the ways."

Jenny Lind, "the Swedish Nightingale," made an extraordinarily successful tour of the United States; one of the songs with which she was identified was "Home, Sweet Home."

George Sand published the novel *François le Champi*.

Grace Aguilar published the novel *A Mother's Recompense*.

b. Elizabeth Thompson Butler (1850–1933), British painter and writer.

d. Marie Grasholtz Tussaud (1761–1850), Swiss artist and entrepreneur, who worked in wax and developed her Wax Museum.

## 1851

### POLITICS/LAW/WAR

Confronting men who tried to shout her down at the Akron Women's Rights Convention, Sojourner Truth responded with the speech "Ain't I a Woman?", which became a centerpiece of the emerging woman's movement.

Harriet Tubman, who had escaped from slavery herself (1849), traveled back into slave country to guide some members of her family north to freedom; it would be the first of 19 trips as a conductor on the Underground Railroad, directly rescuing more than 300 slaves and inspiring countless others; the reward offered for her capture would reach $40,000.

b. Elizabeth Dmitrieva (1851–1910), Russian socialist, active in Britain and France.

b. Ida A. Harper (1851–1931), American writer and suffragist.

### RELIGION/EDUCATION/EVERYDAY LIFE

Elizabeth Smith Miller, among the first American women to adopt for everyday use the "reform dress" of knee-length skirt and loose trousers, introduced the style to Elizabeth Cady Stanton, her cousin, and to Amelia Bloomer. When Bloomer recommended the costume in her journal, the *Lily*, and published a woodcut of herself wearing it, the reform dress was dubbed the "Bloomer costume." Many women's rights advocates adopted it, glorying in the freedom of the loose clothes, but largely abandoned the style within a few years as the dress controversy threatened to overshadow more substantive questions of suffrage and social equality.

"On the Enfranchisement of Women" was published anonymously in the *Westminster Review*; it is believed to have been written by Harriet Taylor.

Mary Carpenter published her influential essay "Reformatory Schools for the Children of the Perishing and Dangerous Classes and for Juvenile Offenders."

Daniel Stern (Marie d'Agoult) published *Histoire de la Révolution de 1848*.

b. Anna (Garlin) Spencer (1851–1931), American minister, writer, and reformer.

d. Emma Bullock Martin (1812–1851), British writer and midwife best known for her wide-ranging, freethinking lectures.

d. Eliza Hart Spalding (1807–1851), American missionary.

---

## Ain't I a Woman?

The man over there says women need to be helped into carriages and lifted over ditches, and to have the best place everywhere. Nobody ever helps me into carriages or over puddles, or gives me the best place—and ain't I a woman? Look at my arm! I have ploughed and planted and gathered into barns, and no man could head me—and ain't I a woman? I could work as much and eat as much as a man—when I could get it—and bear the lash as well! And ain't I a woman? I have born 13 children, and seen most of them sold into slavery, and when I cried out with my mother's grief, none but Jesus heard me—and ain't I a woman?

— Sojourner Truth, responding to male hecklers at the Akron Women's Rights Convention (1851)

### SCIENCE/TECHNOLOGY/MEDICINE

Marie Zakrzewska became director of the Royal Hospital Charité in Berlin, after two years as her predecessor's assistant, but was criticized as too young for the position and emigrated to America, obtaining her medical degree from Cleveland (Western Reserve) University in 1856.

Elizabeth Blackwell set up medical practice in New York, opening a small dispensary in a New York City tenement district.

b. Aletta Jacobs (1851–1929), Dutch physician, birth-control advocate, and women's rights campaigner.

b. Lillien Jane Martin (1851–1943), American psychologist.

### ARTS/LITERATURE

Elizabeth Barrett Browning published the poem *Casa Guidi Windows*.

Grace Aguilar published the novel *Woman's Friendship*.

Annette von Droste-Hülshoff published the poetry collection *Geistliche Jahre*.

b. Kate Chopin (Katherine O'Flaherty, 1851–1904), American writer.

b. Mary Augusta Ward (Mrs. Humphrey Ward, 1851–1920), British writer, social reformer, and antisuffragist.

b. Susan Hannah Macdowell Eakins (1851–1938), American painter, photographer, and pianist.

b. Emilia Pardo Bazán (1851–1921), Spanish writer and critic.

d. Mary Wollstonecraft Godwin Shelley (1797–1851), British novelist who created *Frankenstein* (1818); daughter of Mary Wollstonecraft and William Godwin and wife of Percy Bysshe Shelley.

d. Joanna Baillie (1762–1851), Scottish poet and playwright.

## 1852

### POLITICS/LAW/WAR

Maximum hours of employment for women were set by law in Ohio, the first state to do so.

b. Vera Nikolayevna Figner (1852–1942), Russian anarchist and terrorist.

### RELIGION/EDUCATION/EVERYDAY LIFE

Elizabeth Cady Stanton and Susan B. Anthony founded the Women's State Temperance Society, in New York, after several Daughters of Temperance representatives, including Anthony and Mary C. Vaughn, were barred from speaking at a Sons of Temperance convention. This event helped spur them toward developing the women's rights movement. Stanton, who served as WSTS president, made the controversial proposal that women should be able to obtain divorces to protect themselves against alcoholic husbands.

Barbara Leigh-Smith Bodichon founded Portland Hall, a trailblazing coeducational school.

American Women's Education Association was founded by Catharine Beecher to provide aid to women's colleges, seeking to encourage education and "appropriate" employment for women.

Women were first admitted to membership in the Good Templars, a temperance order in New York (founded 1851); among the earliest female members was Amelia Bloomer; many female Templars would come to hold state and national offices.

---

## On Dress Reform

Women are in bondage; their clothes are a great hindrance to their engaging in any business which will make them pecuniarily independent, and since the soul of womanhood never can be queenly and noble as long as it must beg bread for its body, is it not better, even at the expense of a vast deal of annoyance, that they whose lives deserve respect and are greater than their garments should give an example by which woman may more easily work out her emancipation? . . .

— Lucy Stone, in a letter to Susan B. Anthony

---

First American day-care center was believed to have been opened in New York, by a woman who needed to support her own family.

Mormons in Utah publicly stated that polygyny (multiple wives), which they called plural marriage, was part of their religious system.

Sarah Josepha Hale published *Woman's Record: or, Sketches of All Distinguished Women, from 'the Beginning' till A.D. 1850. Arranged in Four Eras with Selections from Female Writers of Every Age.*

British reformer Mary Carpenter founded a liberal boys' reformatory at Kingswood.

Harriet Martindale wrote a wide-ranging body of work for the *London Daily News* (1852–1866).

Elizabeth Lummis Ellet published *Pioneer Women of the West.*

b. Calamity Jane (Martha Jane Cannary Burke, 1852–1903), American frontierswoman.

d. Frances Wright (1795–1852), Scottish-American writer, editor, and social reformer who addressed a wide range of often controversial issues, including birth control, women's emancipation, slavery, communal living, state-supplied education, and "free unions" instead of marriage.

## SCIENCE/TECHNOLOGY/MEDICINE

d. (Augusta) Ada Byron, countess of Lovelace (1815–1852), British mathematician, daughter of Anne Isabella Milbanke and George Gordon, Lord Byron, noted for her work on the analytical engine, a forerunner of the computer. She designed the "punch-card" program used to give instructions to the machine and first formulated the "garbage in, garbage out" (GIGO) principle (1843). The U.S. Department of Defense named a computer programming language ADA after her (1977).

## ARTS/LITERATURE

Harriet Beecher Stowe created Uncle Tom, Simon Legree, Little Eva, and Eliza and her baby in the novel *Uncle Tom's Cabin*, first serialized in the magazine *National Era*, a major contribution to the antislavery movement.

Susanna Moodie published *Roughing It in the Bush; or, Forest Life in Canada.*

Louise Colet published the poetry collection *Ce qui est dans le coeur des femmes.*

Alice Cary published *Clovernook; Or Recollections of Our Neighborhood in the West.*

b. (Isabella) Augusta Persse Gregory (Lady Gregory, 1852–1932), Irish playwright.

b. Gertrude Stanton Käsebier (1852–1934), American photographer.

b. Maria Nikolaijevna Yermolova (1852–1928), Russian actress.

b. Emma B. Steiner (1852–1929), American composer and conductor.

b. Jesse Irene Sargent (1852–1932), American art historian and Arts and Crafts movement leader.

d. Mary Berry (1763–1852), British writer, a social historian, biographer, and playwright.

# 1853

## POLITICS/LAW/WAR

Caroline Norton published *English Laws for Women in the Nineteenth Century*, calling for passage of a Married Women's Property Bill.

b. Alva Erskine Belmont (1853–1933), American feminist, suffragist, and women's rights movement leader.

b. Clementina Black (1853–1922), English feminist, suffragist, writer, and trade unionist.

b. Sofya Lvovna Perovskaya (1853–1881), Russian anarchist and terrorist.

## RELIGION/EDUCATION/EVERYDAY LIFE

Antoinette Brown (later Blackwell) became the first woman ordained as a minister serving in America, as pastor of the Congregational Church in South Butler, New York. That year she was also an official delegate to the World's Temperance Convention in New York but was not allowed to speak.

After three husbands, two divorces, and several notable lovers, Jane Digby went to Syria to tour the archaeological sites of Palmyra, Damascus, and Baghdad. Her guide on these travels was Sheikh Abdul Medjuel El Mezrab, whom she married; adopting local dress, she remained with him for three decades, fighting beside him in local warfare.

Paulina Wright Davis founded the Boston-published feminist magazine *Una* (1853–1855).

Ann Pamela Cunningham, of South Carolina, founded the first nationwide American women's patriotic society, the Mount Vernon Ladies' Association of the Union.

### SCIENCE/TECHNOLOGY/MEDICINE

b. Clara Eaton Cummings (1853–1906), American botanist.

### ARTS/LITERATURE

Charlotte Brontë created Lucy Snowe in the semiautobiographical novel *Villette*.

Rosa Bonheur's painting *The Horse Fair* (1853–1855) won her an international audience.

Susanna Moodie published *Life in the Clearings versus the Bush*.

b. Lillie Le Breton Langtry (1853–1929), British actress.

b. Hedwig Reicher-Kindermann (1853–1883), German soprano.

## 1854

### POLITICS/LAW/WAR

Barbara Leigh-Smith Bodichon published her landmark work *A Brief Summary in Plain Language of the Most Important Laws Concerning Women*, calling for women's property rights, especially in marriage; it became a central document in the campaign for the Married Women's Property Bill (1857).

French feminist Jeanne Deroin published *Almanach des femmes*.

b. Anna Kulisciov (1854–1925), Italian socialist.

### RELIGION/EDUCATION/EVERYDAY LIFE

Cheltenham Ladies College was founded in England.

British reformer Mary Carpenter founded a liberal girls' reformatory, the Red Lodge, funded by Anne Isabella, Lady Noel Byron.

b. Anna Kulisciov (1854–1925), Italian socialist.

b. Susette La Flèsche Tibbles (1854–1903), American advocate of Native American rights.

d. Katy (Catherine) Ferguson (?–1854), African-American educator who ran a school for poor children in New York City; she was born a slave, but her freedom had been bought for $200 when she was 16. New York City's Katy Ferguson Home (founded in 1920) was named for her.

d. Rebecca Pennock Lukens (1794–1854), American industrial executive who ran the Brandywine Rolling Mill, later renamed the Lukens Mill in her honor.

### SCIENCE/TECHNOLOGY/MEDICINE

Reading of the appalling conditions among the wounded of the Crimean War, Florence Nightingale arranged to lead a party of nurses to the Crimea; within a few months, despite open hostility from the male doctors, she and her 38 nurses cut the death rate dramatically.

The "free nursing movement" began in Switzerland, where a nurses' school was founded for independent nurses not bound by contract or religion, as were most other nurses at the time. The

## Woman, Pariah

The revolutionary tempest, in overturning at the same time the throne and the scaffold, in breaking the chain of the black slave, forgot to break the chain of the most oppressed of all—of Woman, the pariah of humanity.

— Jeanne Deroin, in letter from a Paris prison (1851)

idea quickly spread.

Emily Blackwell, sister of Elizabeth Blackwell, received her medical degree from Cleveland (Western Reserve) University, then did postgraduate work in obstetrics in Europe; she had previously been accepted at Chicago's Rush Medical College (1852), but the Illinois Medical Society refused to accept female physicians.

b. Hertha (Phoebe Sarah) Marks Ayrton (1854–1923), British physicist.

b. Anna Botsford Comstock (1854–1930), American naturalist.

b. Anna Tomaszewicz-Dobrska (1854–1918), Polish physician.

### ARTS/LITERATURE

Harriet Martindale's *Autobiography* was published.

Fanny Cerrito created the title role in her own ballet *Gemma*.

Maria Susanna Cummins published the novel *The Lamplighter*.

Susanna Moodie published the novel *Flora Lyndsay*.

b. Clorinda Matto de Turner (1854–1909), Peruvian writer, editor, and social reformer.

b. Fanny Whiteside Brough (1854–1914), British actress.

d. Henriette Walpurgis Sontag (1806–1854), German soprano.

## 1855

### POLITICS/LAW/WAR

National Women's Rights Convention was held in Cincinnati, Ohio.

Caroline Norton published *A Letter to the Queen*, again calling for passage of the Married Women's Property Bill.

### RELIGION/EDUCATION/EVERYDAY LIFE

Lucy Stone and Henry Blackwell were married, making the then-rare agreement, confirmed in writing, that she would keep her own name.

Anne E. McDowell published the weekly *Woman's Advocate*, the first American newspaper produced entirely by women.

The Prayer Union and the General Female Training Institute formed the basis of the Young Women's Christian Association (YWCA) movement in England.

Antoinette Brown (later Blackwell) published *Shadows of our Social System*.

Frances Power Cobbe published *The Theory of Intuitive Morals*.

---

# On Women's Rights

The last speaker alluded to this movement as being that of a few disappointed women. From the first years to which my memory stretches, I have been a disappointed woman. When, with my brothers, I reached further after the sources of knowledge, I was reproved with "It isn't fit for you; it doesn't belong to women." . . . In education, in marriage, in religion, in everything disappointment is the lot of woman. It shall be the business of my life to deepen this disappointment in every woman's heart until she bows down to it no longer. . . .

We are told woman has all the rights she wants; and even women, I am ashamed to say, tell us so. They mistake the politeness of men for rights—seats while men stand in their hall tonight, and their adulations; but these are mere courtesies. We want rights. The flour-merchant, the house-builder, and the postman charge us no less on account of our sex; but when we endeavor to earn money to pay all these, then, indeed, we find the difference.

— Lucy Stone, in an extemporaneous speech before the Cincinnati, Ohio, Women's Rights Convention (1855)

Lydia Maria Child published *A Progress of Religious Ideas*.

b. Annie R. Taylor (1855–1920?), British traveler and missionary.

b. Séverine (Caroline Rémy Guebhard, 1855–1929), French journalist.

d. Mary Haydock Reibey (1777–1855), British-born Australian entrepreneur who at 13, arrested for theft disguised as a boy, was transported to Australia. There she married Thomas Reibey, and together they built a substantial international trading business, which she later ran herself, becoming a noted philanthropist in Sydney.

### SCIENCE/TECHNOLOGY/MEDICINE

Ann Preston became professor of physiology at Philadelphia's Female Medical College, noted for her focus on medical ethics; many of her students became medical missionaries. She became the school's leading advocate after the Pennsylvania Medical Society denied it official recognition (1859).

Eveline Roberts James was among the first American women to practice dentistry, though without a degree; she had learned the skills working with her husband, continuing his practice in Connecticut after his death (1855).

### ARTS/LITERATURE

Elizabeth Gaskell published the novel *North and South*.

b. Olive Schreiner (1855–1920), South African writer.

b. Cecilia Beaux (1855–1942), American painter and teacher.

b. Marie Corelli (Mary Mackay, 1855–1924), British novelist.

d. Charlotte Brontë (1816–1855), British novelist and poet who created *Jane Eyre*; sister of Emily and Anne Brontë.

d. Anne Brontë (1820–1855), British poet and novelist who created *Agnes Grey*; sister of Charlotte and Emily Brontë.

d. Dorothy Wordsworth (1771–1855), British writer, sister of William Wordsworth.

## 1856

### POLITICS/LAW/WAR

India's Widow Remarriage Act allowed Hindu widows to legally remarry, though the rate of remarriage was low, partly because of religious belief, partly because the widow would lose custody of and support for her children.

French feminist Jeanne Deroin, then in exile, published *Lettre aux travailleurs*.

Susan B. Anthony became an agent of the American Anti-Slavery Society (1856–1861).

b. Eleanor Marx-Aveling (1856–1908), British socialist, the daughter of Karl Marx and Jenny von Westphalen Marx.

b. Harriet Stanton Blatch (1856–1940), American feminist, suffragist, and writer, the daughter of Elizabeth Cady Stanton.

b. Marie Stritt (1856–1928), German feminist, suffragist, and women's rights movement leader.

### RELIGION/EDUCATION/EVERYDAY LIFE

Dress Reform Association (ca. 1856–1865) continued to press for more comfortable, rational clothing styles for women. Two magazines supporting reform dress were the *Sibyl, a Review of the Tastes, Errors, and Fashions of Society*, edited by Lydia Sayer Hasbrouck of Middletown, New York, and the *Laws of Life and Woman's Health Journal*, edited by Harriet Austin and James Jackson of "Our Home" Water-Cure in Dansville, New York (the reform dress "bloomer" was commonly worn when taking "water cures").

Mary Ann Patten, who had learned navigation from her captain husband, assumed command of their tea clipper en route from New York via Cape Horn, bringing it safely to San Francisco after he became gravely ill; she was then pregnant with her first child.

Isabella Bird (later Bishop) published *The Englishwoman in America*, describing several months spent there recuperating from an operation.

b. Grace Hoadley Dodge (1856–1914), American welfare worker.

### SCIENCE/TECHNOLOGY/MEDICINE

On her return to England, to popular acclaim, Florence Nightingale, "the Lady with the Lamp," began applying the principles of hygiene to public-health work, advising the first district nursing service, in Liverpool, and supervising the appointment of female health commissioners. The Nightingale School of Nursing at St. Thomas Hospital was established, endowed with £44,000 raised for her from the British public.

Jamaican nurse Mary ("Mother" or "Aunty") Seacole established the British Hotel near Balaclava as a center for officers and soldiers in the Crimean War, setting it up at her own expense after the British army refused her offers of help (ca. 1856). Often personally nursing soldiers on the battlefield, she was left bankrupt at war's end, but British newspapers raised funds from public subscriptions to pay her debts. She wrote of her experiences in *The Wonderful Adventures of Mrs. Seacole in Many Lands* (1857).

Harriot Hunt published *Glances and Glimpses: or 50 Years Social, Including 20 Years Professional Life.*

b. Constance Stone (1856–1902), Australian physician and feminist.

### ARTS/LITERATURE

Elizabeth Barrett Browning published the poem *Aurora Leigh.*

Harriet Beecher Stowe published the novel *Dred: A Tale of the Great Dismal Swamp.*

Fredrika Bremer published the feminist novel *Hertha.*

Harriet Hosmer's sculpture of *Puck* was her first major success.

Susanna Moodie published the novel *Geoffrey Moncton.*

Louise Colet published the feminist *Le poème de la femme.*

b. Kate Douglas Wiggin (1856–1923), American writer.

d. Mme. Vestris (Lucy Elizabeth Bartolozzi, 1788–1856), British actress and manager.

## 1857

### POLITICS/LAW/WAR

The British women's rights movement won a major victory with passage of the first Married Women's Property Bill, recognizing within severe limits the right of women to own property; once established, the principle was ultimately extended to full and free ownership and transfer of property.

Caroline Dexter published *Ladies' Almanack: The Southern Cross or Australian Album and New Year's Gift.*

b. Anita Augspurg (1857–1943), German feminist and women's suffrage leader.

b. Clara Eissner Zetkin (1857–1933), German socialist and then Communist Party leader.

d. Lakshmi Bai (1835–1857), rani of Jhansi, who was killed in action with her troops at Gwalior, attempting to defend her independent state, Jhansi, against British forces during the Indian-British War. Also called the Indian or Sepoy Mutiny, the uprising later became a symbol of Indian independence.

### RELIGION/EDUCATION/EVERYDAY LIFE

Mary Carpenter led the fight for industrial schools in Britain, winning with passage of the Industrial School Acts (1857; 1861; 1866).

National Teachers' Association (later National Education Association) was founded in Philadelphia; women would not be admitted as members until 1866, though two women— H. D. Conrad and A. W. Beecher—signed the original NTA constitution.

Partly in reaction to earlier 19th-century preaching by Methodist women, *The True Woman*, published by Methodist Episcopal church Bishop Jesse Truesdell Peck, proposed that women should instead employ themselves "decorously" in activities such as Sunday school teaching, and in some circumstances in foreign missions.

Catharine Beecher published *Common Sense Applied to Religion.*

Elizabeth Acton published her last book, *The English Bread Book.*

b. Ida Minerva Tarbell (1857–1944), American investigative journalist and writer.

b. Martha Carey Thomas (1857–1935), American educator and feminist.

b. Fannie Merritt Farmer (1857–1915), American cook and educator.

b. Adelaide Hunter Hoodless (1857–1910), Canadian pioneer in home health education.

### SCIENCE/TECHNOLOGY/MEDICINE

Building on her earlier dispensary (1851), Elizabeth Blackwell, along with her sister, Emily Blackwell, and Marie Zakrzewska, all physicians, formally opened the New York Infirmary for Indigent Women and Children.

b. Ida Henrietta Hyde (1857–1945), American physiologist.

b. Williamina Paton Stevens Fleming (1857–1911), Scottish-American astronomer.

b. Anna Winlock (1857–1904), American astronomer.

b. Ethel Gordon Manson Fenwick (1857–1947), British nurse.

d. Mary Morland Buckland (?–1857), British naturalist noted for the illustrations she provided for naturalist books by her husband, William Buckland; she also took notes and dictation and edited his works, despite her husband's disapproval of "women in science."

### ARTS/LITERATURE

Marian (Mary Ann) Evans published her first works of fiction, as George Eliot, in *Blackwood's* magazine: *The Sad Fortunes of the Reverend Amos Barton, Janet's Repentance*, and *Mr. Gilfil's Love-Story*. They appeared in book form as *Scenes of Clerical Life*.

Louisa Atkinson published her novel *Gertrude the Emigrant: A Tale of Colonial Life*.

Harriet Hosmer showed her sculpture *Beatrice Cenci*.

b. Gertrude Atherton (1857–1948), American author.

b. Cécile Louise Stéphanie Chaminade (1857–1944), French pianist and composer.

b. Margaret Deland (1857–1945), American novelist.

b. Matilde Serao (1857–1927), Italian writer.

## 1858

### POLITICS/LAW/WAR

b. Emmeline Goulden Pankhurst (1858–1928), militant British suffragist.

b. Rosa Mayreder (1858–1938), Austrian feminist and pacifist, a writer and artist.

### RELIGION/EDUCATION/EVERYDAY LIFE

Barbara Leigh-Smith Bodichon was a founder of the *English Woman's Journal*.

Marie Bernarde Soubirous (St. Bernadette), then 14 years old, announced that she had seen visions of a woman who identified herself as the Virgin Mary and gave instructions that a chapel was to be built by a nearby spring on the Gave River; as Lourdes, the French site would become one of Europe's largest pilgrimage shrines.

Dorothea Beale became principal of Cheltenham Ladies College, greatly expanding it and making it financially secure.

The Ladies Christian Association, predecessor of the Young Women's Christian Association (YWCA), was founded in New York City.

Louisa Twining became secretary of the Workhouse Visiting Society, associated with the National Association for the Promotion of Social Science; she also published *Workhouses and Women's Work*.

b. Beatrice Potter Webb (1858–1943), British economist, socialist, and writer.

b. Hannah Greenebaum Solomon (1858–1942), American reformer and women's club leader.

b. Julia Clifford Lathrop (1858–1932), American social worker and reformer.

b. Pandita Ramabai (1858–ca. 1920), Indian feminist, social reformer, and writer.

d. Harriet Taylor (1808–1858), British writer and feminist, probable author of "On the Enfranchisement of Women" (1851), whose views much influenced those of her longtime companion and then husband, John Stuart Mill.

### SCIENCE/TECHNOLOGY/MEDICINE

b. Elizabeth Knight Britton (1858–1934), American botanist.

b. Charlotte Angas Scott (1858–1951), British-American mathematician.

b. Rosa Smith Eigenmann (1858–1947), American ichthyologist.

b. Mary Adela Blagg (1858–1944), British astronomer.

d. Jane Haldimand Marcet (1769–1858), British scientific writer most noted for her *Conversations on Chemistry* (1806).

d. Jane Webb Loudon (1807–1858), British botanist and writer on horticulture who often assisted her husband, landscape gardener John Loudon; her popular botany books were written when the couple was low on funds.

### ARTS/LITERATURE

Adelaide Proctor published the poetry collection *Legends and Lyrics*.

b. Eleanora Duse (1858–1924), Italian actress.

b. Selma Lagerlöf (1858–1940), Swedish writer.

b. Ethel Mary Smyth (1858–1944), British composer and women's rights advocate.

b. Edith Anna Oenone Somerville (1858–1949), Irish novelist.

d. Rachel (1820–1858), French actress, a great star in the French theater who also toured on the English-speaking stage, playing in a wide range of classic roles, such as Camille and Phèdre..

## 1859

### POLITICS/LAW/WAR

Women won the right to vote in school-board elections in Kansas.

b. Carrie Chapman Catt (1859–1947), American women's suffrage movement leader and pacifist.

b. Alexandra van Grippenberg (1859–1913), Finnish women's rights movement leader and politician.

### RELIGION/EDUCATION/EVERYDAY LIFE

John Stuart Mill published *On Liberty*, a work much influenced by the ideas of his late wife, Harriet Taylor, sometimes considered an uncredited collaborator.

Russia's "Triumvirate"—Nadezhda Stasova, Mariya Trubnikova, and Anna Filosova—established a philanthropic organization in St. Petersburg, offering schools (including kindergartens), workshops, communal kitchens, and cheap housing, beginning their long careers as political and social reformers.

Maria Rye opened a law stationers' business in London's Lincoln's Inn to employ young women, one of many such ventures she sponsored, some involving training in new technology, such as telegraphy or printing.

Phoebe Palmer published *Promise of the Father*, arguing for an expansion of women's roles in Methodism.

Salvation Army cofounder Catherine Booth published her pamphlet *Female Ministry*.

When Christians in Syria were threatened with massacres, Englishwoman Jane Digby El Mezrab, wife of a local sheikh, helped to defend them.

Women were first allowed to attend courses at the University of St. Petersburg (1859–1861).

b. Florence Kelley (1859–1932), American social reformer, feminist, and civil-rights and consumer advocate.

b. Ellen Gates Starr (1859–1940), American social reformer and bookbinder.

b. Fanny Bullock Workman (1859–1925), American traveler and mountaineer.

b. Mary Morton Kimball Kehew (1859–1918), American union activist.

d. Elizabeth Acton (1799–1859), British cookery writer, author of *Modern Cookery* (1845).

## SCIENCE/TECHNOLOGY/MEDICINE

Florence Nightingale published *Notes on Nursing*, developing the basic principles of modern nursing.

Martha J. Coston perfected and patented a signal flare conceived by her late husband, selling it in America and Europe, under U.S. government contract during the Civil War. The widely used Coston signal light came to be called the Very pistol, after a man who made some minor improvements decades later.

Elizabeth Agassiz published *Actaea: A First Lesson in Natural History*.

Hepsa Ely Silliman published a theory of the origin of meteorites, using new ideas of chemical affinity and electromagnetism.

Almira Hart Lincoln Phelps, educator and author of popular science textbooks, became the second woman ever elected to membership in the American Association for the Advancement of Science.

Elizabeth Blackwell became the first female physician listed on the United Kingdom Medical Register.

b. Alice Eastwood (1859–1953), American botanist.

b. Julia Brainerd Hall (1859–1925), American chemical engineer.

b. Kate Marsden (1859–1931), British traveler and nurse.

b. Marcia Keith (1859–1950), American physicist.

d. Charlotte Heidenreich von Siebold (1788–1859), German physician, the daughter of physicians, who originally trained with her mother, Josepha von Siebold. Charlotte Siebold attended at the births of many notable people across Europe, including Victoria, later queen of England (1819).

## ARTS/LITERATURE

George Eliot (Marian Evans) published the novel *Adam Bede*.

George Sand published the autobiographical novel *He and She*.

Harriet Beecher Stowe published the novel *The Minister's Wooing*.

Harriet Hosmer showed her monumental sculpture *Zenobia in Chains*.

Louisa Atkinson published her novel *Cowanda, the Veteran's Grant*.

Maria Firmina dos Reis, writing as Uma Brasileira, published the novel *Ursula*, Brazil's first abolitionist novel.

Adeline (A. D. T.) Whitney published the poetry-parody collection *Mother Goose for Grown Folks*.

Anne Whitney published *Poems*.

Augusta Jane Evans published the novel *Beulah*.

Louise Colet published the novel *Lui*.

## 1860

### POLITICS/LAW/WAR

Barbara Bodichon, Jessie Boucherett, and Adelaide Ann Procter founded the Society for Promoting the Employment of Women.

Connecticut passed a law against abortion before quickening (the first sign of fetal movement); abortion *after* quickening had previously been banned (1821). Within four decades, every state would have adopted a law restricting or banning abortion.

b. Annie Furujelhm (1860–1937), Finnish feminist, suffragist, social reformer, and politician.

### RELIGION/EDUCATION/EVERYDAY LIFE

Julie-Victoire Daubie demanded and finally won the right to take the *baccalaureat*, the main qualifying examination, previously taken only by men, passing it before a jury from the Faculté des Lettres of Lyon; a key victory for women's higher education in France, about which she wrote in *Du progres dans l'instruction primaire: justice et liberté* (1862).

British Society for Promoting the Employment of Women was founded.

Ellen Demorest and her husband, William Demorest, developed sew-at-home guides, making dress patterns of tissue paper and introducing a sizing system; they published a widely circulated monthly pattern book, *Mme. Demorest's Mirror of Fashion*.

Isabella Beeton began to publish *Mrs. Beeton's Book of Household Management*, containing articles and more than 3,000 recipes, in 30 monthly installments; in book form (1861), it would be a best-seller for decades.

Mary Rice Livermore was the first female news reporter to work at a major American political convention, the Republican Party convention that nominated Abraham Lincoln for president.

Jane Franklin was awarded the Founder's Medal of the Royal Geographical Society.

Lydia Maria Child published *Correspondence between Lydia Maria Child and Governor Wise and Mrs. Mason of Virginia*.

Caroline Wells Dall published *Women's Right to Labor*.

b. Jane Addams (1860–1935), American social worker, women's rights leader, pacifist, and civil libertarian.

b. Charlotte Perkins Gilman (1860–1935), American feminist writer, reformer, and utopian socialist.

b. Juliette Magill Kinzie Gordon Low (1860–1927), American founder of the Girl Scouts.

b. Annie (Phoebe Anne) Oakley (Mozee; Moses) (1860–1926), American sharpshooter.

b. Alice Pestana (Caiel) (1860–1929), Portuguese writer and feminist.

b. Clara Elizabeth Collet (1860–1948), British feminist and economist.

b. Henrietta Szold (1860–1945), American Zionist leader.

b. Lizzie Andrew Borden (1860–1927), American alleged murderer.

d. Anne Isabella, Lady Noel Byron (1792–1860), British philanthropist, briefly married to the poet Lord Byron, mother of mathematician Ada Byron Lovelace and grandmother of traveler Anne Blunt; she founded schools and supported social reform.

### SCIENCE/TECHNOLOGY/MEDICINE

b. Isabel Hampton Robb (1860–1910), Canadian-American nurse and nursing educator.

b. Mary Jane Rathbun (1860–1943), American marine zoologist.

b. Margaret Eliza Maltby (1860–1944), American physicist and educator.

### ARTS/LITERATURE

George Eliot (Marian Evans) created the partly autobiographical Maggie Tulliver and her brother Tom in the novel *The Mill on the Floss*.

Elizabeth Barrett Browning published *Poems before Congress*.

b. Anna Mary Robertson Moses (Grandma Moses, 1860–1961), American painter.

b. Ada Rehan (1860–1916), American actress.

b. Annie (Elizabeth Fredericka) Horniman (1860–1937), British theater manager and patron.

b. Florence Farr (1860–1917), British actress and director.

d. Anna Murphy Jameson (1794–1860), Irish essayist, novelist, and women's rights advocate.

## 1861

### POLITICS/LAW/WAR

At the death of emperor Hs'en Feng, Tz'u Hsi, his concubine, became regent for her nephew and adopted son Tsai-t'ien; she would effectively rule until 1908, presiding over the long decline of the Manchus that culminated in the lost Manchu-Boxer antiforeign war that began as the Boxer Rebellion and ended with the burning and looting of Peking.

During America's Civil War, Sarah Edwards enlisted in the Union Army as Franklin Thompson and served two years until invalided out due to illness.

Catherine Spence published *A Plea for Pure Democracy*, advocating proportional representation in Australia.

## RELIGION/EDUCATION/EVERYDAY LIFE

Thousands of women moved into previously all-male white-collar jobs during the American Civil War (1861–1865); in Washington, they were known as "government girls."

After writing an article defending the new female government employees from charges of inefficiency, Emily Edson Briggs became the first woman to routinely go to the White House as a news reporter, as reporter and columnist for the *Washington Chronicle* and the *Philadelphia Press* (1861–1882), often writing as "Olivia."

Emily Davies became the editor of the *English Women's Journal*.

*Mother Law* (*Das Mutterrecht*) was published by Johann J. Bachofen, among the first to posit an early epoch in which women ruled society.

Concepción Arenal won the Madrid Academy of Moral and Political Science's top prize for her essay on philanthropy, *La beneficencia, la filantropía y la caridad*.

Harriet Clisby and Caroline Dexter published the *Interpreter*, Australia's first journal produced by women.

Maria Rye published *Emigration of Educated Women* and with Jane Lewin founded the Female Middle Class Emigration Society, helping many British women resettle abroad, in Australia, New Zealand, and Canada.

Hester Lynch Thrale's *Autobiography* was published, edited by A. Hayward.

b. Kalliroe Parren (1861–1940), Greek teacher, writer, and women's rights movement organizer.

b. Margaret Llewelyn Davies (1861–1944), British feminist, socialist, pacifist, and social reformer.

b. Daisy Bates (1861–1951), London-born Australian welfare worker.

b. Elizabeth Hawkins-Whitshed (Mrs. Aubrey) Le Blond (1861–1934), British mountaineer.

b. Gertrude Tuckwell (1861–1951), British union activist.

b. Mary Ellen Richmond (1861–1928), American teacher and social worker.

b. Vida Dutton Scudder (1861–1954), American religious scholar and social activist.

## SCIENCE/TECHNOLOGY/MEDICINE

Ann Preston founded the Woman's Hospital, in Philadelphia (later Hospital of the Medical College of Philadelphia), to provide practical experience in medical treatment for Female Medical College students, after the Philadelphia Medical Society barred women from attending teaching clinics in Philadelphia and joining local medical societies. Preston would also later found an associated nurses' training school, the first in America.

Women founded the United States Sanitary Commission, run by men, to coordinate the efforts of thousands of local women's aid societies on the Union side during the Civil War. These societies provided such vital services as trained nurses, under superintendent Dorothea Dix; medical supplies; and transportation for the wounded, laying the basis for modern American nursing.

Sally Tompkins ran a Richmond, Virginia, hospital for Southern soldiers; when other private hospitals were closed, Confederate President Jefferson Davis gave Tompkins an army commission as a captain of cavalry, so she could keep her hospital open.

Thiphena Hornbrook obtained a U.S. patent for a ventilated beehive case.

b. Dorothea Klumpke Roberts (1861–1942), American-born astronomer working in France.

b. Nettie Maria Stevens (1861–1912), American geneticist.

## ARTS/LITERATURE

George Eliot (Marian Evans) published *Silas Marner: The Weaver of Ravenloe*.

Rebecca Harding Davis published *Life in the Iron Mills*.

Harriet Brent Jacobs published the autobiography *Incidents in the Life of a Slave Girl*.

Adah Isaacs Menken starred in the title role of *Mazeppa*.

b. Ernestine Schumann-Heink (1861–1936), Austrian-American contralto.

b. Lillian Russell (Helen Louise Leonard, 1861–1922), American singer and actress.

b. Nellie Melba (Helen Porter Armstrong, 1861–1931), Australian soprano.

b. Lou Andreas-Salomé (1861–1937), Russian writer and psychoanalyst.

d. Elizabeth Barrett Browning (1806–1861), British poet, especially noted for the love poems to her husband, poet Robert Browning.

d. Lola Montez (Maria Dolores Gilbert, 1818–1861), Irish dancer, a celebrity performer with a reputation as a femme fatale.

## 1862

### RELIGION/EDUCATION/EVERYDAY LIFE

Caroline Wells Dall published *Woman's Rights Under the Law.*

b. Ida Bell Wells (Barnett) (1862–1931), African-American antilynching crusader and journalist.

b. Harriet Morison (1862–1925), New Zealand union activist and feminist.

b. Mary Kingsley (1862–1900), British explorer.

### SCIENCE/TECHNOLOGY/MEDICINE

Physician Emeline Horton Cleveland, who had learned hospital administration at the Maternité of Paris, became chief resident at Philadelphia's Woman's Hospital, introducing nurses' training courses and also practical courses for laywomen, prototypes of modern nurses' aides. As a surgeon, she was noted for her skill in removing ovarian tumors, among the first female physicians to perform such operations.

b. Florence Bascom (1862–1945), American geologist and educator.

### ARTS/LITERATURE

Julia Ward Howe published the poem "Battle Hymn of the Republic," which became the Union Army anthem to the music of "John Brown's Body"; first published in the *Atlantic Monthly.*

Elizabeth Barrett Browning's *Last Poems* appeared posthumously.

George Eliot (Marian Evans) published the historical novel *Romola.*

Carolina Rosati made her final starring appearance, creating the title role in Marius Petipa's ballet *La Fille du Pharaon,* opening in St. Petersburg with a cast of almost 400.

Louise Pyne created the role of the Colleen Bawn in Julius Benedict's opera *The Lily of Killarney.*

Christina Rossetti published *Goblin Market and Other Poems.*

Rebecca Harding Davis published the novel *Margaret Howth.*

Mary Elizabeth Braddon published the melodramatic novel *Lady Audley's Secret.*

b. Edith Wharton (1862–1937), American writer.

b. Elizabeth Robins (1862–1952), American actress, translator, and writer.

b. Loie (Louise Mary) Fuller (1862–1928), American dancer.

## 1863

### POLITICS/LAW/WAR

Elizabeth Cady Stanton, Susan B. Anthony, Lucy Stone, and Ernestine Rose took the lead in founding the short-lived National Woman's Loyal League (1863–1864) in New York City, with Stanton as president and Anthony secretary. From the first, the League split: conservative women wanted to limit activities in support of the Union's effort in the Civil War, but Stanton's dominant faction pushed through a campaign for abolition and also spoke for women's rights. The League disbanded in August 1864.

French feminist Maria Deraismes published *Le théâtre chez soi.*

### RELIGION/EDUCATION/EVERYDAY LIFE

Emily Davies successfully worked to open the Cambridge University examination to women.

Ellen Patterson was the first president of the Working Women's Union, formed by New York garment workers.

Russia's "Triumvirate"—Nadezhda Stasova, Mariya Trubnikova, and Anna Filosova—founded the Publishing Artel, a publishing cooperative providing employment for female writers, copyists, editors, and translators.

Eleanor Butterick and her husband, Ebenezer Butterick, developed paper dress patterns, with legal rights taken in his name.

Mary Baldwin took over as principal of Virginia's Augusta Female Seminary, remaining in the post for the rest of her life (1863–1897).

Olympia Brown was ordained a minister by the Northern Universalists, serving in Weymouth, Massachusetts.

b. Margaret Alice Murray (1863–1963), British scholar.

b. Mary (Eliza) Church Terrell (1863–1954), African-American women's rights leader.

### SCIENCE/TECHNOLOGY/MEDICINE

When America's Civil War started, Clara Barton canvassed for supplies for the wounded, which she often personally paid for and distributed (by mule team), acting as an unpaid nurse (ca. 1863). Later in the war, she organized and ran hospitals and also marked graves and gathered information on missing men.

Physician Marie Zakrzewska founded the New England Hospital for Women and Children, the first American hospital with an associated school for nurses and a social service organization; she led it for nearly four decades.

New York Medical College for Women was incorporated through the efforts of physician Clemence Sophia Lozier, who had received her own degree from the Syracuse Eclectic Medical College.

Susie King Taylor, perhaps the first African-American army nurse, began the diary that would later be published as *In Reminiscences of My Life in Camp: Civil War Nurse* (ca. 1863).

Sarah Mossman obtained a U.S. patent for an improved military cap, with a waterproof flap that could be unfolded in bad weather.

b. Annie Jump Cannon (1863–1941), American astronomer.

b. Ellen Churchill Semple (1863–1932), American geographer.

b. Anna Wessel Williams (1863–1954), American physician and bacteriologist.

b. Bertha Van Hoosen (1863–1952), American surgeon, obstetrician, and feminist.

b. Ethel Sargant (1863–1918), British botanist.

b. Florence Merriam Bailey (1863–1948), American naturalist and ornithologist.

b. Margaret Clay Ferguson (1863–1951), American botanist.

b. Mary Whiton Calkins (1863–1930), American psychologist and philosopher.

### ARTS/LITERATURE

Louisa May Alcott published *Hospital Sketches*.

Fanny Kemble published her antislavery *Journal of a Residence on a Georgian Plantation*.

Kate Bateman starred in the title role of Augustin Daly's play *Leah, the Forsaken*.

Adeline (A. D. T.) Whitney published the novel *Faith Gartney's Girlhood*.

Elizabeth Gaskell published the novel *Sylvia's Lovers*.

Ouida published the novel *Chandos*.

d. Frances Trollope (1780–1863), British writer, mother of novelist Anthony Trollope.

d. Charlotte Barnes (1818–1863), American actress and playwright.

## 1864

### POLITICS/LAW/WAR

Anna Elizabeth Dickinson, a popular speaker on women's rights and abolition, addressed the House of Representatives; she is believed to be the first woman to do so. President Abraham Lincoln attended.

Contagious Diseases Acts were passed in Britain (1864; 1866; 1869) requiring registration of prostitutes in towns where military and naval personnel were garrisoned, the aim being to limit the spread of venereal diseases; prostitutes were periodically examined and, if found infected, could be held in hospitals for months. Many people protested that men were exempt from scrutiny or punishment.

b. Helena Sickert Swanwick (1864–1939), British writer, suffragist, and pacifist.

b. Luise Kautsky (1864–1944), Austrian socialist, communist, suffragist, and writer.

b. Margot (Margaret Emma Alice) Tennant Asquith (1864–1945), Scottish writer.

## RELIGION/EDUCATION/EVERYDAY LIFE

Octavia Hill put into operation her plan, sponsored by John Ruskin, of improving three local houses for the poor, managing the program as an investment; she trained her sister Miranda and others to help her as the program expanded.

Edmonia Highgate addressed the all-male National Convention of Colored Citizens of the United States held in Syracuse, New York; she was the first of two women to do so.

Frances Power Cobbe published *Broken Lights*.

b. Mary Kenney O'Sullivan (1864–1943), American feminist and trade union organizer.

d. Eliza Wood Burham Farnham (1815–1864), American feminist, author, and prison reformer, who became matron of the women's prison at Sing Sing (1844). In the year of her death, she published the lightly fictionalized autobiography *Eliza Woodson; Or, the Early Days of One of the World's Workers*.

d. Ann Royall (1769–1864), American journalist.

## SCIENCE/TECHNOLOGY/MEDICINE

Physician Mary Edwards Walker joined the Union Army as an assistant surgeon, the first woman so commissioned in the American armed services.

Rebecca Lee became the first African-American woman to receive her medical degree when she graduated from Boston's New England Female Medical College, setting up practice in Richmond, Virginia, after the Civil War.

Mary Jane Montgomery obtained a U.S. patent for an improved method of planking armed warships to avoid attachment of barnacles.

British educator Lydia Becker published *Botany for Novices*.

b. Elsie (Maude) Inglis (1864–1917), British physician, born in India.

b. Fiammetta Worthington Wilson (1864–1920), British astronomer.

## ARTS/LITERATURE

Hortense Schneider created the title role in Jacques Offenbach's opera *La belle Hélène* (*The Fair Helen*).

Bengali novelist Bankim Chandra Chatterjee published *Rajmohan's Wife*, among the earliest Anglo-Indian novels.

Julia Margaret Cameron shot her portrait photo of *Ellen Terry*.

Elizabeth Cleghorn Gaskell published the novel *Wives and Daughters* (1864–1866).

b. Ricarda Huch (Richard Hugo, 1864–1947), German writer and historian.

b. Camille Claudel (1864–1943), French sculptor.

b. Janet Achurch (1864–1916), British actress.

b. Marguerite Durand (1864–1936), French actress and publisher.

b. Marie Tempest (Mary Susan Etherington, 1864–1942), British actress and singer.

b. Vera Fedorovna Komisarjevskaya (1864–1910), Russian actress and theater manager.

b. Vesta Tilley (1864–1952), British male impersonator, a star in music halls.

d. Adelaide Procter (1825–1864), British poet who wrote as Mary Berwick.

## 1865

### POLITICS/LAW/WAR

Kensington Society was founded by a group of British feminists that included Barbara Leigh-Smith Bodichon, Emily Davies, Helen Taylor, and Elizabeth Garrett Anderson.

General German Women's Association (Allgemeiner Deutscher Frauenverein) was founded, with Luise Otto-Peters as president and editor of its journal *Neue Bahnen*.

Italian Civil Code (Pisanelli Code) confirmed Italian women's legal dependence on men; women from Lombardy and Venice, who had exercised local votes and had other freedoms, lost them under Italian unification.

French feminist Maria Deraismes published *Aux femmes riches*.

Sarah Edwards, who had served in the Union Army disguised as a man, published *Nurse and Spy in the Union Army*.

b. Mary White Ovington (1865–1951), American social worker, reformer, and civil rights advocate.

b. Lily Braun (1865–1916), German radical feminist and socialist.

### RELIGION/EDUCATION/EVERYDAY LIFE

Vassar College opened in Poughkeepsie, New York, funded in 1861 by British-born brewer Matthew Vassar as the first American college established to give women an education as rigorous as that of men, including physical education (partly because some critics of women's education said it weakened them physically). Unlike some other women's colleges, such as Mount Holyoke, students were not required to do domestic work; as at other schools, most early faculty and presidents were male.

As the Civil War ended, female missionaries, teachers, and doctors—many of them associated with the American Missionary Association—began to work in the South aiding former slaves and founding and staffing churches and schools, from primary schools to colleges (most actively from 1865–ca. 1873).

Eliza Farnham posthumously published *Woman and Her Era*, a statement of her feminist views.

Laura Bell, formerly a wild-living courtesan and wife, became a Christian missionary, preaching in London as a "sinner saved through grace" and working with Liberal leader William Gladstone to rescue London's prostitutes (from the 1860s).

Concepción Arenal published *Cortas a los delincuentes*.

Frances Power Cobbe published *Studies of Ethical and Social Subjects*.

b. Edith Hamilton (1865–1963), American classicist and writer.

b. Elizabeth Cochrane Seaman (Nellie Bly, 1865–1922), American investigative reporter.

b. Evangeline Cary Booth (1865–1950), British-American Salvation Army leader.

b. Abala Das Bose (1865–1951), Indian educator.

b. Elsie de Wolfe (Lady Mendl, 1865–1950), American interior decorator.

b. Katherine Gibbs (1865–1934), American entrepreneur and educator.

b. Margaret Murray Washington (1865–1925), American educator.

b. Tsuda Umeko (1865–1929), Japanese educator.

d. Isabella Mayson Beeton (1837–1865), British cookery writer.

### SCIENCE/TECHNOLOGY/MEDICINE

Physician Mary Edwards Walker became the first woman to win the Congressional Medal of Honor, for her service as a surgeon in the U.S. Army during the Civil War. She had been captured and held in a Confederate prison for four months, before being exchanged for a Confederate major "man for man."

Physician Mary Thompson founded the Chicago Hospital for Women and Children, after her death named the Mary Thompson Hospital of Chicago.

Maria Mitchell became professor of astronomy and director of the observatory at just-founded Vassar College in Poughkeepsie, New York, stressing not lectures but small classes and laboratory work.

Refused admission to the universities of London, Edinburgh, and St. Andrews, Elizabeth Garrett Anderson began her medical training by obtaining an apothecary's license through the Apothecaries' Hall.

*Functions and Disorders of the Reproductive Organs*, by William Acton, stated that "the majority of women (happily for them) are not very much troubled with sexual feeling of any kind."

Rachel Bodley was appointed the first chemistry teacher at Philadelphia's Female Medical College (later Woman's Medical College of Pennsylvania), later becoming dean (1874–1888).

Temperance P. Edson obtained a U.S. patent for a self-inflator for raising sunken vessels.

b. Edith Louisa Cavell (1865–1915), British nurse, executed as a spy (1915).

b. Kate Gleason (1865–1933), American mechanical engineer and entrepreneur.

d. James Stuart (possibly Miranda Stuart [Barry], 1795?–1865), British physician, the first woman to practice as a physician in Britain, serving mostly as a military doctor in colonies around the world, rising to inspector general of all British hospitals in Canada. Only after her death was it discovered that she was a woman, after rumors of her sex triggered an autopsy.

### ARTS/LITERATURE

Laura Keene's company was playing in *Our American Cousin* at Washington's Ford Theater when Abraham Lincoln was assassinated there by John Wilkes Booth (April 4).

Malvina Schnorr von Carolsfeld created Isolde opposite Ludwig Schnorr von Carolsfeld as Tristan in Richard Wagner's opera *Tristan and Isolde*.

Louisa May Alcott published the novel *Moods*.

Edmonia Lewis sculpted a bust of Robert Gould Shaw and a medallion of John Brown (ca. 1865).

Adeline (A. D. T.) Whitney published the novel *The Gayworthys*.

b. Mrs. Patrick Campbell (Beatrice Stella Tanner, 1865–1940), British actress.

b. Fay Templeton (1865–1939), American singer.

b. Minnie Maddern Fiske (1865–1932), American actress.

b. Suzanne Marie Clementine Valadon (1865–1938), French painter.

b. Yvette Guilbert (1865–1944), French folksinger and actress.

d. Giuditta Negri Pasta (1797–1865), Italian soprano, a major figure in European opera who created several central roles, including the title role in Gaetano Donizetti's opera *Anna Bolena* (1830) and Amina in Vincenzo Bellini's opera *La sonnambula*.

d. Elizabeth Cleghorn Gaskell (1810–1865), British novelist and biographer, much of whose work focused on the evils of early English industrialism and the development of sentiment for social reform.

d. Fredrika Bremer (1801–1865), Swedish novelist, travel writer, feminist, and women's rights advocate.

## 1866

### POLITICS/LAW/WAR

American Equal Rights Association was founded, with Lucretia Mott as president, heading a group of abolitionist and feminist leaders that included Elizabeth Cady Stanton, Frederick Douglass, Susan B. Anthony, Lucy Stone, and Thaddeus Stevens. Three years of disputes followed between abolitionists, who wished to make African-American rights central, and suffragists who were unwilling to drop their women's rights demands; the friction ultimately resulted in a historic split that generated the National Woman Suffrage Association and the American Woman Suffrage Association.

The suffragists of the Kensington Society, among them Barbara Leigh-Smith Bodichon and Jessie Boucherett, gathered the landmark British mass women's suffrage petition, presenting it to John Stuart Mill, who first introduced it in Parliament (1867).

Maria Deraismes, Paule Mink, Louise Michel, and André Leo founded the Société pour la Revendication des Droits de la Femme.

Jessie Boucherett became editor of the *Englishwoman's Review* (1866–1871).

b. Cornelia Sorabji (1866–1954), India's first woman lawyer.

b. Maud Gonne MacBride (1866–1953), Irish Republican revolutionary and actress.

b. Sophonisba Preston Breckinridge (1866–1948), American lawyer, educator, social reformer, and women's rights advocate.

b. Florence Prag Kahn (1866–1948), American politician.

b. Martha Munger Black (1866–1957), Canadian miner, politician, and writer.

b. Miina Sillanpää (1866–1952), Finnish socialist, feminist, and politician.

b. Nina Bang (1866–1928), Danish socialist and politician.

### RELIGION/EDUCATION/EVERYDAY LIFE

Emily Davies founded and became secretary of the London Schoolmistresses' Association (1866–1888), and published *The Higher Education of Women*.

America's first local Young Women's Christian Association (YWCA) was established, in Boston.

Women were first admitted as members of the National Teachers' Association (later National Education Association).

Troy Collar Laundry Union, led by Kate Mullaney, disbanded after a failed strike.

Julie-Victoire Daubie published *La femme pauvre au XIX siècle*.

b. Anne (Joanna) Sullivan (Macy) (1866–1936), American educator.

b. Mary Burnett Talbert (1866–1923), African-American civil rights and antilynching leader.

d. Evanthia Kairi (1797–1866), Greek educator, who headed a notable girls' school at Kydonies, in Asia Minor, teaching history and classics, and translating into Greek French works on women's education.

### SCIENCE/TECHNOLOGY/MEDICINE

Lucy Hobbs (later Taylor) became the first woman to obtain a degree in dentistry, when she graduated from the Ohio Dental College; some women had practiced dentistry before her, but without gaining a degree.

Ann Preston became dean at Philadelphia's Female Medical College, the first woman to be dean of an American medical college (1866–1872).

Physician Elizabeth Garrett Anderson established St. Mary's Dispensary for Women, forerunner of the New Hospital for Women and Children (1886), in London.

Elizabeth Agassiz published *Seaside Studies in Natural History*.

British educator Lydia Becker published *Elementary Astronomy*.

b. Antonia Caetana de Paiva Pereira Maury (1866–1952), American astronomer.

### ARTS/LITERATURE

George Eliot (Marian Evans) published the novel *Felix Holt, the Radical*.

## Try, Try Again

Lucy Hobbs had originally intended to be a doctor, but officials at the Eclectic Medical College in Cincinnati refused to accept a woman (1859), advising that she try dentistry. She was unable to find a dentist to accept her as a trainee and was refused admission to the Ohio Dental College (1861), though she worked for the college's dean. Only after she had been accepted into the Iowa State Dental Society (1865) was she admitted to the Ohio Dental College, coming in first in the school's final examinations.

Christina Rossetti published *The Prince's Progress and Other Poems*.

Mary Elizabeth Braddon became editor of the magazine *Belgravia*.

b. Beatrix Potter (1866–1943), British writer, illustrator, and biologist.

b. Julia Marlowe (1866–1950), American actress.

b. Violet Hunt (1866–1942), British biographer and novelist.

d. Maria Susanna Cummins (1827–1866), New England novelist and short story writer.

## 1867

### POLITICS/LAW/WAR

Among those campaigning publicly in Kansas for the woman suffrage amendment were Elizabeth Cady Stanton, Lucy Stone and her husband, Henry Blackwell, Susan B. Anthony, and Olympia Brown.

Lydia Becker's essay "Female Suffrage" appeared in Britain's *Contemporary Review*; she also founded and became the first secretary of the Manchester Women's Suffrage Committee.

French feminist Maria Deraismes published *Eve contre M. Dumas fils* and *Nos principes et nos moeurs*.

b. Emmeline Pethick-Lawrence (1867–1954), British social worker, radical feminist, pacifist, and women's suffrage movement leader.

b. Lida Heymann (1867–1943), German feminist and women's suffrage leader.

b. Marie Lacoste Gerin-Lajoie (1867–1945), French-Canadian feminist and writer.

### RELIGION/EDUCATION/EVERYDAY LIFE

John Stuart Mill introduced the first British women's suffrage resolution in Parliament.

Emily Davies opened her pioneeering women's college at Benslow House, at first as a preparatory school for the Cambridge examinations.

North of England Council for Promoting the Higher Education for Women was founded by Anne Clough, who became secretary, and Josephine Butler, president, seeking women's examinations at university level; Emily Davies was simultaneously pressing for women to have the same, not separate, examinations as men.

Elizabeth Palmer Peabody opened America's first publicly funded kindergarten, in Boston; she had traveled to Germany to learn firsthand about Friedrich Froebel's work with kindergartens and persuaded some German kindergarten teachers, notably Maria Kraus-Boelte, Emma Marwedel, and Alma Kriege, to return with her.

Eugenia Konradi submitted a petition that women be allowed to attend the University of St. Petersburg.

Woman's Commonwealth (originally Sanctified Sisters or the True Church Colony) was founded in Belton, Texas (1867?–1983), originally as a purely religious Christian group, but later (partly in response to attacks from the community) widening into a separatist, socialist, celibate, feminist community led by Martha White McWhirter.

Greek women published a women's journal, *Thaleia*.

New York's Knickerbocker Base Ball Club inaugurated the practice of Ladies' Day, offering free admission to wives, daughters, and girlfriends of male fans.

Virginia Lacy Jones became president of the Association of American Library Schools.

Caroline Wells Dall published *The College, the Market, and the Court: or, Woman's Relation to Education, Politics, and Law*.

b. Emily Greene Balch (1867–1961), American pacifist, social reformer, writer, teacher, and social worker.

b. Maggie Lena Walker (1867–1934), African-American fraternal society executive and banker.

b. Margaret Noble (1867–1911), Anglo-Irish educator, Hindu nun, writer, and political activist.

SCIENCE/TECHNOLOGY/MEDICINE

Elizabeth Agassiz published *A Journey in Brazil* (1867), a record of the 1865 expedition she took with her naturalist husband, Louis Agassiz.

Elizabeth Hawks obtained a U.S. patent for a stove with a separate "air chamber" for baking, the first of her two patents for stove improvements.

Emeline Brigham obtained a U.S. patent for an improvement on the pessary, a device to cover the mouth and neck of the uterus to provide support; since it also was used for contraception, the device was soon banned.

Philadelphia's Female Medical College was renamed the Woman's Medical College of Pennsylvania.

Sophia Jex-Blake published *A Visit to Some American Schools and Colleges.*

b. Lillian D. Wald (1867–1940), American public health nurse.

b. Marie (Maria) Sklodowska Curie (1867–1934), Polish physicist and chemist working in France.

b. Mary Orr Evershed (1867–1949), British astronomer.

ARTS/LITERATURE

Julia Margaret Cameron shot her portrait photo of *John Herschel.*

Augusta Jane Evans published the novel *St. Elmo.*

Lydia Maria Child published the novel *A Romance of the Republic.*

Edmonia Lewis sculpted *Forever Free* (ca. 1867).

Ouida published the novel *Under Two Flags.*

Rhoda Broughton published the novel *Cometh up as a Flower.*

b. Käthe Kollwitz (1867–1945), German artist.

b. Violet Augusta Mary Vanbrugh (1867–1942), British actress.

b. Amy Marcy Cheney Beach (1867–1944), American pianist and composer.

d. Fanny Tacchinardi-Persiani (1812–1867), Italian soprano.

## 1868

POLITICS/LAW/WAR

Fourteenth Amendment to the U.S. Constitution (June 16) federally guaranteed newly freed slaves the right to vote but also limited the vote to males. This exclusion of women was seen by leading male abolitionists and other radical Republicans as a necessary compromise; it was greeted by such radical feminists as Elizabeth Cady Stanton and Susan B. Anthony as a betrayal of a settled promise of women's suffrage. They went on to form women-only suffragist organi-

# Women's Work

Working women, throw your needles to the winds; press yourselves into employments where you can get better pay; dress yourselves in costume, like daughters of the regiment, and be conductors in our cars and railroads, drive hacks. If your petticoats stand in the way of bread, virtue and freedom, cut them off. . . . Woman's dress keeps her out of a multitude of employments where she could make good wages. We hear of a family of daughters out West who, being left suddenly to depend on themselves, decided to ignore all woman's work at low wages, so they donned male attire. One went to work in a lumber yard, one on a steamboat, one drove a hack in a Western city, and in a few years with economy they laid up enough to buy a handsome farm where they now live in comfort as women. . . . If women are to have a place in this world they must get right out of the old grooves and do new and grand things. We have looked through the eye of a needle long enough. It is time for *"The Revolution."*

— *The Revolution* (March 9, 1868)

zations that would dominate the American women's movement until suffrage was won in 1920, ultimately swallowing up the more conservative male-female groups that had accepted the betrayal as compromise.

Susan B. Anthony and Elizabeth Cady Stanton founded the women's rights periodical *The Revolution* (1868–1870), with the motto "Men their rights and nothing more; women their rights and nothing less."

While remaining an activist of the International League of Peace and Freedom, Marie Goegg founded the Association International des Femmes (later Solidarité), seeking equal treatment and status for women in political action; this issue, which had in 1848 sparked the historic Seneca Falls conference, was in the same period splitting the American women's movement and would resonate through the end of the 20th century.

New England Woman Suffrage Association (1868–1877) was founded by a group including Paulina Davis and Julia Ward Howe, who became its first president.

In Italy, Gualberta Alaide Beccari established the women's publication *La Donna* (1868–1891).

Myra Bradwell founded the *Chicago Legal News*, winning a landmark special charter from the State of Illinois so that she, a married woman, could function as an independent businesswoman (1868–1894).

Britain's Queen Victoria published *Leaves from the Journal of our Life in the Highlands*.

Lydia Becker made a trailblazing public speech supporting women's suffrage at Manchester's Free Trade Hall.

b. Constance Gore-Booth Markiewicz (Countess Markiewicz, 1868–1927), Irish Republican soldier and politician.

b. Emily Ferguson Murphy (1868–1933), Canadian lawyer, judge, social reformer, writer, and women's rights advocate.

### RELIGION/EDUCATION/EVERYDAY LIFE

Anne Clough and others petitioned Cambridge University for university-level women's examinations, winning a higher-level local examination for women (1869).

Inspired by a New York model, Maria Rye founded a home for poor children in London; many of them would be resettled in Canada, where she also had a home. She would later expand her efforts, inspiring the founding of the Church of England Waifs and Strays Society (1891). In all, she estimated she sent more than 4,000 children to Canada, though she was criticized for dividing families in the process.

Russia's "Triumvirate"—Nadezhda Stasova, Mariya Trubnikova, and Anna Filosova—gathered 4,000 women's signatures on a petition that they be allowed to become full students at the University of St. Petersburg.

Sorosis, the first known women's professional club in America, was founded in New York City.

House of Shelter for females was established by prison reformer Zebulon Brockway as part of the Detroit House of Corrections.

Margaret Van Cott became the first licensed female preacher in the Methodist Episcopal Church.

Frances Power Cobbe published *Dawning Lights*.

b. Gertrude Margaret Lowthian Bell (1868–1926), British traveler, archaeologist, and government official.

b. Margaret Dreier Robins (1868–1945), American reformer and union activist.

b. Annie Turnbo Malone (ca. 1868–1957), African-American entrepreneur and philanthropist.

b. Mary Parker Follett (1868–1933), American political economist and community worker.

b. La Belle Otero (Caroline Puentovalga, 1868–1965), Spanish courtesan.

### SCIENCE/TECHNOLOGY/MEDICINE

Physicians and sisters Elizabeth and Emily Blackwell founded the Women's Medical College, associated with their New York Infirmary for Indigent Women and Children, with Elizabeth as professor of hygiene and Emily as professor of obstetrics and women's diseases; it remained in operation until Cornell University began to accept women as medical students (1899).

Eleanor Ormerod formally began her collection of insects that were harmful or helpful to farmers, gathering them from her family estate, Sedbury Park in Britain, with the aid of agricultural workers there; the collection was sent to the Royal Horticultural Society, which awarded her its Flora Medal (1870); she received further awards for collections sent to Moscow's International Polytechnic Exhibition.

Anna E. Baldwin obtained the first of her five U.S. patents for improving the treatment, separation, and cooling of milk.

Mary E. A. Evard obtained two U.S. patents for improvements in a broiling apparatus and a cooking stove that allowed for cooking several foods at varying temperatures in different sections of the stove.

b. Henrietta Swan Leavitt (1868–1921), American astronomer.

b. Annie Russell Maunder (1868–1947), Irish astronomer.

### ARTS/LITERATURE

Louisa May Alcott published the novel *Little Women, or Meg, Jo, Beth, and Amy*.

Female performers, barred from the Kabuki stage since 1629, returned to it, with the end of Japan's shogunate.

Anna Katherine Green published *The Leavenworth Case*, an early novel in the then-new mystery genre in the United States.

Hortense Schneider created the title role in Jacques Offenbach's opera *La Périchole*.

Rebecca Harding Davis published the novel *Waiting for the Verdict*.

Edmonia Lewis sculpted *Hagar in the Wilderness*.

Elizabeth Phelps published her first and best-known novel, *The Gates Ajar*.

b. Mary Austin (1868–1934), American writer.

b. Maxine Elliott (1868–1940), American actress.

d. Adah Isaacs Menken (Dolores Adios Fuertes, 1835–1868), American actress, always identified with her role in *Mazeppa* (1861).

d. Sophie Schröder (1781–1868), Austrian actress, a major figure in German-language theater as leading actress at Vienna's Burgtheater.

## 1869

### POLITICS/LAW/WAR

Elizabeth Cady Stanton and Susan B. Anthony founded the National Woman Suffrage Association (NWSA), the radical, militant, women-only central vehicle of the American woman suffrage movement, with Stanton as its first president (1869–1890). Later that year (November), as an alternative to the NWSA, the American Woman Suffrage Association (AWSA), with Henry Ward Beecher as its first president, was organized by Lucy Stone, her husband, Henry Blackwell, and others, many of them former abolitionists and members of the Equal Rights Society. Its formation signaled a historic split in the American women's rights movement between those who wanted to continue to focus on African-American emancipation, confine feminism and largely suffragist issues to second place, and work within the Republican Party, and radical feminists, led by Stanton and Anthony, who were attempting to build a mass movement on the whole range of women's issues. In 1869, Stanton was the first woman to be a witness at a hearing before the U.S. Congress, pleading for suffrage.

Arabella Babb Mansfield won the right to take the Iowa bar examination, and passed, becoming the first American woman admitted to the bar, though she did not practice law, instead becoming a college teacher.

Myra Bradwell was prohibited because of her sex from practicing as a lawyer in Illinois, even though she qualified for the state bar.

Women won the right to vote in Wyoming and Utah, both then territories.

Paule Mink founded the French republican periodical *Les mouches et l'araignée*; a feminist weekly, *Le Droit des femmes* (*The Rights of Women*), was also founded by a man, Léon Richer.

Pioneering suffragist Mary Muller published *An Appeal to the Men of New Zealand*, attacking anti-suffragist male sentiment as mindless prejudice and setting the tone and agenda of the suffrage campaign that would be won there 24 years later.

Sarah Bradford published *Harriet Tubman: The Moses of Her People*, with proceeds going to a home for elderly African-Americans that Tubman had founded.

b. Emma Goldman (Red Emma, 1869–1940), American anarchist and women's rights advocate.

b. Vida Goldstein (1869–1949), Australian feminist, social reformer, women's rights movement and suffragist leader, politician, and editor.

b. Constance Georgia Lytton (1869–1923), British social reformer and suffragist.

b. Adelheid Popp (1869–1939), Austrian feminist, socialist, trade unionist, and editor.

b. Flora Drummond (1869–1949), Scottish socialist and suffragist.

b. Helene Stöcker (1869–1943), German feminist, pacifist, and women's rights movement leader.

### RELIGION/EDUCATION/EVERYDAY LIFE

John Stuart Mill published *The Subjection of Women*, his landmark work calling for complete women's equality, inspired by discussions with his late wife, Harriet Taylor; it would become a centerpiece of the emerging worldwide women's movement.

In a precedent-shattering move for the United States, the Typographical Union began to accept women as members.

Josephine Butler became leader of the successful Ladies' National Association campaign against Britain's Contagious Diseases Acts, which were seen as a government-sponsored attack on poor women.

# Opening Doors

Inspired by physician Elizabeth Blackwell, Sophia Jex-Blake, Edith Pechey (later Pechey-Phipson), and three other British women campaigned for acceptance into medical school. At the University of London, they were told that the "existing charter had been purposely so worded as to exclude the possibility of examining women for medical degrees." They then applied to the University of Edinburgh medical program and were provisionally allowed to attend classes (1869). Pechey did well enough to win the Chemistry Prize and the prestigious merit-based £250 Hope Scholarship, only to find it given to a man. After considerable difficulty, a professor was found to teach the women a separate class in anatomy, but then the five women were barred from studying at the Royal Infirmary, which was required for a medical degree.

The University Court offered a settlement (1872): the women would be allowed to attend classes, if they would accept simply "certificates of proficiency" and not attempt to obtain degrees. The five women then sued the university for breach of its implied contract to provide medical degrees. They lost in the courts (1873), but working through the British Parliament finally achieved the Russell Gurney Enabling Act (1876), which allowed women to take degree examinations before medical bodies.

The women also faced harassment from many male students, including yowling and blocking the entrances to the buildings. A small number of male students supported the women, and at one point a riot erupted between the two factions. When a member of the university staff accused Jex-Blake of leading the riot, she sued for libel, winning a farthing (1871), but nothing toward her legal bills of nearly £1,000. The resulting publicity gained the women some public support, but in the meantime university lecturers began to bar women from attending medical classes.

Pechey transferred to Switzerland's Bern University, there gaining her medical degree. In the end Jex-Blake and Pechey were able to gain the legal right to practice medicine in Great Britain only by being accepted to Ireland's Royal College of Physicians (1877).

In her *Woodhull and Claflin's Weekly*, Victoria Woodhull published an exposé of an affair between noted minister Henry Ward Beecher and a married parishioner, Elizabeth Tilden; the circumstance was ironic and some said hypocritical, since Woodhull herself supposedly supported free love.

Women were first formally admitted to the University of St. Petersburg, with a special program of courses introduced for them; other courses were introduced in Moscow (1870); Russian feminist Nadezhda Stasova later became director of the Bestusehz Advanced Courses.

Catharine Beecher's revised and expanded edition of her influential *A Treatise on Domestic Economy*, with additions by Harriet Beecher Stowe, was published as *The American Woman's Home*; a later edition was *The New Housekeeper's Manual* (1873).

Daughters of St. Crispin was founded, the first American national women's labor organization (1869–1876), with Carrie Wilson as its first president.

Margaret Van Cott was the first women licensed to preach in the Methodist Episcopal church.

Women's Foreign Missionary Society was founded by the Methodist Episcopal church, calling many women to serve abroad.

Dorothea Beale published the critique *Report on the Education of Girls*.

Frances Power Cobbe published *The Final Cause of Women*.

b. Madame C. J. Walker (1869–1919), African-American cosmetics entrepreneur.

b. Alexandra David-Neel (1869–1968), French explorer.

b. Evangeline French (1869–1960), British missionary and traveler.

b. May (Margaret Mary Edith) Tennant (1869–1946), Irish reformer.

## Science/Technology/Medicine

Clemence Royer published the first French translation of Charles Darwin's *On the Origin of Species by Means of Natural Selection*; she would later write her own book, *L'origine de l'homme et des sociétés*.

Antoinette Brown Blackwell published *Studies in General Science*, linking scientific knowledge and women's equality.

Mary Somerville published her last book, *On Molecular and Microscopic Science*, a two-volume work on the components and architecture of matter, including atoms, molecules, and microscopic structure.

Sophia Schliemann began her career working with her husband, Heinrich Schliemann, in the excavation of the city of Troy, which he discovered in Turkey; she kept many of the records of this work, which sparked interest in both archaeology and prehistory.

Harriet Morrison Irwin obtained a U.S. patent for a hexagonal house, an improvement on current constructions; she was the first American woman to patent an architectural innovation, though she had no formal training.

b. Alice Hamilton (1869–1970), American physician and social reformer, a pioneer in industrial medicine.

b. (Mary) Agnes Meara Chase (1869–1963), American botanist.

b. Helen Dean King (1869–1955), American biologist.

b. Mary Frances Winston (Newson) (1869–1959), American mathematician and educator.

b. Maude Abbott (Elizabeth Seymour, 1869–1940), Canadian cardiologist.

## Arts/Literature

d. Giulia Grisi (1811–1869), Italian soprano, sister of Giuditta Grisi.

b. Zinaida Nikolayevna Hippius (1869–1945), Russian writer.

## 1870

### Politics/Law/War

Lucy Stone and her husband, Henry Blackwell, founded the suffragist weekly *Woman's Journal* (1870–1917), the journal of the American Woman Suffrage Association (1870–1890), and then of the National American Woman Suffrage Association (1890–1917).

In Britain, the Married Woman's Property Act of 1870 allowed married women to keep their own earnings.

Maria Deraismes founded the French women's rights organization Association pour le Droit des Femmes.

Lydia Becker became editor of the *Women's Suffrage Journal* (1870–1890).

Millicent Garrett Fawcett published *Political Economy for Beginners*.

Victoria Woodhull announced her candidacy for the U.S. presidency, although no campaign eventuated.

Wyoming was the first state to routinely have sexually integrated grand juries.

Marilla Ricker claimed the right to vote, arguing that the 14th Amendment's reference to "elector" should include women; she was denied the vote in 1870 but apparently voted in 1871.

b. Rosa Luxemburg (1870–1919), Polish-German socialist and Communist leader and theoretician.

b. Dorothy Dix (Elizabeth Meriwether Gilmer, 1870–1951), American journalist.

b. Louise Bennett (1870–1956), Irish feminist, writer, suffragist, and trade unionist.

### RELIGION/EDUCATION/EVERYDAY LIFE

Hunter College of the City University of New York opened, originally as a teacher-training institution (Female Normal and High School), the first American college to provide free education for women. It would be the largest women's college in the world, until becoming coeducational in 1964.

Evanston College for Ladies was founded as a Methodist women's college, led by Frances E. Willard (1870–1873), until it was merged into Northwestern University.

Augusta Lewis (later Troup) was elected corresponding secretary of the International Typographical Union, becoming the first female executive of a national American labor union; she had earlier founded and led the Women's Typographical Union (1868), until the ITU began admitting women.

Mary Carpenter founded the National India Association in Britain to support women's education and penal reform in India, topics on which she spoke widely during four visits to the subcontinent (1866–1876).

Greek women published the women's weekly *Evridice* (1870–1873).

Mary Ewing Outerbridge helped popularize lawn tennis in the United States (1870s).

The Marcel wave became a popular women's hairstyle after French hairdresser Marcel Grateau developed the curling iron.

The typewriter, invented in 1829, began to be widely used in business and government offices, bringing women into clerical work previously dominated by men (1870s).

---

# How Did You Come to Invent Machines?

It is only following nature. As a child, I never cared for things that girls usually do; dolls never possessed any charms for me. I couldn't see the sense of coddling bits of porcelain with senseless faces; the only things I wanted were a jack-knife, a gimlet [a hole-boring tool], and pieces of wood. My friends were horrified. I was called a tomboy; but that made little impression on me. I sighed sometimes, because I was not like other girls; but wisely concluded that I couldn't help it, and sought further consolation from my tools. I was always making things for my brothers: did they want anything in the line of playthings, they always said, "Mattie will make them for us." I was famous for my kites; and my sleds were the envy and admiration of all the boys in town. I'm not surprised at what I've done. I'm only sorry I couldn't have had as good a chance as a boy, and have been put to my trade regularly.

— Margaret (Mattie) Knight, from "A Lady in a Machine-Shop," in the *Woman's Journal* (1872), on being asked how a woman untrained in mechanics could invent machines

Frances Victor published *The River of the West*, on Oregon mountain pioneer Joe Meek.

b. Maria Montessori (1870–1952), Italian educator and physician.

b. Helena Rubinstein (ca. 1870–1965), Polish-American cosmetics entrepreneur.

b. Octavie Coudreau (ca. 1870–ca. 1910), French explorer.

b. Yasui Tetsu (1870–1945), Japanese educator.

d. Emma Willard (1787–1870), American educator, founder of the Troy Female Seminary (1821), later the Emma Willard School, and a textbook author.

d. Edmonia Highgate (1844–1870), African-American teacher and lecturer, who after the Civil War traveled widely to raise funds for the Freedman's Association and the American Missionary Association, which were educating freed slaves in the South.

d. Sophia Smith (1796–1870), American philanthropist under whose will Smith College for women was founded, opening in 1875.

### SCIENCE/TECHNOLOGY/MEDICINE

Ellen Swallow (later Richards) began her studies at the Massachusetts Institute of Technology, as a special student in chemistry; she noted that she was, "so far as I know, the first woman to be accepted at any 'scientific school'."

Margaret (Mattie) Knight received her first patent, for her invention of a device attached to a paper-feeding machine, allowing it to fold square-bottomed bags; with refinements, it is still used today.

Mary Harris Thompson was co-founder of the Women's Hospital Medical College in Chicago, becoming professor of clinical obstetrics and diseases of women and performing major surgery. She had received her medical degree from Chicago Medical College, the only woman to do so, but the school thereafter refused to admit other women.

Unable to obtain a medical degree in England because of her sex, Elizabeth Garrett Anderson obtained her M.D. from the University of Paris, when that became possible in France.

Clara Barton worked with the International Committe of the Red Cross to set up hospitals during the Franco-Prussian War (1870–1871).

Mary Carpenter (later Hooper) obtained a U.S. patent for a sewing machine with a self-threading, self-setting needle, one of her many industrial inventions.

University of Michigan became America's first state university to accept women as students in its medical school.

Susan McKinney Steward received her medical degree from the New York Medical College and Hospital for Women, becoming one of the earliest African-American female doctors (after Rebecca Lee); in her honor, black female women doctors a century later would name their medical society after her.

Mary Somerville was awarded the Victoria Gold Medal by the Royal Geographical Society.

b. Ida (Sophia) Scudder (1870–1960), American medical missionary.

### ARTS/LITERATURE

Louisa May Alcott published the novel *An Old-Fashioned Girl*.

Mrs. Henry Wood published the novel *East Lynne*.

Pauline Viardot premiered Johannes Brahms's *Alto Rhapsody*.

Helen Hunt Jackson published *Verses by H. H.*

b. Olga Knipper (-Chekhova) (1870–1959), Russian actress.

b. Henrietta Robertson Richardson (Henry Handel Richardson, 1870–1946), Australian novelist.

b. Alice Hegan Rice (1870–1942), American author.

b. Jessie Tarbox Beals (1870–1942), American photographer.

b. Marie Lloyd (1870–1922), British music-hall star.

b. Mary Johnston (1870–1936), American author.

## 1871

### POLITICS/LAW/WAR

Victoria Woodhull was the first suffragist to testify before the House Judiciary Committee, taking the position that women's suffrage was already a matter of constitutional right, a position that would be decisively rejected by the U.S. Supreme Court in *Minor v. Happersett* (1874). She also published *Origin, Tendencies and Principles of Government*, a collection of controversial articles written for the *New York Herald* (1870) advocating a utopian socialist society she called Pantarchy, with common property, free love, and no marriage.

Myra Bradwell won her battle for admission to the Illinois bar when the state legislature outlawed sex discrimination in career or employment. Founder-editor of the *Chicago Legal News*, she had earlier been denied admission to the Illinois bar (1870) and lost her U.S. Supreme Court appeal.

Julia Ward Howe became president of the American branch of the Women's International Peace Association.

During the short-lived Paris Commune, socialist Elizabeth Dmitrieva founded and led the Women's Union for the Defense of Paris.

Matilde Bajer and her husband, Fredrik Bajer, founded the Danish Women's Association.

Abigail Duniway founded the women's rights weekly *New Northwest*.

Paulina Davis published *A History of the National Woman's Rights Movement*.

Phoebe Couzins was the first American woman to receive a law degree, from Washington University in St. Louis.

b. Chrystal Macmillan (1871–1937), Scottish feminist, suffragist, women's rights activist, lawyer, and pacifist.

d. Cristina Trivulzio (1808–1871), Italian writer and democratic revolutionary, active in the revolutions of the late 1840s.

### RELIGION/EDUCATION/EVERYDAY LIFE

Merton Hall was founded for female students, offering a series of lectures leading to newly established examinations for women at Cambridge University; starting with five students, and with Anne Clough as its first head (1871–1891), it would become Newnham Hall (1875) and then Newnham College (1880).

The first state girls' high school in the Southern Hemishere, Otago Girls' High School, opened in New Zealand, the model for many more founded within a few years; it was largely sparked by Learmonth White Dalrymple, who also that year organized a petition that women be admitted into the projected new University of New Zealand.

---

# On Social Freedom

. . . To love is a right *higher* than Constitution or laws. It is a right which Constitutions and laws can *neither give* nor take, and with which they have nothing whatever to do . . .

The proper sphere of government in regard to the relations of the sexes, is to enact such laws as in the present conditions of society are necessary to *protect each* individual in the *free* exercise of his or her *right* to love, and also to protect each individual from the forced interference of *every other* person, that would compel him or her to submit to *any* action which is against their *wish* and *will*. . . . It is therefore a strictly legitimate conclusion that where there is *no* love as a basis of marriage there should be *no* marriage. . . I repeat a frequent reply. . . "Yes, I am a Free Lover. I have an *inalienable, constitutional*, and *natural* right to love whom I may, to love as *long* or as *short* a period as I can; to *change* that love *every day* if I please, and with *that* right neither *you* nor any *law* you can frame have *any* right to interfere. . ."

— Victoria Woodhull (1871)

---

Victoria Woodhull gave her famous and controversial address, "Principles of Social Freedom," in New York City; her radical views, notably her support of "free love," caused splits in the women's rights movement.

Julie-Victoire Daubie passed the *licence*, an advanced examination previously taken only by men; that year she also published *L'émancipation de la femme*.

British mountaineer Lucy Walker became the first woman to climb the Matterhorn.

Celia C. Burleigh became the first woman to be ordained a minister in the Unitarian church, serving in Brooklyn, Connecticut.

Mary Andrews Ayres became the first woman to direct the American Association of Advertising Agencies.

Catharine Beecher published *Woman Suffrage and Woman's Profession*, outlining her antisuffragist views.

Helena Blavatsky published *Isis Unveiled*.

b. Annie Carroll (1871–1961), American children's librarian and writer.

b. Francesca French (1871–1960), British missionary and traveler.

b. Lottie (Charlotte) Dod (1871–1960), British tennis player.

d. Henriette d'Angeville (1795–1871), French mountaineer, the first woman to organize her own climb of Mont Blanc (1838).

### SCIENCE/TECHNOLOGY/MEDICINE

Mary Putnam (later Jacobi) received her medical degree from Paris's École de Médécin. She had been admitted only by special permission, after two years of failed applications, even though she already held degrees from the Woman's Medical College of Pennsylvania (1864) and the New York School of Pharmacy (1863). Returning to America, she became a professor at the Women's Medical College of the New York Infirmary, remaining there for 25 years, while also working in private practice and doing volunteer work in the slums.

Women's Education Association of Boston ran a seaside biological laboratory at Annisquam, Massachusetts (1871–1886), the precursor of the Woods Hole Laboratory (1888).

b. Florence Rena Sabin (1871–1953), American anatomist and histologist.

b. Harriet Boyd Hawes (1871–1945), American archaeologist.

b. Margaret Floy Washburn (1871–1939), American psychologist.

b. Anne Sewell Young (1871–1961), American astronomer.

b. Lilian Murray (Lindsay) (1871–1959), British dentist.

### ARTS/LITERATURE

George Eliot (Marian Evans) created Dorothea Brooke in the novel *Middlemarch: A Study of Provincial Life* (1871–1872).

Louisa May Alcott published the novel *Little Men*.

Vinnie Ream completed her statue of Abraham Lincoln for the Capitol Rotunda; he had sat for her (1864–1865).

*Coo-ee: Tales of Australian Life by Australian Ladies*, the first Australian female writers' anthology, was published, edited by Harriette Anne Martin.

Emma Lazarus published *Admetus and Other Poems*.

b. Marie Dressler (1871–1934), Canadian vaudeville singer and film actress.

b. Emily Carr (1871–1945), Canadian painter.

b. Grazia Deledda (1871–1936), Italian novelist.

b. Luisa Tetrazzini (1871–1940), Italian soprano.

d. Alice Cary (1820–1871), American author, who created notable portrayals of the life of American frontier women.

## 1872

### POLITICS/LAW/WAR

Many women's organizations, generally described as the "social purity" movement, supported passage of the antipornography Comstock Law ("An Act for the Suppression of Trade in, and Circulation of, Obscene Literature and Articles of Immoral Use"), named after its chief proponent, Anthony Comstock. Comstock himself became a government-sanctioned witch-hunter in the guise of a special postal inspector. Some women's groups, including the Women's Christian Temperance Union, campaigned successfully for the passage of state ("Little Comstock") antipornography laws through the rest of the 19th and into the 20th century.

In Italy, Aurelia Cimino Folliero De Luna established the publication *La Cornelia* (1872–1880), calling for reform in family law and education and women's access to professions.

Susan B. Anthony and her colleagues dropped the highly visible and controversial Victoria Woodhull from the leadership of the National Woman Suffrage Association.

Matilde Bajer and her husband, Fredrik Bajer, founded a women's vocational training institute in Copenhagen.

b. Alexandra Mikhaylovna Kollontai (1872–1952), Russian Bolshevik, feminist, writer, politician, and diplomat.

b. Emily Wilding Davison (1872–1913), militant British feminist.

b. Mary Anderson (1872–1964), American trade unionist and government official.

b. Mary Sheepshanks (1872–1958), British social worker, educator, suffragist, and pacifist.

### RELIGION/EDUCATION/EVERYDAY LIFE

The Women's Tea Company, founded by American inventor Ellen Demorest and feminist-philanthropist Susan King, sent a ship, *Madame Demorest*, with an all-woman crew on a tea-importing mission. Demorest commented: "I do not claim that all women, or a large portion of them, should enter into independent business relations with the world, but I do claim that all women should cultivate and respect in themselves an ability to make money."

Kalliopi Kehajia founded the Society for Promoting Women's Education, offering Greek women educational classes and skills training.

Swiss women waged a successful campaign to gain admission to Switzerland's Geneva University.

Women's educational opportunities improved in St. Petersburg, as some general education programs were established for women.

b. Eleanor Rathbone (1872–1946), British reformer, feminist, and politician.

### SCIENCE/TECHNOLOGY/MEDICINE

Mary Putnam Jacobi founded the Association for the Advancement of the Medical Education of Women, seeking full entry for women in established medical schools; like Elizabeth and Emily Blackwell, she deplored the "separate but equal" policy that had necessitated the founding of the Women's Medical College, which closed when Cornell University offered admittance to women (1899).

Emily Warren Roebling is regarded as the first American woman to be a field engineer, taking over day-to-day supervision of the construction of the Brooklyn Bridge (1872–1883) after her husband, Washington Augustus Roebling, who had trained her in mathematics and engineering, became largely deaf, blind, mute, and paralyzed.

Marie E. Zakrzewska and Susan Dimock founded the first permanent American nursing school at the New England Hospital for Women and Children.

Jane Wells, of Chicago, patented the still widely used "baby jumper" that "can be operated by an infant from the time it can sit erect until it walks, giving it the ability to dance, swing, and turn itself in any direction, affording it healthy and safe amusement." She and her husband founded a company to make and sell the jumpers.

b. Mary Coffin Ware Dennett (1872–1947), American suffragist, pacifist, and advocate of birth control and sex education.

b. Mary Engle Pennington (1872–1952), American chemist.

d. Mary Greig Fairfax Somerville (1780–1872), Scottish writer on science, largely self-taught, who had wide-ranging interests in astronomy, mathematics, physics, chemistry, and geography, and a notable power to convey scientific principles to others; one of Oxford University's first two women's colleges was named for her, and hers was the first name on the women's suffrage petition presented to Britain's Parliament by John Stuart Mill (1866).

d. Ann Preston (1813–1872), American physician and educator who founded Woman's Hospital in Philadelphia (1861) and was the first woman to be dean of a medical college, at the Female Medical College in Philadelphia (1866); she had been in its first graduating class (1851).

### ARTS/LITERATURE

Christina Rossetti published *Sing-Song: A Nursery Rhyme Book.*

Edmonia Lewis sculpted *Old Arrow Maker and His Daughter.*

Harriet Beecher Stowe published the novel *My Wife and I.*

Marius Petipa's ballet *La Camargo,* a tribute to Marie Camargo, opened in St. Petersburg.

Mrs. Henry Wood published the novel *Within the Maze.*

b. Maude Adams (1872–1953), American actress.

b. Dorothy Richardson (1873–1957), British novelist.

b. Irene Vanbrugh (1872–1949), British actress.

b. Jessie Bonstelle (1872–1932), American actress and theater manager.

b. Clara Ellen Butt (1872–1936), British contralto.

d. Louisa Atkinson (1834–1872), Australian novelist and naturalist, the first Australian-born woman novelist.

## 1873

### POLITICS/LAW/WAR

An amendment to the 1872 Comstock Law added birth-control information to the "obscene" materials that could not legally be circulated by mail; "social purity" and "antipornography" laws were then used by witch-hunters to attack the rights of the women allegedly being protected against the spread of pornography. That line of development was noted by civil libertarians opposing feminist antipornographers and allied witch-hunters a century later.

Association for the Advancement of Women, a moderate feminist group, was founded by journalist Mary Rice Livermore, its first president, and astronomer Maria Mitchell, a later president.

Russian socialist Vera Zasulich assassinated St. Petersburg police general Trepov, was acquitted, and fled abroad.

Oregon Equal Suffrage Association was founded.

b. Elena Dmitrievna Stasova (1873–1966), Russian Bolshevik leader.

b. Gertrude Baumer (1873–1954), German politician, teacher, nationalist, socialist, and feminist.

d. Sarah Moore Grimké (1792–1873), American abolitionist and feminist, coauthor with her sister Angelina Grimké of the notable *Letters on the Equality of the Sexes and the Condition of Women* (1838); both were major figures in the antislavery and women's rights movements.

### RELIGION/EDUCATION/EVERYDAY LIFE

Emily Davies's Benslow House women's college moved to Cambridge, with Davies as its mistress.

Having studied Friedrich Froebel's schools in Europe, Susan Blow opened the first public kindergarten in America, in St. Louis.

Women's Crusade (1873–1874) against the drinking of alcoholic beverages brought women to the forefront of the temperance movement, and helped spur the formation of the Women's Christian Temperance Union.

Fanny Baker Ames and her husband, Charles G. Ames, founded the Relief Society of Germantown, Pennsylvania, establishing the pattern of volunteer social workers.

*Sex in Education; or, a Fair Chance for the Girls*, by Edwin H. Clarke, a former professor of medicine at Harvard University, warned that women scholars who studied "in a boy's way" were at risk of sterility, insanity, death, and atrophy of the uterus and ovaries.

Mormon women began publishing the journal *Woman's Exponent*.

Elizabeth Palmer Peabody published *Kindergarten Messenger* (1873–1875).

b. Motoko Hani (1873–1957), Japanese reporter and educator.

b. Emily Post (1873–1960), American writer on etiquette.

b. Margaret Grace Bondfield (1873–1953), British trade unionist, socialist, and politician.

b. Teresa of Lisieux (Thérèse Martin, 1873–1897), French nun and saint.

d. John Stuart Mill (1806–1873), British economist, philosopher, writer, and women's rights activist, author of the landmark *The Subjection of Women* (1869), and an early supporter of women's suffrage.

### SCIENCE/TECHNOLOGY/MEDICINE

Physician Elizabeth Garrett Anderson became the first female member of the British Medical Association (1873–1892).

Amanda Theodosia Jones obtained a U.S. patent for the first of her many inventions in canning, a vacuum process that would be the basis of the Woman's Canning and Preserving Company.

Helen Augusta Blanchard obtained the first of her many U.S. patents for improvements in the sewing machine, this one an overseaming machine to both sew and trim, ancestor of the later zigzag models.

Anna Nichols became the first women to be a patent examiner for the U.S. government.

Hannah Mountain obtained a U.S. patent for a mattress/life preserver.

b. Josephine (Sara) Baker (1873–1945), American physician and public-health worker.

### ARTS/LITERATURE

Louisa May Alcott published the autobiographical novel *Work: A Story of Experience*.

Louise Colet published the poetry collection *Les dévotés du grand mond*.

b. Willa Cather (1873–1947), American writer.

b. Colette (Sidonie Gabrielle Claudine Colette, 1873–1954), French writer.

b. Lilian Braithwaite (1873–1948), British actress.

d. Laura Keene (1820–1873), British-American actress and one of the first women to become a theater manager in the United States.

## 1874

### POLITICS/LAW/WAR

In the landmark case of *Minor v. Happersett*, the U.S. Supreme Court ruled that the equal protection clause of the 14th Amendment did not extend to women, ruling against Virginia Minor of the National Woman Suffrage Association in a case argued by her lawyer husband, Francis Minor. The ruling, a binding precedent throughout the country, decisively ended a mass legal challenge by suffragists, including Susan B. Anthony, who beginning in 1872 had voted or had sued voting registrars who denied them the vote.

Helen Blackburn became secretary of Britain's National Society for Women's Suffrage (1874–1895).

b. Inesse Steffane Armand (1874–1920), Russian revolutionary, a Bolshevik activist and Marxist feminist.

### RELIGION/EDUCATION/EVERYDAY LIFE

Emily Davies's women's college at Cambridge University became Girton College, with help from Barbara Leigh-Smith Bodichon; Davies remained a central figure at the college for three decades.

Women's Christian Temperance Union (WCTU) was founded in Cleveland, Ohio, growing directly out of the Women's Crusade (1873–1874) against alcohol, with Annie Wittenmyer as its first president (1874–1879). The first major nationwide women's organization—drawing from both North and South—after the Civil War, the WCTU would later become a major women's suffrage and women's rights organization as well, after suffrage was won narrowing again to its temperance focus. It also campaigned against smoking and narcotic drugs.

Writing in *Labour News*, Emma Paterson proposed a general union of female workers, and then founded the Women's Protective and Provident League (later Women's Trade Union League), organizing British women in different trades, among them bookbinding, dressmaking, millinery, and upholstery.

British social reformer Annie Besant was elected vice-president of the National Secular Society after publicly declaring her atheism.

Boston Woman's Club, under Aba Woolson, began a more gradual approach to modifying women's clothing, after the more radical "reform dress" (ca. 1849) had proven socially unacceptable.

Women were once again admitted to Italy's universities; they would later also be admitted to previously all-male high schools and teacher-training colleges (1880s).

Catharine Beecher published *Educational Reminiscences*.

Frances Power Cobbe published *Doomed to be Saved*.

b. (Sarah) Margery Fry (1874–1958), British prison reformer, human rights advocate, and death-penalty opponent.

b. Madeleine (Anne) Pelletier (1874–1939), French physician and feminist.

d. Julie-Victoire Daubie (1824–1874), French feminist and educational pioneer, almost totally self-educated, who demanded and finally gained the right to take the *baccalaureat* (1860).

d. Zilpah P. Grant (1794–1874), American educator who built influential early girls' schools.

## SCIENCE/TECHNOLOGY/MEDICINE

Sonya Kovalevsky received her doctorate in absentia from the University of Göttingen—believed to be the first mathematics Ph.D. granted to a woman—on the basis of three mathematical treatises, on partial differential equations, Abelian integrals, and the rings of Saturn. Unable to attend university lectures at the University of Berlin because of her sex, she had been tutored privately in mathematics by noted professor Karl Weierstrass (1871–1875), but on graduation could find no teaching position at any European university.

Sophia Jex-Blake founded the London School of Medicine for Women, but soon clashed with Elizabeth Garrett Anderson, who was named dean.

b. Christine Murrell (1874–1933), British physician.

b. Dorothy Reed Mendenhall (1874–1964), American physician.

b. Carlotta Maury (1874–1938), American geologist.

## ARTS/LITERATURE

Marie Geistinger created the role of Rosalinda in Johann Strauss's opera *Die Fledermaus*.

Rebecca Harding Davis published the novel *John Andross*.

Eliza Orzeszkowa published the novel *Eli Makower*.

Elizabeth Butler showed her painting *Calling the Role after an Engagement, Crimea*.

b. Amy Lowell (1874–1925), American poet.

b. Ellen Glasgow (1874–1945), American writer.

b. Gertrude Stein (1874–1946), American writer.

b. L. M. (Lucy Maud) Montgomery (1874–1942), Canadian writer.

b. Marguerite (Marie Charlotte) Long (1874–1966), French pianist.

b. Mary Garden (1874–1967), Scottish-American soprano.

b. Romaine Goddard Brooks (1874–1970), American artist.

b. Lilian Mary Baylis (1874–1937), British theater manager.

b. Theresa Serber Malkiel (1874–1949), American writer, socialist, and feminist.

## 1875

### POLITICS/LAW/WAR

Austrian feminist Marianne Hainisch published *Die Brötfrage der Frau*, advocating better educational and work opportunities for women.

b. Hilda Martindale (1875–1952), British feminist, civil servant, and women's rights advocate.

b. Franciska Plamnikova (1875–1942), Czech feminist, women's rights leader, and politician.

b. Jessie Wallace Hughan (1875–1955), American pacifist, socialist, and feminist.

b. Kate Barnard (1875–1930), American social reformer, teacher, labor organizer, and politician.

### RELIGION/EDUCATION/EVERYDAY LIFE

Smith College opened in Northampton, Massachusetts, aiming to provide women with an education comparable to that of men, while allowing them to maintain "traditional femininity"; women had to pass the same entrance exam as that used at Harvard University. Funded by the will of Sophia Smith, it would—at its century mark—be the largest independent women's college in the world.

Wellesley College was founded to give women an education equal to that of men; founder Henry F. Durant, himself Harvard-educated and a trustee of Mount Holyoke College, from the start stressed staffing Wellesley with a female faculty, unlike other women's colleges.

Emma Paterson was the first woman to serve as a delegate to Britain's Trades Union Congress, fighting for female factory inspectors but opposing protective legislation, seeking instead equality of employment.

Annie Besant published *The Fruits of Philosophy*, proposing that population growth should be checked. She also coedited the *National Reformer* with Charles Bradlaugh. Prosecuted for her radical reviews, Besant lost custody of her daughter, though she eventually won her case on appeal.

Calamity Jane joined General George Crook's expedition against the Sioux but was forced to return when it was learned she was a woman. Dressed as a man, she had earned her living as a mule skinner and scout from the early 1870s.

Helena Blavatsky founded the Theosophical Society in the United States, claiming links with ancient occult traditions; her "miracles" (many later shown to be fraudulent) won her many followers.

Mary Baker (later Eddy) published *Science and Health*, propounding her ideas of Christian Science.

Josephine Shaw Lowell became the first woman to serve on New York's State Board of Charities.

Kalliopi Kehajia founded the Zappeion School for girls in Constantinople (now Istanbul), serving as head for 15 years.

Isabel Burton published *The Inner Life of Syria*.

b. Mary McLeod Bethune (1875–1955), African-American educator, women's leader, and presidential advisor.

b. Evelyn Underhill (1875–1941), British religious writer and lecturer.

b. Margaret Scott (1875–?), British golfer.

b. Katharine Dexter McCormick (1875–1967), American philanthropist.

d. Jane Griffin Franklin (Lady Franklin, 1795–1875), British reformer and traveler who explored New Zealand, Australia, and Tasmania, and later more widely. She was the first woman to climb Mount Wellington and to travel overland from Melbourne to Sydney.

### SCIENCE/TECHNOLOGY/MEDICINE

Ellen Swallow Richards convinced the Massachusetts Institute of Technology to establish a Woman's Laboratory, to teach chemical analysis, industrial chemistry, mineralogy, and biology; it opened in 1876. Within a few years, women were accepted as regular students at MIT, and the laboratory, no longer needed, would be closed (1883); but the life science courses, up until then regarded as not appropriate for teaching in scientific schools, would form the basis of MIT's biology department.

Physician Emeline Horton Cleveland is believed to be the first woman to perform an ovariotomy, to remove an ovarian tumor, becoming a specialist in the surgical procedure.

Antoinette Brown Blackwell published *The Sexes Throughout Nature*.

Isabella Bird (later Bishop) published *The Hawaiian Archipelago*, based on a visit made on her return from Australia, New Zealand, and the Pacific.

b. Harriet Quimby (1875–1912), American pilot.

b. Angeliki Panajiotatou (1875–1954), Greek microbiologist.

b. June Etta Downey (1875–1932), American psychologist.

d. Harriot Kezia Hunt (1805–1875), American physician who focused on medical problems of women, especially on "physical maladies growing out of concealed sorrows."

### ARTS/LITERATURE

Vinnie Ream began work on her statue of Admiral David G. Farragut, for which she had won a $20,000 commission, the first U.S. government commission awarded a female artist.

Celestine Galli-Marié created the title role in Georges Bizet's opera *Carmen*.

Female art students won equal treatment with the landmark opening of New York's Art Students League.

Louisa May Alcott published the novel *Eight Cousins*.

Elizabeth Butler published *An Autobiography*.

Helen Mathers published the novel *Comin' thro the Rye*.

Alice Meynell published the poetry collection *Preludes*.

b. Alice Guy-Blaché (1875–1968), French filmmaker.

b. Carlotta Zambelli (1875–1968), Italian ballerina.

b. Mistinguett (Jean-Marie Bourgeois, 1875–1956), French singer and comedian.

## 1876

### POLITICS/LAW/WAR

Elizabeth Cady Stanton and Matilda Gage wrote their Declaration of the Rights of Women, distributed at the Philadelphia Centennial Exposition celebrating the anniversary of the Declaration of Independence, saying, "We ask justice, we ask equality, we ask that all the civil and political rights that belong to citizens of the United States, be guaranteed to us and our daughters forever."

Britain's Queen Victoria was given the title Empress of India.

General German Women's Association ran a petition campaign (1876–1888) seeking reform of marriage laws that discriminated against women.

Emily Dilke became active in the Women's Protective and Provident League (later Women's Trade Union League).

b. (Agnes) Maude Royden (1876–1956), British preacher, feminist, suffragist, editor, and pacifist.

b. Gertrude Simmons Bonnin (Zitkala Sa; Redbird, 1876–1938), Sioux (Dakota) Indian rights leader and writer.

b. Kate Richards O'Hare (1876–1948), American socialist, social reformer, writer, and lecturer.

b. Konkordiya Samoilova (1876–1921), Russian socialist and Communist activist and editor.

b. Mata Hari (Margaretha Geertruida Zelle, 1876–1917), Dutch dancer and reputed German spy.

d. Paulina Kellogg Wright Davis (1813–1876), American feminist journalist, a founder of the New England Woman Suffrage Association (1868) and contributor to the *Revolution*.

### RELIGION/EDUCATION/EVERYDAY LIFE

Mary Baker (Eddy, from 1877) founded the Christian Science Association, which would grow into the Christian Science movement, formally founded in 1879 with the establishment of the First Church of Christ Scientist.

At the Philadelphia Centennial Exposition, a Women's Pavilion was planned, funded by innumerable benefits and "Martha Washington tea parties" and run entirely by women, sparked by Elizabeth Duane Gillespie (Benjamin Franklin's granddaughter).

Emma Paterson began editing the *Women's Union Journal*, a British monthly covering suffrage, education, women's rights, and dress reform. Inspired by Emily Faithful, she learned printing and founded the Women's Printing Society.

Inspired by foreign trade school exhibits at Philadelphia's 1876 Centennial Exposition, Fannie Jackson Coppin began developing industrial education courses at the Quaker-sponsored Institute for Colored Youth (later Cheyney State College), where she was principal (from 1869); courses included dressmaking and millinery (for girls); bricklaying, plastering, carpentry, shoemaking, printing, and tailoring (for boys); and cooking, typing, and stenography (for girls and boys). Her new courses were widely adopted in the United States.

Juliet Corson opened the New York Cooking School, perhaps the first in the United States, the following year publishing her *Cooking Manual*.

b. Edith Abbott (1876–1957), American labor economist, educator, writer, editor, feminist, and social reformer.

b. Mary Ritter Beard (1876–1958), American historian and political economist.

b. Edith Pye (1876–1965), British Quaker nurse, relief worker, and pacifist.

b. Eglantyne Jebb (1876–1928), British philanthropist.

b. Elinore Pruitt Rupert Steward (1876–1933), American homesteader.

## SCIENCE/TECHNOLOGY/MEDICINE

Physician Mary Putnam Jacobi won Harvard University's Boyleston Prize for *The Question of Rest for Women during Menstruation*; it was one of numerous works on women's ailments and their relationship to boredom and celibacy.

Lydia Pinkham, who had begun selling her home herbal remedy locally after her husband lost his money in an 1873 financial crash, patented the compound and began to distribute more widely her "Lydia E. Pinkham's Vegetable Compound," promoting it as a "cure for female complaints." With Pinkham's picture on the label (from 1879), it became widely popular and was sold for a century. She also founded an advice department to answer the many letters she received, a practice that continued long after her death.

Elizabeth Bragg was the first woman to graduate from an American university in engineering, with her civil engineering degree from the University of California at Berkeley.

Physician Sarah Stevenson was the first woman to become a member of the American Medical Association, as a delegate from the Illinois State Medical Society.

Under Britain's Russell Gurney Enabling Act, female medical students were, for the first time, allowed to take their degree examinations before the established medical bodies.

b. Edith Marion Patch (1876–1954), American entomologist.

## ARTS/LITERATURE

George Eliot (Marian Evans) published her final novel, *Daniel Deronda*.

Helen Hunt Jackson published the novel *Mercy Philbrick's Choice*, often described as a fictional treatment of the life of her friend Emily Dickinson.

Louisa May Alcott published the novel *Rose in Bloom* and the essay collection *Silver Pitchers and Independence*.

Clorinda Matto de Turner founded the women's periodical *El Recreo*.

Frances Ritter published the article "Woman as a Musician: An Art-Historical Study," in the *Woman's Journal*.

Mrs. Henry Wood published the novel *Edina*.

b. Anna Vaughn Hyatt (1876–1973), American sculptor.

b. Mary Roberts Rinehart (1876–1958), American writer.

b. Sibilla Aleramo (Rina Pierangeli Faccio, 1876–1960), Italian writer.

d. George Sand (Amandine Lucile Aurore Dupin, 1804–1876), French writer.

d. Harriet Martineau (1802–1876), British rationalist and feminist, a writer and political economist who became a major figure in the emerging women's movement of her time.

d. Marie de Flavigny d'Agoult (1805–1876), French writer who wrote as Daniel Stern.

d. Charlotte Saunders Cushman (1816–1876), American actress.

d. Louise Colet (1810–1876), French poet, novelist, and women's rights advocate.

## 1877

### POLITICS/LAW/WAR

Eudora Clark Atkinson became superintendent of the first state reformatory for women, in Sherborn (later Framingham), Massachusetts.

b. Hannah Sheehy-Skeffington (1877–1946), Irish feminist and independence movement activist.

b. Lizzie (Elizabeth) Wallace Ahern (1877–1969), Australian feminist, socialist, and pacifist.

b. Rosika Schwimmer (1877–1948), Hungarian journalist, union activist, feminist, pacifist, and diplomat.

b. Teresa Billington-Grieg (1877–1964), English teacher, feminist, and suffragist.

b. Martha De Kerchove Bol Poel (1877–1956), Belgian feminist.

b. Annette Abbott Adams (1877–1956), American lawyer, judge, and federal official.

### RELIGION/EDUCATION/EVERYDAY LIFE

Anthropologist Lewis Henry Morgan published *Ancient Society*, in which he posited the existence of early matriarchies, especially among the Iroquois.

Hannah Solomon and her sister Henriette were the first Jewish women admitted to the prestigious Chicago Women's Club.

Kate Edger became the first woman to graduate from the University of New Zealand, taking her degree in mathematics.

Minerva Saunders is credited with being the first American librarian to end age restrictions on access to books (1877) and to provide a special collection and reading area for children, at the Pawtucket Public Library, in Rhode Island.

Helen Magill (later White) was the first woman to receive a Ph.D. degree in America, from Boston University, with a dissertation on Greek drama.

Annie Besant published *The Gospel of Atheism*.

The YWCA in New York City established the first known typing course for women; newspaper advertisements for women typists were appearing by at least 1875.

Sarah Emery published her most notable work, *Seven Financial Conspiracies Which Have Enslaved the American People*.

b. Mary Cromwell Jarrett (1877–1961), American social worker and educator.

b. Isabelle Eberhardt (1877–1904), Russian-born traveler and writer.

b. Josephine (Clara) Goldmark (1877–1950), American social reformer.

d. Mary Carpenter (1807–1877), British social reformer especially interested in reform schools for young people.

### SCIENCE/TECHNOLOGY/MEDICINE

Eleanor Ormerod privately printed the pamphlet "Notes for Observations of Injurious Insects," the first of what would be a series of *Annual Reports of Observations of Injurious Insects* (1877–1900), gathering information from various sources.

Sophia Jex-Blake and Edith Pechey (later Pechey-Phipson) became the first women legally allowed to practice medicine in Great Britain, after being accepted by Ireland's Royal College of Physicians.

Agnes Clerke published "Copernicus in Italy," the first of her many literary articles on astronomy, many (like the first) appearing in the prestigious *Edinburgh Review*.

American sculptor Caroline Brooks obtained a U.S. patent for making plaster casts; an intermediate stage, a sculpture in butter, was a hit at the Women's Pavilion at the Philadelphia Centennial (1876).

British nurse Kate Marsden traveled to Bulgaria to nurse Russian soldiers wounded in the Russo-Turkish war, making her first contact with sufferers from leprosy.

d. Louise Büchner (1821–1877), German nurse and women's rights activist, sister of playwright Georg Büchner.

## ARTS/LITERATURE

Harriet Martineau's *Autobiography* was published posthumously.

Anna Sewell published the novel *Black Beauty, The Autobiography of a Horse*.

Frances Hodgson Burnett published the novel *That Lass o' Lowrie's*.

b. Laura Knight (1877–1970), British painter.

b. Louise A. Boyd (1877–1972), American photographer and Arctic explorer.

d. Caroline Elizabeth Sarah Sheridan Norton (1808–1877), British writer, a campaigner for married women's rights, granddaughter of Richard Brinsley Sheridan, and probably the model for George Meredith's *Diana of the Crossways*.

d. Karoline Unger (1803–1877), Austrian contralto, who sang at the premieres of Beethoven's *Ninth Symphony* and *Missa Solemnis* (both 1824), later a notable figure in Italian opera, creating several major roles.

## 1878

### POLITICS/LAW/WAR

The long fight for the Woman Suffrage Amendment to the U.S. Constitution began, with its first formal introduction into Congress; it became known as the Anthony Amendment, after Susan B. Anthony, leader of the fight.

British Matrimonial Causes Act provided that some battered wives might legally gain separation and maintenance from their husbands.

Hubertine Auclert founded the French women's rights group Droit de la Femme, and published *Le Droit politique des femmes*.

b. Angelika Balabanoff (1878–1965), European socialist and writer, active in Russia and Italy.

b. Kathleen D'Olier Courtney (1878–1974), British feminist, suffragist, and pacifist.

### RELIGION/EDUCATION/EVERYDAY LIFE

Emma M. Nutt became the first woman to work as a telephone operator in America, for the Telephone Dispatch Company in Boston (1878–1911).

The *Monthly Register*, the first nationwide American journal of social work, was edited by Mary Richmond; it was the journal of the Society for Organizing Relief and Repressing Mendicancy (1878–1880).

The Presbyterian church's Women's Executive Committee of Home Missions was formed to work with the Board of Home Missions, with F. E. H. Haines as president; this was the first American denominational women's board.

Anne Blunt published *The Bedouin Tribes of the Euphrates*, based on a desert journey with her husband, Wilfred Scawen Blunt.

Colombian writer Soledad Acosta de Samper founded and edited the feminist journal *La mujer* (1878–1881).

Aline Valette became secretary of the new Teachers' Union in Paris.

Helene Lange, a Berlin teacher, published an article urging higher education for girls.

Mary Elizabeth Braddon became editor of the magazine the *Mistletoe Bough* (1878–1892).

b. Grace Abbott (1878–1939), American social worker, feminist, writer, teacher, and social reformer.

b. (Alice) Mildred Cable (1878–1952), British missionary and traveler.

b. Dorothea Douglass (Mrs. Lambert Chambers, 1878–1960), British tennis player.

b. Margaret Gillespie Cousins (1878–1954), Irish educator and feminist.

d. Catharine Esther Beecher (1800–1878), American educational reformer and writer, sister of Harriet Beecher Stowe and Henry Ward Beecher; she expanded women's education, though opposing women's suffrage.

## SCIENCE/TECHNOLOGY/MEDICINE

Sophia Jex-Blake set up practice in Edinburgh, becoming the first female physician in Scotland; she founded a dispensary that became the Edinburgh Hospital for Women and Children (1886).

Sarah Whiting, two years into her long tenure at Wellesley College, opened only the second undergraduate physics laboratory in the United States.

Christine Ladd-Franklin gained special permission to attend some classes at the Johns Hopkins University graduate school, not then open to women; gradually more professors allowed her to attend their classes.

Physician Marie Zakrzewska founded the New England Hospital (Women's) Medical Society, believed to be the world's first medical society formed by a woman, becoming its president.

Physician Elizabeth Blackwell published *Counsel to Parents on the Moral Education of Their Children*.

b. Lillian Evelyn Moller Gilbreth (1878–1972), American industrial engineer.

b. Lise Meitner (1878–1968), Austrian-born physicist.

b. Mary Emily Sinclair (1878–1955), American mathematician and educator.

b. Mary Lee Jobe Akeley (1878–1966), American explorer and photographer.

## ARTS/LITERATURE

Ellen Terry joined Henry Irving's company, forming an enduring partnership that generated many of her major roles (1878–1902).

Mary Cassatt showed her painting *Little Girl in a Blue Armchair*.

Lydia Maria Child published *Aspirations of the World*.

b. Emmy Destinn (1878–1930), Czech soprano.

b. Isadora Duncan (1878–1927), American dancer.

b. Ruth St. Denis (Ruth Dennis, 1878–1968), American dancer and choreographer.

b. Akiko Otori Yosano (1878–1942), Japanese poet.

b. Constance Collier (Laura Constance Hardie, 1878–1955), British actress.

b. Eva Tanguay (1878–1947), American vaudeville singer.

b. Mary Abastenia St. Leger Eberle (1878–1942), American sculptor.

b. Rachel Crothers (1878–1958), American playwright.

d. Anna Claypoole Peale (1791–1878), American painter, largely of portraits in miniature.

# 1879

## POLITICS/LAW/WAR

Belva Lockwood won her fight for the right of female lawyers to practice before America's highest courts, becoming the first female lawyer admitted to practice before the U.S. Supreme Court.

Emmeline Pankhurst and her husband, barrister Richard Pankhurst, became activists working in Manchester, England, for women's suffrage and married women's property rights.

French feminist Hubertine Auclert published *L'égalité sociale et politique*.

Vera Figner joined the People's Will anarchist-terrorist organization, working in Odessa and planning to assassinate the czar.

b. Annie Kenney (1879–1953), British suffragist and trade unionist.

b. Nancy Langhorne Astor (1879–1964), American-born British Conservative politician.

b. Emilie Gourd (1879–1946), Swiss feminist, suffragist, writer, and editor.

b. Ho Hsiang-ning (1879–1972), Chinese revolutionary feminist.

b. Sarojini Chattopadhyaya Naidu (1879–1949), Indian poet and independence movement leader.

d. Angelina Emily Grimké (1805–1879), American abolitionist and feminist, best known as coauthor of the landmark *Letters on the Equality of the Sexes and the Condition of Women* (1838), with her sister and lifelong colleague, Sarah Grimké, both major figures in the antislavery and women's rights movements.

## RELIGION/EDUCATION/EVERYDAY LIFE

Elizabeth Agassiz founded the school for women that would later become Radcliffe College (1894), associated with Harvard University; she had studied Oxford and Cambridge universities for models.

Frances E. Willard became national president of the Women's Christian Temperance Union and the group's best-known leader, remaining president until her death. During her tenure (1879-1898), she expanded the WCTU's activities to include campaigning for women's rights reforms, with the motto "Do Everything." One argument for women's suffrage advanced by the WCTU was that women could then vote for prohibition.

Susette La Flèsche acted as interpreter for Chief Standing Bear on his campaign for land rights for the Poncas, alongside journalist-lecturer Thomas Henry Tibbles, whom she married; the campaign drew many supporters, including Helen Hunt Jackson, and spurred passing of the Dawes Act (1887), granting Native Americans citizenship and land rights.

Annie Oakley defeated Frank Butler in a shooting match; they later married (1880) and became touring partners.

Mary Foot Seymour founded the Union School of Stenography in New York City, the first all-female secretarial school.

As the Sanctified Sisters' separatist tendencies intensified, female members renounced all financial support from male relatives.

Brazil's universities were opened to women.

Isabella Bird (later Bishop) published *A Lady's Life in the Rockies*, including a description of her friend "Rocky Mountain Jim."

Learmonth White Dalrymple published *The Kindergarten*, which helped spread Friedrich Froebel's ideas in New Zealand.

Louisa Twining became secretary of the Association for Promoting Trained Nursing in Workhouse Infirmaries.

b. Mabel Dodge Luhan (1879–1962), American social reformer and salon hostess.

d. Sarah Josepha Buell Hale (1788–1879), American editor and author, the editor of *Godey's Lady's Book* and *American Ladies' Magazine*.

d. Bernadette of Lourdes (Marie Bernarde Soubirous, 1844–1879), French Catholic saint whose vision led to the founding of the chapel and pilgrimage site at Lourdes.

## SCIENCE/TECHNOLOGY/MEDICINE

Aletta Jacobs received her medical degree from the University of Groningen, becoming the Netherlands' first female doctor; she had been among the first women to attend a Dutch university (1874), obtaining permission from the prime minister to do so. After graduation, Jacobs went into private practice with her physician father, running a clinic for the poor and offering courses on hygiene and child care.

Williamina Fleming began her long career working at the Harvard Observatory, brought there by its director, Edward Pickering, in whose home she had been working as a maid after a failed marriage.

Ellen Swallow Richards was elected to the American Institute of Mining and Metallurgical Engineers, the first woman so honored.

Inspired by Edward Pickering of the Harvard Observatory, Sarah Whiting introduced astronomy ("applied physics") courses at Wellesley College, at first with only primitive equipment.

Vilma Hugonnai (later Hugonnai-Wartha) completed the requirements for her medical degree in Zürich, Switzerland, but, because she was a woman, was given only a midwife's certificate.

b. Margaret Louise Higgins Sanger (1879–1966), American public-health nurse and birth-control campaigner.

b. Agnes Robertson Arber (1879–1960), British botanist.

b. Carolyn Conant Van Blarcom (1879–1960), American nurse and midwife.

d. Lydia Folger Fowler (1822–1879), American physician, the second woman and the first American woman to receive a medical degree in the United States (1850); she was especially interested in phrenology and hydropathic medicine.

### ARTS/LITERATURE

Fru Hennings starred in Henrik Ibsen's play *A Doll's House*.

Emilia Pardo Bazán published the novel *Pascual López*.

Fanny Kemble published her autobiographical *Records of Girlhood*.

b. Ethel Barrymore (Edith Blythe, 1879–1959), American actress.

b. Wanda Landowska (1879–1959), Polish harpsichordist.

b. Alla Nazimova (1879–1945), Russian actress.

b. Vanessa Stephen Bell (1879–1961) British artist.

b. Dorothy Canfield (1879–1958), American novelist.

b. Jane Darwell (Patti Woodward, 1879–1967), American actress.

b. Miles (Stella Marian Sarah) Franklin (1879–1954), Australian writer.

d. Julia Margaret Cameron (1815–1879), pioneering British portrait photographer, a major figure in the history of photography.

## 1880

### POLITICS/LAW/WAR

Russian anarchists Elizaveta Kovalskaya and Saltykov Schchedrin co-founded the terrorist Union of Russian Workers of the South, headquartered in Kiev. They were captured (1881), imprisoned (1881–1903), and then exiled (1903–1917).

French feminists Eugénie Potonie-Pierre, Léonie Rouzade, and Marguerite Tinayre founded the Union des Femmes.

Lydia Becker became secretary of the London Central Committee for Women's Suffrage.

French feminist Jenny d'Hericourt published *La femme affranchie*.

Catherine Spence published *The Laws We Live Under*.

b. Christabel Pankhurst (1880–1958), militant British suffragist.

b. Jeannette Pickering Rankin (1880–1973), American social worker, pacifist, women's suffrage leader, and politician.

b. Edith How-Martyn (1880–1943), British feminist and social reformer.

b. Marie Juhacz (1880–1956), German socialist, feminist, and politician.

b. Rosa Manus (1880–1942), Dutch suffragist and pacifist.

b. Wilhelmina (1880–1962), queen of the Netherlands (r. 1898–1948).

### RELIGION/EDUCATION/EVERYDAY LIFE

Anna Howard Shaw was the first woman to be ordained as a minister in the Methodist Protestant church. She had given her first sermon while in high school (1870), been licensed as a Methodist preacher (1871), and graduated from Boston University's divinity school, supported by the Women's Foreign Missionary Society and "substitute preaching." Earlier in 1880, the Methodist Episcopal church's General Conference had denied applications by Shaw and Anna Oliver for full ordination and also prohibited previously licensed women from preaching. Shaw then left the Methodist Episcopal church for the Methodist Protestants.

Francesca Cabrini founded the Missionary Sisters of the Sacred Heart in Italy.

Newnham College for women became incorporated as part of Cambridge University.

Concepción Arenal published *La cuestión social*.

Isabella Bird Bishop published *Unbeaten Tracks in Japan*.

b. Helen Adams Keller (1880–1968), American campaigner for the blind.

b. Anne O'Hare McCormick (1880–1954), American journalist.

b. Avra Theodoropoulou (1880–1963), Greek musician, writer, and women's rights advocate.

b. Mary Reid MacArthur (1880–1921), Scottish trade unionist.

d. Lucretia Coffin Mott (1793–1880), American Quaker minister, abolitionist, and pioneer women rights leader, co-organizer with Elizabeth Cady Stanton of the landmark Seneca Falls Women's Rights Convention (1848), also an organizer of the Underground Railroad.

d. Susan King (1818–1880), American businesswoman who founded the highly successful Woman's Tea Company.

### SCIENCE/TECHNOLOGY/MEDICINE

Emily Stowe became the first woman licensed to practice medicine in Canada, when she was admitted to the College of Physicians and Surgeons in Ontario; it was the culmination of a 13-year fight, conducted since she had earned her medical degree from the New York College of Medicine for Women (1867).

Charlotte Scott, a Girton College student, won eighth place in the overall mathematics examinations at Cambridge University, but she was passed over, as women were not then given degrees; when at the graduation ceremony (from which she was barred) a man's name was read out as "eighth wrangler," students shouted "Scott of Girton!"

Rosa Smith (later Eigenmann) published the first of her 20 scientific papers; as the first woman to become a member of the San Diego Society of Natural History, she read a paper describing a new species of fish.

Sophia Jex-Blake founded the Edinburgh School of Medicine for Women, running it until Edinburgh Medical School admitted women (1894).

Mary Putnam Jacobi was the first woman elected to membership in the New York Academy of Medicine (1880), later chairing its neurology section.

Rubber gloves were introduced into operating rooms after nurse Caroline Hampton developed a skin allergy to the antiseptic solutions used; when postoperative infections dropped dramatically, such gloves became part of the surgical team's standard uniform.

b. Marie Charlotte Carmichael Stopes (1880–1958), British geologist, botanist, and geographer, best known as a sex education and birth-control advocate.

b. Sylvia May Moore Payne (1880–1974), British psychoanalyst.

### ARTS/LITERATURE

Berthe Morisot showed her painting *Jeune femme au bal*.

b. (Marguerite) Radclyffe Hall (1880–1943), British novelist and poet.

b. Cora Sandel (1880–1974), Norwegian novelist.

---

# WCTU Suffrage Resolution

Believing that it is the part of wisdom to place temperance legislation upon the firm foundation of constitutional law, both State and Nations, that shall prohibit the manufacture and sale of intoxicating beverages; and recognizing the fact that the varying conditions of communities must, in a large measure, determine our line of action, wisdom dictates the do-every-thing-policy constitutional amendment, where the way is open for it; Home Protection, when Home Protection is the strongest rallying cry; equal franchise, where the vote of woman joined to that of men can alone give stability to Temperance legislation.

d. George Eliot (Marian or Mary Ann Evans, 1819–1880), one of the great Victorian novelists, a major figure in the history of English literature, and a leading woman of her age.

d. Lydia Maria Francis Child (1802–1880), American writer and editor, a leading abolitionist.

# 1881

## Politics/Law/War

Helen Blackburn became editor of *The Englishwoman's Review* (1881–1890).

Vera Figner became head of the anarchist-terrorist group People's Will, in Russia, after a series of arrests following an assassination had decimated the organization's leadership.

African-American domestic workers in Atlanta engaged in a failed strike for higher wages.

Anna Maria Mozzoni founded the League to Promote Female Interest, in Milan.

French feminist Hubertine Auclert edited the periodical *La Citoyenne* (1881–1892).

French feminist Maria Deraismes founded the periodical *Le Républicain de Seine et Oise*.

Harriet Hanson Robinson published *Massachusetts in the Woman Suffrage Movement*.

b. Crystal Eastman (1881–1928), American lawyer, feminist, and pacifist.

b. Marion Phillips (1881–1932), British feminist, socialist, and politician.

d. Sofya Lvovna Perovskaya (1853–1881), Russian anarchist and terrorist, a key figure in the assassination of Czar Alexander II (February 1881). She was quickly arrested (March) and executed (April).

d. Jenny (Julia Joan Bertha) von Westphalen (1814–1881), German socialist, wife and aide of Karl Marx, and mother of Eleanor Marx-Aveling.

## Religion/Education/Everyday Life

Women's Christian Temperance Union (WCTU), at its national convention and with a strong split in its membership, adopted a resolution supporting women's suffrage.

Helen Hunt Jackson campaigned against the mistreatment of Indians in the West, and wrote a history of the Indian Wars, *A Century of Dishonor*.

Leonora Kearney Barry became women's general organizer for the Knights of Labor (1881–1991).

Grace Dodge established a discussion group for young women working in factories; out of this grew a state and then a national Association of Working Girls' Societies, with Dodge as director (from 1896).

University of Melbourne became the first Australian college to admit women.

Anne Blunt published *A Pilgrimage to Nedj*.

Helen Blackburn published a *Handbook for Women Engaged in Social and Political Work*.

b. Helene Weber (1881–1962), German social worker and politician.

# On Working Women

. . . Equity draws no lines of difference between the sexes. Our Order is based upon equity and must do the same in order to make the words "equal pay for equal work" a living truth. . . Only those who will work for small wages are employed in many occupations. It is not an uncommon thing to see whole factories in which women, children, and old men are employed. . . Unity of purpose, strength of will, and a determination not to part for trifles wins not only battles on the tented field alone, but on the broad field of labor as well. These elements will eventually win for the working man the right to control the machine which now makes the woman the medium through which man's wages are reduced. We must assist to elevate her, or through her helplessness she will make it impossible for man to help either her or himself. . .

—Terence Powderly, General Master Workman of the Knights of Labor (1881)

b. Mother Gerald Barry (1881–1961), nun and educator.

d. Jane Digby El Mezrab (1807–1881), British adventurer and traveler, noted for her divorces and affairs, who became the wife of Sheikh Abdul Medjuel El Mezrab.

d. Maria-Dominica Mazarello (1836–1881), Italian Catholic nun who founded the Daughters of Mary Auxiliatrix.

## SCIENCE/TECHNOLOGY/MEDICINE

Clara Barton organized the American branch of the International Red Cross and was its first president (1881–1904), successfully campaigning for United States acceptance of the Geneva Treaty (1882), which contained provisions for relief during peacetime disasters, such as floods or earthquakes.

American botanist Elizabeth Knight Britton published the first of her 346 scientific papers (1881–1930), focusing on the study of mosses.

Rachel Bodley, dean of the Woman's Medical College of Pennsylvania, conducted a statistical survey about the careers of her school's graduates, published as the pamphlet *The College Story*, one of the earliest studies of women in the professions.

b. Alice Evans (1881–1975), American microbiologist.

b. Hilda Clark (1881–1955), British Quaker physician, relief worker, and pacifist.

b. Myra Breckenridge (1881–1965), American nurse-midwife.

d. Mary (Jane) Seacole (1805–1881), Jamaican nurse and hotel owner with nursing experience in the Caribbean who as "Mother" or "Aunty" Seacole established a nursing center for soldiers in the Crimea (ca. 1856).

## ARTS/LITERATURE

Sarah Bernhardt created the role of Marguerite in Alexandre Dumas's play *La dame aux camélias*.

Elisavet Moutza-Martinengou's autobiography was published posthumously.

Augusta Holmès composed the choral work *Les Argonautes*.

Christina Rossetti published *A Pageant and Other Poems*.

Elizabeth Butler showed her painting *Scotland for Ever*.

Marie Sittová created the title role in Bedrich Smetana's opera *Libuse*.

b. Bess Streeter Aldrich (1881–1954), American novelist.

b. Natalia Sergeyevna Goncharova (1881–1962), Russian painter and set designer.

# 1882

## POLITICS/LAW/WAR

In Britain, the Married Woman's Property Act of 1882 allowed married women to keep possession of their own property, acquired before or during the marriage.

The Ligue Francaise pour les Droites des Femmes (French League for the Rights of Women) was founded by a man, Léon Richer.

Elizabeth Blackwell published *Christian Socialism*.

b. Frances (Fannie Coralie) Perkins (1882–1965), American teacher, social worker, economist, and administrator.

b. Sylvia Pankhurst (1882–1960), British suffragist, artist, socialist, and anti-war activist.

b. Margery Corbett Ashby (1882–1982), English feminist, suffragist, and pacifist.

## RELIGION/EDUCATION/EVERYDAY LIFE

American Federation of Labor (AFL), formed in 1881, invited women's labor organizations to join the federation "upon an equal footing" with men. Mrs. Charlotte Smith, president of the Women's National Industrial League, attended the 1883 AFL convention and held a seat at the 1884 convention, at which "An Address to Worker Girls and Women" was proposed. It urged female workers to support the federation, saying that "equal amounts of work should bring the same prices whether performed by man or woman."

Association of Collegiate Alumnae was founded in Boston (January 14), the first organization of university women in the United States, by 65 women, sparked by Ellen Swallow Richards, Marion Talbot, Emily Firbanks Taylor, Alice Freeman (Palmer), and Alice Hayes. Among their first projects was to conduct and publish research refuting the idea, then being popularized by Dr. Edward Clarke, that college education ruined women's health. The ACA would become the American Association of University Women (AAUW), after merging with the Southern Association of College Women and the Western Association of Collegiate Alumnae (1921).

Society for the Collegiate Instruction of Women was begun in Cambridge, Massachusetts, regularizing informal women's education that had developed into a full course of study under the "Harvard Annex," drawing faculty and resources from Harvard University; although prominent women raised over a quarter of a million dollars to fund the course, the female students were unable to obtain a Harvard degree; this would eventually lead to the formation of Radcliffe College (1894).

Inexpensive evening classes began to be offered by Philadelphia's New Century Club, developing into the New Century Guild for Working Women, led by Eliza Sproat Turner.

Martha Carey Thomas received a doctorate with distinction from the University of Zürich; she had, after graduation from Cornell University (1877), been admitted (by special vote) to the graduate program at Johns Hopkins University but was not allowed to attend seminars. Trying Europe, she was barred from degree programs at Leipzig and Göttingen, before turning to Zürich.

Pandita Ramabai founded the Sharada Sadan, a home for Indian widows, some not yet even in their teens.

Women's National Press Association was founded, with Emily Edson Briggs as its first president.

Jane Harrison published *Myths of the Odyssey in Art and Literature*.

b. Huda Sh'arawi (1882–1947), Egyptian educator and women's rights activist.

b. Jessie Redmon Fauset (1882–1961), African-American editor and author.

b. Rose (Rachel) Schneiderman (1882–1972), Polish-American trade union leader and social reformer.

## SCIENCE/TECHNOLOGY/MEDICINE

Physician Aletta Jacobs established the world's first birth-control clinic, in Amsterdam.

Christine Ladd-Franklin completed the work for her doctorate in mathematics at Johns Hopkins University. Her dissertation was published with those of the male students, but she was not actually awarded her Ph.D. until 44 years later, in 1926, though she was a lecturer on logic and philosophy at Johns Hopkins (1904–1909) and later taught at Columbia University (1914–1927).

Eleanor Ormerod was appointed consulting entomologist to Britain's Royal Agricultural Society, largely because of her special report on the turnip fly, which had ravaged crops in 1881; she remained there for 10 years.

After her husband's death, Mary Anna Palmer Draper established the Henry Draper Memorial fund at the Harvard College Observatory, which employed many women as astronomers and produced notable achievements, especially in stellar spectroscopy.

In the first speech by a woman before the American Society of Civil Engineers, Emily Warren Roebling successfully argued against replacement of her husband as formal director of construction on the Brooklyn Bridge; she had been actual supervisor of the project for some years, since he became physically incapacitated.

Physician Anna Tomaszewicz-Dobrska became chief of Warsaw's Lying-In Hospital No. 2 (1882–1911).

Sarah Plummer Lemmon discovered a new genus of plants, which botanist Asa Gray later named in her honor, *Plummera floribunda*.

b. Emmy (Amalie) Noether (1882–1935), German mathematician.

b. Melanie Reizes Klein (1882–1960), Austrian-British child psychoanalyst.

### ARTS/LITERATURE

Sarah Bernhardt created the title role in Victorien Sardou's play *Fedora*.

Emma Lazarus published the poetry collection *Songs of a Semite*, including "Dance to Death."

Mary Cassatt showed her painting *La Loge*.

Fanny Kemble published her autobiographical *Records of Later Life*.

Emilia Pardo Bazán published the novel *La tribuna*, about a female tobacco-industry worker.

Matilde Serao published the novel *Fantasia*.

b. Virginia Woolf (Adeline Virginia Stephen, 1882–1941), British writer.

b. Anna Pavlova (1882–1931), Russian ballerina.

b. (Agnes) Sybil Thorndike (1882–1976), British actress.

b. Sigrid Undset (1882–1949), Norwegian writer.

b. Lois Weber (1882–1939), American film director, writer, producer, and actress.

b. Susan Glaspell (1882–1948), American director, novelist, and playwright.

b. Amelita Galli-Curci (1882–1963), Italian soprano.

b. Geraldine Farrar (1882–1967), American singer and actress.

b. Mary Carlisle Howe (1882–1964), American composer.

d. Céline Céleste (1814–1882), French dancer and pantomimist.

d. Margaretta Angelica Peale (1795–1882), American painter, largely of still lifes; sister of Sarah and Mary Peale.

## 1883

### POLITICS/LAW/WAR

French feminist Hubertine Auclert's Droit de la Femme was renamed the Société de Suffrage des Femmes, but pressed for far more than women's suffrage, developing a full women's rights agenda that also included equal employment and professional opportunities, equal pay, and enhanced civil and marital rights.

Physician Aletta Jacobs tried to place her name on the voting list, but the Dutch government negated that possibility by adding "male" to the voting regulations.

In Finland, a Vagrancy Law required that all unmarried women be forced to work, as the only way to obtain legal protection.

Mary F. Hoyt received the top score on the first U.S. Civil Service examination and became the first woman (and second person) hired under the new Civil Service Act.

People's Will leader Vera Figner was captured in Russia and imprisoned for 21 years (1883–1904).

Sarah Winnemucca (Hopkins) published her autobiography, *Life Among the Paiutes: Their Wrongs and Claims*, edited by Mary Mann.

Australian feminist Henrietta Dugdale published *A Few Hours in a Far-off Age*.

b. Halide Edib Adivar (1883–1964), Turkish feminist, writer, educator, and politician.

b. Jessie Daniel Ames (1883–1972), American feminist, reformer, suffragist and civil rights activist.

b. Ona Brazauskaité Masiotene (1883–1949), Lithuanian feminist and nationalist.

d. Sojourner Truth (Isabella Van Wagener, ca. 1797–1883), African-American abolitionist and women's rights advocate, born into slavery, who became free, also freeing one of her children in a landmark case; she became a leading evangelical preacher, abolitionist, and women's rights crusader. Her biography was *The Narrative of Sojourner Truth*.

### RELIGION/EDUCATION/EVERYDAY LIFE

Matilda Joslyn Gage published *Woman, Church, and State*, a landmark attack on patriarchal, anti-woman church doctrines and practices.

Annie Taylor joined the China Inland Mission, traveling widely around the country, not only seeking to make Christian converts but also urging women to end the practice of footbinding.

Western Association of Collegiate Alumnae was founded in Chicago, establishing a bureau of correspondence to foster links between American and European university women, and a scholarship fund for women. It would merge with two other organizations to become the American Association of University Women (1921).

Aline Valette published *La journée de la petite ménagère*, a popular book on home management.

Flora Darling published *Mrs. Darling's Letters, or Memories of the Civil War*.

Isabella Bird Bishop published *The Golden Chersonese*.

b. Catherine Bramwell Booth (1883–1987), British Salvation Army Leader.

b. Coco (Gabrielle) Chanel (ca. 1883–1971), French couturier.

b. Constance Applebee (1883–1981), British hockey player.

### SCIENCE/TECHNOLOGY/MEDICINE

Physician Elizabeth Garrett Anderson helped found the London School of Medicine for Women and was elected its first dean (1883–1902); during that time it became fully accepted as a college of the University of London.

With the help of her mentor, Karl Weierstrass, Sonya Kovalevsky was appointed lecturer in mathematics at the University of Stockholm, where the department said it wanted to hire the "first great woman mathematician." She became a full professor (1884), then a life professor (1889).

Working through the Medical Women for India Fund, Edith Pechey (later Pechey-Phipson) went to Bombay, directing the new Cama Hospital for women and children; she also set up a private practice (1884) and later founded a nursing school.

Mary Anna Palmer Draper founded the Henry Draper Medal, awarded by the National Academy of Sciences for original work in astronomical physics, named for her late husband.

b. Edith Clarke (1883–1959), American mathematician and electrical engineer.

b. Anna Johnson Pell Wheeler (1883–1966), American mathematician.

b. Alice Middleton Boring (1883–1955), American cytologist, geneticist, and zoologist.

d. Lydia Estes Pinkham (1819–1883), American medicine developer and distributor, who marketed her home herbal remedy as a "cure for female complaints."

### ARTS/LITERATURE

Emma Lazarus published the sonnet "The New Colossus," which would be inscribed on the Statue of Liberty (1903).

Olive Schreiner, writing as Ralph Iron, published the novel *Story of an African Farm*.

After Richard Wagner's death, Cosima Wagner became director of the Bayreuth Festival (1883–1906), also later publishing abridged versions of the diaries she had kept during their years together.

Julia Ward Howe published the biography *Margaret Fuller*.

Mary Hallock Foote published the novel *The Led-Horse Claim*.

Mrs. Humphrey Ward published the novel *Robert Elsmere*.

b. Imogen Cunningham (1883–1976), American photographer.

b. Sara Allgood (1883–1950), Irish actress.

b. Asta Nielsen (1883–1972), Danish actress.

## 1884

### POLITICS/LAW/WAR

Belva Lockwood campaigned for the American presidency as the candidate of the National Equal Rights Party.

Divorce was legalized in France; the Code Napoléon (1804) had canceled liberalizations in divorce gained in the Revolution (1789).

New Zealand adopted a reform Married Women's Property Act.

Henrietta Dugdale became the president of the first Women's Suffrage Society in Victoria, Australia.

Britain's Queen Victoria published *More Leaves*.

Ida Harper, then living in Terre Haute, Indiana, home of socialist Eugene V. Debs, wrote regularly for Debs's union publication, the *Locomotive Firemen's Magazine*.

Sarah Edwards won a soldiers' pension for her Civil War service in the Union Army, disguised as a man (Franklin Thompson).

b. (Anna) Eleanor Roosevelt (1884–1962), American social reformer and political leader, wife of President Franklin Delano Roosevelt.

d. Caroline Harper Dexter (1819–1884), Australian feminist, writer, and editor.

### RELIGION/EDUCATION/EVERYDAY LIFE

Emily Malbone Morgan founded the Society of the Companions of the Holy Cross, a lay Episcopalian community of women sharing a focus on communal worship, intercession through prayer, literature and the arts as part of the spiritual experience, and social justice.

Louisa Twining served as a Poor Law Guardian in London (1884–1890) and later in Tunbridge Wells (1893–1896).

*The Origin of the Family, Private Property and the State*, a central Marxist work by Friedrich Engels, incorporated some of Lewis Henry Morgan's thinking on the existence of earlier matriarchies.

Frances Victor collaborated with Hubert Howe Bancroft (1884–1890) on the multivolume series *History of the Pacific States*, writing the volumes on Oregon, Washington, Idaho, Montana, Nevada, Colorado, and Wyoming and contributing to those covering California, the Northwest coast, and British Columbia.

b. (Mary) Gertrude Denman (1884–1954), British voluntary organizer.

b. Elizabeth Arden (Florence Nightingale Graham, 1884?–1966), Canadian beautician and cosmetics entrepreneur.

b. Te Puea (1884–1952), Maori princess.

### SCIENCE/TECHNOLOGY/MEDICINE

Ellen Swallow Richards was appointed instructor in sanitary chemistry at the Massachusetts Institute of Technology.

Hertha Marks (later Ayrton) invented and patented an instrument to divide a line into any number of equal parts; her early study and inventing work was financed by feminist and philanthropist Barbara Leigh-Smith Bodichon, after whom she would later name her daughter.

Mary Jane Rathbun began work at the division of marine invertebrates at the National Museum in Washington, D.C., assisting her brother Richard, the curator; she became a full-time employee, organizing the cataloguing of the museum's collection, standardizing and clarifying cate-

## Founder of Ecology

Ellen Swallow Richards, who had been the first female student at the Massachusetts Institute of Technology and then an unofficial (and probably unpaid) instructor, was formally made instructor of sanitary chemistry and head of the associated laboratory. Already noted for her environmental analyses, she would for the rest of her career (1884-1911) study and teach sanitary engineering, including techniques of water, air, and sewage analysis. She is also noted for developing the world's first water-purity tables, as well as tables that allowed testers to establish early-warning systems of water pollution. With her emphasis on the interplay between organisms and their environment— physical, biological, and social—she is also regarded as a founder of ecology. In fact, Richards introduced the term *oekology* (ca. 1892), at the time including the intertwining of consumer and environmental concerns. These would gradually split apart, with the environmental branch of *ecology* becoming male-dominated. The consumer branch would be female-dominated, later called *domestic science* or *home economics*, of which Richards was also a key founder.

gories and nomenclature in the field, and often effectively running the department, though officially rising no higher than assistant curator (1907–1914).

British nurse Alice Fisher was brought in to reorganize the nursing services at Blockley (now Philadelphia) General Hospital; she set up the Philadelphia Training School for Nurses, following Florence Nightingale's approach.

Eleanor Ormerod published *Guide to the Methods of Insect Life*, based on her series of talks at Britain's Royal Agricultural College and at the South Kensington Museum.

British nurse Kate Marsden, on a visit to New Zealand, became Lady Superintendent of Wellington Hospital.

Physician Elizabeth Blackwell published *The Human Element in Sex*.

b. Helene Deutsch (1884–1982), Polish-American psychoanalyst.

d. Almira Hart Lincoln Phelps (1793–1884), American educator who wrote popular science textbooks, sister of educator Emma Willard. Though supporting educational equality, Phelps opposed women's suffrage and was active in the Woman's Anti-Suffrage Association.

### ARTS/LITERATURE

Helen Hunt Jackson published the novel *Ramona*, dramatizing the oppression of Indians in the American West.

Marie Heilbronn created the title role in Jules Massenet's opera *Manon*.

Sarah Orne Jewett published the novel *A Country Doctor*.

Clorinda Matto de Turner published *Elementos de Literature, Para el uso del bello sexo*, a reading guide for women.

Susan Eakins showed her painting *Kate Lewis*.

b. Ivy Compton-Burnett (1884–1969), British novelist.

b. Laurette Taylor (Helen Laurette Cooney Taylor, 1884–1946), American actress.

b. Ruth Draper (1884–1956), American actress.

b. Sara Teasdale (1884–1933), American poet.

b. Sophie Tucker (Sonia Kalish, 1884–1966), American singer and actress.

b. Jane Cowl (1884–1950), American actress and playwright.

d. Marie Taglioni (1804–1884), a major figure in the history of ballet, daughter of dancer-choreographer Filippo Taglioni and sister of dancer-balletmaster Paul Taglioni.

d. Fanny Elssler (1810–1884), Austrian dancer, a leading ballerina from the mid-1820s, a star at the Paris Opéra from the mid-1830s, and among the first great ballerinas to tour North America, in the early 1840s.

## 1885

### POLITICS/LAW/WAR

Norwegian National Women's Suffrage Association was founded, with Gina Grog as its first president.

Eleanor Marx-Aveling published *The Woman Question*.

b. Alice Paul (1885–1977), American social worker, lawyer, and militant women's rights leader.

b. Adela Constantia Pankhurst Walsh (1885–1961), British-Australian pacifist, feminist, and later fascist, the third daughter of Emmeline Pankhurst, sister of Christabel and Sylvia Pankhurst.

d. Maria Weston Chapman (1806–1885), American teacher, editor, and a leading abolitionist from the 1830s.

### RELIGION/EDUCATION/EVERYDAY LIFE

Bryn Mawr School for Girls in Baltimore (later Bryn Mawr College for Women) was founded, with Mary Elizabeth Garrett as its main financial supporter and president of the board of trustees. Among the school's cofounders was Martha Carey Thomas, who became dean and professor of English, later its president.

Dorothea Beale founded St. Hilda's College at Cheltenham for training women to be secondary school teachers; it was named for St. Hilda of Whitby.

Annie Peck was the first woman admitted to the American School of Classical Studies in Athens.

Committee of Presbyterian Women for Foreign Missions was formed by regional American-sponsored foreign missionary societies, which had previously operated independently.

Lucy Maynard Salmon introduced the German-developed seminar approach in her history courses at Vassar College (1880s).

Annie Oakley and her partner-husband, Frank Butler, joined Buffalo Bill's Wild West Show, touring widely in North America and Europe (1885–1901).

Matilda Evans Stevenson was founder and first president of the Women's Anthropological Society of America.

The Sanctified Sisters expanded from their single household to take over the Central Hotel in Belton, Texas.

Jane Harrison published *Introductory Studies in Greek Art*.

b. Anna Louise Strong (1885–1970), American journalist.

### SCIENCE/TECHNOLOGY/MEDICINE

Agnes Clerke published her first book, *A Popular History of Astronomy during the Nineteenth Century*.

Charlotte Scott became professor and chairman of the mathematics department at then-new Bryn Mawr College (1885–1925), heading a staff of five males; she had earlier that year received her doctorate from the University of London.

Clara Eaton Cummings published her catalogue of North American mosses and liverworts.

Elizabeth Agassiz wrote *Louis Agassiz, His Life and Correspondence*, a biography of her husband, who had died in 1873.

b. Elizabeth Lee Hazen (1885–1975), American microbiologist and mycologist.

b. Ethel Nicholson Browne Harvey (1885–1965), American biologist.

b. Karen Clementine Danielson Horney (1885–1952), German-born American psychoanalyst.

b. Susan Fairhurst Brierley Isaacs (1885–1948), British child psychologist.

### ARTS/LITERATURE

Sarah Orne Jewett published the novel *A Marsh Island*.

Mary Cassatt showed her painting *Lady at the Tea Table*.

Bertha Skram published the novel *Constance Ring*.

Matilde Serao published the novel *Conquista di Roma*.

b. Isak Dinesen (Karen Christence Dinesen Blixen, 1885–1962), Danish writer.

b. Sonia Delaunay (Sophia Terk, 1885–1979), French artist.

b. Tamara Platonovna Karsavina (1885–1978), Russian ballerina.

b. Billie Burke (1885–1970), American actress.

b. Pastora Imperio (Pastora Rojas; La Emperaora, ca. 1885/1894–1961), Spanish dancer and choreographer.

d. Helen Maria Fiske Hunt Jackson (1830–1885), American novelist, poet, essayist, children's book writer, and social reformer, author of the novel *Ramona* (1884), a major figure in the fight for Native American rights.

d. Sarah Miriam Peale (1800–1885), American artist, largely a portraitist, sister of Margaretta and Mary Peale.

d. Susanna Strickland Moodie (1803–1885), Canadian writer, best known for her works on Canadian frontier life.

# 1886

### POLITICS/LAW/WAR

British feminists scored a major victory with repeal of the Contagious Diseases Acts, which had provided for government regulation and prosecution of suspected prostitutes without any reference to male clients and pimps.

Woman Suffrage (Anthony) Amendment to the U.S. Constitution was first brought to a vote in the U.S. Congress—and overwhelmingly defeated. In 1920 it would become the 19th Amendment.

Susan B. Anthony, Elizabeth Cady Stanton, and Matilda Joslyn Gage published the three-volume work *The History of Woman Suffrage*, a valuable source of documents and insight on the early years of the movement. Three further volumes, taking the story through 1920, were later published by others.

Austrian pacifist Bertha von Suttner lectured to the London International Peace Association.

Clementina Black became secretary of Britain's Women's Protective and Provident League (1886–1888).

French feminist Maria Deraismes published *Les droits des enfants.*

Matilde Bajer founded the Danish Women's Progress Association, with a broad women's rights agenda and special focus on woman suffrage.

b. Raicho Hiratsuka (1886–1971), Japanese feminist, editor, and writer.

### RELIGION/EDUCATION/EVERYDAY LIFE

The national Young Women's Christian Association (YWCA) was founded in America, its first president being Mrs. Henry Fowl Durant. The same year the Young Women's Hebrew Association (YWHA) was founded as an auxiliary of the men's YMHA, with Julia Richman as president.

Japan's Women's Christian Temperance Union was founded by Yajima Kajiko and Mary C. Leavitt; its Osaka branch would be the first Japanese women's organization to seek women's suffrage; the WCTU later also campaigned in Japan against prostitution.

Emily Dilke succeeded founder Emma Paterson as president of the Women's Protective and Provident League (later the Women's Trade Union League, WTUL), emerging as a major figure in the British social-reform and trade union movements.

Elizabeth Rodgers was the first woman to become master workman (head) of a Knights of Labor district assembly, covering the greater Chicago region.

Harriet Hubbard Ayer began to make and sell her "beauty cream," made from a formula purchased from her chemist, who alleged that it was the cream used by Madame Récamier, a notable beauty in Napoléon's court. The business laid the foundation for the modern cosmetics industry, though Hubbard later lost it in a family wrangle.

Anna A. Nevins is believed to have been the world's first female wireless operator, working at the top of the New York's Waldorf-Astoria Hotel.

Séverine became editor of the periodical *Cri du peuple* (1886–1888).

Susette La Flèsche Tibbles toured England, lecturing on Native American culture.

b. Ida (Kaganovich) Cohen Rosenthal (1886–1973), Russian-American inventor and manufacturer.

b. María (Liana) Cadilla de Martínez (1886–1951), Puerto Rican educator, writer, folklorist, and feminist.

b. Constance Spry (1886–1960), British entrepreneur, writer, and educator.

d. Emma (Anne) Smith Paterson (1848–1886), British trade unionist who founded the Women's Protective and Provident League (1874) and was the first woman to serve as a delegate to the Trade Union Congress (1875). She was succeeded as League president by Emily Dilke.

### SCIENCE/TECHNOLOGY/MEDICINE

Elizabeth Garrett Anderson built and staffed the New Hospital for Women and Children (1886), associated with the London School of Medicine for Women, serving there until 1892; building on her earlier dispensary, it was later renamed the Elizabeth Garrett Anderson Hospital.

Winifred Edgerton received her Ph.D. from Columbia University, becoming the first American woman to receive a doctorate in mathematics (Christine Ladd-Franklin had earned one from Johns Hopkins University in 1882, but would not receive it until 1926). Edgerton's was also the first Columbia degree granted to a woman in any subject.

Martha J. Coston published *Signal Success: The Work and Travels of Mrs. Martha J. Coston*, the story of her success in selling her patented signal flare internationally, building a considerable fortune.

After her husband's death, Isabella Bird Bishop studied medicine, going as a medical missionary to India, where she founded several hospitals.

Carrie J. Everson patented an improvement on the flotation system used in mining to separate a desired ore from other raw materials.

Sophia Jex-Blake published *Medical Women*, about the experiences of herself and other women attempting to become physicians.

b. Leta Stetter Hollingworth (1886–1939), American educational psychologist.

## ARTS/LITERATURE

Frances Hodgson Burnett published the children's novel *Little Lord Fauntleroy*.

Louise Bethune became the first woman to be a member of the American Institute of Architects.

Sarah Orne Jewett published the short-story collection *A White Heron*.

Helen Hunt Jackson published *Sonnets and Lyrics*.

Emilia Pardo Bazán published *The Son of the Bondswoman*.

Marie Corelli published the novel *A Romance of Two Worlds*.

Mary Hallock Foote published the novel *The Last Assembly Ball*.

b. Ma Rainey (Gertrude Pridgett, 1886–1939), American blues singer.

b. Hilda Doolittle (H. D., 1886–1961), American poet.

b. Mary Wigman (1886–1973), German dancer.

b. Zoë Akins (1886–1958), American playwright and poet.

b. Margaret Ayer Barnes (1886–1967), American novelist and playwright.

b. Marie Laurencin (1886–1956), French painter, poet, and set designer.

d. Emily Elizabeth Dickinson (1830–1886), American poet, a major figure in American literature who wrote almost 2,000 poems, only two of them published in her lifetime. The rest were published posthumously, beginning in the 1890s.

d. Mary Boykin Miller Chesnut (1823–1886), American writer, whose Confederate-era diaries were published in the 1980s.

d. Patience Lovell Wright (1825–1886), American portrait sculptor.

## 1887

### POLITICS/LAW/WAR

Women lost the right to vote in Utah territorial elections, under the federal Edmunds-Tucker Act, prohibiting Mormon polygamy; it would not be reinstated until statehood (1896).

Alice Fletcher became a special agent for the U.S. Indian Bureau, implementing the Dawes Act, under which Native Americans were granted land; she had (from 1879) been working for the cause of Indian rights, pressing for division of reservations into individual homesteads, a policy later considered exploitative.

By U.S. federal law, the age of consent (for heterosexual relations) was raised from the generally accepted age of 10 to 16.

Britain's Queen Victoria celebrated the 50th year of her reign.

b. Frances M. Witherspoon (1887–1973), American peace and civil liberties advocate, writer, and feminist.

b. Louise Schröder (1887–1957), German socialist and politician.

### RELIGION/EDUCATION/EVERYDAY LIFE

Helen Keller, deaf and blind from 19 months old, learned to communicate using a manual alphabet taught her by Annie Sullivan (as told in the film *The Miracle Worker*); Keller would attend Radcliffe College and become a well-known writer and speaker, with Sullivan as her key interpreter (until her death in 1936), and Polly Thompson as her secretary (1914–1960).

New Century Guild for Working Women began publishing the *Working Woman's Journal*, offering articles about work from the employees' point of view.

American reporter Nellie Bly (Elizabeth Cochrane Seaman) published her exposé *Ten Days in a Mad-House*.

Lottie (Charlotte) Dod won the women's singles tennis title at Wimbledon, the youngest winner ever, at 15 years, 10 months.

Florence Kelley published her translation of Friedrich Engels's *Condition of the Working Class in England in 1844*.

Greek journalist and novelist Kallirroi Parren began publishing the *Ladies' Newspaper* (1887–1917).

Suzanna Madora Salter became the first known American female mayor, of Argonia, Kansas.

The first national women's tennis tournament in America was held at the Philadelphia Cricket Club.

b. Ruth Fulton Benedict (1887–1948), American anthropologist.

b. Mary (Evaline) Madeleva Wolff (1887–1964), American poet, scholar, and educator.

b. Louise Bryant (1887–1936), American writer, social reformer, and suffragist.

d. Dorothea Lynde Dix (1802–1887), American social reformer, especially focusing on improved treatment of the mentally ill, superintendent of female nurses during the Civil War (from 1861).

d. Nakayama Miki (1798–1887), Japanese religious leader, called "Beloved Parent," who founded the Tenrikyo religious movement.

### SCIENCE/TECHNOLOGY/MEDICINE

Dorothea Klumpke (later Roberts) became the first woman to work at the Paris Observatory (1887–1901) and later its director.

Smith College Observatory was founded, with Mary Emma Byrd as its first director, though with little funding.

Christine Ladd-Franklin published the first of what would be many papers on physiological optics.

b. Fanny Carter Edson (1887–1952), American geologist.

### ARTS/LITERATURE

Sarah Bernhardt created the title role in Victorien Sardou's play *La Tosca*.

Emma Lazarus published the poem "By the Waters of Babylon."

Bertha Skram published the tetralogy *Hellemyrsfolket* (1887–1898), about the failing fortunes of a family living on the land.

Cecilia Beaux exhibited her painting *The Last Days of Childhood* at the Paris Salon.

Clorinda Matto de Turner founded *El Peru Illustrado*.

b. Georgia O'Keeffe (1887–1986), American painter.

b. Lynn Fontanne (Lillie Louise Fontanne, 1887–1983), British-American actress.

b. Edith Sitwell (1887–1964), British poet and critic.

b. Edna Ferber (1887–1968), American writer.

b. Marianne Moore (1887–1972), American poet.

b. Nadia Boulanger (1887–1979), French music teacher and conductor.

b. Malvina Cornell Hoffman (1887–1966), American sculptor.

b. Marguerite Thompson Zorach (1887–1968), American artist.

b. Sylvia Beach (1887–1962), American bookseller and publisher in Paris.

b. Maria Jeritza (1887–1982), Czech soprano.

b. Marion Eugenie Bauer (1887–1955), American composer.

d. Jenny (Johanna Maria) Lind (1820–1887), Swedish soprano, popularly known as "the Swedish Nightingale."

d. Emma Lazarus (1849–1887), American poet, best known for her poem "The New Colossus" (1883), inscribed on the Statue of Liberty (1903). Among her final works was the poem "By the Waters of Babylon" (1887).

## 1888

### POLITICS/LAW/WAR

National Council of Women of the United States was founded by a wide range of leading women, including Susan B. Anthony, Frances E. Willard, May Wright Sewell, Elizabeth Cady Stanton, Lucy Stone, Julia Ward Howe, and Clara Barton. They also sparked the founding of the International Council of Women (ICW), of which the NCW was an American affiliate; a century later the international umbrella organization had grown into a network of more than 75 national women's councils.

Belva Lockwood again was the presidential candidate of the National Equal Rights Party.

b. Marie-Elizabeth Luders (1888–1966), German political economist, anti-Nazi leader, feminist, and politician.

### RELIGION/EDUCATION/EVERYDAY LIFE

Clementina Black sparked the historic Equal Pay Resolution at the British Trade Union Congress of 1888.

The London Match Girls Strike was a turning point in the long fight for women's equal pay and equal workplace rights; Annie Besant was a key organizer.

Southern Baptist Woman's Missionary Society (Union) was founded by the merger of many individual groups, with Annie Armstrong as first corresponding secretary (1888–1906); they raised funds to support missionary work and developed missionary education programs for all levels, from preschool through adult, for use in America and abroad.

Gertrude Bell was the first woman to obtain first-class honors in history, graduating from Lady Margaret Hall, Oxford.

National Farmers' Alliances, local cooperative organizations founded in rural areas of America, admitted both men and women as members (1888–ca. 1895) and offered women unusual leadership opportunities.

Auguste Schmidt became head of the Allgemeiner Deutscher Frauenverein (General German Women's Association).

Despite fears that they would create a separate "women's church," women in the Presbyterian Church in the U.S.A. organized independent activities; Jennie Hanna and Mrs. Josiah Sibley formed the first "presbyterial."

Elizabeth Morgan was a founder and first president of the Ladies Federal Labor Union.

Kalliopi Kehajia toured the United States, on her return to Greece writing notable articles on women's position and education abroad.

Lottie Dod, still only 16, defended her women's singles tennis title at Wimbledon, defeating Blanche Bingley (later Hillyard).

Methodist Episcopal church's General Conference refused to admit Frances E. Willard and four other women as lay delegates but recognized a new order of deaconesses, offering service, but having no authority.

Frances Power Cobbe published *The Scientific Spirit of the Age*.

Kalliroe Parren founded the *Women's Newspaper*.

b. Ida Pruitt (1888–1985), American missionary and educator.

## SCIENCE/TECHNOLOGY/MEDICINE

Marine Biological Laboratory was established at Woods Hole, sparked by the Women's Education Association of Boston and using equipment from its earlier laboratory (1871–1886). Woods Hole became a prime site for the study of ocean and freshwater life; among the key women associated with it were Ellen Swallow Richards and Cornelia Clapp.

Sonya Kovalevsky was awarded the Prix Bordin by the French Academy of Sciences for her work on the rotation of a solid body about a fixed point.

Nature-study expert Anna Botsford Comstock engraved scientific illustrations for *Introduction to Entomology*, by her husband, Henry Comstock.

b. Winifred Goldring (1888–1971), American paleontologist.

b. Helena (Rosa) Lowenfeld Wright (1888–1982), British physician and birth-control campaigner.

b. Jewell Jeannette Glass (1888–1966), American mineralogist.

b. Libbie H. Hyman (1888–1969), American zoologist.

d. Clemence Sophia Lozier (1813–1888), American physician who successfully campaigned for incorporation of the New York Medical College for Women (1863).

d. Rachel Bodley (1831–1888), American chemist and botanist, noted as a teacher and college administrator.

## ARTS/LITERATURE

Cécile Chaminade composed the choral work *Les amazones*.

Sarah Orne Jewett published the short-story collection *The King of Folly Island*.

b. Katherine Mansfield (Kathleen Beauchamp-Murry, 1888–1923), New Zealand-born British short story writer.

b. Antonia Mercé (La Argentina, 1888–1936), Argentina-born Spanish dancer.

b. Lotte Lehmann (1888–1976), German-American soprano.

b. Edith Mary Evans (1888–1976), British actress.

b. Marie Rambert (Cyvia Rambam, 1888–1982), British choreographer and ballet director.

b. Cathleen Nesbitt (1888–1982), British actress.

b. Elisabeth Schumann (1888–1952), German soprano.

b. Florence Smith Price (1888–1953), African-American composer.

b. Gladys Cooper (1888–1971), British actress.

d. Louisa May Alcott (1832–1888), American writer who created *Little Women* (1868).

## 1889

### POLITICS/LAW/WAR

Australian feminist and editor Louisa Lawson founded the periodical the *Dawn* (1889–1906), which focused on women's suffrage and a wide range of other feminist and social-reform issues.

In France, the Union Universelle des Femmes and La Ligue Socialiste des Femmes were founded, the latter by Eugénie Potonie-Pierre. The French and International Congress of Women's Rights, organized by Maria Deraismes, was also held.

Rosa Luxemburg published *Reform or Revolution*.

Clara Zetkin edited the periodical *Gleichheit* (*Equality*, 1892–1916).

b. Marthe Betenfeld Ricard (1889–1982), French feminist, politician, and spy in two wars.

b. Mabel Walker Willebrandt (1889–1963), American lawyer and federal official.

### RELIGION/EDUCATION/EVERYDAY LIFE

College Settlement opened on New York's Lower East Side; it was the second settlement house in America and the first to be established wholly by women; the educational-recreational-social-reform organization sprang initially from an 1887 Smith College reunion. Other Eastern women's colleges joined in, and also founded additional settlements, notably Boston's Denison House and College Settlements in Philadelphia and Baltimore.

Jane Addams and Ellen Gates Starr founded their famous Hull House, the third and probably best-known settlement house in America, to enrich the lives of poor people in Chicago's immigrant community; modeled on London's Toynbee Hall, it was to become central to the developing American social work movement.

Barnard College was established for women, drawing on Columbia College for instruction, but independent of Columbia on nonacademic matters; it later became part of Columbia University (1900).

American reporter Nellie Bly (Elizabeth Cochrane Seaman) carried out her most sensational exploit, circling the globe alone in 72$1/4$ days (1889–1890), besting the fictional Phileas Fogg in Jules Verne's *Around the World in 80 Days*. She described her trip in *Nellie Bly's Book: Around the World in 72 Days* (1890).

Annie Besant was converted to theosophy by Helena Blavatsky, soon moving into a leading role in the movement; she also contributed to *Fabian Essays*, edited by George Bernard Shaw.

Bertha von Suttner published her controversial *Die Waffen nieder* (*Lay Down Your Arms!*), inspiring Alfred Nobel to establish his Peace Prize.

Francesca Cabrini immigrated to New York City to work with poor Italian immigrants.

Margaret Davies became General Secretary of the British Women's Co-operative Guild.

American markswoman Annie Oakley shot a cigarette from the mouth of Germany's Kaiser William II.

Clara Collet contributed to Charles Booth's classic *Life and Labour of the People of London*.

Harriet Morison, a garment worker and daughter of a tailor, helped found the Tailoresses' Union, New Zealand's first women's union, becoming its secretary (1890).

Henrietta Szold founded a Baltimore school to teach Russian Jewish immigrants about American language and culture, easing their adjustment to their new land; it was the model for many other schools elsewhere.

Louisa Woosley, of the Cumberland Presbyterian Church, was ordained as a Presbyterian minister, but her ordination was quickly invalidated.

Mary Seymour Foot founded the *Business Woman's Journal* for the ranks of new female office workers.

Helena Blavatsky published *The Key to Theosophy*.

b. Eileen Power (Edna Le Poer, 1889–1940), British historian.

b. Lila Acheson Wallace (1889–1984), American publisher, art collector, and patron.

b. Sadie Delany (Sarah Delany; 1889– ), American home economics teacher, the first in New York City's public schools. She and her younger sister, dentist Bessie (Annie Elizabeth) Delany, would publish the bestselling oral history *Having Our Say: The Delany Sisters' First Hundred Years* (1993), when they were 104 and 102 years old, respectively.

d. Belle Starr (1848–1889), American outlaw, linked with the James and Younger gangs in Missouri and then in Arkansas, where her cabin near Fort Smith was a notorious bandit hideout; she made several sensational court appearances, during the last of which she was shot in the back, possibly by a son.

d. Elizabeth Twining (1805–1889), British reformer and educator, sister of Louisa Twining, of the tea family, who originated "Mother's Meetings" in London; one of the founders of Bedford College.

d. Prudence Crandall (1804–1889), American teacher and abolitionist, originally a Quaker from Rhode Island.

## SCIENCE/TECHNOLOGY/MEDICINE

Isabel Hampton (later Robb) organized and led the Johns Hopkins University Nursing School, beginning to set the pattern for modern nursing, including limitation of hours (when 16-hour tours were not uncommon) and three-year courses (when some medical schools had less).

Nurses at the Mayo Clinic in Rochester, Minnesota, began to administer anesthesia, leading to the specialty of nurse-anesthetist, though some critics protested that female nurses were poaching on the territory of male doctors.

Charles Martin Hall obtained a series of patents for a method of producing electrolytic aluminum, a process he had developed working with his sister, Julia Brainerd Hall; they formed the Pittsburgh Reduction Company (later Aluminum Corporation of America, or ALCOA) to produce aluminum by this method. Her record of the development of their invention, summarized in her "History of C. M. Hall's Aluminum Invention" (1887), was key to their later winning a patent suit.

Gertrude Jekyll met architect Edward Lutyens; she would design the gardens for many of his houses. Jekyll was much influenced by the French Impressionists, notably in their bold use of color, and by cottage gardens, favoring more natural alternatives to formal gardens.

Marcia Keith became the first full-time instructor in the physics department at Mount Holyoke College, influencing a generation of female students.

b. Hélène Bruhl Metzger (1889–ca. 1944), French chemist and writer on the history of science and philosophy.

b. Mildred Leonora Sanderson (1889–1914), American mathematician.

d. Maria Mitchell (1818–1889), American astronomer, the first woman elected a member of the American Academy of Arts and Sciences (1848) and the first head of Vassar College's astronomy department and observatory (1865); a crater on the moon was named after her.

## ARTS/LITERATURE

Harriet Robinson wrote the pro-women's suffrage play *The New Pandora*.

Fanny Burney's *Early Diary, 1768–1778* was published.

Clorinda Matto de Turner published the novel *Aves sin Nido*, focusing on the mistreatment of Andean Indians.

Edith Somerville and Martin Ross (Violet Martin) published *An Irish Cousin*, the first of their novels.

Eliza Orzeszkowa published the novel *Cham*.

Emma B. Steiner's opera *Fleurette* premiered in San Francisco.

Mary Catherwood published the novel *The Romance of Dollard*.

b. Gabriela Mistral (Lucila Godoy Alcayaga, 1889–1957), Chilean poet.

b. Anna Akhmatova (Anna Gorenko, 1889–1966), Russian poet.

b. Enid Bagnold (1889–1981), British author.

b. Helen Traubel (1889–1972), American soprano.

b. Pearl White (1889–1938), American actress.

b. Rose Macaulay (1889–1958), British writer.

b. Elsie Janis (1889–1956), vaudeville singer.

b. Fannie Hurst (1889–1968), American writer.

b. Ida Cox (1889–1967), African-American blues singer.

b. Liubov Eding Popova (1889–1924), Russian artist.

# 1890

## POLITICS/LAW/WAR

National American Woman Suffrage Association (NAWSA) was founded, with Elizabeth Cady Stanton as president (1890–1892), merging the larger, militant National Woman Suffrage Association with the more conservative American Woman Suffrage Association and healing the historic breach in the American women's rights movement (1869).

Alice B. Sanger became stenographer for President Benjamin Harrison, the first woman employed in the U.S. executive offices.

Wyoming gained statehood and reaffirmed the right of women to vote in all elections, becoming the first state to do so.

*Remonstrance*, an antisuffrage periodical, began publication (1890–1920).

Italian feminist Anna Kulisciov organized "Il monopolio dell'uomo," a conference exploring economic and social discrimination against women.

b. Agnes Campbell MacPhail (1890–1954), Canadian teacher, reformer, and politician.

b. Elizabeth Gurley Flynn (1890–1964), American anarchist and then Communist Party leader.

b. Rose Fitzgerald Kennedy (1890–1995), American political figure, mother of President John Fitzgerald Kennedy, Senator Robert (Bobby) Francis Kennedy, and Senator Edward (Ted) Kennedy.

d. Lydia Ernestine Becker (1827–1890), British educator, writer, and suffragist, long a leader of the woman suffrage movement.

## RELIGION/EDUCATION/EVERYDAY LIFE

Daughters of the American Revolution (DAR) was founded by Mary Smith Lockwood, Ellin Hardin Walworth, and Eugenia Washington, after the 1890 convention of the Sons of the American Revolution refused full membership to women. The DAR's first president-general was Caroline Scott Harrison, wife of President Benjamin Harrison.

General Federation of Women's Clubs (GFWC) was organized, after Jane Cunningham Croly invited other women's clubs to join in celebrating the 21st anniversary (1889) of her own women's literary club, Sorosis.

Mary Burke was a founder and first president of the Retail Clerks International. She was also the first formal female delegate to the American Federation of Labor (AFL), introducing a resolution that women be used to help organize female workers. Mary Kenney (later O'Sullivan) was appointed as a women's organizer (1892).

General German Association of Women Teachers (Allgemeiner Deutscher Lehrerinneverein) was founded by Helen Lange to promote better education for girls.

Mary Morton Kehew became director of Women's Educational and Industrial Union, which she had joined in 1886. She was later its president (1892–1913; 1914–1918), expanding the organization's role in education, notably, by adding schools of dressmaking (1895), housekeeping (1897), and salesmanship (1905).

Josephine Shaw Lowell was president of the first Consumer League (1890–1896), co-founded with Maud Nathan.

Matilda Joslyn Gage organized the National Woman's Liberal Union, focusing on discrimination against women in church doctrines, attitudes, and institutions.

Anna Kulisciov organized a conference in Italy, *Il monopolio dell'uomo*, in which she tackled the question of women's economic and social inferiority.

Clara Collet published *The Economic Position of Educated Working Women*.

A women's teacher-training college was established in Egypt.

Under pressure from the federal government, the Mormon church ceased to sanction further plural marriages in the United States.

b. Agnes Smedley (1890–1950), American writer.

b. Aimée Semple McPherson (1890–1944), Canadian-American religious leader.

b. Elsa Schiaparelli (1890–1973), French fashion designer.

d. Catherine Mumford Booth (1829–1890), British religious leader, co-founder of the Salvation Army with her husband, William Booth, credited with establishing women's equality in the organization.

## SCIENCE/TECHNOLOGY/MEDICINE

Williamina Fleming published the *Draper Catalogue of Stellar Spectra*, a work classifying over 10,000 stars; she had supervised the classification project from 1886. She also edited the Observatory's *Annals* and other publications.

Ellen Swallow Richards opened the New England Kitchen in Boston, demonstrating ways of preparing nutritious low-cost meals; it would spark other such projects around the country. Richards also advised the U.S. Department of Agriculture on its nutrition publications.

British nurse Kate Marsden, in St. Petersburg to receive a decoration from the Russian Red Cross, made her way by sledge to Siberian settlements of people with leprosy; she reported on her findings to the Venereological and Dermatological Society in Moscow and began raising money for a hospital.

b. Elsie Eaves (1890–1983), American civil engineer.

b. Mary Bailey (1890–1960), British aviator.

b. Olive Clio Hazlett (1890–1974), American mathematician.

b. Pearl Luella Kendrick (1890–1980), American microbiologist and physician.

## Arts/Literature

Kate Chopin published the novel *At Fault.*

Gemma Bellincioni created the role of Santucca in Pietro Mascagni's opera *Cavalleria Rusticana.*

b. Agatha Christie (1890–1976), British author.

b. Katherine Anne Porter (1890–1980), American writer.

b. Myra Hess (1890–1965), British pianist.

b. Theda Bara (Theodosia Goodman, 1890–1955), American actress.

b. Hallie Flanagan (1890–1969), American WPA theater organizer and theater historian.

b. Delmira Agustini (1890–1914), Uruguayan poet.

b. E. M. Delafield (1890–1943), British writer.

b. Victoria Ocampo (1890–1978), Argentinian editor and publisher.

d. Frances Raymond Ritter (1840–1890), American musician, writer, and teacher.

# 1891

## Politics/Law/War

French feminists Maria Martin and Eugénie Potonie-Pierre founded Le Groupe de la Solidarité des Femmes. The Fédération Française des Sociétés Féministes, a federation of feminist groups, was also established.

French feminist Maria Deraismes published *Eve dans l'humanité.*

Australian women's rights leader Rose Scott founded the Womanhood Suffrage League.

b. Ellen Cicely Wilkinson (Red Ellen, 1891–1947), British socialist, trade unionist, feminist, writer, and politician.

d. Sarah Winnemucca (Hopkins) (Thoc-me-tony; Shell-flower, 1844–1891), Paiute Indian rights advocate, author, and interpreter, the daughter of Chief Winnemucca, who spent her life fighting for restoration of Paiute lands.

## Religion/Education/Everyday Life

Mary Katharine Drexel founded the Sisters of the Blessed Sacrament for Indians and Colored People, the motherhouse of the order being in Pennsylvania.

May Tennant began work for the Royal Commission on Labour, becoming one of Britain's first female factory inspectors, focusing on safety, other working conditions, and illegal overtime.

New Century Guild for Working Women opened a School of Women's Trades, offering full-time training and professional certification in dressmaking and millinery. Inspired by its success, A. J. Drexel opened Drexel Institute (now Drexel University).

Women's Protective and Provident League became the Women's Trade Union League, still led by Emily Dilke.

After two years away from competition, Lottie Dod again won the women's singles tennis title at Wimbledon, successfully defending it in 1892 and 1893.

Anna Spencer became an ordained minister of the Unitarian church, serving in Providence, Rhode Island (1891–1905); she was widely known as a speaker on social issues and later became a leader of the New York Society for Ethical Culture.

Jane Club (1891–1938) was founded in association with Chicago's Hull House, intended by Jane Addams and Mary Kenney (later O'Sullivan), its director, as inexpensive cooperative housing for young working women facing possible homelessness during a layoff or strike.

Leaving her husband in Naples, partly to demonstrate that women could travel on their own, May Sheldon traveled widely in Africa, where she was known in Swahili as Bébé Bwana (Lady Boss). She published *Sultan to Sultan*, a book about her experiences, and was elected a fellow of the Royal Geographical Society, among the first women so honored.

b. Mary Stocks (Baroness Stocks of Kensington and Chelsea, 1891–1975), British educator.

b. Edith Stein (1891–1942), German nun.

b. Bessie Delany (Annie Elizabeth Delany; 1891–1995), American dentist and writer.

d. Barbara Leigh-Smith Bodichon (1827–1891), British feminist educator, writer, and artist, a central figure in the British women's rights movement, most notably on the issues of women's property rights, education, and suffrage.

d. Helena Petrovna Blavatsky (1831–1891), Russian religious leader, founder of modern theosophy who later settled in America; daughter of novelist Helena Hahn.

SCIENCE/TECHNOLOGY/MEDICINE

Dorothea Klumpke (later Roberts) became the first woman to direct the Bureau of Measurements in Paris (1891–1901), supervising the cataloguing and charting of stars.

Mary Whiton Calkins founded the first psychology laboratory at a women's college, at Wellesley.

b. Marion E. Kenworthy (ca. 1891–1980), American psychoanalyst, psychiatric social worker, and educator.

b. Katherine Stinson (Otero) (1891–1977), American aviator.

d. Sonya (Sofya) Vasilyevna Korvin-Krukovsky Kovalevsky (1850–1891), Russian mathematician whose work focused on partial differential equations; she is believed to be the first woman to receive a Ph.D. in mathematics (1874).

d. Amalie Nelle Dietrich (1821–1891), German naturalist introduced to specimen-collecting and preparation by her husband, Wilhelm Dietrich; after their separation she collected, prepared, and sold specimens, most notably from Australia and New Guinea (from 1863).

ARTS/LITERATURE

Elizabeth Robins began her introduction of Ibsen to English-speaking audiences, gaining the English-language rights to many of his plays, translating some, and playing the lead in many. Among the Ibsen roles she created in English were Mrs. Linden in *A Doll's House* (1891); the title role in *Hedda Gabler* (1891); Hilda in *The Master Builder* (1893); Rebecca West in *Rosmersholm* (1893); and Ella Bentheim in *John Gabriel Borkman* (1896).

Selma Lagerlöf published the novel *Gösta Berling's Saga*.

Clorinda Matto de Turner published the novel *Indole*, on Indian rights themes.

Fanny Kemble published her autobiographical *Further Records*.

b. Bronislava Nijinska (1891–1972), Russian dancer and choreographer, sister of Vaslav Nijinsky.

b. Fanny Brice (Fanny Borach, 1891–1951) American singer and actress.

b. Nelly Sachs (1891–1970), German Jewish writer.

b. (Margaret) Storm Jameson (1891–1983), British writer.

b. Esther Forbes (1891–1967), American novelist and historian.

## 1892

POLITICS/LAW/WAR

Elizabeth Cady Stanton delivered her celebrated speech "The Solitude of Self" at the 1892 convention of the National American Woman Suffrage Association.

Adelheid Popp became editor of the Austrian socialist women's periodical *Arbeiterinnen-Zeitung*.

b. Ch'ing-ling Soong (Madame Sun Yat-sen, 1892–1981), Chinese political figure, wife of Sun Yat-sen.

RELIGION/EDUCATION/EVERYDAY LIFE

Dorothea Beale founded St. Hilda's Hall, Oxford, to give female teachers a year of university experience; it later became one of Oxford University's colleges; she also founded a College Guild, which established a settlement called St. Hilda's East in London.

University of Chicago opened, from the start coeducational, originally incorporated and funded by John D. Rockefeller (1890). Early classes were sex-segregated, an approach soon abandoned as unworkable.

The first immigration station opened on Ellis Island in New York Harbor, and the first immigrant who came through it was Annie Moore, from Ireland's County Cork. She would be followed by millions of others through a succession of stations on the island.

Aline Valette and Eugenie Potonie-Pierre cofounded the Federation Française des Sociétés Feministes, working for women's rights.

Adelaide Hoodless opened a school of domestic science at the Hamilton, Ontario, Young Women's Christian Association (YWCA), of which she was president; she had been teaching classes there since 1889, after one of her sons died from contaminated milk and government authorities had ignored requests for more public home-health education.

International Kindergarten Union (IKU) was founded by kindergarten teachers seeking to have their work seen as a profession; Sarah Ingersoll Cooper was its first president.

Mary Kenney O'Sullivan became the first female organizer of the American Federation of Labor, but for only five months.

Women's Christian Temperance Union militant Carry Nation began her career as a violent temperance campaigner, often taking apart saloons with an ax.

After her parents' death, Mary Kingsley began her travels in West Africa (1892–1896), returning to England with a collection of insects, reptiles, and fish (three would be named after her), which she donated to the British Museum.

Lizzie Borden was accused of murdering her father and stepmother with an ax; she claimed to have been in the barn when the killings took place. She was acquitted, but widespread belief in her guilt was reflected in still-persistent folk rhymes about her role in the crime; the murders remained unsolved.

Women began playing basketball at Smith College, where Senda Berenson, director of physical education, later drew up women's rules for the game (1899).

Alice Pestana, writing as Caiel, published *What Should Women's Secondary Education Be?*

Mary Baker Eddy published *Retrospection and Introspection*.

b. Gordon Hamilton (1892–1967), American social worker and educator.

d. Anne Jemima Clough (1820–1892), British educator, the first head of what would become Newnham College, Cambridge (1871–1892).

d. Ernestine Rose (1810–1892), Polish-American social reformer and pioneering women's rights advocate.

SCIENCE/TECHNOLOGY/MEDICINE

Harriet R. Tracy obtained a U.S. patent for one of her many sewing machine improvements, which included the Tracy Lock and Chain Stitch Machine.

Isabella Bird Bishop became the first female fellow of Britain's Royal Geographical Society.

Christine Ladd-Franklin presented her theory of color vision before the International Congress of Psychology in London.

Victoria Woodhull and her daughter Zula Maud Woodhull published the *Humanitarian*, a journal devoted to eugenics (1892–1901).

Agnes Clerke was awarded the Actonian Prize by the governors of Britain's Royal Institution.

Clara Eaton Cummings edited *Decades of North American Lichens*, later reissued as *Lichenes Boreali-Americani* (1894).

b. Marion Rice Hart (1892–1990), American aviator.

b. Alva Ellisor (1892–1964), American petroleum geologist.

**ARTS/LITERATURE**

Mary Cassatt showed her painting *The Bath*.

Charlotte Perkins Gilman published the semiautobiographical story *The Yellow Wallpaper*.

Loie Fuller choreographed the dance *Butterfly*.

Mary Hallock Foote published the novel *The Chosen Valley*.

b. Edna St. Vincent Millay (1892–1950), American poet.

b. Pearl Buck (1892–1973), American author.

b. Rebecca West (Cicely Isabel Fairfield, 1892–1983), British writer and critic.

b. Mae West (1892–1980), American actress and writer.

b. Margaret Rutherford (1892–1972), British actress.

b. Vita (Victoria) Sackville-West (1892–1962), British writer.

b. Djuna Barnes (1892–1982), American writer.

b. Germaine Tailleferre (1892–1984), French composer.

b. Lydia Vasilievna Lopokova (1892–1981), Russian ballerina.

b. Marina Ivanovna Tsvetayeva (1892–1941), Russian poet.

b. Rosalinde Fuller (1892–1982), British actress.

# 1893

**POLITICS/LAW/WAR**

Women won the right to vote and be elected to office in New Zealand.

Julia Ward Howe resumed her presidency of the New England Woman Suffrage Association (1893–1910).

Cornelia Sorabji was the first woman allowed to take the Bachelor of Civil Law examination at Oxford University, by special permission from the vice-chancellor; it would be three decades before other women could follow her.

*Die Frau*, the main journal of the moderate German women's rights movement, was established, overseen for many years by Helene Lange.

Dr. Emily Stowe organized the Dominion Woman Suffrage Association, becoming its first president.

Ida B. Wells toured Britain (1893; 1894), her speeches there spurring formation of a British Anti-Lynching Society.

Women won the right to vote in Colorado.

b. Florence Hancock (1893–1974), British trade union official.

b. Louise Weiss (1893–1983), French writer, editor, film director, suffragist, and feminist.

b. Mabel Howard (1893–1972), New Zealand social reformer and politician.

b. Margaret Isabel Postgate Cole (1893–1980), British historian, writer, teacher, and socialist.

b. Ana Pauker (1893–1956), Romanian Communist.

b. Dorothy Detzer (Dorothy Detzer Denny, 1893–1981), American pacifist.

b. Fatima Jinnah (1893–1967), Pakistani politician, sister of the founder of Pakistan, Ali Jinnah.

b. Fusaye Ichikawa (1893–1981), Japanese feminist and politician.

b. Georgia Lee Witt Lusk (1893–1971), American politician.

d. Lucy Stone (1818–1893), American editor, abolitionist, and feminist, an organizer of the American Equal Rights Association (1866) and the American Woman Suffrage Association (1869), noted for keeping her own name after her marriage (1855). Her daughter, Alice Stone, succeeded her as editor of the *Woman's Journal*.

**RELIGION/EDUCATION/EVERYDAY LIFE**

Nurses Lillian Wald and Mary Brewster established the Henry Street Nurses' Settlement on New York's Lower East Side; there Wald developed her notable visiting nurse service, which provided home care for poor families.

Alexandra David-Neel began her long series of journeys in Central Asia, which would occupy her life and about which she wrote many books.

At the Chicago's World's Fair (World's Columbian Exposition), honoring the 400th anniversary of Christopher Columbus's arrival in the New World, the Woman's Building was designed, decorated, and managed by women; the Children's Building and the Woman's Dormitory were among the structures built and run by women. Also held in Chicago was the first World Congress of Women.

Hannah Solomon founded the National Council of Jewish Women and became its first president (1893–1905).

Matilda Gage published her classic feminist analysis *Woman, Church, and State*.

Mount Holyoke Seminary became Mount Holyoke College.

Henrietta Szold was editorial secretary of the Jewish publication society (1893–1916).

Ladies' Golf Union was formed in Britain, in a time when women played on separate courses from men. During its first three years (1893–1895), Lady Margaret Scott was champion; she then retired, having made golf "respectable" for women.

With Buffalo Bill's Wild West Show, Calamity Jane toured England and later the United States.

Alice Cunningham Fletcher published *A Study of Omaha Music*, a pioneer work in the field of American ethnomusicology.

Angela Burdett-Coutts edited *Woman's Work in England*.

Annie Besant published *An Autobiography*.

Josephine Shaw Lowell wrote *Industrial Arbitration and Conciliation*.

Séverine published a collection of her articles in *Pages rouges*.

b. Dhanvanthi Rama Rau (1893–1987), Indian social worker.

b. Dorothy Thompson (1893–1961), American journalist.

b. Florence Hancock (1893–1974), British trade union official.

d. Concepción Arenal (1820–1893), Spanish social scientist and journalist with special interests in penal science, international law, and public education. Two of her works on women, *La mujer del parvenir* and *La mujer de su casa*, were published posthumously (1895).

d. Mary Ann Shadd (1823–1893), African-American antislavery and women's rights movement activist, teacher, writer, and editor of the *Provincial Freeman*.

d. Mary Seymour Foot (1846–1893), American publisher and entrepreneur, who launched *Business Woman's Journal* (1889) and founded a business school to teach women office skills.

SCIENCE/TECHNOLOGY/MEDICINE

Dorothea Klumpke (later Roberts) was the first woman to obtain a doctoral degree in mathematics at the Sorbonne. That same year she presented before the Congress of Astronomy and Physics a work on the charting of heavenly bodies, which won a prize from France's Académie des Sciences.

Kate Gleason helped her father perfect a machine that more quickly and cheaply produced beveled gears, building the family firm on sales to the fledgling auto industry; Henry Ford referred to the Gleason gear planer as "the most remarkable machine work ever done by a woman," crediting her rather than her father with the invention.

Alice Eastwood succeeded Katharine Brandegee as curator of botany in the herbarium at the California Academy of Sciences in San Francisco; she also edited the academy's journal *Zoe* and published her own book, *A Popular Flora of Denver, Colorado*.

Americans Margaret Maltby and Mary Winston and Briton Grace Chisholm were the first women admitted as regular students in a Prussian university, when they registered to study mathematics at Göttingen University.

Bertha Lamme received her degree in mechanical engineering "with an option in electricity" from Ohio State University, becoming the first woman to obtain an American degree in engineering other than civil. She worked at Westinghouse and later, with her husband and brother, helped develop the power system at Niagara Falls.

British Nurses' Association became the first British professional women's group to be granted a royal charter; its prime founder, Ethel Fenwick, was its first president. Fenwick was also instrumental in getting nurses included in the international Hospital and Medical Congress held at the Chicago World's Fair.

Florence Bascom received a Ph.D. in geology from Johns Hopkins University; she was the first woman to receive a doctorate there, and by special dispensation, since women were not officially admitted until 1907. Christine Ladd-Franklin's degree, earned in 1882, would not be granted until 1926.

Isabel Hampton (later Robb) organized the Society of Superintendents of Training Schools for Nurses of the United States and Canada (later National League for Nursing), serving as its first president.

Though invited to do research in the University of Strasbourg's zoology department, and funded by a fellowship from the Association of Collegiate Alumnae (later American Association of University Women), Ida Hyde was not allowed to take a Ph.D. examination there.

Lillian Wald organized home nursing classes for New York City's immigrant families.

Williamina Fleming published the paper "A Field for Woman's Work in Astronomy," stressing both women's aptitude for astronomical work and the contributions women had already made.

British nurse Kate Marsden published *On Sledge and Horseback to Outcast Siberian Lepers.*

b. Cicely (Delphine) Williams (1893–1992), British physician.

b. Margaret Pyke (1893–1966), British birth-control campaigner.

d. Marie (Josefina Mathilde) Durocher (1809–1893), French-Brazilian obstetrician, one of Latin America's first female doctors, who practiced for 60 years.

## Arts/Literature

Sarah Orne Jewett published the short-story collection *A Native of Winby.*

Mrs. Patrick Campbell created the title role in Arthur Wing Pinero's play *The Second Mrs. Tanqueray.*

Cesira Ferrani created the title role in Giacomo Puccini's opera *Manon Lescaut.*

Frances Hodgson Burnett published her autobiography, *The One I Know Best of All.*

Gabrielle Réjane created the title role in Victorien Sardou's play *Madame Sans-Gêne.*

Katherine Lee Bates composed "America the Beautiful."

Christina Rossetti published *Verses.*

Ethel Smyth composed her *Mass in D.*

Marie Corelli published the novel *Barabbas.*

b. Vera Brittain (1893–1970), British feminist, pacifist, and writer.

b. Anita Loos (1893–1981), American writer.

b. Dorothy Leigh Sayers (1893–1957), British mystery writer.

b. Mary Pickford (Gladys Marie Smith, 1893–1979) American actress.

b. Dorothy Parker (1893–1967), American writer and critic.

b. Hanya Holm (Johanna Eckert, 1893–1992), German dancer, choreographer, and teacher.

b. Irene Foote Castle (1893–1969), British dancer, partnered with her husband, Vernon Castle.

b. Katharine Cornell (1893–1974), American actress-manager.

b. Martha Graham (1893–1991), American choreographer and dancer.

b. Sylvia Townsend Warner (1893–1978), British writer.

b. Joan Rosita Forbes (1893–1967), British travel writer.

b. Dorothy Schofield Dickson (1893–1995), American singer, dancer, and actress.

d. Fanny Kemble (1809–1893), British actress, daughter of theater manager Charles Kemble and a star on the London and New York stages in his company (1829–1834).

## 1894

### POLITICS/LAW/WAR

Helene Lange founded the Berlin Women's Association, becoming a leader of the moderate wing of the women's movement, with Gertrude Baumer, in the Federation of German Women's Associations (Bund Deutscher Frauenverein), founded the same year.

Dutch physician Aletta Jacobs founded the Association for Women's Suffrage, becoming its president in 1903.

French feminist Paule Mink became editorial secretary of *La question sociale* (1894–1897).

Kalliroe Parren founded the Greek Union for the Emancipation of Women.

Mary Putnam Jacobi presented the lecture "Common Sense Applied to Woman Suffrage," later published in book form.

b. Elizabeth Eloise (Kirkpatrick) Dilling (1894–1966), American ultraconservative politician and writer.

b. Josepha Abiertas (1894–1929), Philippine feminist.

b. Margaret Hodgson Ballinger (1894–1980), South African historian and liberal politician.

d. Jeanne Deroin (1810–1894), French feminist and socialist, a writer, editor, and the first woman to be a candidate for France's National Assembly (1849).

d. Myra Colby Bradwell (1831–1894), American lawyer, social reformer, and feminist, founder-publisher of the *Chicago Legal News* (1868), which she had developed into a lawbook and forms publisher. Her daughter, Bessie Bradwell, succeeded her as publisher (1894–1925).

d. Maria Deraismes (1828–1894), French feminist, women's rights leader, and writer.

### RELIGION/EDUCATION/EVERYDAY LIFE

Radcliffe College received its formal charter (March) as a women's college associated with Harvard University, unique in that it had no faculty of its own. Elizabeth Agassiz was Radcliffe's first president (until 1903); she had sparked informal women's education efforts (from 1879) and founded the Society for the Collegiate Instruction of Women (1882) that became Radcliffe.

Auguste Schmidt became first president of the Bund Deutscher Frauenverein (Federation of German Women's Associations), seeking to improve women's employment opportunities and legal and civil status, but eschewing radical aims and tactics.

Kate Richards O'Hare Cunningham became the first woman to be a member of the International Order of Machinists; she was apprenticed to her father.

Martha Carey Thomas, dean and professor of English at Bryn Mawr College, became its president (1894–1922).

Sarah Jane Farmer began the first of her Greenacre Summer Conferences, focusing on philosophy, religion, art, and current social problems.

British Women's Industrial Council was founded, to press for improvement in women's working conditions and educational opportunities; Clementine Black, one of its founders, was later its president.

Paule Mink became editor of the periodical *La question sociale* (1894–1897).

United Daughters of the Confederacy was founded, sparked by Caroline Meriweather Goodlett of Nashville and Anna Davenport Raines of Savannah; among the most popular Southern voluntary associations, it sponsored many projects centered on commemoration of the South's "lost cause."

Beatrice Potter Webb and Sidney Webb published *The History of Trade Unionism*.

Bertha von Suttner edited the journal (1894–1900) of the International Peace League, which she had founded.

British trade union activist Gertrude Tuckwell published *The State and Its Children*.

Gertrude Bell published *Safar Nameh*, a volume of travel sketches.

Isabella Bird Bishop published *Journeys in Persia and Kurdistan*.

Octavie Coudreau traveled with her husband, Henri Coudreau, to French Guiana.

b. Anne Loughlin (1894–1979), British trade unionist.

b. Dora (Winifred) Black Russell (1894–1986), British feminist, educator, and social reformer.

b. Fanny Durack (1894–1960), Australian swimmer.

b. Stella (Charnaud), dowager marchioness of Reading (1894–1971), British voluntary organizer.

d. Amelia Jenks Bloomer (1818–1894), American reformer and feminist, who popularized the "Bloomer" costume in her temperance paper, the *Lily* (1849–1855).

d. Elizabeth Palmer Peabody (1804–1894), American author and educator, a key figure in bringing to America the idea of the kindergarten, developed in Germany by Friedrich Froebel.

d. Laura (Eliza Jane Seymour) Bell (1829–1894), Irish courtesan and missionary.

### Science/Technology/Medicine

Anna Wessel Williams developed the first antitoxin against diphtheria, which would make the dreaded and once-common disease rare.

Ethel Fenwick established the Matrons' Council of Great Britain and Ireland, using it to lobby for state registration of matrons, opposed by Florence Nightingale. As an aid to waging the registration campaign (1904–1914), Fenwick and her husband, physician Bedford Fenwick, bought the *Nursing Record* (later the *British Journal of Nursing*).

Isabella Bird Bishop traveled as a missionary to China, Japan, and Korea, founding three hospitals in Szechuan; three books would result: *Korea and Her Neighbours* (1898), *The Yangtze Valley and Beyond* (1899), and *Chinese Pictures* (1900), her last.

Annie Russell Maunder became first editor of the British Astronomical Association's journal (1894–1896; 1917–1930); her husband, Edward Maunder, was a founder of the association and worked with her to start the journal.

Margaret Washburn received her doctoral degree from Cornell University; her dissertation on visual imagery in judgments of distance and direction was published in Germany. She had transferred to Cornell from Columbia University, where she was allowed only as an auditor.

### Arts/Literature

Emma Calvé created the title role in Jules Massenet's opera *The Girl from Navarre*.

Frances Harper published the poetry collection *The Martyr of Alabama*.

Kate Chopin published the short-story collection *Bayou Folk*.

Sybil Sanderson created the title role in Jules Massenet's opera *Thaïs*.

Gertrude Atherton published the novel *Before the Gringo Came*.

Harriet Hosmer's sculpture *Queen Isabella* was shown in San Francisco.

Mary Hallock Foote published the novel *Coeur d'Alene*.

Edith Somerville and Martin Ross (Violet Martin) published the novel *The Real Charlotte*.

Mrs. Humphrey Ward published the novel *Marcella*.

b. Beatrice Lillie (1894–1988), Canadian-British actress and singer.

b. Bessie Smith (1894 or 1898–1937), American blues singer.

b. Bryher (Annie Winifred Ellerman, 1894–1983), British writer and editor.

b. Jean Rhys (Gwen Williams, 1894–1979), British writer.

b. Jeanne Eagels (1894–1929), American actress.

b. Pola Negri (Apollonia Chalupiec, 1894–1987), Polish-born film actress.

b. Fay Compton (1894–1978), British actress.

b. Teresa Deevy (1894–1963), Irish playwright.

d. Christina Georgina Rossetti (1830–1894), British poet, long associated with the pre-Raphaelites; sister of Dante Gabriel and William Michael Rossetti.

d. Marietta Alboni (1823–1894), Italian contralto, a major figure in European opera in the 1840s and early 1850s.

## 1895

### POLITICS/LAW/WAR

Catherine Spence founded the Australian Effective Voting League.

Massachusetts antisuffrage organization was founded.

Millicent Garrett Fawcett published the biography *Life of Queen Victoria*.

Mary Lease published *The Problem of Civilization Solved*.

b. Dolores Ibarruri (La Pasionara, 1895–1991), Spanish Communist Party leader.

b. Larissa Mikhailovna Reisner (1895–1926), Russian writer, a Bolshevik soldier, commissar, and diplomat.

b. Xiang Jingyu (1895–1928), Chinese feminist and Communist leader.

d. Louise Michel (1830–1895), French teacher and writer, an anarchist allied with socialists who became a leading woman of the Paris Commune (1871), was imprisoned until the general amnesty (1881), and was imprisoned again (1883–1889).

d. Luise Otto-Peters (1819–1895), German novelist and women's rights movement leader.

### RELIGION/EDUCATION/EVERYDAY LIFE

Elizabeth Cady Stanton published *The Woman's Bible,* her feminist interpretation of the Bible (1895–1898). The National American Woman Suffrage Association quickly declared itself (1896) "non-sectarian, being composed of persons of all shades of religious opinion" and stated that it had "no official connection with the so-called *Woman's Bible* or any theological publication."

National Federation of Afro-American Women (NFAAW) was organized at a Boston conference led by Josephine St. Pierre Ruffin, becoming the first national organization of black women's clubs (1895–1896); among the founders were Mary Church Terrell, Fannie Barrier Williams, and Margaret Washington, its first president.

Annie Peck won wide attention by climbing the Matterhorn, dressed in a tunic and knickerbockers. She followed this with numerous other ascents, notably in the Alps and in Central and South America.

Ida B. Wells published "Red Record," her famous study of lynching, the earliest comprehensive work in the field, supported by statistical data; it would be followed by numerous writings and speeches in her lifelong antilynching campaign.

---

# On Black Women's Clubs

All over America there is to be found a large and growing class of earnest, intelligent, progressive colored women, women who, if not leading full useful lives, are only waiting for the opportunity to do so, many of them warped and cramped for lack of opportunity, not only to do more but to *be* more . . . Now for the sake of the thousands of self-sacrificing young women teaching and preaching in lonely southern backwoods, for the noble army of mothers who have given birth to these girls, mothers whose intelligence is only limited by their opportunity to get at books, for the sake of the fine cultured women who have carried off the honors in school. . . it is "mete, right and our bounden duty" to stand forth and declare ourselves and principles, to teach an ignorant and suspicious world that our aims and interests are identical with those of all good aspiring women. . . Year after year southern women have protested against the admission of colored women into any national organization on the ground of the immorality of these women. . . Now with an army of organized women standing for purity and mental worth, we in ourselves deny the charge and open the eyes of the world. . .

— Josephine St. Pierre Ruffin, at the organizing conference for the
National Federation of Afro-American Women (1895)

---

Jane Addams published *Hull House Maps and Papers*, a detailed study of conditions in the Chicago immigrant district the settlement house served.

Octavia Hill, who had long campaigned for the preservation of green areas, helped found Britain's National Trust.

Troy Female Seminary became the Emma Willard School.

Virginia's Augusta Female Seminary was renamed the Mary Baldwin Seminary, after its longtime principal, who at her death (1897) heavily endowed the school.

Fanny Workman published *Algerian Memories* and went on a series of cycling tours (1895–1899) with her husband, William Workman, later writing about them.

Florence Kelley became the first woman to lead a state factory-inspection service, in Illinois (1895–1897).

In Germany, girls were allowed to take the *Abitur*, the graduating exam at the end of secondary school, though girls' secondary schools (*Lyzeums*) would not be opened until 1908.

Octavie Coudreau traveled with her husband, Henri Coudreau, to Pará in northern Brazil (1895–1899), co-authoring six books about their journeys.

British reformer Louisa Twining published *Recollections of Life and Work*.

Ellen Key published *Individualism och Socialism*.

b. Flora Benenson Solomon (1895–1984), Russian-born British social reformer.

b. Susanne Knauth Langer (1895–1985), American philosopher.

d. Nadezhda Stasova (1822–1895), Russian feminist and social reformer who helped formally open the University of St. Petersburg to women (1869), active in various philanthropic ventures, founding four of the earliest Russian child nurseries; Elena Stasova was her niece.

d. Sarah Elizabeth van de Vort Emery (1838–1895), American writer on economics and social reform issues.

## SCIENCE/TECHNOLOGY/MEDICINE

Lilian Murray became Britain's first licensed female dentist, when she graduated from Edinburgh Dental School. She had originally applied to London's National Dental Hospital, where she was not even allowed to enter the building, but was interviewed in the street and advised to try Edinburgh.

Physicist Margaret E. Maltby became the first American woman to receive a Ph.D. from Göttingen University, in mathematics.

Trinidad Tescon founded a field hospital and developed a body of nurses during the Philippine Revolution.

Physician Elizabeth Blackwell published *Pioneer Work in Opening the Medical Profession to Women*.

Nature-study expert Anna Botsford Comstock engraved scientific illustrations for *Manual for the Study of Insects*, by her husband, Henry Comstock.

b. Anna Freud (1895–1982), Austrian-British psychoanalyst.

b. Dorothy Russell (1895–1983), Australian-born British pathologist.

b. Esther Applin (1895–1972), American petroleum geologist.

b. Margaret D. Foster (1895–1970), American mineralogist.

d. Mary Harris Thompson (1829–1895), American physician, the leading female doctor in 19th-century Chicago, who founded the Chicago Hospital for Women and Children (1865), later renamed after her, and the Women's Hospital Medical College (1870).

## ARTS/LITERATURE

Eleanora Duse and Sarah Bernhardt appeared in London in separate productions of Suderman's *Magda* (*Heimat*), highlighting their contrasting theatrical styles.

Lou Andreas-Salomé published the novel *Ruth*.

Clorinda Matto de Turner published the novel *Herencia*, on Indian-rights themes.

Cecilia Beaux became a faculty member at the Pennsylvania Academy of the Fine Arts.

b. Alberta Hunter (1895–1984), American blues singer.

b. Doris Humphrey (1895–1958), American dancer, choreographer, and teacher.

b. Dorothea Lange (1895–1865), American photographer.

b. Encarnación Lopez Julves (La Argentinita, 1895–1945), Spanish dancer.

b. Kirsten Malfrid Flagstad (1895–1962), Norwegian soprano.

b. Babette Deutsch (1895–1982), American poet.

b. Juana Morales de Ibarbourou (1895–1979), Uruguayan poet.

b. Olga (Alexandrovna) Spessivtseva (1895–1991), Russian dancer.

b. Blanche Sweet (1895–1986), American actress.

b. Jelly d'Arányi (1895–1966), Hungarian violinist.

d. Berthe Morisot (1841–1895), French painter, a leading Impressionist whose works were regularly exhibited at the Impressionist exhibitions and at the Salon.

## 1896

### POLITICS/LAW/WAR

Ellen Spencer Mussey founded the Washington College of Law, in response to discrimination against women in admission to law schools, specifically against her own students by Columbia University.

Utah became a state and reinstated woman suffrage, lost in 1887.

Women won the right to vote in Idaho.

Kalliroe Parren founded the Union of Greek Women.

Kate Sheppard became the first president of the New Zealand National Council of Women.

New York State antisuffrage organization was founded.

### RELIGION/EDUCATION/EVERYDAY LIFE

National Association of Colored Women (NACW) was formed by a merger of the National Federation of Afro-American Women and the Colored Woman's League, becoming the main national organization for black women's clubs, its motto "Lifting As We Climb." Mary Church Terrell was its first president (1896–1901).

Fannie Merritt Farmer, famed as principal of the Boston Cooking School, published the *Boston Cooking School Cook Book*, introducing precise measurements and instructions to cooking and earning the nickname "Mother of Level Measurement." Periodically revised and renamed the *Fannie Farmer Cookbook*, it would remain a standard through the 20th century through many editions.

Mary Morton Kehew and Mary Kenney (later O'Sullivan) founded the Union for Industrial Progress (1896–1901), to organize bookbinders, laundry and tobacco workers, and female clothing workers.

Women played their first intercollegiate basketball game, between the University of California at Berkeley and Stanford University; no males were allowed at the Berkeley game.

British feminists Helen Blackburn and Jessie Boucheret published *The Condition of Working Women*.

Cosmetics entrepreneur Harriet Hubbard Ayer joined the *New York World* as a beauty columnist for its Sunday supplement (1896–1903), becoming the first coordinator of a "woman's page."

Ellen Key published *Missbrukad Kvinnokraft* (*The Strength of Women Misused*), attacked as a work fostering free love and atheism, although motherhood was central to Key's view of women's position.

Harriet Robinson published *Loom and Spindle, or Life Among the Early Mill Girls, with a Sketch of "The Lowell Offering" and Some of Its Contributors*.

Josephine Butler published the autobiography *Personal Reminiscences of a Great Crusade*.

Mary Follett published an innovative study, *The Speaker and the House of Representatives*, even before receiving her degree in political economy from Radcliffe (1898).

b. Helen Merrell Lynd (1896–1982), American sociologist.

b. Sophia Heath (1896–1936), American athletics administrator and aviator.

b. Wallis Warfield Simpson, duchess of Windsor (1896–1986), American wife of Britain's King Edward VIII, for whom he would give up his throne (1936).

d. Anne Ayres (1816–1896), English-American nun who founded the Sisters of the Holy Communion (1845).

d. Isabel Arundell Burton (1831–1896), British traveler who traveled widely with her husband, Richard Burton, whose biography was her last book.

## SCIENCE/TECHNOLOGY/MEDICINE

Physiologist Ida Hyde graduated from Heidelberg University, becoming the first woman to receive a Ph.D. in science from a German university, having been barred because of her sex from taking the doctoral examination at the University of Strasbourg. She then worked as a research fellow at Radcliffe College (1896–1897), becoming the first woman to do research at Harvard Medical School.

Mary Winston received her mathematics degree magna cum laude from Göttingen University, among the first American women to receive a Ph.D. from a foreign university. In her final year of study she had been supported by a fellowship from the Association of Collegiate Alumnae (later American Association of University Women).

After five years of study at Harvard University, having met all the requirements for a Ph.D. in psychology, Mary Whiton Calkins was denied a Harvard degree; she declined to accept a degree from Radcliffe College.

After obtaining her Ph.D. from the University of Chicago, Cornelia Clapp became professor of zoology at Mount Holyoke College (1896–1916), where she had earlier taught gymnastics and mathematics (from 1872).

Annie Jump Cannon became an assistant at the Harvard College Observatory, where she would work until her retirement in 1940.

Florence Bascom became the first woman to be employed as a geologist by the American Geological Survey.

Mary Orr (later Evershed) published *Southern Stars: A Guide to the Constellations Visible in the Southern Hemisphere*.

Isabel Hampton Robb founded the Nurses' Associated Alumnae of the United States and Canada, becoming its first president (1896–1901).

b. Gerty Theresa Radnitz Cori (1896–1957), Czech-American medical biochemist.

b. Ida (Eva) Tacke Noddack (1896– ), German engineer and nuclear physicist, codiscoverer with her husband, Walter Noddack, of the element rhenium (1925); she first suggested the possibility that an atom's nucleus might be broken apart (1933).

b. Bessie Coleman (1896–1926), African-American pilot.

## ARTS/LITERATURE

Alice Guy-Blaché produced and directed her first film, *La Fee aux Choux*, perhaps the first story film ever made.

Sarah Bernhardt produced Oscar Wilde's *Salome* in Paris, after the play had been banned in Britain.

Sarah Orne Jewett published the collection of sketches *The Country of the Pointed Firs*.

Amy Beach composed her *Gaelic Symphony*.

# Old Prejudice

Of all the old prejudices that cling to the hem of the woman's garments and persistently impede her progress, none holds faster than this. The idea that she owes service to a man instead of to herself, and that it is her highest duty to aid his development rather than her own, will be the last to die.

—Susan B. Anthony, in *The Status of Women, Past, Present, and Future* (1897)

Christina Rossetti published *New Poems* posthumously.

Elizabeth Butler showed her painting *Steady the Drums and Fife*.

Maude Nugent composed the song "Sweet Rosie O'Grady."

b. Ethel Waters (1896–1977), American singer and actress.

b. Lillian Gish (1896–1994), American actress.

b. Mari Sandoz (1896–1966), American author.

b. Marjorie Kinnan Rawlings (1896–1953), American writer.

b. Vicki Baum (1896–1960), Austrian writer and editor.

d. Clara Wieck Schumann (1819–1896), German pianist, composer, and teacher, daughter of composer Friedrich Wieck and wife of composer Robert Schumann, whose works she edited and published after his death.

d. Harriet Beecher Stowe (1811–1896), American writer and women's rights leader, famed for her *Uncle Tom's Cabin* (1852).

## 1897

### POLITICS/LAW/WAR

National Union of Women's Suffrage Societies (NUWSS) was founded in Britain, as a national coalition of regional moderate women's suffrage groups, with Millicent Garrett Fawcett as its first president (1897–1919).

Harriet Tubman finally won a $20-per-month pension for her Civil War service to the Union as soldier, spy, scout, and nurse.

Britain's Victoria celebrated her 60th year as queen.

b. Margaret Chase Smith (1897–1995), American politician, a four-time Republican senator from Maine.

b. Mei-ling Soong (Madame Chiang Kai-shek, 1897– ), Chinese political figure, who married General Chiang Kai-shek (1927), becoming a key figure in the Chinese Republic. She was the sister of Ching-ling Soong (Madame Sun Yat-sen) and Chinese financier T. V. Soong.

### RELIGION/EDUCATION/EVERYDAY LIFE

Adelaide Hoodless founded a Women's Institute at Stoney Creek, Ontario, the first of many designed to bring home-health education to rural Canadian women.

After a "mothers' congress" in Washington, D.C., the National Congress of Mothers was founded by Phoebe Apperson Hearst and Alice McLellan Birney, its first president; this would later become the National Parent-Teacher Association.

Beatrice Potter Webb and Sidney Webb published *Industrial Democracy*.

Motoko Hani became Japan's first full-time female reporter, covering women, education, and religion for the newspaper *Hochi shimbun*.

Isabelle Eberhardt first went to West Africa, where she and her mother converted to Islam; after her mother's death, she traveled the Algerian Sahara disguised as a male Arab student, returning to write sensational stories under a pseudonym.

Marguerite Durand founded the women's newspaper *La Fronde*.

White Rose Mission was founded and headed by Victoria Earle Matthews, president of the Woman's Loyal Union, as a nondenominational mission to aid black women coming from the South to New York City. It provided inexpensive lodging, protection from exploitation, and travelers' aid representatives.

American physician Mary Edwards Walker founded a colony for women called Adamless Eden.

Fanny Workman published *Sketches Awheel in fin de siècle Iberia*, about her cycling tour.

Mary Kingsley published *Travels in West Africa*.

b. Barbara Frances Adam Wootton (Baroness Wootton, 1897–1988), British social scientist and educator.

b. Charlemae Rollins (1897–1979), African-American librarian and author.

b. Dorothy Day (1897–1980), American journalist, pacifist, socialist, and Catholic reform-movement leader.

b. Edith Elizabeth Lowry (1897–1970), American religious leader and organizer.

b. Margaret Fogarty Rudkin (1897–1967), American entrepreneur and baker.

d. Mariya (Vasilevna) Trubnikova (1835–1897), Russian feminist and educator who was part of the "Triumvirate" that sparked mid-19th-century Russia's feminist movements, providing help for poor women (1859) and helping to open Russia's universities to women (1869).

d. Teresa of Lisieux (Thérèse Martin, 1873–1897), French nun and saint, who at 15 joined the Carmelite convent of Lisieux in Normandy with two sisters, dying of tuberculosis at 24; noted for her *Histoire d'une âme*, the posthumously published recollections of her life, she became a patron saint of France.

### SCIENCE/TECHNOLOGY/MEDICINE

Beatrix Potter, later famous as a children's author, discovered that lichen was not a kind of plant but a symbiotic relationship between algae and fungi; her paper on the topic was read (by a male assistant) at the Linnaean Society but was so ill-received that she did not publish it and abandoned her scientific studies in the field. Her discovery would not be accepted for another decade.

Johns Hopkins University's medical school became the first major American medical school to accept women as students—after receiving a large contribution from Mary Elizabeth Garrett on condition that it do so.

Antonia Maury published a catalogue classifying stars according to their spectra, in the *Annals of the Harvard College Observatory*, laying the basis for modern astrophysics.

Hungary's Ministry of Culture recognized Vilma Hugonnai-Wartha as having a medical degree from the University of Zürich, although it had allowed her only a midwife's degree (1879); like other female doctors, however, she could practice in Hungary only with a male physician (until 1913).

Anna Botsford Comstock was made an assistant in nature study at Cornell University; she had earlier lectured on nature study at other universities, notably Stanford, Columbia, and Virginia.

British nurse Kate Marsden opened a hospital for people with leprosy in Viluisk, Siberia, having raised public money to help these outcasts.

Harriet Boyd (later Hawes), a specialist in Greek archaeology, served as a volunteer nurse in Thessaly during the Greco-Turkish War.

Marie Curie published her first paper, on the magnetism of tempered steel, the year her daughter Irène was born.

b. Amelia Earhart (1897–1937), American aviator.

b. Irène Joliot-Curie (1897–1956), French physicist.

### ARTS/LITERATURE

Käthe Kollwitz created her etching series *The Weavers' Revolt* (1897–1898).

Olga Knipper created the role of Elena in Anton Chekhov's *Uncle Vanya*.

Kate Chopin published the short-story collection *A Night in Acadie*.

Ellen Glasgow published the novel *The Descendant*.

Grazia Deledda published the novel *Tesore*.

b. Gloria Swanson (Gloria Josephine Swenson, 1897–1983), American actress.

---

The labor of women in the house, certainly, enables men to produce more wealth than they otherwise could: and in this way women are economic factors in society. But so are horses.

—Charlotte Perkins Gilman, in *Women and Economics* (1898)

b. Marian Anderson (1897–1993), American contralto.

b. Brenda Colvin (1897–1981), British landscape architect.

b. Lillian Smith (1897–1966), American novelist.

b. Louise Bogan (1897–1970), American writer and critic.

b. Rosa Ponselle (1897–1981), American soprano.

d. Margaret Wilson Oliphant (1828–1897), Scottish writer.

## 1898

### POLITICS/LAW/WAR

Ida Harper published the first two volumes of her authorized biography of her friend and suffragist colleague Susan B. Anthony.

b. Golda Meir (Golda Meyerson, 1898–1978), Russian-American-Israeli Zionist and political leader.

d. Eugénie Potonie-Pierre (1844–1898), French feminist and socialist, a leader of the French women's rights movement.

d. Sarah (Emma Evelyn) Edwards (Franklin Thompson, 1841–1898), American soldier, who served disguised as a man in the Union Army during the Civil War.

### RELIGION/EDUCATION/EVERYDAY LIFE

Charlotte Perkins Gilman published *Women and Economics*, her classic study of sexual discrimination, calling for an end to women's sole responsibility for work in the home in favor of communal sharing and equality between women and men in home and child-raising tasks.

Annie Besant founded the Central Hindu College at Benares, India, herself learning Sanskrit and translating the *Bhagavad Gita*.

Gertrude Dudley was made director of women's athletics and women's gymnasium at the University of Chicago, becoming a major figure in American collegiate athletics for women.

American librarian Anne Carroll Moore introduced courses on working with children, at the Pratt Institute in Brooklyn.

First Phi Beta Kappa chapter at an American women's college was founded at Vassar.

Margaret Noble traveled to India to become a follower of Ramakrishna; she became a nun, called Sister Nivedita (she who has been dedicated), founded a girls' school in Calcutta, and later wrote about Indian culture.

Marie Manning, writing as Beatrice Fairfax, developed the first "advice-to-the-lovelorn" column, in the *New York Evening Journal*.

The Sanctified Sisters moved to Washington, D.C., incorporating as the Woman's Commonwealth (1902), with a new constitution.

Under Lillian M. N. Stevens (1898–1914), successor of Frances Willard, the Women's Christian Temperance Union focused on campaigning for national prohibition, along with other temperance groups, such as the Anti-Saloon League.

Alice Pestana, writing as Caiel, published *Women and Peace: Appeal to Portuguese Mothers*.

British reformer Louisa Twining published *Workhouses and Pauperism*.

Dorothea Beale coauthored *Work and Play in Girls' Schools*.

b. Theresa Neuman (1898–1962), Austrian religious figure.

d. Frances E. Willard (1839–1898), American reformer, educator, and temperance advocate, head of Evanston College for Ladies (1870–1873) and influential president of the Women's Christian Temperance Union (1879–1898).

d. Matilda Joslyn Gage (1826–1898), American women's rights organizer and writer, longtime coworker with Elizabeth Cady Stanton and Susan B. Anthony on a wide range of suffrage and other women's rights issues.

SCIENCE/TECHNOLOGY/MEDICINE

Marie Curie coined the term "radioactivity" to describe the aspects of physics she was exploring with her husband, Pierre Curie.

Williamina Fleming was appointed curator of astronomical photographs at the Harvard Observatory, the first female to receive a corporation appointment at Harvard University; she led a team of other women astronomers.

After practicing as a physician for 20 years, Agnes McLaren converted to Catholicism and joined the Third Order of Dominicans; through her efforts, many female physicians were placed in Catholic missions, though women in Catholic religious orders were (until 1936) officially forbidden to become physicians.

Florence Bascom began her long association with Bryn Mawr College, where she founded the geology department, influencing generations of women students.

Army Nurse Corps (ANC) was created, to provide trained military nurses to the armed forces during the Spanish-American War, notably through the efforts of Dr. Anita Newcomb McGee; its first superintendent was Mrs. Dita Kenney.

British physicist Hertha Ayrton was elected to the Institution of Electrical Engineers, becoming its first female member.

Dorothy Reed (later Mendenhall) and Marguerite Long became the first two women employed in a U.S. Navy hospital, at the Brooklyn Navy Yard's bacteriological laboratory.

During the Spanish-American War, Clara Barton once again organized private relief for the wounded, often herself driving mule wagons of supplies, as she had during the Civil War.

Eleanor Ormerod published her book *Handbook of Insects Injurious to Orchard and Bush Fruits, with Means of Prevention and Remedy*.

Agnes Meara Chase became a protégée of bryologist Ellsworth Hill, moving from amateur to professional in botanical illustrations of new species of mosses he was discovering.

Smith College Observatory, previously underfunded, received an endowment from Elizabeth Haven.

b. Helen Brooke Taussig (1898–1986), American pediatric cardiologist.

b. Katherine Burr Blodgett (1898–1979), American physicist.

b. Rachel Fuller Brown (1898–1980), American biochemist.

b. Katherine Esau (1898–1997), American botanist specializing in the effects of viruses on plants.

ARTS/LITERATURE

Eleanora Duse created the title role in Gabriele D'Annunzio's play *La Gioconda*.

Olga Knipper starred as Arkadina in Anton Chekhov's *The Seagull*.

Sarah Bernhardt starred in her own play, *L'aveu*.

Ellen Glasgow published the novel *Phases of an Inferior Planet*.

Gertrude Atherton published the novel *The Californians*.

Pierini Legnani created the title role in Marius Petipa's ballet *Raymonda*.

Gemma Bellincioni created the title role in Umberto Giordano's opera *Fedora*.

Ethel Smyth composed the opera *Fantasio*.

b. Berenice Abbott (1898–1991), American photographer.

b. Lotte Lenya (1898–1981), Austrian actress and singer.

b. Gertrude Lawrence (Alexandra Lawrence-Klasen, 1898–1952), British actress.

b. Judith Anderson (Frances Margaret Anderson, 1898–1992), Australian actress.

b. Lil (Lillian) Hardin Armstrong (1898–1971), American jazz pianist, singer, and bandleader.

b. Gracie Fields (Grace Stansfield, 1898–1979), British singer, comedian, and actress.

b. Lily Pons (Alice Josephine Pons, 1898–1976), French soprano.

b. Marilyn Miller (Mary Ellen Reynolds, 1898–1936), American singer, dancer, and actress.

b. Bessie Love (Juanita Horton, 1898–1986), American actress.

b. Dorothy Gish (1898–1968), American actress.

b. Peggy Guggenheim (1898–1979), American art collector.

b. Vilma Banky (Vilma Lonchit, 1898–1955), Hungarian actress.

b. Winifred Holtby (1898–1935), British writer, pacifist, and feminist.

d. Helen Faucit (1817–1898), British actress, leading lady in William Macready's Covent Garden company (1837–ca. 1844).

## 1899

### POLITICS/LAW/WAR

By U.S. federal law, the age of consent (for heterosexual relations) was raised from 16 to 21.

Marie Stritt was elected president of the Federation of German Women's Associations.

Marianne Hainisch founded and was first president of the General Austrian Women's Association.

Vida Goldstein founded the monthly the *Australian Woman's Sphere*.

Women Lawyers' Club was founded; it would become the Women's National Bar Association (1908).

International Council of Women met in London.

b. Bertha Lutz (1899–1976), Brazilian zoologist, feminist, suffragist, and women's rights movement leader.

d. Marie Pouchoulin Goegg (1826–1899), Swiss feminist and democratic revolutionary, founder of the Association International des Femmes (1868).

### RELIGION/EDUCATION/EVERYDAY LIFE

National Consumers' League was founded, seeking protective legislation for American workers, especially to ban child labor and sweatshops, and to better working conditions for female retail clerks, also pressing for laws and inspections to ensure safe manufacturing and packaging of consumer products. Florence Kelley became its executive secretary (1899–1932), during her lifelong campaign to reform working conditions.

Margaret Bondfield, representing the Shop Assistants Union, was the first woman to become a delegate to Britain's Trades Union Congress.

Through the Chicago Women's Club, Hannah Solomon sparked the establishment of Cook County's pioneering juvenile court.

After the death of her husband and traveling partner, Octavie Coudreau completed her exploration of the Trombetas, a tributary of the Amazon, and published *Voyage au Trombetas*. Employed by Brazilian states, she explored the Amazon region (1899–1906), publishing two other books about her journeys.

Daisy Bates emigrated to western Australia to investigate treatment of the aboriginal population, remaining among them for 35 years and becoming known as *Kabbarli* (Grandmother).

---

# Child Labor and Women's Suffrage

To-night while we sleep, several thousand little girls will be working in textile mills, all the night through, in the deafening noise of the spindles and the looms spinning and weaving cotton and woolen, silks and ribbons for us to buy. . . We do not wish this. We prefer to have our work done by men and women. But we are almost powerless. Not wholly powerless, however, are citizens who enjoy the right of petition. For myself, I shall use this power in every possible way until the right to the ballot is granted. . . What can we do to free our consciences? There is one line of action by which we can do much. We can enlist the workingmen on behalf of our enfranchisement just in proportion as we strive with them to free the children. . .

—Florence Kelley, leader of the National Consumers' League (1905)

---

Fanny Workman and her husband, William Workman, began exploring in the Himalayas (ca. 1899), naming and surveying various peaks.

French physician Madeleine Pelletier became the first woman appointed to the staff of the Assistance Publique.

*Harriet Hubbard Ayer's Book: A Complete and Authentic Treatise on the Laws of Health and Beauty* was published.

Mary Kingsley published *West African Studies*.

b. Frances Amelia Yates (1899–1982), British cultural historian.

b. Suzanne Lenglen (1899–1938), French tennis player.

d. Aline Valette (1850–1899), French teacher, writer, and union activist who became a voluntary labor inspector, among the first in Paris (1880s), and cofounder of the Federation Française des Sociétés Feministes (1892).

## SCIENCE/TECHNOLOGY/MEDICINE

Ellen Swallow Richards chaired a series of summer conferences at Lake Placid, stemming from the work she had generated on ways of bettering the home environment, especially on making the home easier to care for and meals more nutritious, inexpensive, and easy to prepare. The new field she led was dubbed "home economics."

Elsie Inglis received her medical degree in Edinburgh, having successfully fought for women's right to study surgery along with men; after graduation she cofounded, with Jessie MacGregor, the first all-woman maternity center in Scotland.

Anna Botsford Comstock was named assistant professor of nature study at Cornell University, becoming its first female professor. The school's trustees reversed the appointment (1900), forcing her back to the status of lecturer; she would become assistant professor again (1913), then full professor (1920).

Cornell University began to accept women at its medical school, after which Elizabeth and Emily Blackwell closed their Women's Medical College.

Margaret Huggins and her husband, William Huggins, published their *Atlas of Representative Stellar Spectra*.

Taking advantage of the International Council of Women meeting in London, Ethel Fenwick helped organize and became first president of the International Council of Nurses, the first such organization for women working as health professionals.

Viennese psychiatrist Sigmund Freud published his famous *Studies in Hysteria*, putting the case for extreme repression of women's sexuality as a key factor in many sociopsychological ills.

American physicist Marcia Keith was one of the founders of the American Physical Society.

b. Charlotte Auerbach (1899–1994), German geneticist, a specialist in mutation research, who emigrated to Scotland after the Nazis took power (1933).

b. Janet (Maria) Vaughan (1899–1993), British physician, a specialist in the effects of radiation and longtime university principal of Somerville College (1945–1967).

## ARTS/LITERATURE

Kate Chopin published the novel *The Awakening*, controversial because of its sexual frankness and interracial themes.

Olga Knipper created the role of Elena in Anton Chekhov's *Uncle Vanya*.

Julia Marlowe created the title role in Clyde Fitch's play *Barbara Frietchie*.

Minnie Maddern Fiske starred in the title role in Langdon Mitchell's play *Becky Sharpe*.

Edith Somerville and Martin Ross (Violet Martin) published *Some Experiences of an Irish RM*.

Ida Emerson introduced the song "Hello Ma Baby," cowritten with her husband, Joseph E. Howard.

b. Elizabeth Bowen (1899–1973), Anglo-Irish writer.

b. Eva Le Gallienne (1899–1992), British-American actress and director.

b. (Edith) Ngaio Marsh (1899–1982), New Zealand mystery writer and theater producer.

b. Nadezhda Mandelstam (1899–1980), Russian writer.

b. Anne Green (1899– ), American writer long resident in France.

b. Leontine Schlesinger Sagan (1899–1974), Austrian actress and director.

b. Lotte Reiniger (1899–1981), German animated-film maker.

d. Carlotta Grisi (1819–1899), Italian dancer, one of the leading ballerinas of the 1840s and early 1850s, who created several major roles.

d. Rosa Bonheur (1822–1899), French artist, teacher, and women's rights advocate, best known as an animal painter and sculptor.

## 1900

### POLITICS/LAW/WAR

Carrie Chapman Catt succeeded Susan B. Anthony as president of the National American Woman Suffrage Association (1900–1903).

Japan's Security Police Law banned women from political meetings or memberships; its civil code also affirmed exclusion of women from most higher education and, while allowing women to own property, barred them from managing it themselves.

French feminist Hubertine Auclert published *Les femmes arabes en Algérie*.

German feminist Lida Heymann was a founder of the Women's Welfare Association.

German Union of Progressive Women's Associations was organized; among its founders were Anita Augsburg and Minna Cauer.

Maud Gonne (later MacBride) founded the Daughters of Ireland (Inghindhe Na Eireann).

b. Helen Gahagan Douglas (1900–1980), American actress and politician.

b. Vijaya Lakshmi Pandit (Madame Pandit, 1900–1991), Indian independence movement leader and diplomat, the sister of Jawaharlal Nehru.

b. Axis Sally (Mildred Gillars, 1900–1988), American-born Nazi broadcaster during World War II.

b. Elizabeth Angela Marguerite Bowes-Lyon (1900– ), Britain's Queen Mother—more popularly, "Queen Mum"—who would become the wife of George VI of England and the mother of Elizabeth II. She and the rest of the royal family would win popular affection for staying in London through the Blitz, even after Buckingham Palace was hit (1940).

b. Georgia Neese Clark Gray (1900–1995), American politician, actress, and banker, the first woman to be treasurer of the United States (1949–1953).

b. Teresa Noce (1900– ), Italian socialist, writer, and editor of various periodicals, including the antifascist *La voce della donne* (1934).

d. Paule (Paulina) Mekarska Mink (1839–1900), French writer, editor, and socialist women's rights movement leader.

### RELIGION/EDUCATION/EVERYDAY LIFE

International Ladies Garment Workers Union (ILGWU) was founded, with a membership largely composed of women, many of them recent immigrants—and a leadership composed wholly of men.

At a convention of the General Federation of Women's Clubs (GFWC), African-American leader Josephine St. Pierre Ruffin carried credentials representing three organizations: the New England Woman's Club, the Massachusetts State Federation of Women's Clubs, and the Woman's Era Club. The GFWC refused to accept the credentials for the Woman's Era Club, because it was a black club, and Ruffin refused to be seated representing the white clubs only.

---

There are two kinds of restrictions upon human liberty—the restraint of law and that of custom. No written law has ever been more binding than unwritten custom supported by popular opinion.

— Carrie Chapman Catt, in the speech "For the Sake of Liberty" (1902)

---

Barnard College was formally incorporated into the Columbia University system.

Mildred Cable joined Evangeline French at a mission in China's Shanxi province, there later joined by Evangeline's sister, Francesca, in running a girls' school, a base for their Asian travels as "the trio."

On a visit to Persia, Sarah Jane Farmer was converted to the Baha'i religion; on her return she began to turn her Greenacre Summer Conferences and Monsalvat School of Comparative Religion toward the Baha'i movement. Greenacre would formally become the Institute of the Baha'i National Spiritual Assembly in 1928, after her death.

Women were allowed to compete in the modern Olympics for the first time; they had been barred from the first modern games, held in Athens in 1896.

Charlotte Perkins Gilman published *Concerning Children*.

Chicago's African-American Alpha Suffrage Club was founded.

Elizabeth Le Blond is believed to have been the first "woman's rope," climbing Piz Palu in Italy with Evelyn McDonnel; in the higher stretches, she removed her skirt, climbing in breeches; she took a lady's maid with her as far as possible.

Ellen Key published her best-known book, *Barnhets ahrundrade* (*The Century of the Child*), exploring female roles and educational theories.

Fanny Workman published *In the Ice World of the Himalaya*.

Ella Flagg Young was named to head the new Chicago Normal School.

b. Miriam O'Brien Underhill (ca. 1900– ), American mountaineer who pioneered a new route through the Dolomites (1927) and made the first women-only ascent of the Matterhorn (1932), with Alice Damesme.

b. Kitamura Sayo (1900–1967), Japanese religious leader.

d. Mary Kingsley (1862–1900), British explorer, niece of the writer Charles Kingsley; from 1892, she traveled widely, especially in West Africa, and wrote several books.

## SCIENCE/TECHNOLOGY/MEDICINE

Sister Mary Alphonsa Lathrop (Rose Hawthorne) and Alice Huber founded the Dominican Congregation of St. Rose of Lima, the Servants of Relief for Incurable Cancer, the first free American hospice for the terminally ill.

Sarah Whiting established and became director of the Whitin Observatory at Wellesley College, funded by a Wellesley trustee, Mrs. John Whitin.

Agnes Meara Chase provided botanical illustrations for the Field Museum of Natural History (Chicago) publications *Plantae Utowanae* (1900) and *Plantae Yucatanae* (1904).

b. Cecilia Payne-Gaposchkin (1900–1979), British-American astronomer.

b. Honor (Bridget) Fell (1900–1986), British cell biologist.

b. Marion Milner (1900– ), British psychoanalyst who, sometimes writing as Joanne Field, has explored the psychological value of various means of self-expression, notably writing and art.

d. Lucy Hobbs (Taylor, 1833–ca. 1900), American dentist, the first woman to obtain a degree in dentistry (1866).

## ARTS/LITERATURE

Beatrix Potter published *Peter Rabbit*.

Colette published *Claudine at School*, first of the five "Claudine" novels.

Hericlea Darclée created the title role in Giacomo Puccini's opera *Tosca*.

Marthe Rioton created the title role in Gustave Charpentier's opera *Louise*, controversial at the time for its women's liberation theme.

Sarah Bernhardt created the role of Napoléon's son in Edmond Rostand's play *L'Aiglon*.

Ellen Glasgow published the novel *Voice of the People*.

Mrs. Patrick Campbell starred in Max Beerbohm's play *The Happy Hypocrite*.

Grazia Deledda published the novel *Il vecchio della montagna*.

Mary Johnston published the novel *To Have and to Hold*.

Maria Machado de Assis published the novel *Dom Casmurro*.

Marie Corelli published the novel *The Master Christian*.

Mary Elizabeth Braddon published the melodramatic novel *The Infidel*.

b. Helen Hayes (Helen Hayes Brown, 1900–1993), American actress.

b. (Edith) Norma Shearer (1900–1983), Canadian actress.

b. Helen Morgan (Helen Riggins, 1900–1941), American singer.

b. Katina Paxinou (Katina Constantopoulos, 1900–1973), Greek actress, director, and translator.

b. Louise Nevelson (Louise Berliawsky, 1900–1988), American sculptor.

b. Madeleine Renaud (1900–1994), French actress and director.

b. Margaret Mitchell (1900–1949), American writer.

b. Nathalie Sarraute (ca. 1900– ), multifaceted French writer, a leading figure in French cultural life after World War II.

b. Alice Neel (1900–1984), American painter.

b. Anna Reiling Seghers (Netty Radvanyi, 1900–1983), German writer.

b. Dorothy Arzner (1900–1979), American film editor, writer, and director.

b. Elisabeth Bergner (1900–1986), Austrian actress.

b. Helen Edna Hokinson (1900–1949), American cartoonist.

b. Helena Niemirowska Syrkius (1900–1982), Polish architect.

b. Joan Cross (1900–1993), British soprano, producer, and educator.

b. Mildred Dunnock (1900–1991), American actress.

b. Zelda Sayre Fitzgerald (1900–1948), American writer, wife of writer F. Scott Fitzgerald.

b. Meridel LeSueur (1900–1996), American writer, largely on populist themes.

## 1901

### POLITICS/LAW/WAR

Women won the right to vote and be elected to office in Australia.

Lily Braun published the strongly feminist *Die Frauenfrage*, rejecting the view that the triumph of socialism was a necessary precondition for the winning of women's freedom, and precipitating her expulsion from the Social Democratic Party. Disagreements about the importance of women's equality versus other social issues had earlier split the American women's and abolitionist movements after the Civil War and would split the American women's and New Left movement during the early 1970s.

Franciska Plamnikova founded the Women's Club of Prague.

Helene Lange and Gertrude Baumer edited the five-volume *Handbuch der Frauenbegung* (1901–1906).

b. Edith Clara Summerskill (1901–1980), British doctor, socialist, women's rights advocate, and politician.

d. Victoria (1819–1901), queen of England (r. 1837–1901), who succeeded her uncle, William IV, presiding over the expansion of the British Empire and setting her stamp on an era.

### RELIGION/EDUCATION/EVERYDAY LIFE

Constance Applebee introduced field hockey to the United States, the first game being played at Harvard with ice hockey sticks.

Anna Kulisciov opposed the majority of the Italian Socialist Party in demanding that the party make women's suffrage one of its demands.

Calamity Jane starred as a Western "character" at the Pan-American Exposition in Buffalo, New York.

Gertrude Bell gained fame on Alpine expeditions (1901–1904).

Japan Women's College was founded; it offered "bridal training" classes, as did many "finishing schools" for young women that followed.

With her new husband, Soshikazu Hani, Motoko Hani founded the magazine *Fujin no Tomo* (*Woman's Friend*), advocating self-reliance for women.

Emily Murphy published *Janey Canuck Abroad*, a book about the Old World as seen by a clear-eyed Canadian social reformer.

Gertrude Bonnin wrote *Old Indian Legends*.

b. Tillie Lewis (1901– ), American entrepreneur, who during World War II made the Italian tomato a prime commercial crop in California and later developed the first artificially sweetened canned fruit. She was the first woman to direct the massive Ogden Corporation.

b. Kotani Kimi (1901–1971), Japanese religious leader and faith healer.

### SCIENCE/TECHNOLOGY/MEDICINE

American archaeologist Harriet Boyd (later Hawes) discovered and excavated a Minoan site at Gournia on Crete (1901–1904), describing her work in a national lecture tour (1902) and becoming the first woman to speak before the Archaeological Institute of America.

British physicist Hertha Ayrton's paper "The Mechanism of the Electric Arc" was read before the Royal Society by a male fellow, since she was barred from reading it herself.

Dorothy Reed (later Mendenhall) identified the cell that causes Hodgkin's disease, called the Reed or Reed-Sternberg cell.

U.S. Army created its first formal nurse corps, the first women's corps in the American armed forces, led by Anita Newcomb McGee.

American Federation of Nurses was formed by the merger of two other nursing organizations.

Florence Sabin published *An Atlas of the Medulla and Mid-brain*, a standard text.

b. Margaret Mead (1901–1978), American anthropologist.

b. Dorothy Hansine Andersen (1901–1963), American pathologist and pediatrician.

b. Ruth Roland Nichols (1901–1960), American aviator.

b. Sophia Josephine Kleegman (1901–1971), American gynecologist and obstetrician.

d. Eleanor Anne Ormerod (1828–1901), British economic entomologist noted for her work on identifying insects that were harmful or helpful in agriculture.

### ARTS/LITERATURE

Olga Knipper created the role of Masha in Konstantin Stanislavsky's Moscow Art Theatre production of *The Three Sisters*, by Anton Chekhov, her husband.

Ethel Barrymore had her first starring role, in Clyde Fitch's play *Captain Jinks of the Horse Marines*.

Alice Hegan Rice published the children's story *Mrs. Wiggs of the Cabbage Patch*.

Akiko Yosano published the poetry collection *Midaregami*.

Miles Franklin published the autobiographical novel *My Brilliant Career*.

Sarah Orne Jewett published the novel *The Tory Lover*.

Selma Lagerlöf published the novel *Jerusalem* (1901–1902).

b. Irene Dunne (1901–1990), American actress.

b. Marlene Dietrich (1901–1990), German actress and singer.

b. Ruth Crawford Seeger (1901–1953), American composer.

b. Zora Neale Hurston (1901–1960), African-American writer and folklorist.

b. Barbara Cartland (1901– ), British romance writer.

b. Helen Kalvak (1901–1984), Canadian Inuit artist.

b. Helene Weigel (1901–1971), German actress and director.

b. Jeannette MacDonald (1901–1965), American singer and actress.

b. Laura Riding (Laura Reichenthal, 1901–1991), American poet.

b. Sylvia Crowe (1901–1997), British landscape architect.

# 1902

## POLITICS/LAW/WAR

Germany's Union for Women's Suffrage was founded by a group including Lida Heymann, Minna Cauer, and Anita Augspurg, its first president.

Helen Blackburn published *Women's Suffrage: A Record of the Movement in the British Isles.*

Italy's Parliament passed its first protective legislation covering women and children, after a campaign launched by Milanese women in the socialist newspaper *Avanti!* (1897) was taken up by the Female Union (Unione Femminile, 1901).

Dutch physician Aletta Jacobs helped spark foundation of the international suffrage movement, in meetings at Washington, D.C. (1902), and Berlin (1904).

French-Canadian feminist Marie Gerin-Lajoie published *Traité de droit usual.*

Vida Goldstein made the first of her four unsuccessful runs for a seat in Australia's Parliament.

b. Alva Reimer Myrdal (1902–1986), Swedish teacher, social welfare worker, politician, diplomat, and peace activist.

b. Anna Lederer Rosenberg (1902–1993), American government official and public relations executive.

b. Gertrud Scholtz-Klink (1902– ), German propagandist and organizer, the chief Nazi women's leader, who was imprisoned for only 18 months during the postwar period.

d. Elizabeth Cady Stanton (1815–1902), American and worldwide women's rights movement leader, with Lucretia Mott organizer of the landmark Seneca Falls Women's Rights Convention (1848); writer of the historic Declaration of Sentiments and Resolutions (1848) and the Declaration of the Rights of Women (1876); founder and first president of the National Woman Suffrage Association (1869) and the National American Woman Suffrage Association (1890).

d. Louisa Lawson (1848–1902), Australian feminist, editor, and suffragist, founder of the periodical the *Dawn* (1889).

d. Mary Muller (1820–1902), pioneeering New Zealand suffragist and writer on a wide range of women's rights issues, who contributed greatly to the very early winning of suffrage in New Zealand (1893) and made a major contribution to the world suffrage movement as well.

## RELIGION/EDUCATION/EVERYDAY LIFE

Annie Turnbo Malone developed her scalp treatment solution, designed to grow and straighten hair; she marketed a line of products under the trade name Poro, establishing a major business in St. Louis, Missouri, where she was active in community affairs.

Florence Kelley founded the National Child Labor Committee.

Jane Addams published *Democracy and Social Ethics*, powerfully linking democracy and social justice.

Annie Peck was among the founders of the American Alpine Club.

Fannie Farmer founded the Miss Farmer School of Cookery, offering courses on nutrition for nurses and children, and also advising the Harvard Medical School on diets.

The Young Women's Hebrew Association (YWHA) became an independent organization, led by Mrs. Israel Unterberg.

Clara Collet published *Educated Working Women.*

Josephine Goldmark published *Child Labour Legislation Handbook.*

b. Beryl Markham (1902–1986), Anglo-Kenyan aviator and racehorse trainer.

d. Auguste Schmidt (1833–1902), German educator and moderate feminist, longtime head of the Women's Teacher Training College in Leipzig, who became head of the General German Women's Association (1888) and first president of the Federation of German Women's Associations (1894).

d. Clemence (Augustine) Royer (1830–1902), French scholar who wrote, lectured, and published widely, notably on political economy and theories of evolution.

d. Frances Auretta Fuller Victor (1826–1902), American historian and author, best known for her work *History of the Pacific States.*

### SCIENCE/TECHNOLOGY/MEDICINE

British physicist Hertha Ayrton published *The Electric Arc*, which became the standard work in the field. She was proposed as a fellow of the Royal Society, but the organization's board reported "it had no legal power to elect a married woman to this distinction."

During an outbreak of typhoid fever in Chicago, physician Alice Hamilton analyzed the water, discovering the source of contamination.

Lillian Wald founded the first American public school nursing program.

Alice Fletcher was among the founders of the American Anthropological Association.

American medical missionary Ida Scudder established the Mary Taber Schell Memorial Hospital in India.

Florence Sabin became the first female professor at Johns Hopkins University, as an assistant in anatomy.

Ida Hyde was the first woman elected to be a member of the American Physiological Society.

b. Barbara McClintock (1902–1992), American geneticist.

b. Frida (Henrietta Wilfrida) Avern Leakey (1902–1993), British archaeologist and paleontologist.

b. Sidnie Milana Manton (1902–1979), British zoologist.

d. Marie Elizabeth Zakrzewska (1829–1902), German-born Polish-American physician who helped found the New York Infirmary for Indigent Women and Children (1857) and the New England Hospital for Women and Children (1863).

d. Constance Stone (1856–1902), Australian physician and feminist, the first woman to practice as a physician in Victoria.

### ARTS/LITERATURE

Maud Gonne (later MacBride) starred in William Butler Yeats's *Cathleen ni Houlihan* in Dublin.

Alice Guy-Blaché produced and directed the very early feature film *Passion*.

Anne Whitney completed her Boston memorial to abolitionist and radical Republican Charles Sumner, begun in 1875.

Edith Wharton published the novel *The Valley of Decision*.

Mary Garden created the role of Mélisande in Claude Debussy's opera *Pelléas et Mélisande*.

Photographer Gertrude Käsebier joined the Photo-Secession movement, led by Alfred Stieglitz.

Augusta Gregory published a Gaelic-to-English translation of *Guchulain of Muirthemne*.

Alice Pestana, writing as Caiel, published the novel *Desgarrada* (*The One Who Went Astray*).

Ethel Smyth composed the opera *Der Wald*.

Lillian Russell popularized John Stromberg's song "Come Down Ma Evenin' Star."

Marie Tempest created the title role in *The Marriage of Kitty*, then took the play on a world tour.

Retiring from Buffalo Bill's Wild West Show after an injury (1901), Annie Oakley toured in the title role of the melodrama *The Western Girl*.

b. (Ellen) Miriam Hopkins (1902–1972), American actress.

b. Cheryl Crawford (1902–1986), American director, producer, and actress.

b. Cornelia Otis Skinner (1902–1979), American actress.

b. Ding Ling (1902–1986), Chinese writer.

b. Flora Robson (1902–1984), British actress.

b. Stevie (Florence Margaret) Smith (1902–1971), British writer and illustrator.

b. Leni (Helene Bertha Amalie) Riefenstahl (1902– ), German director, actress, and Nazi propagandist.

b. Stella Adler (1902–1993), American actress, daughter of Jacob Adler.

d. Mary Jane Peale (1827–1902), American painter, sister of Margaretta and Sarah Peale.

# 1903

### POLITICS/LAW/WAR

Emmeline and Christabel Pankhurst founded the Women's Social and Political Union (WSPU), in Manchester; it would be the main militant, direct-action organization of the British women's suffrage movement.

Vida Goldstein founded the Australian Women's Federal Political Association.

b. Kamaldevi Chattopadhyay (1903– ), Indian socialist, independence leader, social reformer, and politician.

d. Helen Blackburn (1842–1903), Irish-English feminist, suffragist, social reformer, writer, and editor, a major figure in the British women's suffrage and labor movements.

### RELIGION/EDUCATION/EVERYDAY LIFE

National Women's Trade Union League (NWTUL) was founded at the American Federation of Labor (AFL) convention by a group including Mary Kenney O'Sullivan, Mary Morton Kehew, its first president, and Jane Addams, its vice-president; they aimed to form a united front among women for better wages, pensions, and working conditions, the NWTUL's motto being "The Eight-Hour Day; A Living Wage; to Guard the Home."

Agnes Nestor was the first woman elected president of an international labor union, the International Glove Workers Union.

Charlotte Perkins Gilman published *The Home: Its Work and Influence*, her classic study of women's roles.

Dorothea Douglass won the first of what would be seven women's singles tennis titles at Wimbledon (1903, 1904, 1906, 1910, 1911, 1913, 1914); she might have had more, but Wimbledon was not held for five years during World War I; even so Douglass returned to the finals in 1919 and 1920.

Helen Keller published her first book, *The Story of My Life*.

Independent Order of St. Luke, an African-American fraternal society led by Maggie L. Walker, founded St. Luke Penny Savings Bank in Richmond, Virginia, with Walker as president (1903–1929). She later (1929) became board chairman of its successor, the Consolidated Bank and Trust Company.

Josephine Goldmark became research director for Florence Kelley's National Consumers' League and researched the medical and sociological background to the famous "Brandeis Brief," presented by her brother-in-law Louis Brandeis (later a Supreme Court justice) in *Muller v. Oregon* (1908); it helped to establish the constitutional validity of protective legislation in industry.

Southern Association of College Women (SACW) was formed; it would merge with two other organizations to become the American Association of University Women (1921).

Mary MacArthur became Secretary of the Women's Trade Union League in Britain.

Helen Blackburn published *Women under the Factory Acts*.

Jane Harrison published *Prologomena to the Study of Greek Religion*.

b. Gladys Aylward (1903–1970), British-Chinese missionary.

b. Jessie Ravitch Bernard (1903–1996), American sociologist.

b. Joan Violet Maurice Robinson (1903–1986), British economist.

b. Olive Ann Beech (1903–1993), American aviation entrepreneur who, during World War II, converted a small commercial airplane operator into a major defense contractor, supplying 90 percent of the planes used in training American fighter pilots and their crews.

b. Simone Weil (1903–1943), French philosopher, educator, and writer.

d. Calamity Jane (Martha Jane Cannary Burke, 1852–1903), American frontierswoman, who often dressed as a man and who later toured with Buffalo Bill's Wild West Show; writing as M. C. Burke, she published her autobiography, *Life and Adventures of Calamity Jane: By Herself*.

d. Harriet Hubbard Ayer (1849–1903), American cosmetics entrepreneur, the first woman to build a fortune on beauty products.

d. Maria (Susan) Rye (1829–1903), British social reformer and women's rights advocate, a key figure in the fight for the Married Women's Property Bill (1856), active in women's employment and education and later in the resettlement of poor children, many abroad.

d. Susette La Flèsche Tibbles (1854–1903), American advocate of Native American rights, granddaughter of a French fur trader and daughter of an Omaha chief.

## SCIENCE/TECHNOLOGY/MEDICINE

Marie Curie received the Nobel Prize (her first of two) for physics, shared with her husband, Pierre Curie, and with Henri Becquerel. (Pierre Curie declined an offered Legion of Honor because it was restricted to men.) She also completed her doctoral dissertation on radioactivity, receiving her degree in physical science *très honorable* from the Sorbonne.

Emily Dunning (later Barringer) was the first American woman to become an ambulance surgeon, in New York City, after initially being turned down because of her sex. To climb onto the high horse-drawn city ambulance, she developed a special costume with a divided long riding skirt.

Agnes Meara Chase began her long tenure as botanical artist with the U.S. Department of Agriculture (1903–1939), collaborating on several published works.

Margaret Huggins and Agnes Mary Clerke were made honorary members of the Royal Astronomical Society; women were still not yet allowed to become fellows of the society.

Margaret Washburn founded and headed the psychology department of Vassar College.

Ellen Churchill Semple published *American History and Its Geographic Conditions*, on the geographical influences on American history.

b. Gladys Anderson Emerson (1903– ), American biochemist and nutritionist who first isolated vitamin E.

b. Irmgard Flügge-Lotz (1903–1974), German engineer and mathematician.

b. Kathleen Yardley Lonsdale (1903–1971), Irish-British crystallographer, physicist, and chemist.

b. Amy Johnson (1903–1941), British aviator.

d. Emily Howard Jennings Stowe (1831–1903), Canadian physician and suffrage advocate, the first woman licensed to practice medicine in Canada (1880) and organizer of the Dominion Woman Suffrage Association (1893).

---

# The New Colossus

Not like the brazen giant of Greek fame,
With conquering limbs astride from land to land;
Here at our sea-washed, sunset gates shall stand
A mighty woman with a torch, whose flame
Is the imprisoned lightning, and her name
Mother of Exiles. From her beacon-hand
Glows world-wide welcome; her mild eyes command
The air-bridged harbor that twin cities frame.
"Keep, ancient lands, your storied pomp!" cries she
With silent lips. "Give me your tired, your poor,
Your huddled masses yearning to breathe free,
The wretched refuse of your teeming shore.
Send these, the homeless, tempest-tost to me,
I lift my lamp beside the golden door!"

— Emma Lazarus (1883)

---

## ARTS/LITERATURE

After a campaign and funding from Georgina Schuyler, Emma Lazarus's sonnet "The New Colossus" (1883) was inscribed on a plaque inside the Statue of Liberty, overlooking the immigrant station at Ellis Island, in New York harbor.

Ethel Barrymore played the title role in Hubert Henry Davies's play *Cousin Kate*.

Kate Douglas Wiggin published the novel *Rebecca of Sunnybrook Farm*.

Beatrix Potter published *The Tailor of Gloucester*.

Grazia Deledda published the novel *Elias Portolu*.

Bertha Kalich starred in Jacob Gordin's play *God, Man, and Devil*.

Maxine Elliott starred in Clyde Fitch's *Her Own Way*.

Mrs. Humphrey Ward published the novel *Lady Rose's Daughter*.

b. Claudette Colbert (Claudette Lily Chauchoin, 1903–1996), French-American actress.

b. (Jocelyn) Barbara Hepworth (1903–1975), British sculptor.

b. Anaïs Nin (1903–1977), American writer.

b. Clare Boothe Luce (1903–1987), American actress, writer, editor, and politician.

b. Marguerite Yourcenar (Marguerite de Crayencour, 1903–1987), French writer, translator, and critic.

b. Greer Garson (1903–1996), British actress.

b. Rosamond Lehmann (1903–1990), British writer.

b. Tallulah Bankhead (1903–1968), American actress.

b. Beatrix Lehmann (1903–1979), British actress.

b. Priaulx Rainier (1903–1986), South African composer.

b. Ruth Etting (1903–1978), American torch singer.

b. Marcia Davenport (1903–1996), American novelist, music critic, and editor.

d. Augusta Holmès (1847–1903), French composer.

d. Soledad Acosta de Samper (1833–1903), Colombian writer and editor.

## 1904

### POLITICS/LAW/WAR

Helene Stöcker founded the League for the Protection of Motherhood and Sexual Reform (Mutterschutz League), which advocated among other things sexual freedom and birth control; it was quickly disowned by many in the German women's movement for advocating "free love."

International Woman Suffrage Alliance (IWSA) was founded by Carrie Chapman Catt and Susan B. Anthony, as a suffrage-focused organization split off from the multi-issue International Council of Women. Catt was its first president (1904–1923).

Anna Howard Shaw became president of the National American Woman Suffrage Association (1904–1915), succeeding and then succeeded by Carrie Chapman Catt.

In Italy, women mounted a campaign for the vote (1904–1911), through a Pro-Suffrage Commitee drawing from several organizations, including the Consiglio Nazionale Donne Italiane and the Unione Femminile.

International Alliance of Women was founded in Germany; among its organizers were Lida Heymann, Anita Augspurg, Adele Schreiber, and Minna Cauer.

Japan's government sponsored the Patriotic Women's Society, during the Russo-Japanese War (1904–1905).

People's Will leader Vera Figner was released from prison into Siberian exile and escaped abroad, settling in Switzerland, temporary home of many Russian exiles.

b. Jennie Lee (1904–1988), British socialist and Labour Party leader.

b. Barbara Salt (1904–1975), British diplomat.

b. Deng Yingchao (1904–1992), Chinese Communist leader, the wife of Zhou Enlai.

b. Marie-Hélène Postel Vinay Lefaucheux (1904–1964), French feminist, women's rights activist, and Resistance leader during World War II.

### RELIGION/EDUCATION/EVERYDAY LIFE

American public-health nurse Lillian Wald cofounded the National Child Labor Committee.

Ida Tarbell published her *History of the Standard Oil Company*, a highly critical, very influential anti-monopoly study based on a series of stories published in *McClures*, a magazine of which she was assistant editor.

International Congress of Women was held in Berlin.

Mary McLeod Bethune founded the Daytona Normal and Industrial Institute for girls, in Florida; it would merge with a boys' school to become Bethune-Cookman College (1923), with her as president (1923–1942; 1946–1947).

The first American vocational high school for girls was founded in Boston, with Florence M. Marshall as first principal.

The Mormon church began excommunicating those who continued to practice plural marriage, which the federal government had forced the church to abandon (1890).

Women's Athletic Association was founded at the University of Chicago, the oldest American women's athletic advocacy organization.

Adelaide Hoodless founded the Macdonald Institute, focusing on domestic science (home economics), attached to the Ontario Agricultural Institute at Guelph.

An unnamed young woman invented the ice cream cone at the Louisiana Purchase Exposition in St. Louis, Missouri, when she folded a cookie wafer around the bottom of her ice cream sandwich to keep it from dripping.

Annie Peck made the first ascent of Bolivia's Mt. Sorata.

Annie Taylor joined the Younghusband expedition in Lhasa as a nurse; she had been working in Tibet as a missionary and unofficially helping Britain to establish relations with Tibet.

Gertrude Tuckwell became president of Britain's Women's Trade Union League (1904–1921).

Tennis star Lottie Dod became British Ladies Golf Champion.

Woman's Commonwealth began to break up, at the death of leader Martha White McWhirter, though a core remained in Washington, D.C.

Fannie Farmer published *Food and Cooking for the Sick and Convalescent*.

Fanny Workman published *Through Town and Jungle: 14,000 Miles Awheel Among the Temples and Peoples of the Indian Plain*.

Margaret Davies published *The Women's Co-operative Guild 1883–1904*.

b. Mary Caperton Bingham (1904–1995), American publisher, editor, and philanthropist.

d. Emily (Emilia Francis Strong) Dilke (1840–1904), British feminist, social reformer, art critic, and writer, who became president of the Women's Trade Union League (1902), also publishing books on art criticism. She and her first husband, Mark Pattison, were reputedly the models for Dorothea and Casaubon in George Eliot's novel *Middlemarch*.

d. Frances Power Cobbe (1822–1904), Irish writer, feminist, social reformer, and suffragist.

d. Isabelle Eberhardt (1877–1904), Russian-born traveler and writer, raised as a boy, who converted to Islam (1897), a lifelong passion and the subject of many of her writings; she died in a flash flood while reporting on a Moroccan military campaign for an Algerian newspaper.

### SCIENCE/TECHNOLOGY/MEDICINE

American ethnologist Alice Fletcher published *The Hako: A Shawnee Ceremony*, the first complete description of a Plains Indian ceremony.

Bertha Van Hoosen began experimenting with use of scopolamine-morphine anesthesia in childbirth, popularizing the use of "twilight sleep" in America.

Physicist Hertha Marks Ayrton became the first woman ever to read a paper before Britain's Royal Society, presenting her "The Origin and Growth of Ripple Marks."

Marie Stopes became the first woman on the science faculty of Britain's Manchester University, specializing in the study of fossil plants.

b. Lu Gwei-Djen (1904–1991), Chinese biochemist, teacher, and historian of science.

b. Adele Davis (1904–1974), American nutrition writer.

b. Grace Arabell Goldsmith (1904–1975), American physician, nutritionist, and educator.

d. Isabella Lucy Bird Bishop (1831–1904), British naturalist, geographer, explorer, travel writer, and medical missionary, the first woman to become a fellow of Britain's Royal Geographical Society (1892).

d. Anna Winlock (1857–1904), American astronomer, largely self-taught, long associated with the Harvard Observatory (1875–1904), her major work being a joint star catalogue.

## ARTS/LITERATURE

Maude Adams played the title role in James M. Barrie's *Peter Pan*.

Rosina Storchio created the title role in Giacomo Puccini's opera *Madama Butterfly*.

Augusta Gregory became a codirector of Dublin's Abbey Theatre.

Beatrix Potter published *The Tale of Benjamin Bunny*.

Elizabeth Robins published the novel *The Magnetic North*.

Ida Emerson introduced the song "Good Bye, My Lady Love," by Joseph E. Howard, her husband.

b. Alexandra Danilova (1904–1997), Russian dancer, a leading ballerina in Sergei Diaghilev's Ballets Russes company and in the Ballets Russes de Monte Carlo.

b. Anna Neagle (Marjory Robertson, 1904–1987), British actress.

b. Betty Smith (1904–1972), American novelist.

b. Constance Bennett (1904–1965), American actress.

b. Joan Crawford (Lucille Fay Le Sueur, 1904–1967), American actress.

b. Fumiko Hayashi (1904–1951), Japanese novelist.

b. Germaine Richier (1904–1959), French sculptor.

b. Nancy Freeman Mitford (1904–1973), British writer.

d. Kate Chopin (Katherine O'Flaherty, 1851–1904), American writer.

d. Francesca Romana Maddalena Janauschek (1830–1904), Czech actress, one of the leading tragedians of her time on the German and English-speaking stages.

## 1905

### POLITICS/LAW/WAR

Christabel Pankhurst and Annie Kenney were arrested and briefly imprisoned for creating a public pro-suffrage disturbance at a Liberal Party meeting, signaling a new, militant stage of the British woman suffrage movement.

Eleanor Roosevelt, niece of President Theodore Roosevelt, married her cousin, Franklin Delano Roosevelt, beginning a partnership that would ultimately generate the New Deal, a tremendous flow of social legislation, and take the United States through the Great Depression and World War II.

Alexandra Kollontai published *On the Question of the Class Struggle*.

Alliance of Lithuanian Women was founded by Ona Masiotene and others.

Flora Drummond became a Women's Social and Political Union militant, winning the nickname "General Drummond" as the uniformed leader of a band during WSPU demonstrations for women's suffrage.

Polish revolutionary Rosa Luxemburg fought in Warsaw during the Russian Revolution of 1905 and was imprisoned for her role in the revolt.

Franciska Plamnikova founded the Czech Committee for Women's Suffrage.

b. Begum Liaquat Ali Khan (1905– ), Pakistani politician and diplomat, founder of the All Pakistan Women's Association (1949), who became Pakistan's first female provincial governor, in Sind (1973).

b. Oveta Culp Hobby (1905–1995), American politician and businesswoman, the first head of the Women's Army Corps (1942).

b. Helen Pennell Joseph (1905–1992), white South African antiapartheid crusader.

b. Maggie Kuhn (Margaret E. Kuhn, 1905–1995), American feminist, founder of the Gray Panthers (1971).

b. Federica Montseny (1905– ), Spanish anarchist, a Republican leader during the Spanish Civil War.

d. Jessie Boucherett (1825–1905), English feminist and suffragist, a founder of the Society for Promoting the Employment of Women (1860).

## RELIGION/EDUCATION/EVERYDAY LIFE

Bertha von Suttner was the first woman to receive the Nobel Peace Prize; her 1889 book on pacifism had inspired its establishment.

Association of Collegiate Alumnae (later American Association of University Women) passed a resolution stating that home economics did not belong in a college curriculum for women. In this period, many women's colleges did, however, begin to offer courses in "domestic science," an alternative name for the new field.

Elsie de Wolfe decorated the Colony Club, New York City's first club for women, establishing herself as a top interior decorator.

Fanny Workman became the second woman to address Britain's Royal Geographical Society, after Isabella Bird Bishop (1897), later speaking there regularly.

Madeleine Pelletier became secretary of Le Groupe de la Solidarité des Femmes, employing the militant tactics of the Pankhursts across the English Channel.

"Permanents" became popular among women, after Charles Nestle (Karl Nessler) developed the permanent-wave process for curling hair.

Through the Chicago Women's Club, Hannah Solomon sparked the establishment of the Illinois Industrial School for Girls and was also a founding member of the Illinois Federation of Women's Clubs.

Teresa Billington-Grieg became a national organizer of the Women's Social and Political Union (1905–1906).

Florence Kelley published *Some Ethical Gains Through Legislation.*

Madame C. J. Walker invented a hair softener and a straightening comb, along with a line of facial cosmetics, developing these into the highly successful "Walker System" of treating hair.

Octavia Hill and Beatrice Webb were on Britain's Poor Law Commission (1905–1908).

b. Clara Hale (Mother Hale, 1905–1992), African-American child-care provider, founder of Harlem's Hale House.

b. Helen N. Wills Moody (1905– ), American tennis player who won her first title at Forest Hills (1922), later dominating the game (1926–1938).

b. Margaret Cahill (1905–1995), the first Miss America (1921).

d. Josephine Shaw Lowell (1843–1905), American social reformer, the first woman on New York's State Board of Charities (1875) and president of the first Consumer Council (1890–1896); a radical abolitionist, she was the sister of Robert Gould Shaw, leader of Massachusetts' black regiment in the Civil War.

d. Kalliopi Kehajia (1839–1905), Greek educator, the London-trained head of Athens's Hill School for girls, founder of the Zappeion School for girls (1875) and of the Society for Promoting Women's Education (1872).

## SCIENCE/TECHNOLOGY/MEDICINE

Nettie Maria Stevens reported her major discovery: that sex is determined by a particular chromosome.

Anna Wessel Williams developed a method for diagnosing rabies in the laboratory, which became standard; in 1896 she had brought from Paris a rabies culture used in developing a rabies vaccine (1896–1898).

Alice Fletcher became president of the American Folk-Lore Society.

Mary Whiton Calkins became president of the American Psychological Association, its first female head.

## Arts/Literature

Edith Wharton published the novel *The House of Mirth*.

Frances Hodgson Burnett published the novel *The Little Princess*.

Marie Wittick created the title role in Richard Strauss's opera *Salome*.

Mary Cassatt showed her pastel *Mère et enfant*.

Mary Elizabeth Braddon published the melodramatic novel *The Rose of Life*.

b. Greta Garbo (Greta Louise Gustafsson, 1905–1990), Swedish actress.

b. Myrna Loy (Myrna Williams, 1905–1993), American actress.

b. Jean Arthur (Gladys Georgianna Greene, 1905–1991), American actress.

b. Lillian Hellman (1905–1984), American playwright.

b. Agnes De Mille (1905–1994), American dancer and choreographer.

b. Ayn Rand (1905–1982), Russian-American writer, exponent of Objectivist philosophy.

b. Clara Bow (1905–1965), American actress.

b. Mary Renault (Mary Challans, 1905–1983), British novelist.

b. Dolores Del Rio (Lolita Dolores Negrette, 1905–1983), Mexican actress.

b. Gracie Allen (1905–1964), American actress and comedian.

b. Margaret Webster (1905–1972), British actress and director.

b. Muriel Baker Box (1905–1991), British screenwriter, film director, and producer, and an active feminist.

b. Sylvia Ashton-Warner (1905–1984), New Zealand teacher and writer.

b. Helen Becker Tamiris (1905–1966), American dancer and choreographer.

b. Phyllis McGinley (1905–1978), American poet.

d. Carolina Rosati (Carolina Galletti, 1826–1905), Italian dancer, one of Europe's leading ballerinas from the mid-1840s through the early 1860s.

d. Bertha Amalie Alver Skram (1847–1905), Norwegian novelist.

d. Mary Mapes Dodge (1831–1905), American author.

The massive suffrage petition of 1906, organized by Clementina Black and others, was a British suffrage-movement landmark; Emily Davies, who four decades earlier had been one of the organizers of the historic British suffrage petition (1866), led yet another delegation to Parliament in support of women's suffrage.

## 1906

### Politics/Law/War

Annie Kenney became the London organizer of the Women's Social and Political Union; arrests multiplied as militants developed direct-action tactics.

Edith How-Martyn became secretary of the Women's Social and Political Union (1906–1907).

Teresa Billington-Grieg published *Towards Women's Liberty*.

Emma Goldman founded and edited the magazine *Mother Earth* (1906–1917).

Women won the right to vote and be elected to office in Finland.

Beatrice Potter Webb and Sidney Webb published the nine-volume *English Local Government* (1906–1929).

Rosa Luxemburg published *The Mass Strike, the Political Party, and the Trade Unions*.

Belva Lockwood won a trailblazing $5 million settlement for the Eastern Cherokees in their claim against the federal government.

b. Esther Peterson (1906–1997), American consumer advocate, an adviser to several presidents from 1964.

d. Susan B. Anthony (1820–1906), American women's rights movement leader, social reformer, temperance movement activist, and abolitionist, a key leader of the long, successful fight for American women's suffrage. Lifelong associate of Elizabeth Cady Stanton, she was a founder of the worldwide women's movement at the Seneca Falls Convention (1848), the originator of the Anthony Amendment on women's suffrage, and a founder of the International Council of Women (1888), the united National American Woman Suffrage Association (1890), and the International Woman Suffrage Alliance (1904).

## RELIGION/EDUCATION/EVERYDAY LIFE

Fanny Workman, at age 47, set a women's altitude record of 6,930 meters on Pinnacle Peak, where she planted a "Votes for Women" poster.

In Britain, Gertrude Tuckwell, Mary MacArthur, Adelaide Anderson, and others organized the Sweated Goods Exhibition, as part of their campaigns against white-lead poisoning and sweated trades; this led to the Trade Boards Act (1909).

Britain's National Federation of Women Workers was organized; among its founders were Mary MacArthur and Margaret Bondfield.

French physician Madeleine Pelletier was the first woman allowed to qualify to work in a mental hospital.

Jessie (Celestia Josephine) Field (Shambaugh) founded a series of Corn Clubs and Home Clubs in the Page County schools of which she was superintendent; these Iowa clubs would spark the 4-H Club movement, sponsored nationally by the U.S. Department of Agriculture.

Emily Edson Briggs's letters on current social and political issues, written for newspapers under the name "Olivia," were published in book form as *The Olivia Letters.*

b. Hannah Arendt (1906–1975), German-American political philosopher and writer.

b. Gertrude (Caroline) Ederle (1906– ), American swimmer, the first woman to swim the English Channel (1926).

b. Pauline Frederick (ca. 1906–1990), American news broadcaster.

d. Dorothea Beale (1831–1906), British educator and feminist, principal of Cheltenham Ladies College (1858), who founded St. Hilda's College at Cheltenham (1885) and also St. Hilda's Hall, Oxford (1892), to train women as teachers.

d. Josephine Gray Butler (1828–1906), British feminist and social reformer, who led the successful fight against the Contagious Diseases Acts.

d. Learmonth White Dalrymple (1827–1906), New Zealand educator and feminist who fought for women's education and helped introduce the kindergarten to New Zealand.

d. Angela (Georgina) Burdett-Coutts (1814–1906), British philanthropist known as the Queen of the Poor.

## SCIENCE/TECHNOLOGY/MEDICINE

After her husband's accidental death, Marie Curie succeeded to his chair at the Sorbonne, the first woman to teach there.

Anna Botsford Comstock (writing as Marian Lee) published her *Confessions to a Heathen Idol,* on the social structure of Cornell University.

After the California Academy of Sciences herbarium was destroyed in the San Francisco earthquake, Alice Eastwood rebuilt it from botanical collections throughout America and Europe.

American astronomer Williamina Fleming was elected a member of the Royal Astronomical Society.

Charlotte Scott became vice-president of the American Mathematical Society, the first woman in that position; the second would not come for another 70 years.

Physicist Hertha Ayrton received the Hughes Medal of Britain's Royal Society, the first ever given to a woman.

b. Maria Goeppert Mayer (1906–1972), Polish-American nuclear physicist.

b. Grace Brewster Murray Hopper (1906–1992), American mathematician and computer scientist.

b. Kathleen Mary Kenyon (1906–1978), British archaeologist.

b. Florence Hawley Ellis (1906– ), American archaeologist specializing in the Southwest, who pioneered the use of statistics in archaeology.

d. Mary Corinna Putnam Jacobi (1842–1906), American physician and social reformer, who did pioneer work on psychosomatic illnesses in women and helped expand women's medical education. She self-diagnosed the brain tumor that caused her death.

d. Clara Eaton Cummings (1853–1906), American botanist long associated with Wellesley College.

d. Ellen Mary Clerke (1840–1906), Irish writer on astronomy, like her sister, Agnes Mary Clerke; she also wrote poetry and fiction.

## ARTS/LITERATURE

Anna Pavlova became premier ballerina at St. Petersburg's Maryinsky Theatre.

Fay Templeton starred opposite Victor Moore in George M. Cohan's Broadway musical *Forty-five Minutes from Broadway*.

Russian actress Alla Nazimova emerged as a Broadway star in the title role of Henrik Ibsen's *Hedda Gabler*.

Ruth St. Denis choreographed and danced *Radha*, on Indian dance themes.

Gertrude Atherton published the novel *Rezánov*.

Margaret Anglin starred in William Vaughan Moody's play *The Great Divide*.

Margaret Deland published the novel *The Awakening of Helena Richie*.

Sibilla Aleramo published the autobiographical novel *A Woman*.

b. Anne Spencer Morrow Lindbergh (1906– ), American writer, pilot, and explorer.

b. Mary Astor (Lucille Vasconcellos Langhanke, 1906–1987), American actress.

b. Janet Gaynor (Laura Gainor, 1906–1984), American actress.

b. Josephine Baker (1906–1975), American-French singer, dancer, and actress.

b. Madeleine Carroll (Marie-Madeleine Bernadette O'Carroll, 1906–1987), British actress, a 1930s film star in *The 39 Steps* (1935) and several other British and American films.

b. Louise Brooks (1906–1985), American actress and dancer.

b. Margaret Bourke-White (1906–1971), American photographer.

b. (Agnes) Elisabeth Lutyens (1906–1983), British composer.

b. Grace Mary Williams (1906–1977), Welsh composer.

b. Louise Talma (1906–1996), American composer and teacher.

d. A. D. T. (Adeline Dutton Train) Whitney (1824–1906), American novelist.

d. Adelaide Ristori (1822–1906), Italian actress.

## 1907

### POLITICS/LAW/WAR

British militant suffragists mounted a landmark London parade and demonstration, called the "Mud March" because it was held in a rainstorm.

Christabel Pankhurst became a London-based organizer for the Women's Social and Political Union (WSPU).

Women's Freedom League was founded by British feminists Teresa Billington-Grieg, Charlotte Despard, and Edith How-Martyn, who was secretary (1907–1911), then head of the "political and militant department," seeking women's suffrage.

Emmeline Pethick-Lawrence and her husband, Frederick Lawrence, founded the British periodical *Votes for Women*.

Margery Ashby emerged as a leading British suffragist, becoming organizing secretary of the National Union of Women's Suffrage Societies.

Anita Augspurg and Lida Heymann, working through the German Women's Suffrage League, developed mass action in support of women's suffrage, on the British and American models.

Clara Zetkin was a founder of the International Socialist Women's Congress.

Despite an all-male electorate, Kate Barnard won a statewide office, as Oklahoma's commissioner of charities and corrections; she was re-elected in 1910.

Women won the right to vote and be elected to office in Norway.

Australian pacifist Rose Scott became president of the Peace Society and later opposed Australian participation in World War I.

Kate Sheppard published *Women's Suffrage in New Zealand*.

Miina Sillanpää began her 40-year career as a member of the Finnish Parliament (1907–1947).

## RELIGION/EDUCATION/EVERYDAY LIFE

Maria Montessori founded her Child's House, in Rome, where she would develop the teaching techniques that would transform early-childhood education, spread around the world in Montessori schools.

Annie Besant became president of the Theosophical Society (1907–1933), also becoming active in the campaign for Indian self-rule.

National Consumers' League (NCL) began placing white labels on clothing produced by garment manufacturers whose labor practices met the League's "Standard of a Fair House"; this practice grew out of the group's earlier "White List" campaign, focusing on stores employing women as retail clerks.

As president of the Women's Trade Union League, Margaret Dreier Robins worked with Rose Schneiderman, notably in organizing garment workers' strikes in New York, Philadelphia, and Chicago (1909–1911).

Ladies' Alpine Club was founded; among its first members were Elizabeth Le Blond, its first president, and Lucy Walker, its second.

Anna M. Jarvis began her campaign for the establishment of Mother's Day, after the death of her own mother.

Dorothy Tyler won a horse race in Joplin, Missouri, against experienced male riders, becoming America's first female jockey.

Grace Dodge founded the New York Travelers Aid Society.

Mary MacArthur established the journal *Woman Worker*.

Under an international agreement, Japanese and Korean (but not Chinese) men in the United States (including Hawaii) were allowed to bring from their homelands brides chosen by photograph under the *omaiaikekkon*, or arranged marriages custom; more than 41,000 such "picture brides" were brought to America (1907–1921).

British trade union leader Gertrude Tuckwell published *Women in Industry*.

Clementina Black published *Sweated Industry and the Minimum Wage*.

Gertrude Bell published *The Desert and the Sown*, on her Syrian travels.

Madame Cama, a Bombay-born Parsi living in Europe, is credited with creating India's green, yellow, and red national flag.

b. Germaine (Marie Rosine) Tillion (1907– ), French ethnologist, director of studies at the École Pratique des Hautes Etudes (1957); she also headed a Resistance group (1940–1942), was captured and imprisoned, and later served on postwar commissions.

d. Elizabeth (Cabot) Cary Agassiz (1822–1907), American educator and scientist, the founder and first president of Radcliffe College (1893–1903); she had worked closely with her husband, Swiss naturalist Louis Agassiz, until his death (1873).

d. Harriet Farley (1813–1907), American textile worker, teacher, writer, and editor of the periodical the *Lowell Offering*.

## SCIENCE/TECHNOLOGY/MEDICINE

Emmy Noether received her Ph.D. in mathematics, summa cum laude, from the University of Erlangen, Germany.

Nurses with Florence Nightingale–style training took over Paris's major hospital, the Hôtel Dieu; the Augustinian Sisters who had run it for centuries had resisted modern medical training. They and other religious nursing orders soon reversed course and accepted training.

Mary Engle Pennington was hired as a bacteriological chemist for the U.S. Department of Agriculture; Harvey Wiley, head of the USDA's Bureau of Chemistry, had advised her to take the civil service examination as "M. E. Pennington," so that he could hire her before the civil service officials realized she was a woman.

American home economist Isabel Bevier introduced the use of a thermometer for meat cooking.

Esther Pohl Lovejoy became the first woman to direct the board of health of a major American city, Portland, Oregon.

British nurse Edith Cavell became head of nursing at the first Belgian nurses' training school, at the Birkendael Medical Institute in Brussels.

Canadian cardiologist Maude Abbott began the *Bulletin of the International Association of Medical Museums*, serving as editor.

Mary Adela Blagg was engaged to standardize the names given to features on the moon; her list became the standard authority in the field.

Mary Sinclair published key papers on the calculus of variations (1907–1909).

Mary Whiton Calkins published *The Persistent Problems of Philosophy*.

b. Rachel Louise Carson (1907–1964), American ecologist and science writer.

b. Ivy Parker (1907– ), American chemist and engineer working in the petroleum industry.

d. Agnes Mary Clerke (1842–1907), Irish writer on astronomy; she and her sister were memorialized in Margaret Huggins's privately published *Agnes Mary Clerke and Ellen Mary Clerke*.

## ARTS/LITERATURE

Anna Pavlova introduced *The Dying Swan* (*La Mort du cygne*), her signature role, a solo created for her by Michel Fokine to music from Camille Saint-Saëns's *Carnival of Animals*.

Augusta Gregory wrote the play *The Rising of the Moon*.

Georgette Leblanc created the role of Ariadne in Paul Dukas's opera *Ariadne and Bluebeard*.

---

# No Easy Path

When German mathematician Emmy Noether began attending classes at the University of Erlangen, women were allowed only as auditors; they had gained the right to matriculate by the time she graduated (1907). However, despite receiving her Ph.D. in mathematics summa cum laude, Noether was unable to find employment. She worked without pay at the Mathematical Institute at Erlangen (1908–1915), occasionally lecturing at the university in place of her father, a research mathematician. At her father's death, mathematician David Hibbert invited her to the University of Göttingen but was unable to secure a formal appointment for her, though she occasionally gave lectures announced under his name. Not until 1922 was Noether given a formal appointment at Göttingen, and then only as "unofficial associate professor," for a tiny salary. There she remained, pursuing her own lines of research (original enough so that her followers were later called the "Noether School"), except for visiting professorships to Moscow (1928-1929) and Frankfurt (1930), until she and other Jewish professors were dismissed by the Nazis (1933). She then immigrated to the United States and was warmly welcomed at Bryn Mawr College and at the Institute for Advanced Study in Princeton, New Jersey, but died suddenly in 1935 from complications of an operation for an ovarian cyst.

Elizabeth Robins wrote the play *Votes for Women!*

Sara Teasdale published *Sonnets to Duse and Other Poems.*

Sarah Bernhardt published her autobiography, *My Double Life.*

Selma Lagerlöf published the children's story collection *The Wonderful Adventures of Nils.*

Delmira Agustini published the poetry collection *El libro blanco.*

Pamela Coleman Smith exhibited at New York's 291, the visual-arts gallery founded by Alfred Stieglitz.

Dorothy Canfield published the novel *Gunhild.*

b. Katharine Hepburn (1907– ), American stage and screen star, a major figure in world cinema and a four-time best actress Academy Award winner.

b. Peggy (Edith Margaret Emily) Ashcroft (1907–1991), British actress.

b. Barbara Stanwyck (Ruby Stevens, 1907–1980), American actress.

b. Daphne du Maurier (1907–1989), British writer.

b. Jessie Matthews (1907–1981), British actress, singer, and dancer.

b. Rumer Godden (Rumer Haynes Dixon, 1907– ), British novelist and children's book author, much of whose work is set in India, her early home.

b. Shirley Booth (Thelma Booth Ford, 1907–1992), American actress.

b. Edith Head (1907–1981), American film costume designer.

b. Elizabeth Maconchy (1907–1994), British composer.

b. Irene Rice Pereira (1907–1971), American artist.

b. Wanda Jakubowska (1907– ), Polish filmmaker.

d. Lucile Grahn (1819–1907), Danish ballerina, ballet master, and choreographer, a leading dancer in European ballet (1834–1856).

# 1908

## POLITICS/LAW/WAR

Emmeline Pankhurst was arrested for the first time, as the Women's Social and Political Union moved toward more confrontational tactics, including illegal acts of defiance and crimes against property.

Florence Kelley and the National Consumers' League led the campaign for state minimum-wage laws for women, achieving passage in 14 states and the District of Columbia until the U.S. Supreme Court overturned the District of Columbia law in *Adkins v. Children's Hospital* (1923).

Harriet Stanton Blatch organized the militant feminist American Political Union.

In *Muller v. Oregon*, the U.S. Supreme Court established the constitutionality of protective laws and regulations for women.

Britain's first female physician, Elizabeth Garrett Anderson, became the nation's first woman to serve as mayor, when she was elected Mayor of Aldeburgh.

British Anti-Suffrage League was founded, with Mrs. Humphrey Ward (Mary Augusta Ward) as its first president.

Chrystal Macmillan was the first woman to address Britain's House of Lords, unsuccessfully arguing that, as a graduate of Edinburgh University, she had a right to vote in the Scottish Universities parliamentary contest.

Alexandra Kollontai published *The Social Basis of the Women's Question.*

American antisuffragist periodical was published (1908–1911).

French feminist Hubertine Auclert published *La vote des femmes.*

Ida Harper published the third and final volume of her biography of Susan B. Anthony.

Maude Royden became editor of the feminist periodical the *Common Cause* (1912–1914).

The first All-Russian Women's Congress convened, chaired by Anna Filosova.

The Woman's National Committee of the Socialist Party of America was founded (1908–1915), serving as a coordinating and organizing body for women's committees in the party's local organizations.

b. Ana Figuero (1908–1970), Chilean feminist, teacher, and diplomat.

b. Annabelle Rankin (1908–1986), Australian politician and diplomat.

d. Tz'u Hsi (1835–1908), dowager empress of China, who had abdicated earlier in the year. She had ruled China since the death of Emperor Hs'en Feng (1861); she was formally succeeded by Hsüan T'ung (Henry P'u Yi), with the Chinese Revolution only three years away.

d. Eleanor Marx-Aveling (1856–1908), British socialist, the daughter of Karl Marx and Jenny von Westphalen Marx, a speaker and writer for a variety of socialist causes.

## RELIGION/EDUCATION/EVERYDAY LIFE

Immigrant Protective League was founded in Chicago by Jane Addams, Sophonisba Breckinridge, and Grace Abbott, its first director (1908–1917); a model for many other organizations formed to help single immigrant women reach their American destinations, without being victimized en route, it soon extended its activities to the whole range of immigrant-aid matters.

Grace Abbott and Edith Abbott joined Jane Addams at Chicago's Hull House.

Ida B. Wells organized the Negro Fellowship League, becoming its first president.

International Congress of Women was held in the United States.

Annie Peck made the first ascent of the south peak of Huascarán in the Peruvian Andes; the north peak would later be named for her (1927).

Harriet Morison headed the Women's Employment Bureau (1908–1913) for New Zealand's Labour Department.

Helena Rubinstein, who had earlier founded a business in Australia selling "creme valaz" as a treatment for sunburned skin, opened Britain's first beauty salon, in London.

Susan Blow published *Educational Issues in the Kindergarten*.

Women were admitted to Prussian universities.

Women were barred by law from fighting on foot in the bullring in Spain (1908–1973).

Madeleine Pelletier published *La femme en lutter par ses droits*.

Mary Baker Eddy published *Rudimental Divine Science* and *Unity of Good*.

b. Simone de Beauvoir (1908–1986), French philosopher, writer, and feminist.

b. (Josephine) Estée Mentzer Lauder (1908– ), American entrepreneur who, with her husband-partner Joe Lauder, built a cosmetics empire, starting with a face cream made by her Hungarian uncle, and pioneering in developing hypoallergenic products.

## SCIENCE/TECHNOLOGY/MEDICINE

Angeliki Panajiotatou was employed as lecturer at her alma mater, the Athens University Medical School, but male students boycotted her classes and yelled "back in the kitchen!" Forced to resign, she became a professor at Cairo University and director of the general hospital in Alexandria, returning to Athens's medical school as a professor only in 1938.

Lise Meitner and longtime collaborator Otto Hahn discovered thorium C; because she was barred from established experimental laboratories, they had converted a carpenter's workshop into their laboratory for studying radiation.

Mary Engle Pennington was appointed chief of the U.S. Food Research Laboratory (1908–1919). Focusing on food handling and storage, she devised methods of preparing, packaging, and storing to prevent or retard spoilage of foods, including the then-new technique of freezing, and established standards for railroad refrigerator cars.

American physician Josephine Baker founded the Bureau of Child Hygiene after visiting mothers on New York City's Lower East Side.

Canadian Nurses' Association was founded; in the United States, African-American women formed the National Association of Colored Graduate Nurses.

German housewife Melitta Bentz invented a system for filtering coffee; it would become the widely sold Melitta coffee-making system.

Mary Sinclair became the first woman to receive a Ph.D. in mathematics from the University of Chicago.

Harriet Mann, writing as Olive Thorne Miller, published her popular *The Bird Our Brother: A Contribution to the Study of the Bird as He Is in Life.*

Margaret Washburn published *The Animal Mind: A Textbook of Comparative Psychology.*

U.S. Navy created its first formal nurse corps.

b. Yvette Cauchois (1908– ), French physicist, a specialist in X-ray spectroscopy of solids, longtime professor at the University of Paris, and director of the Laboratoire de Chimie-Physique.

b. Miriam (Louisa) Rothschild (1908– ), British zoologist and parasitologist, home-educated daughter of Baron Rothschild; the first person to analyze the jumping mechanism of fleas, she published more than 200 papers on fleas and natural history in general.

b. Myra Adele Logan (1908–1977), American physician and surgeon.

d. (Mary) Edith Pechey-Phipson (1845–1908), British physician and suffragist who long served in India (1883–1905), where she established and endowed the Pechey-Phipson Sanitorium for women and children.

## ARTS/LITERATURE

Käthe Kollwitz created her etching series *The Peasants' War* (1908–1910).

Anna Pavlova created the title role opposite Vaslav Nijinsky in Michel Fokine's ballet *Cléopâtre.*

L. M. Montgomery published the novel *Anne of Green Gables.*

Elizabeth Robins published the pro-suffrage novel *The Convert.*

Mary Roberts Rinehart published *The Circular Staircase,* her first mystery novel.

Hilda Trevelyan, Gerald du Maurier, Lillah McCarthy, and Edmund Gwenn starred in James M. Barrie's play *What Every Woman Knows.*

American actress Maxine Elliott opened New York's Maxine Elliott's Theatre.

Grazia Deledda published the novel *Conere.*

Loie Fuller choreographed the dance *Ballet of Light.*

Henry Handel Richardson (Henrietta Robertson Richardson) published her first novel, *Maurice Guest.*

b. Bette (Ruth Elizabeth) Davis (1908–1989), American actress.

b. Anna Magnani (1908–1973), Italian actress.

b. Carole Lombard (Jane Alice Peters, 1908–1942), American actress.

b. Olivia Manning (1908–1980), British writer.

b. Celia Johnson (1908–1982), British actress.

b. Rosalind Russell (1908–1976), American actress.

b. Lee Krasner (1908–1984), American painter.

b. Brigit Ragnhild Cullberg (1908– ), Swedish choreographer and dancer.

d. Harriet Goodhue Hosmer (1830–1908), American sculptor, who worked for much of her career in Britain.

d. Marie Louise de la Ramée (1839–1908), popular British romance and adventure novelist who wrote as Ouida.

## 1909

### POLITICS/LAW/WAR

International Ladies Garment Workers Union (ILGWU) organized a successful strike by 20,000 New York City shirtwaist makers (1909–1910); 80 to 85 percent of them were women, and most of these young immigrant women. Their strike pledge, taken by 3,000 Jewish-American and Italian-American workers together on the eve of the strike, was, "If I turn traitor to the cause I now pledge, may this hand wither from the arm I now raise!"

Mary White Ovington led a biracial group of reformers in founding the National Association for the Advancement of Colored People (NAACP), originally the National Negro Committee; she would be active in the NAACP in many roles (1909–1947), including as chairman (1919–1932). Other founding members included Ida B. Wells, Florence Kelley, Mary Church Terrell, and Lillian Wald.

Australian feminist Vida Goldstein founded the periodical the *Woman Voter*.

Women's rights movement leader Alexandra van Grippenberg was elected to the Finnish Diet.

British writer Cicely Hamilton published *Marriage as a Trade*.

Helena Swanwick became editor of the periodical the *Common Cause* (1909–1912)

Lizzie Ahern founded the Australian Women's Socialist League.

b. Juliana (1909– ), queen of the Netherlands (r. 1948–1980), serving in the now largely ceremonial post after the abdication of her mother, Wilhelmina. Juliana herself later abdicated in favor of her daughter, Beatrix.

## RELIGION/EDUCATION/EVERYDAY LIFE

American Home Economics Association was founded; it had grown out of a series of Lake Placid conferences (from 1899) seeking to define the new discipline and find a place for it in the educational system; the conferences and association were both sparked by Ellen Swallow Richards, who had virtually invented the field and who personally funded the association's *Journal of Home Economics*.

Beatrice Potter Webb published her celebrated *Minority Report*, as a member of the Royal Commission on the Poor Laws.

Charlotte Perkins Gilman founded and became first editor of the magazine the *Forerunner* (1909–1916).

Ella Flagg Young was appointed superintendent of the Chicago city school system (1909–1915), the first woman to head a major urban school district.

Jane Addams became first woman to serve as president of the National Conference of Charities and Corrections; she also published *The Spirit of Youth and the City Streets*.

Taking the name Elizabeth Arden, Florence Nightingale Graham opened her first beauty salon, on New York's Fifth Avenue, introducing the concept of matching makeup shades to skin tone and clothing and introducing the first nongreasy skin cream.

Emily Davies published *Thoughts on Some Questions Relating to Women 1860–1908*.

Helen Keller published *The World I Live In*.

African-American educator Nannie Burroughs founded the National Training School for Women and Girls in Washington, D.C.

Ellen Key published *Kvinnororeisen*, her study of the women's movement.

Clementina Black published *Makers of Our Clothes: A Case for Trade Boards*.

Eleanor Rathbone published *How the Casual Labourer Lives*, the year she became the Liverpool City Council's first female member.

Gertrude Bell published *The Thousand and One Churches*, on excavating Byzantine archaeological sites.

The first all-woman auto race was run, a round trip from New York City to Philadelphia and back.

## SCIENCE/TECHNOLOGY/MEDICINE

Alice Hamilton and others discovered the danger to workers in match factories, where exposure to phosphorus led to destruction of the teeth and jaws; a different, harmless substance was substituted.

Ethel Browne (later Harvey) published a paper describing the first successful induction of new differentiated growth from specific tissue, work whose value was unrecognized for many years.

American archaeologist Harriet Boyd (later Hawes) published a monograph on her excavations at Gournia (1901–1904).

*The Scientific Papers of Sir William Huggins and Lady Huggins* was published, edited by Margaret Huggins.

Wellesley professor Mary Whiton Calkins published her popular text, *A First Book in Psychology.*

b. Rita Levi-Montalcini (1909– ), Italian neurobiologist who shared the 1987 Nobel Prize for physiology or medicine for her codiscovery of nerve growth factor (1954).

b. Virginia Apgar (1909–1974), American physician and anesthesiologist.

b. Amalia Coutsouris Fleming (1909?–1986), Greek-British physician and political activist.

b. Jean Gardner Batten (1909–1982), New Zealand aviator.

b. Marguerite Catherine Perey (1909–1975), French physicist.

## ARTS/LITERATURE

Selma Lagerlöf was the first woman to receive the Nobel Prize for literature.

Sarah Bernhardt starred in her own play, *Un coeur d'un homme.*

Ernestine Schumann-Heink created the role of Klytemnestra in Richard Strauss's opera *Elektra.*

Augusta Gregory became manager of the Abbey Theatre (1909–1932).

Gertrude Stein published her first work, *Three Lives,* consisting of the stories "The Good Woman," "Melanctha," and "The Gentle Lena."

Ruth St. Denis choreographed and danced *Cobras.*

Elsie Janis starred in George Ade's play *The Fair Co-Ed.*

b. Eudora Welty (1909– ), American writer, whose novels and short stories are set mainly in her home state of Mississippi.

b. Jessica Tandy (1909–1994), British-American stage and screen star.

b. Ethel Merman (Ethel Zimmerman, 1909–1984), American singer and actress.

b. Joan Blondell (1909–1979), American actress.

b. Gabrielle Roy (1909–1983), French-Canadian writer.

b. Annabella (Suzanne Georgette Charpentier, 1909–1996), French actress, a film star in France, Britain, and Hollywood.

b. Grazyna Bacewicz (1909–1969), Polish composer, violinist, and writer.

d. Fanny Cerrito (1817–1909), Italian dancer and choreographer, a leading European ballerina (early 1830s–late 1850s).

d. Helena Modjeska (1840–1909), Polish-American actress, a star in Poland who emigrated to the United States (1876), becoming a leading tragedian, notably in Shakespeare.

d. Sarah Orne Jewett (1849–1909), American writer, a novelist, poet, and short story writer whose work is largely set on her native Maine seacoast.

d. Augusta Jane Evans (1835–1909), American author.

d. Clorinda Matto de Turner (1854–1909), Peruvian writer, editor, and social reformer, a notable campaigner for the rights of Andean Indians.

## 1910

### POLITICS/LAW/WAR

A Women's Social and Political Union (WSPU) demonstration at Britain's House of Commons was violently broken up by the police, on what British feminists came to call "Black Friday."

Adopting the confrontational tactics favored by Emmeline and Christabel Pankhurst's militant wing of the British women's suffrage movement, New York feminists, led by Harriet Stanton Blatch, mounted the first massive American women's suffrage parade.

Emma Goldman published *Anarchism and Other Essays.*

Adele Schreiber founded the German Association for the Rights of Mothers and Children.

Alice Stebbins Wells joined the Los Angeles police department, the first American city police department to regularly hire women, and began her long campaign to bring women into police work.

International Women's Day (March 8) was established by socialist organizations; it later became a Soviet holiday, and later still, in the 1960s, lost its socialist and communist connotations, being adopted by a wide range of women's groups.

German Union for Women's Suffrage organized massive street demonstrations for women's suffrage.

Gertrude Baumer became president of the League of German Women's Associations (1910–1919); she would support the German government during World War I, organizing the National Women's Service.

The Mann ("White Slavery") Act outlawed the transportation of women across state lines for purposes of prostitution or other "immoral" acts.

Australian women's rights leader Rose Scott became president of the League for Political Education.

Inesse Armand contributed articles to the Bolshevik publication the *Woman Worker*.

Marilla Ricker filed as a candidate for governor of New Hampshire but was rejected as unable to be elected because she was unable to vote.

b. Millicent Fenwick (1910–1992), American liberal Republican congresswoman and feminist.

b. Dori'a Shafiq (1910–1975), Egyptian feminist and suffragist.

b. Ekaterina Furtseva (1910–1974), Russian politician.

d. Julia Ward Howe (1819–1910), American abolitionist, social reformer, writer, and women's rights leader, best known by far as the author of "The Battle Hymn of the Republic" (1862).

d. Elizabeth Dmitrieva (1851–1910), Russian socialist, active in Britain, and in France during the Franco-Prussian War and Paris Commune.

**RELIGION/EDUCATION/EVERYDAY LIFE**

American librarian Frances Jenkins Olcott opened the first comprehensive children's department in America, at the Carnegie Library of Pittsburgh, about which she wrote in *Rational Library Work with Children and the Preparation for It* (1910).

College Alumnae Club was founded by a group of African-American women, led by Mary Church Terrell, to help raise standards of education and professionalism and to work for women's suffrage. It later became the National Association of College Women (1924), then the National Association of University Women.

Ella Flagg Young was elected president of the National Education Association, the first woman so honored.

Jane Addams published *Twenty Years at Hull House*, a central document of the new American social-work movement, as well as a luminous memoir of her early days as a pioneering social worker in Chicago.

Frances Witherspoon and Tracy Mygatt established a New York City child-care center for working mothers and carried out "church raids" to open church facilities as shelters for unemployed and homeless people (ca. 1910–1914).

Camp Fire Girls was founded by Charlotte Vetter Gulick and others, as a nonsectarian, interracial girls' organization.

Edith Abbott published her pioneering book *Women in Industry: A Study in American Economic History*.

Huda Sh'arawi opened a school for girls in Egypt, focusing on general education, instead of practical skills such as midwifery.

# Emancipation

Merely external emancipation has made of the modern women an artificial being . . . Now, woman is confronted with the necessity of emancipating herself from emancipation, if she really desires to be free.

— Emma Goldman, in "The Tragedy of Women's Emancipation," in *Anarchism and Other Essays* (1910)

Margaret Cousins, treasurer of the Irish Women's Franchise League, was a delegate to the "Parliament of Women" in London and was held briefly for allegedly throwing stones at 10 Downing Street.

Rose Schneiderman became full-time organizer for the important New York branch of the Women's Trade Union League, working with Mary Dreier Robins.

Fanny Workman published *The Call of the Snowy Hispar*.

Mary Ritter Beard edited the suffragist periodical the *Woman Voter* (1910–1912), leaving it to work with the Wage Earners' League.

Helen Keller published *Song of the Stone World*.

Henrietta Szold became secretary of the Federation of American Zionists.

Madame C. J. Walker built a factory in Indianapolis to manufacture her beauty products.

b. Mother Teresa (Agnes Gonxha Bejaxhia, 1910–1997), Yugoslavian-born Albanian religious leader who founded the Missionaries of Charity (1948); she won the Nobel Peace Prize (1979).

b. Sonja Henje (Henie, 1910–1969), Norwegian-American ice skater and film actress.

b. Jacquetta Hawkes (1910–1996), British archaeologist and author.

b. Bonnie Parker (1910–1934), American outlaw.

d. Mary Baker Eddy (1821–1910), American religious leader, founder of the Christian Science movement (1876).

d. Adelaide Hunter Hoodless (1857–1910), Canadian pioneer in home health education, who began her campaign after one of her sons died from contaminated milk.

d. Emily Edson Briggs (Olivia) (1830–1910), American newspaper reporter, first president of the Women's National Press Association (1882).

d. Flora Adams Darling (1840–1910), American women's club leader who who helped found several patriotic societies, including the Daughters of the American Revolution, the Daughters of the Revolution, and U.S. Daughters of 1812.

d. Octavie Coudreau (ca. 1870–ca. 1910), French explorer noted for her travels in Latin America, notably French Guiana (1894) and northern Brazil (1895–1899).

## SCIENCE/TECHNOLOGY/MEDICINE

Williamina Fleming reported on her discovery of "white dwarfs," extremely dense stars in a late stage of stellar evolution.

Marie Curie published her *Treatise on Radioactivity*; she was also elected a member of the Swedish Academy of Sciences, only the second woman so honored, the first being in 1748.

Physician Alice Hamilton was appointed director of Illinois's Occupational Disease Commission, the first state survey of work hazards, and then took the same role for the U.S. government. Her work led to recognition of the danger of many industrial substances and helped develop pressure for their elimination or at least control.

Bessica Raiche was the first woman to fly solo; Blanche Stuart Scott had taken off into the air solo earlier in the year, lifted by a gust of wind while taxiing, but her flight was considered "accidental." Raiche adopted riding breeches after her long skirt became tangled in the plane's controls.

American inventor Amanda Theodosia Jones published *A Psychic Autobiography*, exploring what she believed were the spiritual origins of her canning inventions.

Lillian Wald established a Department of Nursing and Health at Columbia University, and also the Town and Country Nursing Service, under the Red Cross.

Marie Stopes published *Ancient Plants*.

b. Dorothy Crowfoot Hodgkin (1910–1994), British scientist, who would win the 1964 Nobel Prize for chemistry.

b. Jacqueline Cochran (1910–1980), American aviator.

b. Joy Gessner Adamson (1910–1980), Austrian conservationist and writer.

b. Marjorie Ferguson Lambert (1910– ), American archaeologist and ethnologist specializing in the Southwest, among the first American woman to become a museum curator, at the Museum of New Mexico.

b. Onnie Lee Logan (1910–1995), Alabama midwife and writer.

d. Elizabeth Blackwell (1821–1910), British-American physician, the first woman to graduate from an American medical school (1849), older sister of Emily Blackwell, also a physician; she was cofounder of the New York Infirmary for Indigent Women and Children (1857) and the London School of Medicine for Women (1869).

d. Emily Blackwell (1826–1910), British-American physician who was co-founder of the New York Infirmary for Indigent Women and Children (1857); younger sister of physician Elizabeth Blackwell, she was the among the first women to work extensively as a surgeon.

d. Florence Nightingale (1820–1910), British nurse and administrator who founded modern nursing during the Crimean War; she was the first woman appointed to the Order of Merit, by Queen Victoria.

d. Isabel Hampton Robb (1860–1910), Canadian-American nurse and nursing educator, who founded and directed the Johns Hopkins nursing school and also founded the two earliest nursing school organizations, one for superintendents (1893), the other for all nurses (1896), and was first president of both.

## ARTS/LITERATURE

Ida Rubinstein created the title role opposite Vaslav Nijinsky in Michel Fokine's ballet *Shéhérazade*, and Tamara Karsavina and Fokine danced the leads in Fokine's ballet *The Firebird*, both productions with Sergei Diaghilev's Ballets Russes company.

Anna Pavlova founded her own dance company.

Emmy Destinn created the role of Minnie in Giacomo Puccini's opera *The Girl of the Golden West*.

Geraldine Farrar created the role of the Goose Girl in Engelbert Humperdinck's opera *Königskinder*.

Laurette Taylor starred opposite H. B. Warner in Paul Armstrong's play *Alias Jimmy Valentine*.

Lucy Arbell created the role of Dulcinée in Jules Massenet's opera *Don Quichotte*.

Cornelia B. Sage Quinton became director of the Albright (later Albright-Knox) Art Gallery in Buffalo (1910–1924), the first American woman in such a post.

Ethel Smyth composed the opera *The Wreckers*.

Laura Knight painted *Daughters of the Sun*.

Marina Tsvetayeva published her first poetry collection, *Evening Album*.

Theresa Serber Malkiel published the novel *Diary of a Shirtwaist Striker*.

Zinaida Hippius published her *Collected Poems*.

Delmira Agustini published the poetry collection *Cantos de mañana*.

b. Alicia Markova (Lillian Alicia Marks, 1910– ), British dancer, who emerged in the 1930s as her country's first international star ballerina.

b. Galina Ulanova (1910– ), Russian ballerina, during the Soviet period a leading dancer with the Kirov Ballet and then the Bolshoi Ballet, from the mid-1940s prima ballerina of the Soviet Union.

b. Katherine Dunham (1910– ), American dancer, choreographer, director, and teacher.

b. Sylvia Sidney (Sophia Kosow, 1910– ), American actress, a dramatic star of Hollywood's Golden Age, in such Depression-era films as *An American Tragedy* (1931) and *Dead End* (1936).

b. Frida Kahlo (1910–1954), Mexican painter.

b. Joan Bennett (1910–1990), American actress.

b. Joyce Irene Grenfell (1910–1979), British actress.

b. Kinuyo Tanaka (1910–1977), Japanese actress and director.

d. Vera Fedorovna Komisarjevskaya (1864–1910), Russian actress and theater manager.

d. Rebecca Harding Davis (1831–1910), American writer.

d. Eliza Pawlowska Orzeszkowa (1841–1910), Polish novelist.

d. Elizabeth Stuart Phelps (1844–1910), American novelist and social reformer.

d. Pauline Garcia Viardot (1821–1910), French mezzo-soprano.

## 1911

### POLITICS/LAW/WAR

Japan's Bluestocking Society was founded by Raicho Hiratsuka, who also edited the journal *Bluestocking* (*Seito*), dealing with women's issues at home, and translated the works of feminists from abroad, including Ellen Key and Emma Goldman.

Militant British suffragist Constance Lytton published *Prisons and Prisoners: Some Personal Experiences by C. Lytton and Jane Wharton, Spinster*. She had repeatedly been imprisoned but then released because she was the daughter of Lord Lytton; she managed finally to achieve equal treatment in jail by using the pseudonym Jane Wharton and was partially paralyzed for the rest of her life by a stroke suffered because of that treatment, including force-feeding of hunger strikers.

The revolution that brought the Chinese Republic radically changed life for women in China. Girls' schools were started, many more women became active in politics, and the practice of footbinding, which had crippled many women from at least the 11th century, was outlawed.

During Portugal's First Republic (1910–1926), the constitution granted women the right to work.

National Association Opposed to Woman Suffrage was founded, with Josephine Dodge as its first president.

Emily Wilding Davison attempted suicide at Holloway prison, as a protest against the force-feeding of imprisoned feminist hunger strikers.

British suffragist Teresa Billington-Grieg published *The Militant Suffrage Movement*.

Emma R. H. Jentzer became the first female special agent (1911–1919) in the Bureau of Investigation, later the Federal Bureau of Investigation; her husband, Harry R. Jentzer, had been the bureau's first agent (1908).

German feminist Marianne Hainisch published *Frauenarbeit*.

Jessie Wallace Hughan published *American Socialism of the Present Day*.

Luisa Capetillo published *My Opinion on the Liberties, Rights, and Obligations of the Puerto Rican Woman*.

b. Barbara Castle (1911– ), British socialist, feminist, and politician, holder of numerous ministerial posts, who chaired the Labour Party (1958–1959).

b. Helga Pedersen (1911– ), Danish lawyer, judge, and politician, the first woman to serve as a judge on the European Court of Human Rights (1971).

b. Lilian Ngoyi (1911–1980), South African antiapartheid leader.

d. Harriet Hanson Robinson (1825–1911), American feminist, suffragist, and writer, founder of the National Women's Suffrage Association of Massachusetts.

### RELIGION/EDUCATION/EVERYDAY LIFE

New York City Triangle Shirtwaist Company fire (March 25) killed 146 workers, mostly young immigrant women trapped in a locked sweatshop; substantial new state health and safety laws resulted, though major abuses persisted.

National Federation of Settlements was founded by Jane Addams, of Chicago's famed Hull House, its first president (1911–1935); after 1979 it would become the United Neighborhood Centers of America.

After ascending Peru's Mt. Coropuna at age 61, Annie Peck planted a sign at the summit: "Votes for Women." She also published *A Search for the Apex of America* (*High Mountain Climbing in Peru and Bolivia*).

Charlotte Perkins Gilman published *The Man-Made World, or Our Androcentive Culture*.

Mary White Ovington published *Half a Man: The Status of the Negro in New York*.

The first mothers' pension laws were passed in Kansas City, Missouri, and then statewide in Illinois.

Theresa West Elmendorf became the first woman to serve as president of the American Library Association.

Avra Theodoropoulou founded the School for Working Women.

Bertha von Suttner published her autobiographical *Memoiren*.

Evelyn Underhill published *Mysticism*, her exploration of religious experience, and *The Path of Eternal Wisdom*.

Clara Collet published *Women in Industry*.

Gertrude Bell published *Amurath to Amurath*, on travels in Turkey.

Madeleine Pelletier published *L'emancipation sexuelle de la femme*.

Olive Schreiner published *Women and Labour*.

b. Eirlys (Rhiwen Cadwalader) Roberts (1911– ), British consumer campaigner, who founded the Consumers' Association (1957), serving as editor of *Which?* (1961–1977), then moving to consumer affairs roles in the European Economic Community.

b. Helen Vlachos (1911–1995), Greek newspaper publisher.

d. Carry Amelia Moore Nation (1846–1911), American temperance activist, a highly visible media celebrity known for her hatchet-wielding direct-action antisaloon campaigns.

d. Margaret Noble (1867–1911), Anglo-Irish educator, writer, political activist, and Hindu nun, known as Sister Nivedita.

## SCIENCE/TECHNOLOGY/MEDICINE

Marie Curie received her second Nobel Prize, this one for chemistry, for her discovery of two new elements: radium and polonium, named for her homeland. Earlier that year she was rejected for membership in the French Academy of Science; their first female member would not be appointed until 1979.

Clara Dutton Noyes founded the first American school for midwives, at New York's Bellevue Hospital.

Harriet Quimby was the first American woman to receive a pilot's license.

Annie Jump Cannon succeeded Williamina Fleming as curator of the Harvard College Observatory's astronomical photographs.

Ellen Churchill Semple published her major work, *Influences of Geographic Environment, on the Basis of Ratzel's System of Anthropo-geography*.

Alice Fletcher published *The Omaha Tribe*, best known of her more than 40 scholarly monographs.

Anna Johnson Pell (later Wheeler) published *Biorthogonal Systems of Functions*, her mathematics doctoral dissertation.

American Nurses' Association was founded.

d. Ellen Swallow Richards (1842–1911), American chemist, ecologist, and home economist, the first female student at the Massachusetts Institute of Technology, who remained there as a teacher; she is regarded as the founder of home economics and of ecology.

d. Williamina Paton Stevens Fleming (1857–1911), Scottish-American astronomer, long attached to the Harvard Observatory, who discovered 10 of the 24 novae then known and over 200 variable stars.

## ARTS/LITERATURE

Tamara Karsavina danced opposite Vaslav Nijinsky in the premieres of Michel Fokine's ballets *La Spectre de la Rose* and *Petrushka*.

Edith Wharton published the novel *Ethan Frome*.

Actresses, barred from the Chinese stage in the mid-19th century, were able to return as performers after the Chinese Republic was established.

Ethel Smyth composed the suffragist anthem *March of the Women*.

Sigrid Undset published the novel *Jenny*.

Frances Hodgson Burnett published the novel *The Secret Garden*.

Ivy Compton-Burnett published the novel *Dolores*.

Sophie Tucker introduced "Some of These Days," her signature song.

Mary Johnston published the novel *The Long Roll*.

b. Ginger Rogers (Virginia Katherine McMath, 1911–1995), American film star.

b. Lucille Ball (1911–1989), American actress.

b. Mahalia Jackson (1911–1972), American gospel singer.

b. Margaret Sullavan (Margaret Brooke, 1911–1960), American actress.

b. Hortense Calisher (1911– ), American novelist and short story writer.

b. Elizabeth Bishop (1911–1979), American poet.

b. Jean Harlow (Harlean Carpenter, 1911–1937), American actress.

b. Paulette Goddard (Marion Levy, 1911–1990), American actress.

b. Hannah Dormer Weinstein (1911–1984), American filmmaker and political activist.

b. Phyllis Margaret Tate (1911–1987), British composer.

d. Edmonia Lewis (active 1843–after 1911), American sculptor.

d. Frances Ellen Harper (1825–1911), American poet, abolitionist, and social reformer.

d. Rose Ettinge (1835–1911), American actress.

# 1912

### POLITICS/LAW/WAR

Emmeline and Christabel Pankhurst took complete control of the Women's Social and Political Union (WSPU), which some former colleagues would call dictatorial. They summarily expelled from the organization Emmeline Pethick-Lawrence and her husband, Frederick Lawrence, key figures in the British women's suffrage movement, who moved to the United Suffragists and continued their work. To avoid trial and imprisonment, and so remain free to orchestrate the women's suffrage campaign, Christabel Pankhurst went into exile in Paris, editing the *Suffragette* and directing the WSPU from abroad (1912–1913).

Substantial numbers of women participated in the successful Lawrence, Massachusetts, textile-industry strike, the high-water mark of its sponsor, the Industrial Workers of the World. The bleak working conditions and impoverishment of many of the women and children affected by the strike stirred considerable sympathy and public support for the strikers.

Sylvia Pankhurst founded the East London Federation branches of the Women's Social and Political Union (WSPU, 1912–1913), a period in which she was repeatedly arrested, went on hunger strikes, and was force-fed while in prison.

Theodore Roosevelt's Progressive Party was the first major political party to endorse women's suffrage, which was part of his Bull Moose platform.

Women's suffrage was won in Oregon; Abigail Duniway, author and co-signer of Oregon's suffrage proclamation, was her state's first woman registered as a voter.

American anarchist Voltairine de Cleyre published *Anarchism and American Traditions*.

Millicent Garrett Fawcett published *Women's Suffrage*, a history of the British women's suffrage movement.

*Woman's Protest*, an antisuffrage periodical, was published (1912–1918).

Inesse Steffane Armand worked underground in St. Petersburg for the Bolshevik party.

Konkordiya Samoilova was a founding editor of the Russian newspaper *Pravda*.

b. Odette Marie Céline Brailey Hallowes (1912–1995), French spy for Britain in German-occupied France during World War II.

b. Electra Apostoloy (1912–1944), Greek communist organizer.

b. Eva Braun (1912–1945), Adolf Hitler's lover (1931–1945).

b. Harriet Fleischl Pilpel (1912–1991), American women's rights and civil liberties lawyer.

b. Kang Keqing (1912–1992), Chinese soldier and Communist Party leader.

d. Anna Diagileva Filosova (1837–1912), Russian social reformer and feminist, a leader of the Russian women's education movement, who chaired the first All-Russian Women's Congress (1908).

## RELIGION/EDUCATION/EVERYDAY LIFE

U.S. Children's Bureau was established by President Theodore Roosevelt at the urging of American public-health nurse Lillian Wald. Julia Lathrop was its first director, focusing on such central concerns as child labor, infant and maternal mortality, and the juvenile-justice system, also preparing and distributing information on child care, and (from 1916) overseeing enforcement of child-labor laws. Her trailblazing programs would be continued under her successor, Grace Abbott.

First American Girl Guides troops (from 1915, Girl Scouts) were founded and led by Juliette Low, modeled on Britain's Girl Guides; the first member was Low's niece, Daisy Gordon. While visiting in Britain, Low had earlier organized some troops of Girl Guides in London and one in Scotland.

Hadassah, the Women's Zionist Organization of America, was formed in New York City by a dozen women, led by Jewish scholar Henrietta Szold; its aims were to foster Jewish religious and social ideals and to provide public-health aid to Palestine, serving not only Jews but also Muslims, Christians, and others.

Australian swimmer Fanny Durack won the women's 100-meter freestyle (the only women's swimming event) at the Stockholm Olympics, setting the first of her nine world records (1912–1918); at that time the Ladies Amateur Swimming Association of New South Wales, to which she belonged, prohibited women from swimming in the presence of men.

Margaret Washington became president of the National Association of Colored Women, founding the publication *National Notes*, which encouraged women to go into business for themselves.

Marie Jenney Howe led in the founding of Heterodoxy, a Greenwich Village–based women's organization (1912–1942), as a place for free-ranging discussions by the era's "new woman," often explored through a series of public forums.

Presbyterian Church in the U.S.A. established a denomination-level superintendent for women's activities, over stiff opposition, with Hallie Paxson Winsborough first taking the post.

Sophonisba Breckinridge and Marion Talbot published *The Modern Household*. Breckinridge and Edith Abbott also published *The Delinquent Child and the Home*.

British mountaineer Lucy Walker, at age 76, became second president of the Ladies' Alpine Club.

Coco Chanel opened her first shop, selling hats of her own design, in Deauville, France.

Helena Rubinstein opened a beauty salon in Paris.

American mountaineer Annie Peck published *The South American Tour*.

Ida Tarbell published *The Business of Being a Woman*.

Anna Kuliscov helped build Italy's Unione Femminile and edited a paper for working-class women, *La digesa delle lavoratrici*.

Evelyn Underhill published *The Spiral Way*.

Anna Spencer published her historical overview *Woman's Share in Social Culture*.

Jane Harrison published *Themis*.

b. Barbara Wertheim Tuchman (1912–1989), American historian and writer.

b. Julia McWilliams Child (1912– ), American cookery writer best known for her television series *The French Chef* (1963–1973), cofounder of the cooking school L'Ecole des Trois Gourmandes (1953).

b. Armi Ratia (1912–1979), Finnish designer and entrepreneur.

b. Virginia Lacy Jones (1912–1984), African-American librarian.

d. Octavia Hill (1838–1912), British reformer best known for her successful programs to improve housing for the poor, also a cofounder of the National Trust; she wrote *Homes of the London Poor* and *Our Common Land*.

d. Louisa Twining (1820–1912), British reformer and feminist, sister of Elizabeth Twining, of the famous tea family, who helped establish nursing sisterhoods in poor areas (1840s) and became secretary of the Workhouse Visiting Society (1858).

d. Caroline Wells (Healey) Dall (1822–1912), American author, who focused on the economic, legal, and educational disadvantages of women.

## SCIENCE/TECHNOLOGY/MEDICINE

The Sorbonne and the Pasteur Institute agreed to build an Institute of Radium, to be directed by Marie Curie.

Nurses working in the field of public health, rather than hospital or private-duty nurses, formed their own National Organization for Public Health Nursing; Lillian Wald, who had coined the label "public health nursing," became its first president.

Entertainer Lillian Russell designed and patented a dresser-trunk containing drawers, hooks, brackets, hinges, lights, and mirrors that all readily folded up for easy shipping.

British botanist Agnes Arber published *Herbals: Their Origin and Evolution*.

b. (Alice) Josephine (Mary Taylor) Barnes (1912– ), British obstetrician and gynecologist, the British Medical Association's first female president (1979).

d. Sophia Jex-Blake (1840–1912), British physician, the first female doctor in Scotland, who helped open medical education to other women, founding the London School of Medicine for Women (1874) and the Edinburgh School of Medicine for Women (1888).

d. Clara (Clarissa Harlowe) Barton (1821–1912), American nurse and founder of the American branch of the International Red Cross.

d. Harriet Quimby (1875–1912), American flyer, the first licensed American female pilot, the first woman to fly across the English Channel (April 16, 1912), and the first authorized to carry the U.S. mail; she was killed during a Boston air meet.

d. Nettie Maria Stevens (1861–1912), American geneticist associated with Bryn Mawr College (1903–1912), who discovered that chromosomes are paired structures and that a particular chromosome determines a person's sex.

## ARTS/LITERATURE

Amy Lowell published her first poetry collection, *A Dome of Many-Coloured Glass*.

Anna Akhmatova published the poetry collection *Evening*.

Maria Jeritza created the title role in Richard Strauss's opera *Ariadne on Naxos*.

Laurette Taylor emerged as a star in the title role of the long-running play *Peg o' My Heart*, by J. Hartley Manners, her second husband.

Harriet Monroe began publishing *Poetry: A Magazine of Verse*.

Mary Austin published the novel *A Woman of Genius*.

Tamara Karsavina and Vaslav Nijinsky premiered Michel Fokine's ballet *Daphnis and Chloe*.

Dorothy Canfield published the novel *The Squirrel-Cage*.

Gertrude Atherton published the novel *Julia France and Her Times*.

Indian poet and feminist Sarojini Naidu published the poetry collection *The Bird of Time*.

Harriet Hosmer's *Letters and Memories*, edited by Cornelia Carr, were published posthumously.

Lilian Baylis became manager of London's Victoria Theater and began to develop what became the Old Vic Company.

Turkish feminist writer Halide Adivar published the novel *Handan*.

b. Wendy Hiller (1912– ), British stage and screen star, a major figure for six decades in both forms, from her stage role in *Love on the Dole* (1935) and her film creation of Eliza Doolittle in *Pygmalion* (1937).

b. Alice Faye (Alice Jean Leppert, 1912– ), American musical film star of Hollywood's Golden Age.

b. Elsa Morante (1912–1985), Italian writer.

b. Mary McCarthy (1912–1989), American writer and critic.

b. Elizabeth Taylor (Elizabeth Coles, 1912–1975), British writer.

b. Kathleen Ferrier (1912–1953), British contralto.

b. Minnie Pearl (Sarah Ophelia Colley, 1912–1996), American actress and singer.

b. Mary Lavin (1912–1996), Irish writer.

b. Peggy Glanville-Hicks (1912–1990), Australian composer.

## 1913

### POLITICS/LAW/WAR

Alice Paul, Lucy Burns, Crystal Eastman, and others founded the Congressional Union for Woman Suffrage (1913–1916), a radical, militant spin-off from the National American Woman Suffrage Association, though formally a NAWSA affiliate. The organization published the weekly *Suffragist*.

The Women's Social and Political Union (WSPU) intensified its confrontation with the British government; Emmeline Pankhurst was arrested more than a dozen times, going on repeated hunger strikes and being force-fed in prison; her health was severely affected, as was that of other WSPU activists.

Konkordiya Samoilova was one of six founding editors of the journal *Rabotnitsa* (*Woman Worker*); all were later arrested (1914), but the journal was later revived (1917).

Helena Swanwick published *The Future of the Women's Movement*.

Rosa Luxemburg published *The Accumulation of Capital*.

German feminist Marianne Hainisch published *Die Mutter*.

Irish suffragist Hannah Sheehy-Skeffington chaired the Irish Franchise League.

Jessie Wallace Hughan published *The Facts of Socialism*.

Louise Bennett was a founder and secretary of the Irishwomen's Suffrage Federation.

Rosa Mayreder published the essay collection *A Survey of the Woman Problem*.

Teresa Billington-Grieg published *Women and the Machine*.

b. Rosa Parks (1913– ), African-American civil rights activist, whose refusal to give up her seat to a white bus passenger generated the landmark Montgomery, Alabama, bus boycott (1955) and helped spark the modern civil rights movement.

d. Harriet Tubman (ca. 1821–1913), African-American abolitionist, an Underground Railroad conductor, who led many slaves to freedom (from 1851); during the Civil War she served the Union as soldier, spy, scout, and nurse.

d. Emily Wilding Davison (1872–1913), militant British feminist, a Women's Social and Political Union activist who practiced arson and violence in pursuit of women's suffrage. She died of injuries suffered when she deliberately jumped before the horse of Britain's King George V at the Epsom Derby, and was treated as a martyr by the militant branch of the British women's suffrage movement.

---

# On Women's Militancy

You have to make more noise than anybody else, you have to make yourself more obtrusive than anybody else, you have to fill the papers more than anybody else, in fact you have to be there all the time and see that they do not snow you under, if you are really going to get your reform realized.

— Emmeline Pankhurst in the speech "When Civil War Is Waged by Women" (1913)

---

d. Alexandra van Grippenberg (1859–1913), Finnish women's rights movement leader and politician, a suffragist who also stressed a wide range of other women's rights issues.

## RELIGION/EDUCATION/EVERYDAY LIFE

Mary Cromwell Jarrett began developing the social service department of Boston Psychopathic Hospital, applying the social casework method there, laying the foundations of what she would name psychiatric social work (1916).

American Federation of Labor endorsed the concept of the woman-only minimum wage.

National Federation of Temple Sisterhoods was formed, as an adjunct to Reformed Judaism's Union of American Hebrew Congregations.

The upper division of the Moravians' Young Ladies Seminary, in Bethlehem, Pennsylvania, became accredited as a college, the Moravian Seminary and College for Women.

Winifred Holt and her sister, Edith Holt, founded Lighthouses for the Blind.

Eleanor Rathbone published *The Conditions of Widows under the Poor Law in Liverpool*.

Elinore Steward published *Letters of a Woman Homesteader*, her memoirs of life as a settler on a Wyoming ranch.

Jane Harrison published *Ancient Art and Ritual*.

Elsie de Wolfe published *The House in Good Taste*, a compilation of her magazine articles.

Georgia (Tiny) Broadwick became the first American woman to parachute from an airplane.

b. Alice Marble (1913–1990), American tennis player.

b. Elizabeth Janeway (1913– ), American writer and feminist, whose *Man's World, Woman's Place* (1971) made her a major voice in the renascent American women's movement.

b. Sylvia Field Porter (1913–1991), American financial writer.

d. Fannie Jackson Coppin (1836–1913), African-American pioneer in industrial education, long associated with Philadelphia's Institute for Colored Youth (later Cheyney State College, then University).

## SCIENCE/TECHNOLOGY/MEDICINE

Henrietta Leavitt completed the "north polar sequence," the first phase of a project using precise measurement of the brightness of stars to establish a standard astronomical reference; she would work on the project until her death.

In a paper published in *Monthly Notices of the Royal Astronomical Society*, Mary Orr Evershed described electric and magnetic forces as acting on the sun's surface.

Mildred Sanderson presented her theorem on modular variants, later known as "Miss Sanderson's Theorem," to the American Mathematical Society.

Female physicians in Hungary were allowed to establish their own medical practices; previously they could practice only with a male doctor.

Carolyn van Blarcom published *The Midwife in England*, as part of her campaign for the training and licensing of American midwives, including the use of silver nitrate solution to prevent blindness in newborns.

Christabel Pankhurst published *The Great Scourge and How to End It*, about venereal diseases.

Louisa King was among the founders of the Garden Club of America.

British astronomer Fiammetta Wilson was the first to spy Westphal's Comet on its return.

Marie Stopes published her two-volume catalogue of fossil plants, *Cretacious Flora* (1913–1915).

b. Chien-Shiung Wu (Madame Wu, 1913– ), Chinese-American nuclear physicist, long at Columbia University, noted for proving the theory of nonconservation of parity among atomic particles (1957).

b. Mary Leakey (Mary Douglas Nicol Leakey, 1913–1996), British anthropologist and paleontologist.

d. Agnes McLaren (1837–1913), Scottish physician and nun, a convert to Catholicism, who helped gain appointments for many female doctors in Catholic missions, despite the rule that women in Catholic orders could not be physicians (until 1936).

## ARTS/LITERATURE

Willa Cather published the novel *O Pioneers!*

Anna Akhmatova published the poetry collection *The Rosary*.

More than 40 female artists, including Marguerite Zorach, participated in the notable 1913 Armory Show in New York City.

Radclyffe Hall published the poetry collection *Songs of Three Counties*.

Sybil Thorndike opened in London in the title role of St. John Irvine's play *Jane Clegg*.

Tamara Karsavina and Vaslav Nijinsky danced in the premiere of Nijinsky's ballet *Jeux*.

Ellen Glasgow published the novel *In Virginia*.

Lilli Lehmann published the autobiography *My Path through Life*.

b. Vivien Leigh (Vivian Mary Hartley, 1913–1967), British actress.

b. Barbara Pym (Crampton, 1913–1980), British writer.

b. Loretta (Gretchen Michaela) Young (1913– ), American actress, a film star in the 1930s and 1940s, and later the star of her own long-running television show (1953–1961).

b. Mary Martin (1913–1990), American singer and actress.

b. Hedy Lamarr (Hedvig Kiesler, 1913– ), Austrian actress, a celebrity after her nude scene in the Czech film *Ecstasy* (1933) and then a Hollywood star of the 1930s and 1940s.

b. Muriel Rukeyser (1913–1980), American writer, feminist, and social reformer.

b. Risë Stevens (1913– ), American mezzo-soprano.

b. May Swenson (1913–1990), American poet and editor.

b. Licia Albanese (1913– ), American soprano.

b. Margaret Bond (1913–1972), African-American composer.

b. Vivian Fine (1913– ), American pianist, composer, and teacher.

# 1914

## POLITICS/LAW/WAR

With the coming of World War I, Emmeline and Christabel Pankhurst abruptly terminated their portion of the women's suffrage campaign, fully supporting the British war effort and openly renouncing militant action for the duration of the war. Widespread reports indicated a covert government pledge of postwar women's suffrage in return for support of the war. Many members left the Women's Social and Political Union, including Sylvia Pankhurst, who founded the pacifist and socialist *Worker's Dreadnought* (1914–1924). Emmeline Pankhurst published *My Own Story*.

Annette Abbott Adams became the first American female federal prosecutor, appointed as assistant United States attorney in northern California by President Woodrow Wilson, for whom she had campaigned.

Jeannette Pickering Rankin became legislative secretary of the National American Woman Suffrage Association.

British nurse Flora Sandes went to Serbia with a nursing unit (1914), working with the Serbian Red Cross and the 2nd Infantry Regiment, then becoming an active soldier against the Bulgarians. Invalided home briefly (1916), she fought in the mountains for seven years and was decorated for bravery. Remaining with the army after the war, she later became a captain (1926).

Emilie Gourd became president of the Swiss Women's Association (1914–1928).

Finnish feminist Annie Furujelhm was elected to the parliament (Diet) of newly independent Finland (1922–1929).

In Germany, women's support of the war effort was mainly directed through the National Women's Service (Nationaler Frauendienst, or NFD), organized by Gertrude Baumer.

People's Will leader Vera Figner returned to Russia, now a Socialist Revolutionary rather than an anarchist-terrorist.

b. Jiang Qing (1914–1991), Chinese actress and politician.

b. Sushila Nayar (1914– ), Indian doctor, independence-movement leader, and politician, who became Speaker of the Delhi Legislative Assembly (1952–1956); she was Mahatma Gandhi's medical attendant.

b. Anna Mikhailovna Larina (1914–1996), Russian author, the wife of Communist leader Nicolai Bukharin.

## RELIGION/EDUCATION/EVERYDAY LIFE

National Women's Trade Union League (NWTUL) established one of the earliest education programs for working women, particularly those in industry (ca. 1914); the International Ladies Garment Workers Union (ILGWU) began its own program of education for women working in the garment trades.

During World War I, American expatriates, mostly women, led by Edith Wharton, established a system of Workrooms (*Ouvroirs*, ca. 1914–1918) to aid civilians in war-ravaged Europe, providing pay, medical care, midday meals, and coal during the winter. Expatriate women were also active in other relief organizations, including the American Fund for French Wounded (for whom Gertrude Stein and Alice B. Toklas drove a truck), American Hostels for Refugees, the Franco-American General Committee, the Children of Flanders Rescue Committee, and the American Distributing Service.

Quaker relief worker Edith Pye, assisted by Hilda Clark, organized care for women and children near the front in France during World War I (1914–1918), establishing a maternity hospital that later became permanent at Châlons. Pye was later awarded France's Legion of Honor.

Mother's Day was established by a joint resolution of the U.S. Congress, the observance later spreading to dozens of other countries.

In the United States, the General Federation of Women's Clubs first formally endorsed women's right to vote.

Polly (Mary Phelps) Jacobs (later known as Caresse Crosby) patented the "backless brassiere," designed to minimize the bustline, to suit the fashion of the day; she founded a manufacturing company and later licensed the brassiere to others.

Louella Oettinger Parsons began writing her syndicated movie column, the first woman to do so.

Margaret Bondfield became secretary of the National Foundation of Women Workers.

May Tennant advised Britain's Ministry of Munitions on women's welfare issues (1914–1918).

Rosika Schwimmer worked in London as a correspondent for several European newspapers.

Smith-Lever Act of 1914 encouraged coeducational state "land grant" colleges and universities to include home economics in their curricula, through federal aid.

Heterodoxy, the Greenwich Village–based women's discussion organization, sponsored the public forum "What Is Feminism?"

Gertrude Bell published *The Palace and Mosque of Ukhaidir.*

Madeleine Pelletier published *L'education feministe des filles.*

b. "Babe" (Mildred Ella) Didrikson Zaharias (1914–1956), American athlete.

b. Barbara Ward (Baroness Jackson of Lodsworth, 1914–1981), British economist.

b. Margery Berney Hurst (1914– ), British entrepreneur, founder of the Brook Street Bureau, a chain of employment agencies.

d. Bertha Felicie Sophie Kinsky von Suttner (1843–1914), Austrian novelist and pacifist whose pacifist writings led Alfred Nobel to establish his Peace Prize, which she later won (1905).

d. Grace Hoadley Dodge (1856–1914), American welfare worker who helped found the Association of Working Girls' Societies and established the New York Travelers Aid Society.

## SCIENCE/TECHNOLOGY/MEDICINE

Margaret Sanger coined the term *birth control,* publishing her classic 16-page pamphlet, *Family Limitation,* in defiance of government bans on dissemination of birth control information; her husband, William Sanger, was arrested with a copy of the pamphlet, leading to a sensational trial in which he was convicted and sentenced to 30 days in jail. Margaret Sanger founded the magazine *Woman Rebel*, which carried articles on contraception, and was herself indicted; the indictment was later dropped.

After World War I began, Marie Curie and her daughter Irène (later Joliot-Curie) toured the battlefields, setting up X-ray stations; they also converted France's newly built but still empty Institute of Radium into a school for training young women to take X rays. In Germany, radiation physicist Lise Meitner served as a radiographer and nurse with the Austrian army.

British physician Hilda Clark published a paper urging use of the new tuberculin injection. When war began, she cofounded the Friends War Victims Relief (War Vics) with Edmund Harvey and was medical organizer of their first team in France.

Physician Elsie Inglis organized the Scottish Women's Hospitals (SWH), fielding all-woman medical teams that served in France and Serbia.

Physician Mary Scharlieb helped form a Women's Medical Service for India during World War I (ca. 1914–1918).

During World War I, British physicist Hertha Ayrton developed the Ayrton fan to drive away poisonous gases, replacing them with fresh air, and also standardized the British military's searchlights (ca. 1914–1918).

Physician Alice Hamilton, studying hazards in the explosives industry, found that many workers were being exposed to toxic, and sometimes lethal, levels of nitrous compounds.

Alice Gertrude Bryant and Florence West Duckering became the first two female members of the American College of Surgeons.

Lillian Gilbreth published *The Psychology of Management*, which pioneered in recognizing management as a province for psychology.

Louisa King was among the founders of the Women's National Farm and Garden Association, serving as its first president (1914–1921).

Mary Orr Evershed published *Dante and the Early Astronomers*.

b. (Hannah) Marie Wormington (1914–1994), American archaeologist, a pioneer in using mixed male-and-female crews at excavations; a specialist in Paleo-Indian studies, she was long associated with the Denver Museum.

b. Dixy Lee Ray (Margaret Ray, 1914–1994), American marine biologist, administrator, and politician.

b. Virginia Satir (1914–1989), American family therapist.

d. Margaret (Mattie) E. Knight (1838–1914), American inventor best known for her patented paper-bag-making machine (1870), who patented numerous automotive engineering and household devices.

d. Mary Anna Palmer Draper (1839–1914), American benefactor of astronomy.

d. Mildred Leonora Sanderson (1889–1914), American mathematician whose promising career was cut short by an early death.

### ARTS/LITERATURE

Mrs. Patrick Campbell created the classic Eliza Doolittle role in the first English-language production of George Bernard Shaw's *Pygmalion*, opening in London opposite Herbert Beerbohm Tree as Henry Higgins.

Amy Lowell published the poetry collection *Sword Blades and Poppy Seed*.

Lidia Quaranta, Umberto Mozzato, and Bartolomeo Pagano starred in *Cabiria*, Giovanni Pastrone's Italian epic silent film.

---

No woman can call herself free who does not own and control her body. No woman can call herself free until she can choose consciously whether she will or will not be a mother.

—Margaret Sanger (1913)

---

Mary Pickford starred in the title role of *Tess of the Storm Country*, Edwin S. Porter's classic silent film.

Pearl White created the title role in the long-running, enormously popular silent film serial *The Perils of Pauline*.

Selma Lagerlöf became the first female member of the Swedish Academy.

Augusta Gregory published *Our Irish Theatre: A Chapter of Autobiography*.

Julia Sanderson and Donald Brian introduced Jerome Kerns's first hit song, "They Didn't Believe Me," in *The Girl from Utah*.

Lois Weber wrote the screenplay and codirected a film version of Shakespeare's *The Merchant of Venice*, also starring as Portia.

Marie Dressler, Charles Chaplin, and Mabel Normand starred in *Tillie's Punctured Romance*, Mack Sennett's classic silent film.

Blanche Sweet, Mae Marsh, Lillian Gish, and Dorothy Gish starred in D. W. Griffith's silent film *Judith of Bethulia*.

Gabriela Mistral published *Sonnets of Death*.

Geraldine Farrar created the role of Louise in Gustave Charpentier's opera *Julien*.

b. Gypsy Rose Lee (Rose Louise Hovick, 1914–1970), American actress, dancer, and writer.

b. Geraldine Fitzgerald (1914– ), Irish actress, a star in the Broadway theater who played strong supporting roles in films.

b. Jane Wyman (Sarah Jane Faulks, 1914– ), American film star of the post–World War II period, in such movies as *The Lost Weekend* (1945), and in her Oscar-winning role as the deaf-mute young woman in *Johnny Belinda* (1948); later a television star.

b. Marguerite Duras (Margaret Donnadieu, 1914–1996), French playwright, filmmaker, and novelist, a major figure in French cultural life from the early 1950s.

b. Dorothy Lamour (Mary Leta Dorothy Kaumeyer, 1914–1996), American actress and singer.

b. Joan Maud Littlewood (1914– ), British director, the founder and manager of the Theatre Workshop.

b. Joy Batchelor (1914–1991), British artist, animator, and filmmaker.

b. Rosalyn Tureck (1914– ), American instrumentalist, conductor, writer, and teacher.

d. Vinnie Ream (Hoxie) (1847–1914), American sculptor, whose works included a full-length statue of Abraham Lincoln (1871) that was the first federal government commission to go to a woman.

d. Delmira Agustini (1890–1914), Uruguayan poet.

d. Fanny Whiteside Brough (1854–1914), British actress.

# 1915

## POLITICS/LAW/WAR

Jane Addams was a founder and first president of the pacifist Women's Peace Party, organized to oppose American participation in World War I or any other war; it was the percursor of the Women's International League for Peace and Freedom; Addams also chaired the first Women's Peace Congress, at The Hague.

While serving as a foreign correspondent in London, Rosika Schwimmer became an active pacifist, convincing Henry Ford to sponsor a "peace ship," the SS *Oscar II*, to visit the enemy nations, in a vain effort to promote peace; she served as vice-president of the Women's Peace Party.

Women won the right to vote and be elected to office in Denmark and Iceland.

Alice Stebbins Wells founded the International Association of Policewomen, which became the main vehicle of the campaign to open police work to women.

Inesse Steffane Armand represented the Bolshevik party at the International Women's Socialist Conference and at internationalist conferences at Zimmenwald and Kienthal (1915–1916).

Gertrude Bell joined Britain's new Arab intelligence bureau in Cairo, which aimed to gather information useful in mobilizing the Arabs against Turkey; traveling widely from India to Iraq, she became assistant political officer in Basra.

International Congress of Women was held at The Hague.

Adela Pankhurst Walsh published the pacifist *Put up the Sword*.

Ellen Wilkinson became an organizer for the British Amalgamated Union of Co-operative Employees.

Jessie Wallace Hughan founded the pacifist Anti-Enlistment League (1915–1917).

b. Ethel Greenglass Rosenberg (1915–1953), American political and union activist, executed as a spy for the Soviet Union.

b. Rani Gaidinliu (1915– ), Naga independence activist, who in her late teens led guerrilla forces in northern India during the continuing low-level insurrection against British colonial rule.

b. Soia Mentschikoff (1915–1984), American lawyer.

d. Abigail Jane Scott Duniway (1834–1915), American women's rights advocate, a leading Western suffragist, publisher of the weekly *New Northwest* (1871).

## RELIGION/EDUCATION/EVERYDAY LIFE

Maud Howe Elliott and Laura Howe Richards published a biography of their mother, *Julia Ward Howe, 1819–1910*, winning a Pulitzer Prize (1916).

Aimée Semple McPherson began conducting revival meetings in a Pentecostal mission in Ontario, Canada; increasingly noted for her skill in preaching, "speaking in tongues," and faith healing, she then toured in tent revivals across North America.

Charlotte Perkins Gilman published the utopian novel *Herland*, about a socialist matriarchy, a work that endured far beyond her time.

Girl Scouts of America organization was founded, its first president Juliette Low, who had formed the first American Girl Guides troops (1912).

Rose Schneiderman became a national organizer for the International Ladies Garment Workers Union.

The Sisters of the Blessed Sacrament for Indians and Colored People, a Roman Catholic order, founded Xavier University, in New Orleans.

Helena Rubinstein opened her Maison de Beauté in Manhattan, making America the base for her cosmetics empire.

Mary Roberts Rinehart became the first American correspondent to report from the front during World War I and the first to interview Britain's Queen Mary.

Women's Executive Committee of Home Missions, under president Katherine Bennett, became the first American women's organization to report directly to the Presbyterian church's General Assembly.

Antoinette Brown Blackwell published *The Social Side of Mind and Action*.

Clementina Black published *Married Women's Work*.

Elinore Steward published further Wyoming memoirs, *Letters on an Elk Hunt by a Woman Homesteader*.

Margaret Davies published *Maternity: Letters from Working Women*.

## If Only It Were So . . .

I find that men welcome women scientists provided they have the proper knowledge. It is absurd to suppose that anyone can have useful knowledge of any subject without a great deal of study. When women have really taken the pains to fit themselves to assist or to do original work, scientific men are willing to treat them as equals. It is a matter of sufficient knowledge. That there is any wish to throw hindrances in the way of women who wish to pursue science I do not for a moment believe. The lady doctors had a great fight, it is true, but that is old history now, and there were special ancient prejudices involved.

—Margaret Huggins

d. Fannie Merritt Farmer (1857–1915), American cook and educator, principal of the Boston Cooking School and author of the famous cookbook (1896) named after the school, and then after her.

## SCIENCE/TECHNOLOGY/MEDICINE

National Birth Control League (NBCL), the first American birth control organization, was founded by Mary Dennett, campaigning for legal dissemination of contraceptive information.

American Medical Women's Association (AMWA) was founded, with Bertha van Hoosen as first president; composed of women doctors and medical students, its purposes were to further the interests and influence of women in the medical profession and to improve women's health care.

Katherine Stinson (later Otero) and her family founded the Stinson Flying School in San Antonio, Texas; she and her sister Marjorie Stinson were the primary flight instructors. That year Katherine Stinson became the first woman to skywrite and to fly at night.

In the National Negro Health Movement (1915–1950), sparked by Booker T. Washington at Alabama's Tuskegee Institute, African-American physicians, nurses, social workers, and other health workers—many of them women—coordinated in providing health services to the poorly served black community.

Lillian Wald published *The House on Henry Street*.

Lou Andreas-Salomé published the essay "Anal-und Sexual."

Mary Adela Blagg was elected to Britain's Royal Astronomical Society.

Lillien Martin became head of the psychology department of Stanford University, the first woman-to head a department there.

d. Edith Louisa Cavell (1865–1915), British nurse, shot by the Germans as a spy in Belgium, who became a martyr in Britain. She had converted her Belgian nurses' training school into a Red Cross hospital, treating wounded soldiers from both sides; it was also an "underground rail-way" stop for French and British soldiers en route to the Netherlands.

d. Margaret Lindsay Murray Huggins (1848–1915), Irish astronomer, a specialist in spectroscopy, who generally worked in partnership with her husband, William Huggins.

## ARTS/LITERATURE

Susan Glaspell founded and was first director of the Provincetown Players (1915–1929), which would present most of Eugene O'Neill's early plays and the works of several other major American playwrights.

Virginia Woolf published her first novel, *The Voyage Out*.

Blanche Sweet starred opposite James O'Neill in *The Warrens of Virginia*, Cecil B. DeMille's silent film.

Mary Pickford starred in *A Girl of Yesterday*, Allen Dwan's silent film.

Ruth St. Denis and Ted Shawn founded the Denishawn school and dance company.

Dorothy Richardson began to publish *Pilgrimage* (1915–1938), a 12-volume series of "stream of consciousness" novels.

Theda Bara emerged as a silent film star in *A Fool There Was*.

Djuna Barnes published graphics and poetry in *Book of Repulsive Women*.

Lois Weber wrote and directed the film *Hypocrites*.

Dorothy Canfield published the novel *The Bent Twig*.

b. Billie Holiday (Eleanora Fagan, 1915–1959), American jazz singer.

b. Edith Piaf (Giovanna Gassion, 1915–1963), French singer.

b. Ingrid Bergman (1915–1982), Swedish actress.

b. Elisabeth Schwarzkopf (1915– ), German soprano, a leading interpreter of the operas of Mozart and Strauss.

b. Anna Sokolow (1915– ), American dancer and choreographer.

b. Betty Comden (1915– ), American composer and singer, who with her longtime collaborator, Adolph Green, created several classic American theater musicals.

b. Judith Wright (1915– ), Australian poet.

b. Jean Stafford (1915–1979), American novelist.

d. Anne Whitney (1821–1915), American sculptor and writer, an abolitionist, feminist, and social reformer, whose concerns were reflected in the choice of subjects for her portrait busts.

d. Mary Elizabeth Braddon (1837–1915), British writer, a playwright, poet, editor, and prolific producer of melodramatic novels.

## 1916

### Politics/Law/War

Montana Republican Jeannette Pickering Rankin became the first woman to be elected to the House of Representatives (serving 1917–1919).

Carrie Chapman Catt returned to the presidency of the National American Woman Suffrage Association (NAWSA), and in the next three years led the successful fight for the passage of the 19th (Woman Suffrage, or Anthony) Amendment.

Congressional Union for Woman Suffrage, led by Alice Paul, changed its name to the National Woman's Party and intensified its militant campaign for women's suffrage.

Emily Ferguson Murphy was appointed magistrate in a Canadian juvenile court, the first female magistrate in the British Empire, but her legal right to rule was immediately challenged under a British law of 1876, under which women (along with children, criminals, and "idiots") were not classed as persons. Murphy's position was soon legally upheld, but the case sparked a landmark reevaluation of women's legal status throughout the British Empire (1916–1929).

Constance Markiewicz fought with Irish Citizen Army forces during the Easter Rising, holding the Royal College of Surgeons building in Dublin. She was sentenced to death, had her sentence commuted, and was freed (1917).

Rosa Luxemburg was imprisoned in Germany for opposing World War I.

Inesse Armand did Russian-to-French translations of some of the works of Bolshevik leader V. I. Lenin.

Louise Bennett became chief organizer and soon general secretary of the Irish Women Workers' Union (1916–1955).

b. Sirimavo Ratwatte Bandaranaike (1916– ), Sri Lankan socialist politician, the world's first woman to serve as prime minister (1960–1965; 1970–1977).

b. Tokyo Rose (Iva Ikuko Toguri D'Aquino, 1916– ), American woman who broadcast Japanese propaganda to American forces in the South Pacific during World War II.

d. Lily Braun (1865–1916), German radical feminist and socialist who refused to subordinate women's freedom issues to socialist issues.

### Religion/Education/Everyday Life

Annie Besant organized and led the Home Rule India League; she also edited *New India*, a Madras daily.

Gertrude Denman chaired a subgroup of Britain's Agricultural Organization Society (1916–1946) that founded the first Women's Institutes, which by the 1950s would number 8,000 and boast more than 450,000 members.

Helene Weber became head of the German Catholic Women's Federation social-work school.

Margaret Cousins became the first non-Indian member of the Indian Women's University, Poona.

Mary Talbert became president of the National Association of Colored Women.

Vassar College introduced a course on the family, the first at an American women's college.

María Cadilla de Martínez became professor of Hispanic history and literature at the University of Puerto Rico.

Virginia's Mary Baldwin Seminary became Mary Baldwin Junior College.

Women's International Bowling Congress was founded in St. Louis, Missouri, sponsoring its first women's bowling tournament (1917).

Josephine Goldmark published *Women in Industry*.

b. Hélène Ahrweiler (1916– ), French historian and archaeologist, the first woman to head the Sorbonne's department of history (1967) and to be president of the Sorbonne (1976); she was later chancellor of the Universities of Paris (1982).

b. Betty Furness (Elizabeth Mary Furness, 1916–1994), American consumer advocate, actress, and journalist.

d. Aikaterini Laskaridou (1842–1916), Greek educator, philanthropist, and writer who opened Greece's first nursery schools, modeled on those in Western Europe. She also introduced gymnastics into girls' schools, founded training workshops for poor women, and wrote widely on women's education and child raising.

d. Hetty (Henrietta Howland Robinson) Green (1834–1916), American financier who turned a $1 million inheritance into an estimated $100 million. She was nicknamed by the media for her personal eccentricities the "witch of Wall Street."

d. Sarah Jane Farmer (1847–1916), religious leader, a founder of the American Baha'i movement.

d. Lucy Walker (1836–1916), British mountaineer, the first woman to climb the Matterhorn (1871).

d. Susan Elizabeth Blow (1843–1916), American educator who founded the first public kindergarten in America (1873).

## SCIENCE/TECHNOLOGY/MEDICINE

Margaret Sanger founded the first American birth control clinic, in Brooklyn's poor Brownsville neighborhood; many of her clients were recent immigrants.

American archaeologist Harriet Boyd Hawes arrived in Corfu bearing supplies for ailing and wounded Serbian solders, much of them donated by the American Distributing Service, but some provided personally; on her return, she gave fund-raising lectures, organized the Smith College Relief Unit, and went with it to France.

Elsie Inglis and other members of the all-woman Scottish Women's Hospital medical teams were repatriated to Britain; they had remained, continuing to serve in their Serbian field hospitals, after their camp was taken by Austrian and Bulgarian troops.

American archaeologist Hetty Goldman became a fellow of the American School of Classical Studies; she would be the first woman to lead an official school expedition.

Leta Hollingworth received her doctorate in psychology from Columbia University, with a dissertation challenging popular theories of male superiority. After three years in clinical work, she returned to Columbia as an assistant professor, becoming a full professor in 1929.

Britain's Royal Geographical Society made Kate Marsden a Free Life Fellow; she had since 1892 been on their list of "well-qualified ladies."

Hazel Hook Waltz invented the bobby pin, though someone else patented an improvement, making a fortune from it.

Margaret Washburn published *Movement and Mental Imagery*.

Landscape architect Beatrix Jones Farrand designed the Graduate College gardens at Princeton University.

## ARTS/LITERATURE

Amy Lowell published the poetry collection *Men, Women, and Ghosts*.

Lois Weber and Phillips Smalley, her partner and husband, codirected the trailblazing film *Where Are My Children?* about birth control. She also wrote and codirected the silent film *The Dumb Girl of Portici*, starring ballerina Anna Pavlova in her only feature film.

Ethel Smyth composed the opera *The Boatswain's Mate*.

Georgia O'Keeffe showed her painting *Blue Lines*.

H. D. (Hilda Doolittle) published the poetry collection *Sea Garden*.

Gertrude Käsebier, Clarence White, and Alvin Langdon Coburn founded the Pictorial Photographers of America.

(Flora) Elizabeth Burchenal founded and led the American Folk Dance Society.

Margaret Deland published the novel *The Rising Tide*.

b. Olivia de Havilland (1916– ), American film star, who emerged as a major dramatic actress in the postwar period, in her Oscar-winning roles in *To Each His Own* (1946), *The Snake Pit* (1948), and *The Heiress* (1949).

b. Shirley Jackson (1916–1965), American writer.

b. Irene Worth (1916– ), American actress, a leading player on the English-speaking stage in Britain, the United States, and Canada from the mid-1940s.

b. Betty (Elizabeth Ruth) Grable (1916–1973), American actress.

b. Natalia Levi Ginzburg (1916–1991), Italian novelist, essayist, and translator.

b. Eleanor Steber (1916–1990), American soprano.

b. Françoise Giroud (1916– ), French editor and writer, a leading journalist, founder of *Elle* (1945) and *L'Express* (1953).

d. Janet Achurch (1864–1916), British dramatic actress, a notable early English-language interpreter of Ibsen, also highly regarded for her roles in Shakespeare and Shaw.

d. Ada Rehan (1860–1916), American actress, a star in England and America from the mid-1870s through the turn of the century.

## 1917

### POLITICS/LAW/WAR

National Woman's Party activists instituted a direct-action campaign in support of women's suffrage, picketing the White House and other federal installations; more than 200 women were arrested (June) and almost 100 jailed. Those jailed mounted hunger strikes, while a mass campaign developed for their release. All were freed by October, and all sentences were later overturned by a federal appeals court.

Women won the right to vote in Canada.

A Parliamentary Conference recommended that British women gain the right to vote.

Alexandra Kollontai became Bolshevik Commissar for Public Welfare.

Antiwar Socialist Party leader Kate Richards O'Hare was convicted under the Espionage Act and served 14 months of a five-year prison sentence, emerging as a campaigner for prison reform.

Frances Witherspoon and several other Women's Peace Party activists organized the New York Bureau of Legal First Aid (later the New York Bureau of Legal Advice), the first organization providing free legal aid to conscientious objectors and draft resisters during World War I (1917–1920). Witherspoon and Tracy Mygatt edited the Women's Peace Party's antiwar journal *Four Lights*.

During a brief period, women were recruited to serve in the U.S. Navy in mostly clerical duties; the first female enlistee was Loretta Walsh. More than 11,000 women served in the U.S. Navy and Marine Corps during World War I (1917–1918).

Emma Goldman was sentenced to a five-year prison term for opposing the World War I military draft.

Women won the right to vote in party primaries in Arkansas.

Clara Zetkin led representatives of various women's groups, meeting at The Hague, then at Zimmerwald, Switzerland, in opposing the war.

Gertrude Bell published *The Arab of Mesopotamia*.

In Britain, the Women's Social and Political Union, now a small organization, became the Women's Party.

Ona Masiotene founded the Lithuanian Women's Freedom Association.

b. Indira Gandhi (1917–1984), Indian prime minister, the daughter of Jawaharlal Nehru.

b. Fannie Lou Hamer (1917–1977), African-American civil rights activist and Mississippi politician.

b. Helen Gavronsky Suzman (1917– ), white South African politician, an economist and antiapartheid activist, cofounder of the Progressive Party (1959).

b. Marietta Peabody Tree (1917–1991), American diplomat.

d. Belva Bennett Lockwood (1830–1917), feminist, suffragist, women's rights movement leader, and pacifist, the first woman admitted to practice law before the U.S. Supreme Court (1879); she was the presidential candidate of the National Equal Rights Party (1884) and a leading member of the International Council of Women.

d. Liliuokalani (Lydia Kamekeha; 1838–1917), the last queen of Hawaii (1891–1893). She composed the song "Aloha Oe" ("Farewell to Thee"; 1898).

d. Mata Hari (Margaretha Geertruida Zelle, 1876–1917), Dutch dancer who was executed as a German spy by the French (October 15) during World War I.

d. Amelia Jane "Amie" Hicks (1840–1917), British feminist, socialist, and trade unionist, a leading figure in the late-19th-century and early-20th-century British social reform movement.

### RELIGION/EDUCATION/EVERYDAY LIFE

Annie Besant, interned for some months because of her Indian self-rule campaign, became fifth president of the Congress Party (1917–1923); her opposition to civil disobedience later cost her that leadership role, as the growing independence movement, led by Mahatma Gandhi, turned to nonviolent mass action.

Catherine Booth became international secretary for the Salvation Army in Europe, leading war-relief efforts for children after World War I, as she would do after World War II.

Smith-Hughes Act of 1917 established the Federal Board for Vocational Education to encourage secondary schools to establish training in vocational subjects, including home economics, agriculture, commerce, and trade skills, and also fostering student organizations such as the Future Homemakers of America and Future Farmers of America; such training tended to direct girls in sex-segregated directions, unlike the more general college-preparation curricula.

Mabel Gillespie founded the Stenographers' Union, becoming its first president.

Annie Oakley returned for the farewell season of Buffalo Bill's Wild West Show.

Margaret Cousins helped found the Indian Women's Association.

President Woodrow Wilson appointed Anna Howard Shaw to chair the Woman's Committee of the Council of National Defense during World War I.

Kate Gleason served as president of the First National Bank of Rochester (1917–1919), while the male president served in World War I.

Mary Ellen Richmond published *What Is Social Casework?*

b. Katharine Meyer Graham (1917– ), American newspaper proprietor, longtime publisher of the *Washington Post*, her family's newspaper.

d. (Maria) Francesca (Xavier) Cabrini (Mother Cabrini, 1850–1917), Italian-born American nun and saint, founder of the Missionary Sisters of the Sacred Heart (1880), and noted for her work with poor immigrants; the first American saint (1946).

d. Anne King Blunt (1837–1917), British traveler, daughter of Ada Byron, countess of Lovelace and wife of poet-diplomat Wilfred Scawen Blunt; she was among the first Englishwomen to explore the Arabian peninsula.

---

# On the Importance of Women's Suffrage

I regard the concurrence of the Senate in the constitutional amendment proposing the extension of the suffrage to women as vitally essential to the successful prosecution of the great war of humanity in which we are engaged. . . . It is vital to the right solution of the great problems which we must settle, and settle immediately, when the war is over. We shall need then a vision of affairs, which is theirs, and, as we have never needed them before, the sympathy and insight and clear moral instinct of the women of the world. . . . Without their counsellings we shall be only half wise. . .

— U.S. President Woodrow Wilson, speaking before the U.S. Senate (September 1918)

---

SCIENCE/TECHNOLOGY/MEDICINE

American bacteriologist Alice Evans first reported that brucellosis (undulant fever) was a single disease, not many, caused by a bacterium that could be killed through pasteurization of milk. Her theories were ill received and not confirmed for years, since fresh, unpasteurized milk was regarded as healthy; only in the 1930s was pasteurization of milk made mandatory.

American Women's Hospitals Service (AWHS) was founded as a committee of the Medical Women's National Association (later, American Medical Women's Association), chaired by Dr. Rosalie Slaughter Morton. Not allowed to serve in the armed forces, women physicians, through the AWHS, fielded all-women teams of doctors, nurses, and ambulance drivers, serving in and near France's war zone.

Margaret Sanger published *What Every Woman Should Know* and was arrested for disseminating birth control information and jailed for 30 days, but freed on appeal. The landmark New York State Court of Appeals decision enabled doctors to legally supply their patients with birth control information.

Lise Meitner and her longtime collaborator, Otto Hahn, discovered the new element protactinium.

Florence Sabin became professor of histology at Johns Hopkins University, their first female full professor.

Mary Orr Evershed and John Evershed published *Memoirs of the Kodaikanal Observatory*, where he was director, in India.

More than 8,500 women would serve in the Army Nurse Corps as part of American armed forces during World War I.

b. Jacqueline (Marie-Thérèse Suzanne Donet) Auriol (1917– ), French aviator, the world's first female test pilot.

d. Elizabeth Garrett Anderson (1836–1917), Britain's first female physician, who helped found and ran the London School of Medicine for Women (1883) and New Hospital for Women (1886); later Britain's first female mayor (1908).

d. Elsie (Maude) Inglis (1864–1917), India-born British physician, who co-founded Scotland's only all-woman maternity center, later named for her; she died en route home from a second trip to Serbia, having fielded and led all-woman Scottish Women's Hospital teams.

ARTS/LITERATURE

Edna St. Vincent Millay published *Renascence and Other Poems.*

Helen Hayes starred in the play *Pollyanna*, based on the Eleanor Porter novel.

Henry Handel Richardson (Henrietta Robertson Richardson) published the novel *Australia Felix*, the first in the trilogy *The Fortunes of Richard Mahony* (1917–1930), which also included *The Way Home* and *Ultima Thule.*

Mary Pickford starred in *Poor Little Rich Girl* and in *Rebecca of Sunnybrook Farm*, Marshall Neilan's silent film version of Kate Douglas Wiggin's novel.

Anna Akhmatova published the poetry collection *The White Flock.*

Mistinguett starred in her own *Revue Mistinguett.*

Katherine Mansfield published the autobiographical work *Prelude.*

Maria Chabelska and Leonid Massine danced the leads in the premiere of Massine's ballet *Parade.*

Sara Teasdale published the poetry collection *Love Songs.*

Theda Bara starred in the title role of *Cleopatra*, J. Gordon Edwards's silent film.

Mary Austin published the novel *The Ford.*

Ina Claire starred on Broadway in *Polly with a Past*, George Middleton and Guy Bolton's stage comedy.

Mary Hallock Foote published the novel *Edith Bonham.*

b. Ella Fitzgerald (1917–1996), American jazz and popular singer.

b. Carson McCullers (1917–1967), American writer.

b. Joan Fontaine (Joan de Havilland, 1917– ), American film star of the 1940s and 1950s, most notably opposite Laurence Olivier in *Rebecca* (1940) and Cary Grant in her Oscar-winning *Suspicion* (1941).

b. Lena Horne (1917– ), American singer, actress, and dancer, a pioneering African-American entertainer.

b. Dinah Shore (Frances Rose Shore, 1917–1994), American singer.

b. Gwendolyn Brooks (1917– ), African-American poet, whose work focuses on black Americans' experiences.

b. Jessica Lucy Mitford (1917–1996), British-American writer.

b. Pamela Brown (1917–1975), British actress.

d. Florence Farr (1860–1917), British actress and director, an early exponent of Ibsen, Shaw, and Yeats.

d. Kate Josephine Bateman (1842–1917), American actress, who created and was long associated with the title role in *Leah the Forsaken*.

d. Maria Firmina dos Reis (1825–1917), African-Brazilian teacher, novelist, and poet who wrote as Uma Brasileira (A Brazilian).

## 1918

### POLITICS/LAW/WAR

President Woodrow Wilson came out in support of the Woman Suffrage Amendment. Militant suffrage organizations, such as the Congressional Union, had campaigned against him in 1916. The House of Representatives passed it (January 10), but it failed in the Senate by two votes.

Women won the right to vote and be elected to office in Germany, Ireland, Poland, and Sweden, and the right to vote in party primaries in Texas.

Anne Henrietta Martin was the first woman to run for the U.S. Senate, from Nevada, but was defeated twice (1918; 1920).

Japanese feminists, among them Fusaye Ichikawa and Raicho Hiratsuka, founded the New Women's Association and began to campaign for the elementary right to participate in the political life of their country.

Pacifist Jeannette Pickering Rankin, who opposed American participation in World War I, lost her bid for a Montana Senate seat.

Rosika Schwimmer was elected to Hungary's National Council of Fifteen and was then appointed minister to Switzerland, believed to be the world's first woman to serve as an ambassador; but as incompatible governments came to power she resigned (1919) and fled Hungary for the United States (1920), though there she was branded a Bolshevik spy.

Annette Abbott Adams became the first American woman to serve as assistant attorney general, in Washington, D.C.

German Communist Party was founded by, among others, Rosa Luxemburg and Clara Zetkin.

Inesse Armand became the first director of the Soviet government's Women's Bureau.

Nina Bang was the first female member of Denmark's Upper House of Parliament.

Alexandra Kollontai published *The New Morality and the Working Class*.

Constance Markiewicz was elected an Irish member of Britain's Parliament but with other Irish MPs did not take her seat.

Czech women's rights leader Franciska Plamnikova was elected to the Prague municipal council.

Harriet Stanton Blatch published *Mobilizing Woman-Power*.

Larissa Reisner fought with Bolshevik forces and became a Red Army political commissar.

Lida Heymann and Anita Augspurg founded the magazine *Die Frau im Staat* (1918–1933); it was discontinued when they fled Nazi Germany.

Louise Weiss founded the political periodical *L'Europe Nouvelle*.

Margaret Postgate and G. D. H. Cole married, making a lifelong commitment of the working partnership they had started in 1916.

Millicent Garrett Fawcett published *Women's Victory and After*.

Opha M. Johnson became the first known female member of the U.S. Marine Corps Reserve.

b. Eva Lundegaard Kolstad (1918– ), Norwegian feminist, women's rights leader, and politician, who became president of the Norwegian Association for the Rights of Women (1956–1968) and of Norway's Liberal Party (1974–1976).

b. Elena Ceausescu (1918–1989), Romanian chemist and political partner of Romanian dictator Nicolae Ceausescu, her husband.

b. Maria Groza (1918– ), Romanian Communist politician, a spokesperson for the Ceausescu regime on matters affecting women.

d. Henrietta Dugdale (1826–1918), Australian feminist, social reformer, suffragist leader, and writer.

### Religion/Education/Everyday Life

American swimmer Gertrude Ederle set her first world record in the 880-yard freestyle at age 12; she used the six-beat crawl introduced by the New York Women's Swimming Association.

Henrietta Szold became education director of the just-founded Zionist Organization of America. In the same year, the Henrietta Szold Hadassah School of Nursing, established by the Jewish women's organization Hadassah, opened with 30 students in Palestine.

For opposing American participation in World War I, Emily Greene Balch lost her teaching position at Wellesley College.

Kathryn Sellers was the first female head judge in an American juvenile court, in Washington, D.C. (1918–1934).

Linda A. Eastman was elected director of the Cleveland Public Library, the first woman to head a major American library system.

Mary Cromwell Jarrett founded the first psychiatric social workers' training program, at Smith College.

Rose Schneiderman became president of the New York branch of the Women's Trade Union League (1918–1949).

Louise Bryant published *Six Red Months in Russia*.

Tokyo Women's College was founded; its graduates were nicknamed "Marx girls" because they studied political (not home) economics.

Women's League of the United Synagogue of America was founded by prominent women in Conservative Judaism.

Annie Oakley demonstrated marksmanship to the American troops in Europe.

Mary Follett published *The New State*.

b. Fanny (Francina) Blankers-Koen (1918– ), Dutch track and field athlete, noted for her four gold medals at the 1948 London Olympics.

d. Ella Flagg Young (1845–1918), American educator, the first woman to head a major urban school district (1909) and to be president of the National Education Association (1910).

d. Mary Morton (Kimball) Kehew (1859–1918), American union activist long associated with the Women's Educational and Industrial Union.

d. Deguchi Nao (1837–1918), Japanese religious leader who founded the Omoto religious movement.

### Science/Technology/Medicine

National Birth Control League (NBCL) was reorganized as the Voluntary Parenthood League by Mary Dennett, seeking a moderate alternative to Margaret Sanger's more radical stance. Dennett also published a sex education article that challenged government obscenity laws.

Dorothy Reed Mendenhall introduced the "Nutrition Series for Mothers," a correspondence course through the University of Wisconsin, later developing the first course in sex hygiene at an American college (1920s).

Newly married Marie Stopes published the first of the best-selling works that would make her a public figure in sex and birth control education: *Married Love* and *Wise Parenthood*.

After World War I ended, the American Women's Hospitals Service (AWHS) focused its attention on reconstruction and on southeastern Europe, especially Serbia. Physician Esther Pohl Lovejoy began her 48 years as chair, succeeding physician Mary M. Crawford.

American Committee for Devastated France involved many women in postwar European disaster relief, including Myra Breckenridge and its head, Anne Morgan.

Austrian physicist Lise Meitner was made head of the physics department of the Kaiser Wilhelm Institute, leading a team researching radioactivity.

Bertha Van Hoosen became the first woman to head a medical division of a coeducational university, as head of obstetrics at Loyola University Medical School (1918–1937).

American medical missionary Ida Scudder founded the Vellore Christian Medical College in India, to train Indian women to become physicians, especially to care for women in purdah.

Lillian Wald chaired the Nurses Emergency Council during the influenza epidemic.

Frances Elliott (later Davis) became the first African-American nurse officially enrolled with the American National Red Cross.

Kate Gleason became the first female member of the American Society of Mechanical Engineers.

Mary Whiton Calkins was elected president of the American Philosophical Association, the first woman to head the group.

b. Gertrude Elion (1918– ), American biochemist, long associated with Burroughs Wellcome (1944–1983), who helped develop numerous drugs to treat diseases such as gout, leukemia, heart disease, and AIDS, notably acyclovir and AZT; she and George H. Hitchings shared the 1988 Nobel Prize for physiology or medicine.

b. Ruth Sager (1918–1997), American geneticist who first demonstrated that genes exist outside the cell nucleus (1963); professor at Hunter College (1966–1975), then at Harvard University.

b. Alla Genrikhovna Massevitch (1918– ), Russian astronomer specializing in the internal structure and evolution of stars.

d. Anna Tomaszewicz-Dobrska (1854–1918), Polish physician, the second Polish woman to become a physician and the first to practice in Poland.

d. Ethel Sargant (1863–1918), British botanist, the first woman on the council of the Linnean Society; at her death, she was president of Britain's Federation of University Women.

d. Harriet Mann (1831–1918), American writer of nature studies and children's books, as Olive Thorne Miller.

## ARTS/LITERATURE

Geraldine Farrar created the title role in Giacomo Puccini's opera *Suor Angelica*.

Lillian Gish starred opposite Robert Harron in *Hearts of the World*, D. W. Griffith's silent film.

Willa Cather published the novel *My Antonia*.

E. M. Delafield published her semiautobiographical novels *The Pelicans* and *The War Workers*.

Georgia O'Keeffe painted *Red Flower*.

Rachel Crothers's play *A Little Journey* was produced in New York.

Selma Lagerlöf published the novel *The Outcast*.

Rebecca West published the novel *The Return of the Soldier*.

Theda Bara starred in the silent film *Salomé*.

Adella Hughes became the first woman to manage a major American symphony orchestra, the Cleveland Orchestra, serving for 15 years.

b. Ida Lupino (1918–1995), British-American actress, director, writer, and producer; daughter of Stanley Lupino, of Britain's Lupino stage family.

b. Muriel Spark (1918– ), a multifaceted British writer, best known as a major novelist.

b. Birgit Nilsson (1918– ), Swedish soprano, in the 1960s and 1970s a fixture at the Metropolitan Opera, especially in Wagner.

b. Pearl Bailey (1918–1990), American singer, dancer, and actress.

b. Rita Hayworth (Margarita Carmen Cansino, 1918–1987), American dancer and actress.

b. Susan Hayward (Edythe Marrener, 1918–1975), American actress.

## 1919

### POLITICS/LAW/WAR

The 19th (Woman Suffrage, or Anthony) Amendment was passed by both houses of Congress, reading that "the right of citizens of the United States to vote shall not be denied or abridged by the United States or by any state on account of sex."

American-born Nancy Langhorne Astor became the first female member of Parliament in Britain (1919–1945).

Women won the right to vote in the Netherlands; limited rights to vote in Tennessee; and the right to vote and be elected to office in Luxembourg.

Women's International League for Peace and Freedom, which developed out of the Women's Peace Party (1915), was founded, with Jane Addams as first president and Emily Greene Balch as first secretary; Addams also chaired the second Women's Peace Congress, in Zurich.

Anarchists Emma Goldman and Alexander Berkman were deported to the Soviet Union. Soon disillusioned with communist authoritarianism, Goldman left the Soviet Union; unable to return to the United States, she spent the rest of her life in exile.

Constance Markiewicz became minister for labour in the Irish Parliament, banned by the British from functioning.

Fanny Garrison Villard founded the pacifist, nonviolent Women's Peace Society.

Hiratsuka Raicho and Ichikawa Fusae and their New Woman's Association won early successes in overturning the ban on women attending political meetings in Japan.

Frances Perkins became the first female member of the New York State Industrial Commission (1919–1933), ultimately moving up to become state industrial commissioner (1928–1933).

In Italy, the Sacchi Law granted married women's property rights and opened many professions to women, except the judiciary, the military, and the upper bureaucracy. Bills for women's suffrage and liberal divorce were introduced but failed to pass, partly because of opposition from the conservative Catholic women's organization Unione Donne de Azione Cattolica.

Mary White Ovington became chairman of the board of directors of the National Association for the Advancement of Colored People (1919–1932); she was the first woman to hold that position. Another woman would not hold the job until 1975 when Margaret Bush Wilson became the second, and the first African-American, woman to chair the NAACP.

Britain's National Union of Women's Suffrage Societies became the National Union of Societies for Equal Citizenship, with Eleanor Rathbone succeeding Millicent Fawcett as president.

Lida Heymann became a vice-president of the League for Peace and Freedom.

Mary H. Donlon became the first woman to serve as chief editor of a law review, at Cornell University Law School.

Zhenotdel, the women's section of the Soviet Communist Party, was established, its first director being Inesse Armand (1919–1920).

b. Evita (Maria Eva) Duarte Perón (1919–1952), Argentinian actress and politician, the wife of Juan Perón.

b. (Mary) Eugenia Charles (1919– ), Dominican lawyer and politician, who became prime minister (1980).

b. Annemarie Renger (1919– ), German socialist, feminist, and politician who became president of the German Bundestag (1972–1976).

b. Ella Tambussi Grasso (1919–1981), American politician.

b. Notsikelelo Albertina Sisulu (1919– ), black South African freedom movement leader, often arrested and restricted; a longtime officer of the African National Congress, United

Democratic Front, and Federation of South African Women, she is the wife of ANC leader Walter Sisulu.

d. Rosa Luxemburg (1871–1919), Polish socialist and communist leader and theoretician, a founder of the Polish Socialist and Communist parties, and of the German Communist Party and Sparticist League. With Karl Liebknecht, she led the failed German Spartacist (Communist) revolution (January 1919); both were murdered by right-wing Freikorps troops (January 15). Luxemburg's *The Crisis in the German Social Democracy* was published posthumously.

d. Vera Zasulich (1849–1919), Russian revolutionary, early in her career a political assassin (1873) and later a Menshevik (Social Democrat) who opposed the Bolshevik Revolution.

## RELIGION/EDUCATION/EVERYDAY LIFE

Jessie Redmon Fauset became editor of the periodical the *Crisis*, organ of the National Association for the Advancement of Colored People (1919–1926).

Business and Professional Women (National Federation of Business and Professional Women's Clubs) was founded, as an umbrella organization for a national network of local clubs. Founder Lena Madeson Phillips was quoted as saying: "Make no small plans. They have no power to stir the blood."

After the passage of the 18th Amendment to the Constitution, bringing Prohibition, the Women's Christian Temperance Union, under president Anna Gordon (1914–1925), turned its attention to child welfare, immigrants, and "social purity."

Suzanne Lenglen won her first Wimbledon title; until she turned professional (1926), she would dominate the game.

Working to aid war victims in the Balkans, British philanthropist Eglantyne Jebb founded the Fight the Famine Council, soon renamed the Save the Children Fund.

Abala Bose organized the Nari Shiksha Samiti to foster education among women throughout India.

British historian Alice Clark published *The Working Life of Women in the 17th Century*.

In Germany, Marie Juchacz founded the Workers' Welfare (Arbeiterwohlfahrt) organization, associated with the Social Democratic Party (SPD), providing a wide range of services to the poor and ill, including prenatal care and child-care centers.

Margaret Cousins became first head of the National Girls' School at Mangalore (1919–1920).

British physician and relief worker Hilda Clark worked in Vienna, notably with Edith Pye, to aid starving war victims.

Margery Fry became secretary of the British Penal Reform League.

Evangeline Booth published *The War Romance of the Salvation Army*.

b. Florence Chadwick (1919– ), American swimmer, the first woman to swim from England to France (1951) and from Los Angeles to Catalina Island (1952).

b. (Gertrude) Elizabeth (Margaret) Anscombe (1919– ), British philosopher long associated with Oxford University's Somerville College (1946–1970), then with Cambridge University.

b. Claude Kogan (1919–1959), French mountaineer.

d. Anna Howard Shaw (1847–1919), British-born American minister and suffragist, the first female minister of the Methodist Protestant Church (1880), and president of the National American Woman Suffrage Association (1904–1915).

d. Madame C. J. Walker (1869–1919), African-American cosmetics entrepreneur who developed the "Walker System" of hair treatment; she also made many notable contributions to charity.

## SCIENCE/TECHNOLOGY/MEDICINE

Physician Alice Hamilton became the first woman to teach at Harvard Medical School (1919–1935), as professor of industrial medicine, a field she had largely pioneered. She had to promise not to use the all-male Harvard Club, to claim football tickets, or to sit on the platform at commencement.

Mary Ware Dennett and the Voluntary Parenthood League mounted a failed campaign in Congress for the Dennett Bill, to legalize dissemination of birth control information (1919–1924).

Margaret Sanger also continued to campaign for the right of doctors to prescribe contraceptive devices and supply birth control information.

American physician and pathologist Louise Pearce and three colleagues developed a compound to cure sleeping sickness (trypanosomiasis), testing it successfully on victims in the Congo.

Medical Women's International Association was founded, with Esther Pohl Lovejoy as its first president (1919–1924). Lovejoy also published *The House of the Good Neighbor*, about her work in war-torn Europe for the American Red Cross.

Sophia Heath became the world's first female commercial airline pilot, employed by Royal Dutch Airlines, breaking the International Commission for Air Navigation's previous ban on women as commercial aviators.

Edith Clarke was the first woman to receive a master's degree in engineering from Massachusetts Institute of Technology.

Helen Dean King began her project of domesticating the Norway rat (1919–1949), which became the standard laboratory animal.

Marion E. Kenworthy founded the first mental hygiene clinic in the Young Women's Christian Association (YWCA).

b. Jane C. Wright (1919– ), American physician specializing in cancer chemotherapy, who became director of the Harlem Hospital Cancer Research Foundation (1952) and the first African-American woman in medical administration, as associate dean and professor of surgery at New York Medical College (1967). Her younger sister, Barbara P. Wright, became a physician specializing in industrial medicine.

b. Julia Bowman Robinson (1919–1985), American mathematician.

d. Mary Edwards Walker (1832–1919), American physician, suffragist, and advocate of dress reform, the first woman to be a surgeon in the U.S. Army and the first to win the Congressional Medal of Honor (1865); she was noted for wearing men's attire.

## ARTS/LITERATURE

Helen Westley starred opposite Dudley Digges in Jacinto Benavente's play *The Bonds of Interest*, the first production of New York's Theatre Guild.

Lillian Gish starred opposite Richard Barthelmess in *Broken Blossoms*, D. W. Griffith's silent film.

Ethel Barrymore starred on Broadway as Lady Helen Haden in Zoë Akins's play *Déclassé*.

Lotte Reiniger made the world's first full-length animation film, *The Adventures of Prince Achmed*.

Mary Pickford, Charles Chaplin, Douglas Fairbanks, and D. W. Griffith founded the major film production company United Artists.

Tamara Karsavina and Leonid Massine danced the leads at the premiere of Massine's ballet *The Three-Cornered Hat*.

Virginia Woolf published the novel *Night and Day*.

Georgia O'Keeffe painted *From the Plains I*, *Music—Pink and Blue I*, *Red Canna*, and *Orange and Red Streak*.

Pianist Marguerite Long premiered Maurice Ravel's *Tombeau de Couperin*.

Sylvia Beach opened her Paris bookshop, Shakespeare and Company.

Pola Negri starred in the title role opposite Emil Jannings in *Madame Dubarry (Passion)*, Ernst Lubitsch's German silent film.

Babette Deutsch published the poetry collection *Banners*.

Edith Day starred in the title role of the long-running Broadway musical *Irene*.

Juana de Ibarbourou published the poetry collection *Las lenguas de diamante*.

Ethel Smyth published the autobiography *Impressions that Remained*.

Fannie Hurst published the short-story collection *Humoresque*.

Storm Jameson published *The Pot Boils*, the first of her more than 40 novels.

b. Margot Fonteyn (Peggy Hookam, 1919–1991), British dancer.

b. (Jean) Iris Murdoch (1919– ), British writer and philosopher.

b. Doris Lessing (1919– ), British novelist and short story writer, often on feminist and leftist radical themes.

b. Uta Hagen (1919– ), German-American actress, who played leading roles on Broadway from the mid-1930s through the late 1940s, and then became a leading American acting teacher.

b. Vera Lynn (Vera Welch, 1919– ), British singer, who in World War II would sing "We'll Meet Again." She was called "the Forces' Sweetheart."

b. Celeste Holm (1919– ), American stage and screen actress, who early in her career created the Ado Annie role on stage in *Oklahoma*.

b. Jennifer Jones (Phyllis Isley, 1919– ), American film star of the 1940s and 1950s, who won an Oscar for her creation of the title role in *The Song of Bernadette* (1943).

b. Pauline Kael (1919– ), American film critic.

b. Tamara Toumanova (1919–1996), Russian-American dancer and actress.

b. Pearl Primus (1919–1994), African-Caribbean-American dancer.

d. Adelina Patti (1843–1919), Italian singer, long the leading soprano at Covent Garden.

## 1920

### POLITICS/LAW/WAR

The 19th (Woman Suffrage) Amendment to the U.S. Constitution, also called the Anthony Amendment, was ratified by Tennessee, the needed 36th state (August 26). Thereafter, some American women's groups began to celebrate August 26th as Equality Day.

Women won the right to be elected to office in Canada, and women over 30 won the right to vote in Britain.

With passage of the 19th Amendment, the National American Woman Suffrage Association (NAWSA) dissolved, its long single-issue fight won. Its successor organization was the multi-issue League of Women Voters (LWV), with Maud Wood Park its first president (1919–1924).

Women's Joint Congressional Committee was founded by many women's organizations, sparked by the League of Women Voters, to coordinate and lobby the U.S. Congress on women's issues.

Among those voted into Germany's Reichstag were Clara Zetkin (1920–1932), Gertrude Baumer (1920–1933), and Louise Schröder (1920–1933).

Jane Addams and Helen Keller, along with Roger Baldwin, were among the key founders of the American Civil Liberties Union.

Alexandra Kollontai became director of the Zhenotdel, the women's section of the Soviet Communist Party (1920–1922); she also published *Communism and the Family*.

Harriet Stanton Blatch published the pacifist work *A Woman's Point of View*.

Margery Ashby became secretary of the International Alliance of Women.

Gertrude Tuckwell became the first female justice of the peace for the County of London.

Ho Hsiang-ning became one of the first Chinese women to bob her hair, as a gesture of independence (1920s).

Rose Tyler Barrett became the first-known American city manager, in Warrenton, Oregon.

Swiss feminist Emilie Gourd published a biography of Susan B. Anthony.

Margot Asquith began publishing her two-volume *Autobiography* (1920–1922).

b. Bella Savitzky Abzug (1920– ), American feminist, lawyer, and politician.

d. Anna Maria Mozzoni (1837–1920), Italian socialist and feminist, a leading organizer and theoretician of the Italian women's rights movement, who founded La Lega Promotrice degli Interessi Femminili.

d. Eugénie (Marie Eugénie de Montijo de Guzman, 1826–1920), wife of Napoléon III of France, credited with helping to maintain papal independence in Italy; in exile in Britain after France's defeat in the Franco-Prussian War (1871).

d. Inesse Steffane Armand (1874–1920), Russian revolutionary, a Bolshevik activist and Marxist feminist.

## RELIGION/EDUCATION/EVERYDAY LIFE

After ratification of the 19th amendment, Congress directed the establishment of a Women's Bureau within the Department of Labor, to help improve the working conditions, welfare, and employment opportunities of working women. Mary Anderson became its first director (1920–1944), in that position playing a major role in the development of protective legislation and regulations for working women.

Avra Theodoropoulou founded the Greek League for Women's Rights, serving as president for 37 years and, with her colleagues, founding orphanages, a night school for girls, holiday camps for working women, and the Papastrateio School of Crafts.

Coco Chanel introduced the chemise dress, most notable of the looser styles of the 1920s, free of corsets and other such constrictions.

In Memphis, Tennessee, black and white women together created the landmark Women's Committee of the Commission on Interracial Cooperation.

Mary Ritter Beard resigned from the Wage Earners' League, in a disagreement over protective legislation, which she felt to be better for women than an equal rights amendment.

Mother Mary Joseph Rogers founded and led (1925–1947) the Foreign Mission Sisters of St. Dominic, better known as the Maryknoll Sisters; she had earlier founded the Pious Society of Women for the Foreign Missions (1914).

Already known as a floral arranger, Constance Spry opened a florist's shop in London, which in the 1930s would be the base for her school of floristry.

Child Welfare League of America (CWLA) was founded, focusing on the care of dependent children; an umbrella organization for a national network of child-care agencies.

Jeannette Rankin became secretary of the National Consumers' League, working with Florence Kelley.

Librarian Sarah Byrd Askew developed the first bookmobile, in New Jersey.

Mary Cromwell Jarrett founded the Psychiatric Social Workers Club (later American Association of Psychiatric Social Workers).

The first women's association in Egypt was founded, led by Huda Sh'arawi.

Union of Orthodox Jewish Women's Organizations of America was established.

b. Helen A. Thomas (1920– ), American reporter, the first woman to head a major news service's White House bureau (1974), who has long traditionally asked the first question at presidential news conferences.

d. Pandita Ramabai (1858–ca. 1920), Indian feminist, social reformer, and writer, a leading women's rights advocate.

d. Annie R. Taylor (1855–1920?), British traveler and missionary, primarily in China and Tibet (from ca. 1883).

## SCIENCE/TECHNOLOGY/MEDICINE

Marie Curie established the Curie Foundation to explore medical uses of radioactivity. She had long recognized the potential of radioactivity for treating cancer but was not fully aware of the dangers of exposure to herself and others.

American journalist Marie Meloney began a subscription campaign to provide money to buy radium needed for France's underfunded Institute of Radium; as part of the campaign, Marie Curie and her two daughters, Irène and Eve, visited America, where President Warren Harding presented them with a gram of the precious radium.

Emmy Noether and W. Schmeidler coauthored a key paper on noncommutative algebra, a field Noether pioneered.

Mary Adela Blagg was appointed to the International Astronomical Union's Lunar Commission, which would name a lunar crater for her, posthumously (1944).

Leta Hollingworth published *Psychology of Subnormal Children*, spurring development of special classes for "slow learners."

Margaret Sanger published *Woman and the New Race*, arguing for fully voluntary motherhood.

Landscape architect Beatrix Jones Farrand designed the gardens at Dumbarton Oaks (ca. 1920–ca.1940), in Washington, D.C., working with her friend, Mildred Bliss, the owner.

Women in the U.S. Army Nurse Corps first won "relative rank," meaning their officers would hold rank comparable to male officers in the army and navy, though not comparable pay or benefits. Previously the nurses' status was like that of a cadet.

Marie Stopes published *Radiant Motherhood*.

British botanist Agnes Arber published *Water Plants: A Study of Aquatic Angiosperms*.

Mary Scharlieb became one of Britain's first female magistrates.

b. Rosalind Elsie Franklin (1920–1958), British molecular biologist and physical chemist.

b. (Eleanor) Margaret Peachey Burbidge (1920– ), British astronomer.

d. Fiammetta Worthington Wilson (1864–1920), British astronomer who observed over 10,000 meteors.

d. Mary Katharine Layne Brandegee (1844–1920), American botanist and physician, specializing in materia medica, plants of medicinal value; two new plant species were named for her: *Astragalus layneae* and *Mimulus layneae*.

## ARTS/LITERATURE

Edith Wharton published her novel *The Age of Innocence*, winning the Pulitzer Prize for fiction (1921), the first woman to do so.

Agatha Christie published *The Mysterious Affair at Styles*, her first novel, introducing detective Hercule Poirot.

Zona Gale adapted her own novel into the play *Miss Lulu Bett*, starring Carroll McComas in the title role; Gale won the Pulitzer Prize for drama for the play, the first woman to do so.

Edna St. Vincent Millay published the poetry collection *A Few Figs from Thistles*.

Fanny Brice sang "My Man," which became her signature song, in the *Ziegfeld Follies of 1920*.

Marilyn Miller introduced the song "Look for the Silver Lining" in the title role of Jerome Kern's musical *Sally*.

Sigrid Undset published the trilogy *Kristin Lavransdatter* (1920–1922).

Mary Pickford played the title role of the silent film *Pollyanna*.

Lynn Fontanne starred as Anna Christie in Eugene O'Neill's play *Chris Christopherson*, an early version of his *Anna Christie*.

Käthe Kollwitz created the poster *Bread!*

Georgia O'Keeffe painted *Zinnias* and *Red Cannas*.

Katherine Mansfield published *Bliss and Other Stories*.

Lillian Gish starred in *Way Down East*, D. W. Griffith's silent film.

Alice Guy-Blaché founded Solax, her own American film production company.

Singer Vaughan DeLeath, the "first lady of radio," originated the soft, murmuring crooning style of early radio, necessitated by the delicate transmitter tubes of the new technology.

Tamara Karsavina and Leonid Massine danced the leads in the premiere of Massine's ballet *Pulcinella*.

Colette published *Cheri*, the first novel in her Cheri series.

Grazia Deledda published the novels *L'incendio dell'oliveto* and *La madre*.

Rose Macaulay published the novel *Potterism*.

Janet Velie starred on Broadway in the title role of the musical *Mary*.

b. Giulietta Masina (Giulia Anna Masina, 1920–1994), Italian film star, Gelsomina in *La Strada* (1954).

b. Lana Turner (1920–1995), American actress.

b. Michèle Morgan (Simone Roussel, 1920– ), French actress, an international film star of the 1930s and 1940s.

b. Betty Evelyn Box (1920– ), British film producer.

b. Gene Tierney (1920–1991), American actress.

b. Peggy Lee (Norma Deloris Engstrom, 1920– ), American singer, composer, and actress, who emerged as a leading popular singer with Benny Goodman's band (1943).

b. Amy Clampitt (1920–1994), American poet.

b. Viveca Lindfors (Elsa Viveca Torstendsdotter Lindfors, 1920–1995), Swedish actress and American stage and screen star.

d. Olive Schreiner (1855–1920), South African writer, a feminist and pacifist.

d. Mary Augusta Ward (Mrs. Humphrey Ward, 1851–1920), British writer, social reformer, and antisuffragist.

## 1921

### POLITICS/LAW/WAR

Agnes MacPhail became the first female member of Canada's Parliament, as a United Farmers of Ontario representative (1921–1940).

Women's Peace Union (WPU) was founded as a pacifist, nonviolent group that sought to literally outlaw war by constitutional amendment and unilateral renunciation of violence; its leaders were convinced that the United States could successfully lead by example. As fascist attacks on their neighbors increased during the 1930s, the WPU seemed to lose relevance, dissolving in 1941.

Clara Zetkin became head of the International Women's Secretariat of the Communist International, and a member of its executive committee.

Alva Belmont became president of the National Woman's Party.

The trailblazing Sheppard-Towner Maternity and Infancy Protection Act provided federal funds for the establishment of prenatal clinics and public-health centers, as recommended by the U.S. Children's Bureau, and also for training and certification of midwives, who would then begin to replace America's uncertified "granny midwives."

Women won the right to vote and be elected to office in Czechoslovakia.

Angelika Balabanoff broke with the Bolsheviks, leaving the Communist Party, her post as Soviet commissioner of foreign affairs, and the Soviet Union to work and write as a moderate European socialist.

Gertrude Bell published *Review of the Civil Administration in Mesopotamia*, becoming adviser to Feisal, whom she had helped bring to the throne of newly independent Iraq.

Japan's Women's Christian Temperance Union formed a women's suffrage auxiliary, led by Kubushiro Ochimi and Gauntlett Tsune.

Mabel Walker Willebrandt became the second American woman to serve as a federal prosecutor, succeeding Annette Abbott Adams as assistant attorney general in Washington, D.C., during the Harding administration.

War Resisters League was founded by a group including Frances Witherspoon and Jessie Wallace Hughan.

In Italy's Fascist Party, women's activities were largely confined to the women-only Fasci Femminili, supporting home as woman's place.

Larissa Reisner became the first Soviet ambassador to Afghanistan.

People's Will leader Vera Figner published her memoirs, written while in prison, later titled *Memoirs of a Revolutionary*.

Sylvia Pankhurst published *Soviet Russia As I Saw It* (1921), about her 1920 trip to Russia.

b. Betty Goldstein Friedan (1921– ), American feminist, a leading 20th-century social reformer, whose book *The Feminine Mystique* (1963), with its call for women to reject dependent roles and reach for independent status and fulfillment, sparked the modern feminist movement. She was founder and first president of the National Organization for Women (NOW, 1966).

b. Constance Baker Motley (1921– ), African-American lawyer, politician, and judge who became the first African-American woman to serve as a federal judge (1966); as an NAACP attorney she was a key figure in the fight to open Southern universities to black students.

b. Aduke Alakija (1921– ), Nigerian lawyer and women's rights leader.

b. Hannah Senesh (1921–1944), Hungarian-Israeli soldier.

b. Jeanne Marjorie Holm (1921– ), American feminist and air force major general.

d. Konkordiya Samoilova (1876–1921), Russian socialist and Communist activist, an editor of *Pravda* (1912) and one of the leading women of the Bolshevik Revolution.

d. Nathalie Lemel (1827–1921), French socialist, an activist of the Paris Commune (1871).

## RELIGION/EDUCATION/EVERYDAY LIFE

Bryn Mawr Summer School for Women Workers (1921–1928) and Brookwood Labor College inaugurated the American workers' education movement.

American Association of University Women (AAUW) was formed by a merger of the Association of Collegiate Alumnae and Southern Association of College Women (SACW); Ada Comstock was first president (1921–1923).

Grace Abbott became head of the U.S. Children's Bureau (1921–1934).

Lucy Stone League was founded and led by Ruth Hale, its main aim to advocate that women keep their own names on marriage, as did Lucy Stone when marrying Henry Blackwell (1855). In 1934, a married woman's birth name was used in a real estate deed, a breakthrough.

Ida Pruitt founded and chaired the Department of Social Services at the Peking Union Medical College (1921–1939).

Lila Acheson Wallace and her husband, DeWitt Wallace, founded the *Reader's Digest* in a Greenwich Village basement; together they would build it into an international publishing empire.

Margaret Murray published *The Witch-Cult in Western Europe*, which held the widespread persecution of alleged witches to have been an attack by patriarchy on old, woman-centered religions; she also published *The God of the Witches*.

Margaret Davies was a founder of the International Women's Co-operative Guild.

Britain's Women's Trade Union League, long led by Gertrude Tuckwell (1904–1921), merged into the Trades Union Congress (TUC).

Motoko Hani and her husband, Sochikazu Hani, founded Jiyu Gakuen, a liberal private school, drawing on both Protestant and traditional Japanese ethics.

The first Miss America Pageant was held, with 16-year-old Margaret Gorman, of Washington, D.C., winning the title, her prize a Golden Mermaid statue worth $5,000. Initially a device to keep tourists in Atlantic City after Labor Day weekend, it grew into the most famous of the women's beauty contests.

Gertrude Bonnin wrote *American Indian Stories*.

# Gentlemen, It Can't Be Done

American petroleum geologist Esther Applin presented a paper to the Geological Society (1921) suggesting that microfossils could be used to provide information on oil-bearing geological formations. Among the responses was this from a Professor J. J. Galloway: "Gentlemen, here is this chit of a girl, right out of college, telling us that we can use Foraminifera to determine the age of a formation. Gentlemen, you know that it can't be done." Working with Alva Ellisor and Hedwig Kniker, Applin would four years later publish a paper showing that it could indeed be done. Analysis and correlation of microfossils became a vital tool in oil drilling, in which many women specialized.

Evelyn Underhill became lecturer on the philosophy of religion at Manchester College, Oxford.

Jane Harrison published *Epilogomena to the Study of Greek Religion*.

María Cadilla de Martínez received the gold medal from the Société Académique d'Histoire Internationale, at Paris's Sorbonne, for her essay "Ethnography of Puerto Rico."

b. Juanita Morris Kreps (1921– ), American economist, writer, and teacher, who became the first woman to be director of the New York Stock Exchange (1972) and U.S. secretary of commerce (1977).

b. Toni Stone (Marcenia Lyle Stone, 1921–1996), American baseball player, the first woman to play in a men's professional league (1953).

b. Tina (Argentina) Schifano Ramos Hills (1921– ), Italian-American publisher of *El Mundo* (from 1960).

d. (Sarah) Emily Davies (1830–1921), British feminist, educator and suffragist, founder of Henslow House (1867), the women's school that became Cambridge's Girton College (1874), which she led.

d. Antoinette Brown Blackwell (1825–1921), American reformer, minister, and women's rights advocate, the first woman ordained a minister in the United States (1853); sister-in-law of Elizabeth Blackwell and Lucy Stone.

d. Mary (Reid) MacArthur (1880–1921), Scottish trade unionist who founded the National Federation of Women Workers (1906), conducting notable campaigns for clothing workers, homeworkers, and chain makers.

## Science/Technology/Medicine

Margaret Sanger founded the American Birth Control League to foster dissemination of birth control information and establishment of clinics, making available lists of doctors willing to dispense contraceptive devices.

Marie Stopes founded a birth control clinic, Britain's first. When Dr. Halliday Sutherland accused her of a "monstrous crime" in disseminating contraceptive information (1922), she instituted and eventually won a libel suit against him. The Malthusian League's Walworth Clinic was also founded.

Bessie Coleman beame the first African-American woman in the world to earn her pilot's license, from France's Fédération Aéronautique Internationale, since she could not gain admittance to an American flying school.

Emmy Noether published her most important paper, "Theory of Ideals in Rings."

Kate Gleason, who had developed a method of pouring concrete, began selling the first concrete box houses in her low-cost housing development in East Rochester, New York, model for many later suburban developments.

Kate Marsden published *My Mission to Siberia: A Vindication*, about the hospital she built there for people with leprosy.

Lillian Gilbreth was made an honorary member of the Society of Industrial Engineers.

Margaret Washburn was elected president of the American Psychological Association.

b. Rosalyn Sussman Yalow (1921– ), American nuclear physicist, codeveloper of radioimmunoassay (1950), the second woman to win the Nobel Prize for medicine (1977).

b. Marija Gimbutas (1921–1994), Lithuanian-American archaeologist.

b. Xie Xide (1921– ), American-trained Chinese physicist who founded the Modern Physics Institute (1977); long associated with Fudan University, of which she became president (1983).

d. Henrietta Swan Leavitt (1868–1921), American astronomer long associated with Harvard Observatory (1902–1921), who discovered more than 2,400 Cepheid variable stars and established standard sequences of stars for reference.

d. Mary Watson Whitney (1847–1921), American astronomer who worked with Maria Mitchell (1881–1888) at Vassar College, then succeeded her as professor of astronomy and observatory director (1888–1910). She reportedly said, "I hope when I get to Heaven I shall not find the women playing second fiddle."

## ARTS/LITERATURE

Pauline Lord created the title role in Eugene O'Neill's play *Anna Christie*.

Constance Talmadge starred as the feminist politician in the silent film *Woman's Place*, a story very unusual for its time, written by Anita Loos and John Emerson, and directed by Victor Fleming.

Amy Lowell published the poetry collection *Legends*.

Edna St. Vincent Millay published the poetry collection *Second April*.

In a scandal that rocked the film industry, actress Virginia Rappe died of a ruptured bladder after having allegedly been raped by actor Fatty Arbuckle; although Arbuckle was acquitted on a manslaughter charge, his film career abruptly ended.

Eva Le Gallienne starred opposite Joseph Schildkraut in the first American production of Ferenc Molnar's play *Liliom*.

Fanny Brice sang "Second Hand Rose" in the *Ziegfeld Follies of 1921*.

Lynn Fontanne emerged as a star on Broadway in the title role of *Dulcy*, George S. Kaufman and Marc Connelly's comedy.

Gloria Swanson starred in *The Affairs of Anatol*, Cecil B. DeMille's film based on Arthur Schnitzler's play.

Katharine Cornell starred in Clemence Dane's *A Bill of Divorcement*.

Greta Garbo starred in *Gösta Berling's Saga*, Mauritz Stiller's silent film based on the Selma Lagerlöf novel.

H. D. (Hilda Doolittle) published the poetry collection *Hymen*.

Marianne Moore published *Poems*.

Dorothy Silk created the title role in Gustav Holst's opera *Savitri*.

Georgia O'Keeffe painted *Lake George with Crows*.

Gertrude Atherton published the novel *The Sisters-in-Law*.

Nadia Boulanger began teaching at the American Conservatory at Fontainebleau; she would become one of the most highly regarded composition teachers of her time.

Dorothy Canfield published the novel *The Brimming Cup*.

Luisa Tetrazzini published the autobiography *My Life in Song*.

b. Simone Signoret (Simone Kaminker, 1921–1985), French actress.

b. Alicia Alonso (Alicia Ernestina Martinez Hoyo, 1921– ), Cuban dancer, who would become artistic director and prima ballerina of Cuba's national ballet company.

b. Deborah Kerr (1921– ), British actress, a film star in Britain and America from the early 1940s through the mid-1960s.

b. Ada Louise Huxtable (1921– ), American architecture critic.

b. Carmen Diaz Laforet (1921– ), Spanish writer.

b. Donna Reed (1921–1986), American actress.

b. Joan Greenwood (1921–1987), British actress.

b. Vivian Blaine (Vivian Stapleton, 1921–1995), American stage and screen musical star.

b. Ruth Gipps (1921– ), British composer and conductor.

b. Sawako Ariyoshi (1921–1984), Japanese novelist.

d. Emilia Pardo Bazán (1851–1921), Spanish writer and critic.

# 1922

## POLITICS/LAW/WAR

Bertha Lutz founded and became president of the Brazilian Federation for the Advancement of Women (Federaçao Brasileira pelo Progresso Feminino).

Ida A. Harper published the final two volumes of the six-volume *History of Woman Suffrage*.

Maud Gonne founded the Republican Women's Prisoners' Defence League in Ireland.

Rebecca Ann Latimer Felton served in the U.S. Senate for a single day, filling out the term of Thomas Watson, an isolationist whose election she had supported in a series of articles in the *Atlanta Sunday American* (1920).

b. Jeanne (Benoit) Sauvé (1922– ), Canadian journalist and politician, longtime broadcast journalist (1952–1972) who then entered Parliament, holding various ministerial posts before becoming Speaker of the House of Commons (1980–1984) and then the first woman to be governor general of Canada (1983).

b. Wang Guangmei (1922– ), Chinese politician.

d. Clementina Black (1853–1922), English feminist, suffragist, writer, and trade unionist, a leader in the fight against sweatshops and for equality of women in the workplace.

d. Minna (Wilhelmine) Cauer (1841–1922), German radical feminist, suffragist, and pacifist, a major women's movement leader before World War I.

## RELIGION/EDUCATION/EVERYDAY LIFE

Helen Wills Moody won the first of her many women's singles tennis titles, at Forest Hills (1922).

Margaret Davies became the first woman to be president of Britain's Co-operative Congress.

Mary Talbert became director of the Anti-Lynching Crusaders (1922–1923).

Reformed Judaism's Central Conference of American Rabbis resolved to seek complete equality between men and women, including ordination, but the first female rabbi would not be seen for 50 more years.

Eileen Power published *Medieval English Nunneries c. 1275–1535.*

Emily Post published *Etiquette: The Blue Book of Social Usage*, her influential guide to contemporary manners.

Inspired by a biography of Teresa of Ávila, Jewish-born Edith Stein became a Catholic nun.

Sophia Heath founded the Women's Amateur Athletic Association.

Mary Cromwell Jarrett and E. E. Southard published *Kingdom of Evils*, explorations in industrial psychiatry.

Mary Ellen Richmond published *Social Diagnosis.*

b. Daisy Gatson Bates (1922– ), African-American civil rights leader and Little Rock, Arkansas, newspaper publisher, who led the landmark campaign to desegregate Little Rock Central High School (1957).

b. Conchita Verrill Cintrón (1922– ), American-born, Peruvian-raised bullfighter, working in Latin America and Europe.

d. Elizabeth Cochrane Seaman (Nellie Bly, 1865–1922), American investigative reporter, noted for exposés of conditions in prisons, sweatshops, and asylums and also for her round-the-world trip (1889–1890).

## SCIENCE/TECHNOLOGY/MEDICINE

Carolyn Van Blarcom published *Obstetrical Nursing*, her classic textbook, and the more popular *Getting Ready to Be a Mother.*

Margaret Sanger published *Women, Morality, and Birth Control.*

Amelia Earhart set her first world record, flying higher than any other woman, in her own plane.

Annie Jump Cannon received the Nova Medal from the American Association of Variable Star Observers.

b. Valérie André (1922– ), French army doctor who, commissioned as a helicopter pilot (1950), flew 150 medical missions during the siege of Dienbienphu (1954) in the French-Vietnamese war; she became France's first female general.

b. Qian Zhangying (1923– ), Chinese engineer and government official.

d. Vilma Hugonnai-Wartha (1847–1922), Hungarian physician specializing in pediatrics.

## Arts/Literature

Sisters Lillian and Dorothy Gish starred in *Orphans of the Storm*, D. W. Griffith's epic silent film set in the French Revolution.

Sylvia Beach began the process of publishing James Joyce's landmark modernist novel *Ulysses*.

Alla Nazimova starred as Nora in *A Doll's House*, Charles Bryant's film of Henrik Ibsen's play.

Jeanne Eagels created the Sadie Thompson role in *Rain*, John Colton and Clemence Randolph's play based on the Somerset Maugham short story.

Bronislava Nijinska choreographed Igor Stravinsky's *Le Renard*.

Ellen Glasgow published the novel *One Man in His Time*.

Käthe Kollwitz sculpted *Father and Mother*, a tribute to her son Peter, killed in World War I.

Katherine Mansfield published the short-story collection *The Garden Party*.

Mary Pickford played the title role in the silent film *Tess of the Storm Country*.

Willa Cather published the Pulitzer Prize–winning novel *One of Ours*.

Asta Nielsen was the title character in the silent film *Miss Julie*.

Dorothy Arzner edited James Cruze's classic silent film *The Covered Wagon* and also the bullfight scenes in *Blood and Sand*.

Fumiko Hayashi published the autobiographical novel *Journey of a Vagabond*.

Gabriela Mistral published her first poetry collection, *Desolation*.

Helen Menken starred opposite George Gaul in Austin Strong's play *Seventh Heaven*.

Marie Carroll starred in the title role of Anne Nichols's long-running Broadway play *Abie's Irish Rose*.

German feminist Helene Stöcker published the novel *Liebe*.

Juana de Ibarbourou published the poetry collection *Raíz salvaje*.

Rebecca West published the novel *The Judge*.

Vita Sackville-West published the short-story collection *The Heir*.

b. Judy Garland (Frances Gumm, 1922–1969), American actress and singer.

b. Ava Gardner (1922–1990), American actress.

b. Judy Holliday (Judith Tuvim, 1922–1965), American actress.

b. Renata Tebaldi (1922– ), Italian soprano who sang leading roles at the Metropolitan Opera from 1955.

b. Doris Day (Doris Kappelhoff, 1922– ), American popular singer of the 1940s who became a film star in the 1950s and later had her own television show (1968–1973).

b. Grace Paley (1922– ), American writer, whose work focuses on the everyday lives of women, as seen from her feminist point of view.

b. Audrey Meadows (Audrey Cotter, 1922–1996), American actress, television's Alice Kramden in *The Honeymooners*.

b. Margaret Leighton (1922–1976), British actress.

b. Jay Presson Allen (1922– ), American screenwriter, film producer, and playwright.

d. Lillian Russell (Helen Louise Leonard, 1861–1922), American singer and actress, a great star in the musical theater.

d. Alice Meynell (1847–1922), British writer.

d. Marie Lloyd (1870–1922), British music-hall entertainer.

## 1923

### Politics/Law/War

In *Adkins v. Children's Hospital*, the U.S. Supreme Court declared unconstitutional a federal minimum-wage law for women in the District of Columbia, holding that social changes, including women's suffrage, had negated the need for special state protection for women.

National Woman's Party head Alice Paul proposed the first version of the Equal Rights Amendment (ERA), which read "Men and women shall have equal rights throughout the United States and every place subject to its jurisdiction." It divided women's rights advocates, between those who supported the ERA and those who supported labor legislation protective of women, including most of the major women's rights organizations of the day.

Chrystal Macmillan became secretary of the International Alliance of Women (1913–1921), a major pacifist organization. Opposed to protective legislation as a limitation of women's rights, she also founded the Open Door Council, calling for entirely equal rights for women in Britain.

Mae Ella Nolan was the first woman to replace her husband in the U.S. Congress, winning a race for his seat after he died.

Constance Markiewicz was elected to the Irish Parliament, from a Dublin district.

In Italy, Benito Mussolini's government fired all government employees hired after 1915, mostly women, and increasingly restricted women's access to work and education.

Women won the right to vote and be elected to office in Mongolia.

Alexandra Kollontai became Soviet trade representative to Norway (1923–1925).

Franciska Plamnikova was a founder and first chair of the Czech Council of Women.

French feminist Hubertine Auclert published *Les femmes au gouvernal*.

Socialist Marie Juchacz was elected to Germany's Reichstag (1923–1933).

Jessie Wallace Hughan published *A Study of International Government*.

Mabel Walker Willebrandt's division of the federal attorney general's office broke a major bootleg liquor ring, the Big Four of Savannah.

---

# Equal Rights Amendment vs. Protective Legislation: Two Views

**For the Equal Rights Amendment** The whole question of restrictive legislation applied to adult women workers is obscured by a fogginess of thought. . . Back of the whole question lie ages of prejudice against any freedom for women, any acknowledgment of their right to function as independent, self-determining citizens. . . My first protest is against classing grown women with children under the law [protective labor legislation]. . . What I am trying to urge. . . is that unequal wages and bad factory conditions, and not special laws for adult women workers, are the things in which we all should interest ourselves. . . When we limit women's opportunities to work [by passing protective labor laws], we simply create more poverty, and we postpone the day when equal pay for equal work will be universal. Without equal work there can be no equal pay, nor anything like a fair field for men and women alike.

— Rheta Childe Dorr, author of *What Eight Million Women Want*

**For Laws Protecting Women** The whole question, it seems to me, comes down to this: Shall we let women continue working longer hours than men, for less pay than men, and continue doing two jobs to their husbands' one? And is that sort of thing to continue in the name of some principle of equality? Or shall we agree that the reality of better conditions is more important, both to health and to industrial equality, than is a cherished theory?

Women who are wage-earners with one job in the factory and another in the home have little time and energy left to carry on the right to better their economic status. They need the help of other women, and they need labor laws. . .

— Mary Anderson, chief of the Women's Bureau, U.S. Department of Labor
(Both excerpts from the *Woman Voter*, February 15, 1923)

Margery Ashby became president of the International Alliance of Women.

Rosa Mayreder published *Geschlecht und Kultur.*

b. Yelena Bonner (1923– ), Russian doctor who, with her husband, nuclear physicist Andrei Sakharov, was a leading dissident during the final years of the Soviet Union's Communist dictatorship.

b. Agatha Barbara (1923– ), Maltese politician, Malta's first female member of parliament (1946), later in ministerial posts, then its first president (1982).

b. Elizabeth Havers Butler-Sloss (1923– ), British judge, the first woman appointed to the Court of Appeal (1987).

b. Gertrud Sigurdsen (1923– ), Swedish socialist, trade unionist, and politician in ministerial posts.

d. Constance Georgia Lytton (1869–1923), British social reformer and militant suffragist, who had been partially paralyzed and made a lifelong invalid by a stroke suffered because of her treatment while imprisoned for suffragist activities.

### RELIGION/EDUCATION/EVERYDAY LIFE

Charlotte Perkins Gilman published *His Religion and Hers: A Study of the Faith of Our Fathers and the Work of Our Mothers.*

Aimée Semple McPherson established a permanent base for her new Pentecostal "Church of the Foursquare Gospel" at the Angelus Temple near Los Angeles; that year she also published *This Is That.*

America's Amateur Athletic Union first admitted women, acceptable sports being basketball, swimming, handball, gymnastics, and track and field.

International Conference of Women was held in Rome.

Margaret Bondfield became the first woman to chair Britain's Trades Union Congress.

Evangeline French, her sister Francesca French, and Mildred Cable received permission to travel as missionaries into the Gobi Desert (1923–1939), learning to speak local dialects and wearing Chinese dress. When on leave in Britain, they reported to geographical societies on their discoveries.

Ida Rosenthal and her husband, William, established the Maidenform Brassiere Corporation, to manufacture the new style of brassiere she had invented; the basis for the modern bra, it was the first to use cups for uplift and to come in a range of sizes.

American journalist Louise Bryant published *Mirrors of Moscow,* based on her firsthand experiences of the early Soviet Union, just after the revolution (1917).

British physician and relief worker Hilda Clark led efforts to aid Greek refugees (1923–1930).

Edith Pye led Quaker relief workers in the postwar Ruhr.

Dora Russell and her husband, Bertrand Russell, collaborated on *The Prospects of Industrial Civilisation.*

Gertrude Bell founded the National Museum of Baghdad (1923–1926) and became Iraq's director of Antiquities.

Josephine Goldmark became secretary to the Rockefeller Committee, producing the notable report *Nursing and Nursing Education in the United States.*

The women's division of the National Amateur Athletic Federation was founded, under the sponsorship of First Lady Lou Henry Hoover.

Theresa Neuman's seemingly miraculous recovery from injuries suffered in a 1918 fire, a recovery that coincided with the beatification, then canonization of Teresa of Lisieux (1923; 1925), made her village of Könnersreuth a pilgrimage center.

---

Personally I do not agree with sex being brought into science at all. The idea of "women and science" is entirely irrelevant. Either a woman is a good scientist, or she is not; in any case she should be given opportunities, and her work should be studied from the scientific, not the sex, point of view.

— Hertha Ayrton

Virginia's Mary Baldwin Junior College became a four-year college, the oldest Presbyterian women's college in America.

White House conference was held on women's athletics.

Anna Spencer published *The Family and Its Members*.

b. (Alice) Louise Brough (1923– ), American tennis player.

d. Mary Burnett Talbert (1866–1923), African-American civil rights and antilynching leader, a president of the National Association of Colored Women (1916), director of the Anti-Lynching Crusaders (1922–1923), and leader of the National Association for the Advancement of Colored People (NAACP), the first woman to win its Spingarn Award.

## SCIENCE/TECHNOLOGY/MEDICINE

Gladys Dick and her husband, George Dick, discovered the streptococcus bacteria that caused scarlet fever, then quickly developed the Dick test, a diagnostic skin test, and an antitoxin for treatment, used until the advent of antibiotics in the mid-1940s.

Margaret Sanger founded the Birth Control Clinical Research Bureau, the first doctor-staffed birth control clinic, dispensing information and devices such as vaginal diaphragms and lactic-acid jelly.

American Women's Hospitals Service (AWHS) continued its overseas work, most notably treating thousands of Greek refugees from Turkey.

British physician Christine Murrell published *Womanhood and Health*.

Marie Stopes published *Contraception: Its History, Theory and Practice*.

d. Hertha (Phoebe Sarah) Marks Ayrton (1854–1923), British physicist noted for her work on the electric arc and sand ripples and for her inventions, including the sphygmograph, to measure the pulse.

d. Alice Cunningham Fletcher (1838–1923), American ethnologist and archaeologist long associated with the Peabody Museum, a crusader for Indian rights who sparked interest in America's pre-Columbian cultures.

d. Sarah Plummer Lemmon (1836–1923), American botanist noted as a collector and illustrator; she discovered a new plant genus (1882).

## ARTS/LITERATURE

Edna St. Vincent Millay published *The Harp-Weaver and Other Poems*, winning the Pulitzer Prize for poetry, the first woman to do so.

Winifred Lenihan created the title role in the Theatre Guild premiere of George Bernard Shaw's play *Saint Joan*.

Bessie Smith, accompanied by Clarence Williams, recorded "Downhearted Blues," her first popular hit.

Bronislava Nijinska's ballet *Les Noces*, with music by Igor Stravinsky, premiered with Sergei Diaghilev's Ballet Russes company.

Katherine Mansfield published the short-story collection *The Dove's Nest*.

Blanche Sweet starred in the title role of *Anna Christie*, a film version of the Eugene O'Neill play; John Wray directed.

Alla Nazimova starred in the silent film *Salome*.

Dorothy L. Sayers published the mystery *Whose Body?* introducing detective Lord Peter Wimsey.

Gloria Swanson created the title role in the silent film *Zaza*, the first of her eight films directed by Allan Dwan.

Edith Evans created the roles of the She-Ancient and the Serpent in George Bernard Shaw's play *Back to Methuselah*.

Georgia O'Keeffe painted *Calla Lily*.

Helen Westley starred opposite Dudley Digges in Elmer Rice's play *The Adding Machine*.

Laurette Taylor starred in the title role of King Vidor's silent film *Peg O' My Heart*.

Lillian Gish starred opposite Ronald Colman in *The White Sister*, Henry King's film based on Francis Marion Crawford's novel.

Alexandra Kollontai published the short-story collection *Love of Worker Bees*.

Djuna Barnes published *A Book*, containing a potpourri of her poetry, plays, and graphics.

Edna May Oliver starred opposite Willard Robertson in Owen Davis's play *Icebound*.

Germaine Tailleferre composed the ballet *Le marchand d'oiseaux*.

Louise Bogan published the poetry collection *Body of This Death*.

Gertrude Atherton published the novel *Black Oxen*.

Ketty Layeyrette created the title role in Albert Roussel's opera *Padmavati*.

Gertrude Whitney showed her sculpture *Chinoise*.

Marina Tsvetayeva published the poetry collections *After Russia* and *Craft*.

Mary Pickford created the title role in Ernst Lubitsch's silent film *Rosita*.

Pola Negri created the title role in Malcolm St. Clair's silent film *A Woman of the World*, based on Carl Van Vechten's novel *The Tattooed Countess*.

Rose Macaulay published the novel *Told by an Idiot*.

Vera Brittain published the novel *The Dark Tide*.

Mary Madeleva Wolff published *Knights Errant, and Other Poems*.

Winifred Holtby published her first novel, *Anderby Wold*.

b. Nadine Gordimer (1923– ), Nobel Prize–winning South African novelist and short story writer, a world figure as an artist, and a longtime white opponent of racism.

b. Siobhan McKenna (1923–1986), Irish actress.

b. Denise Levertov (1923–1997), British-American writer, who emerged as a leading poet and essayist in the postwar period.

b. Diane Arbus (1923–1971), American photographer.

b. Maria Callas (Maria Kalogeropolous, 1923–1977), American soprano.

b. Anne Baxter (1923–1985), American stage and screen actress, notably in the title role of *All About Eve* (1950).

b. Dorothy Dandridge (1923–1965), American actress, singer, and dancer.

b. Victoria de Los Angeles (1923– ), Spanish soprano.

d. Sarah Bernhardt (1844–1923), French actress, a leading tragedian of the French and English-speaking stages.

d. Katherine Mansfield (Kathleen Beauchamp-Murry, 1888–1923), New Zealand–born British short story writer, associated with the Bloomsbury Group.

d. Kate Douglas Wiggin (1856–1923), American writer.

## 1924

### POLITICS/LAW/WAR

Ma (Miriam Amanda) Ferguson was elected governor of Texas, the first American woman elected governor; her husband had earlier been removed from the office for misuse of funds. She would be reelected in 1932 but would lose in 1940.

Mae Ella Nolan was the first woman to chair a committee in the U.S. Congress, on expenditures in the Post Office Department.

Ellen Wilkinson was elected a Labour member of Parliament (1924–1931).

Helena Swanwick published *Builders of Peace* and edited the periodical *Foreign Affairs* (1924–1927).

Edith Nourse Rogers became the first woman to formally deliver the electoral college's votes, as secretary of the presidential electors.

Larissa Reisner published *The Front*, based on her experiences as a Bolshevik soldier and commissar during the Russian Revolution and Civil War.

Millicent Garrett Fawcett published the autobiography *What I Remember*.

Nina Bang became Denmark's Minister of Education.

Sylvia Pankhurst was expelled from the British Communist Party, for declining to devote the *Worker's Dreadnought* wholly to Party interests.

Deng Yingchao joined the Chinese Communist Party, in the same year marrying communist leader Zhou Enlai.

b. Shirley Anita St. Hill Chisholm (1924– ), African-American social worker and politician, the first African-American woman to serve in the House of Representatives (1969–1983).

b. Phyllis Stewart Schlafly (1924– ), American conservative Republican politician, who in the early 1960s organized and led the successful campaign against ratification of the Equal Rights Amendment.

b. Judith Ridehalgh Hart (1924– ), British socialist and politician, long a member of Parliament, who became chair of the Labour Party (1981).

b. Patricia Roberts Harris (1924–1985), American lawyer and politician.

d. Hubertine (Marie-Anne) Auclert (1848–1924), French writer and editor, a socialist, feminist, and leading women's rights movement figure in the late 19th century.

## RELIGION/EDUCATION/EVERYDAY LIFE

Dora Russell founded the Workers' Birth Control Group, campaigning alongside Margaret Sanger, Marie Stopes, and others for birth control and maternity leave.

Hude Sh'arawi founded the Women's Union and its journal *Egyptian Woman*, published in both Arabic and French to reach a wide range of women.

Annie Besant worked with Srinivasa Sastri to found the National Constitutional Convention in India.

Mary Follett published *Creative Experience*, on decision making and labor-management relations in the business world. She also began to lecture on industrial management in the United States, then at Oxford University (1926), the League of Nations and the International Labor Organization in Geneva (1928), and the London School of Economics (1933).

Edith Abbott became dean of the University of Chicago's School of Social Work Administration (1924–1942), a key figure in the development of the social work profession.

Mary McLeod Bethune served as president of the National Association of Colored Women's Clubs (1924–1928).

National Congress of Mothers became the National Congress of Parents and Teachers, later the National Parent-Teacher Association (PTA).

Anna Louise Strong published *The First Time in History*, about the experiences of her first trip to the Soviet Union, with an American Friends Relief Mission (1921).

Eileen Power published her notable study *Medieval People*.

Florence Rood became the first female president of the American Federation of Teachers.

Margaret Petherbridge Farrar, with F. G. Hartswick and A. Prosper Buranelli, all employed at the New York *World*, published the first crossword puzzle book.

Disguising herself as a poor Tibetan, Alexandra David-Neel traveled in Tibet, reaching Lhasa.

Eleanor Rathbone published *The Disinherited Family*.

b. (Helen) Mary Wilson Warnock (Baroness Warnock, 1924– ), British philosopher, educator, and writer, who became mistress of Girton College, Cambridge; she led various commissions on ethical questions, on such matters as animal experiments (1979–1986), environmental pollution (1979–1984), and artificial reproductive techniques (1982–1984).

b. Bess Myerson (1924– ), American politician, the first Jewish Miss America (1945), who later became New York City's commissioner of Consumer Affairs (1969), then Cultural Affairs (1982).

b. Felice N. Schwartz (1924–1996), American women's rights activist.

b. Evelyne (Annie Henriette) Hammel Sullerot (1924– ), French sociologist, feminist, and journalist, founder of a center for the study of mass communications (1960), long a teacher at the Institut Français de la Presse (from 1964). She also founded and led France's key family-planning organizations (1955).

d. Josephine St. Pierre Ruffin (1842–1924), African-American lecturer, journalist, philanthropist, and social activist, involved in many organizations, both white and black; founder of the Woman's Era Club of Boston and editor of its newsletter *Woman's Era* and of the *Boston Courant*, a black weekly.

### SCIENCE/TECHNOLOGY/MEDICINE

Annie Jump Cannon completed *The Henry Draper Catalogue* (1897–1924), classifying more than 200,000 stars; later extended (1925–1949) to cover 350,000 stars. Her work at the Harvard Observatory provided a basis for much 20th-century astronomical research.

Gertrude Caton-Thompson began the First Archaeological and Geological Survey of Northern Fayum (1924–1926), becoming field director for the Royal Anthropological Institute, sometimes joined by another British female archaeologist, E. W. Gardner. Their excavations would take the study of Egyptian culture back as far as 5000 B.C.

Helene Deutsch published the key paper "The Psychology of Women in Relation to the Functions of Reproduction," stressing the supremacy of the penis over the clitoris in terms of power and pleasure, and theorizing that women are masochistically subjugated to the penis.

Lillian Gilbreth succeeded her late husband, Frank Gilbreth, as instructor at Purdue University's School of Mechanical Engineering; actually better qualified than her husband, since she had a Ph.D. and he did not, she became a full professor of management in 1935.

Gertrude Agnes Muller developed a small-scale children's toilet, called the Toidy Seat, and founded her own firm to market it.

Olive Hazlett presented her paper "On the Arithmetic of a General Associative Algebra" before the International Mathematical Congress.

Ruth Nichols was the first woman in the world to obtain an international hydroplane license.

Mary Orr Evershed became a fellow of the Royal Astronomical Society.

Florence Sabin became the first woman to serve as president of the American Association of Anatomists (1924–1926).

Marie Curie published a book about her husband, *Pierre Curie*.

Mary Scharlieb published her *Reminiscences*.

b. Ruth Hoffman Hubbard (1924– ), Austrian-American biology educator, long associated with Harvard University (from 1950), whose work focused on the photochemistry of vision and on women's issues in science and health.

b. Bette Clair McMurray Nesmith Graham (1924–1980), American inventor.

### ARTS/LITERATURE

Mary Blair and Paul Robeson starred as the interracial lovers in Eugene O'Neill's play *All God's Chillun Got Wings*.

Sara Allgood created the title role of Juno Boyle opposite Barry Fitzgerald as Captain Boyle in Dublin's Abbey Theatre production of Sean O'Casey's play *Juno and the Paycock*, set during the Irish Civil War.

Adele Astaire, Fred Astaire, and Jayne Auburn starred in George and Ira Gershwin's musical *Lady, Be Good!*

Beatrice Lillie and Gertrude Lawrence appeared in *Charlot's Revue*, both in their first starring roles, Lawrence introducing "Limehouse Blues."

Bronislava Nijinska's ballet *Les Biches* was premiered by Sergei Diaghilev's Ballets Russes company.

Edna Ferber published her Pulitzer Prize–winning novel *So Big*.

Lotte Lehmann created the role of Christine in Richard Strauss's opera *Intermezzo*.

Käthe Kollwitz created the poster *Never Again War!*

Lillian Gish created the title role in the silent film *Romola*.

Marianne Moore published the poetry collection *Observations*.

Pauline Lord starred opposite Richard Bennett in Sidney Howard's play *They Knew What They Wanted.*

Asta Nielsen played the title role in the silent film *Hedda Gabler.*

Georgia O'Keeffe painted *Corn, Dark, Dark Abstraction, Flower Abstraction,* and *Petunia and Coleus.*

Malvina Hoffman showed her sculpture *Mask of Anna Pavlova.*

H. D. (Hilda Doolittle) published *Helidora and Other Poems.*

Bertha Mahony (later Miller) and Elinor Whitney founded the *Horn Book Magazine,* the first magazine devoted to children's literature.

Cornelia B. Sage Quinton became director of the new California Palace of the Legion of Honor (later Fine Arts Museum of San Francisco).

Jessie Redmon Fauset published the novel *There Is Confusion.*

b. Lauren Bacall (Betty Joan Perske, 1924– ), American actress, who became a star in her first film, *To Have and Have Not* (1944), marrying her costar, Humphrey Bogart.

b. Ruby Dee (Ruby Ann Wallace, 1924– ), African-American stage and screen actress and playwright, one of the leading American actresses of her generation, often playing opposite her husband, Ossie Davis.

b. Janet Frame (1924– ), New Zealand writer best known for her psychologically oriented novels, which seek to portray what she sees as the madness underlying modern life.

b. Sarah Caldwell (1924– ), American opera producer, company director, and conductor, who would be the first woman to conduct New York's Metropolitan Opera (1976).

b. Geraldine Page (1924–1987), American actress.

b. Dinah Washington (Ruth Lee Jones, 1924–1963), American blues singer.

b. Eva Marie Saint (1924– ), American stage and screen actress, a film star in the 1950s and 1960s.

b. Machiko Kyo (Motoko Yano, 1924– ), Japanese actress.

b. Sarah Lois Vaughan (1924–1990), American jazz and popular singer.

d. Eleanora Duse (1858–1924), Italian actress, a major tragedian.

d. Charlotte (Lotta) Crabtree (1847–1924), American actress, as a child a touring player in the West, and in maturity a star of the New York stage.

d. Frances Hodgson Burnett (1849–1924), American novelist and playwright, best known for her children's books.

d. Liubov Eding Popova (1889–1924), Russian artist, a leading Suprematist and Constructivist, and after the Bolshevik Revolution also a theater and textile designer.

d. Marie Corelli (Mary Mackay, 1855–1924), British novelist, most of whose work was on psychic themes.

## 1925

### POLITICS/LAW/WAR

Carrie Chapman Catt founded the National Committee on the Cause and Cure of War, a coalition of a dozen organizations.

Florence Prag Kahn was elected to the first of her six terms in the House of Representatives as a conservative Republican from San Francisco (1925–1937).

The first American federal prison for women was opened at Alderson, West Virginia, through the efforts of assistant attorney general Mabel Walker Willebrandt, who handpicked the first superintendent, Mary Belle Harris.

Mary T. Hopkins Norton was the first woman after the vote was gained to be elected to the U.S. Congress on her own, not succeeding her husband.

Naval Reserve Act made it once again impossible for women to work in the U.S. armed forces. During World War I, more than 11,000 women had worked for the navy and marines as clerical and telephone workers, although not by law allowed to join the armed forces.

Sarojini Naidu was elected to the presidency of the Indian National Congress, the second woman to hold the post.

Alexandra Kollontai became Soviet trade representative to Mexico (1925–1927).

Pattie Field was accepted into the U.S. State Department's consular service, its first woman, serving as vice-consul in Amsterdam (1925–1929).

Soviet writer Larissa Reisner published several works, including *Afghanistan, Hamburg at the Barricades*, and *Coal, Iron and Lively People*.

b. Margaret Hilda Roberts Thatcher (1925– ), British chemist, barrister, and Conservative politician, as prime minister (1979–1991) one of the most powerful and highly visible women of her time, and the longest-serving British prime minister of the 20th century.

b. Barbara Pierce Bush (1925– ), American author and wife of U.S. President George Bush.

b. Ruth First (1925–1982), South African Communist Party and African National Congress activist, editor, and writer.

d. Anna Kulisciov (1854–1925), Italian socialist who took the position that women's emancipation would follow a victory for working-class socialism.

d. Rose Scott (1847–1925), Australian feminist, suffragist, and pacifist, founder or president of several Australian women's movement organizations.

## RELIGION/EDUCATION/EVERYDAY LIFE

Women's World Fair—the World Exposition of Women's Progress—was held at Chicago, organized by Grace Coolidge, wife of U.S. President Calvin Coolidge. Judith Waller, director of Chicago radio station WMAQ, broadcast live from the fair during its full week.

Dora Russell's *Hypatia; or Women and Knowledge*, which espoused sexual freedom and criticized marriage, became a best-seller after Britain's *Sunday Express* called for its banning.

Harriet Chalmers Adams founded the Society of Women Geographers, becoming its first president.

Teresa of Lisieux was named a saint, taken as an indication that sainthood was within reach of even ordinary people; she became (with Joan of Arc) a patron saint of France.

In Italy, the Opera Nazionale Maternita ed Infanzia (ONMI) was founded to provide aid to mothers and young children; various women's groups (*fasci femminili*) were also involved in welfare work.

Abala Bose established a home for widows; as a child, her family had been ostracized and forced to move from their home (1870) for advocating that widows be allowed to remarry.

Coco Chanel introduced the collarless cardigan jacket.

b. Laura Ashley (1925–1985), British designer and entrepreneur.

d. Fanny Bullock Workman (1859–1925), American traveler and mountaineer who with her husband, William Workman, took cycling tours (1895–1899) and then explored in the Himalayas, writing about their experiences.

d. Harriet Morison (1862–1925), New Zealand union activist and feminist who helped found her country's first women's union (1889) and headed the Women's Employment Bureau (1908–1913); she was also among the first women to preach in New Zealand.

d. Margaret Murray Washington (1865–1925), American educator, wife and partner of Tuskegee Institute's Booker T. Washington; she was first president of the National Federation of Afro-American Women (1895), later also heading its successor, the National Association of Colored Women (1912).

d. Henrietta Chamberlain King (1832–1925), American manager of Texas's sprawling King Ranch.

## SCIENCE/TECHNOLOGY/MEDICINE

Cecilia Payne (later Payne-Gaposchkin) received the first doctorate in astronomy from Harvard Observatory, with a notable thesis relating classes of stars to their actual temperatures. Her work helped women move more into astronomy's mainstream, beyond the tedious cataloguing and calculating that had become low-paid (or no-paid) "women's work."

Myra Breckenridge founded the Kentucky Committee for Mothers and Babies, with nurse-midwives traveling on horseback to remote rural areas, greatly lowering infant and maternal deaths; it became the Frontier Nursing Service (1928).

Anna Freud gave a notable series of lectures on childhood behavior (1925–1927), which led to the *Kinderseminar*.

German engineer Ida Tacke (later Noddack) and Walter Noddack discovered the element rhenium, naming it after the Rhine River.

Hélène Metzger won the Prix Bordin in philosophy for *Les concepts scientifiques*, her most notable work on the philosophical bases of science.

Lise Meitner and C. D. Ellis published a key paper on the nature and characteristics of gamma and beta rays.

Vienna Psychoanalytic Institute was founded by disciples of Sigmund Freud, with Helene Deutsch as director (1925–1933) and Anna Freud as secretary (1925–1938).

Alice Hamilton published her landmark *Industrial Poisons in the United States*.

Christine Murrell became president of Britain's Medical Women's Federation.

Florence Sabin became the first woman elected to the National Academy of Sciences.

British botanist Agnes Arber published *Monocotyledons*.

b. Mary Beth Stearns (1925– ), American physicist who worked on magnetism in solids, long the head research scientist at Ford Motor Company.

d. Julia Brainerd Hall (1859–1925), American chemical engineer who helped her brother develop the process for producing electrolytic aluminum (1889).

## ARTS/LITERATURE

Josephine Baker emerged as a star in Paris cabaret in *La Revue Negro*.

Amy Lowell published the poetry collection *What O'Clock*.

Elisabeth Bergner starred in Germany in Max Reinhardt's theater production of *The Circle of Chalk*, adapted from the Chinese work.

Selma Lagerlöf published the trilogy *The Ring of the Lowenskölds* (1925–1928).

Ellen Glasgow published the novel *Barren Ground*.

Sigrid Undset published her four-part novel *Olaf Audunsson* (*The Master of Hestvikken*, 1925–1927).

Virginia Woolf published the novel *Mrs. Dalloway*.

Anita Loos published the novel *Gentlemen Prefer Blondes*.

Carol Dempster played the title role in D. W. Griffith's silent film *Sally of the Sawdust*.

Ethel Leginska became the first woman to conduct a major American orchestra, making her debut with the New York Symphony; that year she also organized an all-woman symphony orchestra.

Gabriela Mistral published the poetry collection *Tenderness*.

Georgia O'Keeffe painted *New York with Moon, Petunia, Lake George*, and *Purple Petunias*.

Gloria Swanson starred in the title role in Léonce Perret's silent film *Madame Sans-Gene*, shot in France.

H. D. (Hilda Doolittle) published her *Collected Poems*.

Ivy Compton-Burnett published the novel *Pastors and Masters*.

Marilyn Miller starred in the title role of Jerome Kern's stage musical *Sunny*.

Vilma Banky starred opposite Ronald Colman in George Fitzmaurice's silent film *The Dark Angel* and opposite Rudolph Valentino in Clarence Brown's *The Eagle*.

Mary Pickford starred in the title role of the silent film *Little Annie Rooney*.

Gertrude Stein published the novel *The Making of Americans*.

Wanda Landowska founded the School of Ancient Music, near Paris (1925–1940).

Babette Deutsch published the poetry collection *Honey Out of the Rock*.

Lillie Langtry published the autobiography *The Days I Knew*.

Belle Bennett starred opposite Ronald Colman in *Stella Dallas*, Henry King's film version of the 1923 Olive Higgins Prouty novel.

Malvina Hoffman showed her sculpture *England*.

Marguerite Zorach founded the New York Society of Women Artists.

Joan Forbes published *Red Sea to Blue Nile*.

María Cadilla de Martínez, writing as Liana, published *Cuentos a Lillian*, a collection of Puerto Rican folk tales.

Pauline Smith published the novel *The Little Karoo*.

b. (Mary) Flannery O'Connor (1925–1964), American writer.

b. Melina Mercouri (1925–1994), Greek classical actress, best known internationally for her role as a prostitute in Never on Sunday (1960). In exile from the late 1960s, she returned home to become a cabinet minister in the mid-1980s.

b. Angela Lansbury (1925– ), British stage and screen actress, a four-time Tony winner who became a television star late in her career, as author-detective Jessica Fletcher in the long-running series *Murder, She Wrote* (1984–1996).

b. Maya Plisetskaya (1925– ), a leading Russian ballerina of the Soviet period, from 1943 in leading roles at the Bolshoi Ballet.

b. Julie (Julia Ann) Harris (1925– ), American stage and screen star; she won the first of her four Tony Awards on Broadway in *A Member of the Wedding* (1950).

b. Mai Zetterling (1925–1994), Swedish actress, director, and writer.

b. (Lois) Maureen Stapleton (1925– ), American actress, who emerged as a star by creating Serafina in Tennessee Williams's play *The Rose Tattoo* (1951).

b. Irina Arkhipova (1925– ), Russian mezzo-soprano.

b. Maria Tallchief (1925– ), American ballerina.

b. Maxine Kumin (1925– ), American poet and novelist.

d. Amy Lowell (1874–1925), American poet.

# 1926

### POLITICS/LAW/WAR

Bertha Knight Landes became the first woman to serve as mayor of a major America city, Seattle.

Alexandra Kollontai wrote her *Autobiography of a Sexually Emancipated Woman*; it would be published posthumously.

Constance Markiewicz was reelected to the Irish Parliament, this time as a Fianna Faill member.

During the General Strike in Britain, Marion Phillips was head organizer of the Women's Committee for the Relief of Miners' Wives and Children.

Nina Bang became Denmark's Minister of Commerce.

Olive Hoskins was the first U.S. Army warrant officer, a skilled technician ranked between enlisted individuals and commissioned officers.

Dutch suffragist Rosa Manus became a vice-president of the International Federation for Women's Suffrage.

Turkish feminist writer Halide Adivar published her *Memoirs*.

b. Elizabeth II (Elizabeth Alexandra Mary, 1926– ), queen of the United Kingdom (1952– ), daughter of George VI and Elizabeth (the Queen Mother).

b. Gaositwe Keagakwa Tibe Chiepe (ca. 1926– ), Botswana government official and diplomat.

d. Larissa Mikhailovna Reisner (1895–1926), Russian writer, a Bolshevik soldier and commissar who fought through the Russian Revolution and Civil War and then became a Soviet diplomat.

### RELIGION/EDUCATION/EVERYDAY LIFE

At the Seven College Conference, the women's colleges Mount Holyoke, Vassar, Wellesley, Smith, Radcliffe, Bryn Mawr, and Barnard forged a formal affiliation, so being called the "Seven Sisters."

Aimée Semple McPherson disappeared after swimming in the Pacific Ocean near Los Angeles, resurfacing in Mexico a month later and claiming, with little evidence, that she had been kidnapped; after international publicity, she then went on a new revival tour, including Britain and Paris.

Gertrude Ederle became the first woman to swim the English Channel, from Cap Grix-Nez in France to Dover, England (August 6), also setting a record at 14 hours 39 minutes.

Helen Wills Moody began her domination of women's tennis, garnering 31 titles (1926–1938), including a then-record eight women's singles titles at Wimbledon.

Gertrude Bonnin founded the National Council of American Indians, becoming its first president (1926–1938).

Rose Schneiderman became national president of the Women's Trade Union League.

The Lucy Stone League led a successful campaign to allow married women to take out copyrights in their birth names.

American Association of University Women established the Margaret E. Maltby Fellowships in honor of the Barnard College professor who had long been active in seeking scholarship funds for female graduate students.

Catherine Booth led the Women's Social Work division of the Salvation Army, working with unwed mothers and abused children.

Margaret Murray became a fellow of Britain's Royal Anthropological Institute.

Portuguese women won the right to teach in all-male high schools.

Beatrice Potter Webb published her autobiographical *My Apprenticeship*.

d. Gertrude Margaret Lowthian Bell (1868–1926), British traveler, archaeologist, writer, and government official, who traveled widely in the Near East, becoming involved in intelligence and political affairs.

d. Annie (Phoebe Anne) Oakley (Mozee; Moses, 1860–1926), American sharpshooter known for her shooting matches with partner-husband Frank Butler, who toured widely in the Buffalo Bill Wild West Show (1885–1901); model for the musical *Annie Get Your Gun*, she had shot game for her family's food after her father's death (1870).

d. Ellen Key (1849–1926), Swedish feminist, who wrote and lectured widely on women's rights, roles, and social position.

## SCIENCE/TECHNOLOGY/MEDICINE

Chemist Rachel F. Brown, working for the New York State Department of Health, developed a still-used vaccine for pneumonia.

At age 78, after a lifetime of college teaching, Christine Ladd-Franklin finally received the Ph.D. in mathematics from Johns Hopkins University that she had earned, but not been awarded, 44 years earlier.

Edith Clarke addressed the American Institute of Electrical Engineers convention, believed to be the first woman to do so.

Lise Meitner became professor of physics at the University of Berlin; when she had arrived (1907), women were not allowed in the laboratories.

American Katherine Blodgett became the first woman to receive a doctoral degree in physics from Cambridge University.

Ethel Fenwick and her husband, Dr. Bedford Fenwick, founded the British College of Nurses.

*Ideal Marriage: Its Physiology and Technique*, by Theodor H. Van de Velde, signaled a shift in sexual attitudes, suggesting focus on foreplay and on simultaneous orgasm.

Leta Hollingworth published her standard text *Gifted Children* and worked with the New York City Board of Education to establish special classes for gifted children.

Women in the U.S. Army Nurse Corps first won the right to receive disability benefits.

b. Elisabeth Kubler-Ross (1926– ), Swiss-American psychiatrist best known for her *On Death and Dying* (1969).

b. Christine Jorgenson (George Jorgensen, 1926–1989), American transsexual and entertainer.

d. Bessie Coleman (1896–1926), American flyer, the first licensed African-American pilot; she was killed preparing for a Florida air meet.

## ARTS/LITERATURE

Sara Allgood created the role of Bessie Burgess in *The Plough and the Stars*, Sean O'Casey's play about the Easter Rising of 1916.

Eva Le Gallienne began her seminal Civic Repertory Theater in New York, for the next seven years bringing classical and modern theater to mass audiences at low prices (1926–1933). Le Gallienne, Egon Brecher, and Beatrice Terry starred in Jacinto Benavente's play *Saturday Night*.

Gertrude Lawrence introduced "Someone to Watch Over Me" in the title role of George and Ira Gershwin's musical *Oh, Kay!*

Grazia Deledda was awarded the Nobel Prize for literature.

Lillian Gish starred in Victor Seastrom's silent film *The Scarlet Letter*.

Greta Garbo played her first starring role, in the *The Torrent*.

Margalo Gilbert starred opposite Earle Larrimore in Sidney Howard's play *The Silver Cord*.

Sylvia Townsend Warner published the novel *Lolly Willowes*.

Agatha Christie published the novel *The Murder of Roger Ackroyd*.

Amy Beach was a founder and first president of the Association of American Women Composers.

Barbara Hepworth showed her sculpture *Doves*.

Catherine Hessling starred in the title role of Jean Renoir's French silent film classic *Nana*, based on Émile Zola's novel.

Edna Ferber published the novel *Show Boat*.

Clare Eames starred in the title role opposite Alfred Lunt in Sidney Howard's play *Ned McCobb's Daughter*.

Gertrude Stein published *Composition as Explanation*.

June Walker created the role of Lorelei Lee in *Gentlemen Prefer Blondes*, Anita Loos and John Emerson's play based on Loos's novel.

Marianne Moore became editor of the magazine the *Dial*.

Ninette de Valois founded Britain's Academy of Choreographic Art, which later became the Royal Ballet.

Ruth Crawford Seeger composed her *Violin Sonata* and *Suite for Small Orchestra*.

Georgia O'Keeffe painted *Black Iris*, *City Night*, *Pink Tulip*, the *Shell on Old Shingle* series, *White Sweet Peas*, and *The Shelton with Sunspots*.

Dorothy Parker published the poetry collection *Enough Rope*.

Ellen Glasgow published the novel *The Romantic Comedians*.

Fannie Hurst published the novel *Mannequin*.

H. D. (Hilda Doolittle) published the novel *Palimpsest*.

Mae West starred in the play *Sex*, which she wrote and produced.

Marie Rambert founded the Ballet Rambert.

Radclyffe Hall published the novel *Adam's Breed*.

Vera Brittain published the novel *Not Without Honour*.

Cora Sandel published *Alberta and Jaceb*, the first novel in her Alberta Trilogy, which included *Alberta and Freedom* (1931), and *Alberta Alone* (1935).

Dorothy Canfield published the novel *Her Son's Wife*.

b. Colleen Dewhurst (1926–1991), American actress, a star on stage from the mid-1960s, who played strong supporting roles in films and television.

b. Marilyn Monroe (Norma Jean Mortenson, 1926–1962), American actress.

b. Galina Vishnevskaya (1926– ), Russian soprano; she and her husband, Mstislav Rostropovich, were notable Soviet-era dissidents and prominent reform supporters in democratic Russia.

b. Joan Sutherland (1926– ), Australian soprano, from the early 1960s one of the world's leading opera singers.

b. Alison Lurie (1926– ), American novelist and teacher, whose work is set largely in academic and upper-middle-class spheres.

b. Judith Malina (1926– ), American actress and director, cofounder of the Living Theater.

b. Margaret Laurence (Jean Margaret Wernyss, 1926–1986), Canadian writer.

b. Jan Morris (James Morris, 1926– ), British historian and travel writer, who had a man-to-woman sex-change operation (1972).

b. Alice Adams (1926– ), American author.

b. Dorothy Collins (Marjorie Chandler, 1926–1994), Canadian singer and bandleader.

b. Ana Maria Matute (1926– ), Spanish writer.

b. Patricia Neal (1926– ), American actress.

b. Ingeborg Bachmann (1926–1973), Austrian writer.

d. Mary Cassatt (1845–1926), American painter and graphic artist, a leading Impressionist of the late 19th century.

## 1927

### POLITICS/LAW/WAR

Ho Hsiang-ning, leader of the Women's Department of the Kuomintang, broke with Chiang Kai-shek after the Shanghai Massacre of communists, then went into exile rather than join either side of the Chinese Civil War.

Kamaldevi Chattopadhyay was elected to the All India Congress and became president of the All India Women's Conference.

Miina Sillanpää became Finland's first woman to serve at cabinet level, as minister of Social Affairs.

Alexandra Kollontai again became Soviet trade representative to Norway (1927–1930).

b. Coretta Scott King (1927– ), African-American concert singer and civil rights leader, wife of Rev. Martin Luther King Jr., whose civil rights work she carried on after his 1968 assassination.

b. Simone Jacob Veil (1927– ), French feminist, lawyer, and politician, serving in the French cabinet and European parliament.

b. Gisèle Taieb Halimi (1927– ), French lawyer, feminist, socialist, politician, and diplomat, founder of Choisir, a key organization supporting women's choice in abortion and birth control (1971).

b. Nguyen Thi Binh (1927– ), Vietnamese teacher, politician, and diplomat.

b. Anne Legendre Armstrong (1927– ), American politician and diplomat.

d. Victoria Claflin Woodhull (1838–1927), American feminist, reformer, spiritualist, publisher, sexual-freedom advocate, with her sister the first female broker on Wall Street, and the first woman to declare as a presidential candidate (1870).

d. Constance Gore-Booth Markiewicz (Countess Markiewicz, 1868–1927), Irish Republican soldier and politician who fought with the Irish Citizens Army during the Easter Rising (1916) and with dissident Irish Republican Army forces during the Irish Civil War, later a Fianna Faill member of the Irish parliament (1926). Married to a Polish count, a painter, she was a founder of the Abbey Theatre (1904) and the Gaelic League.

### RELIGION/EDUCATION/EVERYDAY LIFE

Mary Ritter Beard and Charles Beard, her husband, published their major four-volume work *The Rise of American Civilization* (1927–1939).

Robert Briffault published *The Mothers*, positing the existence of early matriarchies, largely based on the "Venus figurines" found in many European archaeological sites, which he—and many others—took to be mother-goddess figures.

Dora Russell and her husband, Bertrand Russell, founded the experimental Beacon Hill School (1927–1939), near Petersfield, England, which she ran alone from 1935. She also published *The Right to Be Happy*, attacking sexual taboos.

Edith Abbott and Sophonisba Breckinridge edited the highly influential *Social Work Review* (1927–1953).

Mildred Cable and Francesca French published *Through the Jade Gate and Central Asia*, the best-known of their more than 20 books on their Asian travels.

Eileen Power founded the *Economic History Review*, in the 1920s also collaborating on *Tudor Economic Documents*, with R. H. Tawney, and on planning the medieval sections of the *Cambridge Economic History of Europe*.

National Congress of Colored Parents and Teachers was founded by Selena Sloan Butler, seeking to improve segregated Southern schools; it would later merge with the National Parent-Teacher Association (PTA, 1970).

American mountaineer Miriam O'Brien (later Underhill) opened the Via Miriam, a new route through the Torre Grande in the Dolomites.

Barbara Wootton became director of adult education studies at the University of London (1927–1944), beginning her long association with the university (to 1957).

Edna Sewell was named first director of the Associated Women of the American Farm Bureau Federation (1927–1950).

Lima Geographical Society named the north peak of Peru's Huascarán for American mountaineer Annie Peck: Cumbre Ana Peck.

British union leader Gertrude Tuckwell founded the Maternal Mortality Committee.

Edith Pye organized Quaker relief efforts in China for the Women's International League.

Egypt's first secondary school for girls was founded, at the urging of Huda Sh'arawi.

Lillian Wald of New York's Henry Street Settlement directed a study of Prohibition for the National Federation of Settlements.

Aimée Semple McPherson published *In the Service of the King*.

Evelyn Underhill became a fellow of King's College, London.

Mary White Ovington published *Portraits in Color*, profiles of black leaders.

Sophonisba Breckinridge published *Public Welfare Administration*.

b. Althea Gibson (1927– ), American tennis player, the first African-American invited to play in the American Lawn Tennis Association championships (1950) and to win at Wimbledon (1957).

d. Juliette Magill Kinzie Gordon Low (1860–1927), American founder of the Girl Scouts.

d. Lizzie Andrew Borden (1860–1927), American alleged murderess.

### SCIENCE/TECHNOLOGY/MEDICINE

British aviator Mary Bailey flew across the Irish Sea, the first woman to do so.

Phoebe Fairgrave Omlie became the first woman to receive a transport pilot's license from the U.S. Department of Commerce, and an aircraft mechanic's license.

Katharine McCormick gave funds to found the Neuroendocrine Research Foundation at Harvard Medical School (1927–1947) and support the journal *Endocrinology*, seeking biochemical bases for psychiatric disorders.

Elsie Eaves became the first female member of the American Society of Civil Engineers.

Lillian Gilbreth published *The Home-Maker and Her Job*.

Margaret Sanger organized the first World Population Conference.

---

# On Being Alone

For many years I was almost alone in college work in this line [physics] meeting the somewhat nerve-wearing experience of constantly being in places where a woman was not expected to be, and doing what women had not at that time conventionally done.

— Sarah Whiting

---

b. Elizabeth Dexter Hay (1927– ), American embryologist and educator, an expert on tissue regeneration, long associated with Harvard Medical School (1960–1993).

b. Sheila (Christine) Hopkins Scott (1927–1988), British aviator.

d. Sarah Frances Whiting (1847–1927), American physicist and astronomer, long associated with Wellesley College as professor of physics (1876–1912) and director of the Whitin Observatory (1900–1916).

## ARTS/LITERATURE

Edna Ferber's novel *Show Boat* was the basis of Oscar Hammerstein and Jerome Kern's musical, starring Norma Terriss, Howard Marsh, Jules Blesoe, and Helen Morgan.

Janet Gaynor starred opposite Charles Farrell in Frank Borzage's silent-film classic *Seventh Heaven*, for which she would win a 1928 Academy Award (the first awarded), and opposite George O'Brien in F. W. Murnau's equally classic silent film *Sunrise*.

Virginia Woolf published the novel *To the Lighthouse*.

Evelyn Ellis and Frank Wilson opened on Broadway in *Porgy*, Dorothy and Dubose Heyward's play, based on Dubose Heyward's novel.

Greta Garbo starred opposite John Gilbert in Clarence Brown's silent *Flesh and the Devil* and in Edmund Goulding's *Love*, the first two of four Garbo-Gilbert films.

Helen Hayes created the title role in *Coquette*, George Abbott and Ann Preston Bridgers's play.

Martha Graham founded her School of Contemporary Dance.

Barbara Stanwyck starred on Broadway opposite Hal Skelly in *Burlesque*, by George Manker Watters and Arthur Hopkins.

Clara Bow starred in the silent film *It*; studio publicity saw to it that she was forever afterward the "It girl."

Georgia O'Keeffe painted *Abstraction—White Rose No. 2*, *Black Abstraction*, *Red Poppy*, and *Radiator Building—Night, New York*.

Willa Cather published the novel *Death Comes for the Archbishop*.

Gertrude Stein and Virgil Thomson collaborated on the opera *Four Saints in Three Acts*.

Olga Spessivtseva created the title in George Balanchine's ballet *Le Chatte*.

Dorothy Arzner directed the film *Fashions for Women*.

H. D. (Hilda Doolittle) published the play *Hippolytus Temporizes*.

Dorothy L. Sayers published the novel *Unnatural Death*.

Elizabeth Bowen published the novel *The Hotel*.

Janet Lewis published the poetry collection *The Wheel in Midsummer*.

Miriam Hopkins starred opposite Eric Dressler in John McGowan's play *Excess Baggage*.

Jean Rhys published *The Left Bank and Other Stories*.

Norma Talmadge starred in the title role of Fred Niblo's silent film *Camille*, based on Alexandre Dumas's play *La Dame aux Camélias*.

Josephine Baker starred in the film *La Sirène des tropiques*.

Laura Riding and Robert Graves published *A Survey of Modernist Poetry*.

Rosamond Lehmann published the novel *Dusty Answer*.

Winifred Holtby published the novel *Green Ginger*.

b. Leontyne Price (1927– ), American soprano, one of the world's leading singers and one of the first African-Americans to emerge as a world figure in grand opera.

b. Ruth Prawer Jhabvala (1927– ), British novelist, best known for her scripts for Ismail Merchant-James Ivory films.

b. Cleo (Clementina Dinah) Laine (1927– ), British singer and actress.

b. Gina Lollobrigida (1927– ), Italian actress.

b. Helen Gurley Brown (1927– ), American writer and editor in chief of *Cosmopolitan* magazine (1965–1997).

b. Janet Leigh (Jeannette Morrison, 1927– ), American actress.

d. Isadora Duncan (1878–1927), American dancer and teacher, a key figure in the development of the modern dance.

## 1928

### POLITICS/LAW/WAR

Full women's suffrage was won in Britain; women with high school degrees won the right to vote in Portugal.

Jennie Lee became a Labour member of Parliament (1928–1931), its youngest member.

The Women's International League for Peace and Freedom supported the Kellogg-Briand Pact, which aimed to outlaw war and foster international disarmament; in the United States, under executive secretary Dorothy Detzer (later Denny), the group would during the interwar period press for neutrality, attempting to keep America from being drawn into the coming Second World War.

Genevieve Cline was the first female judge on the U.S. Customs Court (1928–1953).

Kang Keqing joined Chinese Communist forces led by Zhu De, later her husband, in the Chingkang Mountains of western Kiangsi (1928), retreated north to Yenan on the Long March, and fought until Communist victory (1949).

Ray Strachey published *The Cause: A Brief History of the Women's Movement*.

Flora Drummond became commander in chief of the conservative Women's Guild of Empire.

Helene Lange published the two-volume *Kampfeitzen*.

b. Takako Doi (1928– ), Japanese lawyer, socialist, and politician who become the first woman to lead a major political party (1986).

b. Angie (Elizabeth) Brooks-Randolph (1928– ), Liberian feminist, lawyer, and diplomat, the second woman to be president of the United Nations General Assembly (1969–1970).

b. Aisha Rateb (1928– ), Egyptian lawyer and diplomat.

d. Emmeline Goulden Pankhurst (1858–1928), militant British suffragist, a central figure in the long fight for women's suffrage, cofounder of the Women's Social and Political Union (1903); she was the mother of suffragist leaders Christabel and Sylvia Pankhurst.

d. Crystal Eastman (1881–1928), American lawyer, feminist, and pacifist, a founder of the Congressonal Union for Woman Suffrage (1913) and a pacifist leader during World War I.

d. Marie Stritt (1856–1928), German feminist, suffragist, and women's rights movement leader, who strongly supported the program of the League for the Protection of Motherhood and Sexual Reform, and as a direct consequence lost her leading position in the German women's movement, including the presidency of the Federation of German Women's Associations.

d. Nina Bang (1866–1928), Danish socialist and politician, the first woman in Denmark's Upper House of Parliament (1918), later minister of education (1924) and commerce (1926).

d. Xiang Jingyu (1895–1928), Chinese feminist and Communist leader, a founder of the Communist Party of China and first director of her party's Women's Department. She was executed by Kuomintang forces.

d. Trinidad Tescon (1848–1928), Philippine soldier and nurse, a figure in the Philippine Revolution.

### RELIGION/EDUCATION/EVERYDAY LIFE

Sonja Henje won the first of her three Olympic gold medals for ice-skating (1928; 1932; 1936); the year before (1927) she had won the first of her ten world skating championships.

Affiliated Schools for Women Workers was founded to provide national coordination of educational programs for working women and to disseminate information about them.

Eileen Power published her translation of *Le ménagier de Paris*, a medieval husband's advice for his young wife.

L'Ecole de Mannequins, the first American models' school, was founded in Chicago.

The first Egyptian-Arab women were admitted to Cairo's Egyptian National University.

Anna Louise Strong published *China's Millions*, on Chiang Kai-shek's break with Moscow.

British feminist Dora Marsden published *The Definition of Godhead*.

Evangeline Booth published *Towards a Better World*.

b. Mary Daly (1928– ), American feminist theologian, a former Catholic who ultimately moved into spiritual feminism and developed a body of radical feminist theology.

b. Mary (Georgene Wells Berg) Lawrence (1928– ), American advertising executive, who in 1966 formed her own firm, Wells, Rich, Greene Inc.

d. Eglantyne Jebb (1876–1928), British philanthropist who founded the Save the Children Fund (1919).

d. Jane (Ellen) Harrison (1850–1928), British classical scholar who became director of the British School of Archaeology in Rome.

d. Mary Ellen Richmond (1861–1928), a teacher and social worker, a key figure in the American Charity Organization Society Movement, who laid out the theory, principles, and techniques of social work for the organization's "friendly visitors."

### SCIENCE/TECHNOLOGY/MEDICINE

British archaeologist Gertrude Caton-Thompson excavated the ruins of Zimbabwe (1928–1929), its importance reflected in the later choice of the name for the nation previously called Rhodesia.

Margaret Mead published *Coming of Age in Samoa*.

American journalist Marie Meloney spearheaded another visit to America by Marie Curie, again to raise money for Curie's Institute of Radium.

During their marriage (1928–1936), Frida Avern Leakey explored human origins in East Africa with her husband, archaeologist and paleontologist Louis Leakey; she provided illustrations for some of his early books.

Myra Breckenridge founded the Frontier Graduate School of Midwifery.

Olive Hazlett presented her paper "Integers as Matrices" at the International Congress of Mathematicians.

Reichs League for Birth Control and Sexual Hygiene (Reichsverband für Geburtenregelung und Sexual-hygiene) was founded in Germany.

British aviator Mary Bailey made a solo flight from Britain to South Africa and back, the first woman to do so; in the same month, their trips partly overlapping in time, Sophia Heath flew solo from South Africa to Britain.

A year after Charles Lindbergh's famous solo crossing, Amelia Earhart was the first woman to cross the Atlantic Ocean by plane, from Newfoundland to Ireland, with enormous publicity, though she was a passenger, not the pilot.

Alice Evans became the first woman to serve as president of the Society of American Bacteriologists (later American Society for Microbiology).

American naturalist Florence Merriam Bailey published her book *Birds of New Mexico*.

Dorothea Klumpke Roberts published *A Celestial Atlas*.

Leta Hollingworth published *Psychology of the Adolescent*.

Marie Stopes published *Enduring Passion*.

b. Vera Cooper Rubin (1928– ), American astronomer, long associated with the Carnegie Institution of Terrestrial Magnetism (1965–)

### ARTS/LITERATURE

Louise Brooks starred as Lulu, an extraordinarily free-spirited woman, in G. W. Pabst's *Pandora's Box*, based on the Franz Wedekind plays *Earth Spirit* and *Pandora's Box*.

Radclyffe Hall published the novel *The Well of Loneliness*, her pioneering work on lesbian themes, long banned.

Sigrid Undset was awarded the Nobel Prize for literature.

Lynn Fontanne starred in Eugene O'Neill's play *Strange Interlude.*

Virginia Woolf published the novel *Orlando.*

Lotte Lenya as Jenny sang "Pirate Jenny" in Kurt Weill and Bertolt Brecht's *The Threepenny Opera.*

Edna St. Vincent Millay published the poetry collection *The Buck in the Snow* and the poem "Justice Denied in Massachusetts," her protest on the miscarriage of justice in the Sacco-Vanzetti case.

Adelaide Hall starred opposite Bill "Bojangles" Robinson in *Blackbirds of 1928,* singing "I Can't Give You Anything But Love."

Gloria Swanson starred as the prostitute opposite Lionel Barrymore as the preacher in *Sadie Thompson,* Raoul Walsh's silent film, based on Somerset Maugham's short story "Rain."

Ethel Barrymore starred in Martinez Sierra's *The Kingdom of God,* the opening production in her own Ethel Barrymore Theatre.

Maria Falconetti played the title role in *The Passion of Joan of Arc,* Carl Dreyer's French silent-film classic.

Dolores Del Rio played the title role in the silent film *Ramona.*

Janet Gaynor starred opposite Charles Farrell in Frank Borzage's silent film *Street Angel.*

Doris Humphrey and Charles Weidman founded the Humphrey-Weidman dance school and company.

Edith Wharton published four novellas as *Old New York.*

Margalo Gillmore starred opposite Alfred Lunt in Eugene O'Neill's *Marco Millions.*

Georgia O'Keeffe painted *Black Night, Black Petunia, White Calla Lilies with Red Anemone, Shell I, East River from the Shelton* (1927–1928), and *Hickory Leaves with Daisy.*

Architect Elizabeth Whitworth Scott designed the Shakespeare Memorial Theatre at Stratford-upon-Avon.

Mae West starred on stage in *Diamond Lil,* which she wrote and produced.

Ziat Hohann starred in Sophie Treadwell's play *Machinal.*

Pola Negri starred as French actress Rachel in the film *Loves of an Actress.*

Bess Streeter Aldrich published the novel *A Lantern in Her Hand.*

Djuna Barnes published the novel *Ladies' Almanack* and the single-character play *Ryder.*

H. D. (Hilda Doolittle) published the novel *Hedylus.*

Laura Riding and Robert Graves published *Against Anthologies.*

b. Shirley Temple (Shirley Temple Black, 1928– ), American actress, who became a child star and worldwide phenomenon, and in adulthood a diplomat.

b. Grace Kelly (1928–1982), American actress.

b. Helen Frankenthaler (1928– ), American painter, a leading abstract expressionist of the New York School from the early 1950s.

b. Jeanne Moreau (1928– ), French actress, screenwriter, and director, an international film star from the the late 1940s.

b. Maya Angelou (1928– ), African-American writer, who emerged as a major figure in American literature with her autobiographical works of the 1970s and 1980s.

b. Agnes Varda (1928– ), French photographer, screenwriter, and director.

b. Anne Sexton (1928–1974), American poet.

b. Cynthia Ozick (1928– ), American novelist, short story writer, and essayist, largely on Jewish-identity themes.

b. Lina Wertmuller (1928– ), Italian director, a leading international film figure briefly during the 1970s.

b. Rosemary Clooney (1928– ), American popular singer, with several hit songs in the 1950s.

b. Thea Musgrave (1928– ), Scottish composer and conductor.

d. Ellen Terry (1847–1928), celebrated British actress, long associated with Henry Irving; she was the mother of Edward Gordon Craig and the aunt of John Gielgud.

d. Loie (Louise Mary) Fuller (1862–1928), American dancer and choreographer.

d. Maria Nikolaijevna Yermolova (1852–1928), Russian actress, a leading figure on the Russian stage (1870–1920).

# 1929

## POLITICS/LAW/WAR

Radclyffe Hall's *The Well of Loneliness* was banned by a United States lower court as "obscene," but the ban was reversed on appeal.

Women won the right to vote and be elected to office in Romania.

Britain's Privy Council ruled that the term *persons* covers both women and men, making both equally eligible for legislative or judicial positions, the culmination of a reevaluation sparked by challenges to the legal position of Emily Ferguson Murphy, Canadian magistrate, the first in the British Empire (1916).

In India, the Child Marriage Restraint Act was passed, seeking to end the practice of forced marriages of young girls.

Margaret Bondfield was appointed minister of Labour, becoming the first British female cabinet minister.

Under the rule of the Chinese Nationalist Party, the Kuomintang, a new civil code (1929–1931) granted women the right to own and inherit property, to obtain a divorce, and to sue husbands for adultery or polygamy.

Mary Dennett was indicted, convicted, and fined under obscenity laws, for open dissemination of a 1918 sex education article, in defiance of a 1922 government ban on doing so. Aided by the American Civil Liberties Union, she appealed the case, arguing that the public has a right to obtain sex education information and that censorship violated civil liberties, winning a significant victory (1930).

A seven-volume edition of Vera Figner's works was published by the Soviet government (1929–1932).

Adela Pankhurst Walsh was a founder of the Australian Women's Guild of Empire and edited the *Empire Gazette* (1929–1939).

Failed six-week United Textile Workers of America organizing strike of rayon workers at the Elizabethton, Tennessee, American Glazstoff plant (March-May) included almost 1,200 women, many of them highly visible in strike activities.

Jeannette Rankin became a Georgia-based organizer of the National Council for the Prevention of War (1929–1939).

Labour Party activist Marion Phillips won election to Britain's Parliament (1929–1931).

Ona Masiotene founded the Council of Lithuanian Women, becoming its first president.

Women's rights leader Franciska Plamnikova was elected to the Czech Senate.

French-Canadian feminist Marie Gerin-Lajoie published *La femme et le code civil.*

María Hernández and her husband, Pedro Hernández, founded the civil rights group Orden Caballeros de America.

b. Jacqueline Lee Bouvier Kennedy Onassis (1929–1994), American photographer and editor, wife of assassinated President John F. Kennedy.

b. Winifred Margaret Ewing (1929– ), Scottish solicitor and politician, a leader of the Scottish Nationalist Party.

b. Yvette Roudy (1929– ), French socialist, feminist, writer, and politician.

d. Millicent Garrett Fawcett (1847–1929), British suffragist, economist, politician, and writer, president of the National Union of Woman Suffrage Societies (1897) and a key figure in the worldwide women's movement; she was the sister of doctor Elizabeth Garrett Andersen.

d. Josepha Abiertas (1894–1929), Philippine feminist and suffragist, the first woman to graduate from Philippine Law School.

## RELIGION/EDUCATION/EVERYDAY LIFE

Helen Merrell Lynd and her husband, Robert Staughton Lynd, published *Middletown,* based on their sociological analyses of Muncie, Indiana.

Maggie L. Walker merged Richmond, Virginia's St. Luke Bank and Trust Company with several other African-American banks, serving as chairman of the Consolidated Bank and Trust Company (1929–1934).

Edith Lowry became director of the Council of Women for Home Missions' program for migrant agricultural workers, where she had worked since 1926.

In Egypt, coeducational university classes began to be offered.

New York's College Settlement, founded by Eastern women's colleges in 1889, moved from the Lower East Side and began to focus entirely on creative-arts activities, as the Art Workshop.

Alexandra David-Neel published *Mystère et magique de Tibet.*

Margaret E. Maltby published *History of the Fellowships Awarded by the American Association of University Women, 1888–1929,* with biographical sketches of the recipients.

b. Fatima Meer (1929– ), South African academic and antiapartheid activist, a sociology professor at Natal University.

d. Séverine (Caroline Rémy Guebhard, 1855–1929), French journalist.

d. Alice Pestana (1860–1929), Portuguese feminist who wrote as Caiel.

d. Tsuda Umeko (1865–1929), Japanese educator who studied abroad, then returned to Japan to found Tsuda College to train women as English teachers.

## SCIENCE/TECHNOLOGY/MEDICINE

Women's Air Derby was held in the United States, the first national aviation event for women; the winner was Louise Thaden. Earlier at least one female pilot, Mabel Cody, had run her own "flying circus."

Ninety-Nines, the first association of female pilots, was founded, so-named for the number of women who responded to a letter proposing such an organization.

American Association of Nurse Midwives was founded by Myra Breckenridge and others from the Frontier Nursing Service.

Anne Morrow Lindbergh served as flight navigator for her pilot husband, Charles Lindbergh, pioneering an air route from New York to Los Angeles.

British cell biologist Honor Fell was named director of the Cambridge Research Hospital, where she would develop the organ-culture method, demonstrating its use in the physiological study of vitamins and hormones in the body.

Katharine Bement Davis published *Factors in the Sex Life of Twenty-Two Hundred Women,* believed to be the first national survey on sexual matters.

Florence Bailey became the first female fellow of the American Ornithologists' Union; she had been the first woman to be an associate member (1885).

Lillien Martin, a consulting psychologist in San Francisco, established perhaps the first counseling center specifically for the elderly.

Pancho (Florence) Lowe Barnes became the first woman to be a motion picture stunt pilot.

Margaret Clay Ferguson became the first woman to serve as president of the Botanical Society of America.

b. Sheila Helena Elizabeth Webster Kitzinger (1929– ), British childbirth educator.

d. Aletta Jacobs (1851–1929), Dutch physician, birth control advocate, and women's rights campaigner, the first Dutch woman to qualify as a doctor (1879). She founded the world's first birth control clinic (1882) and the Dutch Association for Women's Suffrage (1894).

## ARTS/LITERATURE

Virginia Woolf published the feminist essay collection *A Room of One's Own.*

Bronislava Nijinska choreographed the ballet *La Valse;* Ida Rubenstein danced the lead.

Edith Evans created the role of Orinthia in George Bernard Shaw's play *The Apple Cart*.

Greta Garbo starred opposite Lew Ayres in Jacques Feyder's silent film *The Kiss*.

Felia Dubrovska and Serge Lifar danced the leads in George Balanchine's ballet *The Prodigal Son*.

Louise Brooks starred in G. W. Pabst's silent-film classic *Diary of a Lost Girl*.

Mary Pickford starred in her first "talkie," Sam Taylor's film *Coquette*, winning an Academy Award as best actress.

Peggy Wood and Noël Coward sang "I'll See You Again" in Coward's operetta *Bitter Sweet*.

Sylvia Sidney starred in Elmer Rice's play *Street Scene*.

Vicki Baum published the novel *Grand Hotel*, by far her best-known work.

Bessie Smith recorded "Nobody Knows You When You're Down and Out."

Gertrude Vanderbilt founded the Whitney Museum of American Art.

Bessie Love and Anita Page starred in Harry Beaumont's film *Broadway Melody*.

Elizabeth Bowen published the novel *The Last September*.

Georgia O'Keeffe painted *Black Cross with Red Sky*, *Black Cross, New Mexico*, *Black Hollyhock, Blue Larkspur*, *Iris*, *New York Night*, *Ranchos Church, Taos*, and *Yellow Cactus Flowers*.

Gertrude Berg began her 16-year run as Molly Goldberg in radio's *The Goldbergs* (1929–1945).

Jean Rhys published the novel *Quartet*.

Jessie Redmon Fauset published the novel *Plum Bun*.

Louise Bogan published the poetry collection *Dark Summer*.

b. Audrey Hepburn (Audrey Hepburn-Ruston, 1929–1993), British actress.

b. Beverly Sills (Belle Silverman, 1929– ), American soprano, a leading opera singer and opera director.

b. Adrienne Rich (1929– ), American poet and essayist, a leading radical feminist from the mid-1970s.

b. Brigid Antonia Brophy (1929–1995), British writer and critic, a novelist, short story writer, playwright, biographer, and essayist.

b. Jean Simmons (1929– ), British actress, a major star in Britain in the 1940s, whose career survived but did not flourish after a move to Hollywood.

b. Joan Anne Plowright (1929– ), British actress, a leading player on the British stage from the mid-1950s.

b. Toshiko Akiyoshi (1929– ), Manchuria-born American jazz pianist, leader of her own orchestra (from 1984).

b. Christa Wolf (1929– ), German writer.

b. Franca Rame (1929– ), Italian actress, director, and writer.

b. Mariama Ba (1929–1981), Senegalese writer.

b. Shirley Ann Grau (1929– ), American novelist.

d. Lillie Le Breton Langtry (1853–1929), British actress, company manager, and celebrity; a reigning sex symbol in her time, partly because of her relationship with the Prince of Wales.

d. Jeanne Eagels (1894–1929), American actress.

d. Lilli Lehmann (1848–1929), German soprano, a leading interpreter of Wagner.

d. Emma B. Steiner (1852–1929), American composer and conductor.

## 1930

### POLITICS/LAW/WAR

Association of Southern Women for the Prevention of Lynching (1930–1942) was founded by Jessie Daniel Ames, who became its director, responding to a call from black women who stressed that lynching could be ended only by concerted efforts among white women.

Women won the right to vote and be elected to office in South Africa and Turkey.

Italy's criminal code made disseminating birth control information a crime, increased penalties for abortions, and defined women's adultery as more serious than men's.

Indian independence leader Kamaldevi Chattopadhyay was imprisoned, as she would be on several other occasions before independence was won.

Alexandra Kollontai became Soviet trade representative to Sweden (1930–1945).

Zhenotdel, the women's section of the Soviet Communist Party, was abolished by Joseph Stalin.

b. Sandra Day O'Connor (1930– ), American lawyer, politician, an Arizona assistant attorney general, state senator, and judge who became the first woman appointed to the U.S. Supreme Court (1981).

b. Shirley Brittain Williams (1930– ), British socialist, writer, and politician, daughter of Vera Brittain; a Labour Party activist, later cofounder of the Social Democratic Party (1981).

b. Vigdis Finnbogadottir (1930– ), Icelandic theater director, who would become her country's first female president (1980).

b. Maria de Lourdes Pintasilgo (1930– ), Portuguese feminist, politician, and diplomat, who founded and led the Portuguese National Committee on the Status of Women (1970–1974) and was briefly her country's prime minister (1980).

b. Dolores Huerta (1930– ), American union activist who, with César Chávez, helped found and lead the United Farm Workers Union.

b. Imelda Romualdez Marcos (1930– ), wife of Philippine dictator Ferdinand Marcos, notable chiefly for her extravagant lifestyle.

b. Vilma Espin (1930– ), Cuban Communist and feminist, a colleague of Fidel Castro and the wife of his brother, Raul Castro.

d. Helene Lange (1848–1930), German educator and women's rights activist, a moderate leader who founded the German Women Teachers' Association (1889) and the Berlin Women's Association (1894).

d. Kate Barnard (1875–1930), American social reformer, teacher, labor organizer, and Oklahoma politician, a pioneer in child labor, education, and workers' health and safety reform.

d. Mary Harris "Mother" Jones (1830–1930), American teacher and labor organizer, for more than 50 years a considerable figure in the American labor movement.

## RELIGION/EDUCATION/EVERYDAY LIFE

British missionary Gladys Aylward traveled to Shanxi, China, there co-founding the "The Inn of the Sixth Happiness" to draw in local travelers and teach them the gospel; she became a Chinese citizen the following year and, persistently pressing against female footbinding, became the region's official "foot inspector."

African-American entrepreneur Annie Turnbo Malone transferred her business operations to Chicago, buying up a whole city block. She also made major philanthropic contributions, most notably to Howard and Wilberforce universities.

Dorothy Harrison Wood Eustis founded The Seeing Eye, the first American school training guide dogs for the blind, after learning of Germans' use of such dogs for war veterans.

Critical of working conditions in London's Marks & Spencer's, Flora Solomon was given the job of improving them. She developed innovative programs including maternity and sickness benefits, health care, holidays, and lunchrooms.

Ellen Church became the first airline stewardess, having suggested the notion to Boeing Air Transport (later United Airlines); she recruited other stewardesses, originally all, like herself, nurses (until 1942).

Pope Pius XI, in his *Casti connubii*, reaffirmed the Roman Catholic church's condemnation of contraception, though allowing use of the rhythm method.

Readers of Motoko Hani and Sochikazu Hani's magazine *Fujin no Tomo* (*Woman's Friend*) founded the national Friends' Association.

The women's magazine the *Malay Moon* (*Bulan Melayu*) was published by the Malay Women Teachers Association, founded by Hajjah Zainon Sulaiman (Ibu Zain).

Edith Hamilton published *The Greek Way*.

Alexandra David-Neel published *Voyage d'une Parisienne à Lhasa*.

British feminist Dora Marsden published *Mysteries of Christianity*.

British historian Ivy Pinchbeck published *Women Workers in the Industrial Revolution*.

Josephine Goldmark published *Pilgrims of '48*, about the life of her Czech immigrant parents.

Margaret Davies published *Life as We Have Known It*.

Susanne Langer published *The Practice of Philosophy*.

b. Nawa El Saadawi (1930– ), Egyptian doctor, a leading Arab world feminist writer and organizer.

b. Eva Burrows (1930– ), Australian religious leader who became international chief commander of the Salvation Army (1986).

### SCIENCE/TECHNOLOGY/MEDICINE

Anne Morrow Lindbergh and her husband, Charles Lindbergh, broke the transcontinental speed record flying across North America; that year she also became the first American woman to qualify for a glider's license.

National Birth Control Council (later Family Planning Association) was founded in Britain, chaired by Gertrude Denman (1930–1954). As both cofounder and practicing counselor, physician Helena Wright helped introduce new birth control methods, such as the intrauterine device (IUD); she also published the best-selling *The Sex Factor in Marriage*.

Mary Dennett's 1929 conviction under obscenity laws, for disseminating sex education materials, was overturned on appeal, supported by the American Civil Liberties Union.

Amy Johnson made a 17-day solo flight from London to Australia, the first woman to do so, winning a £10,000 prize from Britain's *Daily Mail*.

British archaeologist Gertrude Caton-Thompson conducted excavations at Egypt's Kharga Oasis (1930–1933).

Helene Deutsch published *Psychoanalysis of the Neuroses*.

Margaret Mead published *Growing Up in New Guinea*.

Bertha Van Hoosen founded the first human breast-milk bank, in Chicago.

British zoologist Sidnie Manton coauthored *Practical Vertebrate Morphology*.

Dorothy Weeks was the first woman to receive a doctorate in mathematics from the Massachusetts Institute of Technology.

Edith Patch became president of the Entomological Association of America, its first female head, and of the American Nature Study Society.

Marion E. Kenworthy became the first female psychiatry professor at Columbia University.

Martha Wollstein became the first female member of the American Pediatric Society.

Susan Isaacs published *Intellectual Growth of Young Children*.

Mary Orr Evershed became director of the historical section of the British Astronomical Association (1930–1944).

d. Christine Ladd-Franklin (1847–1930), American mathematician, specializing in logic, and psychologist, focusing on color vision.

d. Mary Ann Bird Scharlieb (1845–1930), British physician serving in England and India, where she founded the Victoria Hospital for women and the Women's Medical Service for India during World War I; also one of England's first female magistrates (1920).

d. Mary Whiton Calkins (1863–1930), American psychologist and philosopher, long at Wellesley (from 1887). She founded the first psychology laboratory at any American women's college (1891), and among the first in the country.

d. Anna Botsford Comstock (1854–1930), American naturalist and illustrator long associated with Cornell University.

### ARTS/LITERATURE

Greta Garbo played the title role in Clarence Brown's film *Anna Christie*, her first "talkie," based on Eugene O'Neill's 1921 play.

Marlene Dietrich starred in two classic Josef von Sternberg films: *The Blue Angel*, opposite Emil Jannings, and *Morocco*.

Agatha Christie introduced amateur detective Jane Marple in her mystery novel *Murder at the Vicarage*.

Dorothy L. Sayers introduced mystery writer and amateur detective Harriet Vane in her mystery novel *Strong Poison*.

Gertrude Lawrence and Noël Coward introduced "Some Day I'll Find You" in Coward's classic comedy *Private Lives*.

Lynn Fontanne and Alfred Lunt starred as Elizabeth and Essex in Maxwell Anderson's blank-verse play *Elizabeth the Queen*.

Margaret Ayer Barnes published her Pulitzer Prize–winning novel *Years of Grace*.

Norma Shearer starred in the film *The Divorcee*, winning a best actress Academy Award for her performance. She also starred opposite Robert Montgomery in Sidney Franklin's screen version of Noël Coward's play *Private Lives*.

Peggy Ashcroft as Desdemona starred opposite Paul Robeson in the title role in a London production of Shakespeare's *Othello*.

Sara Allgood starred as Juno in Alfred Hitchcock's film version of Sean O'Casey's play *Juno and the Paycock*.

Beatrice Lillie starred in *Charlot's Masquerade*.

Ethel Merman played her first starring role, introducing "I Got Rhythm," in George and Ira Gershwin's musical *Girl Crazy*.

Eva Le Gallienne starred in Susan Glaspell's play *Alison's House*, about an Emily Dickinson–like figure.

Juliana Force became the first director of the Whitney Museum (1930–1948), founded by Gertrude Vanderbilt Whitney.

Pearl Buck's first novel was *East Wind, West Wind*.

Babette Deutsch published the poetry collection *Fire for the Night*.

Dorothy Canfield published the novel *The Deepening Stream*.

Edna Ferber published the novel *Cimarron*.

Georgia O'Keeffe painted *Apple Blossoms Black and White*, *Clam Shell*, the *Jack-in-the-Pulpit* series, *Light Iris*, and *Red Rust Hills*.

Dorothy Parker published the short-story collection *Laments for Living*.

Gabriela Mistral published the poetry collection *Questions*.

Irna Phillips wrote a daily radio serial, *Painted Dreams*, regarded as the first radio "soap opera," later writing *Today's Children* and cowriting *The Guiding Light*.

Helen Tamiris became director of the School of American Dance (1930–1945).

Jean Rhys published the novel *After Leaving Mr. Mackenzie*.

Katherine Anne Porter published the short-story collection *Flowering Judas*.

American artist Cecilia Beaux published the autobiography *Background with Figures*.

Anne Green published the novel *The Selbys*.

Juana de Ibarbourou published the poetry collection *La rosa de los vientos*.

b. Anne Frank (1930–1944), Dutch-Jewish diarist.

b. Joanne Woodward (1930– ), American actress, a film, stage, and television star from the mid-1950s.

b. Roberta Peters (1930– ), American soprano, a leading singer who was a fixture at the Metropolitan Opera for more than three decades.

b. Lorraine Hansberry (1930–1965), American playwright.

b. Magdalena Abakanowicz (1931– ), Polish sculptor working primarily with woven and other fiber materials.

b. Elisabeth Frink (1930– ), British sculptor and painter.

b. Grace Ogot (1930– ), Kenyan writer.

b. Oriana Fallaci (1930– ), Italian writer, a leading interviewer.

b. Rosemary Harris (1930– ), British-American actress.

b. Shelagh Delaney (1930– ), British writer.

d. Emmy Destinn (1876–1930), Czech soprano, a leading turn-of-the-century opera singer, who created Minnie in Giacomo Puccini's *The Girl of the Golden West* (1910).

d. (Francesca Gaetana) Cosima Liszt Wagner (1837–1930), daughter of composer-pianist Franz Liszt and Countess Marie D'Agoult, and the wife of composer Richard Wagner, who devoted her life to his career, then to his memory and to the Bayreuth Festival.

d. Virginia Zucchi (1849–1930), Italian dancer and choreographer.

# 1931

## POLITICS/LAW/WAR

Hattie Wyatt Caraway was appointed to the U.S. Senate to fill out the term of her late husband, Thaddeus Caraway; she became the first woman elected to the U.S. Senate, in a special election (1932), then ran for reelection and won, serving until 1944.

Louise Bennett became the first woman to serve as president of the Irish Trades Union Congress (1931–1932).

Women won the right to vote and be elected to office in Chile, Portugal, and Spain.

Sylvia Pankhurst published the *Suffragette Movement*.

b. Isabelita (María Estela) Martínez de Perón (1931– ), Argentinian entertainer, the second wife of Juan Perón; after his death, she was president of Argentina (1974–1976).

b. Haydee Santamaria (1931– ), Cuban revolutionary, a colleague of Fidel Castro and Che Guevara from the early 1950s.

b. Karin Margareta Ahrland (1931– ), Swedish feminist, lawyer, and politician.

b. Shulamit Aloni (1931– ), Israeli teacher and lawyer, a politician and women's rights leader who founded the Civil Rights Party (1973).

d. Ida A. Harper (1851–1931), American writer and suffragist, long closely associated with Susan B. Anthony.

## RELIGION/EDUCATION/EVERYDAY LIFE

Jane Addams and Nicholas Murray Butler were corecipients of the Nobel Peace Prize.

Mary Ritter Beard published *On Understanding Women*.

Beryl Markham became a commercial pilot, transporting mail and passengers throughout East Africa, also pioneering in scouting game from the air.

Emily Post began a radio program and then a syndicated column.

French fashion designer Elsa Schiaparelli introduced clothing with padded shoulders (1931–1932).

Vida Scudder published her major scholarly work, *The Franciscan Adventure*, best-known of her 17 books on religion, literature, history, and politics.

International Kindergarten Union and the National Council of Primary Education merged to form the Association of Childhood Education International.

Helen Hall published *Case Studies of Unemployment*, sponsored by the National Federation of Settlements.

b. Barbara Walters (1931– ), American broadcaster who became a television star with the *Today* show (1963), then the first woman to coanchor an American network evening news program (1976–1978).

b. Barbara Clementine Harris (1931– ), African-American priest, the first woman to serve as bishop of the Episcopal Church (1989).

b. Alice Mitchell Rivlin (1931– ), American economist, the first director of the Congressional Budget Office (1975–1983) and deputy director of Management and Budget in the Clinton administration (1993–1996), later vice-chair of the Federal Reserve Board.

d. Anna (Garlin) Spencer (1851–1931), American minister, writer, and social reformer, an ordained Unitarian preacher (1891); also active in the Ethical Culture movement.

### SCIENCE/TECHNOLOGY/MEDICINE

Britain's National Birth Control Association campaigned for government provision of contraception information and devices to married couples on health grounds. Ealing was the first community to institute monthly birth control sessions.

Irmgard Lotz (later Flügge-Lotz) developed the Lotz method of calculating wingspan in determining lifting force for airplanes, regardless of wing shape.

Margaret Sanger published *My Fight for Birth Control.*

American archaeologist Ann Axtell Morris wrote *Digging in the Yucatan,* about work on the temples at Chichen Itza with her husband, Earl. H. Morris, and Jean Charlot; she also published professional monographs.

American Women's Hospitals Service (AWHS) began to concentrate its efforts in the poor areas of the Appalachians, in the eastern United States.

British archaeologist Margaret Murray published her popular book *The Splendor That Was Egypt.*

Annie Jump Cannon received the Draper Medal from the National Academy of Sciences.

American naturalist Florence Merriam Bailey won the Brewster Medal from the American Ornithologists' Union.

Margaret Washburn became the second woman to be a member of the National Academy of Sciences.

d. Charlotte Angas Scott (1858–1951), British-American mathematician, who founded and headed the mathematics department at Bryn Mawr College (1885–1925).

d. Harriet (Jemima Winifred) Clisby (1830–1931), Australian physician and feminist, late in life founder of L'Union des Femmes in Switzerland.

d. Kate Marsden (1859–1931), British traveler and nurse.

### ARTS/LITERATURE

Barbara Hepworth showed *Pierced Hemisphere Form,* with its pioneering use of inner space.

Pearl Buck published her Pulitzer Prize–winning novel *The Good Earth,* set in China.

Lotte Lenya starred as Jenny opposite Rudolph Forster as Mack the Knife in G. W. Pabst's German film version of Bertolt Brecht and Kurt Weill's *The Threepenny Opera* (1928).

Anna May Wong starred opposite Laurence Olivier in an English-language London production of the classic Chinese play *The Circle of Chalk.*

Sylvia Sidney starred opposite Philips Holmes in Josef von Sternberg's film *An American Tragedy,* based on Theodore Dreiser's 1925 novel, and opposite William Collier Jr. in King Vidor's film version of Elmer Rice's *Street Scene,* reprising her 1929 Broadway role.

Cheryl Crawford, Harold Clurman, and Lee Strasberg founded New York's Group Theater (1931–1941).

Greta Garbo starred as the World War I femme fatale and spy in George Fitzmaurice's film *Mata Hari.*

Lydia Lopokova, Alicia Markova, and Frederick Ashton danced the leads in Ashton's ballet *Façade.*

Martha Graham choreographed *Primitive Mysteries.*

Ninette de Valois founded the Vic-Wells Ballet Company and also choreographed the ballet *Job,* to music by Ralph Vaughan Williams.

Malvina Hoffman sculpted the series of 110 bronzes entitled *The Races of Man,* for the Hall of Man at Chicago's Marshall Field Museum of Natural History.

Lynn Fontanne starred opposite Alfred Lunt in Robert Sherwood's play *Reunion in Vienna*.

Ricarda Huch became the first female member of the Prussian Academy of Literature; she resigned two years later, as an anti-Nazi protest.

Virginia Woolf published the novel *The Waves*.

Adele Astaire and Fred Astaire starred in the Broadway musical *The Band Wagon*.

E. M. Delafield published *The Diary of a Provincial Lady*.

Gracie Fields starred in the film *Sally in Our Alley*, singing "Sally," which became her signature song.

Katharine Cornell starred as Elizabeth Barrett Browning in *The Barretts of Wimpole Street*, Rudolf Besier's play.

Lilian Baylis founded the Sadler's Wells theater.

Marlene Dietrich starred opposite Victor McLaglen in Josef von Sternberg's film *Dishonored*.

Ruth Crawford Seeger composed her *String Quartet*.

Ding Ling published the novel *Flood*.

Ethel Merman sang "Life Is Just a Bowl of Cherries" in *George White's Scandals*.

Georgia O'Keeffe painted *Cow's Skull—Red, White and Blue*, *Horse's Skull with White Rose*, and *Shell on Red*.

Leontine Sagan directed the film *Mädchen in Uniform*, set in a military-style boarding school and notable for its early, open treatment of lesbian themes.

Ivy Compton-Burnett published the novel *Men and Wives*.

Vita Sackville-West published the novel *All Passion Spent*.

Kay Boyle published the novel *Plagued by the Nightingale*.

Victoria Ocampo founded the periodical *Sur*, publishing many new Hispanic authors and translating works from other languages.

Willa Cather published the novel *Shadows on the Rock*.

Fannie Hurst published the novel *Back Street*, later much filmed.

Jessie Redmon Fauset published the novel *The Chinaberry Tree*.

Lou Andreas-Salomé published the autobiography *Mein Dank an Freud*, focusing on her work with Freud.

Miles Franklin published the novel *Old Blastus of Bandicoot*.

Winifred Holtby published the novel *Poor Caroline*.

b. Toni Morrison (Chloe Anthony Wofford, 1931– ), African-American writer and editor, whose body of work would make her one of the leading women of her time; she won the 1993 Nobel Prize for literature.

b. Anne Bancroft (Anna Maria Louisa Italiano, 1931– ), American actress, stage and screen star from the late 1950s.

b. Claire Bloom (1931– ), British actress, who became a stage and screen star in the 1950s; a major figure for more than four decades.

b. Fay Weldon (1931– ), British writer and feminist.

b. Leslie Caron (1931– ), French actress and dancer, a film star in the 1950s and early 1960s, and later a supporting player.

b. Márta Mészarós (1931– ), Hungarian film director.

b. Monica Vitti (Maria Luisa Ceciarelli, 1931– ), Italian actress.

b. Nelly Kaplan (1931– ), French director and writer.

d. Anna Pavlova (1882–1931), Russian dancer, one of the leading ballerinas of the 20th century.

d. Nellie Melba (Helen Porter Armstrong, 1861–1931), Australian soprano, a worldwide figure in opera (1880s–1920s), an extraordinarily popular figure, for whom melba toast and peach melba were named.

# 1932

## POLITICS/LAW/WAR

Congresswoman Mary T. Hopkins Norton was chair of the Labor Committee of the House of Representatives (1932–1947), overseeing passage of the Fair Labor Standards Act, which made sex-based salary distinctions illegal. She was the the first woman to be state chair of a major political party, the New Jersey Democrats.

Women won the right to vote and be elected to office in Thailand.

Alice M. Robertson became the first woman ever to preside over the U.S. House of Representatives, briefly, as a ceremonial honor.

Hilda Martindale became director of Women's Establishments in Britain's Treasury department.

Jessie Wallace Hughan published *The Challenge of Mars and Other Verse.*

b. Wu Wenying (1932– ), Chinese politician.

d. Marion Phillips (1881–1932), British feminist, socialist, and politician, a key figure in the British Labour Party, its leading female officer (from 1918) and a member of Parliament.

## RELIGION/EDUCATION/EVERYDAY LIFE

Dorothy Day and Peter Maurin founded the Catholic Worker Movement.

"Babe" Didrikson (later Zaharias) became the first internationally recognized female athlete, at the 1932 Los Angeles Olympic Games, where she won gold medals in the javelin throw and hurdles and tied for first in the high jump. Earlier that year she had gained publicity as the "Texas Tomboy," winning five gold medals at the Amateur Athletic Union Championships.

Bonnie Parker and Clyde Barrow began their bloody tour of the American South and Midwest, committing numerous robberies and killing 15 people; Parker composed a poem about it, "The Story of Suicide Sal," referring to a nickname given her by a journalist.

Helen Diner (Bertha Eckstein-Diner) published *Mothers and Amazons*, positing the existence and historic primacy of early matriarchies.

American mountaineers Miriam O'Brien (later Underhill) and Alice Damesme reached the top of the Matterhorn, in the first women-only ascent; O'Brien had been defeated on a previous attempt (1931).

Annie Peck made her final ascent, of New Hampshire's Mt. Madison, at age 82, and published *Flying over South America—20,000 Miles by Air.*

Dora Russell wrote about her educational theories in *In Defence of Children.*

Edith Hamilton published *The Roman Way.*

Ella Deloria published *Dakota Texts*, a collection of tales of her people, the Dakotas (Sioux).

d. Florence Kelley (1859–1932), American social reformer, feminist, and civil rights and consumer advocate, longtime executive secretary of the National Consumers' League (1899–1932) and founder of the National Child Labor Committee (1902).

d. Ida Bell Wells (Barnett, 1862–1932), African-American antilynching crusader and journalist.

d. Julia Clifford Lathrop (1858–1932), American social worker and reformer, who was the first director of the U.S. Children's Bureau.

## SCIENCE/TECHNOLOGY/MEDICINE

Amelia Earhart became the first woman to fly solo across the Atlantic Ocean and to receive the Distinguished Flying Cross. On her subsequent tour, she became the first woman to fly from the Atlantic to the Pacific and back.

Spurred by the National Birth Control Association, Plymouth founded Britain's first city-sponsored permanent birth control clinic; in three decades there would be over 500.

American psychologist Florence Goodenough developed the Minnesota Preschool Scale for assessing the mental status of young children.

Emmy Noether became the first woman ever to address a general session of the International Congress of Mathematics.

Marian Cummings became the first American woman to gain her commercial pilot's license.

Ruth Nichols was the first American woman to pilot a commercial passenger plane.

b. Dian Fossey (1932–1985), American primatologist.

d. Ellen Churchill Semple (1863–1932), American geographer who helped establish geography as an academic discipline, focusing on the influences of the physical environment on societies and their history, her last book being *The Geography of the Mediterranean Region: Its Relation to Ancient History*.

d. Gertrude Jekyll (1843–1932), British horticulturalist who helped move gardens from formal to more natural styles.

d. June Etta Downey (1875–1932), American psychologist long associated with the University of Wyoming.

### ARTS/LITERATURE

Marlene Dietrich (as Shanghai Lily), Anna May Wong, and Clive Brook starred in *Shanghai Express*, Josef von Sternberg's classic film set in the Chinese Civil War.

Katharine Hepburn starred opposite John Barrymore in George Cukor's film *A Bill of Divorcement*.

Rosamond Lehmann published the novel *Invitation to the Waltz*.

Clare Boothe (later Luce) and Fred Astaire introduced Cole Porter's song "Night and Day" in *The Gay Divorcée*.

Jean Harlow starred opposite Clark Gable in the film *Red Dust*, emerging as one of the leading "sex symbol" stars of the 1930s.

Joan Crawford starred as the prostitute opposite Walter Huston as the preacher in Lewis Milestone's sound-film version of *Rain*, based on the 1921 Somerset Maugham story.

Amy Beach composed the opera *Cabildo*.

Beatrice Lillie sang "Mad Dogs and Englishmen" in *The Third Little Show*.

Claudette Colbert starred opposite Fredric March in Cecil B. DeMille's Bible epic *The Sign of the Cross*.

Georgia O'Keeffe painted *Bleeding Heart, Cross By the Sea, Canada, Grey Hills II, Nature Forms, Gaspé,* and *The White Trumpet Flower*.

Elisabeth Lutyens composed the ballet *The Birthday of the Infanta*.

Pianist Marguerite Long premiered Maurice Ravel's *Piano Concerto in G*; Ravel conducted.

George Burns and Gracie Allen began their 26-year-long run on the airwaves: first on radio (1932–1950), then television (1950–1958).

Ina Claire starred in S. N. Behrman's play *Biography*.

La Argentenita and Garcia Lorca founded the Ballet de Madrid.

Irene Dunne starred opposite John Boles in *Back Street*, John M. Stahl's film melodrama based on Fannie Hurst's 1931 novel.

Kay Boyle published the novel *Year Before Last*.

Pearl Buck published the novel *Sons*.

Dorothy Arzner directed the film *Merrily We Go to Hell*.

Leni Riefenstahl directed the film *The Blue Light*.

Zelda Fitzgerald published the autobiographical novel *Save Me the Waltz*.

Leontine Sagan directed the film *Men of Tomorrow*.

b. Elizabeth Taylor (1932– ), British-American film star, a major figure as a child then adult actress, and later in her life as a leading anti-AIDS campaigner.

b. Miriam Makeba (1932– ), black South African singer, popular from the early 1950s, banned and forced into exile because of her antiapartheid activities in the late 1950s, long a worldwide symbol of the South African freedom movement.

b. Debbie (Mary Frances) Reynolds (1932– ), American film star of the 1950s and 1960s; mother of author-actress Carrie Fisher.

b. Delphine Seyrig (1932–1990), French actress and feminist.

b. Sylvia Plath (1932–1963), American writer.

b. Billie Whitelaw (1932– ), British actress, best known as an interpreter of Samuel Beckett's work.

b. Cicely Tyson (1932– ), African-American stage and screen star of the 1970s; later largely in supporting roles.

b. Ellen Burstyn (Edna Rae Gilloooly, 1932– ), American stage and screen star; later largely in supporting roles.

b. Harriet Andersson (1932– ), Swedish actress.

b. Lola Beltrán (Maria Lucila Beltrán Ruiz, 1932–1996), Mexican mariachi singer.

b. Shirley Conran (1932– ), British writer, editor, and designer.

d. (Isabella) Augusta Persse Gregory (Lady Gregory, 1852–1932), Irish playwright, translator, and theater director, a founder of Dublin's Abbey Theatre.

d. Minnie Maddern Fiske (1865–1932), American actress, director, and theater company manager, for five decades a major figure in the American theater.

d. Jesse Irene Sargent (1852–1932), American art historian and Arts and Crafts movement leader.

d. Jessie Bonstelle (1872–1932), American actress and theater manager, long a theater proprietor in Detroit (1910–1932).

## 1933

### POLITICS/LAW/WAR

Frances Perkins became Franklin D. Roosevelt's secretary of labor and the first American woman to be a cabinet member (1933–1945).

Eleanor Roosevelt became the first First Lady to hold her own press conference.

Ruth Bryan Owen (Rohde) became America's first female diplomat, appointed by President Franklin Roosevelt as representative to Denmark and Iceland.

Germans opened their first concentration camp for women, at Ravensbrück, north of Berlin.

Minnie D. Craig was the first American woman elected speaker of a state house of representatives, in North Dakota.

Guerrilla leader Rani Gaidinliu was captured in Assam and imprisoned by the British Indian colonial government (1933–1947).

In Italy, Benito Mussolini's government limited women's access to competitive state employment examinations.

Rosika Schwimmer campaigned for world citizenship for people who, like herself, no longer had a country; she had fled Hungary (1920) but had been refused citizenship in the United States (1929) after stating that she would not bear arms in case of war.

Margaret Postgate Cole and G. D. H. Cole published *Review of Europe Today*.

b. (Maria) Corazon Cojuangco Aquino (1933– ), Philippines political leader who, from the assassination of her husband (1983), led the opposition party, then the revolution, becoming democratically elected president of the Philippine Republic (1986–1992).

b. Ruth Bader Ginsburg (1933– ), American lawyer and judge, longtime director of the American Civil Liberties Union's Women's Rights Project, the first tenured female law professor at Columbia Law School (1972–1980), then federal Court of Appeals judge (1980–1993), who became the second woman appointed to the U.S. Supreme Court (1993).

b. Ann Richards (1933– ), American Democratic politician, governor of Texas (1991–1995).

b. Dianne Feinstein (1933– ), American politician; mayor of San Francisco, she was later elected to the U.S. Senate (1992).

b. Anita Gradin (1933– ), Swedish socialist, journalist, and politician.

d. Alva Erskine Belmont (1853–1933), American feminist and suffragist, a society figure best known for much of her life as the wife of William Vanderbilt and then Oliver Belmont; she who emerged as a women's rights movement leader after Belmont's 1908 death.

d. Clara Eissner Zetkin (1857–1933), German socialist and then communist, a founder of the German Communist Party (1918) and key figure in worldwide communist work among women. Her position—and that of her party—was that the advent of socialism was the indispensable precondition for the full equality of women, and that the fight to win socialism necessarily took precedence over the fight for women's freedom; this stance was the exact opposite of that taken by the worldwide women's movement.

d. Emily Ferguson Murphy (1868–1933), Canadian lawyer, judge, social reformer, writer, and women's rights advocate, the first female magistrate in the British Empire (1916), whose legal right to rule was at the center of a landmark reevaluation of women's legal status in Canada and within the entire British Empire.

d. Elizaveta Kovalskaya (1850–1933), Russian anarchist, who spent much of her life imprisoned in Siberia (1881–1903) and in Swiss exile (1903–1917).

d. Mary Clyens Lease (1850–1933), American teacher, labor journalist, feminist, writer, and politician, a populist leader in the mid-South during the 1890s.

### RELIGION/EDUCATION/EVERYDAY LIFE

Dorothy Day and Peter Maurin founded the *Catholic Worker*, the organ of the Catholic Worker Movement.

With repeal of the 18th (Prohibition) Amendment to the Constitution, the Women's Christian Temperance Union declined in influence and power, though continuing to push for total abstinence from alcohol and against smoking and drugs, especially through youth education.

Abala Bose became secretary of the Brahmo Balika Shikshalaya (School for Girls, ca. 1933), remaining there for 26 years, also introducing Montessori teaching methods into India.

Agnes Smedley published *Chinese Destinies* and *China's Red Army Marches*.

Joan Robinson published her first book, *The Economics of Imperfect Competition*.

Mother Mary Gerald Barry became prioress general of the Dominican Sisters of Adrian, Michigan, the Congregation of the Most Holy Rosary (1933–1961).

Restaurateur Ruth Wakefield created the Toll House cookie, the "original" chocolate chip cookie.

Advertisements for sanitary napkins were first accepted in American magazines, starting with a Kotex ad in *Good Housekeeping*.

British social scientist Barbara Wootton published *Twos and Threes*.

Mabel Dodge Luhan published her *Intimate Memoirs* in four volumes (1933–1937).

d. Annie Wood Besant (1847–1933), British suffragist and socialist, who in India (from 1893) became a leading theosophist, educator, and politician, founding a college (1898) and becoming president of the Congress Party (1917–1923).

d. Mary Parker Follett (1868–1933), American political economist and community worker, internationally known for her lectures on industrial relations.

d. Elinore Pruitt Rupert Steward (1876–1933), American homesteader, best known for her autobiographical works (1913; 1915).

### SCIENCE/TECHNOLOGY/MEDICINE

Emmy Noether published her key paper "Nichtkommunutative [Noncommutative] Algebra." That same year she, with other Jewish professors, was dismissed from her university post by the Nazis and emigrated to America.

German researcher Ida Noddack first proposed that puzzling results from experiments with radioactive materials might be explained by the breakup of the nucleus of the material, later called *nuclear fission*.

Gladys Anderson Emerson joined the Institute of Experimental Biology of the University of California at Berkeley (1933–1942), where she would be the first to isolate vitamin E and study its properties.

American archaeologist Ann Axtell Morris published *Digging in the Southwest*.

British child psychologist Susan Isaacs was appointed to head the Department of Child Development at the London Institute of Education (1933–1943). She also published *Social Development of the Young*.

b. Joycelyn Elders (1933– ), American pediatrician who became the Clinton administration surgeon general (1993–1994).

d. Kate Gleason (1865–1933), American mechanical engineer who helped develop the Gleason gear planer (1893) and entrepreneur who expanded her family's machine tool company; the first female member of the American Society of Mechanical Engineers. Funds from her estate helped establish the Rochester Institute of Technology.

d. Christine Murrell (1874–1933), British physician, the first woman elected to the General Medical Council of Great Britain (1933).

## ARTS/LITERATURE

Katharine Hepburn starred opposite Douglas Fairbanks in Lowell Sherman's film *Morning Glory*.

Ginger Rogers and Fred Astaire starred in *Flying Down to Rio*, the first of their 10 dance-film classics.

Anna Neagle and Fernand Gravet starred in *Bitter Sweet*, Herbert Wilcox's film version of Noël Coward's musical.

Greta Garbo starred opposite John Gilbert in the title role of Rouben Mamoulian's film *Queen Christina*.

Ethel Waters, Marilyn Miller, and Clifton Webb starred on Broadway in Irving Berlin's musical *As Thousands Cheer*. Waters also sang "Stormy Weather" in *The Cotton Club Parade*.

Ruby Keeler, Bebe Daniels, Ginger Rogers, Warner Baxter, George Brent, and Dick Powell starred in *42nd Street*, Lloyd Bacon's classic film musical choreographed by Busby Berkeley.

Gertrude Stein published *The Autobiography of Alice B. Toklas*.

Helen Hayes and Helen Menken starred on Broadway in Maxwell Anderson's play *Mary of Scotland*.

Joan Blondell, Ruby Keeler, Dick Powell, and Ginger Rogers starred in Mervyn LeRoy's film musical *Gold Diggers of 1933*, choreographed by Busby Berkeley.

Lynn Fontanne, Alfred Lunt, and Noël Coward starred in Coward's comedy *Design for Living*.

Miriam Hopkins, Fredric March, and Gary Cooper starred in Ernst Lubitsch's film version of Noël Coward's play *Design for Living*. Hopkins also starred in Steven Roberts's screen version of William Faulkner's antilynching novel *The Story of Temple Drake*.

Vera Brittain published *Testament of Youth*, the first of what would become a three-volume autobiography.

Alicia Markova became the prima ballerina of the Vic-Wells Ballet (1933–1935).

Dorothy L. Sayers published *Murder Must Advertise*.

Katharine Cornell starred on Broadway in Sidney Howard's *Alien Corn*.

Dorothy Parker published the short-story collection *After Such Pleasures*.

María Cadilla de Martínez published *La Poesía Popular en Puerto Rico*, her Ph.D. thesis for the Universidad Central of Madrid, which became a popular textbook in Latin America.

Clare Boothe (later Luce) became managing editor of *Vanity Fair* (1933–1934) and published the novel *Stuffed Shirts*.

Dorothy Arzner directed the film *Christopher Strong*.

Edith Evans created the role of Gwenny in Emlyn Williams's play *The Late Christopher Bean*.

Mae West starred in the film farce *She Done Him Wrong*.

Edith Sitwell published *English Eccentrics*.

Fannie Hurst published the novel *Imitation of Life*.

Jessie Redmon Fauset published the novel *Comedy: American Style*.

Marjorie Kinnan Rawlings published the novel *South Moon Under*.

Lou Andreas-Salomé published the autobiography *Grundriss einiger Lebenserinnerungen*.

Winifred Holtby published the novels *Mandea! Mandea!* and *The Astonishing Island*.

b. Brigitte Bardot (Camille Javal, 1933– ) French actress, the "sex kitten" film star of the 1950s, who became a leading environmentalist in the 1980s.

b. Susan Sontag (1933– ), American writer and director, who emerged as a major essayist in the mid-1960s.

b. Kim Novak (1933– ), American film star of the 1950s and 1960s.

b. Elizabeth Montgomery (1933–1995), American actress, Samantha Stevens in television's *Bewitched* (1964–1972).

b. Chryssa (1933– ), American sculptor.

b. Janet Abbott Baker (1933– ), British mezzo-soprano.

b. Nina Simone (Eunice Wayman, 1933– ), American popular singer.

d. Sara Teasdale (1884–1933), American poet.

d. Elizabeth Thompson Butler (1850–1933), British painter and writer, best known by far for her martial paintings.

## 1934

### POLITICS/LAW/WAR

Florence Ellinwood Allen became the first woman to sit on the U.S. Court of Appeals (1934–1959).

Gertrud Scholtz-Klink became head of the Nazi Women's Group and chief Nazi women's leader (*Reichsfrauenführerin*).

Women won the right to vote and be elected to office in Brazil and Cuba.

Italian antifascist women founded the periodical *La voce della donne*; among its noted editors and contributors was Teresa Noce.

Katherine F. Lenrott became head of the U.S. Children's Bureau.

Cornelia Sorabji published *The Memoirs of Cornelia Sorabji* and the autobiographical *India Calling*.

Martha Bol Poel became president of the Belgian National Council of Women.

Elizabeth Dilling published *The Red Network: A Who's Who and Handbook of Radicalism for Patriots*.

b. Winnie Nomzano Mandela (1934– ), black South African social worker and African National Congress leader, wife of Nelson Mandela; she became one of the world's leading women during the course of the long fight for freedom in her country, though she later became embroiled in charges of misuse of power.

b. Carla Anderson Hills (1934– ), American lawyer, who served two Republican administrations, as U.S. secretary of housing and urban development (1975–1977) and U.S. trade representative (1988–1992).

b. Jane Burke Byrne (1934– ), American politician who became mayor of Chicago (1979–1983).

b. Raisa Maksimova Titorenko Gorbachev (1934– ), Russian teacher who in the late 1980s became a symbol of the new Soviet Union as wife of Soviet premier Mikhail Gorbachev.

b. Ulrike Meinhof (1934–1976), German anarchist-terrorist, a leader of the Red Army Faction (Baader-Meinhof Group); captured in 1976, she allegedly committed suicide in her cell while on trial.

b. Kate Millett (1934– ), American radical feminist, writer, teacher, and sculptor, best known for her *Sexual Politics* (1970).

d. Kate Malcolm Sheppard (1848–1934), New Zealand feminist, a leader of the successful fight for women's suffrage and first president of her country's National Council of Women (1896).

d. Matilde Bajer (1840–1934), Danish feminist and suffragist, a leading figure in Danish and European women's rights movements.

### RELIGION/EDUCATION/EVERYDAY LIFE

Ruth Benedict published *Patterns of Culture*, taking the position that cultures follow differing dominant patterns and positing cultural relativity and equality, in direct refutation of racialist theories.

Cissy (Eleanor) Medill Patterson was the first American woman to publish a major daily newspaper, the Washington *Herald*.

Dorothy Day and Peter Maurin founded St. Joseph's House of Hospitality in New York, the first of the network of refuges operated by the Catholic Worker Movement.

Mary Madeleva Wolff was appointed president of St. Mary's College, Notre Dame, Indiana (1934–1961).

Eleanor Rathbone published *Child Marriage: The Indian Minotaur* as part of her widening concern over women's issues in India.

Conchita Cintrón first publicly appeared on horseback in a bullfight ring at age 12, as a *rejoneadora*.

Elizabeth Kingsley invented the double-crostic puzzle, beginning weekly puzzles in the *Saturday Review of Literature*.

María Cadilla de Martínez was elected as the only female member of the Puerto Rican Historical Academy.

Evangeline Booth was chosen as general of international forces of the Salvation Army (1934–1939).

Mary Hirsch became the first American woman licensed to train Thoroughbred horses.

Sophonisba Breckinridge published *The Family and the State*.

Youth Aliyah was founded by members of the Jewish women's organization Hadassah, most notably Recha Freier in Germany and Henrietta Szold, its director in Palestine; it provided aid and resettlement to refugee children.

British social scientist Barbara Wootton published *Plan or No Plan*.

Frances Yates published her first book, *John Florio*.

Jessie Bernard and her husband, Luther Lee Bernard, published *Sociology and the Study of International Relations*.

Mildred Cable and Francesca French published *A Desert Journal*.

Winifred Holtby published *Women and a Changing Civilisation*.

b. Gloria Steinem (1934– ), American writer and feminist, a women's movement celebrity who was a founder and longtime editor of *Ms.* magazine (1971–1989).

b. (Constance) Marie Abraham Patterson (1934– ), British trade unionist, associated with the Transport and General Workers' Union (from 1957) and the Trades Union Congress (TUC, 1963–1984), as chairman (1974–1975; 1977).

b. Mary Quant (1934– ), British designer and entrepreneur who made London a fashion center, best known for her introduction of the miniskirt.

b. Maureen Catherine ("Little Mo") Connolly (1934–1969), American tennis player.

d. Elizabeth Hawkins-Whitshed (Mrs. Aubrey) Le Blond (1861–1934), British mountaineer, the first woman to lead guideless parties on European climbs and first president of the Ladies' Alpine Club (1907–1912; 1932–1934).

d. Bonnie Parker (1910–1934), American outlaw, one of the most notorious gangsters of the early 1930s; killed in a police ambush near Giblans, Louisiana, after a series of robberies and murders with her partner, Clyde Barrow, both Depression-era folk heroes.

d. Katherine Gibbs (1865–1934), American entrepreneur and educator who developed a chain of business schools for women; later criticized by some for directing women to the "pink-collar ghetto" of undervalued, underpaid office work.

d. Maggie Lena Walker (1867–1934), African-American fraternal-society executive and banker.

## SCIENCE/TECHNOLOGY/MEDICINE

Irène Joliot-Curie and Frédéric Joliot-Curie became the first persons ever to artificially induce radioactivity, bombarding an element to cause its transformation into another, with release of particles.

American balloonist Jeanette Ridlou and her husband and partner, French chemist Jean Piccard, flew nearly 58,000 feet high in a balloon; together they made several innovations in balloon technology.

Florence Hawley Ellis pioneered the use of statistics in archaeology, in a work tying the Chaco culture's desertion of sites to ecological change.

Industrial physician Alice Hamilton published her standard text *Industrial Toxicology*, later revised with Harriet L. Hardy (1949).

The National Geographic Society awarded its Hubbard Gold Medal to Charles Lindbergh and Anne Morrow Lindbergh, who served as co-pilot, navigator, and radio operator to her husband, for their mapping of transoceanic air routes.

Dorothea Klumpke Roberts was awarded the Cross of the Legion of Honor for her contributions to French astronomy.

Leta Hollingworth coauthored the book *The Problem of Mental Disorder*.

New Zealand aviator Jean Batten flew solo from England to Australia, beating Amy Johnson's solo record by four days.

British botanist Agnes Arber published *The Gramineae: A Study of Cereal, Bamboo and Grass*.

British psychoanalyst Marion Milner, writing as Joanne Field, published *A Life of One's Own*.

American archaeologist-ethnologist Frederica de Laguna published *The Archaeology of Cook Inlet, Alaska*.

British physician Janet Vaughan published *The Anaemias*.

Helen Richey was the first woman employed for air mail transport.

b. Jane (Van Lawick-) Goodall (1934– ), British zoologist noted for her studies of chimpanzees in East Africa.

d. Marie (Maria) Sklodowska Curie (1867–1934), Polish physicist and chemist working in France, the first person to receive two Nobel prizes, both in science, and the first woman to win a Nobel; she died of leukemia, probably caused by her long exposure to radioactivity.

d. Cornelia Maria Clapp (1849–1934), American zoologist long associated with Mount Holyoke and the Woods Hole Marine Biological Laboratory.

d. Elizabeth Knight Britton (1858–1934), American botanist, specializing in the study of mosses (bryology); 15 species of plants were named for her, as was the moss genus *Bryobrittonia*.

## Arts/Literature

Claudette Colbert starred opposite Clark Gable in Frank Capra's classic film comedy *It Happened One Night*, winning a best actress Academy Award. She also starred as *Cleopatra* in Cecil B. DeMille's film epic.

Käthe Kollwitz created the eight lithographs in her series *Death*, finding the essence of the Nazi regime and portraying the tragedy then befalling humanity (1934–1935).

Isak Dinesen published the short-story collection *Seven Gothic Tales*.

Katherine Emery, Anne Revere, and Florence McGee starred in Lillian Hellman's play *The Children's Hour*, a pioneering work about a charge of lesbian sexual preference that destroyed the careers of two teachers.

Myrna Loy and William Powell played Nora and Nick Charles in W. S. Van Dyke's classic film mystery-comedy *The Thin Man*, based on the 1932 Dashiell Hammett novel; the first of their five "Thin Man" films.

Agatha Christie published the novel *Murder on the Orient Express*.

Dorothy L. Sayers published *The Nine Tailors*, a classic mystery set in the Fen country.

Carole Lombard starred opposite John Barrymore in Howard Hawks's *Twentieth Century*.

Edna St. Vincent Millay published the poetry collection *Wine from these Grapes*.

Ethel Merman starred in Cole Porter's Broadway musical *Anything Goes*, introducing "I Get a Kick out of You" and the title song.

Fay Bainter starred on Broadway opposite Walter Huston in *Dodsworth*, Sidney Howard's stage version of Sinclair Lewis's novel.

Ginger Rogers and Fred Astaire starred in Mark Sandrich's film *The Gay Divorcée*.

Galina Ulanova created the role of Maria in Rostislav Zacharov's ballet *Fountain of Bakhchisaray*.

Jessie Matthews starred in the film version of Victor Saville's stage musical *Evergreen*.

Ninette de Valois's ballet *The Haunted Ballroom* premiered at the Vic-Wells Ballet.

Zora Neale Hurston published the novel *Jonah's Gourd Vine*.

Helen Tamiris choreographed the *Walt Whitman Suite*.

Jane Cowl starred in S. N. Behrman's play *Rain from Heaven*.

Marlene Dietrich starred in the title role of Josef von Sternberg's film *The Scarlet Empress*.

June Walker starred opposite Henry Fonda in *The Farmer Takes a Wife*, Frank B. Elser and Marc Connelly's stage comedy.

Shirley Temple sang "On the Good Ship Lollipop" in the film *Bright Eyes* and starred in the film *Little Miss Marker*.

Tallulah Bankhead created the Judith Traherne role on Broadway in *Dark Victory*.

Anne Green published the novel *Fools Rush In*.

Gertrude Atherton became the first woman to serve as president of the National Academy of Literature.

Isabel Bishop showed her painting *Nude*.

Henry Handel Richardson (Henrietta Robertson Richardson) published the novel *The Young Cosima*.

Jean Rhys published the novel *Voyage in the Dark*.

Marguerite Yourcenar published the novel *A Coin in Nine Hands*.

Rose Macaulay published the novel *Going Abroad*.

b. Shirley MacLaine (Shirley MacLean Beaty, 1934– ) American actress, dancer, and writer, a film star in comedy during the 1950s and 1960s, who then emerged as a major dramatic star.

b. Sophia Loren (Sofia Scicolone, 1934– ) Italian film star, a worldwide sex symbol in the 1950s, who in the 1960s gained recognition as a powerful and versatile actress.

b. Maggie (Margaret Natalie) Smith (1934– ), British stage and screen star, best known internationally for her title role in the film *The Prime of Miss Jean Brodie* (1969).

b. Judi (Judith Olivia) Dench (1934– ), British actress, a leading figure on the British stage from the mid-1960s.

b. Audre Geraldin Lorde (1934– ), American poet.

b. Joan Didion (1934– ), American essayist, novelist, and screenwriter, whose work explores the alienation of many modern women.

b. (Karen) Fleur Adcock (1934– ), New Zealand poet.

b. Barbara Loden (1934–1980), American actress and director.

b. Petula Clark (Sally Olwen, 1934– ), British singer and actress, originally a child star.

b. Shirley Jones (1934– ), American actress and singer.

d. Gertrude Stanton Käsebier (1852–1934), American photographer, a leading figure in photography as it fully emerged as an art form and a member of the Photo-Secession.

d. Marie Dressler (1871–1934), Canadian vaudeville singer and film actress.

d. Mary Austin (1868–1934), American writer.

# 1935

## POLITICS/LAW/WAR

The landmark Social Security Act set up a system of guaranteed retirement benefits for working women and men, and included several long-sought benefits and protections for women and children; it was the basis for the massive American federal-state social welfare system that developed, covering later years, disability, survivors, health care, unemployment compensation, and welfare laws and regulations.

President Franklin D. Roosevelt appointed Anna Rosenberg director of the National Recovery Administration (NRA), the first of her several major New Deal appointments (1935–1945).

Martha Black was elected to represent the Yukon in Canada's Parliament (1935–1940), succeeding her husband, George Black, who later returned to succeed her (1940–1949).

Belgian feminist Martha Bol Poel became president of the International Council of Women (1935–1940).

Carrie Chapman Catt published *Why Wars Must Cease*.

Margaret Postgate Cole and G. D. H. Cole founded the New Fabian Research Bureau, a central resource for the Labour Party through the postwar period.

Jessie Wallace Hughan published *The Beginnings of War Resistance*.

Sylvia Pankhurst published *The Life of Emmeline Pankhurst*.

b. Geraldine Anne Ferraro (1935– ), American lawyer and politician, U.S. congresswoman (1979–1984) who became the first woman major-party vice-presidential candidate (1984).

b. Djamila Bouhired (1935– ), Algerian revolutionary, a terrorist to the French and a national heroine to the Algerians.

b. Fadéla M'rabet (1935– ), Algerian writer and feminist.

### RELIGION/EDUCATION/EVERYDAY LIFE

National Council of Negro Women (NCNW) was founded in New York City by 29 women from 14 organizations, including Mary Church Terrell, Dorothy Ferebee, Mabel Staupers, Charlotte Hawkins Brown, and Mary McLeod Bethune, its first president (1935–1949). The national network sought to coordinate member organizations' activities and improve black women's status.

Mary McLeod Bethune was awarded the Springarn Medal of the National Association for the Advancement of Colored People (NAACP).

Abala Bose started the Women's Industrial Cooperative Home in Calcutta; it later became a relief center for women from East Pakistan (now Bangladesh).

Anne Morrow Lindbergh published *North to the Orient*.

Beatrice Potter Webb and Sidney Webb published *Soviet Communism: A New Civilization?*

Ruth Benedict published *Zuni Mythology*.

b. Lyudmila Yevgenevna Belousova (Protopopov) (1935– ), Russian ice-skater who with her husband, Oleg Protopopov, formed the world's dominant figure-skating pair in the 1960s, with four European, four world, and two Olympic gold medals. She was noted for her "death spiral."

b. Susan Brownmiller (1935– ), American feminist, author of *Against Our Will: Men, Women and Rape* (1975), whose major focus has been on rape and other kinds of sexual violence, which she regards as a tool of woman's subjugation used by all men against all women—literally, not metaphorically. Her strong advocacy of outlawing pornography has given her many conservative allies and brought her into conflict with many other feminists and civil liberties defenders.

b. Pat Harper (Patricia Harper, 1935–1994), American television news anchor.

d. Jane Addams (1860–1935), American reformer, one of the leading women of the late 19th and early 20th centuries, who for almost 50 years took the lead on a wide range of social reform, women's rights, antiwar, and civil liberties issues. Winner of the Nobel Peace Prize (1931), she was a founder of Hull House (1889), the National Federation of Settlements (president 1911–1935), the World War I Women's Peace Party (1915), the Women's International League for Peace and Freedom (1919), and the American Civil Liberties Union (1920).

d. Charlotte Perkins Gilman (1860–1935), American feminist writer, reformer, and utopian socialist, author of highly regarded practical books on women's economic issues and the utopian novel *Herland* (1915).

In our steady insistence on proclaiming sex-distinction we have grown to consider most human attributes as masculine attributes, for the simple reason that they were allowed for men and forbidden to women.

— Charlotte Perkins Gilman, in *Women and Economics* (1898).

d. Martha Carey Thomas (1857–1935), American educator and feminist who became dean and English professor at then-new Bryn Mawr College (1884), then its president (1894–1922).

d. Annie Smith Peck (1850–1935), American mountaineer who became a celebrity with her climb of the Matterhorn (1895), and for whom a peak in Peru was named (1927); she was the first woman admitted to the America School of Classical Studies in Athens (1885).

## SCIENCE/TECHNOLOGY/MEDICINE

Irène Joliot-Curie and Jean Frédéric Joliot-Curie won the 1935 Nobel Prize for chemistry for their work on radioactivity; Irène's mother, Marie Curie, had earlier won two Nobel Prizes, making them the only mother-and-daughter pair of Nobel winners.

Marie Curie's *Radioactivité* was published posthumously.

Physician Alice Hamilton studied health dangers in factories making a new substance, nylon, and produced a special report, *Women Workers and Industrial Poisons*, on hazards faced in trades where women commonly worked, such as pottery, printing, and type founding.

Margaret Mead published *Sex and Temperament in Three Primitive Societies*, a cross-cultural view of women's position in society.

American aviator Jacqueline Cochran flew in the trans-American Bendix Race, the first woman to do so.

New Zealand aviator Jean Batten was the first woman to fly across the Atlantic from England to Brazil, also setting a new speed record.

Agnes Meara Chase published her *First Book of Grasses*.

Marie Stopes published her classic work *Fuel*.

b. Sylvia Earle Mead (1935– ), American marine biologist, who led the first all-woman underwater expedition (1970).

d. Emmy (Amalie) Noether (1882–1935), German mathematician whose work on the general theory of ideals, noncommutative algebra, and abstract algebra was sufficiently original to have inspired a "Noether school."

## ARTS/LITERATURE

Anne Brown and Todd Duncan starred on stage in the title roles of *Porgy and Bess*, George and Ira Gershwin and Dubose Heyward's folk opera, based on Heyward's story.

Peggy Ashcroft was Juliet to both John Gielgud and Laurence Olivier, who alternated as Mercutio and Romeo in the noted London production of *Romeo and Juliet*, directed by Gielgud.

Bette Davis starred in *Dangerous*, winning a 1936 Academy Award for her performance.

Hallie Flanagan was named director of the new Federal Theatre Project (1935–1939), becoming a central figure in the preservation of the American theater during the Great Depression.

Irene Dunne starred with Fred Astaire, Ginger Rogers, and Randolph Scott in William A. Seitzer's film *Roberta*, and opposite Robert Taylor in John M. Stahl's film melodrama *Magnificent Obsession*.

Françoise Rosay starred in Jacques Feyder's French film *Carnival in Flanders*.

Galina Ulanova created the role of Coralie in Rostislav Zacharov's ballet *Lost Illusions*.

Helen Hayes starred in the title role of *Victoria Regina*, Laurence Housman's play.

Greta Garbo played the title role in Clarence Brown's film *Anna Karenina*.

Judith Anderson and Helen Mencken costarred in Zoë Akins's play *The Old Maid*.

Margot Fonteyn danced the lead in Frederick Ashton's version of the ballet *Le Baiser de las Fée*.

Katharine Hepburn starred in George Stevens's film *Alice Adams*, based on the 1921 Booth Tarkington novel.

Laura Ingalls Wilder published the autobiographical children's story *Little House on the Prairie*.

Madeleine Renaud and Jean Gabin starred in Julien Duvivier's French film *Maria Chapdelaine*.

Marianne Moore published her *Selected Poems*.

Ninette de Valois's ballet *The Rake's Progress* premiered with the Vic-Wells Ballet.

Pearl Buck published the novel *A House Divided*.

Ellen Glasgow published the novel *Vein of Iron*.

Alicia Markova and Anton Dolin founded the Markova-Dolin Company.

Edna Ferber published the novel *Come and Get It*.

Dorothy L. Sayers published the mystery novel *Gaudy Night*.

Elizabeth Bowen published the novel *The House in Paris*.

Ginger Rogers and Fred Astaire starred in *Top Hat*, Mark Sandrich's film version of Irving Berlin's musical.

Elsa Lanchester and Boris Karloff starred in James Whale's film *Bride of Frankenstein*.

Ivy Compton-Burnett published the novel *A House and Its Head*.

Mari Sandoz published the biography *Old Jules*.

Georgia O'Keeffe painted *Blue River, Ram's Head with Hollyhock, Rib and Jawbone*, and *Sunflower for Maggie*.

Muriel Rukeyser published the poetry collection *Theory of Flight*.

Mae West starred in the film *I'm No Angel*.

Josephine Baker starred in the film *Moulin Rouge*.

Margaret Ayer Barnes published the novel *Edna, His Wife*.

Marian and Jim Jordan began their 22-year run in radio's *Fibber McGee and Molly* (1935–1957).

Shirley Temple sang "Animal Crackers in My Soup" in the film *Curly Top*.

Marjorie Kinnan Rawlings published the novel *Golden Apples*.

Marlene Dietrich starred in Josef von Sternberg's film *The Devil Is a Woman*.

b. Julie Andrews (Julia Elizabeth Welles, 1935– ), British actress and singer, who originated Eliza Doolittle in *My Fair Lady* (1960) and played Maria von Trapp in the film *The Sound of Music* (1965).

b. Bibi Andersson (1935– ), Swedish actress, who became an international film star in such Ingmar Bergman films as *The Seventh Seal* (1956), *Wild Strawberries* (1957), and *The Magician* (1958).

b. Françoise Sagan (Françoise Quoirez, 1935– ), French writer, whose first and most popular novel was *Bonjour Tristesse* (1954).

b. Furugh Farrukhazad (1935–1967), Iranian writer.

b. Joan Micklin Silver (1935–), American film director.

b. Lee Remick (1935–1991), American actress.

d. Winifred Holtby (1898–1935), British writer, pacifist, and feminist.

## 1936

### POLITICS/LAW/WAR

Communist Party leader Dolores Ibarruri (La Pasionara) became a leading figure in the Spanish Republican government, and a worldwide symbol of antifascist resistance.

Anarchist leader Federica Montseny became Minister of Health in the Spanish Republican government.

A strong antifascist, Irène Joliot-Curie served as under-secretary of state in France's Popular Front government, pressing the Académie des Sciences to accept women as members.

French suffragists, led by Louise Weiss, chained themselves together across Paris's rue Royale, demanding the vote, which would come eight years later.

Eleanor Roosevelt began publishing her newspaper column "My Day," which quickly became widely syndicated.

Women's Emergency Brigade, an unarmed but paramilitary organization, was generated by the women's auxiliary of the United Auto Workers (UAW) during the Flint, Michigan, UAW sit-down strike (December 1936–February 1937).

British Abortion Law Reform Association was founded.

Miina Sillanpää became Speaker of the Finnish parliament (1936–1947).

Elizabeth Dilling published *The Roosevelt Red Record*.

Jane Hoey was appointed first director of the newly established Bureau of Public Assistance, under the Social Security Board.

Sylvia Pankhurst began her full-scale commitment to Ethiopia, advocating British opposition to the Italian invasion and beginning editorship of the periodical *Ethiopian News* (1936–1956).

b. Barbara Charlene Jordan (1936–1996), American civil rights leader, politician, and lawyer.

b. Barbara Mikulski (1936– ), American social worker and Democratic politician from Maryland who served in the House of Representatives (1977–1987), then the Senate.

b. Elizabeth Hanford Dole (1936 – ), American politician and administrator, who was U.S. secretary of transportation (1983–1987) and secretary of labor (1989–1990), then head of the American Red Cross.

d. Marianne Hainisch (1839–1936), Austrian women's rights movement leader and pacifist, a founder and president of the General Austrian Women's Association (1899).

d. Ellen Spencer Mussey (1850–1936), American lawyer, women's rights advocate, and educator, a specialist in commercial and international law, who founded the Washington College of Law (1896).

### RELIGION/EDUCATION/EVERYDAY LIFE

Mary McLeod Bethune was appointed by President Franklin Roosevelt to be director of the Division of Negro Affairs for the National Youth Administration (1936–1944), supervising training programs for some 600,000 young black people. She had a strong influence on Roosevelt administration racial-integration policies and on the thinking of Eleanor Roosevelt.

Anne O'Hare McCormick became the first woman on the *New York Times* editorial board.

Beryl Markham became the first woman to fly across the Atlantic from east to west; after crash-landing in Nova Scotia, she received a ticker-tape welcome in New York.

Edith Abbott's *The Tenements of Chicago* analyzed Depression-era slum life in Chicago and called for major reforms.

Tennis star Alice Marble won the first of her four U.S. singles championships (1936; 1938–1940).

British social scientist Barbara Wootton published *London's Burning*.

Edith Lowry became executive secretary of the Council of Women for Home Missions, remaining co-executive secretary when it merged with the Home Missions Council of North America (1940).

Mirabel Topham took charge of Aintree racecourse, home of Britain's famous steeplechase, the Grand National; she later bought it outright (1949–1973).

b. Iolanda Balas (1936– ), Romanian high jumper.

b. Krystyna Chojnowska-Liskiewicz (1936– ), Polish yachtswoman, the first woman to sail single-handed around the world.

b. Rosemary Radford Ruether (1936– ), American theologian and writer, notably on feminist theory and history.

d. Anne (Joanna) Sullivan (Macy) (1866–1936), American educator, the teacher of Helen Keller, then her interpreter and companion (1887–1936).

d. Sophia Heath (1896–1936), American athletics administrator and aviator, the first female commercial airline pilot (1919), who founded the Women's Amateur Athletic Association (1922).

d. Louise Bryant (1887–1936), American social reformer, suffragist, and radical journalist, who was a war correspondent on the Western Front during World War I and in Russia during the Bolshevik Revolution; she was the wife of radical journalist John Reed, their story told in the film *Reds*.

d. May French Sheldon (1848–1936), American traveler and writer noted for her African travels; one of the first female fellows of the Royal Geographical Society (1892).

## SCIENCE/TECHNOLOGY/MEDICINE

A landmark U.S. Supreme Court decision established that American doctors could legally prescribe and provide birth control devices.

The Catholic rule barring women in religious orders from working as physicians was formally overturned; some had been working as doctors in previous decades, notably through the efforts of Agnes McLaren.

American archaeologist Hetty Goldman was appointed to the Institute of Advanced Studies in Princeton, New Jersey; she was the first female professor there; a second had not been appointed by her death (1972).

After her marriage to anthropologist and archaeologist Louis Leakey, Mary Douglas joined him at work in Tanganyika (now Tanzania), seeking information on human origins.

Louise Thaden was the first female pilot to win the prestigious cross-country Bendix Trophy Race.

Marion Rice Hart, later known as an aviator, sailed around the world with a crew of four (1936–1939).

American archaeologist Florence Hawley Ellis published her standard reference work *Field Manual of Southwestern Pottery Types*.

Canadian miner and politician Martha Black published *Yukon Wild Flowers*.

## ARTS/LITERATURE

Dorothea Lange shot her classic Great Depression photograph *Migrant Mother, Nipomo, California*.

Margaret Mitchell published her Pulitzer Prize–winning only novel, *Gone with the Wind*, set in the Civil War South and told from the Confederate point of view.

Ruth Chatterton, Mary Astor, and Walter Huston starred in William Wyler's film *Dodsworth*, based on the 1929 Sinclair Lewis novel and the 1934 Sidney Howard play.

Irene Dunne, Paul Robeson, Helen Morgan, and Allan Jones starred in James Whale's film of Oscar Hammerstein and Jerome Kern's stage musical *Show Boat* (1927).

Kay Boyle published the novel *Death of a Man* and the story "The White Horses of Vienna."

Leni Riefenstahl shot the Nazi propaganda film *The Triumph of the Will* at the Nuremberg Nazi Party Congress.

Luise Rainer starred in *The Great Ziegfeld*, winning a 1937 best actress Academy Award for her performance.

Margaret Sullavan starred on Broadway in Edna Ferber and George S. Kaufman's play *Stage Door*.

Margot Fonteyn and Robert Helpmann danced the leads in Frederick Ashton's ballet *Apparitions*.

Miriam Hopkins, Merle Oberon, and Joel McCrea starred in Billy Wilder's film *These Three*, based on Lillian Hellman's 1934 play, *The Children's Hour*.

Late in her career, Fanny Brice created the radio character Baby Snooks.

Ginger Rogers and Fred Astaire starred in George Stevens's film *Swingtime*.

Katharine Cornell starred in *Wingless Victory*, Maxwell Anderson's play.

Greta Garbo starred opposite Robert Taylor in George Cukor's film *Camille*, based on Alexandre Dumas's play *La Dame aux Camélias*.

Lynn Fontanne starred opposite Alfred Lunt in Robert Sherwood's antiwar play *Idiot's Delight*.

Margalo Gillmore and Ilka Chase starred in *The Women*, Clare Boothe Luce's comedy.

Margaret Bourke-White's work appeared on the first *Life* magazine cover.

Dorothy Parker published the poetry collection *Not So Deep a Well*.

Anaïs Nin published the novel *The House of Incest*.

Daphne du Maurier published the novel *Jamaica Inn*.

Ayn Rand published the novel *We, the Living*.

Djuna Barnes published the Paris-set novel *Nightwood*.

Ethel Merman starred opposite Bing Crosby in Lewis Milestone's film *Anything Goes*, reprising her Broadway role in Cole Porter's 1934 musical.

Dorothy Arzner directed the film *Craig's Wife*.

Elisabeth Bergner starred in the title role of James M. Barrie's play *The Boy David*.

Georgia O'Keeffe painted *Grey Hill Forms*, *Perdernal*, and *Summer Days*.

Winifred Holtby's novel *South Riding* was published posthumously.

Gracie Fields starred in the film *Queen of Hearts*.

Laura Knight published *Oil Paint and Grease Paint*.

Rebecca West published the novel *The Thinking Reed*.

Shirley Temple starred in the film *Poor Little Rich Girl*.

Mary McCarthy became an editor of the *Partisan Review*.

b. Glenda Jackson (1936– ), British stage, screen, and television star, one of the leading actresses of her time, later a Labour member of Parliament (1992– ).

b. Mary Tyler Moore (1936– ), American actress, a quintessential 1970s American career woman in her *Mary Tyler Moore Show* (1970–1977).

b. Carol Burnett (1936– ), American actress, singer, and variety entertainer.

b. Marge Piercy (1936– ), American poet and novelist, a feminist and social reformer.

d. Ernestine Schumann-Heink (1861–1936), Austrian-American contralto, a leading singer for five decades in opera and recital, and on records.

d. Grazia Deledda (1871–1936), Italian novelist, who received the 1926 Nobel Prize for literature.

d. Antonia Mercé (La Argentina , 1888–1936), Argentina-born dancer, one of the leading Spanish dancers of her time.

d. Marilyn Miller (Mary Ellen Reynolds, 1898–1936), American singer, dancer, and actress, a musical theater star of the 1920s and early 1930s, beginning with *Sally* (1920).

d. Clara Ellen Butt (1872–1936), British contralto, whose signature became Edward Elgar's song "Land of Hope and Glory."

d. Marguerite Durand (1864–1936), French actress and publisher who founded the women's newspaper *La Fronde* (1897).

d. Mary Johnston (1870–1936), American author.

## 1937

### POLITICS/LAW/WAR

Margaret Ballinger was elected to the first of her six terms in the South African parliament (1937–1959).

Women won the right to vote and be elected to office in the Philippines.

Eleanor Roosevelt published the autobiographical *This Is My Story*.

Madame Sun Yat-sen (Ch'ing-ling Soong) returned to China from the Soviet Union, to become a key symbol of support for the Communist side in the Chinese Civil War.

Margaret Postgate Cole and G. D. H. Cole published *The Condition of Britain*.

d. Chrystal Macmillan (1871–1937), Scottish feminist, women's rights activist, suffragist, lawyer, and pacifist, a leader of the National Union of Suffrage Societies and the International Alliance of Women (1913–1921).

d. Annie Furujelhm (1860–1937), Finnish feminist, suffragist, social reformer, and politician, a leading figure in the Finnish and European women's rights movements.

---

## Advice from a Father

When Marjorie Ferguson (later Lambert) decided to enter the field of archaeology, her father advised: "Well, lassie, if you're going to cut off your hair, and if you're going to wear pants, and if you're going to go into a man's field, *be woman enough to take it!*"

---

### RELIGION/EDUCATION/EVERYDAY LIFE

Edith Pye organized Quaker relief work during the Spanish Civil War (ca. 1936–1939); she was active also with the Women's International League for Peace and Freedom and the International Commission for the Assistance of Child Refugees.

Anne O'Hare McCormick won the Pulitzer Prize for foreign correspondence, notably for her reportage on Benito Mussolini.

During the Sino-Japanese War, which became part of World War II, tens of thousands of women and girls, mostly Korean, were forced into prostitution, serving Japanese troops. Not until 1993 did the Japanese government acknowledge and finally apologize for these acts.

Eleanor Rathbone published *War Can Be Averted*, arguing strongly against appeasement of Hitler and the Nazis.

Joan Robinson published *Introduction to the Theory of Employment*, following on from John Maynard Keynes's *General Theory*.

Conchita Cintrón began fighting as a *torera* in Mexico, at age 15; in her career, largely in South America, she killed 400 bulls on foot as a *torera*, and 800 on horseback. *Toreras* were banned in Spain until 1973, so Cintrón had difficulty obtaining entrance to European bullfighting rings.

Doria Kopsky was the first woman to win the National Amateur Bicycle Association tournament.

Helen Merrell Lynd and her husband, Robert Staughton Lynd, published *Middletown in Transition*.

Vida Scudder published her spiritual and intellectual autobiography, *On Journey*.

b. Dawn Fraser (1937– ), Australian swimmer, the first person to win the same title at three successive Olympic Games (1956; 1960; 1964) and the first woman to swim 100 meters and 110 yards in under a minute.

### SCIENCE/TECHNOLOGY/MEDICINE

Marjorie Ferguson (later Lambert) became curator of archaeology at the Museum of New Mexico and began excavations of Rio Grande pueblos.

Leta Hollingworth was appointed director of the Speyer School, New York City's experimental school for "slow learners" and gifted children.

American archaeologist Marie Wormington began her long association with the Denver Museum (1937–1970), as curator of archaeology.

British archaeologist Gertrude Caton-Thompson explored sites at Hureidha in southern Arabia's Hadramaut region.

Irène Joliot-Curie was named a professor at the Sorbonne.

Anna Freud published *The Ego and the Mechanisms of Defence*, her most notable work, the next year emigrating to Britain with her father, Sigmund Freud.

Karen Horney published *The Neurotic Personality of Our Time*.

British psychoanalyst Marion Milner, writing as Joanne Field, published *An Experiment in Leisure*, on the psychological value of writing a journal.

b. Valentina Vladimirovna Nikolayeva Tereshkova (1937– ), Russian cosmonaut who would become the first woman in space (1963).

d. Amelia Earhart (1897–1937), American aviator; she was lost and presumed dead in the western Pacific (July 2), on her second attempt at a round-the-world flight; rumors persisted that she had been captured, held as a spy, and killed by the Japanese. In her final letter to her husband, received after her death, she wrote: "Women must try to do things as men have tried. When they fail, their failure must be but a challenge to others."

### ARTS/LITERATURE

Margaret Bourke-White published her classic Great Depression photo-essay *You Have Seen Their Faces*, shot in the American South, with text by her husband, Erskine Caldwell.

Florence Reece, member of a striking miner's family, wrote "Which Side Are You On?" to the tune of an old song, "Jack Munro."

Sylvia Sidney, Joel McCrea, and Humphrey Bogart starred in William Wyler's film *Dead End*; Lillian Hellman's screenplay was based on the 1935 Sidney Kingsley play.

Virginia Woolf published the novel *The Years*.

Flora Robson played Elizabeth opposite Vivien Leigh and Laurence Olivier in William K. Howard's film *Fire over England*.

Gertrude Lawrence played the title role, a nonsinging one, in Rachel Crothers's comedy-drama *Susan and God*.

Isak Dinesen published her autobiographical *Out of Africa*.

Ginger Rogers and Fred Astaire starred in the films *Shall We Dance* and *Swingtime*.

Janet Gaynor starred opposite Fredric March in William Wellman's film *A Star Is Born*.

Katharine Hepburn starred in *Stage Door*, Gregory La Cava's film of Edna Ferber and George S. Kaufman's play.

Luise Rainer starred opposite Paul Muni, winning a best actress Academy Award in *The Good Earth*, Sidney Franklin's film based on Pearl Buck's 1931 novel set in China.

Stevie Smith published the poetry collection *A Good Time Was Had by All*.

Zora Neale Hurston published the novel *Their Eyes Were Watching God*.

Carole Lombard starred opposite Fredric March in William Wellman's film comedy *Nothing Sacred*.

Louise Bogan published the poetry collection *The Sleeping Fury*.

Marlene Dietrich starred as an aristocrat escaping the Russian Civil War opposite Robert Donat and John Clements in *Knight Without Armour*, Jacques Feyder's film based on James Hilton's novel.

Dorothy L. Sayers published the mystery *Busman's Honeymoon*.

Georgia O'Keeffe painted *From the Faraway Nearby*, *Gerald's Tree I*, *Horse and Feather*, and *Red Amaryllis*.

Hanya Holm choreographed *Trend*.

Grazia Deledda's autobiographical novel *Cosima* was published posthumously.

Ivy Compton-Burnett published the novel *Daughters and Sons*.

Malvina Hoffman published *Sculpture Inside and Out*.

Nuri Hadzic created the title role in Alban Berg's opera *Lulu*.

Shirley Temple starred in the film *Wee Willie Winkie*.

Joan Forbes published *Forbidden Road, Kabul to Samarkand*.

Olivia Manning published the novel *The Wind Changes*.

b. Vanessa Redgrave (1937– ), British stage and screen star, a leading actress on the British stage from the early 1960s, of the notable Redgrave acting family; also a leading British leftist activist.

b. Jane Fonda (1937– ), American film star, a major figure from the late 1960s through the 1980s.

b. Anita Desai (1937– ), Indian novelist and short story writer.

b. Bessie Head (1937–1986), South African novelist.

b. Zhang Jie (1937– ), Chinese writer.

d. Edith Wharton (1862–1937), American novelist, short story writer, and poet best known for her *The Age of Innocence* (1920).

d. Bessie Smith (1894 or 1898–1937), American blues singer, one of the century's greatest singers, called "Empress of the Blues."

d. Jean Harlow (Harlean Carpenter, 1911–1937), American actress, who never recovered after being taken ill while shooting *Saratoga*.

d. Lilian Baylis (1874–1937), British theater manager, founder of the Old Vic theater company and the Sadler's Wells ballet and opera companies.

d. Lou Andreas-Salomé (1861–1937), Russian writer and psychoanalyst.

## 1938

### POLITICS/LAW/WAR

U.S. Fair Labor Standards Act provided new uniform protection in wage and working conditions for both women and men working in interstate commerce, including the minimum wage, a basic workweek beyond which overtime was to be paid by law, an end to under-16 child labor, and an end to sex- and age-based wage differentials. Much of the credit for passage of the new law, which brought enormous and long-sought gains in workplace equality for women, went to Secretary of Labor Frances Perkins.

In Italy, Benito Mussolini's government decreed that women could not exceed more than 10 percent of any public or private work force; this was followed (1939) by lists of jobs "especially suited for women," such as secretaries or switchboard operators, and pay ranges setting women's wages at 35 to 50 percent lower than men's.

Angelika Balabanoff published her autobiography, *My Life as a Rebel.*

Edith Summerskill won election as a Labour Party member of Parliament.

Fatima Jinnah headed the All-India Muslim Women's Committee.

Hilda Martindale published the autobiographical *Women Servants of the State, 1870–1938.*

Martha Black, then representing the Yukon in Canada's Parliament, published *My Life.*

Maud Gonne published her autobiography, *A Servant of the Queen.*

Former Socialist Party leader Kate Richards O'Hare became assistant director of the California Department of Penology.

b. Janet Reno (1938– ), American lawyer, longtime state prosecutor in Florida's Dade County (1978–1993), who became U.S. attorney general in the Clinton administration (1993), the first woman in both positions.

b. Helen Broinowski Caldicott (1938– ), Australian pediatrician and antinuclear activist, a key founder of the Society of Physicians for Social Responsibility (1977), later its president (1978–1983).

b. Gwendoline Konie (1938– ), Zambian diplomat.

d. Gertrude Simmons Bonnin (Zitkala Sa; Redbird, 1876–1938), Sioux (Dakota) Indian rights leader and writer, founder of the National Congress of American Indians (1926–1938).

d. Rosa Mayreder (1858–1938), Austrian feminist and pacifist, a writer and artist.

### RELIGION/EDUCATION/EVERYDAY LIFE

Britain's Home Secretary appointed Stella, dowager marchioness of Reading, to chair the Women's Voluntary Service, which at first recruited women for civil-defense work and during World War II cared for air-raid victims. After the war, it became the Women's Royal Voluntary Service (1966), caring for the poor, infirm, and elderly.

British physician and relief worker Hilda Clark served on the board of directors of the International Commission for Refugee Children (1938–1945), organizing relief work for victims of the Spanish Civil War and later World War II, especially children.

*Helen Keller's Journal* was published, covering the shattering experience of losing Annie Sullivan, her teacher and interpreter.

Margaret Rudkin founded her Pepperidge Farm baking company, starting with loaves of bread and emphasizing natural, healthful ingredients; she soon expanded to pastries and ultimately built a multimillion-dollar business empire.

When China's Shanxi province was overrun by Japanese forces, British-Chinese missionary Gladys Aylward led 100 children on a long trek through the mountains to escape them, then nursed victims of the war.

Mary Stocks became general secretary of the London Council of Social Service and principal of Westfield College (1938–1951).

Barbara Ward published *The International Share-out.*

British social scientist Barbara Wootton published *Lament for Economics.*

Agnes Smedley published *China Fights Back*.

The Miss America Pageant introduced talent as a factor in the competition.

b. Giuliana Benetton (1938?– ), Italian designer and entrepreneur who built a major international knitwear firm starting from a small shop selling her own designs (1955).

d. Suzanne Lenglen (1899–1938), French tennis player who dominated the game from her first Wimbledon title (1919) to turning professional (1926); she also introduced shorter tennis garb, widely adopted by others.

### SCIENCE/TECHNOLOGY/MEDICINE

Dorothy Hansine Andersen reported her discovery that cystic fibrosis is a distinct disease, also developing tests to allow early diagnosis.

Katherine Blodgett's invention of nonreflecting glass was announced by her employer, General Electric; these and later techniques she developed for depositing films on glass also had wide applications in chemistry, biophysics, and solid-state physics.

Thirty years after she was driven from her post by protesting male students, Greek physician Angeliki Panajiotatou returned to Greece as a professor at Athens University Medical School.

Irmgard Flügge-Lotz and her husband, Wilhelm Flügge, both anti-Nazis blocked from academic careers, joined the Deutsche Versuchsanstalt für Luftfahrt (DVL), where they worked through World War II. During that period, she developed the basics of automatic aircraft controls, essential for jets.

American geologist Eleanor Bliss Knopf published *Structural Petrography*, her classic work on the use of texture, orientation of grain, and other mineral properties to analyze rock systems and their history.

American physiologist Ida Hyde published her article "Before Women Were Human Beings . . . Adventures of an American in German Universities in the '90s."

American aviator Jacqueline Cochran won the trans-American Bendix Race.

Cecilia Payne-Gaposchkin was named astronomer of the Harvard Observatory.

Annie Jump Cannon was named William Cranch Bond Astronomer at Harvard University.

Marion Rice Hart's *Who Called That Lady a Skipper* was published, while she herself was still on a round-the-world voyage (1936–1939).

Britain's National Birth Control Association became the Family Planning Association.

b. Sheila Evans Widnall (1938– ), American aeronautics professor and university administrator, long associated with the Massachusetts Institute of Technology, who became the first woman to serve as secretary of the air force (1993–).

d. Carlotta Maury (1874–1938), American geologist who worked largely in South Africa and Brazil, correlating microfossils and rock strata to obtain information on possible oil-bearing formations.

### ARTS/LITERATURE

Pearl Buck was awarded the Nobel Prize for literature.

Virginia Woolf published the essay collection *Three Guineas*.

Wendy Hiller as Eliza Doolittle starred opposite Leslie Howard as Henry Higgins in Anthony Asquith's classic film version of George Bernard Shaw's play *Pygmalion*.

Bette Davis starred opposite Henry Fonda in William Wyler's film *Jezebel*, winning a best actress Academy Award.

Margaret Lockwood, Michael Redgrave, and May Whitty starred in Alfred Hitchcock's film *The Lady Vanishes*.

Marjorie Kinnan Rawlings published her Pulitzer Prize–winning novel *The Yearling*.

Ruth Page and Bentley Stone danced the leads in the ballet *Frankie and Johnny*.

Martha Graham choreographed *American Document*.

Michèlle Morgan starred opposite Jean Gabin in Marcel Carné's film *Port of Shadows*.

Daphne du Maurier published the novel *Rebecca*.

Sybil Thorndike starred opposite Emlyn Williams in Williams's play *The Corn Is Green*.

Ella Fitzgerald recorded her first big hit, "A Tisket, a Tasket."

Stevie Smith published the poetry collection *Tender Only to One* and the novel *Over the Frontier*.

Shirley Temple starred in the film *Rebecca of Sunnybrook Farm*.

Ginger Rogers and Fred Astaire starred in the film *Carefree*.

Leni Riefenstahl filmed the Berlin Olympics for Germany's Nazi government.

Mary Martin sang "My Heart Belongs to Daddy" in *Leave It to Me!*

Vivien Leigh starred opposite Charles Laughton and Rex Harrison in Tim Whelan's film *St. Martin's Lane*.

Gabriela Mistral published the poetry collection *Tala*.

Italian Communist leader Teresa Noce, then in France, published the novel *Gioventù senza sole*.

Muriel Rukeyser published the Depression-era poetry collection *U.S. 1*.

Georgia O'Keeffe painted *Red and Orange Hills, Red Hill and White Shell, Two Jimson Weeds*, and *White Camellia*.

Gracie Fields starred in the film *Keep Smiling*.

Nathalie Sarraute published the novel *Tropisms*.

Sophie Tucker starred opposite Victor Moore in Cole Porter's stage musical *Leave It to Me!*

Taylor Caldwell published the novel *Dynasty of Death*.

Laura Riding published her *Collected Poems*.

Clare Boothe Luce wrote the play *Kiss the Boys Good-bye*.

Edith Head became the first head to a major motion-picture studio's design department.

Penny Singleton as Blondie and Arthur Lake as Dagwood began the 28-film *Blondie* series (1938–1950), based on the Chic Young comic strip.

Elena Stasova edited the Soviet publication *International Literature* (1938–1946).

Peggy Glanville-Hicks composed her *Choral Suite*.

Zinaida Hippius published the poetry collection *Radiances*.

b. Joyce Carol Oates (1938– ), American novelist, short story writer, poet, and critic, whose work often deals with near-mad people in what she perceives as an unstable culture gone over into insanity.

b. Liv Ullmann (1938– ), Norwegian actress, who became an international film star in several Ingmar Bergman films of the late 1960s and 1970s.

b. (Enid) Diana (Elizabeth) Rigg (1938– ), British actress, a leading classical actress best known to worldwide audiences for her role as Emma Peel in the television series *The Avengers* (1965–1967).

b. Natalie Wood (Natasha Gurdin, 1938–1981), American film star, as a child in the 1940s and as an adult from the mid-1950s.

b. Anita Brookner (1938– ), British novelist and art historian.

b. Tina Turner (Anna Mae Bullock, 1938– ), American singer.

b. Caryl Churchill (1938– ), British playwright.

d. Suzanne Marie Clementine Valadon (1865–1938), French painter who began her career as an artist's model; encouraged by Degas and others, she began to show what became a wide range of works in the 1890s.

d. Susan Hannah Macdowell Eakins (1851–1938), American painter, pianist, and photographer, wife of the artist Thomas Eakins.

d. Mary Hallock Foote (1847–1938), American novelist whose work was largely set in the far West.

d. Pearl White (1889–1938), American actress, star of the serial *The Perils of Pauline*.

# 1939

## POLITICS/LAW/WAR

Ellen Wilkinson published the Depression-era *The Town That Was Murdered.*

Jennie Lee published *Tomorrow Is a New Day.*

b. Gro Harlem Brundtland (1939– ), Norwegian doctor and politician, Norway's first female prime minister (1981–1996).

b. Violeta Barrios de Chamorro (1939– ), Nicaraguan political leader who became president of Nicaragua (1990).

b. Miswo Enoki (1939– ), Japanese feminist and politician, who in the 1970s would lead the radical feminist Pink Panthers.

b. Ti-Grace Atkinson (1939– ), American radical feminist leader of the late 1960s and early 1970s, one of the founders of the short-lived group The Feminists (1968).

b. Anna-Greta Leijon (1939– ), Swedish socialist, feminist, and politician.

d. Charlotte French Despard (1844–1939), British social reformer, suffragist, socialist, and activist in the Irish Republican cause, who began her work in London's poorest districts in the early 1890s.

d. Adelheid Popp (1869–1939), Austrian feminist, socialist, trade unionist, and editor, a leader of Austria's women's rights movement.

d. Helena Sickert Swanwick (1864–1939), British writer, suffragist, and pacifist, a leading advocate of disarmament during the interwar period.

## RELIGION/EDUCATION/EVERYDAY LIFE

Gertrude Denman organized the Women's Land Army (1939–1946) in Britain, after the war resigning in protest when they failed to gain pension rights given to other civil-defense and service women.

Flora Solomon developed communal restaurants at London's Marks & Spencer store; when World War II came, the government named her to set up a chain across the country, known as the British Restaurants.

American missionary Ida Pruitt became executive secretary of the American Committee for the Chinese Industrial Cooperatives (1939–1952).

Dorothy Day published *House of Hospitality*, about St. Joseph's House of Hospitality and other Catholic Worker Movement refuges.

Edith Pye organized Quaker relief work among refugees in Britain (from ca. 1939), during the war lobbying the Ministry of Economic Warfare to partially lift the Allied blockade of Europe to prevent starvation.

Rothschild-Hadassah University Hospital, founded by the Jewish women's organization Hadassah, opened in partnership with Hebrew University.

Daisy Bates wrote *The Passing of the Aborigines.*

Edith Lowry became the first woman to speak from the National Radio Pulpit, giving the talk "Women in a Changing World."

Ida Tarbell published *All in the Day's Work.*

Evelyn Underhill published *The Church and War*, on her pacifist views.

Sylvia Porter published *How to Make Money in Government Bonds.*

b. Germaine Greer (1939– ), Australian writer and critic who became a well-known feminist with her book *The Female Eunuch* (1970).

b. Junko Tabei (1939– ), Japanese mountaineer, the first woman to reach the top of Mt. Everest (1975).

b. Marian Wright Edelman (1939– ), American children's rights advocate.

b. Erin Carney Pizzey (1939– ), British social worker and writer, a campaigner against domestic violence.

b. Jael Mbogo (Mama Jael, 1939– ), Kenyan social worker and politician.

b. Julie Palau Tullis (1939–1986), British mountaineer.

d. Grace Abbott (1878–1939), American social worker, feminist, writer, teacher, and a leading 20th-century advocate of social justice. She was director of the Immigrant Protective League (1908–1917), head of the U.S. Children's Bureau (1921–1934), and a powerful exponent of protective legislation for working women and children during the 1930s, often working with her sister, Edith Abbott.

d. Madeleine Anne Pelletier (1874–1939), French physician and feminist who dressed in men's attire and edited the journal *La suffragiste* (from the late 1890s); she was the first woman to join the staff of Assistance Publique (1899). Long a campaigner for legalized birth control and abortion, she was arrested for openly performing abortions (1939). She later died in an asylum.

## SCIENCE/TECHNOLOGY/MEDICINE

Lise Meitner, in a landmark letter cowritten with her nephew Otto Frisch, described the theoretical possibility of splitting an atom to release enormous amounts of energy, a process she named *nuclear fission*, a fundamental concept of the atomic age. Ida Noddack had previously suggested such a process (1933), but Meitner's letter was the first to correctly explain puzzling results from numerous experiments, including many she had conducted with Otto Hahn in Germany before she fled from the Nazis. Hahn and others would receive the 1944 Nobel Prize for their work; Meitner would not be included.

American pediatrician and microbiologist Mattie Elizabeth Alexander successfully developed a serum to treat *Hemophilus influenzae*, which causes bacterial meningitis, especially in young children.

Pearl Kendrick and Grace Eldening developed the pertussis vaccine, for use against whooping cough. Kendrick later developed a combination vaccine, DPT (diphtheria, pertussis, and tetanus).

French physicist Marguerite Perey discovered a natural radioactive element she called "francium" (actirium K).

Dorothy Garrod was elected Disney Professor of Archaeology at Cambridge University, becoming the first female professor in any discipline at either Oxford or Cambridge.

American physician Josephine Baker published her autobiography, *Fighting for Life*.

Hélène Metzger was named head of the library of the history of science at France's Centre Internationale de Synthèse.

Marie Wormington published *Ancient Man in North America*.

Karen Horney published *New Ways in Psychoanalysis*.

Mary Sinclair became head of the mathematics department at Oberlin College (1939–1944).

d. Leta Stetter Hollingworth (1886–1939), American educational psychologist who specialized in the psychology of "slow learners" and gifted children, encouraging the development of special classes for both.

d. Margaret Floy Washburn (1871–1939), American psychologist long associated with Vassar College (1903–1937), whose main work focused on animal behavior, especially color vision.

## ARTS/LITERATURE

Marian Anderson's Easter Sunday concert at the Lincoln Memorial drew 75,000 to 100,000 people; after the Daughters of the American Revolution denied Anderson the use of Constitution Hall because of her race, Eleanor Roosevelt resigned from the DAR and sponsored the Lincoln Memorial event.

Vivien Leigh gave an Oscar-winning performance as Scarlett O'Hara opposite Clark Gable as Rhett Butler in Victor Fleming's film *Gone with the Wind*, adapted by Sidney Howard from Margaret Mitchell's book (1936).

Emily Brontë's novel *Wuthering Heights* was brought to the screen in William Wyler's classic film; Merle Oberon starred as Cathy opposite Laurence Olivier as Heathcliff.

Judy Garland starred as Dorothy, introducing "Over the Rainbow," in Victor Fleming's musical film *The Wizard of Oz*, based on the 1900 Frank Baum novel.

Myra Hess began her long series of lunchtime concerts at London's National Gallery, playing on through the Blitz and throughout the war.

Vera Lynn sang the classic World War II song "We'll Meet Again."

Katharine Hepburn created the Tracy Lord role in Philip Barry's stage comedy *The Philadelphia Story*, in a cast that included Van Heflin, Shirley Booth, and Joseph Cotten. On film, she starred opposite Cary Grant in *Holiday*, George Cukor's film of Barry's 1928 romantic comedy.

Greta Garbo as the Russian trade commissar in Paris starred opposite Melvyn Douglas in Ernst Lubitsch's film comedy *Ninotchka*.

Katherine Anne Porter published three short novels as *Pale Horse, Pale Rider*.

Gertrude Lawrence starred on Broadway in Samson Raphaelson's comedy *Skylark*.

Madeleine Ozeray starred in the title role opposite Louis Jouvet in Jean Giraudoux's play *Ondine*.

Margalo Gillmore, Katharine Cornell, and Laurence Olivier starred in S. N. Behrman's comedy *No Time for Comedy*.

Tallulah Bankhead starred as Regina Giddens in Lillian Hellman's play *The Little Foxes*.

Zora Neale Hurston published the novel *Moses, Man of the Mountain*.

Marlene Dietrich sang "See What the Boys in the Back Room Will Have" as the cabaret entertainer opposite James Stewart in George Marshall's classic film Western *Destry Rides Again*.

Kate Smith introduced "God Bless America," which became her signature song; Irving Berlin wrote it for *Yip Yip Yaphank* (1918), but it was not then used.

Ethel Merman starred opposite Bert Lahr in Cole Porter's stage musical *DuBarry Was a Lady*.

Bette Davis as the incurably ill patient and George Brent as her doctor and lover starred in Edmund Goulding's film drama *Dark Victory*.

Elisabeth Lutyens composed her *First Chamber Concerto*, a serialist work.

Hanya Holm choreographed *Metropolitan Daily*.

Marguerite Yourcenar published the novel *Coup de Grace*.

Myrna Loy and Tyrone Power starred in Clarence Brown's film *The Rains Came*, based on the 1937 Louis Bromfield novel.

Norma Shearer starred opposite Clark Gable in *Idiot's Delight*, Clarence Brown's antiwar film comedy based on the 1936 Robert Sherwood play.

Rumer Godden published her novel *Black Narcissus*.

Alice Faye starred as Fanny Brice in *Rose of Washington Square*, with Al Jolson.

Clare Boothe Luce wrote the play *Margin for Error*.

Edith Evans starred as Lady Bracknell in Oscar Wilde's play *The Importance of Being Earnest*.

Anna Neagle starred as *Nurse Edith Cavell*.

Georgia O'Keeffe painted *Cup of Silver*.

Anna Seghers published the anti-Nazi novel *The Seventh Cross*.

Jean Rhys published the novel *Good Morning, Midnight*.

Muriel Rukeyser published the poetry collection *A Turning Wind*.

Anaïs Nin published the story collection *Winter of Artifice*.

Ruth Lowe wrote the song "I'll Never Smile Again."

Priaulx Rainier composed her *First String Quartet*.

Ruth St. Denis published the autobiography *An Unfinished Life*.

b. Margaret Atwood (1939– ), Canadian novelist, poet, and short story writer, much of whose work speaks to modern women's concerns.

b. Jane Alexander (Jane Quigley, 1939– ), a leading American actress from the late 1960s, and head of the National Endowment for the Humanities (1993–1997).

b. Judy Collins (1939– ), American folk singer and social activist, a major figure from the early 1960s.

b. Margaret Drabble (1939– ), British novelist and editor, whose fiction is often concerned with women taking on new societal roles while remaining very much involved in traditional nurturing roles.

b. Janet Suzman (1939– ), South African actress, from the early 1960s associated with Britain's Royal Shakespeare Company, who also emerged as a director in the late 1980s.

b. Judy Chicago (Judy Cohen, 1939– ), American artist, on feminist themes.

b. Lily Tomlin (1939– ), American actress, comedian, and singer.

d. Lois Weber (1882–1939), American film director, writer, producer, and actress, a major figure during the silent-film era, whose feminism infused her work. Her partner, husband, and often costar and codirector was Phillips Smalley.

d. Ma Rainey (Gertrude Pridgett, 1886–1939), American singer, one of the leading blues singers of her time, on tour and as a recording artist.

d. Fay Templeton (1865–1939), American singer, a star in vaudeville and musical theater for more than six decades.

d. Ethel M. Dell (1881–1939), British novelist.

# 1940

## POLITICS/LAW/WAR

Britain's royal family remained in London through the Blitz of German bombs. Queen Elizabeth (the Queen Mother) won special affection when, after Buckingham Palace was hit by a bomb (September 10), she said: "I'm glad we've been bombed. Now I can look the East End in the face," referring to the hard-hit dock area of London.

Netherlands queen Wilhelmina fled to Britain after the German conquest of her country and helped organize anti-Nazi resistance from exile.

French ethnologist Germaine Tillion led a Resistance group at the Musée de l'Homme (1940–1942) before being arrested and imprisoned at Ravensbruck, about which she wrote in *Ravensbruck* (1973); she received the Légion d'Honneur, Croix de Guerre, and Rosette de la Résistance.

Running on an antiwar platform, Jeannette Pickering Rankin was again elected to the U.S. House of Representatives (1941–1942).

Margaret Chase Smith filled the unexpired House term of her husband, Maine congressman Clyde Smith, who died in office; she would be reelected to the seat four more times.

American Civil Liberties Union leader Elizabeth Gurley Flynn was expelled from the ACLU because she was a Communist Party member.

Louise Weiss published the underground French Resistance periodical *La Nouvelle République* (ca. 1940–1945).

Harriet Stanton Blatch published *Challenging Years*.

Elizabeth Dilling published *The Octopus*.

b. Pat (Patricia Scott) Schroeder (1940– ), lawyer, teacher, and longtime Colorado Democratic congresswoman (1972–1996), who became the senior woman in Congress.

b. Barbara Levy Boxer (1940– ), American politician, in the House of Representatives (1982–1992), then the Senate (1992– ).

b. Chen Muhua (ca. 1940– ), Chinese politician who would hold various ministerial posts.

b. Margrethe II (1940– ), queen of Denmark (1972– ).

b. Juliet Mitchell (1940– ), British teacher and writer, a socialist and feminist.

d. Emma Goldman (Red Emma, 1869–1940), American anarchist and women's rights advocate, one of the most prominent radical women of the early 20th century, who as a writer and editor opposed marriage, advocated birth control information for women, and spoke for and lived her ideal of sexual freedom, anathema in her time.

d. Harriet Stanton Blatch (1856–1940), American feminist, suffragist, and writer, a militant women's rights activist who founded the American Political Union (1908); she was the daughter of Elizabeth Cady Stanton.

## RELIGION/EDUCATION/EVERYDAY LIFE

Ruth Benedict published *Race: Science and Politics*, her attack on the tenets of racism.

Eleanor Rathbone published the highly influential study *The Case for Family Allowances*.

Gordon Hamilton published her *Theory and Practice of Social Case Work*, which became a standard text in social work education, establishing the diagnostic casework approach.

Eliza Gleason became the first African-American to receive a doctorate from the University of Chicago's Graduate Library School.

b. Wilma Glodean Rudolph (1940–1994), American track-and-field athlete noted for her three gold medals at the 1960 Olympics.

d. Eileen Power (Edna Le Poer, 1889–1940), British historian noted for her studies of medieval history, long associated with Girton College (1913–1921), then the London School of Economics.

d. Ellen Gates Starr (1859–1940), American social activist, bookbinder, and cofounder of Hull House (1889).

d. Kalliroe Parren (1861–1940), Greek teacher, writer, and women's rights movement organizer.

## SCIENCE/TECHNOLOGY/MEDICINE

After France fell to the Germans, Irène Joliot-Curie and Jean Frédéric Joliot-Curie ceased their experiments on creating a chain reaction through nuclear fission of uranium, hid their store of uranium, smuggled out of the country their store of the valuable heavy water needed in the process, and remained behind to work in the Resistance.

Grace Goldsmith coauthored a report on vitamin C deficiency, first of many on nutritional deficiency diseases.

American zoologist Libbie H. Hyman began publication of her massive, still-standard five-volume survey *The Invertebrates* (1940–1967).

Helen Richey became the first woman to obtain an instructor's license from the Civil Aeronautics Administration.

Marion Rice Hart published *How to Navigate Today*.

d. Lillian D. Wald (1867–1940), American public-health nurse, founder of the Henry Street Settlement (1895) and the first American public-school nursing program (1902); she coined the phrase "public-health nursing."

d. Maude Abbott (Elizabeth Seymour, 1869–1940), Canadian cardiologist who promoted medical education for women.

## ARTS/LITERATURE

Carson McCullers published the novel *The Heart Is a Lonely Hunter*.

Daphne du Maurier's 1938 novel *Rebecca* was brought to the screen with Joan Fontaine in the title role opposite Laurence Olivier; their costars were Judith Anderson and George Sanders. Alfred Hitchcock directed.

Greer Garson, Laurence Olivier, Maureen O'Sullivan, and Edmund Gwenn starred in Robert Z. Leonard's film version of Jane Austen's novel *Pride and Prejudice*, with a screenplay by Aldous Huxley and Jane Murfind.

Katharine Hepburn starred opposite Spencer Tracy in *Woman of the Year*, the first of their nine film classics together. She also reprised her stage role as Tracy Lord opposite James Stewart and Cary Grant in *The Philadelphia Story*, George Cukor's film version of Philip Barry's play.

Vera Brittain published *Testament of Friendship*, the second volume of her autobiographical trilogy, this one honoring her late friend Winifred Holtby and their shared feminist and pacifist concerns.

Agatha Christie published the novel *And Then There Were None*.

Ginger Rogers played *Kitty Foyle* in Sam Wood's film, winning a best actress Academy Award.

Carole Lombard starred opposite Charles Laughton in Garson Kanin's film *They Knew What They Wanted*.

Galina Ulanova created the role of Juliet opposite Konstantin Sergueyev as Romeo in Leonid Lavrovsky's ballet *Romeo and Juliet*.

Helen Craig starred as the abused young deaf-mute in *Johnny Belinda*, Elmer Harris's stage drama.

Willa Cather published the novel *Sapphira and the Slave Girl*.

Ethel Merman starred in the title role in Cole Porter's stage musical *Panama Hattie*.

Ethel Waters led an African-American cast in *Cabin in the Sky*, Lynn Root and John La Touche's stage musical.

Katherine Dunham produced *Tropics and Le Jazz Hot—From Haiti to Harlem*.

Ninette de Valois's ballet *The Prospect Before Us* was danced by the Sadler's Wells Ballet.

H. D. (Hilda Doolittle) published her *Collected Poems*.

Jessie Royce Landis starred opposite Walter Huston in William Saroyan's play *Love's Old Sweet Song*.

Shirley Booth starred opposite Jo Ann Sayers in the title role in *My Sister Eileen*, the Joseph A. Fields and Jerome Chodorov stage comedy.

Vivien Leigh starred opposite Robert Taylor in Mervyn LeRoy's World War I romantic film *Waterloo Bridge*, based on Robert Sherwood's 1930 play.

Dorothy Arzner directed the film *Dance, Girl, Dance*.

Georgia O'Keeffe painted *Datura and Perdenal*, *Red and Yellow Cliffs*, *Stump on Red Hills*, and *White Place in Shadow*.

Judith Anderson starred in John Gassner's play *The Tower Beyond Tragedy*.

Peggy Guggenheim opened New York's Art of This Century gallery.

Rosalind Russell starred opposite Cary Grant in *His Girl Friday*, Howard Hawks's version of the 1928 Ben Hecht–Charles MacArthur play *The Front Page*.

Taylor Caldwell published the novel *The Eagles Gather*.

Grace Williams composed her *Fantasy on Welsh Nursery Tunes*.

b. Natalia Romanovna Makarova (1940– ), Russian ballerina, a notable Soviet defector in 1970 and then a star in the West.

b. Maeve Binchy (1940– ), Irish novelist and journalist with the *Irish Times*, author of its "The Saturday Column."

b. Angela Carter (1940– ), British writer.

d. Mrs. Patrick Campbell (Beatrice Stella Tanner, 1865–1940), British actress, a star from the early 1890s; she created the Eliza Doolittle role in *Pygmalion* (1914).

d. Selma Lagerlöf (1859–1940), Swedish writer who was awarded the Nobel Prize for literature (1909).

d. Maxine Elliott (Jessie Dermot, 1868–1940), American actress and theater manager.

d. Luisa Tetrazzini (1871–1940), Italian soprano.

# 1941

## POLITICS/LAW/WAR

Pacifist Jeannette Pickering Rankin was the only member of Congress to vote against American entry into World War II (December 8, 1941), saying: "As a woman I can't go to war, and I refuse to send anyone else." The vote ended her political career.

Marie-Hélène Lefaucheux and her husband, Pierre Lefaucheux, became leaders of the French Resistance, based in Paris; she was later awarded the Croix de Guerre and Rosette de la Résistance.

Jennie Lee published *Russia Our Ally*.

Jessie Wallace Hughan published *Pacifism and Invasion*.

## RELIGION/EDUCATION/EVERYDAY LIFE

Margaret Leech published *Reveille in Washington*, becoming the first woman to win the Pulitzer Prize for history (1942).

María Cadilla de Martínez, writing as Liana, published *Raíces de la Tierra*, a collection of Puerto Rican folk tales and essays on folk customs.

Mary Follett published *Dynamic Administration*, based on her lectures in industrial relations.

b. Donna Edna Shalala (1941– ), American political scientist, college president, and Clinton administration secretary of Health and Human Services (1993– ).

b. Robin Morgan (1941– ), American social reformer, radical feminist, writer, and editor, best known for her essay "Goodbye to All That" (1970), later editor of *Ms.* (1990– ).

d. Evelyn Underhill (1875–1941), British religious writer and lecturer.

### SCIENCE/TECHNOLOGY/MEDICINE

Maria Goeppert Mayer published her classic paper "Rare Earth and Transuranic Elements," a key work in solid-state physics and chemistry.

American geneticist Barbara McClintock began her long association with the Cold Spring Harbor Laboratory of the Carnegie Institution (1941–1992).

Approximately 47,000 women served in the Army Nurse Corps with American forces during World War II.

Alma Heflin became the first female test pilot employed by a commercial aircraft firm.

WPA project director Dorothy Cross Jensen organized publication of the massive two-volume work *Archaeology of New Jersey* (1941; 1956).

d. Annie Jump Cannon (1863–1941), American astronomer long associated with Harvard Observatory (1896–1940), who directed the compilation of a catalogue classifying more than 200,000 stars (1897–1924); she herself discovered many stars, providing a key basis for much 20th-century astronomical research.

d. Amy Johnson (1903–1941), British aviator, the first woman to fly across the Atlantic from east to west; she was lost over the Thames Estuary in bad weather, flying planes for the Women's Auxiliary Air Force.

### ARTS/LITERATURE

Ellen Glasgow published her Pulitzer Prize–winning novel *In This Our Life*.

Mady Christians starred opposite Paul Lukas in Lillian Hellman's antifascist play *Watch on the Rhine*.

Virginia Woolf published the novel *Between the Acts*.

Bette Davis starred as Regina Giddens in William Wyler's film version of Lillian Hellman's play *The Little Foxes*, a bitter Deep South family drama.

Alicia Markova and Anton Dolin danced the leads in Michel Fokine's ballet *Bluebeard*.

Billie Holiday introduced the song "God Bless the Child," which she co-wrote with Arthur Herzog Jr.; it became her signature song.

Wendy Hiller starred opposite Rex Harrison in Gabriel Pascal's film version of George Bernard Shaw's 1905 play *Major Barbara*.

Carson McCullers published the novel *Reflections in a Golden Eye*.

Barbara Stanwyck starred opposite Henry Fonda in Preston Sturges's film *The Lady Eve*.

Eudora Welty published the short-story collection *A Circle of Green*.

Gertrude Lawrence starred in *Lady in the Dark*, the Kurt Weill, Moss Hart, and Ira Gershwin musical.

Joan Fontaine starred opposite Cary Grant in Alfred Hitchcock's film thriller *Suspicion*, winning a best actress Academy Award.

Margaret Rambeau and Gene Tierney as the women of a Depression-era Southern farm family starred opposite Charley Grapewin and Dana Andrews in *Tobacco Road*, John Ford's film based on Erskine Caldwell's 1932 novel.

Judith Anderson and Maurice Evans starred in a Broadway production of Shakespeare's *Macbeth*.

Marianne Moore published the poetry collections *The Arctic Ox* and *What Are Years*.

Olivia de Havilland starred opposite Charles Boyer in Mitchell Leisen's film *Hold Back the Dawn*.

Tallulah Bankhead starred opposite Joseph Schildkraut and Robert Ryan in Clifford Odets's play *Clash by Night*.

Helen Hayes starred in *Candle in the Wind*, Maxwell Anderson's play.

Ivy Compton-Burnett published the novel *Parents and Children*.

Josephine Hull and Jean Adair starred opposite Boris Karloff in Joseph Kesselring's dark comedy *Arsenic and Old Lace*.

Margaret Sullavan starred opposite Charles Boyer in Robert Stevenson's film melodrama *Back Street*, based on the 1931 Fannie Hurst novel.

Katharine Cornell starred opposite Raymond Massey on Broadway in George Bernard Shaw's *The Doctor's Dilemma*.

Maureen O'Hara starred opposite Walter Pidgeon in *How Green Was My Valley*, John Ford's film based on Richard Llewellyn's novel set in Welsh mining country.

Tamara Toumanova created the role of the ballerina in George Balanchine's ballet *Balustrade*.

Bette Davis became the first woman to head the Academy of Motion Picture Arts and Sciences.

Edna Ferber published the novel *Saratoga Trunk*.

Dorothy Maguire starred in the title role of Rose Franken's comedy *Claudia*.

Georgia O'Keeffe painted *An Orchid* and *Red Hills and Bones*.

Taylor Caldwell published the novel *The Earth Is the Lord's*.

b. Joan Baez (1941– ), American musician, pacifist, feminist, and social reformer.

b. Julie Christie (1941– ), British actress, an international film star of the 1960s and 1970s; later in starring but less commercially successful roles.

b. Faye Dunaway (Dorothy Faye Dunaway, 1941– ), American film star, from her role as Bonnie Parker in *Bonnie and Clyde* (1967).

b. Twyla Tharp (1941– ), American dancer, a leading choreographer from the mid-1960s.

b. Susannah York (Susannah Yolande Fletcher, 1941– ), British actress, a film star in the 1960s and early 1970s, later in supporting roles.

d. Virginia Woolf (Adeline Virginia Stephen, 1882–1941), leading British writer and feminist, associated with the Bloomsbury Group.

d. Helen Morgan (Helen Riggins, 1900–1941), American singer; she sang "Bill" in *Show Boat*.

d. Marina Ivanovna Tsvetayeva (1892–1941), Russian poet.

## 1942

### POLITICS/LAW/WAR

At the Auschwitz concentration camp, the Germans opened a women's section (Frauenabteilung), its first occupants being from the women's camp at Ravensbrück and Jewish women from Slovakia. From among this group would be drawn women who would serve as much-hated and feared barracks supervisors. An all-woman orchestra was formed led by Alma Rose, niece of Gustav Mahler; one member was Fania Fenelon, who described it in her memoir *Playing for Time* (1979).

(Ann) Leah Fox was the first woman awarded the Purple Heart medal; head nurse at Hickam Field, she had been wounded in the attack on Pearl Harbor, Hawaii (December 7, 1941).

The Women's Army (Auxiliary) Corps (WAAC or WAC) was founded, headed by Oveta Culp Hobby, followed by the navy's WAVES (Women Accepted for Volunteer Emergency Service), led by Mildred Helen McAfee (Horton); Dorothey Stratton became the first director of the U.S. Coast Guard's Women's Corps, named SPARS, after the service motto *Semper Paratus* (Always Prepared). Substantial numbers of women began to enter the armed services.

The Women's Auxiliary Ferrying Squadron was founded under Nancy Harkness Love, composed of women who flew airplanes to coastal points or to the Canadian border, from where they were flown to war zones abroad. Later they would merge with the Women's Air Force Service Pilots (WASPs), led by Jacqueline Cochran.

Angelika Balabanoff published *Traitor or Fascist*.

b. Sarah Kemp Brady (1942– ), leading American gun-control advocate, wife of James Brady, presidential press secretary partially paralyzed in the assassination attempt on Ronald Reagan (1981).

d. Franciska Plamnikova (1875–1942), Czech feminist, women's rights leader, and politician, a leading figure in the Czech women's rights movement. She died in a German death camp.

d. Rosa Manus (1880–1942), Dutch suffragist and pacifist; taken by the Germans early in World War II, she died at Auschwitz.

d. Vera Nikolayevna Figner (1852–1942), Russian anarchist and terrorist, briefly head of the People's Will organization (1881), then long imprisoned (1883–1904) and exiled.

## RELIGION/EDUCATION/EVERYDAY LIFE

U.S. War Manpower Commission campaigned successfully to bring large numbers of female workers into wartime production, calling them "woman power" (1942–1943).

Beryl Markham published *West with the Night*, written with her husband, Raoul Schumacher, on her early days of flying in Africa and across the Atlantic.

Esther Forbes published *Paul Revere and the World He Lived In*, becoming the second woman to win the Pulitzer Prize for history (1943).

Louise Brough and Margaret Osborne won the first of what would be nine successive U.S. doubles tennis titles (1942–1950).

Florence Hancock became chief female officer of the Transport and General Workers' Union (TGWU).

Joan Robinson published *Essay on Marxian Economics*.

Margaret Petherbridge Farrar became first woman to edit the *New York Times* crossword puzzles (1942–1968), originally in the magazine, then (from 1950) in the daily paper.

Jessie Bernard published *American Family Behavior*.

Mildred Cable and Francesca French published *The Gobi Desert*, which won an award from the Royal Central Asian Society.

Susanne Langer published *Philosophy in a New Key: A Study in the Symbolism of Reason, Rite and Art*.

b. Marguerite Ross Barnett (1942–1992), American educational administrator.

b. Vera Caslavska (1942– ), Czech gymnast noted for her Olympics performances (1964; 1968).

b. Xavière Gauthier (1942– ), French feminist literary figure.

d. Edith Stein (1891–1942), German nun, named a saint (1987), who converted from Judaism after reading a biography of Teresa of Ávila (1922); she had fled Nazi persecution but was arrested in the Netherlands and killed in a gas chamber at Auschwitz.

d. Hannah Greenebaum Solomon (1858–1942), American reformer and women's club leader, who founded the National Council of Jewish Women (1893).

## SCIENCE/TECHNOLOGY/MEDICINE

During World War II, General Electric research physicist Katherine Blodgett developed new methods of deicing wings of airplanes and made improvements in smoke screens for troops (ca. 1942–1945).

Planned Parenthood Federation of America was founded, as a successor to Margaret Sanger's first birth control clinic (1916), the American Birth Control League, and the Birth Control Clinical Research Bureau; it would remain the foremost American family-planning and birth control advocacy group.

Gladys Anderson Emerson became head of the department of animal nutrition of the Merck Institute for Therapeutic Research (1942–1956), studying the B complex of vitamins.

Leta Hollingworth's *Children Above 180 I.Q.* was published; it had been completed by her husband after her death from cancer.

American psychologists Florence Goodenough and Katherine Maurer published *The Mental Growth of Children from Two to Fourteen Years*.

Margaret Mead and Geoffrey Bateson, then her husband, produced *Balinese Character*.

Susan Isaacs published *The Family in a World at War*.

Sara Jordan became the first woman to serve as president of the American Gastroenterological Association (1942–1944).

d. Dorothea Klumpke Roberts (1861–1942), American-born astronomer working in France, the first woman to be director of the Bureau of Measurements (1891–1901), to receive a mathematics doctorate from the Sorbonne (1893), and to be elected to the Astronomical Society of France.

## ARTS/LITERATURE

Ingrid Bergman starred opposite Humphrey Bogart in Michael Curtiz's film classic *Casablanca*.

Isak Dinesen published the short-story collection *Winter's Tales*.

Greer Garson starred opposite Walter Pidgeon in William Wyler's wartime family film drama *Mrs. Miniver*, winning a best actress Academy Award, and opposite Ronald Colman in Mervyn LeRoy's *Random Harvest*.

Margot Fonteyn and Robert Helpmann danced the leads in Helpmann's ballet *Hamlet*.

Agnes De Mille, Frederic Franklin, and Casimir Kokitch danced the leads in De Mille's ballet *Rodeo*.

Edna St. Vincent Millay published the anti-Nazi poem "The Murder of Lidice."

Marjorie Kinnan Rawlings published the autobiographical *Cross Creek*.

Mari Sandoz published the biography *Crazy Horse*.

Stevie Smith published the poetry collection *Mother, What Is Man?*

Katharine Hepburn starred opposite Elliott Nugent in Philip Barry's play *Without Love*.

Pearl Buck published the novel *Dragon Seed*, set in wartime China.

Zora Neale Hurston published the autobiographical *Dust Tracks on the Road*.

Edith Sitwell published the poetry collection *Street Songs*.

Georgia O'Keeffe painted *It Was a Man and a Pot*, *The Grey Hills*, and *The White Place in Shadow*.

Mary McCarthy published the novel *The Company She Keeps*.

Daphne du Maurier published the novel *Frenchman's Creek*.

Gertrude Atherton published the novel *The Horn of Life*.

Lynn Fontanne starred opposite Alfred Lunt in S. N. Behrman's comedy *The Pirate*.

Gypsy Rose Lee starred opposite Bobby Clark in the play *Star and Garter*.

Rumer Godden published the novel *Breakfast with the Nikolides*.

Ruth Gipps composed the first of her five symphonies.

Mary Lavin published the first of her many short-story collections, *Tales from Bective Bridge*.

The first all-woman band in the U.S. armed forces was founded in Iowa.

b. Barbra Streisand (Barbara Joan Streisand, 1942– ), American singer, actress, and director, who became an international popular singing star and a film star in the 1960s.

b. Aretha Franklin (1942– ), American soul singer, one of the leading singers of the 1960s and 1970s.

b. Erica Mann Jong (1942– ), American novelist and poet, a popular novelist from publication of her best-selling *Fear of Flying* (1973).

b. Ama Ata (Christina) Aidoo (1942– ), Ghanian writer.

b. Carole King (1942– ), American singer and songwriter.

b. Genevieve Bujold (1942– ), French-Canadian actress.

b. Margarethe von Trotta (1942– ), German actress and director.

b. Susan Hampshire (1942– ), British actress.

b. Tammy Wynette (Virginia Wynette Pugh, 1942– ), American country singer and songwriter.

d. L. M. (Lucy Maud) Montgomery (1874–1942), Canadian writer, who created *Anne of Green Gables*.

d. Carole Lombard (Jane Alice Peters, 1908–1942), American film star, who died in an airplane crash.

d. Violet Augusta Mary Vanbrugh (1867–1942), British actress, like her sister Irene Vanbrugh a leading figure on the British stage for more than 50 years.

d. Akiko Otori Yosano (1878–1942), Japanese poet.

d. Jessie Tarbox Beals (1870–1942), American photographer, a portraitist and photojournalist.

d. Alice Hegan Rice (1870–1942), American author.

d. Cecilia Beaux (1855–1942), American painter and teacher.

d. Mary Abastenia St. Leger Eberle (1878–1942), American sculptor.

d. Marie Tempest (Mary Susan Etherington; 1864–1942), British actress and singer.

d. Violet Hunt (1866–1942), British biographer and novelist.

# 1943

## POLITICS/LAW/WAR

Oveta Culp Hobby became the first director of the Women's Army Corps (WAC), which superseded the Women's Army Auxiliary Corps (WAAC), and in which women received equal status and pay with male reservists.

Marine Corps Women's Reserve was formed; it would later become a permanent part of the Marine Corps, under the Women's Armed Forces Integration Act (1948).

Under the Lanham Act, federal funds were supplied to build and run day-care centers for the children of women working in World War II defense plants, providing too-small but useful day-care help during the war; this did not continue during the anti-female worker reaction that drove most women from the blue-collar work force immediately after the war.

Odette Marie Céline Brailey Hallowes, working as a spy for Britain in Nazi-occupied France, was captured, tortured, and then jailed in Ravensbrück concentration camp (1943–1945).

Mabel Howard won election as a Labour Party member of the New Zealand parliament.

Angelika Balabanoff published *Conquest of Power* and *Tears*.

b. Benazir Bhutto (1943– ), prime minister of Pakistan (1988–1990; 1993–1996) and one of the world's most prominent women. She is the daughter of Zulfikar Ali Bhutto, Pakistani prime minister (1972–1977), who was executed by the military (1979).

b. Brenda Dean (1943– ), British trade unionist official, who joined Sogat (Society of Graphical and Allied Trades) in her teens, becoming its general secretary.

b. Sheila Rowbotham (1943– ), British historian, feminist socialist, and educator.

b. Betty Williams (1943– ), Northern Ireland peace campaigner.

d. Anita Augspurg (1857–1943), German feminist and woman suffrage leader who, with her life-long companion, Lida Heymann, became a foremost radical suffragist, in Germany and internationally; leader of the Federation of German Women's Associations and campaigner against legalized prostitution. She and Heymann were also pacifists whose opposition to World War I cost them much of their women's movement leadership, but who continued to organize for feminist causes during the Weimar period, fleeing Germany when the Nazis came to power.

d. Lida Heymann (1867–1943), German feminist and women's suffrage leader, with her lifelong companion, Anita Augspurg, a leader of the radical wing of the German feminist and suffrage movements, founder of the Women's Welfare Association (1900), and pacifist who opposed World War I and fled Germany after the Nazis took power.

d. Edith How-Martyn (1880–1943), British feminist and social reformer, a leading suffragist and birth control advocate.

d. Helene Stöcker (1869–1943), German feminist, pacifist, and women's rights movement leader, founder of the League for the Protection of Motherhood and Sexual Reform (1904).

## RELIGION/EDUCATION/EVERYDAY LIFE

Ruth Benedict and Gene Welfish published *The Races of Mankind*, an antiracialist statement that generated massive opposition from some racist Southerners in the U.S. Congress.

Arthur and Elizabeth Schlesinger Library at Radcliffe College was established, a major collection of primary and secondary works covering all aspects of American women's history; founded in the same decade was another such archive, the Sophia Smith Collection at Smith College.

All American Girls Baseball League (1943–1954) played in the Chicago area, their story told in the film *A League of Their Own* (1992).

The full curriculum of Harvard College was first opened to women at Radcliffe College; they would not receive Harvard degrees, however, until the early 1960s.

Nellie Neilson was the first woman elected president of the American Historical Association.

Mary Madeleva Wolff established the first American graduate school of sacred doctrine for women, at St. Mary's College, Notre Dame, Indiana.

Anne Loughlin became the first woman to serve as president of Britain's Trades Union Congress; she had been on the TUC General Council since 1929.

Agnes Smedley published *Battle Hymn of China*.

Jessie Bernard and her husband, Luther Lee Bernard, published *Origins of American Sociology*.

b. Billie Jean Moffitt King (1943– ), American tennis player, a key figure in making women's tennis a major sport and the first sportswoman to win more than $100,000 in a single year (1971).

b. Cecilia Danieli (1943– ), Italian industrialist, head of her family's steel company, "Italy's first lady of steel."

d. Beatrice Potter Webb (1858–1943), British economist, a central figure in the Fabian Society and so in British socialism, and a prolific and highly influential author, often in collaboration with her husband, Sidney James Webb.

d. Mary Kenney O'Sullivan (1864–1943), American feminist and union activist, the first female American Federation of Labor organizer (1892), and a founder of the National Women's Trade Union League (1903).

d. Simone Weil (1903–1943), French philosopher, educator, and writer, with strong sympathies for communism, religion, and workers' concerns, who died of tuberculosis while in London with the Free French forces; many of her writings were published posthumously.

### SCIENCE/TECHNOLOGY/MEDICINE

Maria Goeppert Mayer led a team that successfully extracted uranium-235, fissionable material needed for making the atomic bomb, which was being constructed secretly under the Manhattan Project.

Women's Airforce Service Pilots (WASPs) was established in the United States, with women under director Jacqueline Cochran, ferrying all types of aircraft across the United States from factories to the coasts for shipment overseas and handling much of the domestic flying altogether. Earlier in World War II, Cochran and 25 other American women had joined the British Air Transport Auxiliary in England.

Restrictions on female physicians serving in the armed forces were temporarily lifted by the U.S. government; they would be reimposed at war's end; not until the 1950s would female doctors win rank and commission in the U.S. armed forces.

French physicist Yvette Cauchois published a notable paper on X-ray emissions from lead, gold, and thallium.

Antonia Maury received the Annie Jump Cannon Prize from the American Astronomical Society for her system of classifying stars with their spectra, laying the foundation for modern astrophysics.

Edith Clarke published *Circuit Analysis of AC Power Systems, Symmetrical and Related Components*, a classic electrical engineering textbook.

Industrial physician Alice Hamilton published the autobiographical *Exploring the Dangerous Trades*.

b. Jocelyn Bell (1943– ), British astronomer who discovered pulsars (1967), but did not receive the credit (or the Nobel Prize) for the discovery.

d. Lillien Jane Martin (1851–1943), American psychologist long associated with Stanford University (1899–1916), who pioneered in establishing counseling centers for the elderly.

d. Mary Jane Rathbun (1860–1943), American marine zoologist who assisted her brother Richard, curator of marine invertebrates at the National Museum in Washington, D.C., organizing and cataloguing the museum's collection.

### ARTS/LITERATURE

Agnes De Mille's choreography set a new American musical-theater standard in Richard Rodgers's and Oscar Hammerstein's *Oklahoma!*, starring Joan Roberts, Alfred Drake, and Celeste Holm.

Bette Davis and Miriam Hopkins starred in Vincent Sherman's film *Old Acquaintance*. Davis also starred opposite Paul Henreid in Irving Rapper's film drama *Now, Voyager* and opposite Paul Lukas in *Watch on the Rhine*, Herman Shumlin's film of Lillian Hellman's antifascist play (1941).

Deborah Kerr played four roles in *The Life and Death of Colonel Blimp*, all opposite Roger Livesey as the antique British officer.

Ethel Waters and Lena Horne headed an all-African-American cast in Vincente Minnelli's film musical *Cabin in the Sky*.

Ingrid Bergman, Katina Paxinou, and Gary Cooper starred in *For Whom the Bell Tolls*, Sam Wood's film version of Ernest Hemingway's Spanish Civil War story.

Anna Mary ("Grandma") Moses painted *The Thanksgiving Turkey*.

Betty Smith published the novel *A Tree Grows in Brooklyn*.

Dolores Del Rio starred opposite Pedro Armendariz in Emilio Fernandez's Mexican film classic *Maria Candelaria*.

Esther Forbes published the children's historical novel *Johnny Tremain*, which won the Newbery Award.

Jennifer Jones starred opposite Charles Bickford in Henry King's *The Song of Bernadette*, winning a best actress Academy Award.

Margaret Sullavan starred opposite Elliott Nugent in John Van Druten's play *The Voice of the Turtle*.

Mary Martin starred opposite John Boles in Kurt Weill's musical *One Touch of Venus*.

Teresa Wright starred opposite Joseph Cotten in Alfred Hitchcock's film thriller *Shadow of a Doubt*.

Ayn Rand published the novel *The Fountainhead*.

Pearl Primus choreographed *Strange Fruits*.

Eudora Welty published the short-story collection *The Wide Net*.

Lena Horne starred in the film musical *Stormy Weather*.

Georgia O'Keeffe painted *Cliffs Beyond Aliquiu, Cottonwood Tree in Spring, Pelvis with Moon*, and *White Flower on Red Earth*.

Anna Seghers published the novel *Transit*.

Elsa Morante published the novel *House of Liars*.

Joan Cross became director of the Sadler's Wells Opera company (1943–1945).

Greer Garson played the title role in Mervyn LeRoy's *Madame Curie*.

Helen Hayes starred in the title role in *Harriet*, Florence Ryerson and Colin Clements's play.

Ruth Gipps composed her *Violin Concerto*.

Taylor Caldwell published the novel *The Arm and the Darkness*.

Barbara Cartland began publication of her multivolume autobiography, with *The Isthmus Years*.

b. Catherine Deneuve (Catherine Dorléac, 1943– ), French actress, an international film star from the mid-1960s, starting with *The Umbrellas of Cherbourg* (1963).

b. Joni Mitchell (Roberta Joan Anderson, 1943– ), Canadian folksinger, composer, and guitarist, a major folk and blues figure in the 1960s and 1970s.

b. Judith Jamison (1943– ), African-American dancer, leading dancer of the Alvin Ailey Dance Theater (1967–1980), later its director (1990– ).

b. Janis Joplin (1943–1970), a leading American blues singer of the 1960s.

b. Nikki Giovanni (1943– ), American poet.

d. Beatrix Potter (1866–1943), British writer and illustrator who created Peter Rabbit; also an unsung biologist.

d. (Marguerite) Radclyffe Hall (1880–1943), British novelist and poet, author of *The Well of Loneliness* (1928).

d. E. M. Delafield (1890–1943), British writer, a novelist, but best known for *The Diary of a Provincial Lady* (1931).

d. Camille Claudel (1864–1943), French sculptor.

## 1944

### POLITICS/LAW/WAR

Italian socialist and antifascist Teresa Noce, working in the French Resistance, was captured and imprisoned in Ravensbrück (1944–1945).

Women won the right to vote and be elected to office in Bulgaria, France, and Jamaica.

Elizabeth, future queen of the United Kingdom, then 18, served as an Auxiliary Territorial Service driver during World War II.

Dorothy V. Bush became secretary of America's Democratic Party (1944–1989), calling the roll and tallying the vote at nominating conventions.

b. Mary Bourke Robinson (1944– ), Irish liberal, human rights lawyer, and the first woman to be president of Ireland (1990).

b. Sharon Pratt Dixon Kelly (1944– ), American lawyer and politician, the first African-American and first female treasurer of the Democratic National Committee (1984), who became the first African-American woman elected mayor of a major city, Washington, D.C. (1991–1994).

b. Angela Davis (1944– ), African-American philosopher and Communist militant, tried and acquitted in a sensational trial (1972).

b. Bettina Aptheker (1944– ), American teacher, a Marxist and feminist who became a leader of the Berkeley Free Speech Movement (1965).

b. Lombe Phyllis Chibesakunda (1944– ), Zambian lawyer, law officer, and diplomat.

d. Electra Apostoloy (1912–1944), Greek communist organizer, a World War II resistance fighter who was captured and murdered by the Nazis.

d. Hannah Senesh (1921–1944), Hungarian-Israeli soldier, captured and murdered by the Germans after parachuting into Nazi-occupied Eastern Europe; her story, told in her *Life and Diary*, was published posthumously (1945).

d. Luise Kautsky (1864–1944), Austrian socialist, communist, suffragist, and writer, collaborator and wife of socialist writer Karl Kautsky. She died at Dachau.

### RELIGION/EDUCATION/EVERYDAY LIFE

Florence Li Tim Oi became the first woman ever ordained by the Anglican Communion (Anglican Church worldwide), in the Portuguese colony of Macao, partly because male candidates were scarce during World War II.

In Italy, the Unione Donne Italiane (UDI) was founded, its monthly magazine being *Noi Donne*; two women's journals also began publication: *Memoria* and *DonneWomanFemme* (DWF).

Elizabeth Brinton Clark, of the United Presbyterian Church of North America, became a Presbyterian minister, but her ordination was soon invalidated.

Huda Sh'arawi helped found the All Arab Federation of Women.

Jacquetta Hawkes, with then-husband Christopher Hawkes, published the influential *Prehistoric Britain* (1944) and *Early Britain* (1945).

Denny Griswold was founder-publisher of the *Public Relations News*.

b. Ann Oakley (1944– ), British sociologist and writer.

d. Ida Minerva Tarbell (1857–1944), American writer, a leading early 20th-century investigative journalist or "muckraker," best known by far for her 1904 book on the Standard Oil Company.

d. Aimée Semple McPherson (1890–1944), Canadian-American religious leader, founder of the International Church of the Foursquare Gospel, which grew to have some 600 churches worldwide and 20,000 members; she died of an overdose of sleeping pills.

d. Margaret Llewelyn Davies (1861–1944), British feminist, socialist, pacifist, and social reformer, a leading figure in the cooperative movement for more than four decades.

## SCIENCE/TECHNOLOGY/MEDICINE

American pediatric cardiologist Helen Taussig discovered the congenital malformations of the heart that led to the characteristic color of "blue babies"; with her surgeon-colleague Albert Blalock, she devised an operation to correct them, which he first successfully performed.

Helene Deutsch published *The Psychology of Women*, her classic two-volume study of the various stages of women's development, exploring themes of passivity, masochism, and narcissism, and what she felt was the necessary resolution of the Oedipal conflict.

Women in the U.S. Army Nurse Corps won somewhat better pay and, for the first time, ranks roughly equivalent to men doing similar tasks. But substantial, discriminatory pay differentials and lesser benefits remained within those equivalent ranks.

Grace Hopper joined the U.S. Navy as a commander in the WAVES (1944–1946); she would remain on active duty or active reserve until her retirement (1986), as a key computer specialist.

Petroleum-industry engineer Ivy Parker became first editor of *Corrosion* (1944–1965), for the National Association of Corrosion Engineers.

b. Bernardine P. Healy (1944– ), American physician and educator who became the first woman to head the National Institutes of Health (1991–1993).

d. Hélène Bruhl Metzger (1889–ca. 1944), French chemist and writer on the history of science and philosophy; having fled Paris to Lyons, where she worked in the Bureau d'Etudes Israèlites, she was arrested and deported to Auschwitz, where she died.

d. Margaret Eliza Maltby (1860–1944), American physicist and educator long associated with Barnard College (1900–1931), active in seeking graduate scholarships for women.

d. Mary Adela Blagg (1858–1944), British astronomer who was appointed by an international committee to standardize the names of features of the moon (1907).

## ARTS/LITERATURE

Joan Fontaine played the title role opposite Orson Welles in Robert Stevenson's film version of Charlotte Brontë's 1847 novel *Jane Eyre*.

Martha Graham choreographed *Appalachian Spring*.

Lillian Smith published her antilynching novel *Strange Fruit*.

Mady Christians starred in John Van Druten's play *I Remember Mama*.

Barbara Stanwyck as the murderous wife starred opposite Fred MacMurray and Edward G. Robinson in *Double Indemnity*, Billy Wilder's film version of the 1936 James M. Cain novel.

Colette published the novel *Gigi*.

Josephine Hull and Jean Adair starred as the gentle serial murderers in *Arsenic and Old Lace*, Frank Capra's film version of the 1941 Joseph Kesselring play.

Lauren Bacall starred opposite Humphrey Bogart in *To Have and Have Not*; Howard Hawks directed the wartime antifascist film, based on the 1937 Ernest Hemingway novel.

Ingrid Bergman starred opposite Charles Boyer and Joseph Cotten, winning a best actress Academy Award, in George Cukor's film thriller *Gaslight*, based on the 1938 Patrick Hamilton play.

Judy Garland starred in Vincente Minnelli's classic film musical *Meet Me in St. Louis*, set at the 1903 St. Louis World's Fair.

Tallulah Bankhead starred in *Lifeboat*, Alfred Hitchcock's wartime film about survival at sea.

Mary Chase's play *Harvey* starred Josephine Hull and Frank Fay.

Rosamond Lehmann published the novel *The Ballad and the Source*.

Mai Zetterling starred in Alf Sjöberg's film *Torment*.

Celeste Holm starred in the title role of *Bloomer Girl*, Harold Arlen and E. Y. Harburg's musical.

Hilda Simms starred in the title role opposite Earle Hyman in the American Negro Theatre production of Philip Yordan's play *Anna Lucasta*.

Georgia O'Keeffe painted *Aliquiu Country, Flying Backbone, Pelvis III, The Black Place II*, and *The Black Place III*.

Katharine Hepburn and John Huston starred in Jack Conway's film version of Pearl Buck's novel *Dragon Seed*, set in war-torn China.

Edith Sitwell published the poetry collection *Green Song*.

Bette Davis starred opposite Claude Rains in Vincent Sherman's *Mr. Skeffington*.

Helen Hayes starred opposite James Stewart in Mary Chase's play *Harvey*.

Elizabeth Bergner starred opposite Victor Jory in the stage thriller *The Two Mrs. Carrolls*, by Marguerite Vale Veiller, writing as Martin Vale.

Gene Tierney played the title role opposite Dana Andrews in Otto Preminger's romantic thriller *Laura*, based on Vera Caspary's novel.

Grace Williams composed her *Sea Sketches*.

Greer Garson was *Mrs. Parkington*, in Tay Garnett's screen version of the 1942 Louis Bromfield novel.

H. D. (Hilda Doolittle) published the poetry collection *The Walls Do Not Fall*.

Jean Stafford published the novel *Boston Adventure*.

June Havoc starred opposite Bobby Clark in Cole Porter's stage musical *Mexican Hayride*.

Carmen Laforet published the autobiographical novel *Nada*.

b. Diana Ross (1944– ), American singer and actress, a major popular singer in the 1960s and 1970s with the Supremes, and then a solo concert and recording star into the 1990s.

b. Kiri Te Kanawa (1944– ), New Zealand soprano, an international opera star from the early 1970s, and also a highly regarded popular singer and recording artist.

b. Alice Walker (1944– ), African-American novelist, poet, short story writer, biographer, and editor, whose work deals mainly with the experience of African-American women.

b. Jill Clayburgh (1944– ), American film star of the 1970s and early 1980s.

b. Emmylou Harris (1944– ), American country singer and bandleader, a star from the mid-1970s.

b. Jacqueline Bisset (1944– ), British actress.

d. Ethel Mary Smyth (1858–1944), British composer and women's rights advocate who composed the suffragist anthem *March of the Women* (1911).

d. Amy Marcy Cheney Beach (1867–1944), American pianist and composer.

d. Yvette Guilbert (1865–1944), French singer, a leading figure in cabaret.

d. Cécile Louise Stéphanie Chaminade (1857–1944), French pianist and composer.

d. Anne Frank (1930–1944), Dutch-Jewish diarist who died in a German death camp; her diary, kept while in hiding from the Nazis in Amsterdam, was published posthumously and became a key document of the Holocaust.

## 1945

### POLITICS/LAW/WAR

Eleanor Roosevelt became a member of the United States delegation to the United Nations (1945–1953), chairing the U.N. Commission on Human Rights. In a 1952 speech before the U.N., she would comment: "Too often the great decisions are originated and given form in bodies made up wholly of men, or so completely dominated by them that whatever of special value women have to offer is shunted aside without expression."

Marthe Ricard, then a Paris city councilwoman, played a major role in ending legalized prostitution in France (1945–1946). She had been a noted Resistance leader during World War II.

Women won the right to vote and be elected to office in Hungary, Indonesia, Italy, and Japan.

Among the women who were elected to Britain's Parliament were Jennie Lee, once again a Labour member of Parliament (1945–1970), and Barbara Castle (1945–1979). Ellen Wilkinson was appointed minister of education in Britain's postwar Labour government and Edith Summerskill became an undersecretary at Britain's Ministry of Food.

Helen Gahagan Douglas began the first of her three Congressional terms from California.

Oveta Culp Hobby was the first woman awarded the U.S. Army's Distinguished Service Medal, for her service as head of the Women's Army (Auxiliary) Corps.

Anna Rosenberg was awarded the Medal of Freedom.

b. Daw Aung San Suu Kyi (1945– ), Burmese and worldwide human-rights advocate, winner of the Nobel Peace Prize (1991). She is the daughter of Aung San, the founder of modern Burma (now Myanmar), who became his country's first prime minister (1947) but was assassinated in the same year.

b. Alice M. Henderson Harris (1945– ), African-American chaplain in the U.S. Army, its first woman in that position (1974).

b. Shulamith Firestone (1945– ), Canadian-American radical feminist theoretician and organizer of the late 1960s and early 1970s.

b. Wilma P. Mankiller (1945– ), Cherokee leader.

d. Margot (Margaret Emma Alice) Tennant Asquith (1864–1945), Scottish writer, and wife of British prime minister Herbert Asquith.

d. Marie Lacoste Gerin-Lajoie (1867–1945), French-Canadian feminist and writer.

d. Eva Braun (1912–1945), Adolf Hitler's lover (1931–1945); they were probably married before their joint suicide in Berlin (April).

## RELIGION/EDUCATION/EVERYDAY LIFE

Bess Myerson was the first Jewish contestant to become Miss America.

American missionary Ida Pruitt coauthored *A Daughter of Han: The Autobiography of a Chinese Working Woman.*

British social scientist Barbara Wootton published *Freedom Under Planning.*

Françoise Giroud co-founded and was first editor of *Elle* magazine (1945–1952).

Chinese-American Jade Snow Wong published *Fifth Chinese Daughter.*

b. Arlene Blum (1945– ), American mountaineer.

d. Margaret Dreier Robins (1868–1945), American reformer and union activist long associated with the Women's Trade Union League (1904–1922), later serving as president (1907–1922).

d. Henrietta Szold (1860–1945), American Zionist leader who organized the Jewish women's organization Hadassah (1912) and was active in easing passage of Jews to Israel in the 1920s and 1930s.

d. Yasui Tetsu (1870–1945), Japanese educator, Japan's first female college president.

## SCIENCE/TECHNOLOGY/MEDICINE

British physician Janet Vaughan developed ways to treat people with extreme starvation as one of the team of physicians sent, even before World War II ended, to treat survivors of the Nazi concentration camps.

Lise Meitner was elected a member of the Swedish Academy of Sciences. After the atomic bomb was dropped on Hiroshima, Meitner discontinued her work in nuclear fission; she had opposed both the building and use of the bomb.

British crystallographer Kathleen Lonsdale became the first female fellow of the Royal Society.

Karen Horney published *A Constructive Theory of Neurosis.*

d. Ida Henrietta Hyde (1857–1945), American physiologist whose research focused on the physiology of the developing embryo. Only recently acknowledged as having developed the earliest microelectrode, she was long a teacher at the University of Kansas (1898–1920) and was the first woman to receive a Ph.D. in science from a German university (1896).

d. Florence Bascom (1862–1945), American geologist and educator, associated with Bryn Mawr College from 1898, who in the 1880s introduced microscopic analytical techniques to the study of oil-bearing rocks (petrology); she was the first woman to receive her doctorate from Johns Hopkins University, to be employed as a geologist by the U.S. Geological Survey, and to be made a fellow of the Geological Society of America.

d. Harriet Boyd Hawes (1871–1945), American archaeologist, the first woman to lead an archaeological excavation in the Aegean; she taught at Smith College (1900–1906), then Wellesley (1920–1936).

d. Josephine (Sara) Baker (1873–1945), American physician and public-health worker noted for her work in New York's Lower East Side.

ARTS/LITERATURE

Anna Magnani starred in Roberto Rossellini's classic film *Open City*, emerging as an international film star.

Arletty created the role of Garance in *Children of Paradise* (*Les Enfants du Paradis*), opposite Jean-Louis Barrault as the mime Deburau in Marcel Carné's film classic.

Gabriela Mistral was awarded the Nobel Prize for literature.

Celia Johnson and Trevor Howard starred in David Lean's classic film love story *Brief Encounter*, adapted by Noël Coward from his 1936 one-act play *Still Life*.

Laurette Taylor created the Amanda Wingfield role in Tennessee Williams's play *The Glass Menagerie*, which costarred Eddie Dowling and Julie Haydon.

Margaret Bourke-White published her photos of the German death camp at Buchenwald, taken during the Allied liberation; a massive contribution to photojournalism and to history.

Joan Crawford starred in the title role in Michael Curtiz's film *Mildred Pierce*, based on the 1941 James M. Cain novel. She won a best actress Academy Award for her portrayal of a woman whose drive toward an independent life and career destroys her family, in a stereotypical attack on independent women that was part of the temper of the immediate postwar period.

Bette Davis starred opposite John Dall in Irving Rapper's film *The Corn Is Green*, based on Emlyn Williams's 1938 play.

Gabrielle Roy published the novel *The Tin Flute*.

Barbara Bel Geddes starred opposite Gordon Heath in *Deep Are the Roots*, Arnaud d'Usseau and James Gow's pro–civil rights play.

Gwendolyn Brooks published the poetry collection *A Street in Bronzeville*.

Jan Clayton starred opposite John Raitt in *Carousel*, the Richard Rodgers and Oscar Hammerstein musical.

Kay Hammond, Margaret Rutherford, Rex Harrison, Constance Cummings, and Jacqueline Clark starred in *Blithe Spirit*, David Lean's film version of Noël Coward's 1941 stage comedy.

Jessamyn West published the novel *The Friendly Persuasion*.

Wendy Hiller starred opposite Roger Livesey in Michael Powell and Emeric Pressburger's film *I Know Where I'm Going*, a wartime love story set on the Scottish coast.

Joan Cross created the role of Ellen Orford in Benjamin Britten's opera *Peter Grimes*.

Lana Turner starred opposite John Garfield in Tay Garnett's film of *The Postman Always Rings Twice*, based on James M. Cain's 1934 novel.

Betty Field starred opposite Wendell Corey in Elmer Rice's play *Dream Girl*.

Dorothy McGuire, Joan Blondell, Peggy Anne Garner, and James Dunn starred in Elia Kazan's film version of Betty Smith's 1943 novel *A Tree Grows in Brooklyn*.

Edith Sitwell published the poetry collection *Song of the Cold*.

Ingrid Bergman starred opposite Gregory Peck in Alfred Hitchcock's film thriller *Spellbound* and opposite Bing Crosby in *The Bells of St. Mary's*.

Georgia O'Keeffe painted *Cliffs, My Backyard, Dead Tree with Pink Hill, Hills and Mesa to the West, Pelvis Series, Red with Yellow, Red Hills and Blue Sky*, and *Spring Tree No. II*.

Joan Littlewood and Ewan McColl founded the highly experimental, very influential Theatre Workshop (1945–1964; 1970–1975), originally based in Manchester.

Paulette Goddard starred in Jean Renoir's film *Diary of a Chambermaid*.

Elizabeth Taylor published the novel *At Mrs. Lippincott's*.

Gracie Fields starred in the film *Molly and Me*.

Louise Weiss published the novel *La Marseillaise*.

María Cadilla de Martínez, writing as Liana, published *Hitos de la Raza*, a group of Puerto Rican folk tales.

Nancy Mitford published the novel *The Pursuit of Love*.

Mary Lavin published the novel *The House in Clewe Street*.

b. Mia Villiers Farrow (1945– ), American actress, a film star from the late 1960s; she starred in many of Woody Allen's films, until their highly publicized personal and professional breakup (1992).

b. Bette Midler (1945– ), American singer and actress, a recording and cabaret star from the early 1970s and a film star from the early 1980s.

b. Goldie Hawn (1945– ), American actress and comedian who became a popular figure in television's "Laugh-In" (1968–1973), later a film star.

b. Jacqueline Du Pré (1945–1987), British cellist.

b. Jessye Norman (1945– ), American soprano.

d. Käthe Kollwitz (1867–1945), German artist, pacifist, and socialist, who continued to produce her powerful and antifascist graphic work in Germany during the Nazi period, much of it prefiguring the death camp photos that would emerge after the war.

d. La Argentenita (Encarnacíon Lopez Julves, 1895–1945), Spanish dancer; the best-known of the dances she choreographed were *Goyescas* and *Bolero*.

d. Emily Carr (1871–1945), Canadian painter, largely of Native American scenes on the British Columbia coast.

d. Zinaida Nikolayevna Hippius (1869–1945), Russian writer who lived abroad after the Bolshevik Revolution.

d. Ellen Glasgow (1874–1945), American writer.

d. Alla Nazimova (1879–1945), Russian actress, in America from 1905.

d. Margaret Deland (1857–1945), American novelist.

# 1946

## POLITICS/LAW/WAR

Women won the right to vote and be elected to office in Cameroon, Ecuador, North Korea, and Vietnam.

Golda Meir became head of the political department of the Jewish Agency for Palestine.

Louise Schröder, then a deputy mayor of Berlin, became acting mayor of the city.

Soia Mentschikoff became the first woman to teach at Harvard Law School.

Fusaye Ichikawa was elected president of the New Japan Women's League, which focused on women's suffrage and also took up a considerable range of other women's rights matters.

Agatha Barbara became Malta's first female member of parliament.

Annabelle Rankin was elected a Liberal Party member of the Australian Senate (1946–1966).

Barbara Wootton chaired the Metropolitan London Juvenile Courts (1946–1962).

France's new constitution included the principle of equal rights for men and women (as would the 1958 Constitution).

Georgia Lusk was the first New Mexico woman elected to Congress (serving 1947–1948).

Marie-Hélène Lefaucheux became a member of the French Senate (1946–1948) and a French delegate to the first United Nations General Assembly.

Frances Perkins published *The Roosevelt I Knew*.

b. Andrea Dworkin (1946– ), American radical feminist, who as a theoretician has called for a revolution to destroy concepts of male and female, and consequently of male supremacy, and who has focused on the outlawing of pornography as a stimulant to sexual violence against women.

b. Tansu Çiller (1946– ), Turkish educator and politician, the first woman to be prime minister of Turkey (1993–1995), later deputy premier and foreign secretary (1996– ) in a coalition government..

d. Hannah Sheehy-Skeffington (1877–1946), Irish feminist and independence movement activist, a leading suffragist before World War I, who chaired the Irish Franchise League (1913).

d. Emilie Gourd (1879–1946), Swiss feminist, suffragist, writer, and editor, founder of the periodical *Le mouvement féministe*.

## RELIGION/EDUCATION/EVERYDAY LIFE

Emily Greene Balch and John R. Mott were corecipients of the Nobel Peace Prize.

Mary Ritter Beard published *Women as a Force in History*, putting forward the view that women, even in male-dominated societies, have powerfully influenced the course of history, rather than merely being dispossessed victims.

Pauline Frederick was the first woman working in "hard news," as news commentator for ABC (1946–1953), working on early morning radio and evening television news.

As India won independence from Britain, Dhanvanthi Rama Rau was president of the All India Women's Conference (1946–1947).

Catherine Booth led the Salvation Army's war relief efforts for children after World War II, as she had done after World War I.

After World War II, Constance Spry helped found London's Cordon Bleu Cookery School and also ran an exclusive finishing school.

Edith Houghton became a scout for the Philadelphia Phillies, the first woman to scout for a major league baseball team.

Margery Hurst founded an employment agency for temporary secretaries in London's Brook Street, developing the Brook Street Bureau, an international chain, specializing in skilled clerical staff.

Emily Post founded her Institute for the Study of Gracious Living.

Mary Ann Quinn was the first known American woman to be steeplejack, working for Aerial Engineering, a California firm founded by her late husband.

Ruth Benedict published *The Chrysanthemum and the Sword: Patterns of Japanese Culture*.

Mildred Cable published *China, Her Life and Her People*.

b. Connie Chung (Constance Yu-hwa Chung, 1946– ), American broadcaster, who became the second woman and first Asian-American to anchor an American network evening newscast (1993).

b. Karen Gay Silkwood (1946–1974), American atomic worker, who died in highly controversial circumstances.

b. Clare (Mary) Francis (1946– ), British sailor and writer, the first woman to skipper in the Whitbread Round the World Event (1977–1978).

d. Eleanor Rathbone (1872–1946), British reformer, feminist, and politician whose early work focused on the economics of family life, later much concerned with women's issues in India and Jewish refugees.

d. May (Margaret Mary Edith) Tennant (1869–1946), Irish reformer.

## SCIENCE/TECHNOLOGY/MEDICINE

Grace Goldsmith was the first to report on using folic acid to treat vitamin-deficiency anemia; long a professor at Tulane University, she that year became director of nutrition training for medical students there, the first such program in the world.

Irène Joliot-Curie became director of the Radium Institute first led by her mother.

Maria Goeppert Mayer joined the University of Chicago's Institute for Nuclear Studies, though she received no salary because her husband was employed by the university.

Amalia Coutsouris (later Fleming) joined the Wright-Fleming Institute in London, working with Alexander Fleming, discoverer of penicillin, and Robert May, studying the antibiotic streptomycin.

Dorothy Russell published *Observations on the Pathology of Hydrocephalus*.

## ARTS/LITERATURE

Carson McCullers published the novel *The Member of the Wedding*.

Eudora Welty published the novel *Delta Wedding*.

Kathleen Ferrier with Joan Cross starred in Benjamin Britten's opera *The Rape of Lucretia*.

Nelly Sachs published the poetry collection *In the Dwellings of Death*.

Madeleine Renaud and Jean-Louis Barrault, her husband, left the Comédie Française to found the Paris-based Renaud-Barrault repertory company. As its costar and codirector, she further enhanced her position as a leading figure in the French theater.

Margot Fonteyn danced the lead in Frederick Ashton's ballet *Symphonic Variations*.

Vivien Leigh as Cleopatra and Claude Rains as Caesar starred in *Caesar and Cleopatra*, Gabriel Pascal's film based on George Bernard Shaw's 1906 play.

Cheryl Crawford, Eva Le Gallienne, and Margaret Webster organized the American Repertory Theatre, which lasted just one season.

Ethel Merman starred in the title role as Annie Oakley, introducing "There's No Business like Show Business" in Irving Berlin's stage musical *Annie Get Your Gun*.

Ingrid Bergman starred in the title role of Maxwell Anderson's play *Joan of Lorraine*.

Denise Levertov published the poetry collection *The Double Image*.

Irene Dunne and Rex Harrison played the title roles in John Cromwell's film *Anna and the King of Siam*.

Lillian Hellman's play *Another Part of the Forest* starred Patricia Neal, Mildred Dunnock, and Leo Genn.

Lauren Bacall starred opposite Humphrey Bogart in Howard Hawks's film version of the 1939 Raymond Chandler novel *The Big Sleep*.

Louise Nevelson showed her sculpture *Lovers II*.

Olivia de Havilland starred in *To Each His Own*, winning a best actress Academy Award.

Lynn Fontanne starred opposite Alfred Lunt in Terence Rattigan's play *O Mistress Mine*.

Judy Holliday starred as Billie Dawn opposite Paul Douglas and Gary Merrill in Garson Kanin's stage comedy *Born Yesterday*.

Sylvia Sidney starred opposite Robert Young in *The Searching Wind*, William Dieterle's film version of Lillian Hellman's 1944 play.

Katharine Cornell starred opposite Cedric Hardwicke in an American production of Jean Anouilh's *Antigone* and opposite a young Marlon Brando in George Bernard Shaw's *Candida*.

Kay Boyle published *Thirty Stories*.

Mai Zetterling starred in the film *Frieda*.

Pearl Buck published the novel *Pavilion of Women*.

Daphne du Maurier published the novel *The King's General*.

Georgia O'Keeffe painted *A Black Bird with Snow-covered Red Hills*.

Helen Hayes starred in Anita Loos's stage comedy *Happy Birthday*.

Judith Wright published her first poetry collections, *The Moving Image* and *The Double Tree*.

Miles Franklin published the autobiographical novel *My Career Goes Bung*.

Muriel Baker and Sydney Box won a best original screenplay Academy Award for *The Seventh Veil*.

Patricia Jones starred opposite Fredric March in Ruth Gordon's stage comedy *Years Ago*.

Ruby Hill played the title role opposite Rex Ingram and Pearl Bailey in *St. Louis Woman*, Harold Arlen and Johnny Mercer's musical.

Taylor Caldwell published the novel *This Side of Innocence*.

Anaïs Nin published the novel *Ladders of Fire*.

b. Candice Bergen (1946– ), American actress and photographer, star of television's *Murphy Brown*, and the daughter of ventriloquist Edgar Bergen.

b. Cher (Cherilyn LaPierre Sarkisian, 1946– ), American singer and actress, a leading popular singer from the mid-1960s and a film star of the 1980s and early 1990s.

b. Sally Field (1946– ), American actress who became a television situation-comedy star in the 1960s and emerged as a dramatic film star and two-time Oscar winner in the 1970s and 1980s.

b. Diane Keaton (1946– ), American actress, a film star in the 1970s, often in the works of Woody Allen and later in major supporting roles.

b. Dolly (Rebecca) Parton (1946– ), American country singer, songwriter, and actress, a country music star from the early 1970s and a film star from the early 1980s.

b. Helen Mirren (1946– ), British actress known for her *Prime Suspect* television series.

b. Linda Ronstadt (1946– ), American country and popular singer.

b. Liza Minnelli (1946– ), American actress and singer, daughter of Judy Garland and Vincente Minnelli.

b. Patty Duke (Astin) (Anna Marie Duke, 1946– ) American actress who played the young Helen Keller in the film *The Miracle Worker*.

b. Radwa 'Ashur (1946– ), Egyptian novelist.

d. Gertrude Stein (1874–1946), American novelist, poet, and playwright; long resident in France, she was an emblematic avant-garde expatriate in Paris during the interwar period.

d. Henry Handel Richardson (Henrietta Robertson Richardson, 1870–1946), Australian novelist.

d. (Helen) Laurette (Cooney) Taylor (1884–1946), American actress.

# 1947

## POLITICS/LAW/WAR

Women won the right to vote in Mexico, and to vote and be elected to office in Argentina, East Pakistan (later Bangladesh), and Venezuela.

Italy's new constitution affirmed the principles of equality, including equal pay for equal work, equal access to work and advancement, and equal political rights, while defining the woman's family role as essential.

As New Zealand's minister of health and child welfare (1947–1949), Mabel Howard became New Zealand's first female cabinet minister.

Marie-Elizabeth Luders, who had been forced by the Nazis to leave Germany, resumed her political career in the German senate, becoming the Bundestag's senior member by 1953 and becoming honorary president of the Federal Democratic Party (1957).

Marie-Hélène Lefaucheux chaired the United Nations Commission on the Status of Women.

Vijaya Lakshmi Pandit became Indian ambassador to the Soviet Union (1947–1949).

Florence Hancock became president of Britain's Trades Union Congress.

Guerrilla leader Rani Gaidinliu was freed by the newly independent Indian government, under Jawaharlal Nehru.

Louise Bennett served a second term as president of the Irish Trades Union Congress (1947–1948).

Mary White Ovington published *The Walls Came Tumbling Down*, an autobiographical account of her work with the NAACP.

Ana Pauker became foreign minister of Romania.

b. Hillary Rodham Clinton (1947– ), American lawyer, law professor, children's advocate, educational reformer, and women's rights leader, the wife of President Bill Clinton.

b. Kim (Avril Phaedra) Campbell (1947– ), Canadian lawyer and politician, who became Canada's first female prime minister (1993).

b. Carol Elizabeth Moseley-Braun (1947– ), Illinois Democratic senator, the first African-American woman to become a U.S. senator (1993– ), and at that time the only African-American in the Senate.

b. Hazel Rollins O'Leary (1947– ), African-American lawyer and energy company executive, Clinton administration secretary of energy.

b. Madeleine Korbel Albright (1947– ), American international affairs professor and diplomat, the Clinton administration's U.S. ambassador to the United Nations (1993–1997), then the first woman to be U.S. secretary of state (1997– ).

b. Petra Kelly (1947–1992), German environmentalist and politician.

d. Carrie Chapman Catt (1859–1947), American women's suffrage movement leader and pacifist, who led the American women's suffrage movement to victory with passage of the 19th (Anthony) Amendment (1919), granting women the vote.

d. Ellen Cicely Wilkinson (Red Ellen, 1891–1947), British socialist, trade unionist, feminist, writer, and politician, who became a Labour member of Parliament and minister.

## RELIGION/EDUCATION/EVERYDAY LIFE

Agnes Wilson Underwood became the first American woman to be city editor of a major daily newspaper, the *Los Angeles Evening Herald* (later *Herald-Examiner*).

Marynia Farnham and Ferdinand Lundberg published the antifeminist *Modern Woman: The Lost Sex*, as millions of American women were being forced out of war jobs and military service back into domestic roles; it would be almost a generation before a new wave of American women's rights activists would seriously challenge postwar assumptions about women's roles.

Ruth Benedict became president of the American Anthropological Association.

Charlemae Rollins published *We Build Together*, part of her long effort to free children's literature from stereotypical views of black people.

Louise Brough won the U.S. singles tennis title.

Simone Weil's *La Pesanteur et la Grâce* (*Gravity and Grace*) was posthumously published.

British cultural historian Frances Yates published *The French Academies of the Sixteenth Century*.

d. Huda Sh'arawi (1882–1947), Egyptian educator and women's rights activist, who founded Egypt's first women's association (1920) and its first secondary school for girls (1927).

## SCIENCE/TECHNOLOGY/MEDICINE

Gerty Cori became the first American woman to receive the Nobel Prize for physiology or medicine, shared with her husband, Carl Ferdinand Cori, and Bernardo A. Houssay, for their work on the Cori cycle, the series of chemical reactions by which the body converts carbohydrates into energy.

French physicist Yvette Cauchois and her colleague, H. Hulubei, published *Longeurs d'Onde des Emissions X et des Discontinuities d'Absorption X*, their classic work on atomic properties.

Irmgard Flügge-Lotz and her husband, Wilhelm Flügge, left Germany to join the Office National d'Études et de Recherches Aeronautiques (ONERA) in Paris, doing basic aeronautical research, then emigrating the United States to teach at Stanford University (1948).

Alice Chatham handcrafted the helmet worn by Chuck Yeager when he first broke the sound barrier; she would later design helmets for astronauts in the National Aeronautics and Space Administration.

Ann Shaw Carter was the first American woman to receive her helicopter rating.

German-born British archaeologist Elise J. Bäumgartel published *The Cultures of Prehistoric Egypt*, a massive catalogue of the University College of London's Egyptian Neolithic collection.

Adele Davis published her nutrition book *Let's Cook It Right*.

Dorothy Crowfoot Hodgkin was made a fellow of Britain's Royal Society.

Marie Wormington published *Prehistoric Indians of the Southwest*.

b. Elizabeth Meyer Glaser (1947–1994), American AIDS activist, cofounder of the Pediatric AIDS Foundation.

b. Mollie Beattie (1947–1996), American forester and natural resources manager.

d. Mary Coffin (Ware) Dennett (1872–1947), American suffragist, pacifist, and advocate of birth control and sex education, founder of the first American birth control organization, the National Birth Control League (NBCL, 1915).

d. Ethel Gordon Manson Fenwick (1857–1947), British nurse who led campaigns to gain greater recognition for female health professionals, helping to found the British Nurses' Association and other organizations.

d. Annie Russell Maunder (1868–1947), Irish astronomer long associated with the Royal Observatory at Greenwich (1891–1895; 1915–1920) and with the journal of the British Astronomical Association (1894–1896; 1917–1930).

d. Rosa Smith Eigenmann (1858–1947), American ichthyologist, a specialist in fish taxonomy.

### ARTS/LITERATURE

Jessica Tandy created the Blanche DuBois role opposite Marlon Brando as Stanley Kowalski in Tennessee Williams's classic play *A Streetcar Named Desire.*

Judith Anderson starred in the title role opposite John Gielgud as Jason in *Medea,* Robinson Jeffers's adaptation of the Euripides play.

Martha Graham choreographed the dance *Night Journey,* to music by William Schuman.

Cheryl Crawford, Robert Lewis, and Elia Kazan founded the Actors Studio.

Deborah Kerr, Flora Robson, Jean Simmons, and David Farrar starred in *Black Narcissus,* Michael Powell and Emeric Pressburger's film based on Rumer Godden's 1939 novel, set in a Himalayan nunnery.

Claudette Colbert starred opposite Fred MacMurray in Chester Erskine's film *The Egg and I.*

Dolores Del Rio starred in John Ford's film *The Fugitive,* shot in Mexico.

Katharine Hepburn starred opposite Spencer Tracy in Elia Kazan's film version of the 1937 Conrad Richter novel *The Sea of Grass.*

Loretta Young starred in *The Farmer's Daughter,* winning a best actress Academy Award.

Doris Humphrey choreographed the dance *Day on Earth,* to music by Aaron Copland.

Joan Cross created the Mrs. Billows role in Benjamin Britten's opera *Albert Herring.*

Mahalia Jackson recorded "Move on Up a Little Higher."

Wendy Hiller starred opposite Basil Rathbone in the title role of *The Heiress,* Ruth and Augustus Goetz's play, based on Henry James's novel.

Gene Tierney and Rex Harrison played the title roles in Joseph L. Mankiewicz's film comedy *The Ghost and Mrs. Muir.*

Mai Zetterling starred in Ingmar Bergman's film *Night Is My Future.*

Rosalind Russell, Katina Paxinou, Raymond Massey, and Michael Redgrave starred in *Mourning Becomes Electra,* Dudley Nichols's film version of the 1931 Eugene O'Neill trilogy, based on the Oresteia.

Virgil Thomson's opera *The Mother of Us All* was introduced, with libretto by the late Gertrude Stein.

Sarah Vaughan recorded "Tenderly."

Georgia O'Keeffe painted *White Primrose.*

Natalia Ginzburg published the novel *The Dry Heart.*

Nathalie Sarraute published the novel *The Portrait of a Man Unknown.*

Nina Foch starred opposite William Prince in Norman Krasna's stage comedy *John Loves Mary.*

Anne Green published the novel *The Old Lady.*

Brenda Colvin published *Land and Landscape.*

Betty Box produced the film *Dear Murderer.*

b. Glenn Close (1947– ), American actress, an international film star in the 1980s and 1990s.

d. Willa Cather (1873–1947), American novelist, a major figure from publication of her Nebraska-set autobiographical novel, *O Pioneers!* (1913).

d. Ricarda Huch (1864–1947), German writer and historian who wrote as Richard Hugo; her works included books on the life of Garibaldi, the Thirty Years War, Martin Luther, and the Holy Roman Empire, as well as novels and poetry.

d. Eva Tanguay (1878–1947), American vaudeville star, who sang "I Don't Care."

## 1948

### POLITICS/LAW/WAR

Eleanor Roosevelt, heading the United Nations Commission on Human Rights, was the prime mover in the passage of the landmark U.N. Declaration of Human Rights.

Women's Armed Forces Integration Act of 1948 incorporated women's armed service nursing corps into the regular services, further opening military careers to American women. Mary Agnes Hallaren became the first nonmedical female officer in the U.S. Army, director of the Women's Army Corps (WAC); Geraldine Pratt May was first director of Women in the Air Force (WAF).

Representative Margaret Chase Smith was elected a Republican senator from Maine, the first of her four terms (serving 1949–1972). She was the first woman to be elected to the Senate without having completed someone else's term and to serve in both houses of Congress.

Women won the right to vote and be elected to office in Israel and South Korea.

Kamaldevi Chattopadhyay founded the Indian Co-operative Union.

Hilda Martindale published *Some Victorian Portraits.*

Margaret Postgate Cole published *Makers of the Labour Movement.*

b. (Josephine) Bernadette Devlin McAliskey (1948– ), Ulster Catholic Irish socialist and politician.

d. Rosika Schwimmer (1877–1948), Hungarian journalist, union activist, feminist, pacifist, and diplomat, the world's first modern female ambassador (1918), who inspired Henry Ford to sponsor the "peace ship" (1915) and later fought for world citizenship for those who, like herself (1919), were forced from their countries and barred from others.

d. Sophonisba Preston Breckinridge (1866–1948), American lawyer, educator, social reformer, and women's rights advocate long associated with Hull House and with the University of Chicago.

d. Kate Richards O'Hare (1876–1948), American socialist, social reformer, writer, and lecturer, a Socialist Party candidate for the Senate and an anti–World War I activist.

d. Florence Prag Kahn (1866–1948), American politician, a conservative Republican congresswoman (1925–1937).

### RELIGION/EDUCATION/EVERYDAY LIFE

Mother Teresa left her Loreto convent to work among the poor in Calcutta, founding the congregation that would become a new order, the Missionaries of Charity (1950), and spread throughout the world.

Alfred C. Kinsey, Wardell Pomeroy, and Clyde E. Martin published *Sexual Behavior in the Human Male,* first volume of the "Kinsey Report," their landmark study of American sexual attitudes and practices.

Anne Loughlin became general secretary of the Tailors and Garment Workers Union (1948–1953), the first woman to lead a mixed (male and female) British union; she had been a TGWU organizer from 1915.

Patricia J. Martin became the first woman to chair the American Advertising Federation.

Pauline Frederick was the first female broadcaster to cover a U.S. national political convention.

Despite being told she was "too old," Fanny Blankers-Koen won a then-record four gold medals at the London Olympics: 100 meters, 200 meters, 80-meter hurdles, and four-woman 100-meter relay.

Ladies Professional Golf Association was founded by a group of golfers, including "Babe" Didrikson Zaharias.

Flora Solomon was called in to advise Israel's Ministry of Labor about setting up welfare programs for postwar refugees.

Louise Brough won the women's tennis singles title at Wimbledon, as well as doubles and mixed doubles, but lost the U.S. singles tennis title to Margaret Osborne, her doubles partner.

Women's Institute residential center in Berkshire was named Denman College, after Gertrude Denman, who had sparked the Women's Institute movement.

Beatrice Potter Webb's autobiographical *Our Partnership* was published posthumously.

Dorothy Day published *On Pilgrimage*.

d. Ruth Fulton Benedict (1887–1948), American anthropologist noted for her *Patterns of Culture* (1934); long associated with Columbia University (1936–1948) but a full professor only in her final year.

d. Clara Elizabeth Collet (1860–1948), British feminist and economist, who served in many senior civil service positions.

## SCIENCE/TECHNOLOGY/MEDICINE

Maria Goeppert Mayer published her notable paper "On Closed Shells in Nuclei," first describing the now-standard shell theory of nuclear structure, which would win her a Nobel Prize. She and her husband, Joseph Mayer, also published *Statistical Mechanics*, their classic text on the atomic structure of molecules; it was developed from lectures they had given at Johns Hopkins University (ca. 1930–1948), for which she had been unpaid because of the university's nepotism rules.

Dorothy Crowfoot Hodgkin developed the first X-ray photographs of vitamin $B_{12}$ and, using X-ray crystallography, would identify its structure fully by 1955, vital to understanding its workings in the body.

French physicist Yvette Cauchois published the first book focusing wholly on X-ray emission and absorption spectra of solids, based on a series of 1946 lectures she gave to the Société Française de Physique.

Gertrude Rogallo and her husband, Francis Rogallo, patented their flexible kite, which gave rise to the sport of hang gliding, with craft that employ the Rogallo wing.

Edith Clarke was elected a fellow of the American Institute of Electrical Engineers (later Institute of Electrical and Electronics Engineers), the first woman so honored; at that time, she was professor of electrical engineering at the University of Texas, believed to be the first American woman in such a position.

Bonnie Tiburzi was the first American woman employed by a major airline, American Airlines, as a jet pilot.

British physician Cicely Williams was named first head of the Maternal and Child Health Section of the World Health Organization (1948–1951).

Margaret Mead succeeded Ruth Benedict as director of the Columbia University Research in Contemporary Cultures project.

Arkansas University Medical School and Hospital became the first medical school in the former Confederate states to admit an African-American woman as a student.

Susan Isaacs published *Troubles of Children and Parents*.

British zoologist Sidnie Manton was elected fellow of the Royal Society.

b. Barbara Jean Grosz (1948– ), American computer science educator, an expert in natural language processing, a key area of artificial intelligence.

d. Florence Merriam Bailey (1863–1948), American naturalist and ornithologist, noted for her popular books on birds and natural history.

d. Susan Fairhurst Brierley Isaacs (1885–1948), British child psychologist.

## ARTS/LITERATURE

Jane Wyman starred opposite Lew Ayres in Jean Negulesco's film drama *Johnny Belinda*, winning a best actress Academy Award as the young deaf-mute mother.

Agnes De Mille choreographed the ballet *Fall River Legend*; Alicia Alonso created the Lizzie Borden role.

Ingrid Bergman starred opposite Charles Boyer in Lewis Milestone's film version of the 1946 Erich Maria Remarque novel *Arch of Triumph*.

Irene Dunne starred as the memorable San Francisco Norwegian mother in *I Remember Mama*, George Stevens's film version of the 1944 John Van Druten play.

Moira Shearer starred in Michael Powell and Emeric Pressburger's ballet film fantasy *The Red Shoes*. She also created the title role in Frederick Ashton's ballet *Cinderella*.

Joan Cross founded and became director of the British Opera School, later the National School of Opera (1948–1964).

Katharine Hepburn starred opposite Spencer Tracy as the compromised candidate in Frank Capra's film *State of the Union*.

Margaret Phillips starred opposite Tod Andrews in Tennessee Williams's *Summer and Smoke*.

Olivia de Havilland starred as the woman trapped in an inhuman insane asylum in Anatole Litvak's film *The Snake Pit*.

Patricia Morison starred in the title role opposite Alfred Drake in Cole Porter's stage musical *Kiss Me, Kate*.

Joyce Redman was Anne Boleyn opposite Rex Harrison as Henry VIII in Maxwell Anderson's play *Anne of the Thousand Days*.

Rita Hayworth starred as *The Lady from Shanghai* opposite Orson Welles, who wrote, directed, and starred in the film.

Zora Neale Hurston published the novel *Seraph on the Sewanee*.

Judy Garland starred opposite Fred Astaire in *Easter Parade*, Charles Walters's film of Irving Berlin's musical.

Bryher published the historical novel *Beowulf*.

Elisabeth Schumann published *German Song*.

Fay Kanin's stage comedy *Goodbye, My Fancy* starred Madeleine Carroll, Sam Wanamaker, and Conrad Nagel.

Estelle Winwood starred in a New York production of Jean Giraudoux's play *The Madwoman of Chaillot*.

*Myself When Young*, the autobiography of Henry Handel Richardson (Henrietta Robertson Richardson), was published posthumously.

Nancy Walker starred opposite Harold Lang in Hugh Martin's play *Look, Ma, I'm Dancin'*.

Sylvia Townsend Warner published the novel *The Corner That Held Them*.

Wanda Jakubowska made the film *The Last Stop*, about her concentration camp experiences.

Esther Forbes published the historical novel *The Running of the Tide*.

New Zealand writer Ruth Park published the novel *Harp in the South*.

Ruth Crawford Seeger published *American Folk Songs for Children*.

Ruth Gipps composed her *Piano Concerto*.

b. Agnieszka Holland (1948– ), Polish film director.

d. Susan Glaspell (1882–1948), American theater manager, director, novelist, and playwright, the founder and first director of the Provincetown Players.

d. Lilian Braithwaite (1873–1948), British actress, a major figure on the British stage from the turn of the century through the early 1940s.

d. Gertrude Atherton (1857–1948), American author, most notably of several California-based novels.

d. Zelda Sayre Fitzgerald (1900–1948), American writer, wife of writer F. Scott Fitzgerald.

# 1949

## POLITICS/LAW/WAR

United Nations Convention for the Suppression of the Traffic in Persons and of the Exploitation of the Prostitution of Others was a nonbinding declaration of principles opposing prostitution and sexual slavery.

Golda Meir became Israel's first ambassador to the Soviet Union and also began her tenure as Israeli minister of labor (1949–1956).

Georgia Neese Clark Gray was appointed treasurer of the United States by President Harry S. Truman; she was the first woman to hold the position (1949–1953).

(Helen) Eugenie Moore Anderson became the first woman to hold the rank of ambassador, appointed by President Harry Truman as representative to Denmark.

Alva Reimer Myrdal became director of the United Nations and UNESCO social-welfare departments (1949–1956).

Burnita S. Matthews was the first woman to serve as a U.S. federal district judge, in the District of Columbia.

Vijaya Lakshmi Pandit became Indian ambassador to the United States (1949–1951).

Women won the right to vote in Syria and to vote and be elected to office in China.

Edith Summerskill pushed through the British Clean Milk Act.

Federal Republic of Germany's constitution declared women and men to be equal before the law, though discriminatory laws remained.

Eleanor Roosevelt published the autobiographical *This I Remember*.

American-born World War II Nazi broadcaster Axis Sally (Mildred Gillars) was convicted of treason and was imprisoned for 12 years.

Begum Liaquat Ali Khan founded the All Pakistan Women's Association.

Chinese feminist and revolutionary Ho Hsiang-ning, long in exile, joined the new Chinese Communist government as director of the Overseas Chinese Affairs Commission (1949–1959).

b. Nora Astorga (1949–1988), Nicaraguan Sandinista leader.

d. Flora Drummond (1869–1949), Scottish socialist and suffragist, known as "General Drummond" for the uniform she wore leading a band during demonstrations as a militant and often-arrested Women's Social and Political Union organizer before World War I, later head of the conservative Women's Guild of Empire (1928).

d. Sarojini Chattopadhyaya Naidu (1879–1949), Indian poet and independence-movement leader, a president of the Indian National Congress (1925) and colleague of Mahatma Gandhi and Jawaharlal Nehru.

d. Vida Goldstein (1869–1949), Australian feminist, social reformer, women's rights movement and suffragist leader, politician, and editor who founded the Australian Women's Federal Political Association (1903) and the *Woman Voter* (1909).

d. Ona Brazauskaité Masiotene (1883–1949), Lithuanian feminist and nationalist, a founder of several Lithuanian women's organizations.

### RELIGION/EDUCATION/EVERYDAY LIFE

Simone de Beauvoir published *The Second Sex*, a study of women's victimization and marginalization, or "otherness," in male-dominated modern societies, positing the need and possibility of pursuing independent paths. Her book became a central document of the renewed worldwide women's movement that emerged in midcentury.

The first Trappist nunnery in the United States was founded at Wrentham, Massachusetts.

Anna Louise Strong was deported from the Soviet Union, accused of espionage; she had been editor of the *Moscow News* for Americans working there.

Celebrating her marriage, Conchita Cintrón publicly appeared on horseback in a Spanish bullfight ring, then—defying a government prohibition against women fighting on foot—dismounted and made a classic set of passes before the bull but declined to kill him. Arrested for defying the ban, she was pardoned by popular demand.

Hebrew University–Hadassah Medical School, founded by the Jewish women's organization Hadassah, opened in Jerusalem.

Louise Brough won the women's singles tennis title at Wimbledon.

Simone Weil's *L'Enracinement* (*The Need for Roots*) was posthumously published.

Margaret Murray published *The Splendour that Was Egypt*.

Alexandra David-Neel published *Dans le coeur du Hind: le Népal inconnue*.

Jessie Bernard published *American Community Behavior*.

Mary Follett published *Freedom and Coordination*.

b. Irina Rodnina (1949– ), Russian ice skater who, with two different partners, dominated pairs figure skating (1969–1980), then retired and became a coach.

### SCIENCE/TECHNOLOGY/MEDICINE

Chemist Rachel Fuller Brown and Elizabeth Hazen, a mycologist (specialist in the study of fungi), developed *nystatin*, the first safe fungicide, widely used, as in fighting athlete's foot and mildew damage to books and paintings. Some of the royalties from the nystatin patent and license were funneled into scholarships (Brown's to Mount Holyoke College, Hazen's to Mississippi University for Women) and into a foundation to support research in microbiology, immunology, and biochemistry.

Dorothy Crowfoot Hodgkin published her comprehensive analysis of the structure of penicillin, necessary for its large-scale synthesis.

Margaret Mead published *Male and Female*, her study of the interplay of social and biological factors that determine gender roles.

Virginia Apgar became the first full professor of anesthesiology at Columbia University's medical school, also its first female full professor.

Winifred Goldring became the first female president of the Paleontological Society.

d. Mary Orr Evershed (1867–1949), British astronomer.

### ARTS/LITERATURE

After two decades of suppression, Britain finally allowed legal distribution of *The Well of Loneliness*, Radclyffe Hall's 1928 novel on lesbian themes.

Helene Weigel and Bertolt Brecht, her husband, founded the Berliner Ensemble; she became the leading German-language interpreter of Brecht's work, perhaps most notably in *Mother Courage*.

Mary Martin created the Nellie Forbush role opposite Ezio Pinza in *South Pacific*, Richard Rodgers and Oscar Hammerstein's stage musical.

Gwendolyn Brooks published the Pulitzer Prize–winning poetry collection *Annie Allen*.

Olivia de Havilland gave an Oscar-winning performance opposite Ralph Richardson and Montgomery Clift in William Wyler's film *The Heiress*, based on the Henry James novel and the Ruth and Augustus Goetz play.

Carol Channing played Lorelei Lee, introducing "Diamonds Are a Girl's Best Friend," in *Gentlemen Prefer Blondes*, the Jule Styne and Leo Robin stage musical based on the Anita Loos novel.

Eudora Welty published the short-story collection *The Golden Apples*.

Ingrid Bergman left her husband and daughter for film director Roberto Rossellini and for doing so was blacklisted by the American film industry, then deeply in the grip of McCarthyism and associated self-appointed guardians of American morality.

Frida Kahlo painted her *Portrait of Diego*.

Galina Ulanova created the role of Tao-Hoa in Leonid Lavrovsky's ballet *Red Poppy*.

Judy Garland starred in Robert Z. Leonard's film *In the Good Old Summertime*.

Mahalia Jackson recorded "Let the Power of the Holy Ghost Fall on Me."

Nadine Gordimer published the short-story collection *Face to Face*.

Peggy Wood starred in the long-running television series *Mama* (1949–1956), based on the 1944 John van Druten play *I Remember Mama*.

Shirley Jackson published the short-story collection *The Lottery* and the novel *The Road Through the Wall*.

Stevie Smith published the novel *The Holiday*.

Edith Evans starred in James Bridie's play *Daphne Laureola*.

Lilli Palmer starred opposite Cedric Hardwicke in a New York production of George Bernard Shaw's *Caesar and Cleopatra*.

Elizabeth Bowen published the novel *The Heat of the Day*.

Louise Bourgeois showed the sculpture *The Blind Leading the Blind*.

Elizabeth Taylor published the novel *A Wreath of Roses*.

Georgia O'Keeffe painted *Black Place Green*.

Lynn Fontanne starred opposite Alfred Lunt in S. N. Behrman's play *I Know My Love*.

Ginger Rogers and Fred Astaire starred in the film *The Barkleys of Broadway*.

Lillian Hellman wrote the book for the musical *Regina*.

Mary McCarthy published the novel *The Oasis*.

Pearl Primus choreographed *Fanja*.

Nancy Mitford published the novel *Love in a Cold Climate*.

Priaulx Rainier composed her *Barbaric Dance Suite*.

b. Bonnie Raitt (1949– ), American singer, composer, and guitarist, a leading folk and blues figure in the 1970s, who reemerged as a recording star with her album *Nick of Time* (1989).

b. Meryl Streep (Mary Louise Streep, 1949– ), American actress, an international film star from the late 1970s.

b. Sissy Spacek (Mary Elizabeth Spacek, 1949– ), American actress, a film star from the 1980s.

d. Sigrid Undset (1882–1949), Norwegian writer who received the 1928 Nobel Prize for literature.

d. Irene Vanbrugh (1872–1949), British actress, like her sister Violet Vanbrugh a leading figure on the British stage for more than 50 years.

d. Margaret Mitchell (1900–1949), American author who wrote *Gone with the Wind*.

d. Edith Anna Oenone Somerville (1858–1949), Irish novelist who collaborated with her cousin Violet Martin (who wrote as Martin Ross) on a series of light novels set in Ireland (1865–1915).

d. Helen Edna Hokinson (1900–1949), American cartoonist whose satirical work was a staple feature of the *New Yorker*.

d. Theresa Serber Malkiel (1874–1949), American writer, socialist, and feminist.

## 1950

### POLITICS/LAW/WAR

Women won the right to vote in Peru and to vote and be elected to office in India.

Anna Rosenberg was appointed assistant secretary of defense by President Harry S. Truman.

Barbara Castle became a member of the National Executive of Britain's Labour Party (1950–1979).

California Democratic Congresswoman Helen Gahagan Douglas lost her Senate race to Richard Nixon, who successfully smeared her as a communist, driving her out of public life.

Danish judge Helga Pedersen was elected a member of parliament (1950–1964) and was appointed minister of justice (1950–1953).

Odette Hallowes was awarded France's Légion d'honneur, for her services as an Allied spy in occupied France during World War II.

Soia Mentschikoff became the first woman to teach at Chicago Law School.

### RELIGION/EDUCATION/EVERYDAY LIFE

After tennis great Alice Marble wrote an article in *American Lawn Tennis* criticizing a "de facto color line," Althea Gibson was "accepted on her merits," becoming the first African-American to play at Forest Hills.

When various Protestant agencies united to form the National Council of Churches, Edith Lowry became executive director of the division of home missions, throughout her career continuing to personally direct programs for migrant agricultural workers.

Associated Press named "Babe" Didrikson Zaharias "the greatest female athlete of the first half of the twentieth century."

British social scientist Barbara Wootton published *Testament for Social Science*.

Louise Brough won the women's singles tennis title at Wimbledon, as well as doubles and mixed doubles.

Pauline Frederick covered the United Nations Security Council meetings as the Korean War began.

Loula Dunne became the first woman to serve as director of the American Public Welfare Association.

Mildred Cable published *A Journey with a Purpose*.

Simone Weil's *Attente de Dieu* (*Waiting on God*) was posthumously published.

d. Evangeline Cary Booth (1865–1950), British-American Salvation Army leader, youngest child of cofounders Catherine and William Booth; she led Salvation Army activities in Canada, the United States, and then internationally.

d. Josephine Clara Goldmark (1877–1950), American social reformer, active in the National Consumers' League, who provided the research used in the Brandeis Brief (1908).

d. Agnes Smedley (1890–1950), American writer, long a correspondent in Red China.

d. Elsie de Wolfe (Lady Mendl, 1865–1950), American interior decorator, noted for her innovative use of table lamps and brilliantly colored fabrics.

### SCIENCE/TECHNOLOGY/MEDICINE

Nuclear physicist Rosalyn Yalow and internist Solomon A. Berson developed radioimmunoassay (RIA), a method of using radioactive particles to trace and measure minute amounts of substances such as hormones, enzymes, and drugs in blood and body tissues, an enormously important tool in medical diagnosis. She would later win the Nobel Prize for medicine (1977).

George Jorgensen became Christine Jorgenson after a pioneer sex-change operation, performed in Denmark by a medical team under Dr. Christian Hamburger (1950–1952).

Gladys Anderson Emerson did key early work on the relationship between diet and cancer, working at the Sloan-Kettering Institute for Cancer Research (1950–1953).

Marion Donovan, a young New York mother, invented disposable diapers, fashioning the prototype out of a shower curtain and absorbent padding; her early version was called "the Boater." She later also invented an elastic zipper pull and multiple-skirt hanger.

British physician Janet Vaughan became director of the Medical Research Unit for Research on Bone-Seeking Isotopes, studying the effects of radiation.

On her retirement after 57 years as curator of botany at the California Academy of Sciences herbarium, Alice Eastwood was made honorary president of the Seventh International Botanical Congress.

British psychoanalyst Marion Milner published *On Not Being Able to Paint*.

d. Marcia Keith (1859–1950), American physicist long associated with Mount Holyoke College (1885–1903), a founder of the American Physical Society.

### ARTS/LITERATURE

Gloria Swanson starred as the aging silent film star in Billy Wilder's film classic *Sunset Boulevard*.

Bette Davis played aging New York theater luminary Margot Channing in Joseph Mankiewicz's film *All About Eve*, winning a best actress Academy Award, opposite Anne Baxter as Eve.

Cathleen Nesbitt, Alec Guinness, and Irene Worth starred on Broadway in T. S. Eliot's blank verse play *The Cocktail Party*.

Judy Holliday reprised her Broadway role as Billie Dawn in *Born Yesterday*, George Cukor's film version of Garson Kanin's 1946 play, winning a best actress Academy Award, opposite Broderick Crawford and William Holden.

Doris Lessing published the novel *The Grass Was Singing*.

Edna Ferber published the novel *Giant*.

Julie Harris emerged as a star opposite Ethel Waters in Carson McCullers's play *The Member of the Wedding*, based on her 1946 novel.

Katharine Hepburn starred opposite Spencer Tracy in George Cukor's film *Adam's Rib*.

Lilli Palmer starred on Broadway opposite Rex Harrison in John van Druten's comedy *Bell, Book and Candle*.

Shirley Booth starred opposite Sidney Blackmer in William Inge's play *Come Back Little Sheba*.

Louise Bourgeois showed the sculpture *Sleeping Figure*.

Silvano Mangano and Vittorio Gassman starred in Giuseppe de Santis's film *Bitter Rice*.

Uta Hagen starred opposite Paul Kelly and Steven Hill in Clifford Odets's play *The Country Girl*.

Monica Vitti and Gabriele Ferzetti starred in Michelangelo Antonioni's film *L'Avventura*.

Stevie Smith published the poetry collection *Harold's Leap*.

Zelda Fichandler founded the Arena Stage company in Washington, D.C.

Ethel Merman starred in Irving Berlin's musical *Call Me Madam*.

Jane Wyman, Gertrude Lawrence, and Kirk Douglas starred in Irving Rapper's film adaptation of Tennessee Williams's 1945 play *The Glass Menagerie*.

Ida Lupino directed and cowrote the film *Outrage*, beginning her career as one of Hollywood's very few female film directors.

Jean Arthur starred in the title role opposite Boris Karloff in a New York production of *Peter Pan*.

Marguerite Duras published the novel *Un barrage contre le Pacifique* (*The Sea Wall*).

Judith Anderson starred in Robinson Jeffers's play *The Tower Beyond Tragedy*.

Nadia Boulanger became director of the American Conservatory at Fontainebleau.

Barbara Pym published the novel *Some Tame Gazelle*.

Georgia O'Keeffe painted *Poppies* and *White Rose*.

Betty Hutton starred as Annie Oakley in George Sidney's film version of the 1946 Irving Berlin musical *Annie Get Your Gun*.

Elisabeth Lutyens composed *Concertante*, for orchestra.

Brigit Cullberg choreographed a dance version of Strindberg's *Miss Julie*.

Eva Gabor starred opposite Claude Dauphin in Samuel Taylor's comedy *The Happy Time*.

Betty Box produced the film *The Clouded Yellow*.

Helen Hayes starred in Joshua Logan's play *The Wisteria Trees*.

Juana de Ibarbourou published the poetry collection *Perdida*.

Muriel Box directed the film *The Happy Family*.

Anaïs Nin published the novel *The Four-Chambered Heart*.

b. Natalie Cole (1950– ), American singer, the daughter of singer Nat "King" Cole.

b. Jessica Lange (1950– ), American actress.

b. Gloria Naylor (1950– ), African-American writer.

d. Edna St. Vincent Millay (1892–1950), American poet, short story writer, essayist, and social reformer, who emerged as a leading poet in the early 1920s.

d. Sara Allgood (1883–1950), Irish actress, a leading figure in Dublin's Abbey Theatre, who later played many strong supporting roles in Hollywood films.

d. Julia Marlowe (1866–1950), American actress, a star on the New York stage from the mid-1880s through the mid-1920s.

d. Jane Cowl (1884–1950), American actress and playwright, a leading figure in the American theater.

# 1951

## POLITICS/LAW/WAR

Women won the right to vote and be elected in Nepal.

Dori'a Shafiq led 1,500 women in a march on Egypt's parliament, seeking votes for women, granted five years later.

Chilean diplomat Ana Figuero became a special envoy to the United Nations.

Mary Anderson published her autobiography *Woman at Work*.

b. Noor Al-Hussein (Lisa Najeeb Halaby, 1951– ), queen of Jordan, wife of King Hussein, active in charitable projects.

d. Mary White Ovington (1865–1951), American social worker and reformer, a civil rights advocate who sparked the founding of the National Association for the Advancement of Colored People (1909), serving for four decades (1909–1947), as chairman (1919–1932).

## RELIGION/EDUCATION/EVERYDAY LIFE

Hannah Arendt published *The Origins of Totalitarianism*, a seminal work exploring the ethos and social conditions providing environments in which fascist, communist, and other totalitarian regimes might flourish.

Maggie (Marguerite) Higgins was the first woman to win a Pulitzer Prize for international reporting, for her coverage of the Korean War, where she was the only female correspondent.

Florence Chadwick became the first woman to swim across the English Channel from England to France; she had the previous year set a record as the 13th woman to make the easier swim from France to England.

Althea Gibson became the first African-American tennis player to play at Wimbledon, reaching the quarterfinals.

Armi Ratia and her husband, Viljo Ratia, founded Marimekko, which became a world-famous design firm, making a wide range of products with bold, bright, abstract designs; she was managing director (1951–1969; 1971–1979).

Maureen Connolly, at 16, won the U.S. singles tennis title.

Miss Universe pageant was first held, initially founded by Pacific Knitting Mills to advertise its Catalina swimsuits after the reigning Miss America declined to be photographed in a Catalina suit.

Aimée Semple McPherson's autobiographical writings were published posthumously as *The Story of My Life*.

British prison reformer Margery Fry published *Arms of the Law*.

d. Abala Das Bose (1865–1951), Indian educator, who introduced the Montessori teaching methods into India; Abala and her sister Sarla attended Bethune Collegiate School for Girls and were among the first women admitted to Calcutta University.

d. Dorothy Dix (1870–1951), American journalist, whose widely syndicated columns drew an audience of millions.

d. Daisy Bates (1861–1951), London-born welfare worker, working in western Australia (from 1899) on behalf of the Native Australian population.

d. Gertrude Tuckwell (1861–1951), British union activist, long associated with the Women's Trade Union League, and president of the WTUL (1904–1921).

d. María (Liana) Cadilla de Martínez (1886–1951), Puerto Rican educator, writer, and feminist, also a folklorist, writing as Liana.

## SCIENCE/TECHNOLOGY/MEDICINE

Barbara McClintock first publicly presented her discovery that genetic fragments are transposable, which she had recognized as early as the 1930s, long before the structure of DNA had been understood. But her report was so ill-received that for decades she would work without publishing, the value of her work recognized only in the late 1970s.

Rachel Carson published *The Sea Around Us*.

Amalia Coutsouris became chief bacteriologist at Athens's Evangelismos Hospital (1951–1953).

American research physicist Katherine Blodgett received the Garvan Medal from the American Chemical Society.

b. Sally Kristen Ride (1951– ), American astrophysicist and astronaut, the first American woman in space (1983).

d. Margaret Clay Ferguson (1863–1951), American botanist long associated with Wellesley College, head of its botany department (1902–1930).

## ARTS/LITERATURE

Katharine Hepburn starred opposite Humphrey Bogart in *The African Queen*, John Huston's film, adapted by James Agee from the 1935 C. S. Forester novel.

Gertrude Lawrence starred opposite Yul Brynner in *The King and I*, Richard Rodgers and Oscar Hammerstein's musical based on Margaret Landon's novel *Anna and the King of Siam*.

Julie Harris created the Sally Bowles role in John van Druten's play *I Am a Camera*, based on Christopher Isherwood's *Goodbye to Berlin*.

Lucille Ball emerged as one of the world's leading entertainers as Lucy in the long-running television comedy series *I Love Lucy* (1951–1957) and its successors.

Vivien Leigh won a best actress Academy Award playing Blanche DuBois opposite Marlon Brando as Stanley Kowalski in Elia Kazan's film version of the 1947 Tennessee Williams play *A Streetcar Named Desire*.

Marguerite Yourcenar published the novel *Memoirs of Hadrian*.

Maureen Stapleton starred opposite Eli Wallach in Tennessee Williams's play *The Rose Tattoo*.

Barbara Bel Geddes starred opposite Barry Nelson in F. Hugh Herbert's stage comedy *The Moon Is Blue*.

Doris Lessing published the novel *This Was the Old Chief's Country*.

Elisabeth Schwarzkopf created the role of Anne Trulove in Igor Stravinsky's *The Rake's Progress*.

Leslie Caron starred opposite Gene Kelly in Vincente Minnelli's classic film musical *An American in Paris*.

Lillian Hellman's play *The Autumn Garden* starred Florence Eldridge and Fredric March.

Nadine Gordimer published the short-story collection *The Soft Voice of the Serpent*.

Adrienne Rich published the poetry collection *A Change of World*.

Bryher published the historical novel *The Fourteenth of October*.

Hortense Calisher published the short-story collection *In the Absence of Angels*.

Jessica Tandy starred opposite Hume Cronyn in Jan de Hartog's play *The Fourposter*.

Rumer Godden published her children's book *The Mousewife*, inspired by a character in Dorothy Wordsworth's journals.

Judith Malina and Julian Beck founded the highly experimental company The Living Theatre.

Brenda Colvin became president of the British Institute of Landscape Architects (1951–1953).

Carson McCullers published the novel *Clock Without Hands*.

Shirley Booth starred in *A Tree Grows in Brooklyn*, Arthur Schwartz's musical version of Betty Smith's novel.

Deborah Kerr and Robert Taylor starred in *Quo Vadis*, Mervyn LeRoy's epic film.

Georgia O'Keeffe painted *Dry Waterfall* and *Patio Door—Green-Red*.

Ruthanna Boris choreographed the ballet *Cakewalk*.

Irene Pereira published *Light and the New Reality*.

Lou Andreas-Salomé's autobiography, *Lebensrückbild*, was published posthumously.

d. Fanny Brice (Fanny Borach, 1891–1951), American singer and actress, a star of the American musical theater, who also appeared in several films and was radio's "Baby Snooks" late in her career.

d. Fumiko Hayashi (1904–1951), Japanese novelist.

## 1952

### POLITICS/LAW/WAR

Elizabeth II succeeded her father, George VI, to the British throne.

Women won the right to vote and be elected in Ivory Coast.

Indian doctor Sushila Nayar became Speaker of the Delhi Legislative Assembly (1952–1956).

Fusaye Ichikawa became a member of the upper house of Japan's legislature (1952–1970).

Kamaldevi Chattopadhyay chaired All India Handicrafts Limited and was a founder of the World Crafts Council.

Elizabeth Dilling published *The Plot Against Christianity*.

b. Susan Estrich (1952– ), American lawyer, educator, and political strategist, the first female to manage a major presidential campaign (1987).

d. Evita (Maria Eva) Duarte Perón (1919–1952), Argentinian actress and politician, a key figure in the rise and rule of her husband, Juan Perón.

d. Alexandra Mikhaylovna Kollontai (1872–1952), Russian Bolshevik, feminist, writer, politician, and diplomat, a women's rights advocate whose advocacy of sexual emancipation and other views proved unacceptable to Joseph Stalin and the other men in the Soviet leadership.

d. Miina Sillanpää (1866–1952), Finnish socialist, feminist, and politician, Finland's first female cabinet member (1927) and a Speaker of Parliament (1936–1947).

d. Hilda Martindale (1875–1952), British feminist, civil servant, and women's rights advocate, a key figure in securing improved health and working conditions for working women.

## RELIGION/EDUCATION/EVERYDAY LIFE

Florence Chadwick became the first woman to swim the 21-mile channel between Catalina Island and Los Angeles, succeeding at her second attempt.

Maureen Connolly won the women's tennis singles title at her first Wimbledon, successfully defending it in 1953 and 1954, when she also won the U.S. Open women's singles titles.

Claude Kogan was among the climbers making the first ascent of Peru's Sakantay (19,951 feet).

d. Maria Montessori (1870–1952), Italian educator and physician, the first woman doctor in Italy for centuries, who transformed early childhood education from the founding of her Child's House (1907).

d. Te Puea (1884–1952), Maori princess, granddaughter of King Tawhiao, who encouraged her people to revive their arts and other cultural traditions (from the 1920s) and fostered social reforms, founding organizations to aid women and children.

d. (Alice) Mildred Cable (1878–1952), British missionary and traveler known for her travels in Asia (especially 1923–1939).

## SCIENCE/TECHNOLOGY/MEDICINE

Grace Hopper invented the first computer compiler, a special language that allows for automatic writing of repetitive machine instructions, revolutionizing the development of computer programs by eliminating the need to laboriously write basic instructions afresh for each new program.

Kathleen Kenyon began her excavation of Jericho (1952–1958), one of the world's oldest cities, in Jordan.

Virginia Apgar developed the Newborn Scoring System—the Apgar Score—for quickly evaluating the medical condition of newborns and assessing which might need emergency medical attention.

Anna Freud became director of the Hampstead Child Therapy Clinic; she had worked at the clinic and its predecessor from shortly after her 1938 emigration to Britain.

Miriam Rothschild coauthored *Fleas, Flukes and Cuckoos*.

American physician Jane C. Wright became director of the Harlem Hospital Cancer Research Foundation.

Cell biologist Honor Fell became a fellow of Britain's Royal Society.

Gladys Anderson Emerson was awarded the Garvan Medal of the American Chemical Society.

Myra Breckenridge published her autobiographical *Wide Neighborhoods: The Story of the Frontier Nursing Service*.

Optics physiologist (Marie) Gertrude Rand became the first female fellow of the Illuminating Engineering Society of North America; among the projects handled by her and her husband was the lighting for New York City's Holland Tunnel.

National League of Nursing was formed by the merger of various North American nurses' associations.

b. Jeana Yeager (1952– ), American aviator and engineer who co-piloted the first nonstop round-the-world airplane flight (1986).

d. Antonia Caetana de Paiva Pereira Maury (1866–1952), American astronomer who developed a method of classifying stars by their spectra, vital to modern astrophysics.

d. Mary Engle Pennington (1872–1952), American chemist who made key contributions in the science of food handling and storage, including freezing, working first in the government (1908–1919), then as a consultant to private industry (1919–1951).

d. Karen Clementine Danielson Horney (1885–1952), German-born American psychoanalyst, focusing on the psychology of women, who founded the American Institute of Psychoanalysis.

d. Bertha Van Hoosen (1863–1952), American surgeon, obstetrician, and feminist, who helped popularize the use of scopolamine-morphine anesthesia in childbirth.

d. Fanny Carter Edson (1887–1952), American geologist whose analysis and drilling recommendation opened up the major part of Oklahoma's huge Marshall oil pool.

### ARTS/LITERATURE

Anne Frank's diary was published in English; it had been written while she and her family were being hidden from the Germans by a Christian family in Amsterdam during the Holocaust. She died in a German death camp in 1944. The diary had been published in Dutch in 1947.

Helen Frankenthaler created the trailblazing color-field painting *Mountains and Sea*.

Shirley Booth starred opposite Burt Lancaster in Daniel Mann's film version of the 1950 William Inge play *Come Back Little Sheba*, winning a best actress Academy Award. She also starred in Arthur Laurents's play *The Time of the Cuckoo*.

Doriot Anthony Dwyer, great-grandniece of Susan B. Anthony, was appointed first-chair flutist with the Boston Symphony Orchestra, the first woman to occupy a first chair in a major American orchestra.

Agnes De Mille choreographed the ballet *The Harvest According*, to music by Virgil Thomson.

Doris Lessing published the novel *Martha Quest*, on feminist themes.

Edith Evans starred opposite Michael Redgrave in Anthony Asquith's film version of Oscar Wilde's play *The Importance of Being Earnest*.

Flannery O'Connor published the novel *Wise Blood*.

Margaret Sullavan starred in Terence Rattigan's play *The Deep Blue Sea*.

Kinuyo Tanaka starred in the title role of the film *The Life of Oharu*.

Marguerite Duras published the novel *The Sailor from Gibraltar*.

Agatha Christie's play *The Mousetrap* began its long London run (1952– ).

Harriet Andersson starred in the title role opposite Lars Ekborg in Ingmar Bergman's film *Monika*.

Julie Harris, Ethel Waters, and Brandon de Wilde starred in the film version of Carson McCullers's novel and play *The Member of the Wedding*.

Katharine Hepburn starred in a New York production of George Bernard Shaw's *The Millionairess*.

Lilli Palmer starred opposite Rex Harrison in Christopher Fry's play *Venus Observed*.

Beatrice Lillie took her one-woman show, *An Evening with Beatrice Lillie*, on a long-running tour (1952–1956).

Mary McCarthy published the novel *The Groves of Academe*.

Barbara Pym published the novel *Excellent Women*.

Celeste Holm starred in the title role of *Anna Christie*, a New York production of Eugene O'Neill's play, costarring Kevin McCarthy.

Georgia O'Keeffe painted *Wall with Green Door*.

Brigitte Fossey starred opposite Georges Poujouly in René Clement's film *Forbidden Games*.

Grandma Moses published *My Life's History*.

Jean Stafford published the novel *The Catherine Wheel*.

Mary Chase's play *Mrs. McThing* starred Helen Hayes and Brandon de Wilde.

Natalia Ginzburg published the novel *A Light for Fools*.

Ruth Crawford Seeger composed her *Suite for Wind Quintet*.

Sheila Bond and Jack Cassidy starred in Harold Rome's musical *Wish You Were Here*.

Tallulah Bankhead published *My Autobiography*.

Carmen Laforet published the novel *La isla y los demonios*.

Brigit Cullberg became choreographer with the Royal Swedish Ballet (1952–1957).

Clare Boothe Luce wrote the play *Child of the Morning*.

Furugh Farrukhazad published the poetry collection *The Captive*.

b. Anjelica Huston (1952– ), American actress, a film star from the mid-1980s; daughter of John Huston and granddaughter of Walter Huston.

b. Roseanne (Roseanne Barr Arnold, 1952– ), American actress and comedian, a star in television in her show *Roseanne* (1988–1997).

b. Beth Henley (1952– ), American playwright, whose best-known play was the Pulitzer Prize–winning *Crimes of the Heart* (1981).

d. Gertrude Lawrence (Alexandra Lawrence-Klasen, 1898–1952), British actress, a stage and occasionally screen star from the mid-1920s, emerging in *Charlot's Revue* (1924) and long associated with Noël Coward; she died while starring on Broadway in Rodgers and Hammerstein's *The King and I*.

d. Elizabeth Robins (1862–1952), American actress, translator, and writer who introduced many of Ibsen's plays to English-speaking audiences.

d. Elisabeth Schumann (1888–1952), German singer, a leading European soprano from 1909 and a fixture at the Vienna Staatsoper (1919–1938) until the Nazis took Austria, then completing her career in the United States.

d. Vesta Tilley (1864–1952), British male impersonator.

# 1953

## POLITICS/LAW/WAR

Vijaya Lakshmi Pandit became the first female president of the United Nations General Assembly (1953–1954).

Women won the right to be elected to office in Mexico and Syria.

President Dwight D. Eisenhower appointed Oveta Culp Hobby the first-ever secretary of health, education and welfare; she was also the first female cabinet-level appointment by a Republican president.

Lilian Ngoyi became president of the Women's League of the African National Congress.

Indira Gandhi chaired the central Indian Social Welfare Board of India (1953–1957).

Clare Boothe Luce became U.S. ambassador to Italy.

German socialist Annemarie Renger was elected as a Social Democrat to the Bundestag, chairing her party's women's committee.

Margaret Ballinger was a founder and first chair of South Africa's Liberal Party.

The right of a woman to succeed to the throne was established in Denmark.

d. Annie Kenney (1879–1953), British suffragist and trade unionist, a leading associate of the Pankhursts and organizer for the Women's Social and Political Union.

d. Ethel Greenglass Rosenberg (1915–1953), American political and union activist who was executed with her husband, Julius Rosenberg. Both American Communists, they had been arrested (1950) and convicted of spying for and passing atomic secrets to the Soviet Union (1951); a worldwide campaign for clemency failed. Ethel Rosenberg published *Death House Letters* while awaiting execution.

d. Maud Gonn MacBride (1866–1953), Irish Republican revolutionary and actress, a leading figure in the Irish Republican movement, founder of the Daughters of Ireland (1900), known to many through the poems of William Butler Yeats.

## RELIGION/EDUCATION/EVERYDAY LIFE

Florence Chadwick made a "grand slam" of four channel swims in five weeks, each one a record setter: England to France across the English Channel, across the Strait of Gibraltar, across the Bosporus and back, and across the Dardanelles.

Alfred C. Kinsey, Wardell Pomeroy, Clyde E. Martin, and Paul H. Gebhardt published *Sexual Behavior in the Human Female*, the second volume of the landmark "Kinsey Report" on American sexual attitudes and practices, opening the way to a far better understanding and major redefinition of "normal" women's sexual responses, including the clitoral orgasm.

"Babe" Didrikson Zaharias, on learning that she had cancer, went public with the news, to try to help others fighting the disease, also founding the Cancer Research Fund and promoting cancer education.

Maureen Connolly became the first woman to win a Grand Slam in tennis, winning at Wimbledon and at the American, French, and Australian opens.

Pauline Frederick joined NBC, becoming United Nations correspondent; she would become the first woman to be president of the United Nations Correspondents Association.

Toni Stone became the first woman to play as a fully recognized regular on a men's major league baseball team, as a reserve for the Indianapolis Clowns of the Negro League. In 1954 she played second base for the Kansas City Monarchs.

*Women in the Modern World, Their Education and Their Dilemmas*, published by Columbia-Barnard sociologist Mirra Komarovsky, was both a sociological study of contemporary college-educated females and an attack on the new antifeminism of the post–World War II era.

Mary Ritter Beard published *The Force of Women in Japanese History*.

Claude Kogan led a climb of the 23,410-foot Nun in the Himalaya's Nun-Kun massif.

Françoise Giroud cofounded and was first editor of the weekly *L'Express* (1953–1971).

The U.S. National Weather Service began to assign women's names to hurricanes.

Margaret Murray was president of Britain's Folklore Society (1953–1955).

Japanese-American Monica Sone published *Nisei Daughter*.

Susanne Langer published *Feeling and Form*.

d. Margaret Grace Bondfield (1873–1953), British trade unionist, socialist, and politician, the first British female cabinet minister (1929) and the first female delegate to (1899) and chair of (1923) a Trades Union Congress.

## SCIENCE/TECHNOLOGY/MEDICINE

American aviator Jacqueline Cochran broke the sound barrier (May 18), the first woman to do so; French aviator Jacqueline Auriol also did so later that year.

Irmgard Flügge-Lotz published *Discontinuous Automatic Control*, her key work on the basics of automatic flight controls.

American aviator Marion Rice Hart made her first transatlantic flight at age 61 and published her autobiographical *I Fly as I Please*.

Katharine McCormick provided research funds that allowed Gregory Pincus to fully develop the birth control pill on which he had already been working.

Amalia Coutsouris began working in Britain at the Wright-Fleming Institute after her marriage to Alexander Fleming, remaining (after his 1955 death) until 1967, then returning to Greece.

Miriam Rothschild published the six-volume *Catalogue of the Rothschild Collection of Fleas* (1953–1983), detailing her father's collection of 10,000 species of fleas.

Katherine Esau published *Plant Anatomy*.

Margaret Sanger became the first president of the International Planned Parenthood Federation.

d. Florence Rena Sabin (1871–1953), American anatomist and histologist specializing in the functional physiology of living tissue, long associated with the Johns Hopkins Medical School (1902–1925), the school's first female professor, and with the Rockefeller Institute (1925–1938); the first woman elected to the National Academy of Sciences (1925).

d. Alice Eastwood (1859–1953), American botanist associated with the herbarium at the California Academy of Sciences for 57 years.

## ARTS/LITERATURE

Joan Cross created the role of Elizabeth I of England in Benjamin Britten's opera *Gloriana*.

Alice Guy-Blaché received a very overdue French Legion of Honor, in recognition of her contribution to the cinema.

Audrey Hepburn starred opposite Gregory Peck in *Roman Holiday*, winning a best actress Academy Award.

Beatrice Straight created the Elizabeth Proctor role in Arthur Miller's antiwitch-hunting play *The Crucible*.

Deborah Kerr starred as the older woman opposite John Kerr (no relation) in Robert Anderson's play *Tea and Sympathy*.

Brigid Brophy published the novel *Hackenfeller's Ape*.

Doris Humphrey choreographed the ballet *Ruins and Visions* to music by Benjamin Britten.

Edith Sitwell published the poetry collection *Gardeners and Astronomer*.

Gina Lollobrigida starred in Luigi Comencini's film *Bread, Love, and Dreams*.

Kinuyo Tanaka starred in the film *Ugetsu*.

Leslie Caron starred in Charles Walter's film musical *Lili*.

Gwen Verdon starred in Cole Porter's musical *Can-Can*.

Margaret Sullavan created the title role opposite Joseph Cotten in Samuel Taylor's stage comedy *Sabrina Fair*.

Marilyn Monroe and Jane Russell starred in Howard Hawks's film *Gentlemen Prefer Blondes*.

Gwendolyn Brooks published the novel *Maud Martha*.

Rosalind Russell and Edith Adams starred in the Broadway musical *Wonderful Town*, based on the play *My Sister Eileen*.

Rose Macaulay published *The Pleasure of Ruins*.

Vivien Leigh starred opposite Laurence Olivier in Terrence Rattigan's play *The Sleeping Prince*.

Rosamond Lehmann published the novel *The Echoing Grove*.

Jane Bowles's play *In the Summer House* starred Judith Anderson.

Mary Renault published the novel *The Charioteer*.

Nadine Gordimer published the novel *The Lying Days*.

Kathryn Grayson starred opposite Howard Keel in *Kiss Me, Kate*, George Sidney's film version of Cole Porter's 1948 musical.

Nathalie Sarraute published the novel *Martereau*.

Ida Lupino directed and cowrote the film *The Hitch-Hiker*.

Iris Murdoch published the essay *Sartre: Romantic Rationalist*.

Peggy Glanville-Hicks composed her opera *The Transposed Heads*.

Vicki Baum published the novel *Hotel Shanghai*.

b. Rekha (1953– ), Indian actress, a star in Indian films.

d. Marjorie Kinnan Rawlings (1896–1953), American writer, best known for her Pulitzer Prize–winning novel *The Yearling* (1938).

d. Maude Adams (1872–1953), American actress, best known for her creation of the title role in James M. Barrie's *Peter Pan* (1905).

d. Ruth Crawford Seeger (1901–1953), American composer.

d. Kathleen Ferrier (1912–1953), British contralto.

d. Florence Smith Price (1888–1953), African-American composer.

## 1954

### POLITICS/LAW/WAR

Edith Summerskill chaired Britain's Labour Party (1954–1955).

Vijaya Lakshmi Pandit became Indian ambassador to Great Britain (1954–1961).

Begum Liaquat Ali Khan became Pakistan's ambassador to the Netherlands and Belgium.

Marie-Hélène Lefaucheux became president of the French National Council of Women.

d. Emmeline Pethick-Lawrence (1867–1954), British social worker, radical feminist, pacifist, and women's suffrage movement leader, who was treasurer of the Women's Social and Political Union until expelled by the Pankhursts (1912) and later president of the Women's Freedom League.

d. Gertrude Baumer (1873–1954), German politician, teacher, nationalist, socialist, and feminist, president of the League of German Women's Associations (1910–1919).

d. Agnes Campbell MacPhail (1890–1954), Canadian teacher, reformer, and politician, the first female member of the Canadian national Parliament (1921–1940).

d. Cornelia Sorabji (1866–1954), India's first female lawyer and the first woman to take the law examination at Oxford University (1893).

### RELIGION/EDUCATION/EVERYDAY LIFE

Virginia M. Schau won the Pulitzer Prize for spot news photography, the first woman to do so.

Maureen Connolly defeated Louise Brough for the women's singles title at Wimbledon.

d. (Mary) Gertrude Denman (1884–1954), British voluntary organizer, who sparked the Women's Institute movement (chair 1917–1946) and chaired the National Birth Control Council (1930–1954).

d. Margaret Gillespie Cousins (1878–1954), Irish educator and feminist, in India after 1915, the first non-Indian member of the Indian Women's University (1916), a founder of the Indian Women's Association (1919–1920).

d. Mary (Eliza) Church Terrell (1863–1954), African-American women's rights leader, who helped found the National Association of Colored Women, serving as its president (1896–1901).

d. Anne O'Hare McCormick (1880–1954), American Pulitzer Prize–winning foreign correspondent.

d. Vida Dutton Scudder (1861–1954), American religious scholar and social activist.

### SCIENCE/TECHNOLOGY/MEDICINE

Rita Levi-Montalcini and Stanley Cohen codiscovered the nerve-growth factor, which stimulates the growth of nerve cells; they would share a Nobel Prize (1987).

American electrical engineer Edith Clarke received the Achievement Award of the Society of Women Engineers.

American zoologist Libbie H. Hyman was elected to the National Academy of Sciences.

Lillian Gilbreth published *Management in the Home*.

d. Anna Wessel Williams (1863–1954), American physician and bacteriologist who developed the first diphtheria antitoxin (1894) and a method of diagnosing rabies in the laboratory (1905).

d. Angeliki Panajiotatou (1875–1954), Greek microbiologist, the first female medical student (with her sister) at Athens University Medical School; long a professor at Cairo University (1908–1938), then back at Athens, specializing in epidemic and tropical diseases.

d. Edith Marion Patch (1876–1954), American entomologist long associated with the Experimental Station at the University of Maine (1904–1937); the first woman to serve as president of the Entomological Association of America (1930).

### ARTS/LITERATURE

Giulietta Masina starred as doomed Gelsomina in Federico Fellini's film classic *La Strada*, opposite Anthony Quinn as Zampano and Richard Basehart as The Fool.

Eudora Welty published the novel *The Ponder Heart*.

Galina Ulanova created the role of Katerina in Rostislav Zacharov's ballet *Stone Flower*.

Audrey Hepburn played the title role opposite Humphrey Bogart and William Holden in Billy Wilder's film *Sabrina*, and opposite Mel Ferrer in a New York production of Jean Giraudoux's play *Ondine*.

Grace Kelly starred opposite Bing Crosby and William Holden in George Seaton's film version of the 1950 Clifford Odets play *The Country Girl*, winning a best actress Academy Award.

Lotte Lenya reprised her portrayal of Jenny off-Broadway in a long-running English-language version of Bertolt Brecht and Kurt Weill's musical *The Threepenny Opera*.

Françoise Sagan published the novel *Bonjour Tristesse*.

Geraldine Page starred opposite Darrin McGavin in Richard Nash's play *The Rainmaker*,

Alida Valli and Farley Granger starred in Luchino Visconti's film *Senso*.

Iris Murdoch published the novel *Under the Net*.

Joan Cross created the Mrs. Grose role in Benjamin Britten's opera *The Turn of the Screw*.

Mary Martin starred in the title role of *Peter Pan*, the stage musical version of James M. Barrie's play.

Judy Garland starred opposite James Mason in George Cukor's remake of *A Star Is Born*.

Patty McCormack starred as the psychotic child opposite Nancy Kelly in Maxwell Anderson's play *The Bad Seed*.

Simone Signoret and Veral Clouzot starred in Henri-Georges Clouzot's film *Diabolique*.

Ava Gardner starred opposite Humphrey Bogart in Joseph L. Mankiewicz's film *The Barefoot Contessa*.

Bryher published the historical novel *The Roman Wall*.

Dorothy Dandridge, Pearl Bailey, Harry Belafonte, and Brock Peters starred in Otto Preminger's film *Carmen Jones*.

Florence Henderson starred in the title role opposite Ezio Pinza in Harold Rome's stage musical *Fanny*.

Kamala Markandaya published her first novel, *Nectar in a Sieve*.

Janis Paige starred opposite John Raitt in Richard Adler and Jerry Ross's stage musical *The Pajama Game*.

Sylvia Townsend Warner published the novel *The Flint Anchor*.

Julie Andrews starred in Sandy Wilson's musical *The Boy Friend*.

Kinuyo Tanaka starred in *Sansho the Bailiff*.

Shirley Jackson published the novel *The Bird's Nest*.

Georgia O'Keeffe painted *Antelope, From the Plains II*, and *Memory, Late Autumn*.

Agnes Varda wrote and directed her first film, *La pointe courte*.

Betty Box produced the film *Doctor in the House*.

Gabrielle Roy published the novel *The Cashier*.

Mari Sandoz published *The Buffalo Hunters*.

Joy Batchelor and John Halas directed and produced the animated feature film *Animal Farm*.

Louise Bogan published her *Collected Poems*.

Mistinguett published her autobiography, *Toute ma vie*.

b. Louise Erdrich (1954– ), American writer, a poet and novelist, often working with her husband, Michael Dorris.

b. Kathleen Turner (1954– ), American actress, a film star of the 1980s and early 1990s.

b. Irina Ratushinskaya (1954– ), Russian poet.

d. Colette (Sidonie Gabrielle Claudine Colette, 1873–1954), French novelist and short story writer, creator of the Claudine and Cherí series, and of *Gigi* (1944).

d. Frida Kahlo (1910–1954), Mexican painter, who painted a notable portrait of her husband, Diego Rivera.

d. Miles (Stella Marian Sarah) Franklin (1879–1954), Australian writer.

d. Bess Streeter Aldrich (1881–1954), American novelist.

# 1955

## POLITICS/LAW/WAR

African-American Rosa Parks refused to give up her seat on a Montgomery, Alabama, bus to a white passenger, as was the practice at the time (December 1). Accused of violating Alabama's segregation laws, she was arrested and jailed. Within four days, the Rev. Martin Luther King, Jr. and others in the Mongomery Improvement Association had launched a boycott of the city's buses, which attracted national, then worldwide attention. By November 1956, Montgomery's buses were desegrated—and the modern civil rights movement had begun.

Women won the right to vote and be elected to office in Nicaragua.

Agatha Barbara became Malta's education minister (1955–1958).

Margaret Postgate Cole published *Beatrice and Sidney Webb.*

b. Carol Browner (1955– ), American lawyer and environmentalist, Clinton administration head of the Environmental Protection Agency (1993– ).

d. Jessie Wallace Hughan (1875–1955), American pacifist, socialist, and feminist, a founder of the Fellowship of Reconciliation (1919), Anti-Enlistment League (1915–1917), and the War Resisters League (1921).

## RELIGION/EDUCATION/EVERYDAY LIFE

Presbyterian Church in the U.S.A., after numerous rejections of the proposal, finally passed an amendment allowing women to be ordained.

Daughters of Bilitis (DOB), a social and civil rights group for lesbians, was founded in San Francisco.

Louise Brough won the singles tennis title at Wimbledon; she and her doubles partner, Margaret Osborne, also won three successive U.S. doubles tennis titles (1955–1957), on top of their nine previous ones (1942–1950).

Giuliana Benetton opened a small shop to sell brilliantly colored sweaters of her own design, later also selling wholesale, opening factories, and expanding throughout Europe and abroad, within three decades becoming the world's largest knitwear firm.

Mary Quant opened her shop, Bazaar, in London's Chelsea district with two partners, one later her husband, Alexander Plunket-Greene. The popularity of Quant's simple, bold, casual clothing quickly led to expansion and celebrity.

Claude Kogan joined in the first ascent of the 24,300-foot Ganesh Himal in the Himalayas.

Evelyne Sullerot founded France's key organization for family planning, becoming its secretary (1955–1958), then honorary president.

British social scientist Barbara Wootton published *Social Foundations of Wage Policy.*

"Babe" Didrikson Zaharias published *This Life I've Led: My Autobiography.*

Women Involved in Creating Cultural Alternatives (Wicca) was founded in the Philippines.

b. Patricia "Patty" Hearst (1955– ), daughter of publisher Randolph Hearst and granddaughter of William Randolph Hearst, who in 1974 was kidnapped by the Symbionese Liberation Army and later joined them in a bank robbery, for which she served almost two years in jail.

b. Susan Butcher (1955– ), American trail sled dog race champion.

b. Olga Korbut (1955– ), Russian gymnast, star of the 1972 Munich Olympics.

b. Betsy King (1955– ), American golfer.

d. Mary McLeod Bethune (1875–1955), African-American educator who founded what became Bethune-Cookman College (1923) and the National Organization of Negro Women (1935); she became Franklin D. Roosevelt's key adviser on African-American matters, also greatly influencing Eleanor Roosevelt in this area.

## SCIENCE/TECHNOLOGY/MEDICINE

Maria Goeppert Mayer published *Elementary Theory of Nuclear Shell Structure*, coauthored with Hans D. Jensen, who had independently developed a nuclear shell theory; they would later share a Nobel Prize for their work.

Whirly Girls, the first association of American female helicopter pilots, was founded.

American physician Jane C. Wright became associate professor of surgery at New York University's School of Medicine and director of chemotherapy at its Medical Center.

Emma Sadler Moss was the first woman elected president of the American Society of Clinical Pathologists.

The previously all-female U.S. Army Nurse Corps accepted the first male nurses.

d. Hilda Clark (1881–1955), British Quaker physician, relief worker, and pacifist, youngest child of the Clark's Shoes family.

d. Alice Middleton Boring (1883–1955), American cytologist, geneticist, and zoologist, long a teacher in China (1918–1920 at Peking Union Medical College; 1923–1950 at Yenching University).

d. Helen Dean King (1869–1955), American biologist who domesticated the Norway rat and developed it as the standard laboratory animal.

d. Mary Emily Sinclair (1878–1955), American mathematician and educator, the first woman to receive a Ph.D. from the University of Chicago (1908), long associated with Oberlin College (1907–1944), head of the mathematics department from 1939.

## ARTS/LITERATURE

Marian Anderson made her long-overdue debut at New York's Metropolitan Opera, in *Un Ballo in Maschera*, becoming the first African-American artist to sing with that company.

Anna Magnani starred opposite Burt Lancaster in the film version of Tennessee Williams's play *The Rose Tattoo*, winning a best actress Academy Award.

Elizabeth Bishop published her Pulitzer Prize–winning poetry collection, *North and South—A Cold Spring*, including her 1946 collection *North and South*.

Joan Sutherland created the role of Jenifer in Michael Tippett's opera *The Midsummer Marriage*.

Barbara Bel Geddes created the Maggie Pollitt role opposite Burl Ives and Ben Gazzara in Tennessee Williams's play *Cat on a Hot Tin Roof*.

Susan Strasberg starred in the title role in *The Diary of Anne Frank*, Frances Goodrich and Albert Hackett's play based on the diary of the World War II victim of the Nazis.

Anne Morrow Lindbergh published *Gift from the Sea*.

Enid Bagnold's play *The Chalk Garden* starred Gladys Cooper and Siobhan McKenna.

Elizabeth Bowen published the novel *A World of Love*.

Adrienne Rich published the poetry collection *Diamond Cutters*.

Eudora Welty published the short-story collection *The Bride of Innisfallen*.

Gwen Verdon starred opposite Stephen Douglass and Ray Walston in the baseball musical *Damn Yankees*.

Hildegarde Neff starred opposite Don Ameche in Cole Porter's stage musical *Silk Stockings*.

Flannery O'Connor published the short-story collection *A Good Man Is Hard to Find*.

Kim Novak, Rosalind Russell, and Betty Field starred in Joshua Logan's film version of William Inge's 1953 play *Picnic*.

Helen Frankenthaler painted *Blue Territory*.

Julie Harris starred in the title role in the New York production of Jean Anouilh's play *The Lark*.

Kay Boyle published the novel *Seagull on the Step*.

Ruth Gordon was Dolly Levi, the title role, in Thornton Wilder's play *The Matchmaker*.

Kim Stanley, Albert Salmi, and Elaine Stritch starred in William Inge's play *Bus Stop*.

Louise Nevelson showed the sculpture *Black Majesty*.

Martine Carol starred in Max Ophuls's film *Lola Montès*, opposite Anton Walbrook and Peter Ustinov.

Vivien Leigh starred opposite Kenneth More in Anatole Litvak's film version of Terence Rattigan's play *The Deep Blue Sea*.

Louise Bourgeois showed the sculpture *One and Others*.

Ruth Prawer Jhabvala published her first novel, *To Whom She Will*.

Marguerite Duras published the novel *Le square.*

Margaret Sullavan starred opposite Claude Dauphin and Robert Preston in Carolyn Green's stage comedy *Janus.*

Georgia O'Keeffe painted *From the Plains I* and *Patio with Black Door.*

Anna Sokolow choreographed the ballet *Rooms.*

Doris Day starred as singer Ruth Etting opposite James Cagney in Charles Vidor's film *Love Me or Leave Me.*

Thea Musgrave composed the chamber opera *The Abbot of Drimrock.*

Grace Williams composed *Penillion for Orchestra.*

d. Theda Bara (Theodosia Goodman, 1890–1955), American actress, briefly a star in silent films, who was made by studio publicity into "The Vamp."

d. Constance Collier (Laura Constance Hardie, 1878–1955), British actress.

d. Marion Eugenie Bauer (1887–1955), American composer.

# 1956

## POLITICS/LAW/WAR

Women won the right to be elected to office in Peru and to vote and be elected in Egypt, Gabon, and Togo.

Golda Meir became Israel's foreign minister (1956–1966).

Alva Reimer Myrdal became Swedish ambassador to India (1956–1961).

Eva Kolstad became president of the Norwegian Association for the Rights of Women (1956–1968).

Lilian Ngoyi became president of the Federation of South African Women.

Sylvia Pankhurst emigrated to Ethiopia, and was editor of the *Ethiopian Observer* there.

Adele Schreiber was coauthor of *Journey Towards Freedom,* her history of the International Alliance of Women, of which she had been vice-president.

Edith Summerskill published *The Ignoble Art,* an attack on the sport of boxing.

b. Anita Faye Hill (1956– ), American lawyer and law professor who made sexual harassment charges against U.S. Supreme Court nominee Clarence Thomas (1991) that ignited an explosive set of confrontations before a worldwide audience and incidentally revived the women's movement.

d. Annette Abbott Adams (1877–1956), American lawyer and judge, the first American woman to be a federal prosecutor and the first assistant attorney general.

d. (Agnes) Maude Royden (1876–1956), British pioneering interdenominational preacher, feminist, suffragist, editor, and in the 1930s the organizer of the pacifist "Peace Army"; she ultimately supported the British war effort in World War II.

d. Marie Juhacz (1880–1956), German socialist, feminist, and politician, a Social Democratic member of the Weimar Reichstag (1923–1933) who fled the Nazis.

d. Ana Pauker (1893–1956), a founder of the Romanian Communist Party who became postwar Romanian foreign minister in 1947; she was removed from all positions in 1952, though she was not killed.

d. Louise Bennett (1870–1956), Irish feminist, writer, suffragist, and trade unionist, chief architect of the Irish Woman Workers' Union (1916–1955).

d. Martha de Kerchove Bol Poel (1877–1956), Belgian feminist, a leader of her country's women's rights movement.

## RELIGION/EDUCATION/EVERYDAY LIFE

Margaret Towner became the first woman ordained as a minister in the Presbyterian Church in the U.S.A.

Dawn Fraser won the 100-meter freestyle gold medal at the Olympic Games, the first of her three gold medals in the event (1956; 1960; 1964), making her the first person to win the same title in three successive Olympic Games.

Mother Gerald Barry chaired a meeting of the Mothers General in the United States, which developed into the Conference of Major Superiors of Women Religious (later the Leadership Conference of Women Religious).

Charlemae Rollins received the prestigious Grolier Award, the first black person so honored.

Iolanda Balas set a world record in the high jump; she would extend that record 13 more times (1956–1961).

Joan Robinson published *Accumulation of Capital*; she had earlier (1952) published an introduction to Rosa Luxemburg's work of the same title.

b. Martina Navratilova (1956– ), Czech-American tennis champion, nine-time singles titlist at Wimbledon, winner of a record 167 tournaments.

d. "Babe" (Mildred Ella) Didrikson Zaharias (1914–1956), American athlete, best known as a golfer.

## SCIENCE/TECHNOLOGY/MEDICINE

Bette Nesmith (later Graham) invented "Mistake Out," for painting over typing errors, allowing retyping; later that year, she changed the name to "Liquid Paper," becoming a multimillionaire from its sales.

Cecilia Payne-Gaposchkin was made a full professor at Harvard University, the first woman in a Harvard professorship not intended for women only.

Marian Emily (Happy) White became the first woman to receive a doctorate in anthropology from the University of Michigan, becoming a key figure in the development of conservation archaeology.

Dorothy Crowfoot Hodgkin received the Royal Medal from Britain's Royal Society.

Marie Gimbutas published *Bronze Age Cultures in Central and Eastern Europe*.

Ethel Browne Harvey published *The American Arbacia and Other Sea Urchins*.

German-Scottish geneticist Charlotte Auerbach published *Genetics in the Atomic Age*.

d. Irène Joliot-Curie (1897–1956), French physicist, daughter of Marie and Pierre Curie; she and her husband, Jean Frédéric Joliot-Curie, were the first to induce artificial radioactivity (1934), winning the 1935 Nobel Prize for chemistry. Like her mother, she died of leukemia, probably induced by the radioactivity.

## ARTS/LITERATURE

Julie Andrews as Eliza Doolittle and Rex Harrison as Henry Higgins starred in *My Fair Lady*, the Alan Jay Lerner and Frederick Loewe stage musical based on George Bernard Shaw's *Pygmalion*.

Ingrid Bergman starred opposite Yul Brynner and Helen Hayes in the title role of Anatole Litvak's film *Anastasia*, perhaps the last of the Romanovs, winning a best actress Academy Award.

Deborah Kerr as Anna and Yul Brynner as the king starred in Walter Lang's film *The King and I*, based on the long-running 1949 Rodgers and Hammerstein stage musical.

Brigitte Bardot created her "sex kitten" role, and with it a 1950s stereotype, in Roger Vadim's film *And God Created Woman*.

Siobhan McKenna starred in the title role of a New York production of George Bernard Shaw's *Saint Joan*.

Gena Rowlands starred opposite Edward G. Robinson in Paddy Chayevsky's play *Middle of the Night*.

Judy Holliday starred in the Jule Styne, Betty Comden, and Adolph Green stage musical *Bells Are Ringing*.

Giulietta Masina created the title role in *Nights of Cabiria*, as a Roman prostitute in Federico Fellini's film classic.

Marilyn Monroe and Don Murray starred in Joshua Logan's film version of the 1955 William Inge play *Bus Stop*.

Patty McCormack reprised her role as the child in Mervyn LeRoy's film version of Maxwell Anderson's 1954 play *The Bad Seed.*

Grace Paley published the short-story collection *The Little Disturbances of Man.*

Mary Renault published the novel *The Last of the Wine.*

Shirley Jones and Gordon MacRae starred in Henry King's film version of Richard Rodgers and Oscar Hammerstein's stage musical *Carousel.*

Rosalind Russell starred in the title role of *Auntie Mame.*

Simone de Beauvoir published the novel *The Mandarins.*

Rose Macaulay published the novel *The Towers of Trebizond.*

Helen Frankenthaler painted *Eden.*

After the death of her husband and partner, Bertolt Brecht, Helene Weigel took over sole management of the Berliner Ensemble.

Anne Morrow Lindbergh published *The Unicorn and Other Poems.*

Georgia O'Keeffe painted *Patio with Cloud.*

Furugh Farrukhazad published the poetry collection *The Wall.*

Juana de Ibarbourou published the poetry collection *Oro y tormento.*

Sylvia Crowe published *Tomorrow's Landscape.*

d. Mistinguett (Jean-Marie Bourgeois, 1875–1956), French singer and comedian, a star in French music hall and cabaret.

d. Elsie Janis (1889–1956), American singer and actress, a star in vaudeville and musical theater from the turn of the century through the 1920s.

d. Marie Laurencin (1886–1956), French painter, poet, and set designer.

d. Ruth Draper (1884–1956), American mime and monologist, a star from the early 1920s until her death.

## 1957

### POLITICS/LAW/WAR

Women won the right to vote in Southern Rhodesia (now Zimbabwe), and to vote and be elected to office in Malaysia.

Algerian revolutionary Djamila Bouhired was captured by the French and sentenced to death for terrorist activities; after she became a cause célèbre, her sentence was commuted (1958), and after Algerian independence was won (1962) she returned to Algeria a heroine of the revolution.

Anne W. Wheaton was the first woman to be a presidential spokesperson, as associate press secretary for President Dwight D. Eisenhower.

Physician Martha M. Eliot became head of the U.S. Children's Bureau.

Marie-Hélène Lefaucheux became president of the International Council of Women.

d. Martha Munger Black (1866–1957), Canadian miner, politician, and writer, who panned for gold in the Yukon at the turn of the century and represented the Yukon in Parliament (1935–1940).

d. Adele Schreiber (?–1957), Austrian feminist and socialist, a leading women's rights movement leader in Germany from the turn of the century until the beginning of the Nazi period, when she fled into exile.

d. Louise Schröder (1887–1957), German socialist and politician, a Social Democratic legislator during the Weimar period and after World War II.

### RELIGION/EDUCATION/EVERYDAY LIFE

Daisy Gatson Bates, head of the Arkansas chapter of the National Association for the Advancement of Colored People (NAACP), led the successful fight to desegregate Little Rock Central High School.

Tennis player Althea Gibson won both at Wimbledon, the first African-American to do so, and at Forest Hills (1957; 1958), also winning the 1957 doubles title with Darlene Hard; both years, she was named the Associated Press's Woman Athlete of the Year.

Eirlys Roberts founded Britain's Consumers' Association, heading the Research and Editorial Division (1958-1973).

French ethnologist Germaine Tillion became director of studies at the École Pratique des Hautes Etudes.

British philosopher Elizabeth Anscombe published *Intention*.

Jessie Bernard published *Remarriage: A Study of Marriage*.

Susanne Langer published *Problems of Art*.

b. Jayne Torvill (1957- ), British ice skater who, with her partner, Christopher Dean, revolutionized ice dancing, most notably with their performance to Ravel's *Bolero* at the Sarajevo Olympics (1984).

b. Nancy Lopez (1957- ), American golfer who won her first tournament when only nine years old; turning professional (1978), she won the Ladies Professional Golf Association title (1985).

d. Edith Abbott (1876-1957), American labor economist, educator, writer, editor, and feminist who worked on a wide range of social-reform issues, often with her sister Grace Abbott; a key figure in social work education, the longtime dean of the University of Chicago's School of Social Work Administration (1924-1942).

d. Motoko Hani (1873-1957), Japanese journalist and educator, Japan's first full-time female reporter, who founded a progressive school.

d. Annie Turnbo Malone (ca. 1868-1957), African-American entrepreneur and philanthropist whose fortune was built on a scalp treatment she developed.

### SCIENCE/TECHNOLOGY/MEDICINE

Chien-Shiung Wu (Madame Wu) and four coauthors wrote a key letter to the *Physics Review* on their now-classic experiment disproving the widely held theory of conservation of parity, showing that, under certain conditions, atomic particles show "righthandedness" and "lefthandedness."

British astronomer Margaret Burbidge, William Fowler, Fred Hoyle, and Geoffrey Burbidge published a notable paper, "Synthesis of the Elements in Stars." Margaret Burbidge's contribution later won her the Warner Prize (1959).

The drug thalidomide—its dangers then unknown—began to be given to pregnant women; it was widely prescribed in Britain and Germany, experimentally elsewhere.

American geologist Pauline Moyd became the first woman to lead a major symposium for the American Institute of Mining, Metallurgical and Petroleum Engineers.

Helen Sawyer Hogg was elected president of the Royal Astronomical Society of Canada and named professor at the University of Toronto's David Dunlop Observatory; she had long worked there but been barred from an official post because her husband worked there too.

Indian physician Sushila Nayar became Indian Minister of Health (1962-1967).

American botanist Katherine Esau was elected to the National Academy of Sciences.

British crystallographer Kathleen Lonsdale received the Davy Medal of the Royal Society.

Elsie Eaves became the first female member of the American Association of Cost Engineers.

d. Gerty Theresa Radnitz Cori (1896-1957), Czech-American medical biochemist who, with her husband, Carl Ferdinand Cori, discovered the Cori cycle, the series of chemical reactions by which the body converts carbohydrates into energy. They shared a Nobel Prize for physiology or medicine (1947).

### ARTS/LITERATURE

Joanne Woodward starred in Nunnally Johnson's film *The Three Faces of Eve*, winning a best actress Academy Award.

Agatha Christie's 1953 play *Witness for the Prosecution* was filmed by Billy Wilder, starring Marlene Dietrich, Elsa Lanchester, Charles Laughton, and Tyrone Power.

Chinese writer Ding Ling won a Stalin Prize for her novel *Sang-Kan-ho-shang*; that same year she was condemned by her party as "reactionary" and forced into internal exile (1957-1969).

Katharine Hepburn starred opposite Spencer Tracy in Walter Lang's computer-friendly film *Desk Set* and opposite Burt Lancaster in Joseph Anthony's film *The Rainmaker*.

Stevie Smith published the poetry collection *Not Waving but Drowning*.

Marilyn Monroe starred opposite Laurence Olivier in the romantic comedy *The Prince and the Showgirl*, with Olivier directing and reprising his stage role.

Vera Brittain published *Testament of Experience*, the third volume of her autobiographical trilogy.

Janet Frame published the novel *Owls Do Cry*.

Machiko Kyo starred opposite Marlon Brando in the film *The Teahouse of the August Moon*.

Iris Murdoch published the novel *The Sandcastle*.

Maureen Stapleton starred opposite Cliff Robertson in Tennessee Williams's play *Orpheus Descending*.

Nelly Sachs published the poetry collection *And No One Knows Where to Go*.

Isak Dinesen published the short-story collection *Last Tales*.

Susan Strasberg, Helen Hayes, and Richard Burton starred in a New York production of Jean Anouilh's play *Time Remembered*.

Teresa Wright, Pat Hingle, and Eileen Heckart starred in William Inge's play *The Dark at the Top of the Stairs*.

Kim Stanley starred in Arthur Laurents's play *A Clearing in the Woods*.

Mary McCarthy published her autobiography, *Memories of a Catholic Girlhood*.

Simone Signoret starred opposite Yves Montand in Jean-Paul Sartre's French film adaptation of Arthur Miller's 1953 play *The Crucible*.

Gypsy Rose Lee published her autobiograpy, *Gypsy*, basis of the later film and musical.

Helen Frankenthaler painted *Jacob's Ladder*.

Ayn Rand published the novel *Atlas Shrugged*.

Elsa Morante published the novel *Arturo's Island*.

Georgia O'Keeffe painted *Red Hills with White Cloud*.

Lillian Hellman wrote the book for the musical *Candide*.

Nancy Mitford published the biography *Voltaire in Love*.

Ruth Gipps composed her *Concerto for Violin and Viola*.

Elizabeth Maconchy composed the opera *The Sofa*.

Rebecca West published the novel *The Fountain Overflows*.

Elizabeth Taylor published the novel *Angel*.

Furugh Farrukhazad published the poetry collection *Rebellion*.

Juana de Ibarbourou published her *Autobiography*.

d. Gabriela Mistral (Lucila Godoy Alcayaga, 1889–1957), Chilean poet, winner of the 1945 Nobel Prize for literature.

d. Dorothy Leigh Sayers (1893–1957), British mystery writer, creator of detectives Lord Peter Wimsey and Harriet Vane.

d. Dorothy Richardson (1873–1957), British novelist, whose novels were an early exploration of the "stream of consciousness" approach.

## 1958

### POLITICS/LAW/WAR

Marian Anderson became an American delegate to the United Nations.

Barbara Castle chaired Britain's Labour Party (1958–1959), and Jennie Lee joined its National Executive Committee (1958–1970).

Eleanor Roosevelt published the autobiographical *On My Own*.

Women won the right to vote and be elected to office in Laos.

Angie Brooks-Randolph became Liberia's assistant secretary of state (1958–1972).

Italy repealed laws regarding state-controlled prostitution.

Dutch Queen Wilhelmina published her autobiography, *Lonely But Not Alone.*

d. Christabel Pankhurst (1880–1958), British suffragist and writer, co-founder of the Women's Social and Political Union (1903), with her mother Emmeline and sister Sylvia a leader of the militant wing of Britain's women's suffrage movement.

d. Mary Sheepshanks (1872–1958), British social worker, educator, suffragist, and pacifist, who became international secretary of the Women's International League for Peace and Freedom (1920s).

## RELIGION/EDUCATION/EVERYDAY LIFE

Simone de Beauvoir published the four-volume autobiography *Memoirs of a Dutiful Daughter.*

Legalized prostitution was banned in Japan after a long campaign by women (from the 1880s), though illegal prostitutes continued to flourish.

Women's Caravan of Peace, sparked by Dora Russell, traveled from Britain across mainland Europe, protesting the cold war.

b. Belinda Mason (1958–1991), American journalist, AIDS victim, and advocate on AIDS issues.

d. Mary Ritter Beard (1876–1958), American historian and political economist, coauthor of the seminal *The Rise of American Civilization* (1927–1939) and author of *Women As a Force in History* (1946), one of several works dealing with the role of women in history.

d. (Sarah) Margery Fry (1874–1958), British social reformer, for more than three decades a key worldwide penal-reform, human-rights, and anti-death-penalty advocate.

## SCIENCE/TECHNOLOGY/MEDICINE

Xie Xide published *Semi-Conductor Physics.*

Marguerite Perey became director of the Nuclear Research Centre at Strasbourg University.

Marie Wormington became the first female president of the Society of American Archaeology.

Marion E. Kenworthy became the first female president of the American Psychoanalytic Association.

d. Marie Charlotte Carmichael Stopes (1880–1958), British geologist, botanist, and geographer, a specialist on fossil plants, best known as an advocate of sex education and birth control; author of several very popular books on sex education and birth control.

d. Rosalind Elsie Franklin (1920–1958), British molecular biologist and physical chemist whose X-ray photographs of chromosomes (1951) were the key to James Watson and Francis Crick's understanding of the double-helix structure of DNA, but whose contributions were initially unacknowledged; she died before she could have shared in their Nobel Prize (1962).

## ARTS/LITERATURE

Margot Fonteyn created the title role in Frederick Ashton's ballet *Ondine.*

Martha Graham choreographed the ballet *Clytemnestra.*

Anne Bancroft starred opposite Henry Fonda in William Gibson's play *Two for the Seesaw.*

Elizabeth Taylor, Paul Newman, and Burl Ives starred in Richard Brooks's film version of the 1955 Tennessee Williams play *Cat on a Hot Tin Roof.*

Deborah Kerr, David Niven, and Jean Seberg starred in *Bonjour Tristesse,* Otto Preminger's screen version of Françoise Sagan's 1956 novel *A Certain Smile.*

Leslie Caron played the title role of Vincente Minnelli's film *Gigi,* Alan Jay Lerner and Frederick Loewe's musical based on the Colette novel.

Joanne Woodward starred opposite Paul Newman in Martin Ritt's film *The Long Hot Summer,* based on William Faulkner's 1940 Snopes family novel *The Hamlet.*

New Zealand teacher and writer Sylvia Ashton-Warner published her first novel, *Spinster,* about a teacher working with Maori children.

Kim Novak starred as a witch opposite James Stewart in Bill Quine's film version of John van Druten's 1950 play *Bell, Book and Candle.*

Mitzi Gaynor as Nellie Forbush and Rossano Brazzi starred in Joshua Logan's film version of Richard Rodgers and Oscar Hammerstein's 1949 stage musical *South Pacific.*

Kim Stanley, Lloyd Bridges, and Patty Duke starred in *The Goddess*, John Cromwell's film from Paddy Chayevsky's screenplay. Stanley also starred in Eugene O'Neill's play *A Touch of the Poet*.

Louise Nevelson showed the sculpture *Sky Cathedral*.

Mary Renault published the novel *The King Must Die*.

Lynn Fontanne starred opposite Alfred Lunt in Friedrich Dürrenmatt's play *The Visit*.

Nadine Gordimer published the novel *A World of Strangers*.

Australian novelist Nancy Cato published *All the Rivers Run*, first novel of her trilogy under the same title.

Rebecca West published the essay collection *The Court and the Castle*.

Susan Hayward starred in the film *I Want to Live*, winning a best actress Academy Award.

France Nuyen starred in the title role of Paul Osborn's play *The World of Susie Wong*.

Rosalind Russell reprised her stage role as Mame in Morton DaCosta's film version of *Auntie Mame*.

Barbara Pym published the novel *A Glass of Blessings*.

Ana Maria Matute published the novel *Los hijos muertos*, set during the Spanish Civil War.

Djuna Barnes published the verse play *Antiphon*.

Georgia O'Keeffe painted *Ladder to the Moon*.

Bryher published the historical novel *Gate to the Sea*.

Donna Reed began her long run in television's situation comedy *The Donna Reed Show* (1958–1966).

Edna Ferber published the novel *Ice Palace*.

Jean Seberg starred as Joan of Arc in *Saint Joan*, Otto Preminger's film adaptation of George Bernard Shaw's play.

Elizabeth Taylor published *The Blush and Other Stories*.

Laura Knight painted *Bolshoi Ballet Rehearsing*.

Muriel Box produced and directed the film *The Truth About Women*.

Rumer Godden published her novel *The Greengage Summer*.

Shirley Ann Grau published the novel *The Hard Blue Sky*.

b. Madonna (Madonna Louise Ciccone, 1958– ), American singer and actress, a popular music star from the early 1980s.

d. Mary Roberts Rinehart (1876–1958), American mystery novelist, beginning with *The Circular Staircase* (1908); also a playwright and novelist.

d. Doris Humphrey (1895–1958), American dancer, choreographer, and teacher.

d. Rose Macaulay (1889–1958), British novelist from the early 1920s and from *The Pleasure of Ruins* (1953) also a notable travel book writer.

d. Zoë Akins (1886–1958), American playwright, poet, and novelist, best known for her plays, beginning with her first hit, *Déclassée* (1919).

d. Dorothy Canfield (1879–1958), American novelist, short story writer, and essayist.

d. Rachel Crothers (1878–1958), American playwright and director.

## 1959

### POLITICS/LAW/WAR

Helen Suzman was a cofounder of South Africa's antiapartheid Progressive Party, long its only member of Parliament.

Women won the right to vote and be elected in Madagascar and Tunisia.

Judith Hart was elected a Labour member of Parliament in Britain, beginning her long political career.

Conservative Margaret Thatcher was elected to her first term in the British Parliament.

Christabel Pankhurst's book *Unshackled: The Story of How We Won the Vote* was published posthumously.

## RELIGION/EDUCATION/EVERYDAY LIFE

Fatima Meer began teaching sociology at Natal University, where she remained, eventually becoming South Africa's highest-ranking black academic.

Ruth Handler developed the Barbie doll, and later the Ken doll, named after her two children with Elliot Handler, with whom she cofounded Mattel, Inc. Ruth Handler also later developed the Nearly Me line of breast prostheses and swimsuits for women who had had breast-cancer surgery (1970s).

British social scientist Barbara Wootton published *Social Science and Social Pathology*.

Elizabeth Anscombe and her husband, Peter Geach, coauthored *An Introduction to Wittgenstein's Tractatus*.

b. Nicole Brown Simpson (1959–1994), American murder victim, the former wife of football star O. J. Simpson.

b. Rigoberta Menchú (1959– ), Guatemalan Quiché Indian peace activist who won the 1992 Nobel Peace Prize.

d. Claude Kogan (1919–1959), French mountaineer; she and three others died in an avalanche during the Expédition Feminine au Nepal, an all-woman climb of 26,700-foot Cho Oyo.

## SCIENCE/TECHNOLOGY/MEDICINE

Working with her husband, Louis Leakey, in East Africa's Olduvai Gorge, Mary Leakey discovered a skull that revolutionized thinking about human evolution, taking the development of humans back a million years earlier than thought and suggesting that different branches evolved.

Dr. Helen Taussig became the first woman to be a full professor at the Johns Hopkins Medical School, her alma mater; over three decades earlier, she had been informed by the school that she could not intern in internal medicine because that department already had a female intern.

Dorothy Russell published *Pathology of Tumours of the Nervous System*, coauthored with L. Rubenstein.

Gladys Anderson Emerson was given the Certificate Award of the American Association for the Advancement of Science.

d. Edith Clarke (1883–1959), American mathematician and electrical engineer, the first woman to receive a master's degree in engineering from Massachusetts Institute of Technology (1919) and probably the first to teach electrical engineering at the university level (1948).

d. Lilian Murray (Lindsay, 1871–1959), British dentist, the first British woman to gradute from dental school (1895) and to be president of the British Dental Association.

d. Mary Frances Winston (Newson) (1869–1959), American mathematician and educator, the first American woman to receive a Ph.D. in mathematics from a foreign university (1896).

## ARTS/LITERATURE

Mary Martin and Theodore Bikel created the roles of Maria and George von Trapp in *The Sound of Music*, Richard Rodgers and Oscar Hammerstein's stage musical.

Lorraine Hansberry's play *A Raisin in the Sun* starred Claudia McNeil, Sidney Poitier, and Ruby Dee.

Marilyn Monroe as Honey, Tony Curtis, and Jack Lemmon starred in Billy Wilder's classic film comedy *Some Like It Hot*.

Patty Duke and Anne Bancroft starred as the young Helen Keller and her teacher, Annie Sullivan, in William Gibson's play *The Miracle Worker*.

Shirley Jackson published the novel *The Haunting of Hill House*.

Simone Signoret starred in *Room at the Top*, winning a best actress Academy Award.

Emmanuele Riva starred opposite Eiji Okada in *Hiroshima, Mon Amour*, written by Marguerite Duras and directed by Alain Resnais.

Dorothy Dandridge, Sidney Poitier, and Sammy Davis Jr. starred in Otto Preminger's film version of George and Ira Gershwin's folk opera *Porgy and Bess*.

Joanne Woodward, Yul Brynner, and Margaret Leighton starred in Martin Ritt's screen version of William Faulkner's 1929 novel *The Sound and the Fury*.

Denise Duval created the only role in Francis Poulenc's one-character opera *La Voix Humaine*.

Ethel Merman starred in Stephen Sondheim and Jule Styne's stage musical *Gypsy*, on the life of Gypsy Rose Lee.

Geraldine Page starred opposite Paul Newman in Tennessee Williams's play *Sweet Bird of Youth*.

Jean Seberg and Jean-Paul Belmondo starred in *Breathless*, Jean-Luc Godard's "New Wave" film, with screenplay by François Truffaut.

Katharine Hepburn, Elizabeth Taylor, and Montgomery Clift starred in *Suddenly Last Summer*, Joseph L. Mankiewicz's film version of Tennessee Williams's 1958 play.

Denise Levertov published the poetry collection *With Eyes in the Back of Our Heads*.

Katharine Cornell starred as Mrs. Patrick Campbell in *Dear Liar*.

Louise Nevelson showed the sculpture *Dawn's Wedding Feast*.

Marianne Moore published the poetry collection *O to Be a Dragon*.

Kim Novak starred opposite Fredric March in Delbert Mann's film version of Paddy Chayevsky's 1958 play *Middle of the Night*.

Muriel Spark published the novel *Memento Mori*.

Nelly Sachs published the poetry collection *Flight and Metamorphosis*.

Nathalie Sarraute published the novel *Le Planétarium*.

Pamela Hansford Johnson published the novels *The Unspeakable Skipton* and *The Humbler Creation*.

Miriam Makeba starred in the contemporary opera *King Kong*.

Sylvia Beach wrote *Shakespeare and Company*.

Françoise Sagan published the novel *Aimez-vous Brahms?* and wrote the play *Château en Suède*.

Ella Fitzgerald recorded her Grammy-winning album *But Not for Me* (1959).

Georgia O'Keeffe painted *Flagpole with White House* and *It Was Red and Pink*.

Gertrude Berg starred opposite Cedric Hardwicke in Leonard Spiegelgass's stage comedy *A Majority of One*.

Eileen Brennan starred in the title role in Rick Besoyan's stage musical *Little Mary Sunshine*.

Doris Humphrey published *The Art of Making Dances*.

d. Billie Holiday (Eleanora Fagan, 1915–1959), African-American jazz singer, a cabaret and recording star from the mid-1930s through the mid-1940s.

d. Ethel Barrymore (Edith Blythe, 1879–1959), American actress, a star on the New York stage starting with *Captain Jinks of the Horse Marines* (1901), who also appeared in many films; sister of John and Lionel Barrymore.

d. Olga Knipper (1870–1959), Russian actress, star of the Moscow Art Theatre; she originated several classic roles in plays by her husband, Anton Chekhov, including Elena in *Uncle Vanya* (1897) and Masha in *The Three Sisters* (1901).

d. Wanda Landowska (1897–1959), Polish harpsichordist, a major figure in the renaissance of that instrument.

d. Germaine Richier (1904–1959), French sculptor.

## 1960

### POLITICS/LAW/WAR

Sirimavo Bandaranaike became prime minister of Ceylon (later Sri Lanka), succeeding her husband, Solomon Bandaranaike, who had been assassinated (1959). She was the world's first female prime minister (1960–1965; 1970–1977).

The first all-woman U.S. Senate race was held in Maine, when Lucia Marie Cormier challenged Margaret Chase Smith, who was overwhelmingly elected to her third term.

Women won the right to vote and be elected to office in Tonga.

Bella Abzug and Dagmar Wilson founded Women Strike for Peace, which focused on nuclear disarmament, later also opposing the Vietnam War.

Ekaterina Furtseva became the Soviet Union's minister of culture.

Federation of Cuban Women (FMC) was founded, a government-sponsored organization headed by Vilma Espin, wife of Raul Castro and sister-in-law of Cuban leader Fidel Castro.

French lawyer Gisèle Halimi became counsel for the Algerian National Liberation Front.

Ana Figuero became assistant director general of the International Labor Organization.

Ho Hsiang-ning chaired the China Women's Federation, a largely honorary post.

d. Sylvia Pankhurst (1882–1960), British suffragist, artist, socialist, and antiwar activist, with her mother Emmeline and sister Christabel a leader of the militant wing of the British women's suffrage movement until World War I, splitting with them because she opposed the war, which they supported.

### RELIGION/EDUCATION/EVERYDAY LIFE

Simone de Beauvoir published *The Prime of Life.*

Wilma Rudolph won three Olympic gold medals, in the 100 meters, the 200 meters, and the relay.

After the death of her husband, Angel Ramos, Tina Ramos (later Hills) became publisher of *El Mundo*, in San Juan, Puerto Rico (1960–1987); half her workforce were women.

Esther Forbes was elected to the American Antiquarian Society, the first woman to become a member.

Iolanda Balas won an Olympic gold medal and set an Olympic record in the high jump.

Joan Robinson published *Exercises in Economic Analysis.*

British philosopher Mary Warnock published *Modern Ethics.*

d. Evangeline French (1869–1960) and Francesca French (1871–1960), British missionaries and travelers, sisters working in Asia, known for their travels with Mildred Cable (especially 1923–1939).

d. Dorothea Douglass (Mrs. Lambert Chambers, 1878–1960), British tennis player who won seven women's singles tennis titles at Wimbledon (from 1903).

d. Emily Post (1873–1960), American writer best known for her *Etiquette: The Blue Book of Social Usage* (1922).

d. Lottie (Charlotte) Dod (1871–1960), British tennis player, tennis's first prodigy, known at 12 as "the little wonder."

d. Constance Spry (1886–1960), British entrepreneur, writer, and educator, a floral arranger from the 1920s who founded floristry and cooking schools, writing widely in her twin specialties.

d. Fanny Durack (1894–1960), Australian swimmer who set Olympic and world records (1912–1918).

### SCIENCE/TECHNOLOGY/MEDICINE

The first birth control pill, Enovid, went on the market; it had been developed by Gregory Pincus, with funds from the Planned Parenthood Federation of America and from Katharine McCormick.

Jane Goodall began her long study of chimpanzees at the Gombe Stream Game Reserve, in Tanzania (then Tanganyika); she would become famous through her books and photographs and through documentary films created by Dutch naturalist Hugo von Lawick, later her husband.

Joy Adamson published *Born Free*, about her experiences in training the tame lion cub Elsa for a return to the wild.

Dr. Helen Taussig published the two-volume *Congenital Malformations of the Heart* (1960–1961), demonstrating that changes in the heart and lungs could be diagnosed by X rays and fluoroscope.

Irmgard Flügge-Lotz was the first woman appointed engineering professor at Stanford University.

American zoologist Libbie H. Hyman received the Linnean Society's gold medal.

Dorothy Hodgkin became the first Wolfson Research Professor of Britain's Royal Society (1960–1977).

Sophia Josephine Kleegman became president of the American Association of Marriage Counselors.

d. Melanie Reizes Klein (1882–1960), Austrian-British child psychoanalyst focusing on severe mental disorders, who pioneered in using psychoanalysis and play techniques with small children. Her final work was *The Psychoanalysis of Children.*

d. Carolyn Conant van Blarcom (1879–1960), American nurse and midwife, a leader in midwife reform, herself the first licensed American nurse-midwife.

d. Ida (Sophia) Scudder (1870–1960), American medical missionary, one of a family of medical missionaries working in India.

d. Ruth Roland Nichols (1901–1960), American aviator, the first woman to receive a hydroplane license (1924) and the first American woman to obtain a commercial pilot's license (1932).

d. Agnes Robertson Arber (1879–1960), British botanist who published numerous works on plants.

d. Mary Bailey (1890–1960), British aviator.

## ARTS/LITERATURE

Colleen Dewhurst starred opposite Pat Hingle in Tad Mosel's play *All the Way Home*.

Elizabeth Taylor starred opposite Laurence Harvey in *Butterfield 8*, Daniel Mann's film based on the 1935 John O'Hara novel, winning a best actress Academy Award.

Julie Andrews starred opposite Richard Burton in Alan Jay Lerner and Frederick Loewe's musical *Camelot*.

Melina Mercouri starred as the Greek prostitute in Jules Dassin's film *Never on Sunday*.

Lee Remick starred opposite Yves Montand in Tony Richardson's anti-lynching, pro–civil rights film *Sanctuary*, based on William Faulkner's 1931 novel.

Millie Perkins starred in the title role of George Stevens's film *Diary of Anne Frank*, based on the posthumously discovered wartime diaries.

Lillian Hellman's play *Toys in the Attic* starred Maureen Stapleton, Anne Revere, and Jason Robards.

Gwendolyn Brooks published the poetry collection *The Bean Eaters*.

Nadine Gordimer published the short-story collection *Friday's Footprints*.

Olivia Manning published *The Great Fortune*, the first novel in her Balkan trilogy.

Phyllis McGinley published her Pulitzer Prize–winning *Times Three: Selected Verse from Three Decades*.

Ruth Prawer Jhabvala published the novel *The Householder*.

Sylvia Ashton-Warner published the novel *Incense to Idols*.

Tammy Grimes created the title role in Meredith Willson's play *The Unsinkable Molly Brown*.

Flannery O'Connor published the novel *The Violent Bear Took It Away*.

Georgia O'Keeffe painted *White Patio with Red Door, Blue, Black and Grey, It Was Blue and Green*, and *It Was Yellow and Pink III*.

Sophia Loren starred in the title role opposite Peter Sellers in the film *The Millionairess*.

Diana Ross, Florence Ballard, and Mary Wilson organized the Supremes.

Margaret Laurence published the novel *This Side Jordan*, set in East Africa.

Sawako Ariyoshi published the novel *The River Ki*.

Mari Sandoz published the novel *Son of the Gamblin' Man*.

Ana Maria Matute published the trilogy *Los mercaderes* (1960–1969), set during the Spanish Civil War.

Kamala Markandaya published the novel *A Silence of Desire*.

Oriana Fallaci published *The Useless Sex*.

Alicia Markova published the autobiography *Giselle and I*.

Jessica Mitford published the autobiography *Hons and Rebels*.

Phyllis Tate composed the opera *The Lodger*, about Jack the Ripper.

d. Margaret Sullavan (Margaret Brooke, 1911–1960), American actress, a luminous stage and screen star, who committed suicide.

d. Zora Neale Hurston (1901–1960), African-American novelist and folklorist, whose work was rediscovered later in the century, largely by the African-American novelist Alice Walker, who edited an anthology of Hurston's works.

d. Sibilla Aleramo (Rina Pierangeli Faccio, 1876–1960), Italian writer.

d. Vicki Baum (1896–1960), Austrian writer and editor.

## 1961

### POLITICS/LAW/WAR

Marietta Tree was the first woman to become the chief United States delegate to the United Nations.

President John F. Kennedy established the President's Commission on the Status of Women, chaired by Eleanor Roosevelt, with Esther Peterson (who had proposed it) serving as executive vice-chair. Peterson was appointed director of the Women's Bureau of the U.S. Department of Labor.

Women won the right to vote and be elected to office in El Salvador and Rwanda.

Nigerian lawyer Aduke Alakija became a member of the Nigerian delegation to the United Nations (1961–1965).

Elizabeth Gurley Flynn became chairman of the Communist Party of the United States.

d. Adela Constantia Pankhurst Walsh (1885–1961), British-Australian pacifist and feminist, the third daughter of Emmeline Pankhurst, sister of Christabel and Sylvia Pankhurst; she later turned fascist and was interned during World War II.

### RELIGION/EDUCATION/EVERYDAY LIFE

In India, the Dowry Prohibition Act made the asking for a dowry illegal but had little effect, since "presents" could still be legally offered; where the groom's family believed such presents from the bride's family insufficient, they would harass and sometimes kill the bride; this practice, called *dowry murder*, continued into the 1990s, despite protests by India's women's groups.

Tennis player Billie Jean King won a doubles title at Wimbledon; it was the first of what would be 20 Wimbledon titles: singles, doubles, and mixed doubles.

Eirlys Roberts became editor of *Which?* (1961–1971), the product-review journal of Britain's Consumers' Association, which she had founded (1957).

Marianne Means was the first woman assigned full-time to cover the White House, for the Hearst newspapers.

Julia Child, Simone Beck, and Louise Bertholle published *Mastering the Art of French Cooking;* they had earlier founded the cooking school L'Ecole des Trois Gourmandes, in France.

Erin Pizzey published *Scream Quietly or the Neighbours Will Hear*, on domestic violence.

American economist Alice Rivlin published *The Role of the Federal Government in Financing Higher Education*.

Elizabeth Anscombe wrote *Three Philosophers*.

Emily Post's autobiographical *Truly Emily Post* was published posthumously.

b. Diana, Princess of Wales (Diana Frances Spencer, 1961–1997), British kindergarten teacher who in 1981 married Charles, Prince of Wales, heir to the British throne, and who was then a focus of worldwide public attention through the birth of their two sons, their 1992 separation, their 1996 divorce, and her tragic death in an automobile accident.

d. Emily Greene Balch (1867–1961), American pacifist, social reformer, writer, teacher, and social worker, a colleague of Jane Addams at Hull House, a leading advocate of immigration and child welfare reform, first secretary of the Women's International League for Peace and Freedom, and winner of a Nobel Peace Prize (1946).

d. Dorothy Thompson (1893–1961), American journalist who became a leading anti-Nazi while reporting from Germany (1924–1934) until the Germans expelled her, continuing as a major figure throughout her life.

d. Annie Carroll (1871–1961), American librarian and writer, longtime children's library supervisor in the New York Public Library (1906–1941), a pioneer in building public library services for children and gaining professional standing for children's librarians.

d. Mother Mary Gerald Barry (Bridget Catherine Barry, 1881–1961), nun who becamer prioress general of Michigan's Dominican Sisters of Adrian (1933–1961), a strong supporter of higher education for nuns, who established numerous parochial schools and several colleges.

d. Mary Cromwell Jarrett (1877–1961), American social worker and educator, a pioneer in psychiatric social work who founded the Smith College School for Social Work.

d. Jessie Redmon Fauset (1882–1961), African-American editor and author.

### SCIENCE/TECHNOLOGY/MEDICINE

American physician Jane C. Wright led a medical safari, taking a fully equipped "mobile hospital" around Kenya. The trip was sponsored by the African Research Foundation, an organization with which she remained active.

Janet Grame Travell became personal physician to U.S. President John F. Kennedy, the first woman to serve in that post (1961–1965).

Joy Adamson published *Living Free*.

d. Anne Sewell Young (1871–1961), American astronomer, long professor of astronomy at Mount Holyoke College and director of its John Payson Williston Observatory (1899–1936).

### ARTS/LITERATURE

Muriel Spark published the novel *The Prime of Miss Jean Brodie*.

Audrey Hepburn starred opposite George Peppard in Blake Edwards's film version of Truman Capote's 1958 story *Breakfast at Tiffany's*.

Denise Levertov published the poetry collection *The Jacob's Ladder*.

Geraldine Page as Alma starred opposite Laurence Harvey in Peter Glenville's screen version of Tennessee Williams's 1948 play *Summer and Smoke*.

Rita Tushingham starred in the then extraordinarily forthright film *A Taste of Honey*, as a pregnant single woman whose child was fathered by a black sailor, and whose supportive best friend is homosexual.

Sophia Loren starred on film in Vittorio De Sica's *Two Women*, winning a best actress Academy Award, and also in Anthony Mann's *El Cid*, opposite Charlton Heston.

Leslie Caron starred opposite Maurice Chevalier and Charles Boyer in Joshua Logan's film *Fanny*, based on the 1954 stage musical.

Lorraine Hansberry's play *A Raisin in the Sun* was filmed by Daniel Petrie, starring Claudia McNeil, Ruby Dee, Sidney Poitier, and Diana Sands.

Delphine Seyrig starred in Alain Resnais's film *Last Year at Marienbad*.

Jeanne Moreau starred opposite Oskar Werner and Henri Serre in François Truffaut's film *Jules and Jim*.

Marilyn Monroe starred in her last film, *The Misfits*, opposite Clark Gable (also his last film) and Montgomery Clift. John Huston directed from the screenplay by Arthur Miller, then Monroe's husband.

Iris Murdoch published the novel *A Severed Head*.

Janet Frame published the novel *Faces in the Water*.

Margaret Leighton starred opposite Alan Webb in Tennessee Williams's play *The Night of the Iguana*.

Natalie Wood starred opposite Warren Beatty in Elia Kazan's film *Splendor in the Grass*.

Mary Tyler Moore emerged as a television star in *The Dick Van Dyke Show* (1961–1966).

Natalia Ginzburg published the novel *Voices in the Evening*.

Agnes Varda wrote and directed the films *Cleo from 5 to 7* and *Happiness*.

Anna Sokolow choreographed the ballet *Dreams*.

Shirley Ann Grau published the novel *The House on Coliseum Street*.

Googie Withers starred opposite Michael Redgrave in Graham Greene's play *The Complaisant Lover*.

Shirley Booth became a television star in her long-running series *Hazel* (1961–1965).

Barbara Pym published the novel *No Fond Return of Love*.

Furugh Farrukhazad published the poetry collection *Another Birth*.

Judy Collins issued her first album, *A Maid of Constant Sorrow*.

Ellen Stewart founded New York's Café La Mama, a venue for experimental theater.

Hortense Calisher published the novel *False Entry*.

Ingeborg Bachmann published the short-story collection *Das dreissigste Jahr*.

Jean Kerr's play *Mary, Mary* starred Barbara Bel Geddes and Barry Nelson.

Peggy Glanville-Hicks composed her opera *Nausicaa*.

Taylor Caldwell published the novel *A Prologue to Love*.

Pearl Primus choreographed *The Wedding*.

Vita Sackville-West published the novel *No Signposts in the Sea*.

d. Pastora Imperio (Pastora Rojas; La Emperaora, ca. 1885/1894–1961), Spanish dancer and choreographer.

d. Hilda Doolittle (H. D., 1886–1961), American Imagist poet and novelist, long resident in Europe.

d. Vanessa Stephen Bell (1879–1961), British artist, the sister of Virginia Woolf, with whom she was associated in the Bloomsbury Group.

# 1962

## POLITICS/LAW/WAR

Alva Reimer Myrdal became a member of the Swedish parliament (1962–1970), and in part concurrently a delegate to the Geneva Disarmament Conference (1962–1973).

Brazilian feminists won a change in the law that had, previously, considered married women as minors for life.

Vijaya Pandit became governor of Maharastra (1962–1964).

Women won the right to vote in Zambia and to vote and be elected to office in Algeria.

Based on recommendations of the President's Commission on the Status of Women, President John F. Kennedy directed that women and men should be considered on an equal basis for promotions.

Fadéla M'rabet published *La femme algérienne*, profiling many Algerian women just after the Algerian War of Independence.

d. (Anna) Eleanor Roosevelt (1884–1962), American social reformer and political figure, the leading American woman of her time and a world figure, during the presidency of her husband, Franklin Delano Roosevelt (1933–1945) and for the rest of her life. Among her accomplishments was the United Nations Declaration of Human Rights (1948).

d. Wilhelmina (1880–1962), queen of the Netherlands (r. 1898–1948), who during World War II helped organize anti-Nazi resistance from exile in London.

## RELIGION/EDUCATION/EVERYDAY LIFE

Barbara Tuchman published *The Guns of August*, her masterful exploration of the run-up to World War I; she won the Pulitzer Prize for general nonfiction (1963), the first woman to do so.

Joan Robinson published *Essays in the Theory of Economic Growth*.

Stella, dowager marchioness of Reading chaired the Advisory Council on Commonwealth Immigration (1962–1965).

Barbara Ward published *The Rich and Poor Nations*.

Helen Gurley Brown published *Sex and the Single Girl*.

Susanne Langer published *Philosophical Sketches*.

b. Jackie (Jacqueline) Joyner-Kersee (1962– ), American track and field champion, who set a world record in the heptathlon and was a two-time Olympic gold medalist in the event, holding six of the seven over-7,000-point heptathlon performances on record; one of the world's leading athletes.

d. Helene Weber (1881–1962), German social worker and politician, a leading figure in German social work before and after the Nazi period.

d. Mabel Dodge Luhan (1879–1962), American social reformer and salon hostess, active as a patron of the arts and collector of artists in Florence, New York, and Santa Fe.

d. Theresa Neuman (1898–1962), Austrian religious figure, severely injured in a 1918 fire, whose seemingly miraculous recovery (1923–1925) prompted pilgrimages to her village, Könnersreuth.

## SCIENCE/TECHNOLOGY/MEDICINE

Rachel Carson published her landmark *Silent Spring*, on the dangers posed by chemicals in the environment.

Alerted by a German doctor (a former student) that an unusual number of gross malformations were being found among newborn babies, Dr. Helen Taussig traveled to Europe to visit pediatric clinics; she concluded that a new sleeping pill, Thalidomide, was the probable cause, and was the first to warn of its dangers. Not until 1962 it later became clear that it caused major birth defects.

Joy Adamson founded the World Wildlife Fund in the U.S.A. and published *Forever Free*.

Sheila Kitzinger published her highly influential *The Experience of Childbirth*, focusing on reducing pain and fear through relaxation and understanding.

German-Scottish geneticist Charlotte Auerbach published *Mutation Methods* and *The Science of Genetics*.

Xie Xide published *Solid Physics*.

British archaeologist Margaret Murray published her autobiography *Centenary* at age 100.

Margaret Mead published the autobiographical *Blackberry Winter: My Earlier Years*.

Marguerite Perey became the first female member of France's Académie des Sciences.

## ARTS/LITERATURE

Anna Akhmatova's *Poem Without a Hero* became one of the major works of the Soviet period.

Anne Bancroft and Patty Duke reprised their 1959 stage roles in Arthur Penn's film version of *The Miracle Worker*. Bancroft won a best actress Academy Award.

Doris Lessing published her novel *The Golden Notebook*, regarded by many feminists as a seminal work, although she denied any intention to make it so.

Georgia O'Keeffe painted *Sky Above White Clouds I*.

Harriet Andersson starred as the schizophrenic at the center of Ingmar Bergman's *Through a Glass, Darkly*.

Katherine Anne Porter published the novel *Ship of Fools*.

Lee Remick and Jack Lemmon starred as alcoholics on the way down in Blake Edwards's film *Days of Wine and Roses*.

Mary Renault published the novel *The Bull from the Sea*.

Audrey Hepburn, Shirley MacLaine, and James Garner starred in William Wyler's remake of his 1936 film *These Three*, based on Lillian Hellman's play *The Children's Hour*.

Martha Graham choreographed the ballet *Phaedra*.

Kinuyo Tanaka became the first Japanese woman to direct a feature film, *Love Letter*.

Siobhan McKenna starred in *The Playboy of the Western World*, Brian Desmond Hurst's film version of John Millington Synge's play.

Uta Hagen starred opposite Arthur Hill in Edward Albee's play *Who's Afraid of Virginia Woolf?*

Sylvia Plath published the poetry collection *The Colossus*.

Olivia Manning published *The Spoilt City*, the second novel in her Balkan trilogy.

Shirley Jackson published the novel *We Have Always Lived in the Castle*.

Sue Lyon starred in the title role opposite James Mason in *Lolita*, Stanley Kubrick's film version of Vladimir Nabokov's 1955 novel.

Anne Sexton published the poetry collection *All My Pretty Ones*.

Diahann Carroll starred opposite Richard Kiley in Richard Rodgers's stage musical *No Strings*.

Edith Sitwell published the novel *The Outcasts*.

Geraldine Page and Paul Newman reprised their 1957 stage roles in Richard Brooks's film version of Tennessee Williams's play *Sweet Bird of Youth*.

Barbra Streisand starred opposite Elliott Gould in Harold Rome's play *I Can Get It for You Wholesale*.

Hortense Calisher published the short stories *Tale for the Mirror*.

Rosalind Russell and Natalie Wood starred in Mervyn LeRoy's film *Gypsy*, based on Gypsy Rose Lee's autobiography.

Sandy Dennis starred opposite Jason Robards in Herb Gardner's play *A Thousand Clowns*.

Barbara Harris and Jo Van Fleet starred in Arthur Kopit's play *Oh Dad, Poor Dad, Mamma's Hung You in the Closet and I'm Feelin' So Sad*.

Jane Fonda, Tony Franciosa, Jim Hutton, and Lois Nettleton starred in George Roy Hill's film version of Tennessee Williams's 1960 play *Period of Adjustment*.

Brigid Brophy published the novel *Flesh*.

Janet Frame published the novel *The Edge of the Alphabet*.

Maureen O'Sullivan starred opposite Paul Ford in Sumner Arthur Long's stage comedy *Never Too Late*.

Laura Knight published *A Proper Circus Drive*.

Margaret Leighton starred opposite Anthony Quinn in Sidney Michaels's play *Tchin-Tchin*.

Vicki Baum's *Autobiography* was published posthumously.

b. Jodie Foster (1962– ), American actress and director, a child star from the mid-1970s who emerged as an international dramatic film star in the late 1980s.

b. k. d. lang (Kathy Dawn Lang, 1962– ), Canadian popular and country-music singer and composer, who emerged as a star performer in the late 1980s.

b. Paula Abdul (1962– ), American singer, dancer, and choreographer.

d. Marilyn Monroe (Norma Jean Mortenson, 1926–1962), American actress, the leading sex symbol of her time, and a good light comedian. Her death, either suicide or accident, was caused by an overdose of barbiturates.

d. Isak Dinesen (Karen Christence Dinesen Blixen, 1885–1962), Danish short story writer and novelist, long resident in Kenya; a major literary figure from publication of her *Seven Gothic Tales* (1934).

d. Sylvia Beach (1887–1962), American bookseller and publisher in Paris during the interwar period, proprietor of Shakespeare and Company and first publisher of James Joyce's *Ulysses*.

d. Vita (Victoria) Sackville-West (1892–1962), British novelist, poet, essayist, and biographer, long associated with Virginia Woolf and married to diplomat and writer Harold Nicolson.

d. Kirsten Malfrid Flagstad (1895–1962), Norwegian singer, the leading Wagnerian soprano of her time.

d. Natalia Sergeyevna Goncharova (1881–1962), a modernist painter in pre-revolutionary Russia. During and after World War I, she designed several classic sets for Sergei Diaghilev's Paris-based Ballets Russes company, including those for *Le coq d'or*, *Les Noces*, and *The Firebird*.

# 1963

## POLITICS/LAW/WAR

President's Commission on the Status of Women issued the report *American Women*, a central document in the reemergence of the modern women's movement, recommending equality in employment opportunities, wages, and educational opportunities, and a series of special provisions to make these possible for working mothers, including government-assisted daycare centers and government-mandated maternity leave.

The Equal Pay Act was passed by the U.S. Congress, the first federal law against sexual discrimination.

Women won the right to vote and be elected to office in Equatorial Guinea, Iran, Kenya, and Morocco.

Margaret Postgate Cole became president of the Fabian Society.

Federal judge Sarah Tilghman Hughes swore in Lyndon Baines Johnson as U.S. president (November 22), after the assassination of John F. Kennedy.

Joan Baez founded the Institute for the Study of Non-Violence, at Carmel, California.

Ruth First published *South West Africa*; she was also imprisoned for several months by the South African government.

Jennie Lee published *The Great Journey*.

d. Mabel Walker Willebrandt (1889–1963), American lawyer, the second American woman to be a federal prosecutor, who argued over 40 cases before the U.S. Supreme Court; she was dubbed "First Lady in Law" or "Prohibition Portia" for her zealous enforcement of Prohibition.

### RELIGION/EDUCATION/EVERYDAY LIFE

Betty Friedan published *The Feminine Mystique*, a call for modern women to reject roles as dependent and therefore subservient wives and mothers, moving instead to independent wage-earning and professional roles in the wider community. Her book generated enormous response, signaling the regeneration of the American and worldwide women's movements.

Gloria Steinem published the article "I Was a Playboy Bunny," exposing the sexism encountered by women working in the Playboy Club chain.

Barbara Walters joined NBC's *Today* show as an on-screen host (1963–1974), its first woman in the spot, having worked behind the scenes as a writer (1961–1963).

After her husband's death, Katharine Graham took over as president and publisher of the *Washington Post*; her father had bought the paper in 1933, she had worked there as a reporter from 1939, and she and her husband had bought it in 1946.

Dhanvanthi Rama Rau became president of the International Planned Parenthood Federation (1963–1971); she had long worked for the Family Planning Association of India (1949–1963).

Marie Patterson became woman's officer of the Transport and General Workers' Union (1963–1976) and also a member of the General Council of Britain's Trades Union Congress (1963–1984).

Hannah Arendt published *On Revolution*.

Simone de Beauvoir published *Force of Circumstance*.

Dorothy Day published *Loaves and Fishes*.

Julia Child began her influential television series *The French Chef* (1963–1973).

Sylvia Ashton-Warner published *Teacher*.

British philosopher Mary Warnock published *Sartre*.

Margaret Rudkin published her *Margaret Rudkin's Pepperidge Farm Cookbook*.

British social scientist Barbara Wootton published *Crime and the Criminal Law*.

b. Julie (Julieanne) Louise Krone (1963– ), American jockey.

d. Margaret Alice Murray (1863–1963), British scholar, a specialist in Egyptian hieroglyphics, long associated with University College, London, best known for her *The Witch-Cult in Western Europe* (1921); published in her final year were *The Genesis of Religion* and the autobiographical *My First Hundred Years*.

## The Problem That Has No Name

The problem that has no name—which is simply the fact that American women are kept from growing to their full human capacities—is taking a far greater toll on the physical and mental health of our country than any known disease.

— Betty Friedan, in *The Feminine Mystique* (1963)

d. Avra Theodoropoulou (1880–1963), Greek musician, writer, salon hostess, and women's rights advocate, who founded and led the League for Women's Rights (1920) and also founded schools and camps for girls and women.

d. Edith Hamilton (1865–1963), American historian and writer who popularized classical history; sister of physician Alice Hamilton.

### SCIENCE/TECHNOLOGY/MEDICINE

Maria Goeppert Mayer was awarded the Nobel Prize for physics, for her work on the theory of nuclear shell structure, an honor shared with Hans D. Jensen and Eugene P. Wigner; she was the second woman to win the prize in physics, 60 years after Marie Curie.

Soviet cosmonaut Valentina Tereshkova became the first woman in space (June 16), orbiting the Earth 48 times during a 71-hour flight in *Vostok 6*.

American geneticist Ruth Sager first showed that genes (DNA) were not wholly confined to the cell nucleus, but existed outside it as well.

After the death of her husband, fellow balloonist Jean Picard (1963), Jeannette Ridlon became an adviser to the National Aeronautics and Space Administration (NASA).

British zoologist Sidnie Manton was awarded the Linnaean Gold Medal.

d. Dorothy Hansine Andersen (1901–1963), American pathologist and pediatrician who first recognized the disease cystic fibrosis, also a noted expert on congenital heart defects.

d. (Mary) Agnes Meara Chase (1869–1963), American botanist best known as a botanical illustrator, long serving at the U.S. Department of Agriculture (1903–1939).

### ARTS/LITERATURE

Barbara Hepworth showed the sculpture *Square Stones with Circles*.

Carol Channing played Dolly Levi, the title role, in the Broadway musical *Hello, Dolly!*, based on Thornton Wilder's play *The Matchmaker*.

Patricia Neal starred opposite Paul Newman in *Hud*, winning a best actress Academy Award.

Catherine Deneuve starred in Jacques Demy's film *The Umbrellas of Cherbourg*.

Colleen Dewhurst starred opposite Michael Dunn in Edward Albee's play *Ballad of the Sad Café*.

Jean Simmons starred opposite Robert Preston in Alex Segal's film version of Tad Mosel's 1960 play *All the Way Home*, based on James Agee's novel *A Death in the Family* (1957).

Joan Littlefield produced the play *Oh! What a Lovely War*, a powerful antiwar satire set in World War I.

Helen Frankenthaler painted *Blue Atmosphere*.

Nadine Gordimer published the novel *Occasion for Loving*.

Janet Frame published the novel *Scented Gardens for the Blind*.

Gwendolyn Brooks published *Selected Poems*.

Mildred Dunnock starred in Tennessee Williams's play *The Milk Train Doesn't Stop Here Anymore*.

Natalia Ginzburg published the novel *Family Sayings*.

Joan Didion published the novel *Run River*.

Sylvia Ashton-Warner published the novel *Bell Call*.

Bryher published the historical novel *The Coin of Carthage*.

Nathalie Sarraute published the novel *The Golden Fruits*.

Elizabeth Ashley starred opposite Robert Redford in Neil Simon's play *Barefoot in the Park*.

Mary McCarthy published the novel *The Group*.

Shirley MacLaine starred opposite Jack Lemmon in Billy Wilder's film comedy *Irma La Douce*.

Vivian Blaine, Alan Arkin, and Sylvia Sidney starred in Joseph Stein's play *Enter Laughing*.

Anita Desai published the novel *Cry, the Peacock*.

Anne Bancroft starred in the title role of a New York production of Bertolt Brecht's *Mother Courage and Her Children*.

Vivien Leigh starred opposite Jean Pierre Aumont in Lee Pockriss and Anne Crosswell's play *Tovarich*.

Georgia O'Keeffe painted *The Winter Road.*

Jessica Mitford published *The American Way of Death.*

Margaret Bourke-White published *Portrait of Myself.*

Joy Batchelor and John Halas directed and produced the animated feature film *Is There Intelligent Life on Earth?*

b. Whitney Houston (1963– ), a leading American popular singer from the mid-1980s.

d. Edith Piaf (Giovanna Gassion, 1915–1963), French singer, whose signature song was her own "La Vie en Rose."

d. Sylvia Plath (1932–1963), American writer; among the final works before her suicide was the autobiographical novel *The Bell Jar.*

d. Dinah Washington (Ruth Lee Jones, 1924–1963), American gospel and blues singer, who sang with Lionel Hampton's band in the mid-1940s and became a soloist and recording artist.

d. Amelita Galli-Curci (1882–1963), Italian soprano, a leading opera singer of the 1920s.

d. Teresa Deevy (1894–1963), Irish playwright, popular in the 1930s.

## 1964

### Politics/Law/War

Employment discrimination because of sex, race, color, religion, or national origin (but not sexual orientation) was banned by Title VII of the Civil Rights Act of 1964, which also set up the Equal Employment Opportunity Commission (EEOC) as the law's enforcement mechanism. The EEOC would later enforce a considerable range of other antidiscrimination laws, including the 1978 Pregnancy Discrimination Act.

Indira Gandhi was elected to the Indian Parliament and became minister of information and broadcasting (1964–1966).

Marietta Tree became the first woman to serve as permanent U.S. ambassador to the United Nations.

Fannie Lou Hamer was one of the Mississippi Freedom Democratic Party leaders who, at the 1964 Democratic Party national convention, began the ultimately successful challenge of Southern Democratic Party racist convention practices.

Esther Peterson was appointed to chair the President's Committee on Consumer Interests (1964–1967); she was also special presidential assistant on consumer affairs, under Presidents Johnson and Carter, chairing the Consumer Affairs Council.

Barbara Castle became Britain's minister of overseas development (1964–1965).

Women won the right to be elected to office in Zambia.

Helga Pedersen became a Danish Supreme Court judge.

Jennie Lee became Britain's arts minister.

Shirley Williams became a Labour member of Parliament in Britain (1964–1979).

Yvette Roudy became secretary of the Mouvement Démocratique Féminin.

Fatima Jinnah made a failed presidential run against Pakistani president Ayub Khan.

d. Nancy Langhorne Astor (1879–1964), American-born British Conservative politician, the first woman to serve in the British Parliament (1919–1945), a leader of the fascist-oriented Cliveden Set.

d. Elizabeth Gurley Flynn (1890–1964), American anarchist and then communist, a founder of the American Civil Liberties Union (1920), imprisoned as a communist during the McCarthy period, and later chairman of the Communist Party of the United States (1961).

d. Halide Edib Adivar (1883–1964), Turkish feminist, writer, educator, and politician, a leading suffragist and women's education advocate before World War I.

d. Marie-Hélène Postel Vinay Lefaucheux (1904–1964), French feminist, women's rights activist, and Resistance leader, a president of the United Nations Commission on the Status of Women (1947) and the International Council of Women (1957).

d. Mary Anderson (1872–1964), American trade unionist and government official, the first director of the U.S. Women's Bureau (1920–1944).

d. Teresa Billington-Grieg (1877–1964), English teacher, feminist, and militant suffragist in the decade before World War I.

## RELIGION/EDUCATION/EVERYDAY LIFE

Hazel Brannon Smith, publisher of the *Lexington Advertiser* in Mississippi, won a Pulitzer Prize for editorial writing, for her campaign against local political corruption.

Czech gymnast Vera Caslavska won the individual gymnastics title at the Tokyo Olympics and also won gold medals on the beam and vault.

Iolanda Balas won an Olympic gold medal and set an Olympic record in the high jump, the first person to win two gold medals (1960; 1964) in that event.

Carol Doda began a vogue for topless entertainment, dancing with bare breasts at San Francisco's Condor Night Club. She and others were arrested for "lewd conduct" but acquitted (1965).

Marlene Sanders became the first woman to serve as anchor on a major television network's evening newscast, filling in for the regular anchor, Ron Cochran.

Lyudmila Belousova and Oleg Protopopov won the figure-skating pairs' gold medal at the Innsbruck Olympics.

Native American educator Polingaysi Qoyawayma published her autobiography, *No Turning Back*, which describes her life as a Hopi teacher.

Jessie Bernard published her landmark study *Academic Women*.

Presbyterian Church in the U.S.A. rewrote its constitution to delete gender references in relation to qualifications for ordination.

Hunter College, which had been the world's largest women's college and the first to provide free education to all women, went coeducational.

British cultural historian Frances Yates published *Giordano Bruno and the Hermetic Tradition*.

Evelyne Sullerot published *La vie des femmes*.

Mary Renault published *The Lion in the Gateway*, a young reader's history of ancient Greece.

d. Mary (Evaline) Madeleva Wolff (1887–1964), American poet, scholar, and educator, president of St. Mary's College, Notre Dame, Indiana (1934–1961), and earlier Mount Mary-of-the-Wasatch College in Salt Lake City, Utah (1925–1933).

## SCIENCE/TECHNOLOGY/MEDICINE

For her use of X-ray crystallography to study large organic molecules, such as penicillin and vitamin $B_{12}$, Dorothy Crowfoot Hodgkin became the third woman to win the Nobel Prize for chemistry, after Marie Curie and Irène Joliot-Curie; she used her cash award to fund a scholarship and to support peace and famine-relief efforts.

American physiologist Judith Graham Pool developed a now-standard procedure for extracting the blood factor required to treat hemophilia.

Chien-Shiung Wu (Madame Wu) wrote a notable review article "The Universal Fermi Interaction and the Conserved Vector Current in Beta Decay."

French physicist Yvette Cauchois coauthored the first of a series of works for physicists and physical chemists on using radiation as a tool.

Sylvia Earle Mead was the only woman in a 60-person team on the International Indian Ocean Expedition, scuba diving to the ocean depths to study the interrelationships of plants and fish.

Jerrie Mock (Geraldine Fredritz) flew solo around the world, over 29 1/2 days, the first American woman to do so.

Virginia Satir published *Cojoint Family Therapy*, describing the fundamentals of the family therapy approach she had developed.

Indian doctor Sushila Nayar became president of the All-India Institute of Medical Sciences and the Tuberculosis Association of India (1964–1967).

Grace Goldsmith received the American Medical Association's Goldberger Award for Clinical Nutrition.

d. Rachel Louise Carson (1907–1964), American ecologist and science writer best known for her books *The Sea Around Us* (1951) and *The Silent Spring* (1962).

d. Dorothy Reed Mendenhall (1874–1964), American physician who discovered the cell that causes Hodgkin's disease (1901); later an expert in child malnutrition and infant care.

d. Alva Ellisor (1892–1964), American petroleum geologist whose work in micropaleontology, correlating data on microfossils, provided vital information for oil drilling operations.

## ARTS/LITERATURE

Anna Akhmatova published *Requiem*, her homage to the victims of Stalinism.

Glenda Jackson created the Charlotte Corday role in Peter Weiss's play *Marat/Sade*.

Julie Andrews starred in Robert Stevenson's worldwide hit musical film *Mary Poppins*, opposite Dick Van Dyke, winning a best actress Academy Award.

Audrey Hepburn as Eliza Doolittle starred opposite Rex Harrison as Henry Higgins in George Cukor's film version of *My Fair Lady*.

Barbara Hepworth showed her sculpture *Single Form*, for the United Nations Building in New York.

Shirley Ann Grau published the Pulitzer Prize–winning novel *The Keepers of the House*.

Barbra Streisand created the title role of Fanny Brice in Jule Styne's musical *Funny Girl*.

Sophia Loren starred opposite Marcello Mastroianni in Vittorio De Sica's three-part sex comedy *Yesterday, Today, and Tomorrow*.

Barbara Loden and Jason Robards Jr. starred in Arthur Miller's play *After the Fall*.

Brigid Brophy published the novel *The Snow Ball*.

Jeanne Moreau starred in Luis Buñuel's film *Diary of a Chambermaid*.

Deborah Kerr, Richard Burton, Ava Gardner, and Sue Lyon starred in John Huston's film version of Tennessee Williams's 1962 play *The Night of the Iguana*.

Irene Worth starred in Edward Albee's play *Tiny Alice*.

Diana Sands starred opposite Alan Alda in Bill Manhoff's play *The Owl and the Pussycat*.

Iris Murdoch published the novel *The Italian Girl*.

Louise Nevelson showed the sculpture *Black Cord, Silent Music I*.

Rita Moreno starred opposite Gabriel Dell in Lorraine Hansberry's play *The Sign in Sidney Brustein's Window*.

Monica Vitti starred in Michelangelo Antonioni's film *The Red Desert*.

Fleur Adcock published the poetry collection *The Eye of the Hurricane*.

Jessica Tandy starred opposite Hume Cronyn and George Voskovec in Friedrich Dürrenmatt's play *The Physicists*.

Georgia O'Keeffe painted *Above Clouds Again* and *Road Past the View II*.

Ada Louise Huxtable published *Classic New York*.

Mai Zetterling directed and cowrote the film *Loving Couples*.

Margaret Drabble published the novel *The Garrick Year*.

Joyce Carol Oates published the novel *With Shuddering Fall*.

Margaret Laurence published the novel *The Stone Angel*.

Priaulx Rainier composed her *Cello Concerto*.

Márta Mészarós directed the film *The Girl*.

Dottie (Dorothy) March West became the first woman to win a country-music Grammy, for her "Here Comes My Baby."

Muriel Resnik's stage comedy *Any Wednesday* starred Sandy Dennis, Gene Hackman, and Rosemary Murphy.

Edith Piaf's autobiography *Ma Vie* was published posthumously.

d. (Mary) Flannery O'Connor (1925–1964), American novelist and short story writer, much of whose work is set in Georgia.

d. Gracie Allen (1905–1964), American comedian, long partnered with her husband, George Burns, as Burns and Allen.

d. Mary Carlisle Howe (1882–1964), American composer.

# 1965

## POLITICS/LAW/WAR

In *Griswold v. Connecticut,* the U.S. Supreme Court upheld the right of married couples to use contraceptives and further established the doctor-patient right of privacy, in this instance between doctor and married couple.

American Air Force officer Jeanne Holm became director of women in the Air Force (1965–1972) and played a major role in opening Air Force opportunities to women.

Detroit civil rights activist Viola Gregg Liuzzo was murdered by members of the Ku Klux Klan in Selma, Mississippi (March 25); three Klan members were later imprisoned for conspiracy to murder her.

Barbara Castle became Britain's minister of transport (1965–1968).

Dolores Huerta, with César Chávez, led the long United Farm Workers Organizing Committee strike against California table-grape growers (1965–1970), becoming a national officer of the United Farm Workers Union.

Bettina Aptheker was one of the leaders of the Berkeley Free Speech Movement.

Ruth First published the autobiographical *117 Days,* on her imprisonment by the South African government.

d. Frances (Fannie Coralie) Perkins (1882–1965), American teacher, social worker, and economist, who became Franklin D. Roosevelt's secretary of labor and the first female cabinet member (1933–1945).

d. Angelika Balabanoff (1878–1965), European socialist and writer, active in Russia and Italy, who was briefly a Soviet government leader after the Bolshevik Revolution.

## RELIGION/EDUCATION/EVERYDAY LIFE

Helen Gurley Brown published *Sex and the Office,* also becoming editor in chief of *Cosmopolitan* magazine.

Rachel Henderlite became the first woman ordained as a Presbyterian minister in America.

Cecilia Danieli began working in her family's steel company, Danieli of Buttrio, eventually taking over complete control and supplying major clients such as Japan's Mitsubishi and Germany's Krupp.

Jael Mbogo (Mama Jael) became active in Maendelo wa Wanawake, a key Kenyan women's social and cultural organization, in the late 1960s becoming secretary-general of Freedom from Hunger, a branch of the United Nations Food and Agricultural Organization (FAO).

Mary Quant held her first fashion show in America.

Evelyne Sullerot published *Demain les femmes.*

d. Helena Rubinstein (ca. 1870–1965), Polish-American cosmetics entrepreneur who built her business in America (from ca. 1915), developing the first waterproof mascara and medicated skin creams; her autobiographical *My Life for Beauty* was published the year of her death.

d. Edith Pye (1876–1965), British Quaker nurse and pacifist noted for her international relief work.

d. La Belle Otero (Caroline Puentovalga, 1868–1965), Spanish courtesan, whose lovers included kings, kaisers, and prime ministers, from whom she gathered a large fortune, later dissipated in gambling.

## SCIENCE/TECHNOLOGY/MEDICINE

American research chemist Stephanie L. Kwolek invented a stronger-than-steel, polymer-based synthetic fiber called Kevlar, used in everything from spacecraft to radial tires to bulletproof vests.

Vera Cooper Rubin began her long association with the Carnegie Institution of Terrestrial Magnetism (1965– ), exploring the existence of dark matter and galactic rotation with colleague W. Kent Ford.

Sheila Scott flew solo around the world, covering 31,000 miles in 189 flying hours, the longest-ever consecutive flight.

Helen Brooke Taussig was the first woman elected president of the American Heart Association.

Dorothy Crowfoot Hodgkin was awarded Britain's Order of Merit, the first woman so honored since Florence Nightingale.

Katherine Esau published *Vascular Differentiation in Plants.*

Margaret Mead was made curator emeritus of ethnology at the American Museum of Natural History.

Adele Davis published her nutrition book *Let's Get Well.*

Grace Goldsmith became president of the American Institute of Nutrition.

d. Ethel Nicholson Browne Harvey (1885–1965), American biologist specializing in embryology; the first person to induce differentiation from specific tissue (1909).

d. Myra Breckenridge (1881–1965), American nurse-midwife.

## ARTS/LITERATURE

Julie Christie starred opposite Dirk Bogarde and Laurence Harvey in John Schlesinger's film *Darling,* winning a best actress Academy Award. She also starred as Lara opposite Omar Sharif as Zhivago in David Lean's epic film *Doctor Zhivago,* set in the Russian Revolution and Civil War.

Julie Andrews and Christopher Plummer starred as Maria and George von Trapp in *The Sound of Music,* George Wise's film version of Richard Rodgers and Oscar Hammerstein's musical.

Giulietta Masina created the title role in Federico Fellini's film classic *Juliet of the Spirits.*

Katherine Anne Porter published her Pulitzer Prize– and National Book Award–winning *Collected Stories.*

Vivien Leigh, Simone Signoret, Oskar Werner, Jose Ferrer, and Lee Marvin starred in Stanley Kramer's film version of Katherine Anne Porter's 1962 novel *Ship of Fools.*

Barbara Harris and John Cullum starred in Burton Lane and Alan Jay Lerner's musical *On a Clear Day You Can See Forever.*

Georgia O'Keeffe painted *Sky Above Clouds III, Sky Above Clouds IV,* and *The Winter Road.*

Ida Kaminska starred opposite Josef Kroner in *The Shop on Main Street,* a film about Czech acquiescence to German anti-Semitism during World War II.

Barbra Streisand issued the album *My Name is Barbra.*

Jane Fonda starred opposite Lee Marvin in Elliot Silverstein's Western film comedy *Cat Ballou.*

Bea Richards starred in James Baldwin's play *The Amen Corner.*

Diana Rigg starred as a very self-reliant Emma Peel opposite Patrick Magee in the television series *The Avengers* (1965–1967).

Janet Frame published the novel *The Adaptable Man.*

Muriel Spark published the novel *The Mandelbaum Gate.*

Lauren Bacall and Barry Nelson starred in *Cactus Flower,* Abe Burrows's version of Pierre Barillet and Jean Pierre Gredy's French play.

Ruth Prawer Jhabvala wrote the screenplay for *Shakespeare Wallah,* about a British Shakespearean troupe in modern India; James Ivory directed a cast led by Felicity Kendal, Shashi Kapoor, and Geoffrey Kendal.

Maria Callas created the title role in Peggy Glanville-Hicks's opera *Sappho.*

Nadine Gordimer published the short-story collection *Not For Publication.*

Sylvia Plath's poetry collection *Ariel* was published posthumously.

Olivia Manning published *Friends and Heroes,* the third novel in her Balkan trilogy.

Ruth White stared in Samuel Beckett's play *Happy Days.*

Flannery O'Connor published the short-story collection *Everything that Rises Must Converge.*

Marguerite Duras published the novel *The Vice Consul*.

Pauline Kael published her film criticism in *I Lost It at the Movies*.

Margaret Drabble published the novel *The Millstone*.

Anne Bancroft and Jason Robards starred in John Whiting's play *The Devils*.

Faye Dunaway, Ralph Waite, and Tom Ahearne starred in William Alfred's blank-verse play *Hogan's Goat*.

Laura Knight published *The Magic of a Line*.

Anita Desai published the novel *Voices in the City*.

Maxine Kumin published the novel *Through Dooms of Love*.

Taylor Caldwell published the novel *A Pillar of Iron*.

Muriel Rukeyser published the novel *The Orgy*.

Oriana Fallaci published *The Egotists*.

Thea Musgrave composed the opera *The Decision*.

Malvina Hoffman published the autobiography *Yesterday Is Tomorrow: A Personal History*.

d. Jeannette MacDonald (1901–1965), American musical film star, very popular in the 1930s and early 1940s for her long series of starring roles opposite Nelson Eddy.

d. Clara Bow (1905–1965), American actress, a silent film star known as the "It girl."

d. Dorothy Dandridge (1923–1965), American actress, singer, and dancer, who emerged as a breakthrough African-American film star in such films as *Carmen Jones* (1954) and *Porgy and Bess* (1959).

d. Constance Bennett (1904–1965), American film star of the 1930s and 1940s; the sister of actress Joan Bennett and daughter of actor Richard Bennett.

d. Dorothea Lange (1895–1965), American photographer.

d. Lorraine Hansberry (1930–1965), American writer, the first major African-American female playwright, best known for her *A Raisin in the Sun* (1959).

d. Myra Hess (1890–1965), British pianist.

d. Shirley Jackson (1916–1965), American writer.

## 1966

### POLITICS/LAW/WAR

Betty Friedan took the lead in founding and was first president of the National Organization for Women (NOW), one of the leading modern American women's rights organizations, functioning on the whole range of women's issues.

Jiang Qing became a major figure in China's Cultural Revolution, taking and using the authority of her husband, Mao Zedong, becoming (after him) the second most powerful figure in China. Many young women were active in this movement, and many were also among those attacked (1966–1976), including the Women's Federation and its magazine, *Women of China*, both closed down.

Indira Gandhi became prime minister of India.

Alva Reimer Myrdal became Swedish minister for disarmament and church affairs (1966–1973).

Annabelle Rankin became Australia's minister of housing (1966–1971).

Barbara Jordan became the first African-American Texas state legislator (1966–1972) since Reconstruction.

Committee for Equality of Women in Canada (CEW) was founded, leading to a Royal Commission on the Status of Women.

Constance Baker Motley was named U.S. district judge for southern New York, becoming the first African-American woman to serve as federal judge.

Judith Hart became Britain's minister of state for commonwealth affairs, subsequently holding several other cabinet-level posts, including that of minister of overseas development.

Jane Cahill Pfeiffer became the first female White House fellow.

Bettina Aptheker published *Big Business and the American University.*

Juliet Mitchell published *Women: The Longest Revolution*, linking Marxism to women's freedom movement questions.

d. Elena Dmitrievna Stasova (1873–1966), Russian Bolshevik leader, a key member of the Communist organizing group for the Bolshevik Revolution, who occupied a series of Soviet and Comintern posts into the late 1940s.

d. Elizabeth Eloise (Kirkpatrick) Dilling (1894–1966), American politician and writer, an ultra-conservative opponent of the New Deal, an isolationist, segregationist, and anti-Semite, long-time publisher of the *Elizabeth Dilling Bulletin* and author of several widely circulated books.

d. Marie-Elizabeth Luders (1888–1966), German political economist, feminist, and politician, a Reichstag member during the Weimar period, forced into exile by the Nazis, who resumed her political career after the war (1947).

## RELIGION/EDUCATION/EVERYDAY LIFE

Historian Barbara Welter published her notable article "The Cult of True Womanhood," exploring the prescribed role of Victorian American women through the popular literature and artifacts of the time, seeing in the reverence for purity, piety, domesticity, and submission a form of social control used to keep women firmly in "woman's place."

Barbara Tuchman published *The Proud Tower.*

Marie Patterson served on the executive board of the Confederation of Shipbuilding and Engineering Unions (1966–1984), as president (1977–1978).

Barbara Ward published *Spaceship Earth.*

Mary Wells (later Lawrence) established her own advertising company, Wells, Rich, Greene Inc., becoming chairman and chief executive.

British cultural historian Frances Yates published *The Art of Memory.*

French ethnologist Germaine Tillion published *Le harem et les cousins.*

British designer Mary Quant published *Quant by Quant.*

Juanita Morris Kreps edited *Technology, Manpower and Retirement Policy.*

d. Elizabeth Arden (Florence Nightingale Graham, 1884?–1966), Canadian beautician and cosmetics entrepreneur, who developed a chain of over 100 beauty salons, with a full line of cosmetics.

## SCIENCE/TECHNOLOGY/MEDICINE

Lise Meitner was awarded the Atomic Energy Commission's Enrico Fermi Award, the first woman so honored. She shared it with her former colleagues Otto Hahn and Fritz Strassman, who had received the 1944 Nobel Prize for their work, though she had not.

After the Arno River flooded Florence, the antifungal agent nystatin, developed by Rachel Fuller Brown and Elizabeth Hazen, was used to stop the growth of fungus that might otherwise have destroyed precious artworks affected by the floodwaters.

Gabrielle-Émilie Le Tonnelier de Breteuil, marquise du Châtelet's annotated translation of Newton's *Principia* was reprinted in facsimile, 210 years after its original publication.

William H. Masters and Virginia Johnson published *Human Sexual Response*, dissipating many myths associated with sexual life, especially as regarded women's allegedly subservient, pleasureless, passive roles.

Sophia Josephine Kleegman and Sherwin Kaufman published the landmark *Infertility*, studying both male and female fertility problems, most infertility previously being ascribed to the woman.

American aviator Marion Rice Hart made her first solo flight across the Atlantic, at age 74; she would make six more, the last at 83.

At age 60, a year after her retirement, Grace Hopper was recalled to the U.S. Navy to standardize its overall computer operations.

Sylvia Earle Mead was consultant during the building of Florida's Cape Haze Marine Laboratory, of which she became director; later enlarged, it became the Mote Marine Laboratory in Sarasota.

Elizabeth Dexter Hay published *Regeneration*.

Grace Goldsmith became president of the American Board of Nutrition.

d. Margaret Louise Higgins Sanger (1879–1966), American public-health nurse and birth control campaigner who, in the course of winning the long battle for legal contraception, became one of the leading women of the 20th century.

d. Margaret Pyke (1893–1966), British birth control campaigner, long active with the National Birth Control Association (Family Planning Association), secretary from 1938 and chair from 1954.

d. Anna Johnson Pell Wheeler (1883–1966), American mathematician long associated with Bryn Mawr College (1918–1948); the college's mathematics department chairman from 1925, she offered asylum to Emmy Noether in 1933.

d. Jewell Jeannette Glass (1888–1966), American mineralogist who focused on pegmatite minerals and rare earths of economic importance.

d. Mary Lee Jobe Akeley (1878–1966), American explorer and photographer who explored and mapped much of the Canadian Northwest, beginning in 1913, her work winning her a place as a fellow of London's Royal Geographical Society. She and her husband, explorer Carl Akeley, explored and mapped in the then Belgian Congo (1924–1926); she carried on after his death in 1926, and returned to Africa on several further expeditions, through the 1940s, becoming a key figure in the African wildlife conservation movement. Canada named Mt. Jobe after her.

## ARTS/LITERATURE

Elizabeth Taylor starred opposite Richard Burton, winning a best actress Academy Award in *Who's Afraid of Virginia Woolf?*, Mike Nichols's film version of Edward Albee's 1962 play.

Leontyne Price created the role of Cleopatra in Samuel Barber's opera *Antony and Cleopatra*, opening the new Metropolitan Opera House at New York's Lincoln Center.

Anouk Aimee starred opposite Jean-Louis Trintignant in Claude Lelouch's *A Man and a Woman*.

Nelly Sachs and Shmuel Yoseph Agnon shared the 1966 Nobel Prize for literature.

Anne Sexton published her Pulitzer Prize–winning poetry collection *Live or Die*.

Beryl Reid and Eileen Atkins starred in Frank Marcus's play *The Killing of Sister George*.

Susan Sontag published the essay *Against Interpretation*.

Angela Lansbury starred in the title role of *Mame*, the musical version of the play *Auntie Mame*.

Twyla Tharp choreographed the dance work *Re-Moves*.

Vanessa Redgrave played the title role in *The Prime of Miss Jean Brodie*, Jay Presson Allen's stage adaptation of Muriel Spark's novel.

Gwen Verdon starred in the title role in *Sweet Charity*, Cy Coleman, Dorothy Field, and Neil Simon's musical adaptation of Federico Fellini's film *The Nights of Cabiria*.

Jill Haworth created the Sally Bowles role opposite Bert Convy, Joel Grey, and Lotte Lenya in *Cabaret*, Fred Ebb and John Kander's musical, based on John van Druten's play, *I Am a Camera*, and Christopher Isherwood's *Goodbye to Berlin*.

Liv Ullmann and Bibi Andersson starred in Ingmar Bergman's film *Persona*.

Helen Frankenthaler painted *Mauve District*.

Anaïs Nin's *Diary* began publication (1966–1976).

Jessica Tandy starred opposite Hume Cronyn in Edward Albee's play *A Delicate Balance*.

Bryher published the historical novel *The January Tale*.

Lynn Redgrave starred in Silvio Narizzano's film *Georgy Girl*, opposite James Mason, Charlotte Rampling, and Alan Bates.

Mary Martin starred opposite Robert Preston in *I Do! I Do!*, Harvey Schmidt and Tom Jones's Broadway musical.

Julie Christie starred opposite Oskar Werner in François Truffaut's science fiction film *Fahrenheit 451*.

Kamala Markandaya published the novel *A Handful of Rice*.

Louise Nevelson showed *Atmosphere and Environment I*, a "wall" sculpture in aluminum.

Stevie Smith published *The Frog Prince and Other Poems*.

Joanne Woodward, Sean Connery, Colleen Dewhurst, and Jean Seberg starred in Irvin Kershner's film *A Fine Madness*.

Mary Renault published the novel *The Mask of Apollo*.

Nadine Gordimer published the novel *The Late Bourgeois World*.

Rosemary Harris starred as Eleanor of Aquitaine opposite Robert Preston as Henry II in James Goldman's play *The Lion in Winter*.

Margaret Atwood published the poetry collection *The Circle Game*.

Alice Adams published the novel *Careless Love*.

Sawako Arivoshi published the novel *The Doctor's Wife*.

Anita Loos published the autobiography *A Girl Like I*.

Christa Wolf published *The Quest for Christa T.*

Françoise Sagan wrote the play *L'Echardez*.

Chryssa showed her neon work *Ampersand*.

Judith Wright published the short-story collection *The Nature of Love*.

Cynthia Ozick published her first novel, *Trust*.

Grace Ogot published the Tanzania-set novel *The Promised Land*.

Jean Rhys published the novel *The Wide Sargasso Sea*.

Margaret Laurence published the novel *A Jest of God*.

Rebecca West published the novel *The Birds Fall Down*.

Mai Zetterling directed and cowrote the film *Night Games*, based on her own novel.

Sylvia Ashton-Warner published the novel *Greenstone*.

Helen Gurley Brown published *Outrageous Opinions*.

d. Helen Becker Tamiris (1905–1966), American dancer and choreographer who focused on social-protest themes until the mid-1940s, then becoming the choreographer of several Broadway musicals, including *Annie Get Your Gun*.

d. Anna Akhmatova (Anna Andreyevna Gorenko, 1889–1966), Soviet poet.

d. Mari Sandoz (1896–1966), American author.

d. Lillian Smith (1897–1966), American novelist.

d. Malvina Cornell Hoffman (1887–1966), American sculptor.

d. Sophie Tucker (Sonia Kalish, 1884–1966), American singer and actress.

d. Jelly d'Arányi (1895–1966), Hungarian violinist, long resident in Britain.

d. Marguerite (Marie Charlotte) Long (1874–1966), French pianist.

## 1967

### POLITICS/LAW/WAR

Equal Rights Amendment (ERA) was endorsed by the National Organizaton for Women (NOW), which then spearheaded an ultimately unsuccessful campaign for its passage and ratification.

Jennie Lee became chairperson of Britain's Labour Party (1967–1968).

California led the way in liberalizing American abortion laws, passing a bill based on a model statute developed by the American Law Institute (1959); 16 states soon followed, while other state laws began to be declared unconstitutional or liberalized by judicial interpretation.

Britain's National Health Service (Family Planning) Act provided access to contraception and birth control counseling.

Contraception was legalized in France.

In Japan, the League of Single Women (Dokushin Fujin Renmei) was founded, to counter the strong political, economic, and social discrimination directed at single women.

Shulamith Firestone and Pam Allen founded the New York City–based organization Radical Women (1967–1968), which published *Notes from the First Year* before splintering.

Returning to Greece from London, physician Amalia Coutsouris Fleming actively worked against the military leaders who took over in a 1967 coup, finally being forcibly deported by them to Britain in 1971 and stripped of her citizenship. She had during World War II been active in resistance to the Nazis, saved from a sentence of death by Allied troops.

Winifred Ewing became a member of Britain's Parliament.

Edith Summerskill published the autobiographical *A Woman's World*.

d. Fatima Jinnah (1893–1967), Pakistani politician, sister of Pakistan founder Ali Jinnah, who worked with him in the all-Indian independence movement and then in the separatist movement that led to Indian partition and the establishment of India and Pakistan.

### RELIGION/EDUCATION/EVERYDAY LIFE

Daughters of the American Revolution (DAR) barred Joan Baez from singing in Constitution Hall because of her opposition to the Vietnam War, which included a refusal to pay a portion of her federal income taxes. Baez sang outdoors instead, near the Washington Monument, as Marian Anderson had earlier done at the Lincoln Memorial (1939).

Barbara Ward was appointed to the Vatican Commission for Justice and Peace.

Hélène Ahrweiler became the first woman to head the Sorbonne's department of history.

Muriel Siebert became the first woman to own a seat on the New York Stock Exchange.

Opposed to the military junta that had taken control of Greece and was attempting to impose censorship, Helene Vlachou closed her daily newspaper *Kathimerini* and, escaping from house arrest, went abroad to fight from exile.

Laura Ashley and her husband, Bernard Ashley, opened their first shop in Kensington, London, selling clothes that she designed, many of them drawing on 18th- and 19th-century fabric designs; her styles became internationally popular, and at her death the couple had 225 shops and 11 factories in Europe and America.

Tina Schifano Ramos Hills received Columbia University's Maria Moors Cabot Award for her contributions to inter-American relations.

British social scientist Barbara Wootton published *In a World I Never Made*.

Margery Hurst wrote her autobiographical *No Glass Slipper*.

Susanne Langer published the two-volume *Mind: An Essay on Human Feeling* (1967–1972).

Rosemary Ruether published *The Church Against Itself*.

d. Gordon Hamilton (1892–1967), American social worker and educator, long associated with the New York School of Social Work at Columbia University (1923–1957).

d. Katharine Dexter McCormick (1875–1967), American philanthropist who supplied vital funds for the women's suffrage, birth control, and women's higher education movements.

d. Margaret (Fogarty) Rudkin (1897–1967), American entrepreneur who founded the Pepperidge Farm baking company (1938).

d. Kitamura Sayo (1900–1967), Japanese religious leader, noted for wearing men's attire, who founded the Tensho Kotai Jingu Kyo religious movement.

### SCIENCE/TECHNOLOGY/MEDICINE

British astronomer Jocelyn Bell, then a graduate student at Cambridge University, discovered pulsating astronomical objects dubbed pulsars; her professor, Antony Hewish, received the 1974 Nobel Prize for physics for the discovery; Bell did not.

Dian Fossey began working at the Karisoke Research Centre in Rwanda, studying mountain gorillas.

Britain's National Health Service began providing free information on and access to birth control methods.

Grace Goldsmith helped found and became first dean of the Tulane School of Public Health and Tropical Medicine, the first woman to head an American public-health school.

Jane C. Wright became the first African-American woman in medical administration, as associate dean and professor of surgery at New York Medical College, her alma mater.

British aviator Sheila Scott published *I Must Fly*.

German-Scottish geneticist Charlotte Auerbach was awarded a personal chair at the University of Edinburgh.

## ARTS/LITERATURE

Faye Dunaway starred as Depression-era outlaw Bonnie Parker opposite Warren Beatty as Clyde Barrow in Arthur Penn's film *Bonnie and Clyde*.

Katharine Hepburn, Spencer Tracy, Sidney Poitier, and Katharine Houghton starred in Stanley Kramer's film *Guess Who's Coming to Dinner*. Hepburn won a best actress Academy Award.

Barbara Cook starred opposite Elliott Gould in Jules Feiffer's play *Little Murders*.

Catherine Deneuve starred in Luis Bunuel's film *Belle de Jour*.

Joyce Carol Oates published the novel *A Garden of Earthly Delights*.

Fleur Adcock published the poetry collection *Tigers*.

Ingrid Bergman, Colleen Dewhurst, and Arthur Hill starred in Eugene O'Neill's posthumously produced play *More Stately Mansions*.

Janet Frame published the novel *A State of Siege*.

Judith Jamison became the leading dancer of the Alvin Ailey Dance Theater (1967–1980), emerging in that period as one of the world's first-rank dancers, with emphasis on her interpretation of African-American themes.

Geraldine Page, Michael Crawford, and Lynn Redgrave starred in Peter Shaffer's play *Black Comedy*.

Helen Frankenthaler painted *Guiding Red*.

Pearl Bailey starred as Dolly Levi, leading an African-American cast in a production of *Hello, Dolly!*

Carol Burnett emerged as a major television star in her long-running *The Carol Burnett Show* (1967–1979).

Brigit Cullberg founded the Cullberg Ballet, at the Swedish National Theater.

Chryssa showed *Clytemnestra*, a neon work.

Sally Field starred in the television series *The Flying Nun* (1967–1970).

Nelly Kaplan's documentary, *Le regard Picasso*, won a Golden Lion award at the Venice Film Festival.

Sylvia Ashton-Warner published the autobiography *Myself*.

d. Vivien Leigh (Vivian Mary Hartley, 1913–1967), British actress, an international stage and screen star, best known worldwide as Scarlett O'Hara in *Gone With the Wind* and Blanche DuBois in *A Streetcar Named Desire*.

d. Carson Smith McCullers (1917–1967), American novelist and playwright, often on Southern themes; a major literary figure from publication of her first novel, *The Heart Is a Lonely Hunter* (1940).

d. Dorothy Rothschild Parker (1893–1967), American writer, a poet, short story writer, playwright, screenwriter, and journalist.

d. Mary Garden (1874–1967), American soprano, one of the leading opera singers of her time, long at the Chicago Opera (1910–1930).

d. Esther Forbes (1891–1967), American novelist and historian best known for her *Johnny Tremain* (1943).

d. Jane Darwell (Patti Woodward, 1879–1967), American film actress, most notably Ma Joad in *The Grapes of Wrath*.

d. Geraldine Farrar (1882–1967), American soprano, long a leading singer at the Metropolitian Opera (1906–1922).

d. Furugh Farrukhazad (1935–1967), Iranian writer.

d. Ida Cox (1889–1967), African-American blues singer.

d. Joan Rosita Forbes (1893–1967), British travel writer.

d. Margaret Ayer Barnes (1886–1967), American novelist and playwright.

# 1968

## POLITICS/LAW/WAR

Coretta Scott King began the development of Atlanta's Martin Luther King Memorial Center, which became a monument to her murdered husband and also her personal headquarters, as she developed a leading role in civil rights, antiwar, and social-reform movements.

German journalist Ulrike Meinhof helped anarchist-terrorist Andreas Baader to escape from prison; their Baader-Meinhof Group (Red Army Faction) then engaged in murders, bombings, and robberies (1968–1972).

Barbara Castle became Britain's secretary of state for employment and productivity (1968–1970).

Pacifist Jeannette Pickering Rankin led a Washington anti–Vietnam War demonstration, called by its organizers the Jeannette Rankin Brigade.

Frances Witherspoon organized an anti–Vietnam War protest among Bryn Mawr alumnae, with more than 1,000 signing a statement carried in the *New York Times* and *Philadelphia Evening Bulletin*.

The Feminists, a small, utopian, leaderless, anarchist-socialist radical feminist group, was founded and called for the development of a nonpatriarchal, classless society, a merging of radical feminism and anarchism. TiGrace Atkinson was one of the founders of the group.

Eugenia Charles founded the Dominican Freedom Party.

Gaositwe Keagakwa Tibe Chiepe became Botswana's director of education (1968–1969).

Mary Robinson became the youngest law professor ever appointed at Ireland's Trinity College.

Winifred Ewing became a vice-president of the Scottish Nationalist Party.

Margaret Ballinger published *From Union to Apartheid: A Trek to Isolation*.

Margaret Chase Smith published *Gallant Women*, a group of biographies of leading American women.

## RELIGION/EDUCATION/EVERYDAY LIFE

Mary Daly published *The Church and the Second Sex*, attacking many Catholic practices from a feminist point of view.

Czech gymnast Vera Caslavska won four gold and two silver medals at the Mexico Olympics, one gold being for her "Mexican-hat dance" floor routine; her wins were especially notable because she had to train in hiding, as Soviet troops were suppressing the Czech independence movement.

Marian Wright Edelman founded the Washington Research Project.

National Women's Hall of Fame was founded at Seneca Falls, New York, on the site of the landmark 1848 women's rights convention.

Outside the Miss America Pageant, women's liberation protesters threw into garbage cans items of clothing they regarded as sexist and exploitative; a photograph of a burning bra, which gave such protesters the nickname of "bra-burners," apparently was staged by a newspaper photographer.

Women's International Terrorist Conspiracy from Hell (WITCH) was founded, a radical feminist group focusing on theatrical, media-attention-getting demonstrations, beginning with its Halloween New York Stock Exchange protest, in which the demonstrators dressed as witches.

Federally Employed Women (FEW) was founded, as an advocacy group for women in federal employment.

Kathy Kusner was the first American woman granted a jockey's license for racing Thoroughbred horses at major racetracks.

Lyudmila Belousova and Oleg Protopopov won the figure-skating pairs' gold medal in the Grenoble Olympics.

Sonja Henje and her husband, Niels Onstad, established the Sonja Henje–Niels Onstad Art Centre in Oslo, to which they donated their collection of Impressionist and post-Impressionist art.

Venita Walker Van Caspel became the first female member of the Pacific Stock Exchange.

Evelyne Sullerot published *Histoire et sociologie du travail fémininin*.

Jessie Bernard published *The Sex Game*.

d. Helen Adams Keller (1880–1968), American campaigner for the blind, herself blind and deaf from 19 months, who learned to communicate with a manual alphabet (1887) and eventually attended Radcliffe College; later a well-known writer and speaker.

d. Alexandra David-Neel (1869–1968), French explorer who traveled widely in Central Asia (from 1893), most notably in Tibet.

### SCIENCE/TECHNOLOGY/MEDICINE

British X-ray crystallographer Dorothy Crowfoot Hodgkin became a Fellow of the Australian Academy of Science, the first woman so honored.

Nuclear physicist Rosalyn Yalow became chairman of the department of medicine at New York's Mount Sinai School of Medicine.

Helena Wright published *Sex and Society*.

Katherine Esau published *Plants, Viruses and Insects*.

d. Lise Meitner (1878–1968), Austrian-born physicist who first described and named nuclear fission (1939); also the codiscoverer of thorium C (1908) and protactinium (1917). She worked in Germany until the rise of the Nazis forced her to leave (1938), then in Sweden.

### ARTS/LITERATURE

Katharine Hepburn as Eleanor of Aquitaine starred opposite Peter O'Toole as Henry II in the film version of the 1966 James Goldman play *The Lion in Winter*.

Barbra Streisand played Fanny Brice opposite Omar Sharif in *Funny Girl*, William Wyler's musical film version of Isobel Lennart's 1964 play.

Katharine Hepburn and Barbra Streisand tied for the best actress Academy Award (1969).

Jane Alexander created the role of Ellie, a white woman in love with a black man in a bigoted time, opposite James Earl Jones as boxer Jack Jefferson in Howard Sackler's play *The Great White Hope*.

Janis Joplin issued the album *Cheap Thrills*.

Lillian Gish, Hal Holbrook, and Teresa Wright starred in Robert Anderson's play *I Never Sang for My Father*.

Joanne Woodward starred in *Rachel, Rachel*, the first film directed by Paul Newman, her husband.

Audre Lorde published the poetry collection *The First Cities*.

Iris Murdoch published the novel *A Time of the Angels*.

Janet Frame published the novel *Yellow Flowers in the Antipodean Room*.

Alice Walker published the poetry collection *Once*.

Joyce Carol Oates published the novel *Expensive People*.

Louise Bogan published the poetry collection *The Blue Estuaries*.

Maureen Stapleton starred opposite George C. Scott in *Plaza Suite*, a group of three one-act plays by Neil Simon.

Louise Nevelson created *Transparent Sculpture II*, another "wall" sculpture in aluminum (1967–1968).

Mia Farrow starred opposite John Cassavetes in Roman Polanski's horror film *Rosemary's Baby*, based on the Ira Levin novel.

Diana Sands starred opposite Jason Robards in Joseph Heller's play *We Bombed in New Haven*.

Nikki Giovanni published the poetry collections *Black Feeling, Black Talk*, and *Black Judgment*.

Jane Fonda starred in *Barbarella*, a film directed by Roger Vadim, then her husband.

Nelly Kaplan wrote and directed the film *La fiancée du pirate*.

Grace Ogot published the short-story collection *Land Without Thunder*.

Julie Harris played Ann Stanley in the play *Forty Carats*.

Grace Williams composed *Ballads for Orchestra*.

Indian actress Rekha starred in the film *Sawan Bhadon*.

Marisol showed the painting *Portrait of Sidney Janis Selling Portrait of Sidney Janis by Marisol*.

Maxine Kumin published the novel *The Passions of Uxport*.

Ruth Gipps composed her *Horn Concerto*.

d. Alice Guy-Blaché (1875–1968), French filmmaker, the world's first female filmmaker, and creator of probably the first story film (1896).

d. Edna Ferber (1887–1968), American popular novelist, many of whose works became the bases of films or plays, among them *So Big* (1924), *Show Boat* (1926), *Cimarron* (1930), and *Stage Door* (1936).

d. Ruth St. Denis (Ruth Dennis, 1878–1968), American dancer and choreographer, a founder of the modern dance, and with Ted Shawn a founder of the seminal Denishawn School and Dance Company (1915–1931).

d. Tallulah Bankhead (1903–1968), American actress, in leads on the London and New York stages in the 1920s and 1930s. Her film appearances included a starring role in *Lifeboat* (1944).

d. Carlotta Zambelli (1875–1968), Italian ballerina, a fixture at the Paris Opéra (1894–1950), as dancer and later teacher.

d. Dorothy Gish (1898–1968), American actress, the sister of Lillian Gish.

d. Fannie Hurst (1889–1968), American novelist and short story writer.

d. Florence Austral (1894–1968), Australian soprano.

d. Marguerite Thompson Zorach (1887–1968), American artist.

# 1969

## POLITICS/LAW/WAR

Golda Meir became Israel's prime minister (1969–1974).

Liberia's Angie Brooks-Randolph became the second woman to serve as president of the United Nations General Assembly (1969–1970).

Shirley Chisholm became the first African-American woman to be a member of the U.S. House of Representatives (1969–1983).

Catholic Ulster leader Bernadette Devlin (later McAliskey) was elected a member of the British Parliament (1969–1974), at age 21 the house's youngest member since William Pitt. She also published *The Price of My Soul*.

Shulamith Firestone and Ellen Willis founded the radical feminist Redstockings (1969–1970), a splinter of the Radical Women group; Firestone also founded the New York Radical Feminists (1969–1971).

Deng Yingchao became a member of the Central Committee of the Chinese Communist Party (1969–1985).

Jiang Qing became a member of the Politburo of China's Communist Party.

Mary Robinson won election as a Labour member of the Irish Senate (1969–1989).

Nguyen Thi Binh became North Vietnam's foreign minister.

Judith Hart served as chair of Britain's Labour Party (1981–1982).

Takako Doi won election to Japan's parliament, the Diet.

Australia passed a law embodying the principle of "equal pay for equal work," but it had little effect because of extreme sex segregation in occupations.

Action Council for the Liberation of Women (Aktionsrat zur Befreiung der Frau) was founded in Germany.

Indian doctor Sushila Nayar became a member of the Indian parliament (1957–1971).

Coretta Scott King published *My Life with Martin Luther King*.

Yvette Roudy published *La réussite de la femme*.

d. Lizzie (Elizabeth) Wallace Ahern (1877–1969), Australian feminist, socialist, and pacifist, a leading figure in the Australian Socialist Party and an activist in the Labour Party.

## RELIGION/EDUCATION/EVERYDAY LIFE

San Diego State University established America's first degree program in women's studies; within 15 years there would be nearly 450.

Women's International Terrorist Conspiracy from Hell (WITCH) staged its Bridal Fair protest, which was highly and very adversely publicized as a demonstration against brides, rather than against stereotypical sex roles as sold by the bridal industry, effectively destroying WITCH, which soon disbanded.

Irina Rodnina won the first of what would be ten successive world pairs' figure-skating titles, four partnered with Alexei Ulanov (1969–1972) and the rest with Aleksander Zaitsev (1973–1978), whom she married (1975).

Clara Hale started to take the children of drug addicts into her home, beginning the process that would eventuate in Harlem's Hale House.

Women journalists were first admitted into Sigma Delta Chi, a journalists' society; Charlayne Hunter (later Hunter-Gault), then a *New York Times* reporter, was the first African-American woman to become a member.

Lesbian, gay, and bisexual Catholics founded Dignity/USA, focusing on issues of common concern within the Catholic church.

Having made topless entertainment a household phrase, Carol Doda moved on to bottomless— totally nude—dancing, at San Francisco's Condor Night Club. California later that year banned topless dancing; the U.S. Supreme Court upheld revocation of liquor licenses for topless bars (1970).

Penny Ann Early played a single game with the Kentucky Colonels team of the American Basketball Association, the first woman to play professional basketball.

Sharon Sites Adams sailed solo across the Pacific, the first woman to do so.

Vassar College admitted its first male students.

b. Steffi Graf (Stephanie Maria Graf, 1969– ), German tennis champion, in the late 1980s and early 1990s the world's dominant women's tennis player, in one period the top-ranked woman in the world for a record 186 consecutive weeks.

d. Sonja Henje (Henie, 1910–1969), Norwegian-American ice-skater, three-time Olympic gold medalist (1928; 1932; 1936), who became a film actress.

d. Maureen Catherine ("Little Mo") Connolly (1934–1969), American tennis player who was the first woman ever to win a Grand Slam (1953); her career had been cut short by a riding accident (1954).

## SCIENCE/TECHNOLOGY/MEDICINE

Boston Women's Health Collective was organized, one of the earliest, and certainly the best known, women's health information centers.

Elisabeth Kubler-Ross published her landmark *On Death and Dying*, drawn from her work with terminally ill patients and their families.

Gladys Anderson Emerson served as vice-chairman of the White House Conference on Food, Nutrition, and Health (Panel on the Provision of Food as It Affects the Consumer).

Indian doctor Sushila Nayar became director of the Mahatma Gandhi Institute of Medical Sciences and professor of Preventive and Social Medicine.

Chien-Shiung Wu (Madame Wu) published her noted review article "Muonic Atoms and Nuclear Structure," written with Lawrence Wilets.

Joy Adamson published the book *The Spotted Sphinx*, describing Pippa, a cheetah she retrained to live in the wild.

Association for Women in Psychology was founded, splitting off from the American Psychological Association.

British psychoanalyst Marion Milner published *The Hands of the Living God*, her analyses of drawings by Susan, a schizophrenic patient.

d. Libbie H. Hyman (1888–1969), American biologist specializing in invertebrate zoology.

### ARTS/LITERATURE

Maggie Smith starred as the memorable Edinburgh schoolteacher, winning a best actress Academy Award, in the title role of *The Prime of Miss Jean Brodie*, Ronald Neame's film version of Muriel Spark's 1961 novel.

Adrienne Rich published the poetry collection *Necessities of Life and Other Poems*.

Blythe Danner, Keir Dullea, and Eileen Heckart starred in Leonard Gershe's play *Butterflies Are Free*.

Genevieve Bujold starred as Anne Boleyn opposite Richard Burton as Henry VIII in Charles Jarrott's film version of the 1948 Maxwell Anderson play *Anne of the Thousand Days*.

The changing sexual mores of the '60s were featured in Paul Mazursky's film *Bob and Carol and Ted and Alice*, starring Natalie Wood, Robert Culp, Dyan Cannon, and Elliot Gould.

Toni Morrison published the novel *The Bluest Eye*.

Brigid Brophy published the novel *In Transit*.

Jean Stafford published her Pulitzer Prize–winning *Collected Stories*.

Elizabeth Bishop published her National Book Award–winning *Complete Poems*.

Joan Didion published the essay collection *Slouching Toward Bethlehem*.

Babette Deutsch published her *Collected Poems*.

Joyce Carol Oates published the National Book Award–winning novel *them*.

Helen Frankenthaler painted *Commune* and *Stride*.

Anne Sexton published *Love Poems*.

Jane Fonda and Michael Sarrazin starred in Sidney Pollack's film *They Shoot Horses, Dont They?*, set at a Depression-era dance marathon.

Kamala Markandaya published the novel *Coffer Dams*.

Rumer Godden published the novel *In This House of Brede*.

Katharine Hepburn played her first musical role, starring in Alan Jay Lerner's stage musical *Coco*.

Alison Lurie published the novel *Real People*.

Margaret Atwood published the novel *The Edible Woman*.

Lillian Hellman published the autobiographical *An Unfinished Woman*.

Margaret Drabble published the novel *The Waterfall*.

Stevie Smith published the poetry collection *The Best Beast*.

Angela Lansbury starred opposite Milo O'Shea in Jerry Herman's stage musical *Dear World*.

Vanessa Redgrave starred as dancer Isadora Duncan in Karel Reisz's film *Isadora*.

Susan Sontag published the essay collection *Styles of Radical Will*.

Barbra Streisand starred in the title role in *Hello, Dolly!*, Gene Kelly's film version of the 1963 stage musical.

Linda Lavin starred opposite James Coco in Neil Simon's stage comedy *The Last of the Red Hot Lovers*.

Margaret Laurence published the novel *The Fire-Dwellers*.

Shirley MacLaine starred in Bob Fosse's film version of the musical *Sweet Charity*.

Bessie Head published the novel *When Rain Clouds Gather*.

Marge Piercy published the novel *Going Down Fast*.

d. Ivy Compton-Burnett (1884–1969), British novelist.

d. Hallie Flanagan (1890–1969), American WPA theater organizer and theater historian.

d. Grazyna Bacewicz (1909–1969), Polish composer, violinist, and writer.

## 1970

### POLITICS/LAW/WAR

Mouvement de Liberation des Femmes (MLF) began in France, composed of many groups of differing philosophies. Psychanalyse et Politique condemned feminism as reformist and attempted to adopt the MLF name as a trademark; other groups united in protest against that. The *Torchon Brûle* was a feminist journal published by several groups.

In France, a law was passed that gave both parents equal authority over their children and allowed the wife to retain her property from before or during the marriage.

In Britain, the Matrimonial Proceedings and Property Act (1970) and the Matrimonial Causes Act (1973) recognized the principle of "matrimonial property"—assets held jointly by both spouses, however and by whom acquired.

Bella Abzug, a liberal Democrat, was elected to the U.S. House of Representatives from New York City, and was reelected twice (1972; 1974), leaving Congress to make a failed senatorial primary run in 1976.

Andrea Dworkin published *Our Blood: Prophecies and Discourses on Sexual Politics.*

Canada's Royal Commission on the Status of Women made a report, with a National Committee on the Status of Women established to implement its recommendations.

Women's Liberation Conference was held at Oxford University's Ruskin College; a National Coordination Committee was established and other conferences were held, until a radical-socialist feminist split (1978).

Divorce was permitted in Italy.

NOW Legal Defense and Education Fund was founded by the National Organization for Women, as that organization's legal and educational division.

Barbara Castle led the successful fight for passage of the British Equal Pay Act.

California Democrat Dianne Feinstein began her term as member and then president of the San Francisco Board of Supervisors (1970–1978).

Margaret Thatcher became British education and science minister (1970–1974).

North American Indian Women's Association (Naiwa) was founded.

Radicalesbians was formed, a separatist lesbian group that also invited nonlesbian women to join, as stated in the Radicalesbian position paper *The Woman-Identified Woman.*

Shulamith Firestone published *The Dialectic of Sex: The Case for Feminist Revolution,* calling for a revolution that would destroy the biological family, based on the thinking of Karl Marx and Friedrich Engels.

Women were first allowed to join the Secret Service, protecting the U.S. president.

American radical feminist Jo Freeman published "The Bitch Manifesto," defining a *bitch* as a strong woman.

Gaositwe Keagakwa Tibe Chiepe became high commissioner to Britain from Botswana and held several other ambassadorial posts.

Sheila Rowbotham published *Women's Liberation and the New Politics.*

Louise Weiss published her six-volume *Mémoires d'une Européenne* (1970–1976).

Shirley Chisholm published the autobiography *Unbought and Unbossed.*

d. Ana Figuero (1908–1970), Chilean feminist, teacher, diplomat, and United Nations official.

### RELIGION/EDUCATION/EVERYDAY LIFE

Germaine Greer published *The Female Eunuch,* urging individual action by women to achieve independence, including the rejection of marriage and adoption of sexually diverse lifestyles.

Kate Millett published *Sexual Politics,* a book of feminist literary criticism attacking several male authors, including D. H. Lawrence, Norman Mailer, and Henry Miller, as patriarchal woman haters, and also more generally calling for a women's revolution.

Robin Morgan published the anthology *Sisterhood Is Powerful* and the essay "Goodbye to All That," announcing her decision to leave what she felt were the sexist peace and civil rights movements in favor of women-only groups.

Simone de Beauvoir published *The Coming of Age*, about the plight of the aged in modern society.

Billie Jean King won the Virginia Slims singles title and successfully defended it seven times (1971–1977); the high-paying tournaments began to raise women's prize money, which had lagged far behind men's.

Barbara Ward and René Dubos published *Only One Earth*.

Eva Figes published *Patriarchal Attitudes: Women in Society*, a key women's movement work.

Hannah Arendt published *On Violence*, focusing on but not limited to political violence.

First all-woman climb of the Denali summit at Mt. McKinley, in Alaska, was made by a team including Arlene Blum.

Center for Women and Religion was founded at Berkeley, California.

Diane Crump became the first female jockey to ride in the Kentucky Derby.

Helen Vlachou published *House Arrest*, about her opposition to Greece's ruling military junta.

Evelyne Sullerot published *La femme dans le monde moderne*.

Joan Robinson published *Freedom and Necessity*.

British philosopher Mary Warnock published *Existentialism*.

d. Gladys Aylward (1903–1970), British-Chinese missionary who became a Chinese citizen and led a successful campaign against female footbinding; she was portrayed by Ingrid Bergman in *The Inn of the Sixth Happiness*.

d. Anna Louise Strong (1885–1970), American journalist who published numerous pro-Communist works; deported from the Soviet Union (1949), she later settled in Peking (1958), becoming an honorary Red Guard during the Cultural Revolution.

d. Edith Elizabeth Lowry (1897–1970), American religious leader and organizer, an interdenominational Protestant worker noted for her work among migrant agricultural workers.

## Science/Technology/Medicine

Sylvia Earle Mead led four colleagues—America's first all-woman team of aquanauts—in a two-week underwater mission off St. John, in the Virgin Islands, formally titled the Tektite Underwater Research Project, depicted in an educational film, *The Aquamaids of Tektite II*.

Jane Goodall published *In the Shadow of Man*, on the chimpanzees, and *Innocent Killers*, on wild dogs, jackals, and hyenas, both with photos by Hugo von Lawick, then her husband.

William H. Masters and Virginia Johnson published *Human Sexual Inadequacy*.

Margaret Mead published *Culture and Commitment*, exploring generational rifts.

Irmgard Flügge-Lotz was appointed a fellow of the American Institute of Aeronautics and Astronautics, its second woman.

Jacqueline Auriol published *I Live to Fly*.

Janet Vaughan published *The Physiology of Bone*.

d. Alice Hamilton (1869–1970), American physician and social reformer, a pioneer in industrial medicine, the first woman to teach at Harvard Medical School (1919–1935); she was the sister of classicist Edith Hamilton.

---

It is interesting that many women do not recognize themselves as discriminated against; no better proof could be found of the totality of their conditioning.

—Kate Millett, in *Sexual Politics* (1970).

---

d. Margaret D. Foster (1895–1970), American mineralogist who specialized in analyzing water resources, especially for trace minerals; while working with the Manhattan Project during World War II, she developed new methods for analyzing uranium.

## ARTS/LITERATURE

Glenda Jackson gave an Oscar-winning performance opposite Alan Bates, Oliver Reed, and Eleanor Bron in Ken Russell's film version of D. H. Lawrence's 1920 novel *Women in Love*.

Judy Collins issued the album *Whales and Nightingales*, with her renditions of "Amazing Grace" and "Farewell to Tarwathie."

Jane Alexander and James Earl Jones reprised their stage roles in Martin Ritt's film version of Howard Sackler's 1968 play *The Great White Hope*.

Mary Renault published the novel *Fire from Heaven*.

Joan Didion published the novel *Play It as It Lays*.

Maya Angelou published her autobiographical *I Know Why the Caged Bird Sings*.

Ruby Dee starred opposite James Earl Jones in a New York production of Athol Fugard's *Boesman and Lena*.

Alice Walker published the novel *The Third Life of Grange Copeland*.

Sada Thompson starred in Paul Zindel's play *The Effect of Gamma Rays on Man-in-the-Moon Marigolds*.

Audre Lorde published the poetry collection *Cables to Rage*.

Eudora Welty published the novel *Losing Battles*.

Lauren Bacall starred opposite Len Cariou in *Applause*, Charles Strouse and Lee Adams's stage musical.

Nadezhda Mandelstam published the autobiography *Hope Against Hope*.

Nadine Gordimer published the novel *Guest of Honor*.

Sylvia Ashton-Warner published the novel *Three*.

Ada Louise Huxtable received the first Pulitzer Prize for criticism, for her work as the *New York Times* architecture critic (1963–1982).

Mary Tyler Moore played a career woman, much in the temper of quite new times, in television's long-running situation comedy *The Mary Tyler Moore Show* (1970–1977).

Barbara Loden made the film *Wanda*, on feminist themes.

Ama Ata Aidoo published the short-story collection *No Sweetness Here*.

Elaine Stritch starred opposite Dean Jones in Stephen Sondheim's musical *Company*.

Marsha Mason starred opposite Kevin McCarthy in Kurt Vonnegut's play *Happy Birthday, Wanda June*.

Zoë Caldwell and Emlyn Williams starred in Elinor Jones's play *Colette*.

Maureen Stapleton starred in Neil Simon's play *The Gingerbread Lady*.

Alice Neel painted *Andy Warhol*.

Colleen Dewhurst starred in the title role in Bertolt Brecht's play *The Good Woman of Setzuan*.

Sarah Miles starred in the title role in David Lean's film *Ryan's Daughter*, opposite Robert Mitchum and John Mills.

Denise Levertov published the essay collection *Relearning the Alphabet*.

Georgia O'Keeffe painted *Black Rock with Blue III*.

Lotte Reiniger published *Shadow Theaters and Shadow Films*.

Nikki Giovanni published *Poem of Angela Yvonne Davis* and *Re: Creation*.

b. Mariah Carey (1970– ), American singer, who emerged as a star with her popular first album, *Mariah Carey* (1990).

d. Janis Joplin (1943–1970), emblematic American blues singer of the 1960s, who died of a heroin overdose.

d. Billie Burke (1885–1970), American actress who began her long career in turn-of-the-century London and was a star on Broadway from 1907, later also appearing in many films; wife of Florenz Ziegfeld.

d. Gypsy Rose Lee (Rose Louise Hovick, 1914–1970), American actress, dancer, and writer, best known as a stripper in burlesque, whose story was the basis for the musical play and film *Gypsy*.

d. Nelly Sachs (1891–1970), German Jewish poet and playwright, who took the Holocaust as her main theme. She and Schmuel Yoseph Agnon shared the 1966 Nobel Prize for literature.

d. Romaine Goddard Brooks (1874–1970), American artist, a portraitist who lived and worked in Paris during the interwar period.

d. Vera Brittain (1893–1970), British feminist, pacifist, and writer.

d. Laura Knight (1877–1970), British painter, whose later work included notable works on the ballet and circus.

d. Louise Bogan (1897–1970), American poet and critic.

# 1971

## POLITICS/LAW/WAR

U.S. House of Representatives passed the Equal Rights Amendment (ERA).

Danish judge Helga Pedersen was appointed to the European Court of Human Rights; she was that court's first female judge.

The *Manifeste des 343* was made public, in which 343 French women, some of them celebrities, declared publicly that they had had abortions when they were still illegal in France.

Women won the right to vote and be elected to office in Switzerland.

Anne Armstrong became the first woman to co-chair the Republican National Committee (1971–1973).

Aisha Rateb became Egypt's minister of social affairs (1971–1977).

National Women's Political Caucus was founded, to foster the election of women's rights candidates at all levels of American politics.

Wilma Scott Heide became president of the National Organization for Women (1971–1974).

Yelena Bonner married nuclear physicist Andrei Sakharov, both becoming increasingly visible Soviet dissidents in the years that followed.

Annabelle Rankin became Australia's high commissioner to New Zealand (1971–1975).

French lawyer Gisèle Halimi founded the organization Choisir, which became a substantial force for women's choice in such areas as abortion and contraception.

Barbara Mikulski served on the Baltimore City Council (1971–1976).

Agatha Barbara served a second term as Malta's education minister (1971–1974).

Italy's Constitutional Court ruled unconstitutional the law banning dissemination of birth control information.

Jeanne M. Holm was promoted to brigadier general in the U.S. Air Force, the first woman in that post, rising to major general before her retirement (1975).

Angela Davis and Bettina Aptheker published *If They Come in the Morning: Voices of Resistance*.

Kate Millett published *The Prostitution Papers*.

Louise Weiss founded the Strasbourg-based Institute for the Science of Peace.

Native Women's Association of Canada was founded.

---

I have met brave women who are exploring the outer edge of human possibility, with no history to guide them, and with a courage to make themselves vulnerable that I find moving beyond words.

— Gloria Steinem, in "Sisterhood" (1972)

d. Raicho Hiratsuka (1886–1971), Japanese feminist, editor, and writer, founder of the Seitosha (Bluestocking Society, 1914).

d. Georgia Lee Witt Lusk (1893–1971), American politician, three-time New Mexico education commissioner and the first New Mexico woman in Congress (1946).

### RELIGION/EDUCATION/EVERYDAY LIFE

*Ms.* magazine was founded by a group of feminist writers led by Gloria Steinem, who became its first editor (1971–1989); its first issue appeared in January 1972, to quick success.

Elizabeth Gould Davis published *The First Sex*, claiming that a single great matriarchy in the Mediterranean area, which was destroyed by a natural disaster, preceded later patriarchies, and that matriarchy would soon again become the dominant form in human societies.

Elizabeth Janeway published *Man's World, Woman's Place*, a powerful and very well-received call for rejection of the then-standard "home and family" women's roles in favor of a mass move into independent, far freer wage-earning and status-building roles.

Barbara Tuchman published *Stilwell and the American Experience in China*, winning her second Pulitzer Prize for general nonfiction (1972).

Lucinda Franks and Thomas Powers shared the Pulitzer Prize for reporting, for a series of United Press International articles about radical activist Diana Oughton; Franks was the first woman and youngest person to win a Pulitzer for reporting.

Aline B. Louchheim Saarinen was the first woman to head an overseas bureau for a major television network, NBC's Paris bureau.

Barbara Ward became the first woman to address the Vatican Council in Rome.

Chiswick's Women's Aid opened in London, a pioneering shelter for battered women.

National Black Women's Political Leadership Caucus was founded, as a national networking advocacy and educational organization.

Althea Gibson was named to the Lawn Tennis Hall of Fame and Tennis Museum.

Center for American Woman and Politics (CAWP) was founded as part of the Eagleton Institute of Politics at Rutgers University.

Esther Van Wagoner Tufty was the first woman elected to the National Press Club.

Margery Ann Tabankin became the first woman to serve as president of the National Student Association.

Juanita Morris Kreps published *Sex in the Marketplace: American Women at Work* and *Lifetime Allocation of Work and Income*.

British social scientist Barbara Wootton published *Contemporary Britain*.

Joan Robinson published *Economic Heresies*.

Xavière Gauthier published *Surréalisme et sexualité*.

b. Kristi Tsuya Yamaguchi (1971– ), American women's figure-skating champion.

d. Coco (Gabrielle) Chanel (ca. 1883–1971), French couturier who pioneered the loose, liberating clothing of the 1920s, such as the chemise dress, collarless cardigan, and bias-cut dress, as well as flowing scarves.

d. Stella (Charnaud), dowager marchioness of Reading (1894–1971), British voluntary organizer, born in Constantinople, who chaired the Women's Voluntary Service during World War II (from 1938).

d. Kotani Kimi (1901–1971), Japanese religious leader and faith healer, co-founder of the Reiyukai religious movement.

### SCIENCE/TECHNOLOGY/MEDICINE

Brenda Hall became the first female keeper at the National Zoological Park in Washington, D.C.

Jacqueline Cochran was elected to the American Aviation Hall of Fame, the only living woman so honored.

Sheila Scott made the first solo light-aircraft flight around the world, a five-week journey equator to equator, over the North Pole.

Elizabeth Dexter Hay served as editor in chief of *Developmental Biology Journal* (1971–1975).

American botanist Katherine Esau was elected to the Swedish Royal Academy of Sciences.

Czech mathematician Olga Taussky became the first female professor at the California Institute of Technology.

Association for Women in Mathematics (AWM) was founded.

d. Kathleen Yardley Lonsdale (1903–1971), Irish-British crystallographer, physicist, and chemist, working primarily at the University College, London, and the Royal Institute; a key figure in the development of X-ray crystallography, she became president of the International Union of Crystallography and of the British Association.

d. Sophia Josephine Kleegman (1901–1971), American gynecologist and obstetrician, a pioneer in studying and treating infertility and sterility and an early advocate of artificial insemination and sperm banks.

d. Winifred Goldring (1888–1971), American paleontologist long associated with the New York State Museum in Albany, the first woman to be president of the American Paleontological Society.

## ARTS/LITERATURE

Glenda Jackson created a memorable, fiercely independent Elizabeth I of England in the six-part television miniseries *Elizabeth R*. She also starred opposite Peter Finch in John Schlesinger's film *Sunday, Bloody Sunday*.

Jane Fonda starred as prostitute Bree Daniels opposite Donald Sutherland in Alan J. Pakula's film thriller *Klute*, winning a best actress Academy Award.

Julie Christie starred opposite Warren Beatty in Robert Altman's film *McCabe and Mrs. Miller*, as the operator of a frontier house of prostitution, and opposite Alan Bates in Joseph Losey's period love story *The Go-Between*.

Bonnie Raitt issued her first album, *Bonnie Raitt*.

Doris Lessing published the novel *Briefing for a Descent into Hell*, on feminist themes.

Lynn Seymour created the title role in Kenneth MacMillan's ballet *Anastasia*.

Fleur Adcock published the poetry collection *High Tide in the Garden*.

Anne Meara starred opposite William Atherton in John Guare's play *The House of Blue Leaves*.

Janet Frame published the novel *Intensive Care*.

Sylvia Plath's poetry collection *Crossing the Water* was published posthumously.

Lee Grant and Peter Falk starred in Neil Simon's stage comedy *The Prisoner of Second Avenue*.

Shirley Ann Grau published the novel *The Condor Passes*.

Margaret Atwood published the poetry collection *Power Politics*.

Cynthia Ozick published *The Pagan Rabbi and Other Stories*.

Ruby Keeler, Helen Gallagher, Patsy Kelly, and Jack Gilford starred in a Broadway revival of Vincent Youmans's 1925 musical *No, No, Nanette*.

Helen Frankenthaler painted *Chairman of the Board*.

Jessica Tandy, Colleen Dewhurst, George Voskovec, and Betty Field starred in Edward Albee's play *All Over*.

Alexis Smith, Dorothy Collins, and Gene Nelson starred in Stephen Sondheim's stage musical *Follies*.

Georgia O'Keeffe painted *Black Rock with Red* and *Black Rock with Blue Sky and White Clouds*.

Anita Desai published the novel *Bye-Bye Blackbird*.

Denise Levertov published the essays in *To Stay Alive*.

Louise Nevelson created a welded steel sculpture for New York's Seagram Building.

Ingeborg Bachmann published the novel *Malina*.

Judith Wright published her *Collected Poems 1942–1970*.

Bessie Head published the novel *Maru*.

Lynda Benglis showed the sculpture *For Darkness; Situation and Circumstance*.

Nelly Kaplan wrote and directed the film *Papa les petits bateaux*.

Melina Mercouri published the autobiographical *I Was Born Greek*.

Sandy Dennis and Phil Silvers starred in a New York production of Alan Ayckbourn's play *How the Other Half Loves*.

Elizabeth Taylor published the novel *Mrs. Palfrey at the Claremont*.

Erica Jong published the poetry collection *Fruits & Vegetables*.

b. Selena (Selena Quantanilla Perez, 1971–1995), Mexican-American singer, a star in the 1990s.

d. Helene Weigel (1901–1971), German actress and director, the wife of Bertolt Brecht and codirector of the Berliner Ensemble.

d. Margaret Bourke-White (1906–1971), American photographer, a leading photojournalist through the Great Depression, World War II, and the postwar period.

d. Stevie Smith (Florence Margaret Smith, 1902–1971), British poet, novelist, and illustrator from the late 1930s until her death.

d. Diane Arbus (1923–1971), American photographer who turned from fashion photos to the portrayal of grotesques and marginal people later in her career.

d. Lil (Lillian) Hardin Armstrong (1898–1971), American jazz pianist, singer, and bandleader, the first wife and early collaborator of Louis Armstrong.

d. Gladys Cooper (1888–1971), British actress and theater manager, a leading figure on the London and New York stages for half a century.

d. Irene Rice Pereira (1907–1971), American artist.

## 1972

### POLITICS/LAW/WAR

U.S. Senate passed the Equal Rights Amendment (ERA), the 1972 version reading: "Equality of rights under the law shall not be denied or abridged by the United States or by any State on account of sex." The decade-long fight for state ratification began, ultimately failing in 1982.

Discrimination in most federally assisted educational programs and related activities, including sports, was banned in the United States by Title IX of the 1972 Education Act Amendments.

Shirley Chisholm was a candidate for the Democratic presidential nomination, the first woman to carry her candidacy through to the end of a major party convention, receiving 152 delegate votes; she described her experience in *The Good Fight* (1973).

Anne L. Armstrong delivered the keynote speech at the Republican Party's national convention, the first woman to do so for a major party, and was appointed counselor to President Richard Nixon (1972–1974), founding the Office of Women's Programs.

Barbara Jordan was elected to the U.S. House of Representative from Houston, becoming the first African-American woman to serve in Congress (1973–1979) from a state in the old Confederacy.

Colorado Democratic Congresswoman Pat Schroeder won her first term in the U.S. Congress, by the early 1990s becoming the senior woman in Congress.

Fannie Lou Hamer was seated as a Mississippi delegate to the 1972 Democratic Party national convention, signaling the defeat of Southern Democratic Party racist convention practices.

Margrethe II succeeded to the Danish throne, becoming her country's first officially recognized queen of the millennium, the right of women to directly succeed to the throne having been established only in 1953.

Alene B. Duerk was named an admiral in the U.S. Navy, the first woman at that rank; she had been head of the Navy Nurse Corps.

Ruth Bader Ginsburg became the first woman tenured as a law professor at Columbia Law School (1972–1980).

Annemarie Renger became president of the German Bundestag (1972–1976).

Angela Davis was acquitted on charges that she had supplied the guns used by Jonathan Jackson during the Marin County, California, courthouse shooting (1970), in which a judge and two inmates were killed and a district attorney paralyzed.

In Portugal, Maria Teresa Horta, Maria Isabel Barreno, and Maria Velho da Costa had to defend themselves in court after publishing the radically feminist *Novas Cartas Portuguesas*.

Joanne E. Pierce and Susan Lynn Roley were the first two women to become special agents in the Federal Bureau of Investigation; women were allowed to apply only after the death of long-time FBI director J. Edgar Hoover earlier that year.

Australia passed a law mandating equal pay for work of equal value.

German anarchist-terrorists Ulrike Meinhof and Andreas Baader were captured.

Eva Kolstad became Norway's minister of consumer affairs (1972–1973).

Bella Abzug published *Bella: Ms. Abzug Goes to Washington*.

Juliet Mitchell published *Women's Estate*.

Margaret Chase Smith published *Declaration of Conscience*.

Bettina Aptheker published *The Academic Rebellion*.

Ruth First published *The South African Connection: Western Involvement in Apartheid*.

*Erlebtes-Erschautes*, the autobiographical work by German feminists and pacifists Anita Augspurg and Lida Heymann, was published posthumously.

d. Jessie Daniel Ames (1883–1972), American feminist, reformer, suffragist, and civil rights activist, founder of the Association of Southern Women for the Prevention of Lynching (1930–1942).

d. Ho Hsiang-ning (1879–1972), Chinese revolutionary and feminist, a colleague of Sun Yat-sen and Ch'ing-ling Soong, who broke with the Kuomintang after the Shanghai Massacre (1927), a Chinese Communist government official (from 1949).

d. Mabel Howard (1893–1972), New Zealand social reformer and politician, her country's first woman to be a cabinet minister (1947).

## RELIGION/EDUCATION/EVERYDAY LIFE

Phyllis Chesler published *Women and Madness*, arguing that strong, independent women are often called "deviant" and can literally be driven mad in male-dominated society.

Athletic scholarships for American women were first offered, by the University of Chicago, where organized American women's collegiate athletics had effectively started (1898).

Ethel Ann Hoefly was the first woman to become a brigadier general in the U.S. Air Force Nurse Corps.

General Commission on the Status and Role of Women of the United Methodist Church was organized, focusing on ending discrimination against women in the church.

Irina Rodnina and Alexei Ulanov won the pairs figure-skating gold medal at the Sapporo Olympics, the first of her three Olympic pairs gold medals.

Judith Hird became the first parish pastor of the Lutheran Church in America, at Toms River, New Jersey.

Olga Korbut won three gold medals at the Munich Olympics, becoming the first person to do a backward somersault on the uneven parallel bars in competition and the first woman to do a backflip on the balance beam.

British sociologist Ann Oakley published her first book, *Sex, Gender and Society*, a classic survey of women's social position.

Ellen Frankfort published *Vaginal Politics*.

Nawa El Saadawi published *Women and Sex*, emerging as a major and very unusual Muslim feminist.

Simone de Beauvoir published the autobiographical *All Said and Done*.

Elizabeth Janeway published the essay collection *Between Myth and Morning: Women Awakening*.

Sally Preisand became the first woman ordained a rabbi of Reform Judaism.

Association of Women Business Owners (later National Association) was founded.

Bans against advertising feminine-hygiene products on American radio and television were lifted.

Center for Women Policy Studies (CWPS) was founded, as a research and advocacy group focusing on women's issues.

Dorothy Day published *On Pilgrimage: the Sixties.*

Eileen Power's lectures on women in medieval society were published, long after her death (1940), as *Medieval Women,* edited by her husband, Michael Postan.

Juanita Morris Kreps became the first woman to direct the New York Stock Exchange.

Lin Bolen became head of daytime programming at NBC, the first woman in that slot for a major television network.

Ms. Foundation for Women was founded, to supply alternative funding sources for women-generated projects.

National Association of Female Executives was founded, as a networking and funding organization.

National Conference of Puerto Rican Women was founded, to help the integration of Puerto Rican and other Hispanic women into American life.

Sylvia Ashton-Warner published *Spearpoint: Teacher in America.*

*Women's Studies—An Interdisciplinary Journal* was founded; the first American scholarly women's studies journal.

Billie Jean King published her autobiographical *Billie Jean.*

Jessie Bernard published *The Future of Marriage.*

British cultural historian Frances Yates published *The Rosicrucian Enlightenment.*

d. Rose (Rachel) Schneiderman (1882–1972), Polish-American trade union leader and social reformer, most noted for her work organizing for the International Ladies Garment Workers Union (ILGWU), especially from 1909 to 1914; a key activist in the Women's Trade Union League from 1905.

## SCIENCE/TECHNOLOGY/MEDICINE

Nina Felice Tabachnick became the first girl ever to win the grand prize in the prestigious Westinghouse Science Talent Search.

Sylvia Earle Mead acted as chief scientist on *Searcher,* a research vessel analyzing marine life in the Galápagos and Cocos islands.

*The Joy of Sex,* by Alex Comfort, rode a new wave of sexual attitudes, proposing to help people learn how to maximize their sexual pleasure; in a major shift, masturbation and homosexuality were treated as acceptable sexual alternatives.

Margaret Burbidge became the first woman to direct the Royal Observatory at Greenwich, though without the traditional honorary title of Astronomer Royal.

Mary Leakey became director of the excavations in East Africa's Olduvai Gorge after the death of her husband, Louis Leakey.

Dorothy Crowfoot Hodgkin served as president of the International Union of Crystallography (1972–1975).

American research physicist Katherine Blodgett received the Progress Medal of the Photographic Society of America.

Grace Goldsmith became president of the American Society for Clinical Nutrition (1972–1973).

Pamela Chelgren became the first woman in the U.S. National Oceanic and Atmospheric Administration Corps.

Adele Davis published *Let's Have Healthy Children* and *You Can Get Well.*

Ruth Sager published *Cytoplasmic Genes and Organelles.*

d. Maria Goeppert Mayer (1906–1972), Polish-American nuclear physicist who was the second woman to receive the Nobel Prize for physics (1963); developed the shell theory of nuclear structure (1948) and was part of the team that first isolated uranium-235, needed for nuclear fission.

d. Lillian Evelyn Moller Gilbreth (1878–1972), American industrial engineer, a pioneer in time-and-motion studies and scientific management, who taught, wrote widely, and ran a highly influential consulting firm with her husband, Frank Gilbreth, and after his death alone, while raising 12 children (two of whom wrote *Cheaper by the Dozen*).

d. Esther Applin (1895–1972), American petroleum geologist who did key work in micropaleontology, correlating data on microfossils to provide information for oil drilling operations.

## ARTS/LITERATURE

Eudora Welty published the Pulitzer Prize–winning novel *Optimist's Daughter*.

Harriet Andersson, Ingrid Thulin, and Liv Ullmann starred in Ingmar Bergman's film *Cries and Whispers*.

Aretha Franklin recorded the albums *Amazing Grace* and *Young, Gifted and Black*.

Barbara Hepworth showed her sculpture group *Family of Man*.

Maureen Stapleton, Jason Robards, and George Grizzard starred in Clifford Odets's play *The Country Girl*.

Maxine Kumin published her Pulitzer Prize–winning *Up Country: Poems of New England*.

Janet Frame published the novel *Daughter Buffalo*.

Nikki Giovanni published the poetry collection *My House*.

Sylvia Plath's poetry collection *Winter Trees* was published posthumously.

Margaret Atwood published the novel *Surfacing*.

Nadine Gordimer published the short-story collection *Livingstone's Companions*.

Lina Wertmuller directed *The Seduction of Mimi*.

Liza Minnelli starred in *Cabaret*, winning a best actress Academy Award.

Jane Alexander starred opposite Jerry Orbach in Bob Randall's play *6 Rms Riv Vu*.

Louise Nevelson painted *Night Presence IV*.

Anne Morrow Lindbergh published *Bring Me a Unicorn*.

Denise Levertov published the essay collection in *Footprints*.

Carmen Callil founded the British feminist publishing house Virago.

Elisabeth Lutyens published *A Goldfish Bowl*.

Hannah Weinstein produced and directed the film *Claudine*.

Françoise Sagan published the novel *Scars on the Soul*.

Georgia O'Keeffe painted *The Beyond*.

Sawako Ariyoshi published the novel *The Twilight Years*.

Ingrid Bergman starred in George Bernard Shaw's play *Captain Brassbound's Conversion*.

Robin Morgan published the poetry collection *Monster*.

Sylvia Crowe published *Gardens of Moghul India*.

Zoë Caldwell starred opposite George Grizzard in Arthur Miller's play *The Creation of the World and Other Business*.

Caryl Churchill published the play *Owners*.

Elisabeth Frink published *The Art of Elisabeth Frink*.

Karen Riale, a clarinetist, was the first female member of the U.S. Air Force Band.

d. (Ellen) Miriam Hopkins (1902–1972), American actress, a leading player on Broadway who became a dramatic star of Hollywood's Golden Age in such films as *Design for Living* (1933), *These Three* (1936), and *Old Acquaintance* (1943).

d. Mahalia Jackson (1911–1972), American gospel singer, the most popular gospel singer of her time, who emerged as a worldwide symbol of the American civil rights movement of the 1960s with her rendition of "Amazing Grace."

d. Marianne Moore (1887–1972), American Objectivist poet, a major literary figure from the early 1920s.

d. Asta Nielsen (1883–1972), Danish actress, a silent-film star in Germany, most notably in such films as *Miss Julie* (1922) and *Hedda Gabler* (1924).

d. Helen Traubel (1889–1972), American soprano, a fixture at the Metropolitan Opera (1937–1953).

d. Margaret Rutherford (1892–1972), British actress, an early "Miss Marple" on film.

d. Bronislava Nijinska (1891–1972), Russian dancer and choreographer, sister of Vaslav Nijinsky.

d. Margaret Webster (1905–1972), British actress and director, daughter of actor Ben Webster and actress May Whitty.

d. Betty Smith (1904–1972), American novelist, whose work included *A Tree Grows in Brooklyn* (1943).

d. Louise A. Boyd (1877–1972), American photographer and Arctic explorer.

d. Margaret Bond (1913–1972), African-American composer.

# 1973

## POLITICS/LAW/WAR

In the landmark case *Roe v. Wade*, the U.S. Supreme Court legalized abortion in the United States based on the "right of privacy" between a woman and her doctor. Unrestricted abortions were allowed during the first trimester (three months) of pregnancy; states were allowed to regulate abortion in the second trimester, and to regulate or prohibit abortion in the third trimester, except where the mother's life or health were endangered. A series of court decisions over the following decades would modify this decision, making abortions more difficult to obtain, especially for poor women, even while affirming *Roe*'s basic principles.

Amalia Coutsouris Fleming returned to Greece after the military junta fell, becoming the head of the Greek Committee of Amnesty International, a member of the European Human Rights Commission, and later a member of the Greek and European parliaments.

American Air Force officer Jeanne Holm was appointed a major general, until then the highest rank won by a woman in any branch of the armed forces.

Golda Meir's political career essentially ended with her resignation as prime minister, after Israel suffered major losses when surprised by Arab attacks at the beginning of the Fourth Arab-Israeli War (Yom Kippur War).

Isabelita Perón became vice-president of Argentina after her husband, Juan Perón, began his second presidential term.

Begum Liaquat Ali Khan became governor of Sind, the first female provincial governor in Pakistan.

Reba C. Tyler was the first woman to lead a NATO military unit, being appointed a commander at Mannheim, West Germany.

Call Off Your Old Tired Ethics (COYOTE) was formed by prostitutes and their advocates, seeking legalization of prostitution and protection from arrest.

Felda Looper became the first regular female page in the U.S. House of Representatives; Gene Cox, daughter of Congressman Edward Cox, had served one day in 1939.

Nguyen Thi Binh was among the signatories to the agreement ending the Vietnam War.

Sheila Rowbotham published *Woman, Resistance and Revolution, Women's Consciousness, Man's World*, and *Hidden from History: 308 Years of Women's Oppression and the Fight Against It*.

Algerian feminist Fadéla M'rabet published *L'Algérie des illusions*.

Shirley Chisholm published *The Good Fight*.

Gisèle Halimi published *La cause des femmes*.

Judith Hart published *Aid and Liberation: A Socialist Study of Aid Policies*.

Shulamit Aloni founded Israel's Civil Rights Party.

d. Jeannette Pickering Rankin (1880–1973), American social worker, pacifist, women's suffrage leader, and politician, the first woman to be elected to the U.S. House of Representatives (1916).

d. Frances M. Witherspoon (1887–1973), American peace and civil liberties advocate, writer, and feminist, who founded the New York Bureau of Legal Advice (1917–1920) to counsel conscientious objectors and draft resisters.

## RELIGION/EDUCATION/EVERYDAY LIFE

Marian Wright Edelman founded the Children's Defense Fund, serving as its president (1973– ).

American Telephone & Telegraph Company (AT&T), then a unified national company, signed a consent decree with the Equal Employment Opportunity Commission ending sex segregation in its employment.

9 to 5, National Association of Working Women, was founded, to take up the whole range of issues affecting working women, with special emphasis on office workers.

*Washington Post* publisher Katharine Graham was the first woman to win the John Peter Zenger Award, for service to freedom of the press. She also became the first woman to be a member of the Associated Press board.

Barbara Ward became president of the International Institute for Environment and Development (1973–1980), then its chair (1980–1981).

Women's Tennis Association was founded by a group that included Billie Jean King, seeking to have women's pay, perks, and prestige equal that accorded to men. That same year King played in a highly publicized "battle of the sexes" match, besting male challenger Bobby Riggs (1939 Wimbledon champion).

Virginia Lacy Jones received the Melvil Dewey Award for professional achievement in librarianship.

British cultural historian Frances Yates received the Wolfson History Award.

Women were for the first time able to fight as *toreras* on foot in the bullfight ring in Spain, after Spanish bullfighter Angelita (Angela) Hernandez won her fight to do so; from 1908, women *toreras* had been barred, though some had defied the ban.

*Woman Alive!*, a television documentary, was produced by *Ms.* magazine (1973; 1974).

Rosemary Ruether edited *Religion and Sexism.*

Evelyne Sullerot published *Les françaises au travail.*

Joan Robinson published *Introduction to Modern Economics*, coauthored with John Eatwell.

d. Elsa Schiaparelli (1890–1973), French fashion designer who built an international reputation; noted for her use of color and texture, she was among the first to introduce padded shoulders (1931–1932), zippers, and synthetic fabrics.

d. Ida (Kaganovich) Cohen Rosenthal (1886–1973), Russian-American inventor and manufacturer who developed the modern brassiere and founded Maidenform Inc. to manufacture it, in the process helping to develop the "ready-to-wear" mass-production clothing industry.

## SCIENCE/TECHNOLOGY/MEDICINE

Boston Women's Health Collective published their now-classic *Our Bodies, Ourselves.*

Judy Neuffer was the first female U.S. Navy pilot to fly into the eye of a hurricane, the destructive Carmen (August 30–September 1).

Sylvia Earle Mead was chief scientist and aquanaut on a series of diving projects using the underwater laboratory Hydrolab (from 1973).

American Psychological Association established a division focusing on the psychology of women, with its own scholarly journal, *Psychology of Women Quarterly.*

Barbara Grosz began her long association with the Artificial Intelligence Center at Stanford University (1973–1986).

Lois E. Hinson became the first woman to serve as president of the National Association of Federal Veterinarians.

British aviator Sheila Scott published *On Top of the World.*

Janet Vaughan published *The Effects of Irradiation on the Skeleton.*

Psychoanalyst Helene Deutsch published *Confrontations with Myself.*

## ARTS/LITERATURE

Glenda Jackson starred opposite George Segal in Melvin Frank's film *A Touch of Class*, winning a best actress Academy Award.

Glynis Johns, Len Cariou, and Hermione Gingold starred in Stephen Sondheim's stage musical *A Little Night Music*, adapted from Ingmar Bergman's film *Smiles of a Summer Night*.

Katharine Hepburn starred opposite Paul Scofield in Tony Richardson's film version of Edward Albee's 1966 play *A Delicate Balance* and opposite Sam Waterston and Joanna Miles in Anthony Harvey's film version of Tennessee Williams's 1945 play *The Glass Menagerie*.

Liv Ullmann starred opposite Erland Josephson in Ingmar Bergman's film *Scenes from a Marriage*.

Rita Mae Brown published her largely autobiographical radical lesbian novel *Rubyfruit Jungle*.

Lillian Hellman published the autobiographical *Pentimento*.

Barbra Streisand starred opposite Robert Redford in Sidney Pollack's evocative film *The Way We Were*.

Toni Morrison published the novel *Sula*.

Colleen Dewhurst starred opposite Jason Robards in Eugene O'Neill's play *A Moon for the Misbegotten*.

Trish Hawkins starred opposite Judd Hirsch in Lanford Wilson's play *Hot l Baltimore*.

Virginia Capers starred opposite Joe Morton in *Raisin*, Judd Woldin and Robert Brittan's musical adaptation of Lorraine Hansberry's play *Raisin in the Sun*.

Twyla Tharp's ballet *As Time Goes By* premiered with the Joffrey Ballet.

Liv Ullmann starred opposite Max von Sydow, as Swedish-American settlers, in Jan Troell's films *The Emigrants* and the sequel *The New Land*.

Marguerite Duras directed and wrote the film *Nathalie Granger* and wrote the play *India Song*.

Erica Jong published the novel *Fear of Flying* and the poetry collection *Half-Lives*.

Marge Piercy published the novel *Small Changes*.

Marsha Mason starred opposite Christopher Plummer in Neil Simon's play *The Good Doctor*.

Natalia Ginzburg published the novel *No Way*.

Bessie Head published the novel *A Question of Power*.

Michele Lee, Ken Howard, and Tommy Tune starred in *Seesaw*, Cy Coleman and Dorothy Fields's stage musical.

Caryl Churchill published the play *Objections to Sex and Violence*.

Dorothy Loudon, Myrna Loy, Kim Hunter, and Rhonda Fleming starred in *The Women*, a revival of Clare Boothe Luce's 1936 play.

Jean Kerr's comedy *Finishing Touches* starred Barbara Bel Geddes.

Françoise Sagan wrote the play *Zaphorie*.

Thea Musgrave composed the opera *The Voice of Ariadne* and her *Viola Concerto*.

Ingeborg Bachmann published the short-story collection *Simultan*.

Lina Wertmuller directed *Love and Anarchy*.

d. Anna Magnani (1908–1973), Italian variety, stage, and screen actress, who became an international film star after her leading role in *Open City* (1945).

d. Pearl Buck (1892–1973), American writer, author of *The Good Earth*, who won the 1938 Nobel Prize for literature.

d. Katina Paxinou (Katina Constantopoulos, 1900–1973), Greek actress, director, and translator, a leading figure in the Greek theater.

d. Betty (Elizabeth Ruth) Grable (1916–1973), American actress, a star in Hollywood musicals of the 1930s and early 1940s, and during World War II an active armed services entertainer and popular "pinup girl."

d. Elizabeth Bowen (1899–1973), Anglo-Irish novelist, short story writer, and essayist; a substantial literary figure from the late 1920s.

d. Mary Wigman (1886–1973), German dancer, a major figure in the modern dance.

d. Anna Vaughn Hyatt (1876–1973), American sculptor.

d. Ingeborg Bachmann (1926–1973), Austrian writer.

d. Nancy Freeman Mitford (1904–1973), British writer.

## 1974

### POLITICS/LAW/WAR

On the death of her husband, Juan Perón, Isabelita Perón succeeded him as president of Argentina (1974–1976).

Simone de Beauvoir became president of the French League for the Rights of Women.

Karen DeCrow became president of the National Organization for Women (1974–1977).

Agatha Barbara became Malta's minister of labor, culture, and welfare.

Democrat Ella Grasso was elected governor of Connecticut; the first female governor not her husband's successor, she held office until forced to resign because of ill health (1980).

New Jersey Republican Millicent Fenwick began the first of her four terms in the House of Representatives (1974–1982), emerging as a pipe-smoking, extraordinarily quotable feminist and liberal.

Barbara Allen Rainey became the first female pilot in the U.S. Navy.

Alice M. Henderson (later Harris) began as U.S. Army chaplain at Fort Bragg, North Carolina, the first woman in that position.

Maria de Lourdes Pintasilgo was secretary of state for social security and minister for social affairs in the first Portuguese provisional government (1974–1975). She also founded and chaired the Portuguese National Committee on the Status of Women (1970–1974).

Barbara Castle became Britain's secretary of state for social security (1974–1976).

Eva Kolstad became president of Norway's Liberal Party (1974–1976).

Françoise Giroud became France's first secretary of state for women's affairs.

Gaositwe Keagakwa Tibe Chiepe became Botswana's minister of commerce (1974–1977).

Simone Veil became France's minister of health and fought through several new laws on family planning and abortion choice.

Texas Congresswoman Barbara Jordan won wide notice for her keen questioning during the televised House Judiciary Committee hearings on the proposed impeachment of Richard Nixon.

Shulamit Aloni became Israeli minister without portfolio.

U.S. Merchant Marine Academy at Kings Point, New York, began admitting women, the first of the American service academies to do so.

Women won the right to vote and be elected to office in Jordan.

Equal Rights Advocates (ERA) was created by a group of American women's rights lawyers, as a national center that supplied free legal services to poor women, especially those of color.

Federal Republic of (Western) Germany's Reichstag passed a law allowing abortion within the first three months of pregnancy.

Gwendoline Konie was Zambia's ambassador to Sweden, Norway, Denmark, and Finland (1974–1977), then serving in the United Nations and Zambian civil service.

U.S. Congress passed the Child Abuse Prevention and Treatment Act.

*Amazon Odyssey* appeared, a collection of the speeches and papers of radical feminist Ti-Grace Atkinson.

Juliet Mitchell published *Psychoanalysis and Feminism*, an attack on the former which also signaled a turn away from her earlier Marxism.

Andrea Dworkin published *Woman Hating*.

Ruth First published *Libya: the Elusive Revolution*.

Angela Davis published her *Autobiography*.

---

# What Does 40 Look Like?

On publicly celebrating her 40th birthday, Gloria Steinem was told by a male reporter, "You don't look 40." Her reply was "This is what 40 looks like. We've been lying for so long, who would know?" (1974)

Kate Millett published *Sita* and the autobiography *Flying*.

Winifred Ewing was again a member of Britain's Parliament (1974–1979).

d. Kathleen D'Olier Courtney (1878–1974), British feminist, suffragist, and pacifist, a leader in international relief and peace efforts. She was a leader of the Women's International League for Peace after World War I, of the British League of Nations Association during the 1930s, and of the British United Nations Association after World War II.

d. Ekaterina Furtseva (1910–1974), Russian politician, Khrushchev-era minister of culture (1960).

#### RELIGION/EDUCATION/EVERYDAY LIFE

Jacqueline Means was the first woman ordained as an Episcopal priest in America.

Helen Thomas became United Press International's bureau chief, the first woman to head a major news service.

Patricia "Patty" Hearst was kidnapped by the Symbionese Liberation Army, two months later participating with them in a bank robbery; she was captured in 1976 and was later sentenced to a seven-year prison term, serving almost two years.

Houston sportscaster Anita Martini entered the Los Angeles Dodgers' locker room after a game at Houston's Astrodome. She was the first woman to report from a professional men's sports locker room, a practice still controversial in the 1990s.

The newly organized Coalition of Labor Union Women successfully campaigned for the American Federation of Labor (AFL) to reverse its opposition to the Equal Rights Amendment, which had been based on its support of protective legislation for working women.

After the military junta was deposed, Helene Vlachou returned to Greece, resuming publication of the daily newspaper *Kathimerini*; she later became a member of parliament.

Carol Sutton was made managing editor of the Louisville (Kentucky) *Courier-Journal*, the first woman to head a major daily's news staff.

Mary Daly published *Beyond God the Father*, moving away from Catholicism toward an alternative radical feminist theology.

Women's Campaign Fund was founded, to support the political campaigns of pro-choice women running for public office.

Pat Harper coanchored the evening television news on New York's WPIX (1974–1984), with her husband, Joe Harper, until his 1983 death; they won two local Emmy awards.

American tennis player Chris Evert won the first of her three women's singles tournaments at Wimbledon (1974; 1975; 1981).

All-American Girls' Basketball Conference was founded.

Little League baseball was first formally opened to girls.

Marie Patterson became chair of Britain's Trades Union Congress (1974–1975; 1977).

Carol Polis became the first American woman licensed as a boxing judge.

Madeline H. McWhinney was the first president of the First Women's Bank and Trust Company (1974–1976), in New York City.

France's national health insurance began to cover contraception advice and devices.

Barbara Ward received the Jawaharlal Nehru Award for international understanding.

National Association of Women Business Owners was founded as a networking and service organization.

Marie Gimbutas published *Goddesses and Gods of Old Europe*.

Rhoda Hendrick Karpatkin became the first woman to serve as executive director of the Consumers Union.

Tennis star Billie Jean King and her husband, Larry King, founded *WomenSports* (originally *Women's Sports and Fitness*), a magazine later published by the Women's Sports Federation.

Phyllis Ackerman was the first woman to provide sports commentary for a professional basketball team, the Indiana Pacers.

Women's Sports Foundation was founded, to encourage women's participation in sports and combat laws and other influences discouraging participation.

Ann Oakley published *Housewife* and *The Sociology of Housework*.

British social scientist Barbara Wootton published *Incomes Policy: An Inquest and a Proposal*.

Jessie Bernard published *The Future of Motherhood*.

Jacquetta Hawkes was editor of the *Atlas of Ancient Archaeology*.

Marguerite Duras and Xavière Gauthier published *Les parleuses*.

b. Monica Seles (1974– ), Serbian-born Hungarian tennis champion, a leading figure in women's tennis in the late 1980s and early 1990s.

d. Florence Hancock (1893–1974), British trade union official who became president of the Trades Union Congress (1947).

d. Karen Gay Silkwood (1946–1974), American atomic worker, who died in a highly suspicious automobile accident while on her way to meet a *New York Times* reporter regarding her allegations of health and safety hazards at a Kerr-McGee plutonium production plant in Oklahoma.

## SCIENCE/TECHNOLOGY/MEDICINE

Eleanor Maccoby and Carol Jacklin published *The Psychology of Sex Differences*, a reanalysis of hundreds of studies investigating gender-based diferences.

William H. Masters and Virginia Johnson published *The Pleasure Bond: A New Look at Sexuality and Commitment*.

Virginia Satir published *Peoplemaking*, on personal rules and behavioral changes.

British aviator Sheila Scott published *Barefoot in the Sky*.

Cosmonaut Valentina Tereshkova became a member of the Soviet Union's Presidium.

d. Virginia Apgar (1909–1974), American physician and anesthesiologist, the first full professor of anesthesiology (1949) at Columbia University, best known for developing the Apgar Score (1952) for evaluation of newborns; later an expert on birth defects. She never married, stating, "It's just that I haven't found a man who can cook."

d. Irmgard Flügge-Lotz (1903–1974), German engineer and mathematician noted for her aeronautical work, basic to the development of automatic flight controls.

d. Olive Clio Hazlett (1890–1974), American mathematician specializing in linear associative algebra; she taught at Mount Holyoke College, then at the University of Illinois.

d. Sylvia May Moore Payne (1880–1974), British psychoanalyst who became chair of directors of the Institute of Psychoanalysis and president of the British Psychoanalytical Society.

d. Adele Davis (1904–1974), American nutrition writer.

## ARTS/LITERATURE

Ellen Burstyn played Alice, winning a best actress Academy Award, opposite Jodie Foster and Kris Kristofferson, in Martin Scorsese's film *Alice Doesn't Live Here Anymore*.

Doris Lessing published the autobiographical *Memoirs of a Survivor*.

Nadezhda Mandelstam published the autobiography *Hope Abandoned*.

Muriel Spark published the novel *The Abbess of Crewe*.

Jan Morris published *Conundrum*, describing her 1972 sex-change operation and process of change from James to Jan Morris.

Iris Murdoch published the novel *The Sacred and Profane Love Machine*.

Fleur Adcock published the poetry collection *The Scenic Route*.

Liv Ullmann starred in a New York production of Henrik Ibsen's *A Doll's House*.

Margaret Atwood published the poetry collection *You Are Happy*.

Nadine Gordimer published the novel *The Conservationist*.

Maya Angelou published the novel *Gather Together in My Name*.

Grace Paley published the short-story collection *Enormous Changes at the Last Minute*.

Dolly Parton composed the song "I Will Always Love You," a hit that Whitney Houston revived in 1992.

Alison Lurie published the novel *The War Between the Tates*.

Carol Channing starred in the title role of *Lorelei*, Jule Styne and Leo Robin's stage musical.

Anne Baxter, Jessica Tandy, and Hume Cronyn starred in *Noël Coward in Two Keys*.

Helen Frankenthaler painted *Savage Breeze*.

Cicely Tyson starred in the fictional television film *The Autobiography of Miss Jane Pittman*, as a former slave.

Elsa Morante published the novel *The Story*.

Julie Harris, Rex Harrison, and Martin Gabel starred in Terence Rattigan's play *In Praise of Love*.

Zoë Caldwell starred opposite Robert Shaw in August Strindberg's *The Dance of Death*.

Kinuyo Tanaka starred as a prostitute in *Sandakan No. 8*.

Shirley Ann Grau published the novel *Evidence of Love*.

Alice Adams published the novel *Families and Survivors*.

Lynn Redgrave starred opposite George Rose in Charles Laurence's play *My Fat Friend*.

Christa Wolf published the short-story collection *Unter den Linden*.

Lucille Ball starred in Gene Saks's film version of the 1966 Broadway musical *Auntie Mame*.

Marjorie Barkentin's play *Ulysses in Nighttown* starred Zero Mostel and Fionnuala Flanagan.

Lynda Benglis showed the sculpture *Victor*.

Margaret Laurence published the novel *The Diviners*.

Oriana Fallaci published the autobiography *Interview with History*.

d. Katharine Cornell (1893–1974), American actress and manager, a leading figure on the American stage from the mid-1920s through the late 1950s.

d. Anne Sexton (1918–1974), American poet whose work explores her private world, often in bitter and ultimately psychotic terms, perhaps prefiguring her suicide.

d. Cora Sandel (1880–1974), Norwegian novelist.

d. Leontine Schlesinger Sagan (1899–1974), Austrian actress and director.

# 1975

## POLITICS/LAW/WAR

Equal Credit Opportunity Act formally prohibited discrimination by United States lenders on the basis of sex, race, ethnic origin, religion, age, marital status, or welfare status, although covert discrimination continued.

Margaret Thatcher became the first woman to lead a major British political party, succeeding Edward Heath as leader of the Conservative Party.

Attorney Margaret Bush Wilson was elected chairman of the board of directors of the National Association for the Advancement of Colored People (NAACP). She was the first African-American woman to hold this position and the second woman, after Mary White Ovington (1919–1932).

British Sex Discrimination Act was enacted, legally banning sex discrimination in a wide range of public and private practices and institutions, and bringing Britain into compliance with European Economic Community guidelines.

In France, divorce laws were liberalized, allowing for divorce by mutual consent, with custody awarded to either parent, though in practice usually the mother. Abortion was provisionally approved, with numerous restrictions; the law later became permanent (1979).

President Gerald R. Ford signed a bill that allowed women to enter the American armed services academies.

The U.S. Supreme Court ruled in *Taylor v. Louisiana* that it was unreasonable to suggest that jury service was a special hardship for all women, a common argument for all-male juries, and that a jury that automatically exempted women violated the Sixth Amendment guaranteeing a defendant a trial by a cross section of the community.

Women won the right to vote and be elected to office in Mozambique and Papua New Guinea.

Indira Gandhi responded to a campaign to remove her because of electoral fraud by declaring a state of emergency, arresting opposition leaders and ruling by decree until her party was defeated (1977).

Angie Brooks-Randolph was Liberia's representative to the United Nations and concurrently ambassador to Cuba (1975–1977).

Carla Hills became U.S. secretary of housing and urban development (1975–1977).

Julie Roy was the first woman known to have won a suit against her psychiatrist becaue he induced her to have sex with him as part of the "therapy."

Centro da Mulher Brasileira (Brazilian Women's Center) was founded.

European Economic Community (EEC) Council of Ministers directive called for equal pay for work of equal value.

Cuba's Family Code attempted to legislate (without marked success) that men and women should share household chores.

Eugenia Charles became a Dominican member of Parliament and an opposition leader (1975–1980).

Lombe Phyllis Chibesakunda became Zambia's ambassador to Japan.

Maria de Lourdes Pintasilgo became Portuguese ambassador to UNESCO (1975–1979).

Portugal's new constitution affirmed sexual equality in marriage, work, and politics and barred sex discrimination.

Winifred Ewing became a member of the European Parliament, representing the Scottish highlands and islands.

Golda Meir published *My Life*.

Yvette Roudy published *La femme en marge*.

d. Barbara Salt (1904–1975), British diplomat whose wide-ranging career took her to many foreign posts, including Moscow, Tel Aviv, Washington, and New York.

d. Dori'a Shafiq (1910–1975), Egyptian feminist and suffragist, founder of the women's rights organization Daughters of the Nile and a key figure in the successful fight for Egyptian women's suffrage.

## RELIGION/EDUCATION/EVERYDAY LIFE

Midge Mackenzie produced the television documentary and accompanying book *Shoulder to Shoulder*, celebrating Britain's late -9th-and early-20th-century militant women's suffrage movement.

Czech national woman's tennis champion (1972–1975) Martina Navratilova defected to the West and went on to become the top-ranked female tennis player in the world.

Susan Brownmiller published *Against Our Will: Men, Women and Rape*.

American economist Alice Rivlin founded and became first director of the Congressional Budget Office (1975–1983), established to help the U.S. Congress evaluate and shape policy on federal income and spending.

Britain's General Synod of the Anglican Church found the ordination of women unobjectionable theologically, but the issue would remain divisive, even after women's ordination was allowed (1993).

International Women's Year was proclaimed by the United Nations, the start of the "Decade for Women" (1975–1985). A worldwide women's rights summer conference convened at Mexico City, but the conference was destroyed by politicians pursuing a myriad of cold war, Middle East, and other political issues, rather than women's rights.

Helen Thomas was the first woman elected president of the White House Correspondents Association and of the Gridiron Club.

Evelyn Reed published *Woman's Evolution*, positing the existence of early matriarchies and taking a straight-line Marxist developmental view of the evolution of human societies.

Fatima Meer was elected president of South Africa's Black Women's Federation, later banned; Meer herself was detained under the Internal Security Act (1976) and barred from travel or political activity.

Mary McGrory became the first woman to win the Pulitzer Prize for commentary.

Junko Tabei became the first woman to reach the top of Mt. Everest, with a male Sherpa guide; she was deputy leader of the all-woman Japanese expedition. Later in 1975, a Tibetan woman, Phanthog, also climbed to the top of Everest.

Chris Evert won the first of her six U.S Open titles (1975–1978; 1980; 1981).

American tennis star Billie Jean King founded the Women's Professional Softball League.

Barbara Herman became the first female cantor in Reform Judaism.

Kathleen Nolan was elected the first woman president of the Screen Actors Guild, running as an independent.

Reporters Robin Herman and Marcelle St. Cyr were allowed into the male players' locker rooms after a Montreal hockey game; the players' wives later caused women to be barred from the locker rooms.

Mother Teresa published the autobiographical *Gift from God.*

Ms. Foundation for Women Inc. was founded by *Ms.* magazine as a tax-exempt educational and charitable organization to provide direct aid and advisory services to women's projects.

*Signs: Journal of Women in Culture and Society* began publication, becoming a leading American women's studies scholarly journal.

Women's International Network was founded, as an international information and support group for women in developing countries.

Juanita Morris Kreps published *Sex, Age and Work.*

British cultural historian Frances Yates published *Shakespeare's Last Plays.*

Jessie Bernard published *Women, Wives, Mothers.*

Sylvia Porter published *Sylvia Porter's Money Book.*

Julia Child published *From Julia Child's Kitchen.*

d. Hannah Arendt (1906–1975), German-American political philosopher and writer, a refugee from Nazi Germany (1933), whose work probed the causes of the political violence, authoritarianism, and mass murder that had dominated the world in her lifetime.

d. Mary Stocks (Baroness Stocks of Kensington and Chelsea, 1891–1975), British educator, long associated with the London Council of Social Service and Westfield College (both from 1938), in the 1950s noted for her appearances on the BBC radio shows *The Brains Trust* and *Any Questions?*

## SCIENCE/TECHNOLOGY/MEDICINE

Federation of Feminist Women's Health Centers (FFWHC) was founded; an umbrella organization for a network of women's health clinics, focusing on reproductive rights and self-help.

Qian Zhangying became Chinese minister of water conservancy and electric power (1975–1979; 1984–1988).

Rachel Fuller Brown received the Pioneer Chemist Award of the American Institute of Chemists, their first to a woman, "for pioneering the discovery of the fungal antibiotic nystatin, which is an important help to physicians and a boon to mankind."

Jane C. Wright was honored by the American Association for Cancer Research for her research in clinical cancer chemotherapy.

Elizabeth Dexter Hay became chair of the department of anatomy and cellular biology at the Harvard Medical School (1975–1993), where she had taught since 1960.

d. Alice Evans (1881–1975), American microbiologist who discovered brucellosis (undulant fever) and its cure: pasteurization of milk. She was the first woman to be president of the Society of American Bacteriologists (1928).

d. Elizabeth Lee Hazen (1885–1975), American microbiologist and mycologist, codeveloper of the fungicide nystatin (1949).

d. Marguerite Catherine Perey (1909–1975), French physicist, discoverer of francium (1939), the first female member of the Académie des Sciences (1962). Like Marie Curie, with whom she had worked (from 1929), she died of complications from exposure to radiation.

d. Grace Arabell Goldsmith (1904–1975), American physician, nutritionist, and educator noted for her work on vitamin-deficiency diseases.

### ARTS/LITERATURE

Katharine Hepburn starred opposite John Wayne in Stuart Millar's offbeat Western *Rooster Cogburn* and opposite Laurence Olivier in George Cukor's television film *Love Among the Ruins*, based on the 1953 Evelyn Waugh novel.

Isabelle Adjani starred opposite Bruce Robinson in François Truffaut's film *The Story of Adele H.*

Louise Fletcher starred opposite Jack Nicholson in *One Flew over the Cuckoo's Nest*, winning a best actress Academy Award.

Joan Micklin Silver directed the turn-of-the-century East Side Jewish immigrant film *Hester Street*, starring Stephen Keats and Carol Kane.

Donna McKechnie starred opposite Robert LuPone in Michael Bennett's stage musical *A Chorus Line*, which would run for 15 years.

Ellen Burstyn starred opposite Charles Grodin in Bernard Slade's stage comedy *Same Time, Next Year*.

Faye Dunaway starred opposite Robert Redford in Sydney Pollack's film thriller *Three Days of the Condor*.

Gwen Verdon, Jerry Orbach, and Chita Rivera starred in *Chicago*, John Kander and Fred Ebb's Broadway musical.

Julie Christie, Warren Beatty, and Goldie Hawn starred in Hal Ashby's film *Shampoo*.

Margaret Drabble published the novel *The Realms of Gold*.

Kay Boyle published the novel *The Underground Woman*.

Ruth Prawer Jhabvala published the India-set novel *Heat and Dust*.

Louise Nevelson created the sculpture *Transparent Horizon*.

Marguerite Duras directed and wrote the film *India Song*.

Margarethe von Trotta cowrote and codirected the film *The Lost Honour of Katharina Blum*.

Barbra Streisand again starred as Fanny Brice in Herbert Ross's film musical *Funny Lady*, a sequel to *Funny Girl* (1968).

Denise Levertov published the poetry collections *Here and Now* and *The Freeing of the Dust*.

Maggie Smith starred opposite Brian Bedford in Noël Coward's *Private Lives*.

Maxine Kumin published the poetry collection *House, Bridge, Fountain, Gate*.

Deborah Kerr starred opposite Frank Langella in Edward Albee's play *Seascape*.

Nikki Giovanni published the poetry collection *The Women and the Men*.

Anita Desai published the novel *Where Shall We Go This Summer*.

Elisabeth Lutyens composed and wrote the libretto for *The Goldfish Bowl*.

Lynda Benglis showed the sculpture *Bravo 2*.

Rita Moreno starred opposite Jack Weston in Terrence McNally's play *The Ritz*.

Erica Jong published the poetry collection *Loveroot*.

Sheila Hicks showed the sculpture *Communications Labyrinth*.

d. Josephine Baker (1906–1975), American singer, dancer, and actress, resident in France from 1925, who became a major European star in cabaret, musical theater, and films.

d. (Jocelyn) Barbara Hepworth (1903–1975), British sculptor, from the early 1930s a leader of Britain's abstract sculpture movement and a major figure in 20th-century sculpture.

d. Susan Hayward (Edythe Marrener, 1918–1975), American dramatic film star, who died of cancer, like so many others in the film *The Conqueror* (1956) who were exposed to massive atomic test–generated radiation while filming on location downwind of the Nevada Test Site (1954).

d. Pamela Brown (1917–1975), British actress, in leads on the London and New York stages from the early 1940s.

d. Elizabeth Taylor (Elizabeth Coles, 1912–1975), British novelist and short story writer.

d. Marie Lohr (1890–1975), Australian actress, for more than six decades a leading figure on the London stage.

# 1976

## POLITICS/LAW/WAR

The U.S. Military Academy at West Point, New York; the U.S. Naval Academy at Annapolis, Maryland; the U.S. Air Force Academy at Colorado Springs, Colorado; and the U.S. Coast Guard Academy at New London, Connecticut, admitted their first women, under the 1975 law directing them to do so; women had been admitted to the Merchant Marine Academy earlier (1974).

Barbara Jordan made a national reputation as a speaker when she gave one of the two keynote addresses to the Democratic National Convention, the first ever given by a woman to a major party's national presidential convention.

Mairead Corrigan, Betty Williams, and Ciaran McKeaun founded the Northern Ireland Peace Movement. Corrigan and Williams shared the 1976 Nobel Peace Prize.

Federal Republic of (Western) Germany's Federal Constitutional Court ruled unconstitutional the 1974 law liberalizing abortion, which was then allowed only under certain conditions, as when the mother's health was in danger, after a rape, or when the child was physically handicapped.

Françoise Giroud became France's secretary of culture (1975–1976).

In *Planned Parenthood v. Danforth*, the U.S. Supreme Court struck down a law that required a married woman to get her husband's consent before getting an abortion.

Jiang Qing and three others were arrested and later tried and convicted of attempting to take power by coup in China, as the "Gang of Four," turning China, at least for a time, toward more moderate policies.

Isabelita Perón was deposed by coup and imprisoned (1976–1981).

Nguyen Thi Binh became Vietnam's minister of education.

President Gerald Ford appointed Republican political organizer Anne Armstrong ambassador to Great Britain (1976–1977).

Susan Estrich became the first woman to be president of the prestigious *Harvard Law Review*; she later became a law professor at Harvard.

Yelena Bonner was a founder of the Helsinki Human Rights Group in what was then the Soviet Union.

Britain's Parliament passed the Domestic Violence Act and the Sex Offenses Amendment Act, though marital rape was not recognized.

Australia's Family Law Act provided for no-fault divorce.

Shirley Temple Black was appointed chief of protocol by U.S. President Gerald Ford.

Under new laws in India, divorce was allowed among Hindus after a year's legal separation; other religious groups in India were already able to obtain divorces, family law varying in India for the different religious groups.

Alva Myrdal published *The Game of Disarmament*.

Louise Weiss published the autobiographical *Tempête sur l'occident 1945–1975*.

Juliet Mitchell and Ann Oakley edited the essay collection *The Rights and Wrongs of Women*.

Madeleine Albright published *The Role of the Press in Political Change: Czechoslovakia 1968*.

d. Bertha Lutz (1899–1976), Brazilian zoologist and feminist, founder and president of the Brazilian Federation for the Advancement of Women (1922), a prime mover in achieving women's suffrage, and a key figure in the establishment of the United Nations Commission on the Status of Women.

d. Ulrike Meinhof (1934–1976), German anarchist-terrorist, a leader of the Baader-Meinhof Group; captured in 1972 and on trial in 1976, she was found dead in her cell, allegedly having committed suicide (as, allegedly, would Andreas Baader and two other imprisoned group members in 1977).

### RELIGION/EDUCATION/EVERYDAY LIFE

Barbara Walters became the first woman coanchor to an American network evening news program, on ABC, partnered with Harry Reasoner (1976–1978). She also began her occasional series of *Barbara Walters Specials.*

Krystyna Chojnowska-Liskiewicz sailed solo around the world in her yacht *Mazurek* (March 1976–March 1978), writing about her trip in the 1979 book *Pierwsza dook ola Swiata* (*The First One Round the World*).

British sailor Clare Francis, who had previously crossed the Atlantic singlehanded, became the only one of four women (out of 125 entrants) to complete the Royal Western Singlehanded Transatlantic Race, setting a women's record of 29 days, from Falmouth to Newport, Rhode Island.

Hélène Ahrweiler was elected president of the Sorbonne (1976–1981), the first woman so honored in the university's history.

Irina Rodnina and Aleksander Zaitsev won the pairs figure-skating Olympic gold medal; it was her second successive gold medal in the event; she won the first with a different partner.

Merlin Stone published *When God Was a Woman*, positing the existence of early matriarchies worshipping a Great Goddess.

Tennis star Billie Jean King was named *Time* magazine's Woman of the Year.

United Nations Development Fund for Women was organized; originally named the Voluntary Fund for the United Nations Decade for Women, it aimed to help women in the developing world.

Britain's first rape crisis center was established in North London.

Barbara Ward and René Dubos published *The Home of Man.*

Billie Jean King founded the World Team Tennis League.

Betty Friedan published *It Changed My Life: Writings on the Women's Movement.*

International Center for Research on Women (ICRW) was founded, focusing on the status and future of women in developing countries.

Audrey P. Beck became the first woman to serve as president of the American Society of Planning Officials.

Del Martin published *Battered Wives.*

Betsy Warrior published the *Battered Women's Directory.*

Eva Figes published *Tragedy and Social Evolution.*

International Women's Tribune Centre was founded, as an information and support center for those working on women's issues in many countries.

Pauline Frederick acted as moderator for the presidential campaign debate between Jimmy Carter and Gerald Ford.

The first "woman's house" for battered women was established in Germany, in West Berlin.

Phyllis Chesler and Emily Jane Goodman published *Women, Money, and Power.*

Kitty O'Neil was the first woman to become a member of Hollywood's Stunts Unlimited.

Rosemary Ruether published *Christology and Feminism.*

British philosopher Mary Warnock published *Imagination.*

Evelyne Sullerot published *Histoire et mythologie de l'amour.*

Jacquetta Hawkes was editor of the *Atlas of Early Man.*

Xavière Gauthier founded the periodical *Sorcières.*

Juanita Morris Kreps published *Women and the American Economy.*

### SCIENCE/TECHNOLOGY/MEDICINE

Virginia Satir founded the AVANTA network in Menlo Park, California, as a training center for teachers of family therapy; she had earlier founded the Esalen Institute "human-growth" center.

National Women's Health Network was founded, to press for increased women's influence on the American health-care system and to foster education and research on women's health issues.

Nuclear physicist Rosalyn Yalow won the Albert Lasker Basic Medical Research Award, the first woman so honored.

Roberta A. Kankus was the first woman licensed to be a nuclear power plant operator.

British astronomer Margaret Burbidge, long teaching in America, became the first woman to serve as president of the American Astronomical Society (1976–1978).

Elizabeth Dexter Hay was elected president of the American Society for Cell Biology (1976–1977).

Margaret Mead became president of the American Association for the Advancement of Science.

German-Scottish geneticist Charlotte Auerbach published *Mutation Research*.

Marine biologist Sylvia Earle Mead received the NOGI award from the Underwater Society of America.

Suzanne Kennedy became the first female veterinarian at the National Zoological Park in Washington, D.C.

### ARTS/LITERATURE

Faye Dunaway starred opposite William Holden and Peter Finch in Sidney Lumet's film *Network*, winning a best actress Academy Award.

Julie Harris starred as poet Emily Dickinson in William Luce's play *The Belle of Amherst*.

Jane Alexander starred as Eleanor Roosevelt opposite Edward Herrmann as Franklin D. Roosevelt in the television film *Eleanor and Franklin* and the sequel, *Eleanor and Franklin: The White House Years* (1977).

Lillian Hellman published the autobiographical *Scoundrel Time*, focusing on the McCarthy years.

Jodie Foster as a teenage prostitute starred opposite Robert De Niro in Martin Scorsese's film *Taxi Driver*.

Marge Piercy published the novel *Woman on the Edge of Time*.

Jeanne Moreau wrote, directed, and starred in *Lumière*.

Alice Walker published the novel *Meridian*.

Maya Angelou published the novel *Singin' and Swingin' and Gettin' Merry like Christmas*.

Anne Rice published the novel *Interview with the Vampire*.

Sarah Caldwell conducted *La traviata* at New York's Metropolitan Opera, becoming the Met's first female opera conductor.

Trazana Beverley starred in Ntozake Shange's play *For Colored Girls Who Have Considered Suicide When the Rainbow Is Enuf*.

Audre Lorde published the poetry collection *Coal*.

Sarah Miles starred opposite Kris Kristofferson in Lewis John Carlino's film *The Sailor Who Fell from Grace with the Sea*, based on Yukio Mishima's 1965 novel.

Delores Hall starred opposite William Hardy Jr. in the African-American musical *Your Arms Too Short to Box with God*.

Elizabeth Bishop published the ten-poem cycle *Geography III*.

Josephine Premice and Avon Long starred in the African-American musical *Bubbling Brown Sugar*.

Joyce Carol Oates published the novel *The Childwold*.

Judy Collins issued the album *Bread and Roses*.

Katharine Hepburn starred in Enid Bagnold's play *A Matter of Gravity*.

Lee Krasner painted *Present Perfect*.

Margaret Atwood published the novel *Lady Oracle*.

Sissy Spacek and Piper Laurie starred in Brian De Palma's *Carrie*.

Twyla Tharp choreographed the ballet *Push Comes to Shove*.

Vanessa Redgrave starred opposite Pat Hingle in Henrik Ibsen's play *The Lady from the Sea*.

Barbra Streisand starred as a rising young actress opposite Kris Kristofferson as her husband, on his way down, in Frank Pierson's remake of *A Star Is Born*.

Lina Wertmuller directed *Seven Beauties*.

Colleen Dewhurst starred opposite Ben Gazzara in Edward Albee's play *Who's Afraid of Virginia Woolf?*

Diane Ladd starred in Preston Jones's play *A Texas Trilogy*.

Lynn Redgrave, John Heffernan, and Charles Durning starred in *Knock Knock*, Jules Feiffer's stage comedy.

Beverly Sills published *Bubbles: A Self-Portrait*.

Caryl Churchill published the plays *Light Shining in Buckinghamshire* and *Vinegar Tom*.

Elizabeth Taylor's novel *Blaming* was published posthumously.

Christa Wolf published the autobiographical novel *A Model Childhood*, set in Nazi Germany.

Hannah Weinstein produced and directed the film *Greased Lightning*.

Isabel Bishop painted *Recess #3*.

Jackie Winsor showed the sculpture *Cement Piece, #1 Rope*.

Nelly Kaplan wrote and directed the film *Néa*.

Mary Wigman's *The Language of Dance* was published posthumously.

Robin Morgan published the poetry collection *Lady of the Beasts*.

Vivian Fine composed *Meeting for Equal Rights 1866*, on feminist themes.

Ada Louise Huxtable published *Kicked a Building Lately?*

d. Agatha Christie (1890–1976), British novelist, short story writer, and playwright, best known for her mystery novels, beginning with *The Mysterious Affair at Styles* (1910).

d. (Agnes) Sybil Thorndike (1882–1976), British actress, a leading player on the English-speaking stage, perhaps most notably in Shaw and Shakespeare, also appearing in several films.

d. Lotte Lehmann (1888–1976), German soprano, a leading opera and lieder singer of the inter-war period, especially of Richard Strauss, whose *Arabella* she created; in the United States after fleeing the Nazis in 1938.

d. Lily Pons (Alice Josephine Pons, 1898–1976), French soprano, an international opera star for almost three decades following her 1931 Metropolitan Opera debut in *Lucia de Lammermoor* (1931).

d. Imogen Cunningham (1883–1976), American photographer, best known for her nature studies and photos of notables.

d. Edith (Mary) Evans (1888–1976), a leading British stage actress from the early 1920s, who later also appeared in several films.

d. Rosalind Russell (1908–1976), American stage and screen star from the late 1930s through the early 1960s.

## 1977

### POLITICS/LAW/WAR

Patricia Roberts Harris was appointed secretary of housing and urban development by President Jimmy Carter.

Eleanor Smeal became president of the National Organization for Women (1977–1982).

Antinuclear activist Helen Caldicott was a prime founder of the Society of Physicians for Social Responsibility, later its president (1978–1983).

Beverly Gwinn Kelley and Debra Lee Wilson were the first two women to serve with men on an American military vessel.

Chen Muhua became China's minister of economic relations with foreign countries.

Congressional Caucus for Women's Issues was founded as a bipartisan organization of women in Congress, to foster research and legislation on women's legal, health, and economic issues.

Eleanor Holmes Norton became the first woman to chair the Equal Employment Opportunity Commission.

In *Beal v. Doe*, the U.S. Supreme Court ruled that states were not required to use public funds to pay for abortions.

Brazil legalized divorce, originally with a limit of one divorce in a lifetime, a restriction later dropped (1988).

Portugal established the Commission on the Status of Women, its first director being Maria de Lourdes Pintasilgo.

Barbara Mikulski began the first of her five terms in the U.S. House of Representatives (1977–1987).

Eva Kolstad chaired Norway's Government Council on the Equal Status of Men and Women (1977–1978).

Simone Veil became France's minister of health and social security.

Winnie Mandela was sentenced to internal exile for her freedom movement activities and temporarily almost silenced by the South African government.

Gaositwe Keagakwa Tibe Chiepe became Botswana's minister of mineral resources (1977–1984).

Hillary Rodham Clinton founded Arkansas Advocates for Children and Families.

Janna Lambine became the first female pilot in the U.S. Coast Guard.

Kang Keqing became a member of the Communist Party Central Committee (1977–1985).

Lombe Phyllis Chibesakunda became Zambia's high commissioner to Britain (1977–1981).

Miswo Enoki formed the Woman's Party, which fared poorly in the Japanese general elections.

Alva Myrdal published *War, Weapons and Everyday Violence*.

Phyllis Schlafly published *The Power of the Positive Woman*.

d. Alice Paul (1885–1977), American social worker, lawyer, and militant women's rights leader, founder of the National Woman's Party (1916) and framer of the first Equal Rights Amendment proposal (1923).

d. Fannie Lou Hamer (1917–1977), African-American civil rights leader and politician, a former sharecropper who became a leader of the civil rights movement in the 1960s and cofounded the Mississippi Freedom Democratic Party, which charged racist selection practices and disputed the seating of the regular Mississippi Democratic Party delegates at the 1964 and 1968 Democratic National Conventions, and was seated in the offical delegation in 1972.

## RELIGION/EDUCATION/EVERYDAY LIFE

Juanita Morris Kreps was appointed secretary of commerce (1977–1979) by President Jimmy Carter, the first woman in the post and only the fifth woman to serve in the U.S. cabinet.

Beverly Messenger-Harris was the first woman to be rector (in charge of the parish) in the American Episcopal church.

British sailor Clare Francis was the first woman to captain a boat in the Whitbread Round the World Event (1977–1978), coming in fifth with her crew of 11.

Women were first admitted to the Rhodes Scholars program, after passage of Britain's 1975 Sex Discrimination Act.

Saudi Arabia's Princess Misha was convicted of adultery and sentenced to death by stoning; her execution was secretly filmed and widely publicized in the television documentary *Death of a Princess*.

---

The claim that American women are downtrodden and unfairly treated is the fraud of the century.

— Phyllis Schlafly, as quoted in *Ms.* magazine (March 1974)

Shirley Muldowney became the first woman to win the National Hot Rod Association's Winston World Championship of drag racing; she would later win twice more (1980; 1981), the first person to do so.

Janet Guthrie was the first woman to drive in the Indianapolis 500 automobile race.

National Association of Cuban-American Women was founded, as a service organization for Cuban-American and other Spanish-speaking women adjusting to American life.

Organization of Chinese American Women was founded, to help the integration of Chinese-American women into American society.

Mary Driscoll Shane was the first woman to do play-by-play broadcasts of major league baseball, covering Chicago White Sox games.

Mary Maynard was the first woman to become president of a United Mine Workers of America local, in Run Creek, West Virginia.

Eva Shain was the first American woman to judge a world heavyweight boxing match.

Tina Schifano Ramos Hills became the first woman to serve as president of the Inter-American Press Association.

Women and Foundations/Corporate Philanthropy was founded, to help gain funds for women's programs and to enhance the position of women in philanthropic organizations.

Women's Research and Education Institute was founded, as an information clearinghouse and report generator on women's issues.

British philosopher and educator Mary Warnock published *Schools of Thought*.

Xavière Gauthier published *Dire nos sexualités—contre la sexologie*.

### SCIENCE/TECHNOLOGY/MEDICINE

Nuclear physicist Rosalyn Yalow won the Nobel Prize for medicine for her work (with Solomon Berson) in developing radioimmunoassay (1950), using radioactive particles to measure minute amounts of substances such as hormones or vitamins in blood and body tissues. Discussing discrimination against women, Yalow said: "The world cannot afford the loss of the talents of half its people if we are to solve the many problems which beset us."

British gynecologist-obstetrician Patrick Steptoe developed the technology of in vitro (literally, in glass) fertilization; the first baby conceived and born by this innovation was Louise Brown (1978).

American aviator Jacqueline Cochran successfully campaigned in Congress for veterans' benefits for World War II's Women's Air Force Service Pilots (WASPs). She herself had remained in the Air Force Reserve until 1970, retiring with the rank of colonel.

Ann Moore, a young Colorado mother, patented the Snugli baby carrier, inspired by carriers she had seen used in West Africa while serving there in the Peace Corps.

Pamela Chelgren became the first female field-operations officer in the U.S. National Oceanic and Atmospheric Administration Corps, serving on the hydrographic survey ship USS *Pierre*.

Miriam Rothschild hosted the first International Flea Conference, at her family's Northamptonshire home.

Sheila Kitzinger published *Education and Counseling for Childbirth*.

The U.S. Department of Defense named its new high-level computer programming language ADA in honor of Ada Byron, countess of Lovelace, a pioneer of early computing machines.

American geneticist Ruth Sager was elected to the National Academy of Sciences.

British zoologist Sidnie Manton published *Arthropods*.

Cynthia Irwin-Williams became the second woman to serve as president of the Society of American Archaeology (1977–1979), after Marie Wormington (1958).

d. Myra Adele Logan (1908–1977), American physician, the first woman to perform open heart surgery, and the first African-American woman elected a fellow of the American College of Surgeons.

d. Katherine Stinson (Otero) (1891–1977), American aviator, the first woman to loop an aircraft and the first pilot to fly nonstop from San Diego to San Francisco.

## ARTS/LITERATURE

Andrea McArdle played the title role opposite Dorothy Loudon and Reid Shelton in *Annie*, Martin Charnin and Charles Strouse's stage musical based on the "Little Orphan Annie" comic strip.

Diane Keaton starred opposite Woody Allen in Allen's film *Annie Hall*, winning a best actress Academy Award, and also starred in Richard Brooks's *Looking for Mr. Goodbar*.

Jane Fonda starred as Lillian Hellman opposite Jason Robards as Dashiell Hammett and Vanessa Redgrave in the title role of *Julia*, in Fred Zinneman's film based on Lillian Hellman's 1973 autobiography *Pentimento*.

Margot Fonteyn created the role of Juliet opposite Rudolf Nureyev in Kenneth MacMillan's ballet *Romeo and Juliet*.

Anne Bancroft starred as Israeli premier Golda Meir in William Gibson's biography play *Golda*, and opposite Shirley MacLaine in Herbert Ross's film *The Turning Point*.

Marilyn French published the feminist novel *The Women's Room*.

Toni Morrison published the novel *Song of Solomon*.

Vivian Fine composed *The Women in the Garden*, on feminist themes.

Perry Miller Adato directed the documentaries *Echoes and Silences*, on Carl Sandburg, and *Georgia O'Keeffe*, which brought her a Directors Guild of America award, the first to a woman.

Anita Gillette starred opposite Judd Hirsch in Neil Simon's play *Chapter Two*.

Colleen McCullough published the novel *The Thorn Birds*.

Geraldine Fitzgerald, Lawrence Luckinbill, and Simon Oakland starred in Michael Cristofer's play *The Shadow Box*.

Margaret Drabble published the novel *The Ice Age*.

Jessica Tandy starred opposite Hume Cronyn in D. L. Coburn's play *The Gin Game*.

Carole Bouquet starred opposite Fernando Rey in Luis Buñuel's film *That Obscure Object of Desire*.

Joan Didion published the novel *A Book of Common Prayer*.

Liv Ullmann starred in a New York production of Eugene O'Neill's *Anna Christie*.

Marsha Mason starred opposite Richard Dreyfuss in Herbert Ross's film *The Goodbye Girl*.

Simone Signoret starred in Moshe Mizrachi's film *Madame Rosa*.

Louise Nevelson showed the sculpture *Mrs. N's Place*.

Mary Renault published the novel *The Persian Boy*.

Olivia Manning published *The Danger Tree*, the first novel in her Levant trilogy.

Sylvia Sidney starred in Tennessee Williams's play *Vieux Carré*.

Millicent Martin, Julie McKenzie, and David Kernan starred in the stage musical *Side by Side by Sondheim*.

Lynn Redgrave starred in a New York production of George Bernard Shaw's *St. Joan*.

Susan Sontag published the essays in *On Photography*.

Agnes Martin painted *Untitled No. 11, No. 12*.

Thea Musgrave composed the opera *Mary, Queen of Scots*.

Bette Davis was the first woman to receive the American Film Institute's Life Achievement Award.

Lily Tomlin starred in *Appearing Nightly*, her one-woman show.

Estelle Parsons starred in Roberto Athayde's play *Miss Margarida's Way*.

Anita Desai published the novel *Fire on the Mountain*.

Rosemary Harris, Tovah Feldshuh, and Ellen Burstyn starred in a New York production of Anton Chekhov's *The Three Sisters*.

Priaulx Rainier composed her *Violin Duo*.

Ama Ata Aidoo published the novel *Our Sister Killjoy: Reflections from a Black-eyed Squint*.

Margarethe von Trotta directed the film *The Second Awakening*.

Alice Aycock showed the sculpture *Studies*.

Hortense Calisher published the novel *On Keeping Women*.

Erica Jong published the novel *How to Save Your Own Life*.

Bessie Head published the short-story collection *The Collector of Treasures*.

Audrey Flack painted *Marilyn*.

Bessie Love published the autobiography *From Hollywood with Love*.

Anita Loos published *Cast of Thousands*, on film and the film industry.

d. Maria Callas (Maria Kalogeropolous, 1923–1977), American soprano, a highly emotional opera star who drew great media attention during the 1950s.

d. Joan Crawford (Lucille Fay Le Sueur, 1904–1977), American film star, most notably in such dramas as *Rain* (1932), *Mildred Pierce* (1945), and *Daisy Kenyon* (1947).

d. Anaïs Nin (1903–1977), American diarist, novelist, short story writer, and essayist, whose work often focused on sexual identity and experience.

d. Ethel Waters (1896–1977), African-American singer, comedian, and actress.

d. Kinuyo Tanaka (1910–1977), Japanese actress and director.

d. Grace Mary Williams (1906–1977), Welsh composer.

# 1978

## POLITICS/LAW/WAR

Pregnancy Discrimination Act was passed, prohibiting discrimination against women because of pregnancy, childbirth, or related conditions, in firms of 15 or more employees. It was actually an amendment to Title VII of the 1964 Civil Rights Act and, like it, enforced by the Equal Employment Opportunity Commission (EEOC).

After Violeta Chamorro's husband, Pedro Joaquin Chamorro Cardenal, was murdered in Managua, Nicaragua, she participated in the Sandinista revolution. She later served in the first Sandinista government and then moved into opposition to the developing Sandinista dictatorship, replacing her husband as editor of *La Prensa*.

Abortion was legalized in Italy following strong pressure from feminist groups, including the Unione Donne Italiane (UDI); strong protests persisted, including an unsuccessful repeal referendum (1981).

With passage of the Women's Armed Forces Integration Act, women were integrated into the armed forces; the separate womens' corps, dating from their formation during World War II, were dissolved.

Women won the right to be elected to office in Zimbabwe.

Indira Gandhi split away from India's Congress Party, founded the Indian National Party-Indira, won election to parliament, but was imprisoned when she tried to take her seat.

Aisha Rateb became Egypt's Minister of Foreign Affairs.

California Democrat Dianne Feinstein succeeded to the unexpired term of murdered San Francisco Mayor George Moscone, then winning election to two full mayoral terms (1979–1988).

Lois Gibbs led the campaign to close the toxic chemical dump at Love Canal, in Niagara Falls, New York.

Mary Clarke was promoted to major general, the highest rank up to then held by a woman in the U.S. Army; she had been commander of the Women's Army Corps (WAC), which was dissolved and merged into the Army.

Nancy Landon Kassebaum of Kansas won election to the Senate, becoming the first woman elected senator who was not the wife of a former Congressman.

Chen Muhua became a vice-premier of China.

Janet Reno became the Dade County (Florida) state prosecutor, the first woman in the post, and went on to win five reelections (1978–1993).

Margaret A. Brewer was the first woman to reach the rank of brigadier general in the U.S. Marine Corps.

Simone Veil became France's minister of health and family affairs (1978–1979).

Deng Yingchao became a member of the Chinese Communist Politburo (1978–1985).

Joan Baez was a founder of Humanitas, an international human-rights organization.

South African antiapartheid campaigner Helen Suzman won the United Nations Human Rights Award.

Kang Keqing became president of the All-China Women's Federation.

Women were first permitted to join the White House Honor Guard.

Gisèle Halimi sparked and contributed to the collective work *Le programme commun des femmes*, exploring the main legal, medical, educational, and professional needs of women.

Helen Caldicott published *Nuclear Madness*.

Nazi women's leader Gertrud Scholtz-Klink published the autobiographical *Die Frau im Dritten Reich*.

d. Golda Meir (Golda Meyerson, 1898–1978), Russian-American-Israeli Zionist, for more than four decades an Israeli socialist leader, at cabinet level (from 1949) and as Israeli prime minister (1969–1973); one of the world's most highly visible political leaders.

### RELIGION/EDUCATION/EVERYDAY LIFE

Mary Daly completed her move to spiritual feminism and radical feminist theology, publishing *Gyn/Ecology: The Metaethics of Radical Feminism*.

Hanna Holborn Gray was named president of the University of Chicago, the first woman to head a major American university.

Robin Morgan published the essay collection *Going Too Far: The Personal Chronicles of a Feminist*, in which she espoused "metaphysical feminism," a form of religious belief, and called for the development of a worldwide utopia.

Barbara Tuchman published *A Distant Mirror*.

Mary Michael Simpson became the first ordained woman to preach at Britain's Westminster Abbey; she was the first American Episcopal nun to become ordained as a priest (1977).

Tennis star Martina Navratilova won the first of her record-breaking nine Wimbledon women's singles tennis championships.

Arlene Blum organized and led the American Women's Himalayan Expedition to Annapurna. Two women, Irene Miller and Vera Komarkova, with two sherpas, reached the top; two other women, Vera Watson and Alison Chadwick-Onyszkiewicz, died in a second attempt.

British social scientist Barbara Wootton published *Reflections on Fifty Years Experience* and *Crime and Penal Policy*.

Eirlys Roberts became chair of the Research Institute for Consumer Affairs and the European Economic Community's Environment and Consumer Protection subcommittee.

*Canadian Women's Studies* began publication.

Golfer Nancy Lopez won her first championship as a professional, the Bent Tree Classic, later winning a record five consecutive tournaments and also the the European Ladies tournament.

Julia Child began a new television series featuring American cooking, *Julia Child and Company* (1978–1979), and published an accompanying book by the same title.

Margaret Wade Trophy for the best American woman collegiate basketball player was first offered; the first winner was Carol Blazejowski.

National Coalition Against Domestic Violence was founded, as a network of organizations helping battered women and children.

Jane Cahill Pfeiffer was the first woman to chair NBC's board of directors.

Nancy Hays Teeters was the first woman named a member of the Federal Reserve Bank's board of governors.

Native American women founded Women of All Red Nations (WARN), a coalition built around several key land, education, health, and family issues.

Phyllis Chesler published *About Men*.

Salvation Army leader Catherine Booth, at age 95, received Britain's Guild of Professional Toastmasters' Best Speaker award.

French ethnologist Germaine Tillion published *L'Algérie en 1957: Les ennemis complémentaires.*

Jessie Bernard published *Self-Portrait of a Family.*

Evelyne Sullerot edited *Le fait féminin,* papers from a 1978 colloquium of medical and behavioral scientists.

### SCIENCE/TECHNOLOGY/MEDICINE

Toxic shock syndrome, a rare and sometimes fatal bacterial infection most common in menstruating women, was first recognized. By 1980, at its height, the United States alone had over 800 cases and 69 deaths. Incidence dropped after super-absorbent tampons were taken off the market (1981) and women were warned about misuse of contraceptive sponges (1984).

Sally Ride and five other women became the first female astronaut trainees chosen by NASA (National Aeronautics and Space Administration).

Alla Massevitch became president of the Soviet Union's Section Satellite Tracking for Geodesy.

Conservationist Joy Adamson published her *Autobiography.*

Sheila Kitzinger published her comparative cultural study *Women as Mothers.*

American physicist Mary Beth Stearns published a notable historical overview, "Why Is Iron Magnetic?"

d. Margaret Mead (1901–1978), American anthropologist long associated with the American Museum of Natural History (1926–1945), among the first American women to earn a Ph.D. in anthropology; best known for her *Coming of Age in Samoa* (1928).

d. Kathleen Mary Kenyon (1906–1978), British archaeologist who excavated Jericho (1952–1958).

### ARTS/LITERATURE

Glenda Jackson starred as poet Stevie Smith opposite Mona Washbourne in *Stevie,* Robert Enders's film version of Hugh Whitemore's play.

Ingrid Bergman and Liv Ullmann starred in Ingmar Bergman's film *Autumn Sonata.*

Judy Chicago showed her large construction on feminist themes, *The Dinner Party,* symbolically illustrating many women's achievements.

Jill Clayburgh starred in the title role opposite Alan Bates and Michael Murphy in Paul Mazursky's *An Unmarried Woman.*

Susan Sontag published the essay collection *Illness as Metaphor.*

Claudette Colbert starred opposite Rex Harrison in William Douglas Home's play *The Kingfisher.*

Jane Fonda, Jon Voight, and Bruce Dern starred in *Coming Home,* Hal Ashby's film set in the aftermath of the Vietnam War. Fonda won a best actress Academy Award.

Jane Alexander and Henry Fonda starred as Supreme Court justices in Jerome Lawrence and Robert E. Lee's play *First Monday in October.*

Geraldine Page, E. G. Marshall, Maureen Stapleton, and Diane Keaton starred in Woody Allen's film *Interiors.*

Iris Murdoch published the novel *The Sea, the Sea.*

Jacqueline Brookes starred opposite Jay O. Sanders in Sam Shepard's play *Buried Child.*

Elizabeth Taylor starred opposite Len Cariou in Harold Prince's film version of Stephen Sondheim's stage musical *A Little Night Music.*

Joyce Carol Oates published the novel *Son of the Morning.*

Nell Carter starred opposite Andre De Shields in the Broadway musical *Ain't Misbehavin',* a jazz revue based on the work of Fats Waller.

Olivia Newton-John starred opposite John Travolta in Randal Kieser's film version of the 1972 stage musical *Grease.*

Nikki Giovanni published the poetry collection *Cotton Candy on a Rainy Day.*

Olivia Manning published *The Battle Lost and Won,* the second novel in her Levant trilogy.

Aretha Franklin recorded the album *Almighty Fire.*

Carol Hall's stage musical *The Best Little Whorehouse in Texas* starred Carlin Glynn.

Maxine Kumin published the poetry collection *The Retrieval System*.

Glenn Close starred opposite Paxton Whitehead in Paul Giovanni's play *The Crucifer of Blood*.

Madeline Kahn, John Collum, and Kevin Kline starred in *On the Twentieth Century*, Betty Comden and Adolph Green's stage musical.

Adrienne Rich published the poetry collection *The Dream of a Common Language*.

Louise Bourgeois showed the sculpture *Confrontation, Structure III—Three Floors.*

Marian Seldes starred opposite John Wood in Ira Levin's stage thriller *Deathtrap*.

Meryl Streep starred opposite Raul Julia in a New York production of *The Taming of the Shrew.*

The British feminist Women's Press was founded.

Ann Reinking starred in the Broadway musical *Dancin'*, choreographed by Bob Fosse.

Susan Rothenberg painted *For the Light.*

America's first all-woman jazz festival was held, in Kansas City, Missouri.

Audrey Flack painted *Bounty.*

M. M. Kaye published the novel *The Far Pavilions.*

Anita Desai published the novel *Games at Twilight.*

Alice Neel painted *Geoffrey Hendricks and Brian.*

Jennifer Bartlett painted *Summer Lost at Night (for Tom Hess).*

Elizabeth Murray painted *Children Meeting.*

Alice Adams published the novel *Listening to Billie.*

d. Sylvia Townsend Warner (1893–1978), British novelist and short story writer; her novel *Lolly Willowes* was the Book-of-the-Month Club's first main selection.

d. Tamara Platonovna Karsavina (1885–1978), Russian ballerina, a leading dancer of Sergei Diaghilev's Ballets Russes company.

d. Fay Compton (1894–1978), British actress, a leading figure on the London stage from the early 1920s through the 1950s.

d. Phyllis McGinley (1905–1978), American poet, essayist, and children's book writer, whose work was often carried by the *New Yorker.*

d. Ruth Etting (1903–1978), American torch singer.

d. Victoria Ocampo (1890–1978), Argentinian editor and publisher.

## 1979

### POLITICS/LAW/WAR

Conservative Party leader Margaret Thatcher became Britain's first female prime minister.

United Nations Convention on the Elimination of All Forms of Discrimination Against Women was a nonbinding international declaration of principles opposing a wide range of sexual discrimination.

In *Bellotti v. Baird*, the U.S. Supreme Court ruled that teenagers could not be required to obtain a parent's consent before having an abortion unless an alternative was provided, such as obtaining consent from a judge.

Environmentalist Petra Kelly cofounded the Green Party, and soon became a worldwide environmental leader.

Simone Veil became president of the European Parliament (1979–1982).

Barbara Castle became a member of the European Parliament (1979–1989), and leader of the parliament's British Labour Group (1979–1985).

In Japan, the Women's Monument (Onna no Hi) was founded to campaign for women's equal access to government housing, bank loans, social security benefits, and tax reductions.

Jane Byrne was elected mayor of Chicago (1979–1983).

Patricia Roberts Harris was appointed secretary of health, education, and welfare by President Jimmy Carter.

Shirley Mount Hufstedler was named secretary of education in the Carter administration.

Aisha Rateb became Egypt's ambassador to Denmark (1979–1981).

Australia's minimum wage law was extended to cover women.

Beverly Gwinn Kelley became the first woman to command a U.S. Coast Guard vessel at sea.

Harriet Pilpel became general counsel of the American Civil Liberties Union (1979–1986).

Louise Weiss became the oldest member of the European Parliament.

Simone de Beauvoir, Christine Delphy, and Monique Wittig founded the periodical *Questions féministes*.

Wang Guangmei became director of the Foreign Affairs Bureau of the Chinese Academy of Social Sciences.

Yvette Roudy was elected a French deputy to the European Parliament.

Sheila Rowbotham, Hilary Wainwright, and Lynne Segal published *Beyond the Fragments*.

Vijaya Pandit published the autobiographical *The Scope of Happiness*.

## RELIGION/EDUCATION/EVERYDAY LIFE

Mother Teresa received the Nobel Peace Prize, for her worldwide work with the poor.

Barbara Tuchman was the first woman elected president of the American Academy and Institute of Arts and Letters.

Barbara Ward and René Dubos published *Progress for a Small Planet*.

Germaine Greer published *The Obstacle Race: The Fortunes of Women Painters and their Work*.

Nawa El Saadawi published *The Hidden Face of Eve: Women in the Arab World*.

National Center on Women and Family Law was founded to represent poor women and children directly and to serve as a resource and educational center for others working on the same issues; it sponsored the National Battered Women's Law Project.

Barbara Walters became cohost of ABC's *20/20* (1979– ).

Mary Warnock headed the Committee of Enquiry into Human Fertilization (1982–1984), its recommendations outlined in the *Warnock Report*. She also published *Education: A Way Forward*.

Japan's first women's studies program was introduced at Ochanomizu Women's College.

National Committee on Pay Equity was founded as a national coalition seeking pay equity and fighting wage discrimination based on sex and race.

Nancy Lopez published *The Education of a Woman Golfer*.

National Women's Studies Association (NWSA) was founded, holding its first conference.

Phyllis Chesler published *With Child*.

National Displaced Homemakers Network was founded, to help displaced homemakers become financially independent through a wide range of self-help, career-training, and placement programs.

The Oxford-based Christian Women's Information and Resource Service was founded.

Women's International Resource Exchange (WIRE) was founded, as a women's collective focusing on information and advocacy in support of women of the developing world.

Ann Oakley published *Becoming a Mother*.

British cultural historian Frances Yates published her final work, *The Occult Philosophy in the Elizabethan Age*.

d. Anne Loughlin (1894–1979), British trade unionist, a leader in the Tailors and Garment Workers Union from 1915, who became the first woman to serve as president of the Trades Union Congress (1943).

d. Charlemae Rollins (1897–1979), American librarian and author, the first African-American president of the Children's Services Division of the American Library Association, who sought to free children's books from stereotypical portraits of blacks.

d. Armi Ratia (1912–1979), Finnish designer and entrepreneur who co-founded the design firm Marimekko.

## SCIENCE/TECHNOLOGY/MEDICINE

Margaret Rhea Seddon became the first American woman to achieve the rank of astronaut in the National Aeronautics and Space Administration.

Sheila Kitzinger published *Giving Birth: Emotions in Childbirth, Birth at Home, The Experience of Breastfeeding*, and *The Good Birth Guide*.

Josephine Barnes became the British Medical Association's first female president.

Elsie Eaves became the first woman elected as an honorary member of the American Society of Civil Engineers.

Ruth Hubbard edited the books *Women Look at Biology Looking at Women* and *Genes and Gender II*.

d. Cecilia Payne-Gaposchkin (1900–1979), British-American astronomer who pioneered classification of stars by relating their spectral classes to their actual temperatures (1925), playing a key role in opening mainstream astronomy to women.

d. Katherine Burr Blodgett (1898–1979), American physicist who invented nonreflecting glass (1938); a pioneer industrial researcher, long associated with General Electric.

d. Sidnie Milana Manton (1902–1979), British zoologist specializing in crustacean embryology, noted for her beautifully illustrated work.

## ARTS/LITERATURE

Sally Field starred as a Southern textile factory rank-and-file organizer, winning a best actress Academy Award, in Martin Ritt's film *Norma Rae*, opposite Ron Liebman and Beau Bridges.

Angela Lansbury starred opposite Len Cariou in the Stephen Sondheim stage musical *Sweeney Todd, the Demon Barber of Fleet Street*.

Doris Lessing published *Shikasta*, the first novel in her science-fiction series Canopus in Argos.

Fleur Adcock published the poetry collection *The Inner Harbour*.

Jane Fonda, Jack Lemmon, and Michael Douglas starred in James Bridges's nuclear-meltdown film *The China Syndrome*.

Frances Sternhagen starred opposite Tom Aldredge in Ernest Thompson's play *On Golden Pond*.

Lee Remick as Kay Summersby starred opposite Robert Duvall as Dwight D. Eisenhower in the television miniseries *Ike, The War Years*.

Janet Frame published the novel *Living in the Maniototo*.

Liv Ullmann starred in the title role in *I Remember Mama*, Richard Rodgers and Martin Charnin's stage musical.

Patti Lupone starred as Eva Perón in Andrew Lloyd Webber and Tim Rice's bio-musical *Evita*.

Lucie Arnaz starred opposite Robert Klein in *They're Playing Our Song*, Marvin Hamlisch, Carole Bayer Sager, and Neil Simon's Broadway musical.

Meryl Streep starred opposite Dustin Hoffman as the battling New York couple in Robert Benton's film *Kramer vs. Kramer*.

Katharine Hepburn starred opposite Ian Saynor in *The Corn Is Green*, George Cukor's film version of Emlyn Williams's 1938 play.

Nadine Gordimer published the novel *Burger's Daughter*.

Jean Marsh and Tom Conti starred in Brian Clark's play *Whose Life Is It Anyway?*

Joan Didion published the novel *The White Album*.

Muriel Rukeyser published her *Collected Poems*.

Roxanne Hart, Kevin Kline, and Jay O. Sanders starred in Michael Weller's play *Loose Ends*.

Margaret Atwood published the novel *Life Before Man*.

Maya Angelou's 1970 autobiography *I Know Why the Caged Bird Sings* was adapted in a television film, starring Ruby Dee and Diahann Carroll.

Ann Miller and Mickey Rooney starred in *Sugar Babies*, Ralph Allen and Harry Rigby's Broadway musical.

Beverly Sills became director of the New York City Opera.

Alice Adams showed the sculpture *Three Arches*.

Caryl Churchill published the play *Cloud 9*.

Elizabeth Maconchy composed the cantata *Héloïse and Abelard*.

Constance Cummings starred in Arthur Kopit's play *Wings*.

Erica Jong published the poetry collection *At the Edge of the Body*.

Thea Musgrave composed the opera *A Christmas Carol*.

Hilda Doolittle's *End to Torment: A Memoir of Ezra Pound by H. D.* was published posthumously.

Ida Applebroog painted *Sure, I'm Sure*.

Márta Mészarós directed the film *Two Women*.

Susan Rothenberg painted *Pontiac*.

Mia Farrow starred opposite Anthony Perkins in Bernard Slade's play *Romantic Comedy*.

Nelly Kaplan wrote and directed the film *Charles et Lucie*.

d. Cornelia Otis Skinner (1902–1979), American actress, a leading monologist and soloist, who also wrote several light autobiographical works, perhaps most notably *Our Hearts Were Young and Gay* (1942).

d. Mary Pickford (Gladys Marie Smith, 1893–1979), American silent-film star, dubbed "America's Sweetheart."

d. Gracie Fields (Grace Stansfield, 1898–1979), British singer, comedian, and actress, a leading figure in music hall, variety, and radio in the 1920s and 1930s.

d. Jean Rhys (Gwen Williams, 1894–1979), British novelist, whose popular novels of the 1920s and 1930s stressed the financial victimization of women; she found new feminist audiences in the 1960s.

d. Dorothy Arzner (1900–1979), pioneering American film editor, writer, and director.

d. Joan Blondell (1909–1979), American film star, most notably in such films as *Gold Diggers of 1933*, *Gold Diggers of 1937*, and *A Tree Grows in Brooklyn* (1945).

d. Beatrix Lehmann (1903–1979), British actress, a leading figure on the London stage from her appearance in *All God's Chillun Got Wings* (1929).

d. Joyce Irene Grenfell (1910–1979), British mime and monologist, who toured widely in one-woman shows.

d. Elizabeth Bishop (1911–1979), American poet and travel book writer, who emerged as a major literary figure in midcentury.

d. Jean Stafford (1915–1979), American short story writer and novelist, often on themes of adolescent alienation.

d. Juana Morales de Ibarbourou (Juana de America, 1895–1979), Uruguayan poet, whose love poems brought her much popularity.

d. Nadia Boulanger (1887–1979), French music teacher and conductor.

d. Sonia Delaunay (Sophia Terk, 1885–1979), French artist.

d. Peggy Guggenheim (1898–1979), American art collector.

# 1980

## POLITICS/LAW/WAR

Indira Gandhi's Indian National Party-Indira swept the parliamentary elections; she again became prime minister (1980–1984), until her assassination.

The site of the landmark 1848 women's rights convention in Seneca Falls, New York, as well as the home of Elizabeth Cady Stanton, a key organizer, were designated the Women's Rights National Historic Park; the privately funded Women's Hall of Fame is nearby.

In Communist China, revisions in the Marriage Law raised a woman's minimum age for marriage from 18 to 20; women and men alike were pressed to practice birth control, with penalties for those who did not.

In *Harris v. McRae*, the U.S. Supreme Court upheld the constitutionality of the Hyde Amendment, which allowed the states to ban the use of Medicaid to pay for even medically necessary abortions.

Maria de Lourdes Pintasilgo was briefly Portuguese prime minister (1980) and published *Les nouvezux féminismes*.

Jeanne Sauvé, member of Canada's Parliament from 1972, became Speaker of the House of Commons (1980–1984).

Vigdis Finnbogadottir was elected president of Iceland, becoming the first woman to hold the largely honorary position.

Eugenia Charles was elected the Dominican Republic's prime minister, also filling several other cabinet-level positions.

Ruth Bader Ginsburg was appointed to the federal Court of Appeals for the District of Columbia by President Jimmy Carter (1980–1993).

Women won the right to vote and be elected to office in Iraq.

Copenhagen World Conference for Women was a conference meant to report on progress during the United Nations Decade for Women (1975–1985); it fell apart over a wide range of cold war and Middle East political issues.

Sirimavo Bandaranaike was expelled from the Sri Lankan parliament, effectively ending her political career.

Angela Davis published *Women, Race and Class*.

Jennie Lee published the political and personal autobiography *My Life With Nye*.

Bettina Aptheker published *Woman's Legacy: Interpretative Essays in U.S. History*.

d. Edith Clara Summerskill (1901–1980), British doctor, socialist, women's rights advocate, and politician, a leading figure in the Labour Party and in the development of the British social service network.

d. Helen Gahagan Douglas (1900–1980), American actress, a star on Broadway in the 1920s and in films in the 1930s, and a California Democratic congresswoman (1945–1950); she lost her 1950 senatorial campaign to Richard M. Nixon, who implied that she was a Communist.

d. Margaret Hodgson Ballinger (1894–1980), South African historian and liberal pro-integration politician, a founder and first chair of the Liberal Party (1953), who served six terms in the South African Parliament (1937–1959).

d. Margaret Isabel Postgate Cole (1893–1980), British historian, writer, teacher, and socialist, a leading figure in British socialism, with her lifelong partner and husband, G. D. H. Cole.

d. Lilian Ngoyi (1911–1980), South African antiapartheid leader, president of the African National Congress Women's League (1953) and the Federation of South African women (1956).

## RELIGION/EDUCATION/EVERYDAY LIFE

Pat Harper became the first woman in America to be sole anchor of an independent national news program, with her syndicated *USA Tonight*.

National Women's History Project (NWHP) was founded, growing out of a 1978 celebration of International Women's Day (March 8) and its associated National Women's History Week, originally organized by the Commission on the Status of Women in California's Sonoma County. The NWHP provides educational materials and assistance on women's history, since 1981 through its Women's History Resource Service.

Donna Shalala became president of Hunter College (1980–1988).

Elizabeth Janeway published the essay collection *Powers of the Weak*.

Arlene Blum led the Indian-American Women's Expedition to the Gangotri Glacier, near the India-Tibet border; that year Blum published *Annapurna: A Woman's Place* about the 1978 expedition.

Crystal Fields, at age 11, won the Pitch, Hit, and Run Championship, the first girl to win the national baseball playoff open to both sexes.

Australian writer and feminist Dale Spender published *Man Made Language*.

American National Clearinghouse on Marital Rape was founded.

Irina Rodnina and Aleksander Zaitsev again won the pairs figure-skating Olympic gold medals; it was her third successive gold medal in the event, the first title won with a different partner.

Ann Oakley published *Women Confined*.

Jessie Bernard published *The Female World*.

d. Dorothy Day (1897–1980), American journalist, pacifist, socialist, and Catholic reform-movement leader, a cofounder and leading figure in the Catholic Worker Movement (1932) and its publication *Catholic Worker* (1933).

d. Mirabel Topham (?–1980), British racecourse owner, when young (as Hope Hillier) one of the Gaiety Girls at London's Haymarket Theatre, owned by her father. Through marriage, she came to control Aintree racecourse (1936), home of Britain's Grand National.

### SCIENCE/TECHNOLOGY/MEDICINE

Stephanie L. Kwolek received the American Chemical Society Award for creative invention, notably for her invention of Kevlar (1965).

The first American clinic for in vitro (literally, in glass) fertilization opened.

Sheila Kitzinger published *Pregnancy and Childbirth*.

d. Jacqueline Cochran (1910–1980), American aviator, director of the Women's Air Force Service Pilots (WASPs), the first woman to break the sound barrier (1953), later a cosmetics executive.

d. Joy Gessner Adamson (1910–1980), Austrian conservationist and writer, best known for her book *Born Free* (1960).

d. Rachel Fuller Brown (1898–1980), American biochemist, codiscoverer of the antifungal agent nystatin (1949).

d. Bette Clair McMurray Nesmith Graham (1924–1980), American inventor of Liquid Paper.

d. Pearl Luella Kendrick (1890–1980), American microbiologist and physician, codeveloper of the pertussis vaccine (1939).

d. Marion E. Kenworthy (ca. 1891–1980), American psychoanalyst and educator, a pioneer psychiatric social worker, long associated with Columbia University (1921–1957).

### ARTS/LITERATURE

Jane Fonda, Lily Tomlin, and Dolly Parton starred in the feminist office-worker film *Nine to Five*, directed by Colin Higgins.

Phyllis Frelich as the deaf student and John Rubinstein as her teacher starred in Mark Medoff's play *Children of a Lesser God*.

Irina Muravyova, Raisa Ryazonova, and Natalie Vavilova starred as three modern Russian women in Vladimir Menshev's film *Moscow Does Not Believe in Tears*.

Jean M. Auel published the novel *Clan of the Cave Bear*, first of her Earth's Children series, focusing on a strong central woman, Ayla.

Sissy Spacek starred as country singer Loretta Lynn, winning a best actress Academy Award, in Michael Apted's biofilm *Coal Miner's Daughter*.

Vanessa Redgrave, Jane Alexander, Shirley Knight, and Marisa Berenson starred as prisoners forced to play in a women's orchestra at Auschwitz, the German murder camp, in Daniel Mann's television film *Playing for Time*, based on Fania Fenelon's 1979 book.

Amanda Plummer, Elizabeth Ashley, and Geraldine Page starred in John Pielmeier's play *Agnes of God*.

Catherine Deneuve starred in François Truffaut's film *The Last Metro*.

Eudora Welty published the short-story collection *Moon Lake*.

Joyce Carol Oates published the novel *Bellefleur*.

Lee Remick starred as actress Margaret Sullavan in the television film *Haywire*.

Nadine Gordimer published the short-story collection *A Soldier's Embrace*.

Joan Copeland, William Atherton, and John Randolph starred in Arthur Miller's play *The American Clock*.

Olivia Manning published *The Sum of Things*, the third novel in her Levant trilogy.

Rita Dove published the poetry collection *The Yellow House on the Corner*.

Teresa Wright, Maureen O'Sullivan, and Nancy Marchand starred in Paul Osborne's play *Morning's at Seven*.

Wanda Richert, Jerry Orbach, and Tammy Grimes starred in *42nd Street*, the stage musical based on the 1933 film.

Colleen McCullough's 1977 novel *The Thorn Birds* was filmed as a television miniseries, starring Rachel Ward, Barbara Stanwyck, Richard Chamberlain, and Jean Simmons.

Bette Midler starred as a rock singer, modeled on Janis Joplin, in Mark Rydell's film *The Rose*.

Hannah Schygulla starred opposite Gunther Lamprecht in Rainer Werner Fassbinder's film *Berlin Alexanderplatz*.

Ann Beattie published the novel *Falling in Place*.

Priscilla Lopez, Stephen James, and David Garrison starred in *A Day in Hollywood/A Night in the Ukraine*, Dick Vosburgh and Frank Lazarus's Broadway musical.

Shirley Hazzard published the novel *The Transit of Venus*.

Glenn Close starred opposite Jim Dale in *Barnum*, Michael Stewart and Cy Coleman's Broadway musical.

Mariama Ba published her first novel, *So Long a Letter*.

Alice Adams published the novel *Rich Rewards*.

Marguerite Yourcenar became the first woman inducted into the French Academy.

Anita Desai published the novel *Clear Light of Day*.

Barbara Pym published the novel *A Few Green Leaves*.

Hannah Weinstein produced and directed the film *Stir Crazy*.

Nancy Holt showed the sculpture *14 Concrete Discs and Fragments*.

Sylvia Ashton-Warner published the autobiography *I Passed This Way*.

Erica Jong published the novel *Fanny, Being the True History of the Adventures of Fanny Hackabout-Jones*.

d. Barbara Stanwyck (Ruby Stevens, 1907–1980), American actress, a movie star of the 1930s and 1940s and later a television star.

d. Katherine Anne Porter (1890–1980), American short story writer, novelist, and poet, best known for her only novel, *Ship of Fools* (1962).

d. Mae West (1892–1980), American actress and playwright, a star in vaudeville, burlesque, musical theater, and films, often in self-parodying short sexually oriented pieces she had written.

d. Nadezhda Mandelstam (1899–1980), Russian writer, the wife of poet Osip Mandelstam.

d. Muriel Rukeyser (1913–1980), American writer, feminist, and social reformer.

d. Olivia Manning (1908–1980), British writer noted for her Balkan and Levant trilogies.

d. Barbara Pym (Crampton) (1913–1980), British writer.

d. Barbara Loden (1934–1980), American actress and director.

## 1981

### POLITICS/LAW/WAR

Gro Harlem Brundtland became Norway's first female prime minister.

Judge Sandra Day O'Connor became the first woman named a U.S. Supreme Court justice, appointed by President Ronald Reagan.

British female peace activists established the Women's Peace Camp at Greenham Common, at the gates of the Newbury American air base.

Gisèle Halimi was elected as a Socialist deputy to the French National Assembly (1981–1984).

Karin Ahrland became Sweden's minister for public health (1981–1982)

Sarah Kemp Brady became a leading American gun-control advocate after the presidential assassination attempt that partially paralyzed her husband, James Brady, then President Ronald Reagan's press secretary.

Shirley Williams became a founding member of Britain's Social Democratic Party (SDP) and an SDP member of Parliament (1981–1983). She also published *Politics Is for People*.

Yvette Roudy was appointed France's secretary of state for women's rights by François Mitterrand and published *Les métiers et les cajoints*.

Alva Myrdal won the Albert Einstein Peace Prize.

Geraldine Ferraro represented New York in the House of Representatives (1981–1985).

Aisha Rateb became Egypt's ambassador to Germany (1981–1984).

Lois Gibbs founded and led the Citizen's Clearinghouse for Hazardous Wastes, becoming a lobbyist and adviser to communities facing hazardous waste concentrations.

Andrea Dworkin published *Pornography: Men Possessing Women*.

Italy rescinded legal protection for a man's "crime of passion."

Kate Millett published the story of her expulsion from Iran in *Going to Iran*.

Ruth First published *Olive Schreiner*.

d. Ch'ing-ling Soong (Madame Sun Yat-sen, 1892–1981), Chinese political figure who married Sun Yat-sen (1914) and became a key symbolic figure in Communist China. She was the sister of Mei-ling Soong (Madame Chiang Kai-shek) and Chinese financier T. V. Soong.

d. Fusaye Ichikawa (1893–1981), Japanese feminist and politician, a leader of the New Women's Association and the New Japan Women's League, later a member of the Japanese legislature's upper house (1952–1970).

d. Ella Tambussi Grasso (1919–1981), American politician, the first woman elected state governor entirely on her own merits and record (1974), rather than as her husband's successor in office.

d. Dorothy Detzer (Dorothy Detzer Denny, 1893–1981), American pacifist who was longtime executive secretary of the U.S. section of the Women's International League for Peace and Freedom (1924–1946).

### RELIGION/EDUCATION/EVERYDAY LIFE

Betty Friedan published *The Second Stage*, a collection of essays in which she called for equality between women and men in all phases of life and criticized what she felt were negative tendencies in the women's movement, especially in the rejection by some of family relationships.

Jayne Torvill and her partner, Christopher Dean, won the first of their three successive European and world ice-dancing championships (1981–1983).

Diana Spencer married Charles, the Prince of Wales, heir to the British throne, in what was then seen as a "fairy-tale" marriage. As the Princess of Wales, she would remain at the center of media attention, even after their marriage foundered in the 1990s, until her death in 1997.

Guatemalan Quiché Indian peace activist Rigoberta Menchú fled to Mexico, becoming a leader of the Committee for Peasant Unity and a pan–Latin American Indian spokesperson.

Barbara Tuchman published *Practicing History*.

National Women's History Week was proclaimed by Congress.

American radical feminist Jane Alpert published the autobiographical *Growing Up Underground*.

Eva Figes published *Sex and Subterfuge: Women Novelists to 1850*.

Margery Hurst became a member of the Worshipful Company of Marketers, its first woman, and a freeman of the City of London.

National Council for Research on Women was founded as a network of feminist organizations engaged in research, advocacy, and action programs.

*She's Nobody's Baby: American Women in the Twentieth Century*, a television documentary, was produced by *Ms.* magazine.

Melinda Spickard rode three winning horses at Churchill Downs, setting a women's one-day record.

Ann Oakley published *Subject Women*.

d. Barbara Ward (Baroness Jackson of Lodsworth, 1914–1981), British economist and writer, long at Harvard (1957–1968) and Columbia (1968–1973) universities, then with the International Institute for Environment and Development (1973–1981); noted for her writings, the best known being those with René Dubos.

d. Constance Applebee (1883–1981), British hockey player who introduced field hockey to the United States (1901); longtime sports director of Bryn Mawr (1904–1928).

## SCIENCE/TECHNOLOGY/MEDICINE

National Black Women's Health Project was founded, as a self-help and advocacy organization for African-American women.

British astronomer Margaret Burbidge, long resident in America, became president of the American Association for the Advancement of Science.

Elizabeth Dexter Hay was elected president of the American Association of Anatomists (1981–1982).

Doris Malkin Curtis became the first woman to serve as president of the American Geological Institute.

## ARTS/LITERATURE

Katharine Hepburn starred with father and daughter Henry and Jane Fonda in Mark Rydell's film *On Golden Pond*, winning a best actress Academy Award. She also starred opposite Dorothy Loudon in Ernest Thompson's play *The West Side Waltz*.

Diane Keaton as Louise Bryant starred opposite Warren Beatty as John Reed in Beatty's film *Reds*, set before and during the Russian Revolution.

Jacqueline Bisset and Candice Bergen starred as the lifelong friends in *Rich and Famous*, George Cukor's remake of *Old Acquaintance*.

Lauren Bacall starred in the title role of *Woman of the Year*, Fred Ebb and John Kander's stage musical, based on the 1942 film.

Sally Field starred opposite Paul Newman in Sydney Pollack's film *Absence of Malice*.

Margaret Atwood published the novel *Bodily Harm*.

Toni Morrison published the novel *Tar Baby*.

Beth Henley's play *Crimes of the Heart* starred Mary Beth Hurt and Mia Dillon.

Meryl Streep starred opposite Jeremy Irons in Karel Reisz's film *The French Lieutenant's Woman*.

Maya Angelou published the novel *The Heart of Woman*.

Anita Brookner published the novel *A Start in Life*.

Aretha Franklin recorded the album *Love All the Hurt Away*.

National Museum of Women in the Arts was founded, with Wilhelmina Cole Holladay as president of its board of directors; it opened in Washington, D.C., in 1987.

Linda Ronstadt, Kevin Kline, and Estelle Parsons starred in the Gilbert and Sullivan classic *The Pirates of Penzance*.

Jessica Lange starred opposite Jack Nicholson in Bob Rafelson's remake of *The Postman Always Rings Twice*, based on James M. Cain's 1934 novel.

Louise Nevelson created the sculptures *Moon-Star III* and *Moon-Star Zag XIII*.

Mary Renault published the novel *Funeral Games*.

*Mary Chesnut's Civil War* was published, C. Vann Woodward's edition of some Confederate-era diaries.

Zhang Jie published the novel *Leaden Winds*.

Margarethe von Trotta directed the film *Marianne and Juliannne*.

Agnieszka Holland directed the film *A Woman Alone*.

Joanne Woodward starred in the title role of George Bernard Shaw's play *Candida*.

Ingrid Bergman published her *Autobiography*.

Elizabeth Taylor, Maureen Stapleton, and Tom Aldredge starred in Lillian Hellman's play *The Little Foxes*.

Bessie Head published *Serowe: Village of the Rain Wind*.

d. Lotte Lenya (Karoline Blamauer, 1898–1981), Austrian actress and singer, the original Jenny of *The Threepenny Opera*.

d. Anita Loos (1893–1981), American novelist, screenwriter, and playwright, who wrote hundreds of light screenplays starting in 1912 as a writer for D. W. Griffith.

d. Natalie Wood (Natasha Gurdin, 1938–1981), American actress who appeared as a child in films in the 1940s and emerged as an adult star in the mid-1950s, in such films as *Rebel Without a Cause* (1955) and *West Side Story* (1961).

d. Lydia Vasilievna Lopokova (1892–1981), Russian ballerina and actress who danced with Sergei Diaghilev's Ballets Russes company and, after marrying economist John Maynard Keynes, appeared in ballet and theater in Britain.

d. Brenda Colvin (1897–1981), British landscape architect who became president of the British Institute of Landscape Architects (1951).

d. Edith Head (1907–1981), a leading Hollywood costumer who won eight Academy Awards during the course of her long career.

d. Enid Bagnold (1889–1981), British playwright and novelist, best known for her play *The Chalk Garden* (1955).

d. Jessie Matthews (1907–1981), British actress, singer, and dancer, a musical theater and film star of the 1920s and 1930s, most notably in *Evergreen* (1930).

d. Rosa Ponselle (1897–1981), American soprano, long a fixture at the Metropolitan Opera.

d. Lotte Reiniger (1899–1981), German animated-film maker.

d. Mariama Ba (1929–1981), Senegalese writer.

## 1982

### Politics/Law/War

The Equal Rights Amendment failed to win the 38 states necessary for its ratification, with time running out on June 30, 1982. The National Organization of Women and other pro-ERA groups continued to press for passage of an Equal Rights Amendment, but the massive campaign that began in 1972 was over. Anti-ERA forces, notably Phyllis Schlafly's Stop-ERA and Eagle Forum organizations, had prevailed, though many individual states passed their own equal-rights laws.

Alva Reimer Myrdal and Alfonso García Robles shared the Nobel Peace Prize.

Agatha Barbara became president of the Republic of Malta.

Gertrud Sigurdsen became Sweden's minister for public health.

Madeleine Albright became research professor of international affairs and director of Women in Foreign Service at Georgetown University's School of Foreign Service (1982–1992).

California liberal Democrat Barbara Boxer won the first of her five congressional terms.

Anna-Greta Leijon became Sweden's minister of labor (1982–1987).

Chen Muhua became China's minister of foreign trade.

Christine Ama Ata Aidoo became Ghana's secretary of education.

France's national health insurance began to cover abortions.

Ann Richards was elected to the first of her two terms as Texas state treasurer.

d. Marthe Betenfeld Ricard (1889–1982), French feminist and politician, a much-decorated spy for France during World War I and a Resistance leader during World War II.

d. Margery Corbett Ashby (1882–1982), English feminist, suffragist, and pacifist, for more than four decades a key figure in the International Alliance of Women.

d. Ruth First (1925–1982), South African Communist Party (CP) and African National Congress (ANC) activist, editor, and writer, wife of CP and ANC leader Joe Slovo; she was killed by a letter bomb.

### RELIGION/EDUCATION/EVERYDAY LIFE

Israel's two main federations of kibbutzes (collective communities) established a Department for the Advancement of the Equality Between the Sexes, to deal with the persistent problem of unequal sexual division of labor.

Erin Pizzey and Jeffrey Shapiro published *Prone to Violence*, on domestic violence.

Hélène Ahrweiler became chancellor of the Universities of Paris.

North American Chicana women, mostly academics, founded Mujeres Activas en Letras y Cambio Social (MALCS).

Robin Morgan published *The Anatomy of Freedom*.

Helen Gurley Brown published *Having It All*.

d. Frances Amelia Yates (1899–1982), British cultural historian, long associated with the Warburg Institute (1941–1967).

d. Helen Merrell Lynd (1896–1982), American sociologist, best known for coauthoring *Middletown* (1929) and *Middletown in Transition* (1937).

### SCIENCE/TECHNOLOGY/MEDICINE

Qian Zhangying became Chinese minister of power (1982–1984).

Russian astronomer Alla Massevitch became deputy general-secretary of UNISPACE.

Ruth Hubbard edited the book *Biological Woman—The Convenient Myth*.

d. Helene Deutsch (1884–1982), Polish-American psychoanalyist, a Freudian disciple focusing on the psychology of women, director of the Vienna Psychoanalytic Institute (1925–1933).

d. Anna Freud (1895–1982), Austrian-British psychoanalyst, a specialist in childhood behavior; Sigmund Freud's youngest daughter, secretary, companion, and student.

d. Helena (Rosa) Lowenfeld Wright (1888–1982), British physician and birth control campaigner, a founder of the National Birth Control Council (1930).

d. Jean Gardner Batten (1909–1982), New Zealand aviator who set several early solo flight records.

### ARTS/LITERATURE

Alice Walker published her Pulitzer Prize–winning novel *The Color Purple*.

Meryl Streep played the title role in Alan J. Pakula's *Sophie's Choice*, winning a best actress Academy Award as a postwar concentration camp survivor who had emigrated to the United States, based on William Styron's 1979 novel.

Isabel Allende published the novel *The House of the Spirits*.

Jessica Tandy starred opposite Hume Cronyn in *Foxfire*, the play by Susan Cooper, Jonathan Holtzman, and Cronyn.

Julie Andrews starred as a male impersonator opposite Robert Preston as her homosexual manager and friend, and James Garner as her almost-gangster lover in Blake Edwards's film-comedy-with-music *Victor/Victoria*.

The Vietnam Veterans Memorial, created by Maya Lin, opened in Washington, D.C.

Anne Tyler published the novel *Dinner at the Homesick Restaurant*.

Barbara Pym's novel *An Unsuitable Attachment* was published posthumously.

Cher starred opposite Sandy Dennis in Ed Graczyk's play *Come Back to the 5 & Dime, Jimmy Dean, Jimmy Dean*.

Anita Brookner published the novel *Providence*.

Marge Piercy published the poetry collection *Circles in the Water*.

Ellen Taaffe Zwilich composed her first symphony, *Three Movements for Orchestra*; she would become the first woman to win the Pulitzer Prize for music (1983).

Denise Levertov published the poetry collection *Candles in Babylon*.

Harriet Andersson starred opposite Erland Josephson in Ingmar Bergman's film *Fanny and Alexander*.

Mary Oliver published her Pulitzer Prize–winning poetry collection *American Primitive*.

Shelley Long starred opposite Ted Danson (1982–1987) in the long-running television situation-comedy series *Cheers*.

Audre Lorde published *Chosen Poems Old and New*.

Faye Dunaway starred in William Alfred's play *The Curse of an Aching Heart*.

Janet Jackson issued her first album, *Janet Jackson*.

Gail Godwin published the novel *A Mother and Two Daughters*.

Louise Bourgeois showed the sculpture *Femme Couteau*.

Gloria Naylor published the novel *The Women of Brewster Place*.

Susan Sarandon starred in William Mastrosimone's play *Extremities*.

Jean M. Auel published the novel *The Valley of Horses*.

Sigourney Weaver, Linda Hunt (playing a man), and Mel Gibson starred in *The Year of Living Dangerously*, Peter Weir's film set in Indonesia during government-organized massacres.

Judith Ivey starred in Nell Dunn's play *Steaming*.

Sissy Spacek and Jack Lemmon starred in the Constantin Costa-Gavras film *Missing*, a political thriller set in Chile under the dictatorship.

Zoë Caldwell and Judith Anderson starred in the play *Medea*.

Tyne Daly and Sharon Gless starred as a trailblazing female detective team in the long-running television series *Cagney and Lacey*.(1982–1989).

Caryl Churchill published the play *Top Girls*.

Bobbie Ann Mason published *Shiloh and Other Stories*.

Debra Winger starred opposite Richard Gere in Taylor Hackford's film *An Officer and a Gentleman*.

Indian actress Rekha starred in the film *Umrao Jaan*.

Janet Baker published the autobiography *Full Circle*.

Claire Bloom published *Limelight and After: The Education of an Actress*.

Maeve Binchy published the novel *Light a Penny Candle*.

Shirley Conran published the novel *Lace*.

d. Ingrid Bergman (1915–1982), Swedish actress, who became a major international film star in *Casablanca* (1942), was blacklisted in Hollywood during the McCarthy period after leaving her husband for Roberto Rossellini, and came back to win a best actress Academy Award for *Anastasia* (1956).

d. Grace Kelly (1928–1982), American actress, who became a Hollywood star in the 1950s, in such films as *The Country Girl* (1954) and *High Society* (1956), before retiring to marry Prince Rainier III of Monaco.

d. (Edith) Ngaio Marsh (1899–1982), New Zealand mystery writer and theater producer, creator of fictional Scotland Yard detective Roderick Alleyn.

d. Ayn Rand (1905–1982), Russian-American novelist and philosopher, exponent of Objectivist philosophy, stressing the desirability of rational self-interest as a basis of human behavior.

d. Celia Johnson (1908–1982), British actress, a leading figure on the British stage for more than four decades; also a star in several 1940s films, including *Brief Encounter* (1945).

d. Djuna Barnes (1892–1982), American writer, long resident in Paris, much of whose work deals with lesbian themes.

d. Cathleen Nesbitt (1888–1982), British actress, whose long career in the British and American theaters spanned more than seven decades.

d. Babette Deutsch (1895–1982), American poet, essayist, and social reformer.

d. Maria Jeritza (1887–1982), Czech soprano, a leading singer at Vienna Staatsoper and the Metropolitan Opera.

d. Helena Niemirowska Syrkius (1900–1982), Polish architect, with her husband, Simon Syrkius, a leading modernist during the interwar period.

d. Marie Rambert (Cyvia Rambam, 1888–1982), British choreographer and ballet director.

# 1983

## POLITICS/LAW/WAR

After the assassination of her husband, Philippine opposition leader Benigno Aquino, by agents of Ferdinand Marcos's dictatorship, Corazon Aquino replaced him as head of the Liberal Party, beginning the run-up to the Philippine Revolution (1986).

Jeanne Sauvé became the first woman to serve as governor general of Canada.

Petra Kelly and Bastian became Green Party representatives in the West German parliament (1983–1990).

Elizabeth Hanford Dole served as U.S. secretary of transportation (1983–1987).

Hillary Rodham Clinton chaired the Arkansas Education Standards Committee (1983–1984).

Notsikelelo Albertina Sisulu became Transvaal president of the United Democratic Front (1983– ).

France's Law of Professional Equality prohibited sex discrimination in employment and mandated affirmative action programs in hiring and training.

Sheila Rowbotham published *Dreams and Dilemmas.*

Wu Wenying became Chinese minister of the Textile Industry (1983–1993).

Madeleine Albright published *Poland: The Role of the Press in Political Change.*

Ruth First's *Black Gold: The Mozambiquan Miner* was posthumously published.

d. Louise Weiss (1893–1983), French writer, editor, film director, and feminist, a leading suffragist during the 1930s, founder of the feminist group La Femme Nouvelle, and ultimately the oldest member of the European Parliament.

## RELIGION/EDUCATION/EVERYDAY LIFE

Tennis star Martina Navratilova won the first of her four U.S. Open championships (1983, 1984, 1986, 1987).

Gloria Steinem published the essay collection *Outrageous Acts and Other Rebellions.*

Alice Rivlin became director of economic studies at the Brookings Institution (1983–1987).

Rigoberta Menchú published her autobiography *I, Rigoberta Menchú: An Indian Woman in Guatemala.*

Association for Intercollegiate Athletics for Women (AIAW) was disbanded, as women's sports were merged into the National Collegiate Athletic Association; in the same period, many previously separate men's and women's athletics departments were merged, with women often losing jobs in the process.

Dora Russell published *The Religion of the Machine Age*, an attack on the social damage caused by technology, a book begun in the 1930s.

The last surviving member of the Woman's Commonwealth, Martha McWhirter Scheble, died; the Commonwealth was dissolved, and its property transfered to the Washington City Orphan Asylum.

Rosemary Ruether published *Sexism and God Talk.*

## SCIENCE/TECHNOLOGY/MEDICINE

American geneticist Barbara McClintock won the Nobel Prize for physiology or medicine for her work on the transposition of genetic fragments.

Sally Ride became the first American woman in space (June 18), when she blasted off in Space Shuttle 7 as flight engineer.

Dian Fossey's *Gorillas in the Mist*, about her work with mountain gorillas in east-central Africa, was published; it was the basis for the movie of the same name.

Chinese physicist Xie Xide became president of Fudan University, with which she had been associated since 1952, except during the Cultural Revolution.

Marie Wormington received the Distinguished Service Award of the Society of American Archaeology.

Mary Leakey published *Africa's Vanishing Art: The Rock Paintings of Tanzania.*

Ruth Hubbard edited the book *Women's Nature: Rationalizations of Inequality.*

d. Dorothy Russell (1895–1983), Australia-born British pathologist long associated with London Medical College (1946–1960), noted for her work on diseases of the brain.

d. Elsie Eaves (1890–1983), American civil engineer, the first woman to be a member of the American Society of Civil Engineers (1927).

## ARTS/LITERATURE

Shirley MacLaine, Debra Winger, and Jack Nicholson starred in *Terms of Endearment,* James L. Brooks's film based on the 1975 Larry McMurtry novel. MacLaine won a best actress Academy Award.

Julie Christie starred as a modern Western woman visiting India, and Greta Scacchi as her grandmother in an earlier, parallel story, in James Ivory's film *Heat and Dust,* screenplay by Ruth Prawer Jhabvala based on her own 1975 novel.

Marsha Norman's play *'Night, Mother* starred Kathy Bates and Anne Pitoniak.

Angela Lansbury starred in the title role of Jerry Herman's musical version of *Mame.*

Meryl Streep starred as whistle-blowing nuclear plant worker Karen Silkwood opposite Kurt Russell and Cher in Mike Nichols's film *Silkwood.*

Elizabeth Bishop's *The Complete Poems, 1927–1979* was posthumously published.

Sally Field starred opposite John Malkovich in Robert Benton's film *Places in the Heart,* winning a best actress Academy Award.

Janet Frame published the first volume of her autobiography, *To the Island;* it would be followed by *An Angel at My Table* (1983) and *The Envoy from Mirror City* (1985).

Carolyn Kizer published her Pulitzer Prize–winning poetry collection *Yin.*

Dorothy Loudon starred opposite Brian Murray in Michael Frayn's play *Noises Off.*

Elizabeth Taylor starred opposite Richard Burton in Noël Coward's play *Private Lives.*

Fleur Adcock published her *Selected Poems.*

Jessica Tandy played Amanda Wingfield in a New York production of Tennessee Williams's *The Glass Menagerie.*

Margaret Atwood published the novels *Murder in the Dark* and *Unearthing Suite.*

Joan Didion published the novel *Salvador.*

Madonna issued the albums *Madonna* and *Like a Virgin.*

Kamala Markandaya published the novel *Shalimar.*

Twiggy starred opposite Tommy Tune in *My One and Only,* George and Ira Gershwin's stage musical.

Rita Dove published the poetry collection *Museum.*

Caryl Churchill published the play *Fen.*

Amy Clampitt published the poetry collection *The Kingfisher.*

Paula Gunn Allen published *The Woman Who Owned the Shadows,* on Native American themes.

Cynthia Ozick published the novel *The Cannibal Galaxy.*

Jenny Holzer created her performance artwork *Unex Sign #1.*

Colleen Dewhurst, Jason Robards, and Elizabeth Wilson starred in *You Can't Take It with You,* Moss Hart and George S. Kaufman's play.

Sarah Caldwell became artistic director of the New Opera Company of Israel.

Clare Francis published the novel *Night Sky.*

Erica Jong published the poetry collection *Ordinary Miracles.*

Jennifer Bartlett painted *Shadow.*

Lynne Sharon Schwartz published the novel *Disturbances in the Field.*

d. Gloria Swanson (Gloria Josephine Swenson, 1897–1983), American silent-film star, who made an extraordinary comeback as a has-been silent-screen star in Billy Wilder's classic 1950 film *Sunset Boulevard*.

d. Lynn Fontanne (Lillie Louise Fontanne, 1887–1983), British-American actress, stage partner and wife of Alfred Lunt.

d. Mary Renault (Mary Challans, 1905–1983), British historical novelist, popular from the mid-1950s, many of whose works are set in the classical Greek world.

d. Norma Shearer (Edith Norma Shearer, 1900–1983), Canadian actress, a Hollywood star of the 1920s and 1930s, in silents and sound films, as in *The Divorcee* (1930), *The Barretts of Wimpole Street* (1934), and *Marie Antoinette* (1938).

d. Rebecca West (Cicely Isabel Fairfield, 1892–1983), British writer, a journalist, political essayist, and literary critic.

d. Bryher (Annie Winifred Ellerman, 1894–1983), British writer and editor.

d. Gabrielle Roy (1909–1983), French-Canadian writer, best known for her first novel, *The Tin Flute* (1947).

d. (Agnes) Elisabeth Lutyens (1906–1983), British composer, daughter of the architect Edwin Lutyens.

d. (Margaret) Storm Jameson (1891–1983), British writer.

d. Anna Reiling Seghers (Netty Radvanyi, 1900–1983), German writer.

## 1984

### POLITICS/LAW/WAR

Democratic Congresswoman Geraldine Ferraro became the first woman to be a major-party vice-presidential candidate, running with Walter Mondale in an unsuccessful presidential campaign.

Baby Doe law (part of the Child Abuse Amendments of 1984) established the right of all U.S. infants to medical care, including those with major disabilities, deformities, or disorders, regardless of such factors as insurance and ability to pay, outlawing the common practice of allowing such infants to die untreated or inadequately treated.

U.S. Supreme Court ruled, in relation to *Grove City College v. Bell*, that Title IX (covering equality in education) applied only to programs receiving federal funds, throwing many women's academic and athletic programs into limbo.

Esther Peterson became the representative of the International Organization of Consumers Unions at the United Nations Economic and Social Council, helping gain passage of the *Guidelines for Consumer Protection*.

Retirement Equity Act, passed by the U.S. Congress, was designed to protect women's insurance and pension rights, notably in case they are widowed or divorced.

Australia passed a Sex Discrimination Act.

Sharon Pratt Dixon (later Kelly) became the first African-American and first woman to be treasurer of the Democratic National Committee.

Gaositwe Keagakwa Tibe Chiepe became Botswana's minister of external affairs.

Notsikelelo Albertina Sisulu was president of the Federation of South African Women.

Winifred Ewing became a vice-president of the European Democratic Alliance.

Marian Anderson received the first Eleanor Roosevelt Human Rights Award.

Bella Abzug published *Gender Gap: Bella Abzug's Guide to Political Power for Women*.

Daw Aung San Suu Kyi published *Aung San*, a biography of her father.

Helen Caldicott published *Missile Envy*.

Petra Kelly published *Fighting for Hope*.

Barbara Bush published *C. Fred's Story*.

d. Indira Gandhi (1917–1984), Indian politician who became prime minister (1966), the daughter of Jawaharlal Nehru; assassinated by two Sikh members of her personal guard, she was succeeded by her son, Rajiv Gandhi.

d. Soia Mentschikoff (1915–1984), American lawyer, the first woman to teach at Harvard Law School (1946) and at Chicago Law School (1950), later dean of the University of Miami Law School (1974–1982) and the first woman to be president of the Association of American Law Schools.

### RELIGION/EDUCATION/EVERYDAY LIFE

Jayne Torvill and her partner, Christopher Dean, won the gold medal for ice dancing at the Sarajevo Olympics, receiving a perfect 6 points across the board for their revolutionary ice dance interpretation of Ravel's *Bolero*; having shattered ice dancing's "ballroom" image, they turned professional, returning to the Olympics in 1994 with less success.

Pat Harper became coanchor of the evening television news on New York's WNBC (1984–1990). She and Chuck Scarborough won five successive Emmy awards (1984–1989) for outstanding single newscast, and she personally won an Emmy for her reporting on New York's homeless people.

Brenda Dean was elected general secretary of Britain's Society of Graphical and Allied Trades union (Sogat).

Robin Morgan published *Sisterhood Is Global.*

Ann Oakley published the autobiographical *Taking It like a Woman.*

Germaine Greer published *Sex and Destiny: The Politics of Human Fertility.*

Mary Daly published *Pure Lust.*

Flora Solomon published *Baku to Baker Street: The Memoirs of Flora Solomon.*

Helene Hahn became the first female business and legal head of an American motion-picture studio, Walt Disney Pictures.

d. Lila Acheson Wallace (1889–1984), American publisher and patron, who cofounded the *Reader's Digest* (1921); later known for her art collection and her wide-ranging philanthropies, most notably at the Metropolitan Museum of Art, Monet's house and gardens at Giverny, and the Abu Simbel temples on the Nile.

d. Flora Benenson Solomon (1895–1984), Russian-born British social reformer who developed innovative workers' benefits programs, later advising the British and Israeli governments; her son, Peter Benenson, founded Amnesty International.

d. Virginia Lacy Jones (1912–1984), African-American librarian long associated with the Atlanta University School of Library Science.

### SCIENCE/TECHNOLOGY/MEDICINE

Cathleen Synge Morzwetz became the first woman to direct the prestigious Courant Institute of Mathematical Sciences, which she had joined in 1952.

Mary Leakey published the autobiographical work *Disclosing the Past.*

### ARTS/LITERATURE

Anita Brookner published her Booker Prize--winning novel *Hotel du Lac.*

Eudora Welty published the autobiographical *One Writer's Beginnings.*

Alison Lurie published her Pulitzer Prize–winning novel *Foreign Affairs.*

Helen Hooven Santmyer published the novel *"...And Ladies of the Club."*

Angela Lansbury as mystery writer Jessica Fletcher starred in the long-running television series *Murder, She Wrote* (1984–1997).

Marguerite Duras published the autobiographical novel *L'Amant* (*The Lover*), which won the Prix Goncourt.

Louise Erdrich published the novel *Love Medicine.*

*Whoopi Goldberg* was the actress's one-woman Broadway show.

Fay Weldon published the novel *Lives and Loves of a She-Devil*, later adapted for television and film.

Bernadette Peters starred opposite Mandy Patinkin in *Sunday in the Park with George*, Stephen Sondheim's stage musical.

Glenn Close starred opposite Jeremy Irons in Tom Stoppard's play *The Real Thing*.

Marge Piercy published the novel *Fly away Home*.

Joan Didion published the novel *Democracy*.

Maryann Plunkett starred opposite Robert Lindsay in *Me and My Girl*, Noel Gay's musical.

Theresa Merritt starred opposite Charles Dutton in August Wilson's play *Ma Rainey's Black Bottom*.

Meryl Streep and Jack Nicholson starred as 1930s alcoholics in *Ironweed*, Hector Babenco's film version of William Kennedy's 1983 novel.

Irene Worth, Stockard Channing, and Jeff Daniels starred in A. R. Gurney's play *The Golden Age*.

Anita Desai published the novel *In Custody*.

*The Private Mary Chesnut* was published, C. Vann Woodward's edition of more of Chesnut's Civil War–era diaries.

Barbara Pym's autobiography, *A Very Private Eye*, was published posthumously.

Shirley MacLaine mounted her one-woman show *Shirley MacLaine on Broadway*.

Caryl Churchill published the play *Softcops*.

Ellen Gilchrist published the novel *Victory over Japan*.

Irina Ratushinskaya published *Poems*.

Jayne Anne Phillips published the novel *Machine Dreams*.

Liza Minnelli and Chita Rivera starred in Fred Ebb and John Kander's stage musical *The Rink*.

Tess Gallagher published the poetry collection *Willingly*.

Erica Jong published the novel *Parachutes & Kisses*.

Marisol showed the sculpture *Self-Portrait Looking at the Last Supper*.

Toshiko Akiyoshi founded her New York Jazz Orchestra.

Sharon Olds published the poetry collection *The Dead and the Living*.

d. Lillian Hellman (1905–1984), a leading American playwright for three decades.

d. Ethel Merman (Ethel Zimmerman, 1909–1984), American singer and actress, a musical theater star from her appearance in *Girl Crazy* (1930), who also starred in several film musicals.

d. Alberta Hunter (1895–1984), American blues singer, popular from the 1920s through the 1950s, who made a fully successful comeback in 1977.

d. Germaine Tailleferre (1892–1984), French composer, in the 1920s a member of the group of French modernist composers who became known as Les Six.

d. Flora Robson (1902–1984), British actress who emerged as a stage star in the early 1930s and was a leading figure on the British stage through the late 1960s; she also appeared in several films.

d. Lee Krasner (1908–1984), American painter who emerged as a foremost abstract expressionist in the 1950s; she was the wife of Jackson Pollock.

d. Sylvia Ashton-Warner (1905–1984), New Zealand teacher and writer.

d. Alice Neel (1900–1984), American painter, best known for her late portraits of notables.

d. Sawako Arivoshi (1921–1984), Japanese novelist.

d. Hannah Dormer Weinstein (1911–1984), American filmmaker and political activist.

d. Helen Kalvak (1901–1984), Canadian Inuit artist.

## 1985

### POLITICS/LAW/WAR

As worldwide condemnation of apartheid grew, Winnie Mandela began to successfully defy continuing South African government efforts to silence her. That year she also published *A Part of My Soul Went with Him*, about her imprisoned husband, Nelson Mandela.

EMILY's List was founded as a fund-raising organization for Democratic women running for office at the federal and state levels, EMILY being an acronym for Early Money Is Like Yeast—it makes the dough rise.

Eugenia Charles was reelected to a second term as the Dominican Republic's prime minister.

Gertrud Sigurdsen became Sweden's minister for health and social affairs.

Melina Mercouri became Greece's minister of culture and sciences.

Wilma P. Mankiller was the first woman elected to be chief of a major Native American people, the Cherokee.

Penny Harrington became the first woman named police chief of a major American city, Portland, Oregon.

Brazil established its first federal commission on women, Conselho Nacional dos Direitos da Mulher.

Gail Reals became a brigadier general in the U.S. Marine Corps, the first woman to reach that rank in open competition with men; she was later in charge of the Quantico, Virginia, base (1988–1990).

Canada passed a no-fault divorce law and established a National Strategy for Child Care.

New Zealand established a Ministry of Women's Affairs.

Chen Muhua became president of the People's Bank of China.

Portuguese feminist Maria de Lourdes Pintasilgo published *Dimensâo de mudança*.

Susan Estrich published *Dangerous Offenders: The Elusive Target of Justice*.

Yvette Roudy published *A cause d'elles*.

Shirley Williams published *A Job to Live*.

d. Patricia Roberts Harris (1924–1985), American lawyer and politician, secretary of housing and urban development (1977–1979), then of health, education, and welfare (1979–1980).

## RELIGION/EDUCATION/EVERYDAY LIFE

Nairobi Forward-Looking Strategies for the Advancement of Women, a women's rights priorities list, was adopted by the world conference, held in Nairobi, Kenya, that ended the United Nations Decade for Women (1975–1985). Although adopted by the U.N., the list was only advisory, and unenforced.

Lynette Woodard became the first woman to play regularly on a previously all-male professional basketball team, joining the Harlem Globetrotters (1985–1987).

Amy Eilberg became the first American Conservative female rabbi.

Nancy Lopez won the Ladies Professional Golf Association title and set a winnings record with over $416,000.

Libby Riddles became the first woman ever to win Alaska's Iditarod Trail Sled Dog Race.

Mujeres Activas en Letras y Cambio Social (MALCS) began publishing *Trabajos Monograficos: Studies in Chicana/Latina Research*.

British philosopher Mary Warnock published *A Question of Life*.

Marilyn French published the essay collection *Beyond Power: On Women, Men and Morals*.

Tennis star Martina Navratilova published *Martina: Autobiography*, written with George Vecsey.

d. Laura Ashley (1925–1985), British designer and entrepreneur who developed a chain of over 200 shops, selling clothes and fabrics based on 18th- and 19th-century fabric designs.

d. Susanne Knauth Langer (1895–1985), American philosopher long associated with Connecticut College (from 1945), whose work focused on linguistic analysis and aesthetics.

d. Ida Pruitt (1888–1985), American missionary and educator working in China from 1912.

## SCIENCE/TECHNOLOGY/MEDICINE

Elena Ceausescu published *The Science and Progress of Society*.

Mary Leakey published the autobiographical work *Lasting Impressions*.

d. Dian Fossey (1932–1985), American primatologist noted for her studies of mountain gorillas in east-central Africa, described in *Gorillas in the Mist* (1983); local people called her *Nyiramachabelli*, ("the old lady who lives in the forest without a man").

d. Julia Bowman Robinson (1919–1985), American mathematician, the first woman to be president of the American Mathematical Society and the first female mathematician elected to the National Academy of Sciences.

## ARTS/LITERATURE

Helena Bonham Carter, Maggie Smith, Denholm Elliott, and Daniel Day-Lewis starred in James Ivory's film version of E. M. Forster's 1908 novel *A Room with a View*, screenplay by Ruth Prawer Jhabvala.

Meryl Streep as Isak Dinesen starred opposite Robert Redford in Sydney Pollack's film *Out of Africa*, based on Dinesen's 1937 book.

Geraldine Page starred in Peter Masterson's film *The Trip to Bountiful*, winning a best actress Academy Award.

Judy Chicago showed her painting *The Birth Project*, on feminist themes.

Lily Tomlin did a solo starring turn in Jane Wagner's play *The Search for Signs of Intelligent Life in the Universe*.

Glenda Jackson starred as Nina Leeds opposite Edward Petherbridge and Tom Aldredge in Eugene O'Neill's *Strange Interlude*.

Meg Tilly, Jane Fonda, and Anne Bancroft starred in *Agnes of God*, Norman Jewison's film version of John Pielmeier's 1980 play.

Whoopi Goldberg starred in *The Color Purple*, Steven Spielberg's film version of Alice Walker's 1982 novel.

Gloria Naylor published the novel *Linden Hills*.

Linda Hunt starred in Wallace Shawn's play *Aunt Dan and Lemon*.

Grace Paley published the short-story collection *Later the Same Day*.

Norma Aleandro, Analia Castro, and Hector Alterio starred in *The Official Story*, Luis Penzo's film set in Argentina during the period of military dictatorship.

Rita Dove published the short-story collection *Fifth Sunday*.

Barbara Pym's novel *Crampton Hodnet* was published posthumously.

Glenn Close, Sam Waterston, and Mary Beth Hurt starred in Michael Frayn's play *Benefactors*.

Carolyn Chute published the novel *The Beans of Egypt, Maine*.

Anne Tyler published the novel *The Accidental Tourist*.

Bobbie Ann Mason published the novel *In Country*.

Jean M. Auel published the novel *The Mammoth Hunters*.

Christa Wolf published the novel *Kassandra*.

Betty Buckley starred opposite George Rose in *The Mystery of Edwin Drood*, Rupert Holmes's play based on Charles Dickens's unfinished novel.

Claudette Colbert, Rex Harrison, Lynn Redgrave, and Jeremy Brett starred in Frederick Lonsdale's play *Aren't We All?*

Jan Morris published the essay collection *Among the Cities*.

Agnes Varda wrote and directed the film *Vagabonde*.

Clare Francis published the novel *Red Crystal*.

June Jordan published the poetry collection *Living Room*.

Oprah Winfrey began her long-running television talk show (1985– ).

Thea Musgrave composed the opera *Harriet, the Woman Called Moses*, based on the life of Harriet Tubman.

Rosemary Harris starred opposite Patrick McGoohan in Hugh Whitemore's play *Pack of Lies*.

Sherrie Levine began her *Golden Knots* series of paintings.

Maeve Binchy published the novel *Echoes*.

Stockard Channing starred opposite Jim Dale in Peter Nichols's play *Joe Egg*.

Twyla Tharp directed a stage musical adaptation of the film *Singin' in the Rain*.

d. Simone Signoret (Simone Kaminker, 1921–1985), French actress who emerged as an international film star in the 1950s in such films as *La Ronde* (1950), *Diabolique* (1955), and *Room at the Top* (1958).

d. Elsa Morante (1912–1985), Italian novelist, poet, and essayist; wife of writer Alberto Moravia.

d. Louise Brooks (1906–1985), American actress and dancer, a notably independent woman who starred in Germany in two G. W. Pabst film classics: *Pandora's Box* (1928) and *Diary of a Lost Girl* (1929).

d. Anne Baxter (1923–1985), American stage and screen actress, notably in the title role of *All About Eve* (1950).

# 1986

## POLITICS/LAW/WAR

Corazon Aquino led the Philippine Revolution, ousting dictator Ferdinand Marcos and taking power as democratically elected president of the Philippine Rebublic.

Benazir Bhutto returned to Pakistan from exile, as head of the Pakistan People's Party, and quickly became head of the opposition to the military government.

Takako Doi was elected leader of Japan's Socialist Party, becoming the first female to lead a major party in Japan.

Gro Harlem Brundtland began a second term as Norway's first woman prime minister.

In Sweden, Anita Gradin became minister for foreign trade (1986–1991) and Anna-Greta Leijon minister of sexual equality (1986–1987).

Japan's Equal Employment Opportunity Law was passed, though its benefits to women were limited by lack of enforcement.

Australia passed an Affirmative Action (Equal Employment Opportunity for Women) Act.

Nora Astorga became Nicaragua's ambassador to the United Nations.

d. Alva Reimer Myrdal (1902–1986), Swedish teacher, social-welfare worker, politician, diplomat, and peace activist, who shared the 1982 Nobel Peace Prize with Alfonso García Robles. Her husband and often collaborator was Gunnar Myrdal.

d. Annabelle Rankin (1908–1986), Australian politician and diplomat.

## RELIGION/EDUCATION/EVERYDAY LIFE

Eva Burrows was chosen to be chief commander of the Salvation Army, the first woman to be international head since Evangeline Booth.

Alice Rivlin became president of the American Economic Association.

American basketball player Nancy Lieberman played in a men's professional league game, with the Springfield Fame in the U.S. Basketball League.

Gloria Steinem published *Marilyn*, on the life and death of Marilyn Monroe.

Ann Oakley published *Telling the Truth about Jerusalem*.

Estée Lauder published her autobiographical *A Success Story*.

d. Simone de Beauvoir (1908–1986), French philosopher, writer, and feminist, whose book *The Second Sex* (1949) made her one of the central figures in the worldwide mid-20th-century women's movement. With Albert Camus and Jean-Paul Sartre, her companion, she was also at the center of the Existentialist movement.

d. Beryl Markham (1902–1986), Anglo-Kenyan aviator and race-horse trainer best known for her book *West with the Night* (1942), the first woman to fly the Atlantic from east to west (1936).

d. Dora (Winifred) Black Russell (1894–1986), British social reformer and educator, cofounder of Beacon Hill School (1927), long active on feminism, birth control, pacifism, sexual equality, and civil-liberties concerns.

d. Joan Violet Maurice Robinson (1903–1986), British economist long associated with Cambridge (1931–1971); one of the "Cambridge group" of economists, influenced by John Maynard Keynes and Richard Kahn.

d. Julie Palau Tullis (1939–1986), British mountaineer, originally serving as sound recordist and filming assistant to Kurt Diemberger; she died in their third attempt on K2, when their return from the summit was delayed by bad weather. That year saw publication of her *Clouds from Both Sides*.

d. Wallis Warfield Simpson, duchess of Windsor (1896–1986), American wife of Britain's King Edward VIII; after succeeding to the throne (1936), he abdicated to marry her (1937), following her second divorce. They then became the duke and duchess of Windsor.

## SCIENCE/TECHNOLOGY/MEDICINE

Computer scientist Grace Hopper retired from the U.S. Navy after 42 years of service with the rank of rear admiral; at her retirement, she was the oldest serving officer in any of the U.S. armed forces.

When the Space Shuttle *Challenger* exploded on takeoff (January 28), all seven people in the crew were killed, including astronaut Judith Resnik and teacher Christa McAuliffe, who would have been the first civilian in space. Sally Ride, the first American woman in space (1983), was a member of the commission investigating the causes of the explosion.

Jeana Yeager and Dick Rutan made the first nonstop round-the-world airplane flight in the tiny *Voyager*, designed so light that they were able to make the 25,012-mile, nine-day voyage without refueling.

Rosalyn Yalow received the Georg Charles de Henesy Nuclear Medicine Pioneer Award.

Barbara Grosz, an expert in natural language processing, a key area of artificial intelligence, became Gordon McKay professor of computer science at Harvard University.

d. Helen Brooke Taussig (1898–1986), American pediatric cardiologist, who first identified the heart defects that led to cyanosis (blue pallor) in blue babies and codeveloped an operation to correct them (1944), and also first warned of dangers from thalidomide (1962).

d. Amalia Coutsouris Fleming (1909?–1986), Constantinople-born Greek physician, a specialist in bacteriology, wife of Alexander Fleming; she was also active politically in Greece, during and after World War II.

d. Honor (Bridget) Fell (1900–1986), British cell biologist.

## ARTS/LITERATURE

Margaret Atwood published the novel *The Handmaid's Tale*, on feminist themes, and the short-story collection *Bluebeard's Egg and Other Stories*.

Marlee Matlin starred as the deaf student opposite William Hurt as her voice teacher in *Children of a Lesser God*, Randa Haines's film version of the 1980 Mark Medoff play, winning a best actress Academy Award.

Rita Dove published the Pulitzer Prize–winning poetry collection *Thomas and Beulah*.

Diane Keaton, Jessica Lange, and Sissy Spacek starred in *Crimes of the Heart*, Bruce Beresford's film version of Beth Henley's 1981 play.

Mia Farrow, Dianne Wiest, Barbara Hershey, Carrie Fisher, Woody Allen, and Michael Caine starred in Allen's film *Hannah and Her Sisters*.

Ruth Prawer Jhabvala published the novel *The Nature of Passion*.

Whitney Houston issued her first album, the Grammy-winning *Whitney Houston*.

Zoë Caldwell appeared in the one-woman show *Lillian*, based on the three Lillian Hellman autobiographical works.

Louise Erdrich published *The Beet Queen*.

Adrienne Rich published the poetry collection *Your Native Land, Your Life*.

Sigourney Weaver starred as the heroic spaceship crew member in James Cameron's sci-tech monster film *Aliens*.

Bette Midler starred opposite Nick Nolte in Paul Mazursky's *Down and out in Beverly Hills*.

Swoosie Kurtz, Stockard Channing, and John Mahoney starred in John Guare's play *The House of Blue Leaves*.

Debbie Allen starred in the title role in *Sweet Charity*, Cy Coleman, Dorothy Fields, and Neil Simon's stage musical.

Amanda Plummer and Uta Hagen starred in the George Bernard Shaw play *You Never Can Tell*.

Alicia Markova published the autobiography *Markova Remembers*.

Caryl Churchill published the play *Serious Money*.

Jane Kenyon published the poetry collection *The Boat of Quiet Hours*.

Judy Pfaff showed the sculpture *Supermercado*.

Kate Burton, Ian McKellan, and Kathryn Walker starred in Michael Frayn's play *Wild Honey*.

Jean Stapleton, Polly Holliday, and Abe Vigoda starred in Joseph Kesselring's play *Arsenic and Old Lace*.

Margarethe von Trotta directed the film *Rosa Luxemburg*.

Paula Gunn Allen published *The Sacred Hoop*, on Native American themes.

Perry Miller Adato directed *Eugene O'Neill: A Glory of Ghosts*.

Ada Louise Huxtable published *Architecture Anyone?*

d. Georgia O'Keeffe (1887–1986), one of the leading American and world artists of the 20th century; also a favorite subject for her mentor and later husband, photographer Alfred Steiglitz.

d. Siobhan McKenna (1923–1986), Irish actress best known abroad for her leads in George Bernard Shaw's *St. Joan* and John Millington Synge's *The Playboy of the Western World*.

d. Cheryl Crawford (1902–1986), American director, producer, and actress, a founder of the Group Theater, the American Repertory Theater, and the Actors Studio.

d. Ding Ling (Ting Ling, 1902–1986), Chinese writer, a leading Communist cultural figure who was forced into internal exile (1957–1969), imprisoned (1970–1975), largely in solitary confinement, and again in internal exile (1975–1978). She was later "rehabilitated."

d. Margaret Laurence (Jean Margaret Wernyss, 1926–1986), Canadian writer, many of whose novels were set in the fictional western Canadian town of Manawaka.

d. Kate Smith (1907–1986), American singer, whose signature song was Irving Berlin's "God Bless America."

d. Bessie Love (Juanita Horton, 1898–1986), American actress, a star in silent films who made the transition to sound, from the mid-1930s continuing her stage and screen career in Britain.

d. Elisabeth Bergner (1900–1986), Austrian actress, a leading German stage and screen star during the 1920s and early 1930s; she fled the Nazis in 1933, pursuing her career in Britain and America.

d. Blanche Sweet (1895–1986), American silent-film star, in such films as *Anna Christie* (1923) and *Tess of the D'Urbervilles* (1924).

d. Donna Reed (1921–1986), American actress who played the prototypical midcentury American mother in television's *The Donna Reed Show*.

d. Bessie Head (1937–1986), South African novelist, long resident in Botswana.

d. Priaulx Rainier (1903–1986), South African composer.

## 1987

### POLITICS/LAW/WAR

Barbara Mikulski began her first term in the U.S. Senate (1987– ), then the only Democratic woman in the Senate; she would be overwhelmingly reelected in 1992.

Hillary Rodham Clinton chaired the American Bar Association Commission on Women in the Professions (1987–1991).

Gro Harlem Brundtland of Norway chaired the World Commission on Environment and Development, playing a major role in the development of its landmark report *Our Common Future*.

In *California Federal Savings and Loan Association v. Guerra*, the U.S. Supreme Court ruled that states could by law guarantee that the jobs of women on unpaid pregnancy disability leave must be held for them, even though lesser job-protection guarantees were extended to workers with other "disabilities."

In Canada, the Ontario legislature passed a trailblazing law requiring pay equity in both the public and private sectors.

Susan Estrich was appointed manager of Democrat Michael Dukakis's presidential campaign, the first woman in such a position for a major party; she had earlier been an adviser to Edward Kennedy and Walter Mondale.

Anna-Greta Leijon became Sweden's minister of justice (1987–1988).

Elizabeth Havers Butler-Sloss became the first woman appointed to Britain's Court of Appeal.

Molly Yard became president of the National Organization for Women (1987–1989).

Barbara Castle published *Christabel and Sylvia Pankhurst*.

## RELIGION/EDUCATION/EVERYDAY LIFE

National Women's History Month was proclaimed by the U.S. Congress.

Steffi Graf emerged as the world's leading femlale tennis player, with 66 consecutive victories, continuing to dominate women's tennis for long periods through the early 1990s.

Fund for the Feminist Majority was founded by Eleanor Smeal and Peg Yorkin as a research and activist organization on a wide range of women's concerns.

Gayle Sierens was the first woman to do play-by-play coverage of a major league football game, at a Kansas City Chiefs–Seattle Seahawks game for NBC.

Susan Estrich published *Real Rape*; she herself had survived a rape.

British philosopher Mary Warnock published *Memory*.

d. Catherine Bramwell Booth (1883–1987), British Salvation Army leader, daughter of cofounders Catherine and William Booth, who led efforts in Europe and in Britain with unwed mothers and abused children.

d. Dhanvanthi Rama Rau (1893–1987), Indian social worker, one of the first Indian women to attend college, at the University of Madras; her work focused on women's issues, especially family planning and the abolition of child marriage.

## SCIENCE/TECHNOLOGY/MEDICINE

Rita Levi-Montalcini and Stanley Cohen shared the Nobel Prize for physiology or medicine for their codiscovery of nerve-growth factor (1954).

Institute on Women and Technology was founded to study and generate action on a wide range of women's concerns affected by modern technology, in such areas as birth control, reproduction, addictive substances, and the environment.

Sheila Widnall was elected president of the American Association for the Advancement of Science (1987–1988), then chair of the board of directors (1988–1989).

Arkansas governor Bill Clinton appointed Dr. Joycelyn Elders director of the Arkansas Department of Public Health.

British psychoanalyst Marion Milner published *The Suppressed Madness of Sane Man* and also *Eternity's Sunrise, A Way of Keeping a Diary*, on her travels in Greece, India, and Israel.

## ARTS/LITERATURE

Toni Morrison published the Pulitzer Prize–winning novel *Beloved*.

Cher starred opposite Nicolas Cage in Norman Jewison's film *Moonstruck*, winning a best actress Academy Award. Cher, Susan Sarandon, Michelle Pfeiffer, and Jack Nicholson starred in George Miller's film *The Witches of Eastwick*, based on the 1984 John Updike novel.

Sigourney Weaver starred as naturalist and environmentalist Dian Fossey in Michael Apted's film *Gorillas in the Mist*, based on Fossey's book.

Alisa Gyse, Susan Beaubian, and Arnetia Walker starred in *Dreamgirls*, Henry Krieger and Tom Eyen's stage musical.

Iris Murdoch published her Booker Prize–winning novel *The Book and the Brotherhood*.

Stephane Audran, Gudmar Wivesson, Bibi Andersson, and Jarl Kulle starred in *Babette's Feast*, Gabriel Axel's film based on Isak Dinesen's short story.

Maya Angelou published the novel *All God's Children Need Traveling Shoes*.

Linda Ronstadt, Dolly Parton, and Emmylou Harris issued the album *Trio*.

Holly Hunter starred opposite William Hurt in James Brooks's film *Broadcast News*.

Melanie Griffith, Harrison Ford, and Sigourney Weaver starred in Mike Nichols's big-money-oriented film *Working Girl*.

Anne Bancroft starred opposite Anthony Hopkins in *84 Charing Cross Road*, David Jones's film based on Helene Hanff's autobiographical book.

Bernadette Peters starred opposite Tom Aldredge in *Into the Woods*, Stephen Sondheim and James Lapine's stage musical.

Cynthia Ozick published the novel *The Messiah of Stockholm*.

Denise Levertov published the poetry collection *Breathing the Water*.

Joan Didion published the novel *Miami*.

Nadine Gordimer published the novel *A Sport of Nature*.

Anita Brookner published the novel *A Friend from England*.

Joan Allen starred opposite John Malkovich in Lanford Wilson's play *Burn This*.

National Museum of Women in the Arts opened in Washington, D.C.

Anjelica Huston starred in *The Dead*, the last film directed by her father, John Huston, set in Dublin and based on a James Joyce story.

Marge Piercy published the novel *Gone to Soldiers*.

Mary Tyler Moore starred opposite Lynn Redgrave in A. R. Gurney's play *Sweet Sue*.

Amanda Plummer starred as Eliza Doolittle opposite Peter O'Toole as Henry Higgins in George Bernard Shaw's *Pygmalion*.

Clare Francis published the novel *Wolf Winter*.

Shirley Conran published the novel *Savages*.

Erica Jong published the novel *Serenissima*.

Lindsay Duncan starred opposite Alan Rickman in the play *Les Liaisons Dangereuses*.

Melissa Meyer painted *My Father's Sketch Pad*.

Fay Weldon wrote the play *The Heart of the Country*.

Rumer Godden published her autobiography *A Time to Dance, No Time to Weep*.

d. Geraldine Page (1924–1987), American actress, a star on stage from the early 1950s. Her occasional films included an Oscar-winning starring role in *The Trip to Bountiful* (1985).

d. Clare Boothe Luce (1903–1987), American actress, writer, editor, and politician.

d. Anna Neagle (Marjory Robertson, 1904–1987), British film star from the early 1930s through the 1950s, often in biographical films.

d. Marguerite Yourcenar (Marguerite de Crayencour, 1903–1987), French writer, translator, and critic, best known for her historical novels; the first woman to be a member of the French Academy (1981).

d. Rita Hayworth (Margarita Carmen Cansino, 1918–1987), American actress and dancer, a Hollywood star of the 1940s in such films as *Blood and Sand* (1941), *Gilda* (1946), and *The Lady from Shanghai* (1948).

d. Joan Greenwood (1921–1987), British film star of the 1940s and 1950s, in such films as *Tight Little Island* (1949), *The Man in the White Suit* (1950), and *Tom Jones* (1963).

d. Madeleine Carroll (Marie-Madeleine Bernadette O'Carroll, 1906–1987), British film star of the 1930s, most notably in *The 39 Steps* (1939) and *The Secret Agent* (1936).

d. Pola Negri (Apollonia Chalupiec, 1894–1987), Polish actress, a star in German and American silent films during the 1930s.

d. Jacqueline Du Pré (1945–1987), British cellist, her career and life cut short by multiple sclerosis.

d. Phyllis (Margaret) Tate (1911–1987), British composer.

# 1988

## POLITICS/LAW/WAR

After the death of Pakistani military dictator Zia Ul-Haq, Benazir Bhutto's Pakistan People's Party swept the parliamentary elections (December 2), and she became prime minister of Pakistan.

Daw Aung San Suu Kyi returned to Burma (Myanmar) from abroad to nurse her sick mother, who died that year, and stayed on to lead her country's democratic movement during the "Burmese Spring," as head of the nonviolent National League for Democracy. Placed under house arrest and barred from running for office, she was freed during the short-lived republic (August–September 1988), but after an army coup had overthrown the republic, refused to leave Burma, remaining opposition leader, again under house arrest.

In response to the U.S. Supreme Court's 1984 ruling in *Grove City College v. Bell*, Senate Bill 557 was passed, under which Title IX applies to all higher education programs, regardless of whether they draw federal funds.

Ann Richards, then Texas state treasurer, delivered the keynote address at the Democratic National Convention.

The Reagan administration instituted regulations barring federally funded clinics from providing information about abortions to pregnant women; the so-called gag rule was later invalidated by the courts (1992).

Carla Hills became U.S. trade representative (1988–1992).

Progressive Conservative Kim Campbell was elected to the Canadian House of Commons.

Elizabeth Hanford Dole and her husband, Republican Senator Bob Dole, published *Doles: Unlimited Partners*.

d. Jennie Lee (1904–1988), British socialist and Labour Party leader, for more than six decades a major figure on the left in her party, as was her husband, Aneurin Bevan.

d. Nora Astorga (1949–1988), Nicaraguan Sandinista leader, who became her country's ambassador to the United Nations (1986).

d. Axis Sally (Mildred Gillars, 1900–1988), American-born Nazi broadcaster during World War II.

## RELIGION/EDUCATION/EVERYDAY LIFE

Jackie Joyner-Kersee scored a world-record 7,291 points in the heptathlon, winning an Olympic gold medal.

Donna Shalala became chancellor of the University of Wisconsin (1988–1992).

Women's organizations from two branches of America's Presbyterian church united to form Presbyterian Women.

Barbara Tuchman published *The First Salute*.

American economist Alice Rivlin published *Caring for the Disabled Elderly: Who Will Pay?*

Carol Doda, the original topless dancer, inaugurated a sexual-fantasy telephone service, soon widely copied.

d. Barbara Frances Adam Wootton (Baroness Wootton, 1897–1988), British social scientist and educator long associated with the University of London (1927–1957), who published numerous books.

## SCIENCE/TECHNOLOGY/MEDICINE

Gertrude Elion and longtime pharmaceutical research colleague George H. Hitchings shared the 1988 Nobel Prize for physiology or medicine, for their development of drugs to treat diseases such as leukemia, organ-transplant rejection, and AIDS; the award was shared with James White Black.

RU 486, the so-called "abortion pill" developed by Etienne-Emile Baulieu, was approved for use in France, not without controversy; other European countries would also begin using it, though religious-political considerations kept it out of the United States, even for testing, until 1994.

Jeana Yeager and Dick Rutan published *Voyager: The Flying Adventure of a Lifetime*, about their record-breaking flight (1986).

d. Sheila (Christine) Hopkins Scott (1927–1988), British aviator, founder and first governor of the British section of the Ninety Nines.

### ARTS/LITERATURE

Jodie Foster starred as the gang-raped woman willing to face and prosecute her attackers in Jonathan Kaplan's film *The Accused*; she won a best actress Academy Award, opposite Kelly McGillis as her lawyer.

Joan Allen created the title role in Wendy Wasserstein's play *The Heidi Chronicles*.

Lillian Gish and Bette Davis starred in the film *The Whales of August*.

Muriel Spark published the novel *A Far Cry from Kensington*.

Nell Carter, Armelia McQueen, Charlaine Woodard, and Ken Page starred in *Ain't Misbehavin'*, the stage musical based on the music of Fats Waller.

Anne Tyler published the Pulitzer Prize–winning novel *Breathing Lessons*.

Shirley MacLaine starred as the piano teacher in John Schlesinger's London-set film *Madame Sousatzka*.

Nancy Marchand starred in A. R. Gurney's play *The Cocktail Hour*.

Yvonne Bryceland starred opposite Amy Irving in a New York production of Athol Fugard's play *The Road to Mecca*.

Sarah Brightman starred opposite Michael Crawford in *Phantom of the Opera*, Andrew Lloyd-Webber and Charles Hart's stage musical.

Colleen Dewhurst starred opposite Jason Robards in Eugene O'Neill's play *Long Day's Journey into Night*.

Glenda Jackson starred opposite Christopher Plummer in Shakespeare's *Macbeth*.

Isabell Monk starred opposite Morgan Freeman in *The Gospel at Colonnus*, Bob Telson and Lee Breuer's stage musical.

Madonna starred opposite Joe Mantegna and Ron Silver in David Mamet's play *Speed-the-Plow*.

Glenn Close starred opposite John Malkovich in Stephen Frears's film *Dangerous Liaisons*.

Agnieszka Holland directed the film *Angry Harvest*.

Roseanne Barr (later Arnold, then just Roseanne) and John Goodman starred in the long-running television series *Roseanne* (1988–1997).

Kate Nelligan starred opposite Jeffrey de Munn in Michael Weller's play *Spoils of War*.

Miriam Makeba published the autobiography *Makeba, My Story*.

Rebecca Horn showed the sculpture *The Hot Circus*.

d. Louise Nevelson (Louise Berliawsky, 1900–1988), American sculptor, a leading modernist.

d. Beatrice Lillie (1894–1988), Canadian-British actress and singer who became a British musical-theater star in *Charlot's Review* (1924).

d. Doris Humphrey (1895–1988), American dancer and choreographer, co-founder of the Humphrey-Weidman school and company (1928–1944).

## 1989

### POLITICS/LAW/WAR

In *Webster v. Reproductive Health Services*, the U.S. Supreme Court upheld a Missouri law prohibiting use of public hospitals and clinics for abortions.

Elizabeth Hanford Dole served as U.S. secretary of labor (1989–1990), leaving to head the American Red Cross.

Kim Campbell became Canadian minister of state affairs and northern development (1989–1990).

Madeleine Albright became president of the Center of National Policy (1989–1992).

Colorado Democratic Congresswoman Pat Schroeder coauthored *Champion of the Great American Family: A Personal and Political Book*, with Andrea Camp and Robyn Lipner.

Benazir Bhutto published *Daughter of Destiny: An Autobiography*.

d. Elena Ceausescu (1918–1989), Romanian chemist and political partner of Romanian dictator Nicolae Ceausescu, her husband; both were executed by revolutionaries after their regime fell (December 25).

### RELIGION/EDUCATION/EVERYDAY LIFE

African-American Episcopal priest Barbara Clementine Harris was the first woman consecrated as bishop of the Episcopal church, and of the Anglican Communion (Anglican church worldwide).

Women's Environment and Development Organization was founded as an international women's network especially concerned with monitoring governmental Earth Summit commitments.

Julie Croteau became the first woman to play on an American men's college varsity baseball team, at St. Mary's College, Maryland; while in high school in Prince William County, Virginia, she had played on the junior varsity team but lost a lawsuit to join the varsity squad (1988).

Susan Sontag published the essays in *AIDS and Its Metaphors*.

Marie Gimbutas published *The Language of the Goddess*.

d. Barbara Wertheim Tuchman (1912–1989), American historian and writer best known for her *The Guns of August* (1962).

### SCIENCE/TECHNOLOGY/MEDICINE

Antonia C. Novello became the first woman named surgeon general of the U.S. Public Health Service.

Longtime Alabama midwife Onnie Lee Logan published her autobiographical book *Motherwit: An Alabama Midwife's Story*.

d. Virginia Satir (1914–1989), American pioneer in the area of family therapy, who founded the first training program in the field and also developed the Esalen Institute's "human-growth" center.

d. Christine Jorgenson (George Jorgensen, 1926–1989), American transsexual, who underwent a pioneer sex-change operation (1950–1952), later becoming an entertainer.

### ARTS/LITERATURE

Amy Tan published the novel *The Joy Luck Club*, later adapted into the 1993 film.

Jessica Tandy starred in the title role in Bruce Beresford's film *Driving Miss Daisy*, winning a best actress Academy Award opposite Morgan Freeman and Dan Aykroyd.

Bonnie Raitt issued the Grammy-winning album *Nick of Time*.

Alice Walker published the novel *The Temple of My Familiar*.

Pauline Collins starred in Willy Russell's play *Shirley Valentine* and in Lewis Gilbert's film of the play.

Candice Bergen starred in her long-running television series *Murphy Brown* (1989– ).

Annette Bening, Colin Firth, and Meg Tilly starred in Milos Forman's film *Valmont*.

Meg Ryan and Billy Crystal starred in Rob Reiner's film *When Harry Met Sally . . .*

Adrienne Rich published the poetry collection *Time's Power*.

Maya Lin designed the Civil Rights Memorial, at Montgomery, Alabama.

Mercedes Ruehl starred opposite Kevin Conway in Jerry Sterner's play *Other People's Money*.

Holly Hunter starred opposite Richard Dreyfuss in Steven Spielberg's film *Always*.

Iris Murdoch published the novel *The Message to the Planet*.

Jacqueline Bisset starred in Paul Bartel's film *Scenes from the Class Struggle in Beverly Hills*.

Ruth Brown, Linda Hopkins, and Carrie Smith starred in *Black and Blue*, Claudio Segovia and Héctor Orezzoli's stage musical.

Louise Erdrich published *Tracks*.

Betty Garrett, George Hearn, and Donna Kane starred in *Meet Me in St. Louis*, Hugh Martin and Ralph Blane's stage musical.

Rita Dove published the poetry collection *Grace Notes*.

Jane Fonda and Gregory Peck in the title role starred in *Old Gringo*, Luis Puenzo's film based on Carlos Fuentes's novel, set during the Mexican Revolution.

Kate Burton starred opposite Len Cariou in Shakespeare's *Measure for Measure*.

Mia Farrow starred opposite Woody Allen in Allen's film *Crimes and Misdemeanors*.

Tyne Daly starred as Gypsy Rose Lee in *Gypsy*, Jule Styne, Stephen Sondheim, and Arthur Laurents's musical.

Charlotte d'Amboise starred opposite Jason Alexander in the stage musical *Jerome Robbins' Broadway*.

Joan Mitchell painted *Mountain*.

Mary Gordon published the novel *The Other Side*.

Radwa 'Ashur published the novel *Khadgia and Sawsan*.

Cynthia Ozick published the novel *The Shawl*.

Sherrie Levine painted *Untitled (Mr. Austridge: 3; 5)*.

d. Bette (Ruth Elizabeth) Davis (1908–1989), American actress, a dramatic star of Hollywood's Golden Age.

d. Lucille Ball (1911–1989), American actress, a supporting player in film during the 1930s and 1940s, who emerged as a worldwide star in 1951 in television's first situation comedy, *I Love Lucy* (1951–1957), and its several successor series.

d. Daphne du Maurier (1907–1989), British writer, best known for her novel *Rebecca*.

d. Mary Therese McCarthy (1912–1989), American novelist, short story writer, and essayist, a substantial literary figure from the late 1940s.

# 1990

## POLITICS/LAW/WAR

Daw Aung San Suu Kyi's democratic party swept the elections in Burma (Myanmar), but the military rejected the vote, openly held power, and continued to keep her under close house arrest.

Violeta Chamorro was elected president of Nicaragua (February 25), in a free election endorsed by Sandinista leader Daniel Ortega; she then successfully negotiated agreements that ended her country's long civil war.

Benazir Bhutto was removed from office by Pakistani president Ishaq Khan, with the support of the military. Her party lost power in the general elections (October), which she attacked as fraudulent.

In an upset victory, Mary Robinson won the Irish presidential election, then becoming the highly visible, peace and social justice–oriented occupant of what had been a ceremonial position.

In *Ohio v. Akron Center for Reproductive Health*, the U.S. Supreme Court upheld an Ohio law requiring teenagers seeking abortions to notify one parent before doing so.

Democrat Dianne Feinstein was California's first female major-party gubernatorial nominee, but lost the election to Republican Senator Pete Wilson, whose unexpired Senate term she would later fill (1992–1994).

Kim Campbell became Canadian minister of justice and attorney-general of Canada (1990–1993).

Barbara Bush published the best-seller *Millie's Book: As Dictated to Barbara Bush*, a look at Washington life from the viewpoint of Millie, the Bush family's springer spaniel.

## RELIGION/EDUCATION/EVERYDAY LIFE

Dogsled racer Susan Butcher set a new course record in winning her fourth Anchorage-Nome Iditarod Trail Sled Dog Race in five years, further enhancing her worldwide celebrity as a leading figure in a "man's" sport.

Marguerite Ross Barnett became the first female president of the University of Houston, the first African-American woman to head a major American university.

Robin Morgan became editor of *Ms.* magazine.

Sylvia Porter published *Sylvia Porter's Your Finances in the 1990s*.

d. Pauline Frederick (ca. 1906–1990), American news analyst, the first woman to broadcast "hard news" (1946–1953) and to cover a national convention (1948); later longtime United Nations correspondent for NBC (from 1953).

d. Alice Marble (1913–1990), American tennis player who revolutionized women's tennis in the 1930s by introducing the serve-and-volley style, until then used only by men.

## SCIENCE/TECHNOLOGY/MEDICINE

U.S. National Institutes of Health established its Office on Research on Women's Health, to foster research on women's health matters and strengthen the participation of women in biomedical careers; its first director was renal pathologist Vivian Pinn.

Society for the Advancement of Women's Health Research was founded, to combat perceived anti-woman biases in American health research.

The U.S. Patent Office, celebrating its 200th anniversary, mounted a special exhibit, "A Woman's Place Is in the Patent Office," a version of the exhibit later shown at the University of Minnesota.

Doris Malkin Curtis became the first woman to serve as president of the Geological Society of America.

Ruth Hubbard published *The Politics of Women's Biology*.

d. Marion Rice Hart (1892–1990), American aviator who made her first transatlantic flight in 1953, at age 61, and her first solo transatlantic flight in 1966, at 74; also a noted sailor.

## ARTS/LITERATURE

Margaret Atwood's 1986 novel *The Handmaid's Tale* was filmed starring Natasha Richardson, Faye Dunaway, and Robert Duvall; Volker Schlöndorff directed and Harold Pinter wrote the screenplay.

Performance artist Karen Finley was denied a National Endowment for the Arts (NEA) grant for a work on sexual abuse, on the grounds that it was obscene.

Jane Alexander starred opposite Nigel Hawthorne in William Nicholson's play *Shadowlands*.

Stockard Channing, John Cunningham, and Courtney Vance starred in John Guare's play *Six Degrees of Separation*.

Joyce Carol Oates published the novel *Because It Is Bitter, and Because It Is My Heart*.

Kathy Bates, James Caan, and Lauren Bacall starred in *Misery*, Rob Reiner's film based on the Stephen King novel. Bates won a best actress Academy Award.

Maggie Smith and Margaret Tyzack starred in Peter Shaffer's play *Lettice and Lovage*.

Maya Angelou published the poetry collection *I Shall Not Be Moved*.

Shirley MacLaine and Meryl Streep starred as Hollywood star mother and daughter in *Postcards from the Edge*, Mike Nichols's film from a screenplay by Carrie Fisher from her own novel.

Ann Beattie published the novel *Picturing Will*.

Eileen Heckart, Elizabeth Franz, and Doris Belack starred in Ivan Menchell's play *The Cemetery Club*.

Muriel Spark published the novel *Symposium*.

Penny Marshall directed the film *Awakenings*, starring Robert De Niro.

Anne Rice published the novel *The Witching Hour*.

Beryl Bainbridge published the novel *An Awfully Big Adventure*.

Camille Paglia published the essays in *Sexual Personae: Art and Decadence from Nefertiti to Emily Dickinson*.

Glenda Jackson starred in Bertolt Brecht's *Mother Courage*.

Felicity Kendal starred opposite Peter Barkworth in Simon Gray's play *Hidden Laughter*.

Kate Burton, Frances Conroy, Henderson Forsythe, and Nathan Lane starred in Richard Nelson's play *Some Americans Abroad*.

Erica Jong published the novel *Any Woman's Blues*.

d. Greta Garbo (Greta Louise Gustafsson, 1905–1990), Swedish actress, a Hollywood star from the mid-1920s and one of the leading figures in film history, for such movies as *Anna Christie* (1930), *Anna Karenina* (1935), and *Camille* (1937). She retired in 1941.

d. Mary Martin (1913–1990), American singer and actress who originated several classic musical-theater roles, as in *South Pacific* (1949) and *The Sound of Music* (1961); mother of actor Larry Hagman.

d. Irene Dunne (1901–1990), a leading American film star of the 1930s and 1940s, for such films as *Cimarron* (1931), *Roberta* (1935), *Penny Serenade* (1941), and *I Remember Mama* (1948).

d. Ava Gardner (1922–1990), American film star, a sex symbol for much of her career, who later played several strong supporting dramatic roles, in such films as *On the Beach* (1959) and *Seven Days in May* (1964).

d. Pearl Bailey (1918–1990), African-American singer, dancer, and actress, a star in cabaret, in musical theater, and on screen.

d. Eleanor Steber (1916–1990), American soprano, a leading singer at the Metropolitan Opera (1940–1963).

d. Rosamond Lehmann (1903–1990), British novelist and short story writer, best known for such novels as *Invitation to the Waltz* (1932) and *The Ballad and the Source* (1944).

d. Sarah (Lois) Vaughan (1924–1990), American jazz and popular singer, a star from the mid-1940s through the late 1980s.

d. Delphine Seyrig (1932–1990), French actress and feminist, an international film star from her appearance in *Last Year at Marienbad* (1961).

d. May Swenson (1913–1990), American poet and editor, often published in the *New Yorker*, winner of the 1981 Bollingen Prize.

d. Peggy Glanville-Hicks (1912–1990), Australian composer.

## 1991

### POLITICS/LAW/WAR

Anita Faye Hill's sexual harassment charges against U.S. Supreme Court nominee Clarence Thomas were taken up by the Senate Judiciary Committee in open and televised hearings before massive worldwide audiences. Although Thomas, his reputation shattered, was ultimately confirmed by the Senate, the entire set of confrontations—and Hill's treatment by some Republican members of the all-male Judiciary Committee—caused enormous outrage that went far beyond feminist partisans, triggering a powerful revival of the American women's rights movement. One proximate result was the election of large numbers of women to Congress in 1992, the "Year of the Woman" in American politics.

At least 26 women, most of them active-duty naval officers, were sexually assaulted by at least 70 active or retired Navy aviators at a convention of the Tailhook Association at the Hilton Hotel in Las Vegas. One of those attacked, helicopter pilot and admiral's aide Lt. Paula Coughlin, "went public" after her superiors refused to act on her complaint, generating the Tailhook Scandal, which ultimately caused the resignation of a secretary of the navy and the early retirement of several senior officers. However, not one of the assaulting aviators was ever brought to trial—and Lt. Coughlin ultimately resigned from the navy under pressure.

While under house arrest in Burma (Myanmar), human rights leader Daw Aung San Suu Kyi was awarded the Nobel Peace Prize.

British Prime Minister Margaret Thatcher was succeeded by John Major, having been Britain's longest-serving prime minister of the 20th century (1979–1991).

In *Automobile Workers v. Johnson Controls Inc.* the U.S. Supreme Court unanimously ruled that women could not be barred from specific jobs because of their sex.

Patricia Ireland became president of the National Organization for Women (NOW).

Democrat Ann Richards became governor of Texas (1991–1995).

Edith Cresson became the first female prime minister of France.

Sharon Pratt Dixon (later Kelly) became the mayor of Washington, D.C., the first African-American woman elected mayor of a major city.

Winnie Mandela was convicted of kidnapping and assault in connection with a murder committed by her bodyguards and was sentenced to six years in prison but was freed on appeal.

Carol Browner became head of the Florida Department of Environmental Protection.

Lois Gibbs won the Goldman Environmental Prize for her work against hazardous chemicals.

Raisa Gorbachev's long autobiographical interview with writer Georgi Pryakhin was published as the book *I Hope*.

d. Dolores Ibarruri (La Pasionara, 1895–1991), Spanish Communist Party leader, who emerged as a major Republican figure during the Spanish Civil War (1936–1939), later fled to the Soviet Union, and returned to Spain and a parliamentary seat after the death of Francisco Franco (1975).

d. Jiang Qing (1914–1991), Chinese actress and politician, the third wife of Mao Zedong, who became a major political figure during China's Cultural Revolution; after his death, she was accused, tried, and sentenced to life imprisonment, for allegedly attempting to take power as leader of the "Gang of Four."

d. Vijaya Lakshmi Pandit (Madame Pandit, 1900–1991), Indian independence-movement leader and diplomat, the sister of Jawaharlal Nehru; often-jailed from the 1920s, she became a leading Indian diplomat after independence (1947), and the first woman to serve as president of the United Nations General Assembly (1953–1954).

d. Harriet Fleischl Pilpel (1912–1991), American lawyer, long a leader in women's rights, civil liberties, and intellectual property law; a general counsel of the American Civil Liberties Union (1979–1986) and the Planned Parenthood Federation of America, and a federal government adviser.

d. Marietta Peabody Tree (1917–1991), American diplomat, the first woman to be chief American delegate (1961), then permanent ambassador (1964) to the United Nations.

### RELIGION/EDUCATION/EVERYDAY LIFE

Gloria Steinem published *Revolution from Within: A Book of Self-Esteem*, a popular-psychology book for women.

Kate Millett published *The Loony Bin Trip*, charging a long period of persecution, including her unjust commitment to mental hospitals by her family.

Marie Gimbutas published *The Civilization of the Goddess*.

Monica Seles won the first of two successive U.S. Open championships (1991; 1992), in the early 1990s emerging as one of the world's leading tennis players.

Sarah Eileen Williamson was the first girl to be elected mayor of Boys Town, in Omaha, Nebraska.

Susan Faludi published *Backlash: The Undeclared War Against American Women*.

d. Belinda Mason (1958–1991), American journalist, AIDS victim, and leading advocate of more humane treatment for those with AIDS. Mason, who had contracted AIDS from a blood transfusion, founded Kentuckian People with AIDS, was president of the National Association of People with AIDS, and served on the National Commission on AIDS.

d. Sylvia Field Porter (1913–1991), American financial writer for more than five decades.

### SCIENCE/TECHNOLOGY/MEDICINE

Physician Bernardine P. Healy became the first woman to head the National Institutes of Health (1991–1993).

Gertrude Elion was inducted into the National Inventors Hall of Fame for her work in developing many drugs, including acyclovir and AZT.

Through modern reproductive technology, Arlette Rafferty Schweitzer was able to bear her own twin grandchildren, having brought to term fertilized eggs from her daughter, born without a uterus. A South African woman had earlier borne triplets for her daughter (1987).

d. Lu Gwei-Djen (1904–1991), Chinese biochemist, teacher, and historian of science, Joseph Needham's collaborator in the massive, landmark multivolume series *Science and Civilization in China*, and several other works. She and Dr. Needham married in 1990, after the death of his first wife, her lifelong friend.

### ARTS/LITERATURE

Nadine Gordimer was awarded the 1991 Nobel Prize for literature.

Jodie Foster starred opposite Anthony Hopkins in Jonathan Demme's film *The Silence of the Lambs*, winning a best actress Academy Award. Foster also starred in and directed *Little Man Tate*, beginning her directorial career.

Barbra Streisand directed and starred as the psychiatrist opposite Nick Nolte in the film *The Prince of Tides*.

Jane Smiley published the Pulitzer Prize–winning novel *A Thousand Acres*.

Jessica Tandy starred opposite Kathy Bates in the film *Fried Green Tomatoes*, directed by John Avnet and based on the Fannie Flagg novel.

Natalie Cole issued her Grammy-winning album *Unforgettable*, with its electronically engineered "duet" with her late father, Nat "King" Cole.

Amy Tan published the novel *The Kitchen God's Wife*.

Martha Coolidge directed *Rambling Rose*, starring Laura Dern and Robert Duvall.

Susan Sarandon and Geena Davis starred in Ridley Scott's murderous road-buddy film *Thelma and Louise*.

Anna Quindlen published the novel *Object Lessons*.

Mercedes Ruehl starred opposite Mark Blum in Neil Simon's play *Lost in Yonkers*.

Anne Tyler published the novel *Saint Maybe*.

Emma Thompson starred opposite Kenneth Branagh in the thriller *Dead Again*, directed by Branagh.

Joyce Carol Oates published *Heat: And Other Stories* and the novel *The Rise of Life on Earth*.

Adrienne Rich published the poetry collection *An Atlas of the Difficult World: Poems 1988–1991*.

Alice Walker published *Her Blue Body Everything We Know: Earthling Poems 1965–1990 Complete*.

Judith Ivey starred opposite Jason Robards in Israel Horovitz's play *Park Your Car in Harvard Yard*.

Margaret Atwood published the short-story collection *Wilderness Tips*.

Margaret Drabble published the novel *The Gates of Ivory*.

Maryann Plunkett, Martin Sheen, Fritz Weaver, and Michael York starred in Arthur Miller's play *The Crucible*.

Ann Beattie published *What Was Mine: Stories*.

Michelle Pfeiffer starred opposite Al Pacino in *Frankie and Johnny*, Garry Marshall's offbeat romantic film.

Sandra Cisneros published *Woman Hollering Creek: And Other Stories*.

Judith Jamison became artistic director of the Alvin Ailey Dance Theater.

Julie Harris starred in William Luce's play *Lucifer's Child*.

Marsha Norman and Lucy Simon's stage musical *The Secret Garden* starred Daisy Eagen, Mandy Patinkin, and Rebecca Luker.

Alexandra Ripley published the novel *Scarlett: The Sequel to Margaret Mitchell's Gone with the Wind*.

Cynthia Macdonald published the poetry collection *Living Wills*.

Doris Grumbach published the essays in *Coming into the End Zone*.

Maeve Binchy published the novel *Circle of Friends*.

Shulamit Ran became the first woman appointed composer-in-residence at a major American orchestra, the Chicago Symphony.

Tracey Ullman starred in *The Big Love*, Brooke Allen and Jay Presson Allen's play.

Martha Graham's *Blood Memory: An Autobiography*, was published posthumously.

d. Margot Fonteyn (Peggy Hookam, 1919–1991), British ballerina, an international star from the mid-1930s and prima ballerina of the Royal Ballet.

d. Martha Graham (1893–1991), American choreographer and dancer, a leading figure in modern dance.

d. Jean Arthur (Gladys Georgianna Greene, 1905–1991), American film star, most notably in such films as *Mr. Deeds Goes to Town* (1936) and *You Can't Take It with You* (1938).

d. Gene Tierney (1920–1991), American film star of the 1940s and early 1950s, beginning with *Tobacco Road* (1940) and *Laura* (1943).

d. Olga (Alexandrovna) Spessivtseva (1895–1991), Russian dancer, a prima ballerina with the Maryinsky Theater and a leading dancer with Diaghilev's Ballets Russes company.

d. Peggy (Edith Margaret Emily) Ashcroft (1907–1991), British actress; she was Juliet alternately to John Gielgud and Laurence Olivier, Desdemona to Paul Robeson, Hedda Gabler, and more.

d. Lee Remick (1935–1991), American stage and screen star best known for such theatrical films as *The Long Hot Summer* (1958) and *Days of Wine and Roses* (1962).

d. Muriel Baker Box (1905–1991), British screenwriter, film director, and producer, longtime collaborator (1935–1969) with her husband, Sidney Box. An active feminist, she was a founder of the Femina Press.

d. Joy Batchelor (1914–1991), British artist, animator, and filmmaker, often working with her husband and partner, John Halas.

d. Laura Riding (Laura Reichenthal, 1901–1991), American poet.

d. Berenice Abbott (1898–1991), American photographer.

d. Colleen Dewhurst (1926–1991), American actress.

d. Natalia Levi Ginzburg (1916–1991), Italian novelist, essayist, and translator.

## 1992

### POLITICS/LAW/WAR

In *Planned Parenthood v. Casey*, the U.S. Supreme Court specifically reaffirmed the legalization of abortion, from *Roe v. Wade* (1973), while also affirming the states' rights to place restrictions on such abortions, if they do not pose an "undue burden."

In an international cause célèbre, an anonymous 14-year-old girl, pregnant after being raped by a friend of her father's and threatening suicide, was barred from leaving Ireland (February 7) to have an abortion in Britain, as some 4,000 of her countrywomen did annually. Upheld by the High Court, the ruling was overturned by Ireland's Supreme Court, which freed her to travel to Britain for the abortion. The case sparked national and international debate, and later in the year Irish voters passed constitutional amendments allowing women to receive informa-

---

# Rethinking *Roe v. Wade*

It must be stated at the outset and with clarity that Roe's essential holding, the holding we reaffirm, has three parts. First is a recognition of the right of the woman to choose to have an abortion before viability and to obtain it without undue interference from the state. Before viability, the state's interests are not strong enough to support a prohibition of abortion or the imposition of a substantial obstacle to the woman's effective right to elect the procedure. Second is a confirmation of the state's power to restrict abortions after fetal viability, if the law contains exceptions for pregnancies which endanger a woman's life or health. And third is the principle that the state has legitimate interests from the outset of the pregnancy in protecting the health of the woman and the life of the fetus that may become a child. These principles do not contradict one another; and we adhere to each. . .

Men and women of good conscience can disagree, and we suppose some always shall disagree, about the profound moral and spiritual implications of terminating a pregnancy, even in its earliest stages. Some of us as individuals find abortion offensive to our most basic principles of morality, but that cannot control our decision. Our obligation is to define the liberty of all, not to mandate our own moral code. . .

— From *Planned Parenthood v. Casey* (1992), decision jointly written by U.S. Supreme Court Justices Sandra Day O'Connor, Anthony M. Kennedy, and David H. Souter.

---

tion on abortion and to travel to obtain one, but not allowing abortion in Ireland, still barred except where the mother's life is in danger.

21st Century Party was founded; an American national political party initiated by the National Organization for Women with a wide-ranging platform, but a very narrow feminist constituency. With the advent of the women's rights–oriented Clinton administration, the new party did not move forward.

Liberal California Democratic Congresswoman Barbara Boxer won the race for the Senate seat vacated by retiring Alan Cranston; in the same election, former San Francisco mayor Dianne Feinstein was elected to serve in the final two years of California's other Senate seat, making it the first state ever to have two women as senators.

Betty Boothroyd was the first woman elected Speaker of Britain's Parliament.

Mary Robinson made the first state visit of an Irish president to Northern Ireland since 1921 (February 4), and continued to speak out on a wide range of feminist and other social-justice issues, including sexual discrimination, abortion choice, and homophobia.

Aung San Suu Kyi, under house arrest in Burma (Myanmar), published the essay collection *Freedom from Fear*.

d. Petra Kelly (1947–1992), German environmentalist and politician, founder of Germany's Green Party (1979); found shot dead in her home in Bonn, with her companion Gerd Bastian, who allegedly (and highly questionably) killed her and then himself (October 19). Published that year was her *Nonviolence Speaks to Power*.

d. Helen Pennell Joseph (1905–1992), White South African teacher, social worker, and antiapartheid crusader, often imprisoned or otherwise restrained by her government, and a founder of the Congress of Democrats and the United Democratic Front.

d. Deng Yingchao (1904–1992), Chinese Communist leader, a Central Committee member (1969–1985) and a Politburo member (1978–1985); wife of Zhou Enlai until his death (1924–1976).

d. Kang Keqing (1912–1992), Chinese soldier and Communist Party leader, wife of Zhu De; she was a frontline fighter with Communist forces from the Long March (1928) through to victory (1949), later holding several high positions, including membership in the Communist Party Central Committee (1977–1985).

d. Millicent Fenwick (1910–1992), American feminist and liberal Republican congresswoman from New Jersey (1974–1982).

### RELIGION/EDUCATION/EVERYDAY LIFE

Guatemalan Quiché Indian peace activist Rigoberta Menchú was awarded the Nobel Peace Prize.

The Anglican Churches of England and Australia voted to accept the ordination of women as priests. The first Anglican female priests would be ordained in Britain in 1994.

Marilyn French published the *The War Against Women*, charging that most men in all countries have literally been waging all-out war against women since the fourth millennium B.C., the period in which she believes patriarchies won out over earlier matriarchies.

American ice-skater Kristi Yamaguchi won the gold medal for women's figure skating at the Albertville Winter Olympics.

Jackie Joyner-Kersee won an unprecedented second Olympic gold medal in the heptathlon.

Marian Wright Edelman published the best-seller *The Measure of Our Success: A Letter to My Children and Yours*.

American economist Alice Rivlin published *Reviving the American Dream*.

Germaine Greer published *The Change: Women, Aging, and the Menopause*.

Women's Action Coalition was founded, as an action organization on a wide range of women's issues.

Carol Tavris published *The Mismeasure of Women*, on "why women are not the better sex, the inferior sex, or the opposite sex."

Clarissa Pinkola Estes published *Women Who Run with the Wolves: Myths and Stories of the Wild Woman Archetype*.

d. Marguerite Ross Barnett (1942–1992), American educational administrator who became the first woman to serve as president of the University of Houston (1990), the first African-American woman to head a major American university.

d. Clara Hale (Mother Hale, 1905–1992), African-American child-care provider, who founded Harlem's Hale House after retirement (1969) and saw it grow into a highly respected child-care institution.

### SCIENCE/TECHNOLOGY/MEDICINE

*Born to Rebel: The Life of Harriet Boyd Hawes* was published; the biography of the American archaeologist was written by her daughter, Mary Allsebrook, and edited by her granddaughter, Annie Allsebrook.

d. Barbara McClintock (1902–1992), American geneticist who won the 1983 Nobel Prize for physiology or medicine for her work on the transposition of genetic fragments; she was long associated with the Cold Spring Harbor Laboratory of the Carnegie Institution (1941–1992).

d. Grace Brewster Murray Hopper (1906–1992), American mathematician and computer scientist who served in the U.S. Navy for nearly 40 years (1944–1983); a computer pioneer, working with the early ENIAC and UNIVAC computers, she developed the first compiler language (1952) and was coinventor of the COBOL programming language.

d. Cicely (Delphine) Williams (1893–1992), British physician who, while doing public-health work on the Gold Coast (now Ghana), was the first person to describe kwashiorkor as a distinct disease and recognize it as a deficiency disorder.

### ARTS/LITERATURE

Alice Walker published the novel *Possessing the Secret of Joy*, attacking the widespread practice of ritual genital mutilation, inflicted on more than 100 million women worldwide and euphemistically called female circumcision.

Mona Van Duyn became American poet laureate, also winning a Pulitzer Prize for her poetry collection *Near Changes*.

Penny Marshall directed *A League of Their Own*, a film about women's baseball, starring Geena Davis, Tom Hanks, Lori Petty, and Madonna.

Emma Thompson, Vanessa Redgrave, Helena Bonham Carter, and Anthony Hopkins starred in *Howard's End*, James Ivory's film adapted by Ruth Prawer Jhabvala from E. M. Forster's 1910 novel. Thompson won a best actress Academy Award and several other awards.

Catherine Deneuve starred in *Indochine*, Regis Wargnier's film set in French-held Indochina in the 1930s.

Miranda Richardson, Joan Plowright, Josie Lawrence, and Polly Walker starred in Mike Newell's film *Enchanted April*.

Rita Dove published the novel *Through the Ivory Gate*.

Glenn Close, Richard Dreyfuss, and Gene Hackman starred in the New York production of Ariel Dorfman's play *Death and the Maiden*.

Meryl Streep and Goldie Hawn starred as the highly competitive Hollywood beauties opposite Bruce Willis in Robert Zemeckis's film farce *Death Becomes Her*.

Stockard Channing starred opposite James Naughton in John Guare's play *Four Baboons Adoring the Sun*.

Whitney Houston starred opposite Kevin Costner in Mick Jackson's film *The Bodyguard*, reviving Dolly Parton's "I Will Always Love You" as a major hit.

Maryann Plunkett, Tony Randall, Lynn Redgrave, and Rob Lowe starred in Georges Feydeau's play *A Little Hotel on the Side*.

Sharon Stone starred opposite Michael Douglas in Joe Eszterhaus's sex thriller film *Basic Instinct*.

Mia Farrow and Woody Allen costarred in Allen's film *Husbands and Wives*.

Jakuco Setouchi won the Tanizaki prize for her novel *Ask the Flowers*.

Tyne Daly, Jon Voight, and Maryann Plunkett starred in Anton Chekhov's *The Seagull*.

Jessica Lange, Alec Baldwin, and Amy Madigan starred in a Broadway production of Tennessee Williams's *A Streetcar Named Desire*.

Jodi Benson starred opposite Harry Groener in *Crazy for You*, George and Ira Gershwin's stage musical.

Elizabeth Macklin published the poetry collection *A Woman Kneeling in the Big City*.

Camille Paglia published the essays in *Sex, Art, and American Culture*.

Elena Poniatowska published the historical novel *Tinísima*.

Muriel Spark published her autobiography, *Curriculum Vitae*.

d. Marlene Dietrich (1901–1992), German actress and singer, who emerged as a film star in Germany in *The Blue Angel* (1930) and became a leading Hollywood star, later in her career moving into several major dramatic roles.

d. Arletty (Léonie Bathiat, 1898–1992), French film star of the late 1930s and 1940s, a world figure for the single role of Garance opposite Louis Barrault as the mime Deburau in Marcel Carné's classic *Les Enfants Du Paradis* (1945).

d. Hanya Holm (Johanna Eckert, 1893–1992), German dancer, choreographer, and teacher, a central figure in modern dance, and late in her career the choreographer of such musicals as *Kiss Me, Kate* (1948), *My Fair Lady* (1956), and *Camelot* (1960).

d. Shirley Booth (Thelma Booth Ford, 1907–1992), American actress, a stage, screen, and television star, starting with her Tony-winning role in *Come Back Little Sheba* (1950; she won an Oscar for the 1952 film). She later had the title role on television's *Hazel* (1961–1966).

d. Judith (Frances Margaret) Anderson (1898–1992), Australian actress who emerged as a leading figure in the English-speaking theater in the 1930s, her greatest role coming in *Medea* (1947).

d. Dorothy Kirsten (1910–1992), American lyric soprano, a fixture at the Metropolitan Opera (1945–1975).

d. Eve Merriam (1916–1992), American feminist poet and playwright.

d. Molly Picon (1898–1992), Jewish-American actress, a star of the American Yiddish theater.

d. Stella Adler (1901–1992), American actress and teacher.

d. Yvonne Bryceland (Yvonne Hellbuth, 1924–1992), South African actress.

d. Georgia Brown (Lillie Klot, 1933–1992), British singer and actress.

# 1993

## POLITICS/LAW/WAR

Justice Sandra Day O'Connor wrote the landmark, unanimous opinion in *Harris v. Forklift Systems*, ruling that workers charging sexual harassment need not prove that they were unable to perform their tasks or to prove psychological damage, instead applying the rule of "workplace equity."

A family and medical leave bill was signed into law by President Bill Clinton; a similar bill, providing time off for pregnancy or a medical condition, or for care of a sick family member, had been twice passed and vetoed under the previous Bush administration.

Benazir Bhutto and her Pakistan People's Party made a powerful comeback, winning a plurality in the general elections (October 6); she once again became prime minister, heading a coalition government.

Hillary Rodham Clinton emerged as a major figure in American life, as the working partner of President Bill Clinton, openly taking responsibility in several major areas, most notably taking the lead for the Clinton administration on reconstruction of the American health-care system and provision of universal health care.

District of Columbia federal Court of Appeals Judge Ruth Bader Ginsburg became an associate justice of the U.S. Supreme Court (August), replacing retiring Justice Byron R. White. A veteran civil liberties and women's rights lawyer, she had previously won several landmark women's rights cases.

Janet Reno was named U.S. attorney general by President Bill Clinton, the first woman to hold the position.

Aeronautics professor Sheila Widnall became the first woman to serve as secretary of the air force (1993– ).

Tansu Çiller became prime minister of Turkey, the first woman to hold the post, and the first woman to lead an Islamic country without a family or dynastic link to power.

Kim Campbell was named Canada's minister of defence, then succeeded retiring prime minister Brian Mulroney as head of the ruling Progressive Conservative Party, and subsequently became her country's first female prime minister (June 25). She resigned after her party suffered a disaster in the general elections (October 25), emerging with only two House of Commons seats, down from 153, with Campbell failing even to win her Vancouver constituency.

Hazel O'Leary became secretary of energy in the Clinton administration, the first to have worked in the industry she was regulating; she began a highly public investigation of decades of cold war American government–sponsored radiation experiments on humans.

President Bill Clinton signed into law the Brady Handgun Control Law (November 30), an immense personal triumph for Sarah Kemp Brady and her husband, James Brady, partially paralyzed after having been wounded during John Hinckley's 1981 attempt to assassinate President Ronald Reagan.

Florida lawyer and environmentalist Carol Browner became Clinton adminstration head of the Environmental Protection Agency.

Madeleine Albright became Clinton administration U.S. ambassador to the United Nations.

New senators Carol Moseley-Braun and Dianne Feinstein became members of the Senate Judiciary Committee; they were strongly urged to join by Senator Joseph Biden, greatly embarrassed to be chairing an all-male committee during the Anita Faye Hill–Clarence Thomas confrontation (1991). Moseley-Braun was the first African-American woman to become a senator and at the time was the only African-American serving in the Senate.

First known sexual harassment case in Russia was brought by Tatyana L. Smyshlayeva, a physician at a Siberian clinic, against the head physician, for repeated sexual advances and threats of dismissal for resistance; laws against such behavior have never been enforced; this case was dropped by the government during a general amnesty.

Margaret Thatcher published *The Downing Street Years*, the first volume of her autobiography.

d. Anna Lederer Rosenberg (1902–1993), American government official and public relations executive, a key associate of Presidents Roosevelt and Truman.

### RELIGION/EDUCATION/EVERYDAY LIFE

Connie Chung joined Dan Rather as coanchor on the *CBS Evening News*, becoming the second woman (after Barbara Walters in 1976) and first Asian-American to be a nightly news anchor on any of America's big three networks.

Donna Shalala became secretary of health and human services (1993– ) in the Clinton administration.

Alice Walker and Pratibha Parmar made the film *Warrior Marks*, attacking the practice of ritual female genital mutilation, accompanied by the book *Warrior Marks: Female Genital Mutilation and the Sexual Blinding of Women*.

For her humanitarian work in the worldwide fight against AIDS, Elizabeth Taylor was awarded the Jean Hersholt Humanitarian Award at the Academy Awards ceremony.

At a match in Hamburg, an obsessed fan of Steffi Graf stabbed tennis star Monica Seles (April), to keep her from playing; she was injured seriously enough to be forced out of tournament play for over a year.

Betty Friedan published *The Fountain of Age*, exploring the possibility of new roles for older people in a changing society and rejecting the ghettoization of the aged.

First registered rape victims' center and the first crisis line for abused women were opened in Moscow, as sexual abuse continued to rise with the new lawlessness in Russia.

Julie Krone won the Belmont Stakes, becoming the first female jockey to win one of America's "Triple Crown" races; she also won five races in one day at Saratoga (done only twice previously in 126 years).

d. Olive Anne Beech (1903–1993), American aviation entrepreneur.

## SCIENCE/TECHNOLOGY/MEDICINE

Physician Joycelyn Elders, director of the Arkansas Department of Public Health, was appointed U.S. surgeon general, despite conservative opposition to many of her views, including her outspoken support of sex education and child-bearing choice.

At age 11, Vicki Van Meter became the youngest girl to fly across the United States, from Augusta, Maine, to San Diego, California; she handled every aspect of the navigation, though she was accompanied by her instructor, as required by federal regulations for all pilots under age 16.

Ellen Ochoa, the first Hispanic woman in space, was part of the five-person crew of the *Discovery* space shuttle.

Ruth Hubbard and Elijah Wald published *Exploding the Gene Myth*.

d. Janet (Maria) Vaughan (1899–1993), British physician, a specialist in the effects of radiation and longtime university principal of Somerville College (1945–1967).

d. Frida (Henrietta Wilfrida) Avern Leakey (1902–1993), British archaeologist and paleontologist, who worked in East Africa with her husband, Louis Leakey, during their marriage (1928–1936), providing illustrations for some of his early books; later a BBC broadcaster on Africa.

## ARTS/LITERATURE

Toni Morrison was awarded the Nobel Prize for literature, the first African-American woman and second American woman so honored.

Jane Campion's film *The Piano*, starring Holly Hunter, Anna Paquin, Harvey Keitel, and Sam Neill, won the Palme d'Or at the Cannes Film Festival; at the Academy Awards, Hunter was honored as best actress and Paquin as best supporting actress.

Maya Angelou was the first presidential inaugural poet since Robert Frost at John F. Kennedy's inauguration, reading her new poem "On the Pulse of the Morning," before a worldwide audience at President Bill Clinton's inauguration.

Rita Dove became U.S. poet laureate, the first African-American woman and the youngest person in the post.

President Bill Clinton appointed actress Jane Alexander head of the National Endowment for the Arts.

Barbra Streisand issued the album *Back to Broadway*, a collection of songs from the musical theater, and also very successfully returned to the concert stage, after a 27-year absence.

Emma Thompson starred opposite Anthony Hopkins in James Ivory's film *The Remains of the Day*, written by Ruth Prawer Jhabvala, starring as well in *In the Name of the Father* and *Much Ado about Nothing*.

Glenn Close starred as aging film star Norma Desmond opposite Alan Campbell in Andrew Lloyd Webber's stage musical *Sunset Boulevard*, based on the 1950 film; Patti LuPone originated the role in London.

Iris Murdoch published *Metaphysics as a Guide to Morals: Philosophical Reflections* and also the novel *The Green Knight*, a Cain-and-Abel story set in contemporary London.

Michelle Pfeiffer, Daniel Day-Lewis, and Winona Ryder starred in *The Age of Innocence*, Martin Scorsese's film version of Edith Wharton's novel.

Margaret Atwood published the Toronto-set novel *The Robber Bride*, a dark, offbeat comedy about women attacking women.

Anne Rice published the novel *Lasher*, her second work about a New Orleans family of witches.

Debra Winger starred as Joy Gresham opposite Anthony Hopkins as C. S. Lewis in *Shadowlands*, the Richard Attenborough film based on William Nicholson's adaptation of his own play.

Isabelle Allende published the novel *The Infinite Plan*, her first set in the United States and her first with a male central character.

Jodie Foster starred opposite Richard Gere in *Sommersby*, Jon Amiel's post–Civil War film based on *The Return of Martin Guerre*.

Kathy Bates starred in Tony Bill's film *A Home of Our Own*, as a poor, sexually harassed 1960s California woman who, with her six children, sets out to build a new life in Idaho.

Joyce Carol Oates published her novel *Foxfire: Confessions of a Girl Gang*.

Dolly Parton issued the album *Slow Dancing with the Moon*, with such songs as "Put a Little Love in Your Heart," "I'll Make Your Bed," and "Full Circle."

Mariah Carey issued the album *Music Box*, with the songs "Dreamlovers" and "Hero."

Lynn Redgrave starred on Broadway in *Shakespeare for My Father*, her autobiographical one-woman play about her relationship with her father, actor Michael Redgrave.

Natalie Cole issued the album *Take a Look*, a collection of classic songs.

Wynonna (Judd) issued the album *Tell Me Why*.

d. Marian Anderson (1897–1993), American contralto, the first African-American artist to sing at the Metropolitan Opera (1955), to Arturo Toscanini "the voice that comes once in a hundred years." Her Easter Sunday 1939 Lincoln Memorial concert made her a central figure in the American civil rights struggle.

d. Helen Hayes (Helen Hayes Brown, 1900–1993) American actress, a child actress on Broadway, who went on to become a major star in the American theater, in such plays as *Coquette* (1927), *Mary of Scotland* (1933), *Victoria Regina* (1935), and *Time Remembered* (1957).

d. Lillian Gish (Lillian Diana de Guiche, 1893–1993), American actress, who starred in such classic silent films as *Birth of a Nation* (1914) and *Orphans of the Storm* (1922), often co-starring with her sister, Dorothy Gish (1898–1968).

d. Myrna Loy (Myrna Adele Williams, 1905–1993), American actress and social reformer, a great star of Hollywood's golden age, in such classic films as *The Thin Man* (1934) and *The Best Years of Our Lives* (1946).

d. Agnes De Mille (1905–1993), American dancer and the trailblazing choreographer of *Oklahoma*, *Carousel*, *Brigadoon*, and many other works that transformed the American musical theater and helped transform American ballet.

d. Audrey Hepburn (Edda Hepburn-Ruston, 1929–1993), British stage and screen star and humanitarian, best known for such films as *Breakfast at Tiffany's* (1961) and *My Fair Lady* (1964). She was later a goodwill ambassador for the United Nations Children's Fund.

d. Helen O'Connell (1920–1993), American popular singer who became a star with the Jimmy Dorsey band and on records in the 1940s, with such songs as "Green Eyes," "Amapola," and "Tangerine."

d. Alexis Smith (Gladys Smith, 1921–1993) Canadian-American actress, a film star of the 1940s and 1950s.

d. Ruby Keeler (1910–1993), American singer, dancer, and actress, the star of Lloyd Bacon's classic film musical *42nd Street*, *Gold Diggers of 1933*, and *Footlight Parade*; also the wife of singer Al Jolson.

d. Claudia McNeil (1916–1993), African-American actress and singer, who starred as the mother in Lorraine Hansberry's *Raisin in the Sun* and many other powerful stage and screen roles.

d. Adelaide Hall (1901–1993), African-American singer and actress, who starred in *Shuffle Along* (1921) and *Blackbirds of 1928*.

d. Joan Cross (1900–1993), British soprano, producer, and educator.

d. Eleanor Burford Hibbert (1910–1993), prolific British author, who used many pen names, including Jean Plaidy, Victoria Holt, Philippa Carr, Elbur Ford, and others.

## 1994

### POLITICS/LAW/WAR

At the sharply divided United Nations Third International Conference on Population and Development in Cairo, Egypt (September 5–13), an estimated 20,000 attendees met and debated abortion, sexual practices and standards, and other current birth control and family planning issues. The Conference draft plan called for "gender equity and the empowerment of women," and leaders such as Premier Gro Bruntland of Norway called for establishment of a worldwide right to abortion. But the Vatican and many fundamentalist Muslims strongly opposed abortion, called for a return to "sexual morality," and attacked the draft plan. Ultimately, a greatly modified version of the plan was adopted.

Chandrika Bandaranaike Kumaratunga narrowly won election as prime minister of Sri Lanka, and then won by a landslide in the presidential election that followed. She entered into new, but ultimately failed peace negotiations with the Tamil Tigers, aimed at ending the then 13-year-old Sri Lankan Civil War. She is the daughter of Siramovo Bandaranaike, the world's first female prime minister, and was the wife of People's Party co-founder Vijaya Kumaratunga, assassinated in 1988.

In the landmark case of *J.E.B v. T.B.*, the U.S. Supreme Court ruled that jurors could not be disqualified because of their gender by lawyers using peremptory challenges. Retiring Justice Harry A. Blackmun wrote the 5–4 majority opinion, a milestone in the fight for women's rights.

In a second landmark case, *Madsen v. Women's Health Center*, the Supreme Court ruled that anti-abortion activists demonstrating outside a Florida clinic could be restrained by an injunction. Chief Justice William Rehnquist wrote the 6–3 majority opinion. Rehnquist also wrote the unanimous opinion in *National Organization of Women v. Scheidler*, ruling that the federal Racketeer Influenced and Corrupt Organizations Act (RICO) could be a basis for suits by abortion rights organizations against antiabortion groups that had violently attacked clinics.

Former U.S. Navy pilot Paula Coughlin was awarded a total of $6.7 million for sexual assault damages suffered at the September 5–7, 1991, Tailhook Association convention at the Las Vegas Hilton. She had earlier been forced to resign from the navy, while a navy coverup protected those naval officers accused in the scandal, with no convictions and only some early retirements.

The Violence Against Women Act was passed as part of a federal anticrime law; it provided new prohibitions and penalties for violence directed at women and $1.6 billion for enforcement and development of new educational programs.

Women forced into prostitution as "comfort women" by Japanese forces during World War II were denied direct compensation in a ten-year, $1 billion Japanese government plan aimed at atoning for the behavior of Japanese forces during World War II.

Carmen Lawrence was named Australian health and human services minister by Prime Minister Paul Keating.

Legislator Barbara Jordan and National Council of Negro Women president Dorothy Height were awarded U.S. Medals of Freedom.

d. Jacqueline Bouvier Kennedy Onassis (1929–1994), who from 1953 to 1963 had been the very popular wife of President John Fitzgerald Kennedy, and who emerged as one of the most tragic figures in American history on his November 22, 1963, assassination. She was later the wife of Greek shipping magnate Aristotle Onassis, who died in 1975, and then became a New York book editor.

### RELIGION/EDUCATION/EVERYDAY LIFE

The Church of England ordained its first women as priests; in the first group, 32 women were ordained at Bristol Cathedral (March 12), after the British High Court refused to block the ordinations.

In a trailblazing settlement, the United Nations agreed for the first time to pay legal fees and damages to a female employee who charged sexual harassment, in this instance $210,800.

A U.S. federal district court judge ordered the state-supported, all-male Citadel military school, in Charleston, South Carolina, to admit Shannon Faulkner to full student status at the school.

The European Court of Justice ruled that pension payments to men and women must be equal, establishing a principle to be worked out in practice by the individual European Union member nations.

A U.S. federal court ruled that the Army must reinstate Col. Margarethe Cammermeyer, who had been involuntarily discharged in 1992 after stating that she was a lesbian while being directly questioned during a security clearance interview. In 1995, Glenn Close and Barbra Streisand coproduced the award-winning television film *Serving in Silence: The Margarethe Cammermeyer Story*; Close won an Emmy as Cammermeyer.

Ukrainian skater Oksana Baiul won the world women's figure skating gold medal at the 1994 Winter Olympics. American skater Nancy Kerrigan was the silver medalist; she had recovered from a disabling attack on her legs, which had forced her out of the U.S. championship. American skater Tonya Harding was out of Olympic medal contention; she was later stripped of her title and heavily fined for hindering the prosecution of three men accused of being responsible for the attack on Kerrigan.

University of Connecticut forward Rebecca Lobo led her team to a 35–0 unbeaten year, was honored as the most outstanding player of the Final Four, and was consensus National Player of the Year.

Dominique Dawes won the all-around gold medal at the U.S. national gymnastics championships; in the first such sweep in 25 years, she placed first in all four events—the uneven bars, balance beam, vault, and floor exercise.

Kenyan runner Tegla Laroupe was the first black African woman to win a major marathon, winning the New York City Marathon.

Khadra Hassan Farah and her 10-year-old daughter were granted asylum in Canada, after fleeing Somalia to escape ritual genital mutilation.

d. Nicole Brown Simpson (1959–1994), American woman who, with her friend Ronald L. Goldman, was murdered outside her Los Angeles home on June 13. Her former husband, football star and celebrity O. J. Simpson, was accused of her murder, tried in a blaze of publicity, and acquitted in 1995, after a 14-month trial; in 1997 he was convicted of her wrongful death in a civil suit.

d. Wilma Glodean Rudolph (1940–1994), American athlete, a major figure in the history of women's sports. She was the first American woman to win three Olympic gold medals in running, in the 100 and 200 meters, and as anchor of the 400-meter relay at Rome (1960).

d. Betty Furness (Elizabeth Mary Furness, 1916–1994), pioneering American consumer affairs advocate, actress, and broadcast journalist, who in the late 1960s was President Lyndon Johnson's special assistant on consumer affairs.

### SCIENCE/TECHNOLOGY/MEDICINE

China banned the use of ultrasound to determine the sex of fetuses; in male-dominated Chinese life, massive numbers of female babies were being aborted in favor of male babies. Despite worldwide condemnation as human rights violations, new Chinese laws also sought to ban marriages by some people with genetic defects and to force abortions of fetuses with genetic defects.

U.S. Surgeon General and Arkansas pediatrician Joycelyn Elders was fired by President Bill Clinton (December 9). An unswerving advocate on such issues as increased sex education for children and legalization of some drugs, Elders had survived a nine-month-long confirmation process to become Surgeon General in September 1993 but had continued to be a focus of conservative attack.

Vicki Van Meter, age 12, was the youngest woman to fly across the Atlantic Ocean, from Augusta, Maine, to Glasgow, Scotland, with stops en route.

Heart surgeon Dr. Chiaki Naito-Makai became the first Japanese citizen to fly in a spaceship, on the *Columbia* space shuttle (July 8–23).

d. Dorothy Crowfoot Hodgkin (1910–1994), British chemist and academic, one of the most notable scientists of the century, who won the 1964 Nobel Prize for chemistry for her pioneering work in using X-ray crystallography to explore molecular structures. She was also a leading activist against apartheid and nuclear weapons.

d. Dixy Lee Ray (Margaret Ray, 1914–1994), American marine biologist, who headed the U.S. Atomic Energy Commission (1973–1975) and was the first female governor of the state of Washington (1977–1981).

d. Elizabeth Meyer Glaser (1947–1994), celebrated American AIDS activist, a cofounder of the Pediatric AIDS Foundation. She had contracted AIDS from a blood transfusion while pregnant and unknowingly passed it on to her children, one of whom died from AIDS transmitted through her breast milk. She became a national figure after telling her story to worldwide television viewers during her very notable address to the 1992 Democratic National Convention.

d. Marija Gimbutas (1920–1994), Lithuanian-American archaeologist and author, a leading advocate of the theory that before approximately 4000 B.C. European civilization was dominated by goddess-worshipping matriarchies, which were later conquered by patriarchies. Her books included *Goddesss and Gods of Old Europe* (1974) and *The Civilization of the Goddess* (1991).

## ARTS/LITERATURE

Singer Whitney Houston won Grammys for record of the year and best pop vocal for her rendition of "I Will Always Love You," and for the album of the year for the soundtrack of the film *The Bodyguard*, which included the top hit single.

Bangladesh physician, feminist, and writer Taslima Nasrin fled to asylum in Sweden after Islamic fundamentalists accused her of insulting Islam in her 1993 novel *Shame* (*Lajja*) and threatened her with death, while a warrant was issued for her arrest.

Jodie Foster coproduced and starred as the speech-impaired North Carolina backwoodswoman in the film *Nell*, based on Mark Handley's play *Idioglossia* and costarring Liam Neeson and Natasha Richardson.

E. Annie Proulx won the Pulitzer Prize and a National Book Award for her best-selling novel *The Shipping News*.

Whoopi Goldberg became the first woman and the first African-American to host the Academy Awards show.

*Billboard* named singer and songwriter Mariah Carey the top female musical artist of 1994.

South African author Nadine Gordimer published the novel *None to Accompany Me*, set in post-apartheid South Africa.

Actress Meryl Streep starred in the action-thriller *The River Wild*.

Country singer and songwriter Dolly Parton published her autobiography, *Dolly: My Life and Other Unfinished Business*, and issued the album *Heartsounds*.

Joyce Carol Oates published the novel *What I Lived For* and the short-story collection *Haunted: Tales of the Grotesque*.

Singer Toni Braxton received two Grammys, for best new artist and best female rhythm and blues performance, for the single "Another Sad Love Song."

Diana Rigg received a Tony Award as best actress in a play for her performance in the title role in *Medea*.

Singer Natalie Cole received her seventh Grammy, for the album *Take a Look* (1993).

Donna Murphy received a Tony Award as best actress in a musical for her work in *Passion*.

Joanne Whalley-Kilmer starred as Scarlett O'Hara opposite Timothy Dalton as Rhett Butler in *Scarlett*, a television film sequel to *Gone with the Wind*.

d. Jessica Tandy (1909–1994), distinguished British-American actress, on stage in London from 1927, who became a leading Shakespearean actress in the 1930s and created the role of Blanche Du Bois in Tennessee Williams's play *A Streetcar Named Desire* (1947). She was partnered with her second husband, Hume Cronyn, in many plays and several films. Late in her career, she also became a film star, winning a best actress Oscar for her work in the title role in *Driving Miss Daisy* (1989).

d. Giulietta Masina (Giulia Anna Masina, 1920–1994), celebrated Italian film star, who created the classic Oscar-winning role of Gelsomina in *La Strada* (1954), directed by her husband, Federico Fellini. She created classic roles in several other films, most notably in Fellini's *Nights of Cabiria* (1956) and *Juliet of the Spirits* (1965).

d. Madeleine Renaud (1900–1994), noted French stage and screen star and theater director, one of the leading figures of the French theater. After starring in the Comédie-Francaise (1923–1946), she and her husband, Jean-Louis Barrault, founded the Renaud-Barrault repertory company (1946), working together for almost half a century. On screen, she was a star of the Golden Age of French films, creating the title role in *Maria Chapdeleine* (1934).

d. Mai Zetterling (1925–1994), Swedish actress, writer, and director, who emerged on the world scene as the star of the classic film *Frenzy* (*Torment;* 1944), directed by Alf Sjoberg and written by Ingmar Bergman. Much of her later fiction film work was on feminist themes.

d. Dinah Shore (Frances Rose Shore, 1917–1994) American singer and actress, a great star in the 1940s, starting with her rendition of "Blues in the Night" (1942); from the 1950s through the 1970s she was a popular television host.

d. Pat Harper (Patricia Harper, 1935–1994), pioneering, Emmy-winning American broadcast journalist, who in 1980 was the first woman to anchor a nationally syndicated news show, *USA Tonight.*

d. Dorothy Collins (Marjorie Chandler, 1926–1994), Canadian singer and bandleader, who was best known by far as the lead singer of the popular television show *Your Hit Parade* (1950–1957).

d. Pearl Primus (1919–1994), celebrated African-American choreographer, dancer, anthropologist, and teacher, who was awarded a 1981 National Medal of the Arts.

d. Amy Clampitt (1920–1994), American poet, best known for her collections *The Kingfisher* (1983) and *What the Light Was Like* (1985).

d. Elizabeth Maconchy (1907–1994), British composer.

## 1995

### POLITICS/LAW/WAR

In her opening day address to the United Nations Fourth World Conference on Women, held in Beijing, China (September 4–15), Pakistani prime minister Benazir Bhutto sharply attacked worldwide abuse of women and female children, especially focusing on "son preference," as in China and India, which every year results in hundreds of thousands and perhaps millions of abortions of female fetuses and murders of female babies. Many other speakers addressed similar issues. American first lady Hillary Rodham Clinton focused on a wide range of human rights abuses, with China clearly in mind, though she did not attack its record directly. The conference called for many reforms and condemned many specific abuses, among them ritual genital mutilation, domestic violence, sexual harassment, mass rape in wartime, and genocide.

Hillary Rodham Clinton addressed the 180-nation first United Nations World Summit on Social Development in Copenhagen, Denmark (March 6–13), urging world focus on the health and education of women and girls.

The Japanese government set up a fund to compensate an estimated 200,000 World War II "comfort women," most of them Korean, who had been forced into prostitution, serving Japanese occupation forces. Named the Asia Peace and Friendship Foundation for Women, the fund was described as "private," rather than governmental, and was also to solicit private contributions. Many former "comfort women" refused these cash awards, which began to be offered in 1996, because they felt that the "private" nature of the organization was an attempt to avoid Japanese government responsibility for war crimes.

American politician Carol Bellamy was named head of the United Nations Children's Fund (UNICEF) by U.N. Secretary-General Boutros Boutros-Ghali.

Jane Alexander received a special Tony Award on behalf of the National Endowment for the Arts (NEA), for that federal funding organization's contribution to the theater. The award was essentially for Alexander, who in her second year as head of the NEA, continued to battle with congressional conservatives over the future of the NEA.

The Senate Ethics Committee recommended the expulsion of Oregon senator Bob Packwood, on September 6 issuing a 179-page report backed by thousands of pages of evidence that showed a "pattern of sex abuse" of his subordinates that involved at least 17 women. Packwood resigned (September 7), ending one of the most notable sexual harassment cases of the 1990s.

Queen Elizabeth II made her first visit to South Africa since 1947; she had refused to visit the country during the apartheid period, in protest against its racism.

Christine Silverberg became Canada's first woman named a major city police chief, with her appointment as chief of the Calgary Police Service.

Irish voters narrowly voted (50.3 percent to 49.7 percent) to legalize divorce. Ireland has been the last European country still banning divorce.

The European Court of Justice ruled that the use of hiring quotas to increase the hiring and promotion of women was discriminatory.

Laura D'Andrea Tyson, chairwoman of the Council of Economic Advisers, was appointed by President Bill Clinton to chair the National Economic Council.

Children's television figures Joan Ganz Cooney and Peggy Charen were awarded Presidential Medals of Freedom.

d. Margaret Chase Smith (1897–1995), American politician. In 1940, when her husband, Maine congressman Clyde R. Smith, died in office, Margaret Chase Smith won election to his unexpired term, and to four more terms, as well. She then served four terms in the Senate, becoming the first woman to serve in both houses of Congress. An independent and moderate Republican, she ran for the Republican presidential nomination in 1964.

d. Maggie Kuhn (Margaret E. Kuhn, 1905–1995), American feminist who devoted her career to social causes, working with the YWCA, General Alliance of Unitarian Women, and United Presbyterian Church. After retiring in 1970, she founded the Gray Panthers in 1971, and for a quarter of a century was a leading national spokesperson for older Americans, especially on issues vitally affecting older women. She also spoke out on a much wider range of issues, among them sexism and racism, and was a leading opponent of the Vietnam War.

d. Georgia Neese Clark Gray (1900–1995), American actress, bank president, and longtime New Deal Democratic National Committeewoman (1937–1964), a major figure in the Democratic Party for almost three decades. In 1949, President Harry S. Truman appointed her treasurer of the United States; she was the first woman to hold that post (1949–1953).

d. Odette Marie Céline Brailey Hallowes (1912–1995), French-born spy, a legendary World War II British Special Operations executive intelligence agent in France. She was captured by the Germans in 1943, tortured repeatedly by the Gestapo, and sent to the Ravensbrück death camp, where her torture continued; she told them nothing. After the war, she received the British George Cross and the French Legion of Honor. Anna Neagle played her in the film *Odette* (1950).

d. Oveta Culp Hobby (1905–1995), American politician and businesswoman who was the first head of the Women's Army Corps (1942) and became the first woman to be awarded the Distinguished Service Medal (1946). President Dwight D. Eisenhower named her head of the Federal Security Agency (1953); it became the Department of Health, Education, and Welfare and she became its first head and the second woman to become a cabinet member.

d. Rose Fitzgerald Kennedy (1890–1995), child of a Boston political family and herself an astute political adviser; she was the daughter of Boston mayor John "Honey Fitz" Fitgerald, wife of financier and Democratic politician Joseph Kennedy, and the mother of nine children, among them assassinated President John Fitzgerald Kennedy, assassinated presidential candidate Robert (Bobby) Francis Kennedy, and Senator Edward (Ted) Kennedy.

### RELIGION/EDUCATION/EVERYDAY LIFE

After a two-year-long struggle that became one of the key women's rights battles of the 1990s, Shannon Faulkner was admitted to the Citadel military college (August 14), at Charleston, South Carolina. Admission came after the Fourth Circuit Court of Appeals had upheld a federal district court decision and the Supreme Court had refused a final appeal by the school. Exhausted, Faulkner collapsed in 100-degree heat (August 14), was too sick to attend the Citadel, and resigned (August 18). However, the admissions battle had been won; she was followed by scores of other applicants.

In a papal letter (July 10), Pope John Paul II apologized for past discrimination against women, including that of the Roman Catholic Church, and congratulated women's rights activists for gains achieved, while restating Catholic church opposition to abortion, contraception, and the ordination of women priests, the latter a major current issue, especially in the United States. In his 11th encyclical, *Evangelium Vitae* (*The Gospel of Life*), the Pope restated his opposition to abortion and euthanasia, also commenting on several related matters.

The CIA settled a major class action suit involving sexual discrimination, with $990,000 going to 450 women in its Directorate of Operations (secret operations), plus a series of promised promotions.

In the landmark case of *Adarand Constructors v. Pena*, the Supreme Court ruled that the federal government must follow the same standards as the states in carrying out affirmative action programs, reversing the Court's previous position on federal affirmative action programs. Justice Sandra Day O'Connor wrote the 5–4 majority opinion.

Myrlie Evers-Williams became chairperson of the deeply divided, declining, and financially damaged National Association for the Advancement of Colored People (NAACP), replacing Dr. William F. Gibson. She was the widow of Mississippi NAACP leader Medger Evers, murdered by racist Byron De La Beckwith (1963).

Steffi Graf held a No. 1 world singles ranking throughout the year, though she shared it with Monica Seles late in the year. Graf won nine tournaments, three of them Gland Slam titles, despite recurring back and foot injuries and protracted tax and other legal problems in Germany.

Chen Lu became the first Chinese figure skater to win a world championship, with a very notable long program set to music from the film *The Last Emperor*.

The bipartisan U.S. Glass Ceiling Commission reported that women and minority groups continued to be little represented in senior management positions and that the "glass ceiling" remained firmly in place.

Hillary Rodham Clinton published the bestseller *It Takes a Village: and Other Lessons Children Teach Us*.

Diana, the Princess of Wales, became the center of yet another media circus after her tell-all interview with BBC reporter Martin Bashir was televised to an audience of tens of millions. She and her husband, Charles, the Prince of Wales, would divorce in 1996, a year before her death.

d. Helen Vlachos (1911–1995), Greek newspaper publisher who inherited the Greek daily *Kathimerini*, closing it (1967–1974) while working against the military junta; later a member of parliament.

d. Margaret Cahill (1905–1995), American beauty contest winner, who was the first Miss America (1921).

d. Mary Caperton Bingham (1904–1995), American publisher, editor, and philanthropist; the Binghams' family media empire was anchored by the *Louisville Courier-Journal*.

## SCIENCE/TECHNOLOGY/MEDICINE

The Department of Energy, under the direction of Secretary of Energy Hazel O'Leary, concluded its investigation of radiation experiments on humans. It reported that more than 16,000 experiments had been conducted through the late 1970s, some of them on aborted fetuses and on children—and this total did not include an unstated number of experiments by several major government agencies, including the Defense and Health and Human Services departments.

U.S. Air Force Lt. Col. Eileen M. Collins became the first woman to pilot a space shuttle, taking *Discovery* to a rendezvous with the *Mir* space station.

Kenyan archaeologist Maeve Leakey announced a new find, *Australopithecus anamensis*, a biped more than 4 million years old.

The U.S. National Center for Health Statistics reported that the overall breast cancer death rate had dropped by 4.7 percent since 1992.

d. Onnie Lee Logan (1910–1995), Alabama midwife, who practiced in Prichard, Alabama (near Mobile), from 1931 through the early 1990s, despite later state regulations that banned midwifery. She became a national figure with publication of her autobiographical book *Motherwit: An Alabama Midwife's Story* (1989), which set out her recollections, as taped by author Katherine Clark.

## ARTS/LITERATURE

Anne Tyler published the novel *Ladder of Years*, about a woman who leaves her family to begin a new life.

Actress and director Diane Keaton directed the comedy-drama film *Unstrung Heroes*, starring Andie MacDowell and John Turturro.

Amy Tan published her third novel, *The Hundred Secret Senses*, exploring a difficult relationship between two Chinese half-sisters, one America-born and the other China-born.

Anne Rice published the bestselling novel *Memnoch the Devil*, fifth in her *Vampire Chronicles* series.

Carol Ann Shields received a Pulitzer Prize and a National Book Critics Circle Award for her novel *The Stone Diaries*, the fictional biography of a 20th-century woman.

Glenn Close won the best actress Tony Award for her performance as silent screen star Norma Desmond in the stage musical *Sunset Boulevard*, Andrew Lloyd Webber's adaptation of Billy Wilder's 1950 classic film drama.

Indian novelist Anita Desai published the novel *Journey to Ithaca*, about a young European couple in India; it drew heavily from the experience of her parents.

Isabel Allende published the novel *Paula*, an autobiographical work written while her daughter Paula was in the long coma that ended with her death.

Jessica Lange won the best actress Oscar for her work in the film *Blue Sky*.

Joyce Carol Oates published the novel *Zombie*, in which she created and explored the inner thoughts of a serial killer, much like real-life killer Jeffrey Dahmer.

Julie Andrews opened on Broadway in a smash hit stage version of her 1982 hit musical film *Victor/Victoria*, again starring as a down-on-her-luck English singer in 1920s Paris, who becomes a star in cabaret while playing a man who successfully masquerades as a woman.

Margaret Atwood published the poetry collection *Morning in the Burning House*.

Mary Chapin Carpenter's album *Stones in the Road* won a Grammy as best country album of the year, and for the album she won a Grammy for best female country performance of the year.

Meryl Streep starred opposite Clint Eastwood in the film version of Robert James Waller's best-selling novel *The Bridges of Madison County*.

Shirley MacLaine published the best-selling autobiography *My Hollywood Family*.

Singer and songwriter Bonnie Raitt received a best pop album Grammy for *Longing in Their Hearts*.

Singer and songwriter Sheryl Crow won Grammys for best pop vocal performane of the year and best new artist of the year, while her hit single "All I Wanna Do" won the best record of the year Grammy.

Singer Melissa Etheridge won a Grammy for best female rock vocal performance, for "Come to My Window."

Versatile film star Annette Bening starred opposite Michael Douglas in *The American President* and as Queen Elizabeth opposite Ian McKellan in a film version of Shakespeare's *Richard III*.

Yet another generation of Barrymores arrived: Drew Barrymore starred opposite Chris O'Donnell in the film *Mad Love*.

d. Ginger Rogers (Virginia Katherine McMath, 1911–1995), American actress, a film star of Hollywood's Golden Age and beyond. She was best known by far for her roles opposite Fred Astaire in their ten classic film musicals, from *Flying Down to Rio* (1933) to *The Barkeleys of Broadway* (1949). She won a best actress Oscar for her straight dramatic role in *Kitty Foyle* (1941).

d. Ida Lupino (1918–1995), British-American actress, director, writer, and producer, on screen from 1933. She became a Hollywood star following her breakthrough role opposite Ronald Colman in *The Light That Failed* (1940) and her classic role opposite Humphrey Bogart in *High Sierra* (1941). She was the daughter of British actor Stanley Lupino and a member of the great Lupino stage family.

d. Bessie Delany (Annie Elizabeth Delany 1891–1995), American dentist, the second black woman to be a dentist in New York City. She and her sister, Sadie (Sarah) Delany, then 102 and 104 years old, published the best-selling oral history *Having Our Say: The Delany Sisters' First Hundred Years* (1993).

d. Selena (Selena Quantanilla Perez, 1971–1995), Mexican-American popular music star; she was shot and killed at Corpus Christi, Texas (March 31), by Yolande Salvador, chief organizer of Selena's fan club.

d. Elizabeth Montgomery (1933–1995), American actress and television star, who was best known by far for her role as witch Samantha Stevens in the long-running television series *Bewitched* (1964–1972). She was the daughter of movie star Robert Montgomery.

d. Lana Turner (1920–1995), American actress.

d. Vivian Blaine (Vivian Stapleton, 1921–1995), American stage and screen musical star, best known for her role as cabaret singer Adelaide in the hit Broadway musical *Guys and Dolls* (1950), which she reprised in the 1955 film version.

d. Brigid Antonia Brophy (1929–1995), British author, best known for her debut novel *Hackenfeller's Ape* (1953). Though impeded by multiple sclerosis from 1981, she was also a dedicated crusader on many social causes and was president of the British National Anti-Vivisection Society.

d. Dorothy Schofield Dickson (1893–1995), American singer, dancer, and actress, who became a star on the British stage, beginning with her rendition of "Look for the Silver Lining," in the 1921 London stage version of the Jerome Kern musical *Sally*.

d. Viveca Lindfors (Elsa Viveca Torstendsdotter Lindfors, 1920–1995), Swedish actress, who became an American stage and screen star after going to Hollywood in 1946. She made her 1955 Broadway debut in the title role of the play *Anastasia*.

## 1996

### POLITICS/LAW/WAR

Madeleine Albright was nominated U.S. secretary of state by President Bill Clinton (December 5). With her confirmation by the Senate (January 22, 1997), she became the first woman to hold that high post.

Pakistan Prime Minister Benazir Bhutto and her government were dismissed by President Farooq Leghari (November 5). Bhutto and her husband, Asif Ali Zardari, were arrested; she was charged with corruption and other illegal acts, he with complicity in the September murder of her brother. She and her party were decisively defeated at the polls (Febuary 3), though she was again elected to the National Assembly. Many feared for her life; her father, Prime Minister Zulfikar Ali Bhutto, had been executed by the Zia Ul-Haq military government in 1979.

First Lieutenant Kelly Flinn became the U.S. Air Force's first female B-52 bomber pilot. In 1997, she would be forced to accept a general discharge because of an adulterous affair, about which she lied to investigators—although many would charge the armed services with sexual double standards, outmoded regulations, and outright hypocrisy in the wake of the Flinn case.

Following a series of sensational rape and sex abuse charges, the U.S. Army announced a wide range of sexual crime investigations, which continued into 1997, with many rape, sex abuse, and sexual harassment prosecutions and some convictions.

U.S. radical activist Lori Berenson was arrested by the Peruvian government, convicted of treason by a secret military court, and sentenced to life imprisonment. Her case was taken up by international human rights organizations and generated further worldwide criticism of the Peruvian government and of President Alberto Fujimori.

White House public liaison director Alexis Margaret Herman was nominated by President Bill Clinton to succeed outgoing Secretary of Labor Robert Reich (December 20). She would take office on April 30, 1997, after a very long confirmation process.

Rutsuko Nagao was appointed Japanese justice minister by Prime Minister Ryutaro Hashimoto.

Three U.S. servicemen were convicted by a Japanese court of the November 1995 kidnapping and rape of a 12-year-old Okinawan girl, in a case that had aroused a storm of protest and condemnation in Japan.

New York Congresswoman Susan Molinari was the keynote speaker at the Republican National Convention.

d. Barbara Charlene Jordan (1936–1996), American civil rights leader, politician, and lawyer, the first black Texas state legislator (1966–1972) since Reconstruction. She was a Democratic Texas congresswoman (1973–1979), drawing wide attention as the keynote speaker at the 1976 Democratic National Convention. She was later a professor of public service at the University of Texas and in the mid-1990s chaired the federal Commission on Immigration Reform.

d. Anna Mikhailovna Larina (1914–1996), Russian author, the wife of executed (1938) Soviet Communist leader Nicolai Bukharin, who was "posthumously rehabilitated" half a century later (1988), at least partially through her efforts from 1959 to clear his name, though she was long held in internal exile. Her best-selling autobiography was *This I Cannot Forget* (1988).

RELIGION/EDUCATION/EVERYDAY LIFE

At the Atlanta Olympics, the U.S. women's gymnastics team took home their first gold medal. One of the year's enduring television images was that of Kerri Strug completing her final vault on a badly strained ankle to clinch the gold medal and then being carried to the platform for the medal ceremony by her coach, Bela Karolyi. Teammate Shannon Miller became the first American to win a gold medal on the balance beam.

A new era opened in women's basketball, as the U.S. Women's Senior National Team (the "Dream Team"), coached by Tara VanDerveer, became the U.S. Olympic women's basketball team—and capped a 60-game winning record by defeating Brazil 111–87 to win the Olympic gold medal. In the winter of 1996, the new women's American Basketball League (ABL) began play, and in the spring of 1997, the new Women's National Basketball Association (WNBA) began its inaugural season before record-breaking crowds.

American swimmer Amy Van Dyken won four gold medals at the Atlanta Olympics, in the 50-meter freestyle, 100-meter butterfly, 4 x 100 medley relay, and 4 x 100 freestyle relay.

Chinese diver Fu Mingxia won two gold medals at the Atlanta Olympics, successfully defending her 10-meter platform diving title and adding the 3-meter diving title.

U.S. runner Gail Devers won two gold medals at the Atlanta Olympics, successfully defending her 1992 Olympic gold in the 100-meter sprint, and winning a second gold in the 4 x 400-meter relay.

French Guadeloupan runner Marie-José Pérec won two gold medals at the Atlanta Olympics, in the 200 and 400 meters.

Russian runner Svetlana Masterkova won two gold medals at the Atlanta Olympics, in the 800 meters and the 1,500 meters.

Irish swimmer Michelle Smith won three gold medals at the Atlanta Olympics—in the 400-meter freestyle, and the 200- and 400-meter individual medleys—and a bronze, in the 200-meter butterfly.

In a landmark ruling (June 3), the U.S. Board of Immigration Appeals found that Fauzinga Kasinga, who had fled Togo in 1994 to escape ritual genital mutilation, was entitled to asylum under U.S. immigration law. While doing so, the Board stated that her story was true; on arrival she had been imprisoned by the Immigration and Naturalization Service in degrading conditions, and an immigration judge had stated that he did not believe her story. But the American media and worldwide human rights organizations intervened, proved her story true, and forced the reversal.

In the landmark *U.S. v. Virginia* case, Justice Ruth Bader Ginsburg, writing for the majority of the Supreme Court, ruled that the state-funded Virginia Military Institute had violated the 14th Amendment by refusing to admit women as students and must either admit women or go completely private, forfeiting state support. Her ruling also included The Citadel; both schools then announced full compliance with the Court's ruling.

Seven-year-old Jessica Dubroff died in a plane crash on takeoff in a rainstorm, while trying to become the youngest to ever fly from coast to coast. Her father and her flight instructor died with her.

Champion Russian figure skater Ekaterina Gordeeva published the bestseller *My Sergei: A Love Story*, about her life with her husband and figure-skating partner, Sergei Grinkov, which ended with his 1995 fatal heart attack. She began to build a career as a singles skater in 1996.

In the landmark *Romer v. Evans* case, Justice Anthony Kennedy, writing for a 6–3 majority of the Supreme Court, ruled unconstitutional the state of Colorado's recently adopted constitutional amendment 2, which prohibited all governments in the state from passing laws barring discrimination.

Fifteen-year-old American figure skater Michelle Kwan won the world and U.S. national figure skating championships.

Picabo Street won the world downhill women's skiing championship, the first American do so.

A group of feminist organizations organized the first annual Feminist Expo, held in Washington, D.C.

d. Jessica Mitford (1917–1996), British-American author, who was best known by far for her best-seller *The American Way of Death* (1963), an exposè of the American funeral industry.

d. Felice N. Schwartz (1924–1996) American women's rights activist, founder of the organization Catalyst, aimed at advancing women in corporate life. One of her proposals, in 1989, brought great criticism from other feminists, who blamed her (probably in error) for creating the concept of the "mommy track."

d. Toni Stone (Marcenia Lyle Stone, 1921–1996), American baseball player, the first woman to play in a men's professional league (1953).

d. Jessie Ravitch Bernard (1903–1996), American sociologist.

### SCIENCE/TECHNOLOGY/MEDICINE

The U.S. launched the Mars probe *Pathfinder* (December 4), which included the Mars exploration robot vehicle *Sojourner*. It had previously launched the Mars-orbiting probe *Surveyor* (November 7). The *Pathfinder* would land successfully and on schedule (July 4, 1997), with the slower *Surveyor* scheduled to go into orbit around Mars in early September 1997. The entire project, with several further Mars probes scheduled, had been largely developed by Dr. Donna S. Shirley, head of the Mars exploration project at the National Aeronautics and Space Administration's Space Jet Propulsion Laboratory. She also designed the *Sojourner* which captured the imagination of hundreds of millions back on Earth.

American astronaut and biochemist Shannon Lucid set a new woman's record for the longest stay in space, with 188 days on the Soviet space station *Mir*, breaking Elena Kondakova's record of 169 days (1994–1995). She also set a new record for an American in space, breaking Norman Thagard's record of 115 days (1995). Lucid was awarded a Congressional Space Medal of Honor.

Neuroscientist Claudie Andre-Deshays became the first French woman in space, making a shuttle voyage to the Russian space station *Mir* (August 17–September 2).

Two studies indicated that a specific gene mutation was often the cause of breast cancer occurring in young women. In these preliminary studies, the gene seemed especially prevalent among some groups of Jewish women.

The U.S. Food and Drug Administration (FDA) approved the antiabortion drug RU486, accepting the recommendation of an FDA panel.

d. Mary Leakey (Mary Douglas Nicol Leakey, 1913–1996), British anthropologist and paleontologist, who with her husband, anthropologist Louis Leakey, worked in East Africa from 1936. In 1959, at Olduvai Gorge, in Tanzania, they discovered hominid remains 2 million years old, revolutionizing thinking about human evolution. After his death in 1972, she went on to unearth several major new finds, including human footprints 3.7 million years old. Her autobiography was *Disclosing the Past* (1984). She was the mother of conservationist and paleontologist Richard Leakey.

d. Mollie Beattie (1947–1996), American forester and natural resources manager, who was director of the U.S. Fish and Wildlife Service (1993–1996), the first woman to hold that post.

### ARTS/LITERATURE

Polish poet Wislawa Szymborska was awarded the 1996 Nobel Prize for literature.

Susan Sarandon won a best actress Oscar for her performance as Sister Helen Prejean in the film *Dead Man Walking*, about Prejean's work with Death Row inmates.

American country singer LeAnn Rimes, just 13 years old, made a stunning recording debut with the top hit single "Blue," the centerpiece of her equally popular album of the same name.

Comedian and actress Ellen DeGeneres published the best-seller *My Point. . . and I Do Have One*, and prepared to "go public" as to her lesbian sexual preference—which she did on her television series *Ellen* in 1997, accompanied by enormous publicity, becoming the first openly gay lead character in a prime-time network television situation comedy.

Celine Dion opened the Atlanta Olympics, singing "The Power of the Dream" to a worldwide television audience of more than a billion people.

Madonna starred as Evita Perón in the title role of the film musical *Evita*, Alan Parker's screen adaptation of the 1976 Andrew Lloyd Webber–Tim Rice stage musical.

Meg Ryan starred as U.S. helicopter pilot Captain Karen Walden, who died in action (1991) during the Persian Gulf War, in the film *Courage Under Fire*. It focused on an investigation of the circumstances of her death, occurring while she was being considered for a Congressional Medal of Honor.

Canadian composer, singer, and guitarist Joni Mitchell shared the Polar Music Prize with classical composer Pierre Boulez.

Whoopi Goldberg starred in the fact-based film *Ghosts of Mississippi*, as Myrlie Evers, whose husband, civil rights leader Medgar Evers, had been murdered by racist Byron De La Beckwith during the struggle for civil rights—and who after a quarter century of trying saw the case reopened and De La Beckwith convicted.

Jamaica Kincaid published *The Autobiography of My Mother*, a fictionalized account of her mother's life on her home island of Dominica.

Barbra Streisand directed, produced, composed, sang in, and starred in the romantic film comedy *The Mirror Has Two Faces*, opposite Jeff Bridges and Lauren Bacall.

Actress Claire Bloom published the autobiography *Leaving a Doll's House: A Memoir*, focusing on her charges that writer and former husband Philip Roth had treated her abusively during their 15 years together.

Zoë Caldwell was awarded the Tony Award for leading actress in a play for her work in *Master Class*.

Joan Didion published the novel *The Last Thing He Wanted*, set in the United States and during the Nicaraguan Civil War.

Toni Morrison's novel *The Song of Solomon*, originally published in 1977 and reissued in 1995, suddenly became a top seller, after Oprah Winfrey recommended it on her television show.

Julie Christie starred as Gertrude in Kenneth Branagh's version of *Hamlet*, opposite Branagh in the title role.

Margaret Atwood published the novel *Alias Grace*, based on the well-known Marks-McDermott Canadian murder case.

Shirley MacLaine starred again as Aurora Greenway in the film *The Evening Star*, a 15-years-on sequel to *Terms of Endearment* (1983).

Singer and songwriter Sheryl Crow issued her second hit album, *Sheryl Crow*.

Donna Murphy was awarded the Tony Award as leading actress in a musical for her work in *The King and I*.

Louise Erdrich published the novel *Tales of Burning Love*.

Tracy Chapman issued a hit album, *New Beginning*.

d. Ella Fitzgerald (1917–1996), American singer, one of the great jazz and popular singers of the century. Her breakthrough came with her recording of "A Tisket, a Tasket (1938). She was a leading bop and scat singer in the 1940s, then moved back into popular music, most notably in her classic recordings with Louis Armstrong and her equally classic "songbook" recordings, each featuring the works of a notable composer, starting with *Ella Fitzgerald Sings Cole Porter* (1958).

d. Claudette Colbert (Claudette Lily Chauchoin, 1903–1996), French-American stage and screen actress, a great star of Hollywood's Golden Age, whose breakthrough role came in Cecil B. DeMille's *The Sign of the Cross* (1932). She became an international film figure in the classic comedy *It Happened One Night* (1934), a year in which she also starred in *Imitation of Life* and *Cleopatra*. Among her later films were *Skylark* (1940) and *The Egg and I* (1947).

d. Greer Garson (1903–1996), British actress, a Hollywood star from her breakthrough role opposite Robert Donat in *Goodbye, Mr. Chips* (1939). She won a best actress Oscar in the title role of an indomitable wartime heroine in *Mrs Miniver* (1942). She received best actress Oscar nominations for *Blossoms in the Dust* (1941), *Madame Curie* (1943), *Mrs. Parkington* (1944), *The Valley of Decision* (1945), and *Sunrise at Campobello* (1960).

d. Marguerite Duras (Margaret Donnadieu, 1914–1996), French writer and director, whose breakthrough novels were *The Sea Wall* (1950) and *The Sailor from Gibraltar* (1952). Her first screenplay was for the classic *Hiroshima, Mon Amour* (1959). She became an international figure with the best-selling novel *The Lover* (1984), which she adapted for the 1992 film.

d. Annabella (Suzanne Georgette Charpentier, 1909–1996), French actress, a film star of the Golden Age of French films, who scored her breakthrough in Rene's Clair's musical *Le Millione* (1931), followed up with a starring role in his *July 14th* (1933), and later starred in *Hotel du Nord* (1938). In the late 1930s and 1940s she starred in several British and then Hollywood films, among them *Suez* (1938), opposite Tyrone Power, to whom she was married (1939–1948).

d. Audrey Meadows (Audrey Cotter, 1922–1996), American actress, best known by far for her classic television role as Alice Kramden opposite Jackie Gleason in *The Jackie Gleason Show* (1952–1953) and *The Honeymooners* (1955–1956).

d. Minnie Pearl (Sarah Ophelia Colley, 1912–1996), American actress and singer who introduced her comedy act on radio's "Grand Ole Opry" (1940) and for more than half a century was a major figure in country music.

d. Jacquetta Hawkes (1910–1996), British archaeologist and author, long associated with UNESCO (1943–1979), best known for her popular writings on archaeology.

d. Jessica Lucy Mitford (1917–1996), British-American author, who was best known by far for her bestseller *The American Way of Death* (1963), an exposé of the American funeral industry.

d. Dorothy Lamour (Mary Leta Dorothy Kaumeyer, 1914–1996), American actress and singer who played several sex-symbol roles during Hollywood's Golden Age, generally in her trademark sarong, as in *The Hurricane* (1937) and *Aloma of the South Seas* (1941). She was also a fine comedian, playing successfully opposite Bing Crosby and Bob Hope in their seven "road" films, from *Road to Singapore* (1940) to *Road to Hong Kong* (1962).

d. Meridel LeSueur (1900–1996), American writer best known by far for her novel *North Star Country* (1945), set during the settlement of the northern Midwest.

d. Lola Beltrán (Maria Lucila Beltrán Ruiz, 1932–1996), celebrated Mexican mariachi singer, known to her millions of fans as "Queen of the Ranchera."

d. Marcia Davenport (1903–1996), American novelist, music critic and editor, best known for her novels *The Valley of Decision* (1943; basis of the 1945 film), about a Pittsburgh steel family, and *East Side, West Side* (1947; filmed in 1949).

d. Mary Lavin (1912–1996), Irish writer.

d. Tamara Toumanova (1919–1996), Russian-American dancer and actress.

d. Louise Talma (1906–1996), American composer and teacher.

# Select Bibliography*

Adburgham, Alison. *Women in Print: Writing Women and Women's Magazines from the Restoration to the Accession of Victoria*. London: Allen & Unwin, 1972.

Allayson-Jones, Lindsay. *Women in Roman Britain*. London: British Museum Publications, 1989.

Amt, Emilie, ed. *Women's Lives in Medieval Europe: A Sourcebook*. New York: Routledge, 1993.

Anderson, Bonnie S., and Judith P. Zinsser. *A History of Their Own*. New York: Harper & Row, 1988.

Apple, Rima D. *Women, Health and Medicine in America: A Historical Handbook*. New York: Garland, 1990.

Applewhite, Harriet B., and Darline G. Levy. *Women and Politics in the Age of the Democratic Revolution*. Ann Arbor: University of Michigan Press, 1990.

Arjava, Antti. *Women and Law in Late Antiquity*. Oxford: Clarendon Press, 1996.

Arnaud, A. J., and E. Kingdom, eds. *Women's Rights and the Rights of Man*. Aberdeen: Aberdeen University Press, 1990.

Arrom, Silvia Marina. *The Women of Mexico City, 1790–1857*. Stanford: Stanford University Press, 1985.

Backhouse, Frances. *Women of the Klondike*. Vancouver: Whitecap Books, 1995.

Bacon, Margaret Hope. *Mothers of Feminism: The Story of Quaker Women in America*. San Francisco: Harper & Row, 1986.

Bailey, Martha J. *American Women in Science: A Biographical Dictionary*. Denver: ABC-CLIO, 1994.

Bainton, Roland Herbert. *Women of the Reformation, from Spain to Scandinavia*. Minneapolis: Augsburg Publishing House, 1977.

———. *Women of the Reformation in France and England*. Minneapolis: Augsburg Publishing House, 1973.

———. *Women of the Reformation in Germany and Italy*. Minneapolis: Augsburg Publishing House, 1971.

Baldwin, Louis. *Women of Strength: Biographies of 106 Who Have Excelled in Traditionally Male Fields, 61 A.D. to the Present*. Jefferson, NC: McFarland, 1996.

Banks, Olive. *The Biographical Dictionary of British Feminists*. Brighton, UK: Wheatsheaf Books, 1985.

Barber, Elizabeth Wayland. *Women's Work: The First 20,000 Years: Women, Cloth, and Society in Early Times*. New York: Norton, 1994.

*Note: Hundreds of other works and authors significant in women's history are cited in the body of this book, e.g., Mary Wollstonecraft's *Vindication of the Rights of Woman* and Simone de Beauvoir's *The Second Sex*.

Barker-Benfield, G. J., and Catherine Clinton, eds. *Portraits of American Women: From Settlement to the Present*. New York: St. Martin's, 1991.

Bartley, Paula, and Cathy Loxton. *Plains Women: Women in the American West*. Cambridge, UK: Cambridge University Press, 1991.

Bashevkin, Sylvia, ed. *Women and Politics in Western Europe*. London: F. Cass, 1985.

Bataille, Gretchen M. *Native American Women: A Biographical Dictionary*. New York: Garland, 1993.

Bauman, Richard A. *Women and Politics in Ancient Rome*. London: Routledge, 1992.

Baxandell, Rosalyn, et al., eds. *American Working Women: Documentary History*. New York: Vintage, 1976.

Beer, Frances, ed. *Women and Mystical Experience in the Middle Ages*. Rochester, NY: Boydell Press, 1992.

Belford, Barbara. *Brilliant Bylines: A Biographical Anthology of Notable Newspaperwomen in America*. New York: Columbia University Press, 1986.

Bell, Elizabeth S. *Sisters of the Wind: Voices of Early Women Aviators*. Pasadena: Trilogy Books, 1994.

Bhattachariji, Sukumari. *Women and Society in Ancient India*. Calcutta: Basumati Corp., 1994.

Bingham, Marjorie Wall, and Susan Hill Gross. *Women in Japan: From Ancient Times to the Present*. St. Louis Park, MN: Glenhurst Publications, 1987.

Bisilliat, Jeanne, and Michèle Fiéloux. *Women of the Third World: Work and Daily Life*. Rutherford, NJ: Fairleigh Dickinson University Press, 1987.

Blain, Virginia, et al., eds. *The Feminist Companion to Literature in English: Women Writers from the Middle Ages to the Present*. New Haven: Yale University Press, 1990.

Blundell, Sue. *Women in Ancient Greece*. London: British Museum Press, 1995.

Bolt, Christine. *The Women's Movements in the United States and Britain from the 1790s to the 1920s*. Amherst: University of Massachusetts Press, 1993.

Bonta, Marcia. *Women in the Field: America's Pioneering Women Naturalists*. College Station: Texas A&M University Press, 1991.

Bornstein, Daniel, and Roberto Rusconi, eds. *Women and Religion in Medieval and Renaissance Italy*. Chicago: University of Chicago Press, 1996.

Bourdillon, Hilary. *Women as Healers: A History of Women and Medicine*. Cambridge, UK: Cambridge University Press, 1988.

Bowden, Ros. *Women of the Land: Stories of Australia's Rural Women*. Sydney: ABC Books, 1995.

Brooke, George J., ed. *Women in the Biblical Tradition*. Lewiston, NY: E. Mellen, 1992.

Brosius, Maria. *Women in Ancient Persia, 559–331 B.C.* Oxford: Oxford University Press, 1996.

Brunn, Emilie Zum, and Georgette Epiney-Burgard. *Women Mystics in Medieval Europe*. New York: Paragon House, 1989.

Buck, Claire, ed. *The Bloomsbury Guide to Women's Literature*. New York: Prentice Hall, 1992.

Buechler, Steven M. *Women's Movements in the United States: Woman Suffrage, Equal Rights, and Beyond*. New Brunswick: Rutgers University Press, 1990.

Bullough, Vern, and Bonnie Bullough. *Women and Prostitution: A Social History*. Buffalo, NY: Prometheus, 1987.

Caine, Barbara. *Victorian Feminists*. New York: Oxford University Press, 1992.

Campbell, Karlyn Kohrs. *Women Public Speakers in the United States, 1800–1925: A Bio-Critical Sourcebook*. Westport, CT: Greenwood, 1993.

Cant, Bob, and Susan Henning, eds. *Radical Records: 30 Years of Lesbian and Gay History*. London: Routledge, 1988.

Carabillo, Toni, et al. *Feminist Chronicles: 1953–1993*. Los Angeles: Women's Graphics, 1993.

Carmody, Denise Lardner. *Women and World Religions*, 2nd ed. Englewood Cliffs, NJ: Prentice Hall, 1989.

Castro, Ginette. *American Feminism: A Contemporary History*. New York: New York University Press, 1990.

Catt, Helena, and Elizabeth McLeay, eds. *Women and Politics in New Zealand*. Wellington, New Zealand: Victoria University Press, 1993.

Chafe, William H. *The Paradox of Change: American Women in the 20th Century*. New York: Oxford University Press, 1991. A revision of *The American Woman: Her Changing Social, Economic, and Political Roles, 1920–1970* (1972).

Charles, Lindsey, and Lorna Duffin, eds. *Women and Work in Pre-Industrial England*. London: Croom Helm, 1985.

Chaudhuri, Maitryee. *Indian Women's Movement: Reform and Revival*. New Delhi: Radiant Publishers, 1993.

Chesler, Phyllis, et al., eds. *Feminist Foremothers in Women's Studies, Psychology, and Mental Health*. New York: Hawroth, 1995.

Chinoy, Helen Frich, and Linda Walsh Jenkins. *Women in American Theatre*, rev. ed. New York: Theatre Communications Group, 1987.

Claassen, Cheryl, ed. *Women in Archaeology*. Philadelphia: University of Pennsylvania Press, 1994.

Claassen, Cheryl, and Rosemary A. Joyce, eds. *Women in Prehistory: North America and Mesoamerica*. Philadelphia: University of Pennsylvania Press, 1997.

Clark, Elizabeth A. *Women in the Early Church*. Collegeville, MN: Liturgical Press, 1990.

Clark, Gillian. *Women in Late Antiquity: Pagan and Christian Lifestyles*. Oxford: Clarendon, 1993.

———. *Women in the Ancient World*. Oxford: Oxford University Press, 1989.

Clark, Judith Freeman. *Almanac of American Women in the 20th Century*. New York: Prentice Hall, 1987.

Clarke, Jocelyn, and Kate White. *Women in Australian Politics*. Sydney, Australia: Fontana/ Collins, 1983.

Coates, Anne. *Women and Sport*. Hove, UK: Wayland, 1989.

Cohen, Marcia. *The History of Feminism*. New York: Simon & Schuster, 1988.

————. *The Sisterhood: The True Story of the Women Who Changed the World*. New York: Simon & Schuster, 1988. Reprinted as: *The Sisterhood: The Inside Story of the Women's Movement and the Leaders Who Made It Happen*. New York: Columbine, 1989.

Cott, Nancy F., and Elizabeth H. Pleck. *A Heritage of Their Own*. New York: St. Martin's, 1975.

Craik, Elizabeth, ed. *Marriage and Property: Women and Marital Customs in History*. Aberdeen: Aberdeen University Press, 1991.

Crawford, Anne, ed. *The Europa Biographical Dictionary of British Women: Over 1000 Notable Women from Britain's Past*. London: Europa, 1983.

D'Avino, Michele. *The Women of Pompeii*. Napoli: Loffredo, 1967.

D'Oyley, Enid, and Rella Braithwaite, eds. *Women of Our Times*. Toronto: Canadian Negro Women's Association for the National Congress of Black Women, 1973.

Davis, Flora. *Moving the Mountain: The Women's Movement in America Since 1960*. New York: Simon & Schuster, 1991.

Deegan, Mary Jo. *Women in Sociology: A Bio-Bibliographical Sourcebook*. New York: Greenwood, 1991.

Donegan, Jane B. *Women and Men Midwives: Medicine, Morality and Misogyny in Early America*. Westport, CT: Greenwood, 1978.

Donnison, Jean. *Midwives and Medical Men: A History of the Struggle for the Control of Childbirth*, 2nd ed. London: Historical Publications, 1988. Originally published as *Midwives and Medical Men: A History of Inter-Professional Rivalries and Women's Rights*. London: Heinemann Educational, 1977.

Duberman, Martin Bauml, et al., eds. *Hidden from History: Reclaiming the Gay and Lesbian Past*. New York: New American Library, 1989.

DuBois, Ellen Carol. *Feminism and Suffrage: The Emergence of an Independent Women's Movement in America, 1848–1869*. Ithaca: Cornell University Press, 1978.

Duby, Georges, ed. *A History of Private Life*. Cambridge, MA: Belknap, 1988.

Duby, Georges, and Michelle Perrot, gen. eds. *A History of Women*. Cambridge, MA: Belknap.

*Vol. I: From Ancient Goddesses to Christian Saints*, Pauline Schmitt Pantel, ed. 1992.

*Vol. II: Silences of the Middle Ages*, Christiane Klapisch-Zuber, ed. 1992.

*Vol. III: Renaissance and Enlightenment Paradoxes*. Natalie Zemon-Davis and Arlette Farge, eds. 1993.

*Vol. IV: Emerging Feminism from Revolution to World War*. Geneviève Fraisse and Michelle Perrot, eds. 1993.

*Vol. V: Toward a Cultural Identity in the 20th Century*. Françoise Thebaud and Georges Duby, eds. 1994.

Echols, Anne, and Marty Williams. *The Annotated Index of Medieval Women*. New York: M. Wiener Publishers, 1992.

Edmondson, Linda, ed. *Women and Society in Russia and the Soviet Union*. Cambridge, UK: Cambridge University Press, 1992.

Edwards, Julia. *Women of the World: The Great Foreign Correspondents*. Boston: Houghton Mifflin, 1988.

Ehrenberg, Margaret. *Women in Prehistory*. London: British Museum Publications, 1989.

Elshtain, Jean Bethke. *Women and War*. New York: Basic Books, 1987; Chicago: University of Chicago Press, 1995.

Erickson, Amy Louise. *Women and Property in Early Modern England*. London: Routledge, 1993.

Erler, Mary, and Maryanne Kowaleski, eds. *Women and Power in the Middle Ages*. Athens: University of Georgia Press, 1988.

Evans, Richard J. *The Feminists: Women's Emancipation Movements in Europe, America, and Australasia, 1840–1920*. New York: Barnes & Noble, 1977.

Ewing, Elizabeth. *Women in Uniform: Through the Centuries*. London: Batsford, 1975.

Faderman, Lillian. *Odd Girls and Twilight Lovers: A History of Lesbian Life in Twentieth-Century America*. New York: Columbia University Press, 1991.

Faragher, John Mack. *Women and Men on the Overland Trail*. New Haven: Yale University Press, 1979.

Fine, Elsa Honig. *Women and Art—the 15th to the 20th Century*. Montclair, NJ: Allanheld & Schram, 1978.

Fister, Patricia. *Japanese Women Artists 1600–1900*. New York: Harper & Row, 1988.

Foner, Philip S. *Women and the American Labor Movement. Vol. 1: From Colonial Times to the Eve of World War I*, 1979. *Vol. 2: From World War I to the Present*, 1980. New York: Free Press.

Forbes, Malcolm S., with Jeff Bloch. *Women Who Made a Difference*. New York: Simon & Schuster, 1990.

Forbes, Thomas R. *The Midwife and the Witch*. New Haven: Yale University Press, 1966.

Frances, Rae, and Bruce Scates. *Women at Work in Australia: From the Gold Rushes to World War II*. Cambridge, UK: Cambridge University Press, 1993.

Fraser, Antonia. *The Warrior Queens*. New York: Knopf, 1989. Originally published as *Boadicea's Chariot: The Warrior Queens*. London: Weidenfeld & Nicolson, 1988.

Frith, Valerie, ed. *Women and History: Voices of Early Modern England*. Toronto: Coach House Press, 1995.

Frost-Knappman, Elizabeth. *The ABC-CLIO Companion to Women's Progress in America*. Santa Barbara: ABC-CLIO, 1994.

Gacs, Ute. *Women Anthropologists: A Biographical Dictionary*. New York: Greenwood, 1988.

Gardner, Jane F. *Women in Roman Law and Society*. London: Croom Helm, 1986.

Gibson, Wendy. *Women in Seventeeth-Century France*. New York: St. Martin's, 1989.

Gilbert-Falkenburg, Pamela. *Women in Japanese Theatre*. Elizabeth Vale, South Australia: P. Gilbert-Falkenburg, 1985.

Gill, Sean. *Women and the Church of England: From the Eighteenth Century to the Present*. London: SPCK, 1994.

Gilman, Sander L. *Sexuality: An Illustrated History*. New York: Wiley, 1989.

Goldin, Claudia. *Understanding the Gender Gap: An Economic History of American Women*. New York: Oxford University Press, 1990.

Golemba, Beverly E. *Lesser-Known Women: A Biographical Dictionary.* Boulder: Lynne Rienner, 1992.

Gorsline, Douglas. *What People Wore: A Visual History of Dress from Ancient Times to 20th-Century America.* New York: Bonanza Books, 1952.

Green, Rayna. *Women in American Indian Society.* New York: Chelsea House, 1992.

Greenspan, Karen. *The Timetables of Women's History.* New York: Simon & Schuster, 1994.

Greer, Germaine. *The Obstacle Race: The Fortunes of Women Painters and Their Work.* New York: Farrar, Straus & Giroux, 1979.

Greer, Mary K. *Women of the Golden Dawn: Rebels and Priestesses.* Rochester, VT: Park Street Press, 1995.

Grinstein, Louise S., et al., eds. *Women in Chemistry and Physics: A Biobibliographic Sourcebook.* Westport, CT: Greenwood, 1993.

Grinstein, Louise S., and Paul J. Campbell, eds. *Women of Mathematics: A Biobibliographic Sourcebook.* New York: Greenwood, 1987.

Grossman, Susan, and Rivka Haut, eds. *Daughters of the King: Women and the Synagogue: A Survey of History, Halakhah, and Contemporary Realities.* Philadelphia: Jewish Publication Society, 1992.

Guttman, Allen. *Women's Sports: A History.* New York: Columbia University Press, 1991.

Hager, Lori D., ed. *Women in Human Evolution.* New York: Routledge, 1997.

Hahner, June, ed. *Women in Latin American History: Their Lives and Views.* Los Angeles: University of California, 1980.

Haines, Janine. *Suffrage to Sufferance: A Hundred Years of Women in Politics.* North Sydney: Allen & Unwin, 1993.

Hanawalt, Barbara A., ed. *Women and Work in Preindustrial Europe.* Bloomington: Indiana University Press, 1986.

Hardy, Gayle J. *American Women Civil Rights Activists: Biobibliographies of 68 Leaders, 1825–1992.* Jefferson, NC: McFarland, 1993.

Harris, Ann Sutherland, and Linda Nochlin. *Women Artists: 1550–1950.* New York: Knopf, 1989.

Hazou, Winnie. *The Social and Legal Status of Women: A Global Perspective.* New York: Praeger, 1990.

Henriques, Fernando. *Prostitution and Society: A Survey,* 3 vols. London: MacGibbon & Kee, 1962–1968.

Hine, Darlene Clark, et al., eds. *Black Women in America: An Historical Encyclopedia.* Brooklyn: Carlson, 1993.

Hixon, Don L., and Don Hennessee. *Women in Music: An Encyclopedic Biobibliography,* 2nd ed. Metuchen, NJ: Scarecrow, 1993.

Hoehling, A. A. *Women Who Spied.* Lanham, MD: Madison Books, 1993. Original publication: New York: Dodd, Mead, 1967.

Hoff, Joan. *Law, Gender, and Injustice: A Legal History of U.S. Women.* New York: New York University Press, 1991.

Holton, Sandra Stanley. *Suffrage Days: Stories from the Women's Suffrage Movement in Britain.* London: Routledge, 1996.

Hopkins, Lisa. *Women Who Would Be Kings: Female Rulers of the Sixteenth Century.* New York: St. Martin's, 1991.

Hudson, Pat, and W. R. Lee, eds. *Women's Work and the Family Economy in Historical Perspective.* New York: St. Martin's, 1990.

Hughes, Muriel Joy. *Women Healers in Medieval Life and Literature.* Freeport, NH: Books for Libraries, 1968. Originally published 1943.

Hughes, Sarah Shaver, and Brady Hughes. *Women in World History*, Vol. 1. Armonk, NY: M.E. Sharpe, 1995.

Jackson, George F. *Black Women Makers of History: A Portrait.* Oakland, CA: George F. Jackson, 1975. Distributed by National Women's History Project.

Jackson, Guida M. *Women Who Ruled.* Santa Barbara: ABC-CLIO, 1990.

James, Edward T., et al., eds. *Notable American Women: A Biographical Dictionary, 1607–1950*, 3 vols. Cambridge, MA: Belknap, 1971. [See also Sicherman, below.]

James, Janet Wilson, ed. *Women in American Religion.* Philadelphia: University of Pennsylvania Press, 1980.

Jaquette, Jane S., ed. *The Women's Movement in Latin America: Participation and Democracy*, 2nd ed. Boulder: Westview, 1994.

Jeansonne, Glen. *Women of the Far Right: The Mothers' Movement and World War II.* Chicago: University of Chicago Press, 1996.

Jeansonne, Sharon Pace. *The Women of Genesis: From Sarah to Potiphar's Wife.* Minneapolis: Fortress Press, 1990.

Jesch, Judith. *Women in the Viking Age.* Woodbridge, UK: Boydell Press, 1991.

Jewell, Helen M. *Women in Medieval England.* Manchester: Manchester University Press, 1996.

Jones, H. Wendy. *Women Who Braved the Far North: 200 Years of Alaskan Women.* San Diego: Grossmont, 1976.

Just, Roger. *Women in Athenian Law and Life.* London: Routledge, 1989.

Kaptur, Marcy. *Women of Congress: A Twentieth-Century Odyssey.* Washington, DC: Congressional Quarterly, 1996.

Katzenstein, Mary Fainsod, and Carol Mueller, eds. *The Women's Movements of the United States and Western Europe: Consciousness, Political Opportunity, and Public Policy.* Philadelphia: Temple University Press, 1987.

Kay, Ernest, ed. *Foremost Women of the Twentieth Century.* Cambridge, UK: International Biographical Centre, 1988.

Kelly, Linda. *Women of the French Revolution.* London: Hamish Mailton, 1987.

Kenneally, James J. *The History of American Catholic Women.* New York: Crossroad, 1990.

Kennedy, Susan Estabrook. *If All We Did Was to Weep at Home: A History of White Working-Class Women in America.* Bloomington: Indiana University Press, 1979.

Kerber, Linda K. *Women of the Republic: Intellect and Ideology in Revolutionary America.* Chapel Hill: University of North Carolina Press, 1980.

Kersey, Ethel M. *Women Philosophers: A Bio-Critical Source Book.* New York: Greenwood, 1989.

Kinchen, Oscar A. *Women Who Spied for the Blue and the Gray.* Philadelphia: Dorrance, 1972.

King, Margaret L. *Women of the Renaissance.* Chicago: University of Chicago Press, 1991.

Kinnear, Karen L. *Women in the Third World.* Santa Barbara: ABC-CLIO, 1997.

Klein, Laura F., and Lillian A. Ackerman, eds. *Women and Power in Native North America.* Norman: University of Oklahoma Press, 1995.

Kleinberg, S. J. *Women in American Society, 1820–1920.* Brighton, UK: British Association for American Studies, 1990.

Köhler, Carl. *A History of Costume.* New York: Dover, 1963.

Kome, Penney. *Women of Influence: Canadian Women and Politics.* Toronto: Doubleday Canada, 1985.

Kramarae, Cheris, and Paula A. Treichler. *Amazons, Bluestockings and Crones.* London: Pandora Press, 1992. 2nd edition of *A Feminist Dictionary*, 1985.

Krull, Edith. *Women in Art.* London: Studio Vista, 1989.

Kuhn, Annette, with Susannah Radstone, eds. *Women in Film: An International Guide.* New York: Fawcett Columbine, 1991.

LaBastille, Anne. *Women and Wilderness.* San Francisco: Sierra Club Books, 1980.

Langley, Winston E., ed. *Women's Rights in International Documents: A Sourcebook with Commentary.* Jefferson, NC: McFarland, 1991.

Laurence, Anne. *Women in England, 1500–1760: A Social History.* New York: St. Martin's, 1994.

Lefkowitz, Mary R., and Maureen B. Fant, *Women's Life in Greece and Rome: A Source Book in Translation,* 2nd ed. Baltimore: Johns Hopkins University Press, 1992.

Lerner, Gerda, ed. *Women and History,* 2 vols. New York: Oxford University Press, 1986–1993.

Levine, Linda Gould, et al., eds. *Spanish Women Writers: A Bio-Bibliographical Source Book.* Westport, CT: Greenwood, 1993.

Levine, Philippa. *Victorian Feminism, 1850 to 1900.* London: Hutchinson Education, 1987.

Lewenhak, Sheila. *Women and Trade Unions: An Outline History of Women in the British Trade Union Movement.* London: Benn, 1977.

Lister, Margot. *Costume: An Illustrated Survey from Ancient Times to the Twentieth Century.* London: Jenkins, 1967.

———. *Costumes of Everyday Life: An Illustrated History of Working Clothes.* Boston: Plays, 1972.

Litoff, Judy Barrett. *American Midwives: 1860 to the Present.* Westport, CT: Greenwood, 1978.

Lloyd, Trevor. *Suffragettes International: The World-Wide Campaign for Women's Rights.* New York: American Heritage Press, 1971.

Lomax, Judy. *Women of the Air.* London: J. Murray, 1986.

Lucas, Angela M. *Women in the Middle Ages: Religion, Marriage and Letters*. Brighton, UK: Harvester, 1983.

Luchetti, Cathy, with Carol Olwell. *Women of the West*. Berkeley, CA: Antelope Island Press, 1982.

Lutz, Alma. *Crusade for Freedom: Women of the Anti-Slavery Movement*. Boston: Beacon, 1968.

Lynn, Vera, et al. *Unsung Heroines: The Women Who Won the War*. London: Sidgwick & Jackson, 1990.

Macdonald, Anne L. *Feminine Ingenuity: Women and Invention in America*. New York: Ballantine, 1992.

MacIvor, Heather. *Women and Politics in Canada*. Peterborough, Canada: Broadview Press, 1996.

MacMillan, Margaret. *Women of the Raj*. London: Thames and Hudson, 1988.

Mahoney, M. H. *Women in Espionage: A Biographical Dictionary*. Santa Barbara: ABC-CLIO, 1993.

Mandel, William M. *Soviet Women*. Garden City, NY: Anchor, 1975.

Markale, Jean. *Women of the Celts*. Rochester, VT: Inner Traditions, 1986.

Marks, Patricia. *Bicycles, Bangs and Boomers: The New Woman in the Popular Press*. Lexington: University Press of Kentucky, 1990.

Marsh, Rosalind, ed. *Women in Russia and Ukraine*. Cambridge, UK: Cambridge University Press, 1996.

Massey, Mary Elizabeth. *Women in the Civil War*. Lincoln: University of Nebraska Press, 1994. Originally published as *Bonnet Brigades*. New York: Knopf, 1966.

Massey, Michael. *Women in Ancient Greece and Rome*. Cambridge, UK: Cambridge University Press, 1988.

McAuslan, Ian, and Peter Walcot, eds. *Women in Antiquity*. Oxford: Oxford University Press, 1996.

McHenry, Robert, ed. *Liberty's Women*. Springfield, MA: G & C. Merriam, 1980. Reprinted as *Famous American Women: A Biographical Dictionary from Colonial Times to the Present*. New York: Dover, 1983.

McKenzie, Midge. *Shoulder to Shoulder: A Documentary*. New York: Vintage, 1988.

Meale, Carol M., ed. *Women and Literature in Britain, 1150–1500*. Cambridge, UK: Cambridge University Press, 1993.

Mernissi, Fatima. *Women and Islam: An Historical and Theological Enquiry*. Oxford: Blackwell, 1991.

Meyer, Donald. *Sex and Power: The Rise of Women in America, Russia, Sweden, and Italy*, 2nd ed. Hanover, NH: University Press of New England, 1989.

Miles, Rosalind. *The Women's History of the World*. Topsfield, MA: Salem House, 1989.

Miller, Francesca. *Latin American Women and the Search for Social Justice*. Hanover, NH: University Press of New England, 1991.

Murray, Janet. *Strong-Minded Women and Other Lost Voices from 19th Century England*. New York: Pantheon, 1982.

Murray, Margaret. *The Witch-Cult in Western Europe*. Oxford: Clarendon, 1962. Originally published 1921.

Nair, Janaki. *Women and Law in Colonial India: A Social History*. New Delhi: Kali for Women with the National Law School of India University, 1996.

Nelson, Barbara J., and Najma Chowdhury, eds. *Women and Politics Worldwide*. New Haven: Yale University Press, 1994.

Nicholas, Susan Cary, et al. *Rights and Wrongs: Women's Struggle for Legal Equality*, 2nd ed. New York: Feminist Press at the City University of New York, 1986.

O'Connell, Agnes N., and Nancy Felipe Russo, eds. *Women in Psychology: A Bio-Bibliographic Sourcebook*. New York: Greenwood, 1990.

O'Neill, Lois Decker. *The Women's Book of Records and Achievements*. Garden City, NY: Anchor, 1979.

O'Neill, William L. *Feminism in America: A History*, 2nd ed. New Brunswick, NJ: Transaction, 1989.

Ogilvie, Marilyn Bailey. *Women in Science: Antiquity Through the Nineteenth Century: A Biographical Dictionary with Annotated Bibliography*. Cambridge, MA: MIT Press, 1991.

Olsen, Kirstin. *Chronology of Women's History*. Westport, CT: Greenwood, 1994.

Olsen, Kirstin. *Remember the Ladies: A Woman's Book of Days*. Pittstown, NJ: Main Street, 1988.

Osen, Lynn M. *Women in Mathematics*. Cambridge, MA: MIT Press, 1974.

O´ Céirín, Kit, and Cyril O´ Céirín. *Women of Ireland: A Biographic Dictionary*. Kinvara, Eire: Tír Eolas, 1996.

Parry, Melanie, ed. *Chambers Biographical Dictionary of Women*. Edinburgh: Chambers, 1996.

Pendle, Karin, ed. *Women and Music: A History*. Bloomington: Indiana University Press, 1991.

Pomeroy, Sarah B. *Goddesses, Whores, Wives, and Slaves: Women in Classical Antiquity*. New York: Schocken. 1976.

Porter, Cathy. *Women in Revolutionary Russia*. Cambridge: Cambridge University Press, 1988.

Power, Eileen. *Medieval Women*. Cambridge, UK: Cambridge University Press, 1975. Originally published 1940.

Pugh, Martin. *Women and the Women's Movement in Britain, 1914–1959*. London: Macmillan Education, 1992.

Randall, Vicky. *Women and Politics: An International Perspective*, 2nd ed. Houndmills, Basingstoke, UK: Macmillan, 1987.

Ranft, Patricia. *Women and the Religious Life in Premodern Europe*. New York: St. Martin's, 1996.

Read, Phyllis J., and Bernard L. Witlieb. *The Book of Women's Firsts*. New York: Random House, 1992.

Reeves, Minou. *Female Warriors of Allah: Women and the Islamic Revolution*. New York: Dutton, 1989.

Reifert, Gail, and Eugene M. Dermody. *Women Who Fought: An American History*. Norwalk, CA: Dermody, 1978.

Rhoodie, Eschel M. *Discrimination Against Women: A Global Survey of the Economic, Educational, Social and Political Status of Women*. Jefferson, NC: McFarland, 1989.

Robertson, Claire C., and Martin A. Klein, eds. *Women and Slavery in Africa*. Madison: University of Wisconsin Press, 1983.

Rogers, Katharine M. *Feminism in Eighteenth-Century England*. Urbana: University of Illinois Press, 1982.

Rosa, Kumudhini. *Women of South Asia*. Colombo: Friedrich-Ebert-Stiftung, 1995.

Rose, Mary Beth, ed. *Women in the Middle Ages and the Renaissance: Literary and Historical Perspectives*. Syracuse: Syracuse University Press, 1986.

Rose, Phyllis, ed. *The Norton Book of Women's Lives*. New York: Norton, 1993.

Rossiter, Margaret L. *Women in the Resistance*. New York: Praeger, 1986.

Rowbotham, Sheila. *A Century of Women: The History of Women in Britain and the United States*. London: Viking, 1997.

———. *Hidden from History: Three Hundred Years of Women's Oppression and the Fight Against It*. New York: Pantheon, 1975.

———. *Women, Resistance, and Revolution: A History of Women and Revolution in the Modern World*. New York: Pantheon, 1972.

Ruether, Rosemary Radford, and Rosemary Skinner Keller, eds. *Women and Religion in America*, 3 vols. San Francisco: Harper & Row, 1981.

Rule, Babs. *Everyday Life in the Harem*. London: Blond & Briggs, 1983.

Rupp, Leila J. and Verta Taylor. *Survival in Doldrums: The American Women's Rights Movement, 1945 to the 1960's*. New York: Oxford University Press, 1987.

Salem, Dorothy C., ed. *African American Women: A Biographical Dictionary*. New York: Garland, 1993.

Salmon, Marylynn. *Women and the Law of Property in Early America*. Chapel Hill: University of North Carolina Press, 1986.

Salmonson, Jessica Amanda. *The Encyclopedia of Amazons: Women Warriors from Antiquity to the Modern Era*. New York: Paragon House, 1991.

Salokar, Rebecca Mare, and Mary L. Volcansek, eds. *Women in Law: A Bio-Bibliographical Sourcebook*. Westport, CT: Greenwood, 1996.

Sawyer, Deborah F. *Women and Religion in the First Christian Centuries*. London: Routledge, 1996.

Saxenz, T. P. *Women in Indian History: A Biographical Dictionary*. New Delhi: Kalyani Publishers, 1979.

Saxonhouse, Arlene W. *Women in the History of Political Thought: Ancient Greece to Machiavelli*. New York: Praeger, 1985.

Schneir, Miriam, ed. *Feminism: The Essential Historical Writings*, New York: Vintage, 1994.

Scholer, David M., ed. *Women in Early Christianity*. New York: Garland, 1993.

Scott, Joan Wallach. *Feminism and History*. Oxford: Oxford University Press, 1996.

Seagraves, Anne. *Women Who Charmed the West*. Lakeport, CA: Wesanne, 1991.

Sealy, Raphael. *Women and Law in Classical Greece*. Chapel Hill: University of North Carolina Press, 1990.

Seller, Maxine Schwartz. *Women Educators in the United States, 1820–1883: A Bio-Bibliographical Sourcebook*. Westport, CT: Greenwood, 1994.

Shanley, Mary Lyndon. *Feminism, Marriage, and the Law in Victorian England, 1850–1895.* Princeton: Princeton University Press, 1989.

Sharma, Arvind, ed. *Women in World Religions.* Albany: State University of New York Press, 1987.

Sharma, Tripat. *Women in Ancient India: From 320 A.D. to c.1200 A.D.* New Delhi: Ess Ess Publications, 1987.

Shattock, Joanne. *The Oxford Guide to British Women Writers.* Oxford: Oxford University Press, 1993.

Sherrow, Victoria. *Encyclopedia of Women and Sports.* Santa Barbara: ABC-CLIO, 1996.

———. *Women and the Military: An Encyclopedia.* Santa Barbara: ABC-CLIO, 1996.

Shevelow, Kathryn. *Women and Print Culture: The Construction of Femininity in the Early Periodical.* London: Routledge, 1989.

Showalter, Elaine, et al., eds. *Modern American Women Writers.* New York: Scribner's, 1991.

Shreir, Sally, ed. *Women's Movements of the World.* Harlow, UK: Longman: 1988.

Sicherman, Barbara, et al., eds. *Notable American Women: The Modern Period.* Cambridge, MA: Belknap, 1980. [See also James, above.]

Siegel, Patricia Joan, and Kay Thomas Finley. *Women in the Scientific Search: An American Bio-Bibliography, 1724–1979.* Metuchen, NJ: Scarecrow, 1985.

Simon, Rita J., and Gloria Danziger. *Women's Movements in America: Their Successes, Disappointments, and Aspirations.* New York: Praeger, 1991.

Simpson, Helen MacDonald. *The Women of New Zealand,* rev. ed. Auckland: Paul's Book Arcade, 1962.

Smith, Harold L., ed. *British Feminism in the Twentieth Century.* Amherst: University of Massachusetts Press, 1990.

Smith, Sharon. *Women Who Make Movies.* New York: Hopkinson and Blake, 1975.

Solomon, Martha M., ed. *A Voice of Their Own: The Woman Suffrage Press, 1840–1910.* Tuscaloosa: University of Alabama Press, 1991.

Spender, Dale. *Women of Ideas and What Men Have Done to Them.* London: Pandora Press, 1982.

Stefoff, Rebecca. *Women of the World: Women Travelers and Explorers.* New York: Oxford University Press, 1992.

Stienstra, Deborah. *Women's Movements and International Organizations.* New York: St. Martin's, 1994.

Stites, Richard. *The Women's Liberation Movement in Russia: Feminism, Nihilism and Bolshevism, 1860–1930.* Princeton: Princeton University Press, 1991.

Stone, Lawrence. *The Family, Sex and Marriage in England 1500–1800.* New York: Harper & Row, 1979.

Stuard, Susan Mosher, ed. *Women in Medieval History and Historiography.* Philadelphia: University of Pennsylvania Press, 1987.

Tannahill, Reay. *Sex in History.* New York: Stein & Day, 1980.

Taylor, Eric. *Women Who Went to War: 1938-46.* London: Hale, 1988.

Telgen, Diane, and Jim Kamp, eds. *Notable Hispanic American Women.* Detroit: Gale Research, 1993.

Terborg-Penn, Rosalyn, et al., eds. *Women in Africa and the African Diaspora.* Washington, DC: Howard University Press, 1987.

Tierney, Helen, ed. *Women's Studies Encyclopedia.* Westport, CT: Greenwood. *Vol. I: Views from the Sciences,* 1989. *Vol. II: Literature, Arts, and Learning,* 1990. *Vol. III: History, Philosophy, and Religion,* 1991.

Todd, Janet, ed. *British Women Writers: A Critical Reference Guide.* New York: Continuum, 1989.

Towler, Jean, and Joan Bramall. *Midwives in History and Society.* London: Croom Helm, 1986.

Trager, James. *The Women's Chronology.* New York: Holt, 1994.

Trevor-Roper, H. R. *The European Witch-Craze of the Sixteenth and Seventeenth Centuries.* New York: Harper & Row, 1956.

Tuttle, Lisa. *Encyclopedia of Feminism.* New York: Facts On File, 1986.

Uglow, Jennifer S. *The Continuum Dictionary of Women's Biography,* rev. ed. New York: Continuum, 1989.

Upadhyay, Neelam, and Rekha Pandey. *Women in India: Past and Present.* Allahabad, India: Chugh Publications, 1990.

Vare, Ethlie Ann, and Greg Ptacek. *Mothers of Invention: From the Bra to the Bomb, Forgotten Women and Their Unforgettable Ideas.* New York: Quill, 1987.

Vickers, Jeanne. *Women and War.* London: Zed Books, 1993.

*Views from Jade Terrace: Chinese Women Artists 1300–1912.* New York: Rizzoli, 1988.

Wall, Cheryl A. *Women of the Harlem Renaissance.* Bloomington: Indiana University Press, 1995.

Warnicke, Retha M. *Women of the English Renaissance and Reformation.* Westport, CT: Greenwood, 1983.

Warren, Mary Anne. *The Nature of Woman: An Encyclopedia and Guide to the Literature.* Inverness, CA: Edgepress, 1980.

Watterson, Barbara. *Women in Ancient Egypt.* New York: St. Martin's 1991.

Waugh, Norah. *The Cut of Women's Clothes: 1600–1930.* New York: Theatre Arts Books, 1968.

Weatherford, Doris. *American Women's History: An A to Z of People, Organizations, Issues, and Events.* New York: Prentice Hall, 1994.

Western Writers of America. *The Women Who Made the West.* Garden City, NY: Doubleday, 1980.

White, Robert Orr, and Pauline Whyte. *The Women of Rural Asia.* Boulder, CO: Westview Press, 1982.

Wilcox, Helen, ed. *Women and Literature in Britain, 1500–1700.* New York: Cambridge University Press, 1996.

Wilcox, R. Turner. *The Mode in Costume,* 2nd ed. New York: Scribner's, 1958.

Williams, Marty, and Anne Echols. *Between Pit and Pedestal: Women in the Middle Ages.* Princeton: Markus Wiener Publishers, 1994.

Wilson, Katharina M., et al., eds. *Women Writers of Great Britain and Europe: An Encyclopedia.* New York: Garland, 1997.

Witherington, Ben, III. *Women in the Earliest Churches.* Cambridge, UK: Cambridge University Press, 1988.

Wolf, Stephanie Grauman. *As Various as Their Land: The Everyday Lives of Eighteenth Century Americans.* New York: HarperCollins, 1993.

Woloch, Nancy. *Women and the American Experience,* 2nd ed. New York: McGraw-Hill, 1994.

Wood-Clark, Sarah. *Beautiful Daring Western Girls: Women of the Wild West Shows,* 2nd ed. Cody, WY: Buffalo Bill Historical Center, 1991.

Woodrough, Elizabeth, ed. *Women in European Theatre.* Oxford: Intellect Books, 1995.

Woolum, Janet. *Outstanding Women Athletes: Who They Are and How They Influenced Sports in America.* Phoenix: Oryx, 1992.

Yellin, Jean Fagan. *Women and Sisters: The Antislavery Feminists in American Culture.* New Haven: Yale University Press, 1989.

Young, James D. *Women and Popular Struggles: A History of British Working-Class Women, 1560–1984.* Edinburgh: Mainstream Pub., 1985.

Zilboorg, Caroline, ed. *Women's Firsts.* Detroit: Gale, 1997.

Zophy, Angela Howard, with Frances M. Kavenik, eds. *Handbook of American Women's History.* New York: Garland, 1990.

# Index

347, 355, 361, 389, 399
Ashur, Radwa, 297, 410
Asia Peace and Friendship
Foundation for Women,
425
Askew, Anne, 30-31
Askew, Sarah Byrd, 221
Aspasia (physician), 8
Aspasia of Miletos, 3
Asquith, Anthony, 274
Asquith, Margot, 110, 292
Assistance Publique (France),
277
Associated Press, 364
Associated Women of the
American Farm Bureau
Federation, 242
Association for Intercollegiate
Athletics for Women
(AIAW), 395
Association for Promoting
Trained Nursing in
Workhouse Infirmaries,
134
Association for the
Advancement of the
Medical Education of
Women, 124
Association for the
Advancement of Women,
125
Association for Women in
Mathematics, 358
Association for Women in
Psychology, 351
Association for Women's
Suffrage, 159
Association International des
Femmes (later
Solidarité), 116, 169
Association of American Law
Schools, 398
Association of American
Library Schools, 114
Association of American
Women Composers, 240
Association of Childhood
Education International,
253
Association of Collegiate
Alumnae, 139, 164, 182,
224
Association of Southern
Women for the
Prevention of Lynching,
249, 360
Association of University
Women, 139
Association of Women
Business Owners, 361
Association of Working Girls'
Societies, 137, 204
Association pour le Droit des
Femmes, 120
Astaire, Adele, 234, 255
Astaire, Fred, 234, 255, 257,

260, 263, 266-267, 269,
272, 275, 302, 305
Astell, Mary, 43, 48
Astin, Patty Duke, 51
Astor, Mary, 185, 269
Astor, Nancy Langhorne, 133,
217
Astorga, Nora, 303, 402, 407
Astronomical Society of
France, 284
astronomy, 53, 61, 76, 93,
134, 158, 168, 202, 234,
236, 263, 346. *See also
individual astronomers*
astrophysics, 166, 287
Ataulf, 11
Athaliah, queen of Judah, 3
Athayde, Roberto, 379
Athens University Medical
School, 189, 274, 315
Atherton, Gertrude, 103, 160,
168, 185, 200, 226, 232,
264, 285, 302
Athletics. *See Sports*
Atkins, Eileen, 344
Atkins, Eudora Clark, 131
Atkinson, Louisa, 79, 103,
105, 125
Atkinson, Ti-Grace, 276, 348,
366
*Atlanta Sunday American*, 227
Atomic Energy Commission,
343
Attenborough, Richard, 420
Attica, 4
attorneys. *See lawyers*
Atwood, Margaret, 278, 345,
352, 358, 362, 368, 375,
385, 391, 396, 403, 414,
420
*Alias Grace*, 432
*Morning in the Burning
House*, 428
Aubrey, Mrs. (Elizabeth
Hawkins-Whitshed Le
Blond), 107, 172, 186,
262
Auburn, Jayne, 234
Auclert, Hubertine, 90, 132-
133, 137, 140, 171, 188,
229, 233
Audran, Stephane, 406
Audrey (Ethelreda), Saint, 14
Auel, Jean M., 388, 394, 401
Auerbach, Charlotte, 170,
320, 333, 347, 375
Augsburg, Anita, 171, 179,
214, 360
Augusta Female Seminary, 85,
109, 162
Augustinian Sisters, 13, 187
Augustus, Roman emperor, 7
Aumont, Jean Pierre, 336
Aurelian, 9
Auriol, Jacqueline, 213, 313,
354

Auschwitz concentration
camp, 283-284, 290, 388
Austen, Jane, 59, 70-71, 280
Austin, Harriet, 101
Austin, Mary, 117, 200, 213,
264
Austral, Florence, 350
Australia, 87, 106, 173, 308,
350, 360, 384, 397, 402
Australian Academy of
Science, 349
Australian Women's Federal
Political Association,
177, 303
Australian Women's Guild of
Empire, 247
Australian Women's Socialist
League, 191
*Autobiography of My Mother,
The* (Kincaid), 432
automobile racing, 191, 378
*Automobile Workers v. Johnson
Controls Inc.*, 412
Ava, Frau, 18
AVANTA network, 375
*Avanti!* (newspaper), 175
aviation, 194, 200, 213, 219,
225, 234, 242, 245, 248,
251, 254, 256, 263, 266,
274, 280, 282, 287, 301,
310, 313, 317, 329, 341,
343, 357, 378, 420
Avnet, John, 414
Avvaiyar, 11
Axiothea of Phlius, 5
Axis Sally (Mildred Gillars),
171, 303, 407
Ayckbourn, Alan, 359
Aycock, Alice, 380
Ayer, Harriet Hubbard, 94,
145, 163, 177
Aylward, Gladys, 177, 250,
273, 354
Ayres, Anne, 69, 87, 164
Ayres, Mary Andrews, 123
Ayrton, Hertha Marks, 100,
142, 168, 174, 176, 181,
184, 205, 231
Ayrton fan, 205
AZT, 216

**B**
B-52 pilots, first female, 429
Ba, Mariama, 249, 389, 292
Baader, Andreas, 348, 360
Baader-Meinhof Group (Red
Army Faction), 348, 360
Babbage, Charles, 261, 348
Babenco, Hector, 86
Baby Doe law, 397
baby jumpers, 124
Bacall, Lauren, 235, 290, 296,
341, 355, 391, 411
Bacewicz, Grazyna, 192, 352
Bachmann, Ingeborg, 241,